The Civil War
A Narrative

ALL THESE WERE HONOURED IN THEIR GENERATIONS

AND WERE THE GLORY OF THEIR TIMES

THERE BE OF THEM

THAT HAVE LEFT A NAME BEHIND THEM

THAT THEIR PRAISES MIGHT BE REPORTED

AND SOME THERE BE WHICH HAVE NO MEMORIAL

WHO ARE PERISHED AS THOUGH THEY HAD NEVER BEEN

AND ARE BECOME AS THOUGH THEY HAD NEVER BEEN BORN

AND THEIR CHILDREN AFTER THEM

BUT THESE WERE MERCIFUL MEN

WHOSE RIGHTEOUSNESS HATH NOT BEEN FORGOTTEN

WITH THEIR SEED SHALL CONTINUALLY REMAIN

A GOOD INHERITANCE

AND THEIR CHILDREN ARE WITHIN THE COVENANT

THEIR SEED STANDETH FAST

AND THEIR CHILDREN FOR THEIR SAKES

THEIR SEED SHALL REMAIN FOR EVER

AND THEIR GLORY SHALL NOT BE BLOTTED OUT

THEIR BODIES ARE BURIED IN PEACE

BUT THEIR NAME LIVETH FOR EVERMORE

Ecclesiasticus xliv

THE
Civil War
A Narrative

★ ★

RED RIVER
to CHATTAHOOCHEE

★ ★

Another Grand Design

By SHELBY FOOTE

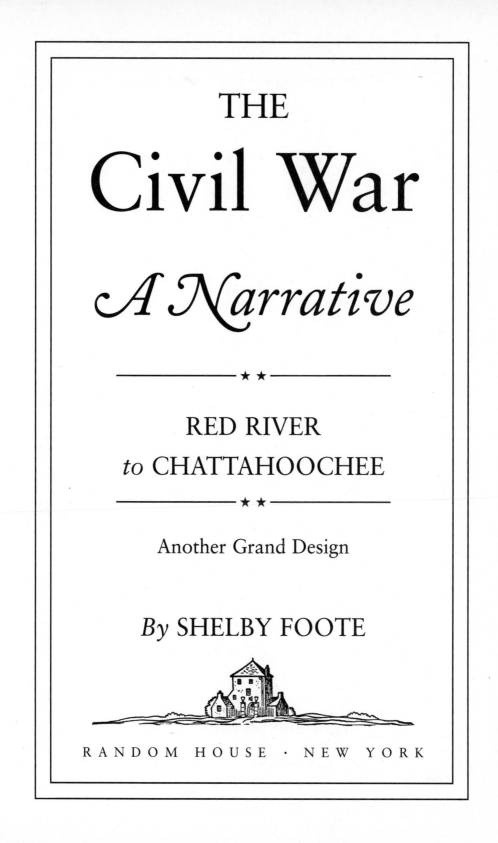

RANDOM HOUSE · NEW YORK

Originally published in slightly different form as
Part 1 of THE CIVIL WAR: A Narrative—Red River to Appomattox
Copyright © 1974 by Shelby Foote
All rights reserved under International and Pan-American Copyright
Conventions. Published in the United States by Random House, Inc., New York, and
simultaneously in Canada by Random House of Canada Limited, Toronto.

Library of Congress Cataloging in Publication Data
Foote, Shelby.
The Civil War.
CONTENTS.—1.   Fort Sumter to Perryville.—
2.   Fredericksburg to Meridian.—3.   Red River to
Appomattox.
1.   United States—History—Civil War.
E468.F7 973.7 58-988
ISBN 0-307-29029-8
Manufactured in the United States of America
10 9 8 7 6 5 4 3 2 1

CONTENTS

★ ✗ ☆

☆

Red River
to
Chattahoochee

☆

GRANT'S PLAN
Early Spring 1864

(Shaded areas represent Federal gains
since start of war.)

ATLANTIC OCEAN

GULF OF MEXICO

Miles
0   200

Another Grand Design

★ ✗ ☆

LATE AFTERNOON OF A RAW, GUSTY DAY
in early spring — March 8, a Tuesday, 1864 — the desk clerk at Willard's Hotel, two blocks down Pennsylvania Avenue from the White
House, glanced up to find an officer accompanied by a boy of thirteen
facing him across the polished oak of the registration counter and inquiring whether he could get a room. "A short, round-shouldered man
in a very tarnished major general's uniform," he seemed to a bystanding
witness to have "no gait, no station, no manner," to present instead, with
his ill-fitting jacket cut full in the skirt and his high-crowned hat set
level on his head, a somewhat threadbare, if not quite down-at-heels,
conglomerate impression of "rough, light-brown whiskers, a blue eye,
and rather a scrubby look withal . . . as if he was out of office and on
half pay, with nothing to do but hang round the entry of Willard's,
cigar in mouth." Discerning so much of this as he considered worth his
time, together perhaps with the bystander's added observation that the
applicant had "rather the look of a man who did, or once did, take a
little too much to drink," the clerk was no more awed by the stranger's
rank than he was attracted by his aspect. This was, after all, the best
known hostelry in Washington. There had been by now close to five
hundred Union generals, and of these the great majority, particularly
among those who possessed what was defined as "station," had checked
in and out of Willard's in the past three wartime years. In the course of
its recent and rapid growth, under the management of a pair of Vermont
brothers who gave it their name along with their concern, it had swallowed whole, together with much other adjacent real estate, a former
Presbyterian church; the President-elect himself had stayed here through
the ten days preceding his inauguration, making of its Parlor 6 a "little
White House," and it was here, one dawn two years ago in one of its
upper rooms, that Julia Ward Howe had written her "Battle Hymn of
the Republic," the anthem for the crusade the new President had begun

to design as soon as he took office. Still, bright or tarnished, stars were stars; a certain respect was owed, if not to the man who wore them, then in any case to the rank they signified; the clerk replied at last that he would give him what he had, a small top-floor room, if that would do. It would, the other said, and when the register was given its practiced half-circle twirl he signed without delay. The desk clerk turned it back again, still maintaining the accustomed, condescending air he was about to lose in shock when he read what the weathered applicant had written: "U.S. Grant & Son — Galena, Illinois."

Whereupon (for such was the aura that had gathered about the name "Unconditional Surrender" Grant, hero of Donelson, conqueror of Vicksburg, deliverer of Chattanooga) there was an abrupt transformation, not only in the attitude of the clerk, whose eyes seemed to start from his head at the sight of the signature and who struck the bell with a force that brought on the double all the bellboys within earshot, but also in that of the idlers, the loungers roundabout the lobby, who soon learned the cause of the commotion in the vicinity of the desk. It was as if the prayers of the curious had been answered after the flesh. Here before them, in the person of this undistinguished-looking officer — forty-one years of age, five feet eight inches tall, and weighing just under a hundred and forty pounds in his scuffed boots and shabby clothes — was the man who, in the course of the past twenty-five months of a war in which the news had mostly been unwelcome from the Federal point of view, had captured two rebel armies, entire, and chased a third clean out of sight beyond the roll of the southern horizon. Now that he made a second visual assessment, more deliberate and above all more informed than the first, the bystander who formerly had seen only an "ordinary, scrubby-looking man, with a slightly seedy look," perceived that there was more to him than had been apparent before the authentication that came with the fixing of the name. The "blue eye" became "a clear blue eye," and the once stolid-seeming face took on "a look of resolution, as if he could not be trifled with."

Such, then, was the effect of the gathered aura. And yet there was a good deal more to it than fame, past or present. There was also anticipation, and of a particular national form. Just last week, on Leap Year Day, the President had signed a congressional act reviving the grade of lieutenant general, and Grant had been summoned east to receive in person his promotion, together with command of all the armies of the Union, which he was expected to lead at last to final victory over the forces that had threatened its destruction. Forgotten now was the small top-floor room his modesty had been willing to accept. Instead, the clerk obsequiously tendered the distinguished guest "the best in the house": meaning Parlor 6, where Abraham Lincoln himself had held court in the days preceding his inauguration, less than one week more than three years ago today.

Grant accepted this as he had the other, with neither eagerness nor protest, which caused a second witness to remark upon "his shy but manly bearing." Still another even saw virtue in the dead-level way he wore his hat. "He neither puts it on behind his ears, nor draws it over his eyes; much less does he cock it on one side, but sets it straight and very hard on his head." A fourth believed he detected something else beneath the general's "rough dignity" of surface. "He habitually wears an expression as if he had determined to drive his head through a brick wall, and was about to do it." Just now though, here in the close atmosphere of the lobby of Willard's — which a disgruntled Englishman complained was compounded, in about equal parts, of "heat, noise, dust, smoke, and expectoration" — what he mainly seemed to desire was an absence of fanfare.

But that was not to be. For a week now the town talk had been of his imminent arrival, and now that the talkers had him within actual reach they intended to make the most of him. Returning downstairs presently for dinner in the main dining room, and holding his son Fred by the hand as if for mutual reassurance, he managed to get as far as his table and even to order the meal before he was recognized by a gentleman from New Orleans who came over for a handshake. Then, as before, all hope of privacy ended. Word of his presence "spread from table to table," according to one who was there; "people got up and craned their necks in an anxious endeavor to see 'the coming man.'" This reached a climax when one of the watchers, unable to contain his enthusiasm, mounted a chair and called — prematurely, for the promotion had not yet been conferred — for "Three cheers for Lieutenant General Grant!" These were given "in the most tremendous manner" and were followed by a pounding that made the glasses and silverware dance on the tables, "in the midst of which General Grant, looking very much astonished and perhaps annoyed, rose to his feet, awkwardly rubbed his mustache with his napkin, bowed, and resumed his seat." For a time, good sense prevailed; "the general was allowed to eat in peace." But when he rose again and began to make his way out, once more with his son in tow, a Pennsylvania congressman took him in hand and began a round of introductions. "This was his first levee," the witness added; after which his retreat through the crowded lobby and up the staircase to his rooms was characterized by "most unsoldierly blushing."

Hard as this was on a man who valued his privacy and was discomfited by adulation, before the night was over he would find himself at storm center of an even worse ordeal. Word of his arrival having spread, he found on his return to Parlor 6 a special invitation to come by the White House, presumably for a conference with the Commander in Chief, whom he had never met although they both were from Illinois and were by now the two most famous men in the country.

If he had known that the President's weekly receptions were held

on Tuesday evenings he would perhaps have postponed his call, but by
the time he completed the short walk up the avenue to the gates of the
executive mansion it was too late. He found himself being ushered up the
steps, through the foyer, down a corridor, and finally into the brightly
lighted East Room, where the reception was in full swing. The crowd,
enlarged beyond the norm tonight by the news that he would be there,
fell silent as he entered, then parted before him to disclose at the far end
of the room the tall form of Abraham Lincoln, who watched him approach, then put out a long arm for a handshake. "I'm glad to see you,
General," he said.

The crowd resumed its "stir and buzz"; there was a spattering of
applause and even "a cheer or two," which struck Navy Secretary
Gideon Welles as "rowdy and unseemly." Lincoln turned Grant over
to Secretary of State William H. Seward for presentation to Mrs
Lincoln, who took his arm for a turn round the room while her husband
followed at a distance, apparently much amused by the general's reaction
to being placed thus on display before a crowd that soon began to get
somewhat out of hand, surging toward him, men and women alike, for
a close-up look and a possible exchange of greetings. Grant "blushed like
a schoolgirl," sweating heavily from embarrassment and the exertion of
shaking the hands of those who managed to get nearest in the jam.
"Stand up so we can all have a look at you!" someone cried from the
rim of the crowd, and he obliged by stepping onto a red plush sofa, looking out over the mass of upturned faces whose eyes fairly shone with
delight at being part of an authentic historical tableau. "It was the only
real mob I ever saw in the White House," a journalist later wrote,
describing how "people were caught up and whirled in the torrent which
swept through the great East Room. Ladies suffered dire disaster in the
crush and confusion; their laces were torn and crinolines mashed, and
many got up on sofas, chairs, and tables to be out of harm's way or to
get a better view of the spectacle. . . . For once at least the President of
the United States was not the chief figure in the picture. The little, scared-
looking man who stood on a crimson-covered sofa was the idol of the
hour."

Rescued from this predicament — or, as the newsman put it,
"smuggled out by friendly hands" — Grant presently found himself
closeted in a smaller chamber, which in time he would learn to identify
as the Blue Room, with the President and the Secretary of War, Edwin
M. Stanton. Lincoln informed him that he would be given his lieutenant
general's commission at a ceremony here next day and would be expected to reply to a short speech, "only four sentences in all, which I
will read from my manuscript as an example which you may follow . . .
as you are perhaps not so much accustomed to public speaking as I
am." For guidance in preparing his reply, he gave him a copy of what
he himself would say, together with two suggestions for remarks which

he hoped the general would incorporate in his response: first, something that would "prevent or obviate any jealousy" on the part of the generals about to come under his command, and second, something that would put him "on as good terms as possible with the Army of the Potomac," to which he was a stranger. "If you see any objection to doing this," Lincoln added as a final sign of consideration for a man about to be cast in an unfamiliar role, "be under no restraint whatever in expressing that objection to the Secretary of War."

Grant expressed no objection, but as he returned to the hotel after midnight for his first sleep in Washington he was perhaps regretful that he had ever left the West, where life was at once less pushy and more informal, and convinced no doubt of the wisdom of his resolution to go back there at the first opportunity.

Returning next day to the White House for the ceremony that would correspond to a laying-on of hands, he brought with him his chief of staff and fellow townsman, Brigadier General John Rawlins, who had come east with him from Nashville in response to the presidential summons, and the thirteen-year-old Fred. Promptly at 1 o'clock, as scheduled, the Galena trio was shown into the presence of the President, the seven members of his Cabinet, his private secretary John Nicolay, and Major General Henry W. Halleck, the present general-in-chief, over whose head the man they had gathered to honor was about to be advanced. Facing Grant, Lincoln handed him the official document and read the speech of which he had given him a copy the night before. "General Grant: The nation's appreciation of what you have done and its reliance upon you for what remains to do in the existing great struggle are now presented with this commission, constituting you lieutenant general in the Army of the United States. With this high honor devolves upon you also a corresponding responsibility. As the country herein trusts you, so under God it will sustain you. I scarcely need to add that with what I here speak for the nation goes my own hearty personal concurrence." Brief as this was, Grant's response was briefer by seven words. He took from his coat pocket a half-sheet of notepaper covered with a hasty lead-pencil scrawl. Either the light was poor or else he had trouble reading his own writing. In any case he read it badly. "Mr President," he replied, groping and hesitant as he strained to decipher the words: "I accept this commission with gratitude for the high honor con-ferred. With the aid of the noble armies that have fought on so many fields, it will be my earnest endeavor not to disappoint your expecta-tions. I feel the full weight of the responsibilities now devolving on me and know that if they are met it will be due to those armies, and above all to the favor of that Providence which leads both nations and men."

The surprise in this, to anyone aware of the Blue Room exchange the night before, was that the general had not incorporated either of the remarks the President recommended for inclusion in his acceptance speech. Nicolay, for one, thought that Grant, in an attempt to establish an independence none of his predecessors had enjoyed, had decided it would be wise to begin his career as general-in-chief by disregarding any suggestions from above. Lincoln himself, on the other hand, seemed not to notice the omission which his secretary considered, if not a downright act of insubordination, then in any case a snub.

Once the congratulations were over, the two leaders had a short talk that began with Grant asking what special service was required of him. The taking of Richmond, Lincoln said, adding wryly that the generals who had been told this in the past "had not been fortunate in their efforts in that direction." Did Grant think he could do it? Grant replied that he could if he had the troops, whereupon Lincoln assured him that he would have them. That ended their first strategy conference, such as it was, and Nicolay observed that nothing was said as to the route or method to be employed, the jump-off date, or the amount of time the operation would require. All Grant said was that he could take Richmond if he had the troops, and Lincoln had been willing to let it go at that; after which the general took his leave. He was going down to Virginia today, specifically to Brandy Station, headquarters of the Army of the Potomac, for a consultation with its commander as a prelude to the planning of his over-all campaign.

One thing remained to be done before he got aboard the train. No truly recognizable photograph had been made of him since the early days of the war, when his beard reached the middle buttons on his blouse, and he had agreed — perhaps without considering that he thus would lose the near-anonymity he had enjoyed among strangers up to now — to an appointment that would remedy the lack. Accompanied by Stanton, who proposed to go to the station to see him off, he rode from the White House, down Pennsylvania Avenue, to the intersection of Seventh Street, where the carriage stopped in front of Mathew Brady's Portrait Gallery. The photographer was waiting anxiously, and wasted no time in getting the general upstairs into what he called his "operating room," where he had four of his big cameras ready for action. It was past 4 o'clock by now and the light was failing; so while Grant took his place in a chair on which the cameras, their lenses two full feet in length and just under half a foot in diameter, were trained like a battery of siege guns, Brady sent an assistant up on the roof to draw back the shade from the skylight directly overhead. To his horror, the fellow stumbled, both feet crashing through the glass to let fall a shower of jagged shards around the general below. "It was a miracle that some of the pieces didn't strike him," the photographer later said. "And if one had, it would have been the end of Grant; for that glass was two inches thick." Still more surprising, in its way, was the general's reaction. He glanced up casually, with "a barely perceptible quiver of the nostril," then as casually back down, and that was all. This seemed to Brady "the most remarkable display of nerve I ever witnessed."

It was otherwise with Stanton, who appeared unstrung: not only for Grant's sake, as it turned out, but also for his own, though none of the splinters had landed anywhere near him. Grasping the photographer by the arm, he pulled him aside and sputtered excitedly, "Not a word about this, Brady, not a word! You must never breathe a word of what happened here today. . . . It would be impossible to convince the people that this was not an attempt at assassination!"

The train made good time from Alexandria, chuffing through Manassas and Warrenton Junction, on to Brandy, a distance of just under sixty miles; Grant arrived in a driving rain, soon after nightfall, to find that the Army of the Potomac, whatever its shortcomings in other respects — there was scarcely a place-name on the landscape that did not mark the scene of one or more of its defeats — knew how to greet a visitor in style. A regiment of Zouaves, snappy in red fezzes and baggy trousers, was drawn up to give him a salute on his arrival, despite the rain, and a headquarters band, happily unaware that Grant was tone-deaf — he once remarked that he only knew two tunes in all: "One was Yankee Doodle. The other wasn't" — played vigorous music by way of welcome as the army commander, Major General George G. Meade, emerged from his tent for a salute and a handshake. He and Grant, six years his junior and eight years behind him at West Point, had not met since the Mexican War, sixteen years ago, when they were lieutenants.

Tall and dour, professorial in appearance, with a hook nose, a gray-shot beard, glinting spectacles, and heavy pouches under his eyes, Meade was one of the problems that would have to be dealt with before other, larger problems could be tackled. Specifically, the question was whether to keep him where he was, a prima donna commander of a prima donna army, or remove him. His trouble, aside from a hair-trigger temper that kept his staff on edge and caused associates to refer to him, behind his back, as "a damned old goggle-eyed snapping turtle," was that he lacked the quality which Grant not only personified himself but also prized highest in a subordinate: the killer instinct. At Gettysburg eight months ago, after less than a week in command, Meade had defeated and driven the rebel invaders from his native Pennsylvania, but then, with his foe at bay on the near bank of a flooded, bridgeless river, had flinched from delivering the coup de grâce which Lincoln, for one, was convinced would have ended the war. Instead, the Confederates, low on ammunition and bled down to not much more than half their strength, had withdrawn unmolested across the rain-swollen Potomac to take up a new defensive position behind the Rapidan, where they still were. Meade had crossed in late November, with the intention of coming to grips with them in the wintry south-bank thickets, but then at the last minute had held his hand; had returned, in fact, ingloriously to the north bank, and ever since had seemed content to settle for the stalemate that resulted, despite practically unremittent prodding from the press and the politicians in his rear. Just last week he had been grilled by Congress's radical-dominated Joint Committee on the Conduct of the War, whose members for the most part, in admiration of his politics and his bluster, favored recalling Major General Joseph Hooker to the post he had lost to Meade on the eve of Gettysburg. Much bitterness had ensued between the Pennsylvanian and his critics; "My enemies," he called them in a letter this week to a kinsman, maintaining that they consisted "of certain politicians who wish me removed to restore Hooker; then of certain subordinates, whose military reputations are involved in the destruction of mine; finally, [of] a class of vultures who in Hooker's day preyed upon the army, and who sigh for a return of those glorious days."

This was accurate enough, as far as it went, but it seemed to Grant — as, indeed, it must have done to even a casual observer — that the trouble lay deeper, in the ranks of the army itself. Partly the reason was boredom, a lack of employment in the craft for which its members had been trained. "A winter in tents is monotonous," one officer complained. "Card playing, horse racing, and kindred amusements become stale when made a steady occupation." Moreover, Grant would have agreed with an assessment later made by a young West Pointer, a newcomer like himself to the eastern theater, that the trouble with the Army of the Potomac, predating both Meade and Hooker, was its "lack of springy formation and audacious, self-reliant initiative. This organic weakness was entirely due to not having had in its youth skillfully aggressive leadership. Its early commanders had dissipated war's best elixir by training it into a life of caution, and the evil of that schooling it had shown on more than one occasion."

Before coming down to Brandy, Grant had rather inclined to the belief that the removal of Meade was a prerequisite to correction of this state of mind in the army he commanded. But once the round of greetings and introductions had ended and the corps and division commanders had retired for the night, leaving the two men alone for a private conference, Meade showed Grant a side of himself that proved not only attractive but disarming. He began by saying that he supposed Grant would want to replace him with some general who had served with him before and was therefore familiar with his way of doing things: Major General William T. Sherman, for example, who had been Grant's mainstay in practically all of his campaigns to date. If so, Meade declared, he hoped there would be no hesitation on his account, since (as Grant paraphrased it afterwards) "the work before us was of such vast importance to the whole nation that the feeling or wishes of no one person should stand in the way of selecting the right men for all positions. For himself, he would serve to the best of his ability wherever placed." Grant was impressed. The offer, he said, gave him "even a more favorable opinion of Meade than did his great victory at Gettysburg," and he assured him, then and there, that he had "no thought of substituting anyone for him," least of all Sherman, who "could not be spared from the West." Now it was Meade who was impressed, and he said as much the following day in a letter to his wife. "I was much pleased with Grant," he wrote, "and most agreeably disappointed in his evidence of mind and character. You may rest assured he is not an ordinary man."

Mutual admiration on the part of the two leaders might be a good and healthy thing for all concerned, but the troops themselves, having paid in blood for the blasting of a number of overblown reputations in the drawn-out course of the war, were unconvinced and noncommittal. While this latest addition to the doleful list of their commanders was on his way eastward, they had engaged in some rather idle speculation as to his professional ability, and it did not seem to them that the mere addition of a third star to each of his shoulders would necessarily increase his military worth.

"Who's this Grant that's made a lieutenant general?"

"He's the hero of Vicksburg."

"Well, Vicksburg wasn't much of a fight. The rebs were out of rations and they had to surrender or starve. They had nothing but dead mules and dogs to eat, as I understand."

About the best thing they could say for him was that he was unlikely to be any worse than John Pope, who had also brought a western reputation east, only to lose it at Bull Run. "He cannot be weaker or more inefficient," a jaundiced New York veteran declared, "than the generals who have wasted the lives of our comrades during the past three years." For one thing, Grant was likely to find a good deal less room between bullets here in Virginia than he had found in the region of his fame. "If he's a fighter," another hard-case infantryman put it, "he can find all the fighting he wants." Then he arrived and some of them got a look at him. What they saw was scarcely reassuring.

"Well, what do you think?" one asked a friend, who replied thoughtfully, having studied the firm-set mouth and the level glance of the clear blue eyes:

"He looks as if he meant it."

Nodding agreement, the first allowed that they would find out for themselves before too long. Meanwhile he was willing to defer judgment, except as to looks. "He's a little 'un," he said.

Talk of Vicksburg brought on the inevitable comparison of western and eastern Confederates, with particular reference to the presence here in the Old Dominion of General Robert E. Lee, the South's first soldier. Grant could never have penned up Lee, as he had done John Pemberton, thereby forcing his surrender by starvation; Lee, they said, "would have broken out some way and foraged around for supplies." Thus the men. And Rawlins, as he moved among the officers on Meade's staff, found a similar respect for the southern commander, as if they took almost as great a pride in having opposed "Mars Robert" as the Virginian's tattered veterans took in serving under him. "Well, you never met Bobby Lee and his boys," they replied when Grant's chief of staff presumed to speak of victories in the West. "It would be quite different if you had." As for the campaign about to open here in the East, they seemed to expect nothing more than another version of the old story: advance and retreat, Grant or no Grant. They listened rather impatiently while Rawlins spoke of past successes, off on the far margin of the map. "That may be," they said. "But, mind you, Bobby Lee is just over the Rapidan."

In any case, whatever opinions had been formed or deferred, the new chieftain and his major eastern army had at least had a look at each other, and next morning, after a second conference at which both past and future campaigns in Virginia were discussed, Grant returned to the station and got aboard the train for Washington. Last night he had received a presidential telegram extending an invitation from Mrs Lincoln for him and Meade "to dine with us Saturday evening," and he had replied by wire that they were pleased to accept. Overnight, however, he changed his mind. Today was Friday, March 11, and he would be leaving at once for the West — but only for a visit of a week or ten days, in order to confer with Sherman and other commanders there; after which, despite his previous resolution to avoid the political snares so thickly strewn about the eastern theater, he would be returning here to stay. Paradoxically, now that he had seen them at first hand, it was just those snares that determined his decision. "When I got to Washington and saw the situation," he later explained, "it was plain that here was the point for the commanding general to be. No one else could, probably, resist the pressure that would be brought to bear upon him to desist from his own plans and pursue others."

Not that the adulation and the invasions of his privacy did not continue to go against his grain. They did indeed. Closeted that afternoon with the President at the White House, he complained that the past three days, in Washington and at Brandy, had been "rather the warmest campaign I have witnessed during the war." Lincoln could sympathize with this, but he was disappointed that the general would not stay on through tomorrow night for the banquet planned in his honor. "We can't excuse you," he protested. "Mrs Lincoln's dinner without you would be *Hamlet* with Hamlet left out." But Grant was firm. "I appreciate the honor Mrs Lincoln would do me," he said, "but time is very important now. And really, Mr Lincoln," he added frankly, "I have had enough of this show business."

He left that evening on a westbound train, with stops for inspection at several points along the way, and reached Nashville in time to keep a St Patrick's Day appointment with Sherman, whose troops were advanced beyond Chattanooga, into northwest Georgia, to confront the main western Confederate army under General Joseph E. Johnston, around Dalton. They traveled together by rail to Cincinnati, the voluble red-head, "tall, angular, and spare, as if his superabundant energy had consumed his flesh" — so an acquaintance saw him at the time — and the new lieutenant general, who had once been described as "a man who could be silent in several languages" and who now seemed doubly reticent by contrast with his talkative companion. In the Ohio city they left the cars and checked into a hotel for privacy and room to spread their maps. There they worked on a preliminary draft of the over-all campaign which Sherman defined long afterwards: "He was to go for Lee and I was to go for Joe Johnston. That was his plan."

That was what it basically was. That was what it came to, in the end. At the outset, however, the plan — which might better have been defined, at this stage, as a plan for a plan — was a good deal more complicated, involving a great many other forces that were thrown, or were intended to be thrown, into action against the South. Grant had under him more than half a million combat soldiers, "present for duty, equipped," about half of them in the ranks of six field armies, three in the East and three in the West, while the other half were scattered about the country in nineteen various departments, from New England to New Mexico and beyond. His notion was to pry as many as possible of the latter out of their garrisons, transfer them to the mobile forces in the field, and bring the resultant mass to bear in "a simultaneous movement all along the line." Long ago in Mexico, during a lull in the war, he had written home to the girl he later married: "If we have to fight, I would like to do it all at once and then make friends." Apparently he felt even more this way about it now that the enemy were his fellow countrymen. In any case, the plan as he evolved it seemed to indicate as much.

"From an early period of the rebellion," he said afterward, looking back, "I had been impressed with the idea that active and continuous operations of all the troops that could be brought into the field, regardless of season and weather, were necessary to a speedy termination of the war." The trouble from the outset, east and west, was that the Federal armies had "acted independently and without concert, like a balky team, no two ever pulling together, enabling the enemy to use to great advantage his interior lines of communication." It was this that had made possible several of the greatest Confederate triumphs, from First Bull Run to Chickamauga, where reinforcements from other rebel departments and even other theaters had tipped the tactical scale against the

Union. "I determined to stop this," Grant declared. Moreover, convinced as he was "that no peace could be had that would be stable and conducive to the happiness of the people, both North and South, until the military power of the rebellion was entirely broken," he held fast to his old guideline; he would work toward Unconditional Surrender. He had it very much in mind to destroy not only the means of resistance by his adversaries, but also the will. The Confederacy was not only to be defeated, it was to be defeated utterly, and not only in the field, where the battles were fought, but also on the home front, where the goods of war were produced. "War is cruelty," Sherman had said four months ago, in response to a southern matron's complaint that his men appeared hardhanded on occasion. "There is no use trying to reform it. The crueler it is, the sooner it will be over." Grant felt much the same way about the matter, and here at the start, in formulating his plan for achieving what he called "a speedy termination," he was determined to be guided by two principles of action: 1) "to use the greatest number of troops practicable," and 2) "to hammer continuously against the armed force of the enemy and his resources, until by mere attrition, if in no other way, there should be nothing left to him but an equal submission with the loyal section of our common country to the Constitution and the laws of the land."

To achieve the first of these, the concentration of fighting men on the actual firing line, he proposed that most of the troops now scattered along the Atlantic coast, in Florida, Georgia, and the Carolinas, be brought to Virginia for a convergent attack on Richmond and the army posted northward in its defense. All down the littoral, various forces of various sizes were attempting to make their way toward various objectives, few if any of them vital to Grant's main purpose. Accordingly, he prepared orders for abandoning all such efforts south of the James, along with as much of the region so far occupied as was not clearly needed to maintain or strengthen the naval blockade. The same would apply in the West, along the Mississippi River from New Orleans to Cairo, where the men thus gained were to be employed in a similar convergence upon Atlanta and the forces likewise posted in its defense. As for the troops held deep in the national rear, serving mainly by their numbers to justify the lofty rank of political or discredited generals assigned to duty there, Grant proposed to abolish some of these commands by merging superfluous departments, thus freeing the men for duty at the front. As for the generals themselves, useless as most of them were for combat purposes, he favored their outright dismissal, which would open the way for just that many promotions in the field. Though this last was rather a ticklish business, verging as it did on the political, he thought it altogether worth a try because of the added opportunities it would afford him to reward the ablest and bravest of his subordinate commanders, even before the fighting got under way, and thus incite the rest to follow their example. By such methods (though little came of the last; out of more than a hundred generals Grant recommended for removal, Lincoln let no more than a handful go, mindful as he had to be of the danger of making influential enemies with the presidential election less than nine months off) he would reduce the ratio of garrison to combat troops from one-to-one to one-to-two, which in itself was a considerable accomplishment, one that no previous general-in-chief, from Winfield Scott through George McClellan to Henry Halleck, had conceived to be possible even as a goal.

As for his method of employing that continuous hammering which he believed was the surest if not the only way to bring the South to her knees, the key would be found in orders presently issued to the commanders involved: "So far as practicable all the armies are to move together, and toward one common center." This was to be applied in two stages. West and East, there would be separate but simultaneous convergences upon respective goals, Atlanta and Richmond, by all the mobile forces within each theater; after which, the first to be successful in accomplishing that preliminary task — the reduction of the assigned objective, along with the defeat of the rebel army charged with its defense — would turn east or west, as the case might be, to join the other and thus be in on the kill, the "speedy termination" for which Grant had conceived his grand design. It was for this, the western half of it at least, that he had come to Tennessee to confer with Sherman, his successor in command of the largest of the three main armies in this and the enormous adjoining theater beyond the Mississippi.

There the commanders of the Departments of the Gulf and Arkansas, Major Generals Nathaniel P. Banks and Frederick Steele, were engaged in the opening phase of a campaign of which Grant disapproved and which they themselves had undertaken reluctantly on orders from Lincoln, issued through Halleck before Grant was given over-all command. Advancing on Shreveport by way of Red River, which would afford them gunboat support, they were charged with the invasion and conquest of East Texas, not because there was much of strategic importance there, but because of certain machinations by the French in Mexico, which Lincoln thought it best to block by the occupation of Texas, thus to prevent a possible link-up between the forces of Napoleon III and those of the Confederacy, with which that monarch was believed to be sympathetic. Grant opposed the plan, not because of its international implications, of which he knew little and understood less, but because of its interference with, or in any case its nonfurtherance of, his design for ending the rebellion by concentrating "the greatest number of troops practicable" against its military and manufacturing centers. None of these was in the Lone Star State, so far at least as he could see, or for that matter anywhere else in the Transmississippi, which he preferred to leave to the incidental attention of Steele alone, while

Banks moved eastward, across the Mississippi, to play a truly vital role in the drama now being cast. Yet here he was, not only moving in the opposite direction, but taking with him no less than 10,000 of Sherman's best soldiers, temporarily assigned by Halleck to assist him in seizing the Texas barrens. Grant found this close to intolerable, and though he could not directly countermand an order issued by authority of the Commander in Chief, he could at least set a limit to the extent of the penetration and, above all, to the amount of time allowed for the execution of the order, and thus ensure that Sherman would get his veterans back in time for the opening of the offensive in northwest Georgia. Accordingly, two days before Sherman joined him in Nashville on March 17, he wrote to Banks informing him that, while he regarded "the success of your present move as of great importance in reducing the number of troops necessary for protecting the navigation of the Mississippi River," he wanted him to "commence no move for the further acquisition of territory" beyond Shreveport, which, he emphasized, "should be taken as soon as possible," so that, leaving Steele to hold what had been won, he himself could return with his command to New Orleans in time for the eastward movement Grant had in mind for him to undertake in conjunction with Sherman's advance on Atlanta. Above all, Banks was told, if it appeared that Shreveport could not be taken before the end of April, he was to return Sherman's 10,000 veterans by the middle of that month, "even if it leads to the abandonment of the main object of your expedition."

Sherman's own instructions, as stated afterward by Grant in his final report, were quite simple and to the point. He was "to move against Johnston's army, to break it up, and go into the interior of the enemy's country as far as he could, inflicting all the damage he could upon their war resources." For the launching of this drive on the Confederate heartland — admittedly a large order — the Ohioan would have the largest army in the country, even without the troops regrettably detached to Banks across the way. It included, in fact, three separate armies combined into one, each of them under a major general. First, and largest, there was George Thomas's Army of the Cumberland, badly whipped six months ago at Chickamauga, under Major General William S. Rosecrans, but reinforced since by three divisions from Meade for the Chattanooga breakout under Thomas, which had thrown General Braxton Bragg back on Dalton and caused his replacement by Joe Johnston. Next there was the Army of the Tennessee, veterans of Donelson and Shiloh under Grant, of Vicksburg and Missionary Ridge under Sherman, now under James B. McPherson, who had been promoted to fill the vacancy created by Sherman's advancement to head the whole. Finally there was the Army of the Ohio, youngest and smallest of the three, takers of Knoxville and survivors of the siege that followed under Major General Ambrose Burnside, who was succeeded now by

John M. Schofield, lately transferred from guerilla-torn Missouri. Made up in all of twenty infantry and four cavalry divisions, these three armies comprised the Military Division of the Mississippi under Sherman, redoubtable "Uncle Billy" to the 120,000 often rowdy western veterans on its rolls. This was considerably better than twice the number reported to be with Johnston around Dalton, but the defenders had a reserve force of perhaps as many as 20,000 under Lieutenant General Leonidas Polk at Demopolis, Alabama, and Meridian, Mississippi, in position to be hastened by rail either to Mobile or Atlanta, whichever came under pressure in the offensive the North was expected to open before long.

That was where Banks came in; that was why Grant had been so insistent that the Massachusetts general finish up the Red River operation without delay, in order to get his army back to New Orleans for an eastward march with 35,000 soldiers against Mobile, which would also be attacked from the water side by Rear Admiral David G. Farragut, whose Gulf squadron would be strengthened by the addition of several of the ironclads now on station outside Charleston, where the naval attack had stalled and which, in any case, was no longer on the agenda of targets to be hit. This double danger to Mobile would draw Polk's reserve force southward from Meridian and Demopolis, away from Atlanta and any assistance it might otherwise have rendered Johnston in resisting Sherman's steamroller drive on Dalton and points south. Later, when Banks and Sherman had achieved their primary goals, the reduction of Mobile and Atlanta, they would combine at the latter place for a farther penetration, eastward to the Atlantic and Lee's rear, if Lee was still a factor in the struggle by that time. "All I would now add," Grant told Banks in a follow-up letter sent two weeks after the first, "is that you commence the concentration of your forces at once. Preserve a profound secrecy of what you intend doing, and start at the earliest possible moment."

Such, then, was the nature of the offensive Grant intended to launch in the West, with Sherman bearing the main tactical burden. Similarly in the East, in accordance with his general plan "to concentrate all the force possible against the Confederate armies in the field," he planned for Meade to move in a similar manner, similarly assisted by a diversionary attack on the enemy rear. But he wanted it made clear from the start that this was to be something more than just another "On to Richmond" drive, at least so far as Meade himself was concerned. "Lee's army will be your objective point," his instructions read. "Wherever Lee goes, there you will go also."

If past experience showed anything, it clearly showed that in Virginia almost anything could happen. Moreover, with Lee in opposition, that *anything* was likely to be disastrous from the Federal point of view. Four of the five offensives so far launched against him — those by McClellan, by Pope, by Burnside, by Hooker — had broken in blood and ended in headlong blue retreat, while the fifth — Meade's own, the previous fall — had managed nothing better than a stalemate; which last, in the light of Grant's views on the need for unrelenting pressure, was barely preferable to defeat. Numerical odds had favored the Union to small avail in those encounters, including Hooker's three-to-one advantage, yet that was a poor argument against continuing to make them as long as possible. Just now, as a result of the westward detachments in September, the Army of the Potomac was down to fewer than one hundred thousand men. By way of lengthening the odds, Grant proposed to bring unemployed Ambrose Burnside back east to head a corps of four newly raised divisions which would rendezvous at Annapolis, thus puzzling the enemy as to their eventual use, down the coast or in Virginia proper, until the time came for the Rapidan crossing, when they would move in support of the Army of the Potomac, raising its strength to beyond 120,000 effectives, distributed among fifteen infantry and three cavalry divisions.

Such assurance as this gave was by no means certain. Lee was foxy. No mere numerical advantage had served to fix him in position for slaughter in the past. But Grant had other provisions in mind for securing that result, involving the use of the other two eastern armies. In the West, the three mobile forces had three separate primary assignments: going for Johnston, taking Mobile, riding herd on Transmississippi rebels. In the East, all three were to have the same objective from the start.

Posted in defense of West Virginia and the Maryland-Pennsylvania frontier, the smallest of these three armies was commanded by Major General Franz Sigel; "I fights mit Sigel" was the proud boast of thousands of soldiers, German-born like himself, who had been drawn to the colors by his example. This force was not available for use elsewhere, since its left lay squarely athwart the northern entrance to the Shenandoah Valley, that classic avenue of Confederate invasion exploited so brilliantly two years ago by Stonewall Jackson, who had used it to play on Lincoln's fears, thereby contributing largely to the frustration of McClellan's drive on Richmond at a time when the van of his army could hear the hours struck by the city's public clocks. To Grant, however, the fact that Sigel's 26,000 troops were not considered withdrawable, lest another rebel general use the Valley approach to serve him as Stonewall had served Little Mac, did not mean that this force was not usable as part of the drive on the Virginia capital and the gray army charged with its defense. It seemed to him, rather, that a movement up the Valley by a major portion of Sigel's command would serve even better than an immobile guard, posted across its northern entrance — or exit — to deny it to the enemy as a channel of invasion. Elaborating on this, he directed that the advance was to be in two columns, one under Brigadier General George Crook, who would march west of the

Alleghenies for a rapid descent on the Virginia & Tennessee Railroad, along which vital supply line he would move eastward, tearing up track as he went, then north for a meeting near Staunton with Sigel himself, who would have led the other column directly up the Valley. There they would combine for a strike at Lee's flank while Meade engaged his front; or if by then Lee had fallen back on Richmond, as expected, they would join in the pursuit, by way of the Virginia Central — another vital supply line — to the gates of the city and beyond.

So much for the task assigned the second of the three Union armies in Virginia. The third, being larger, had a correspondingly larger assignment, with graver dangers and quite the highest prize of all awaiting the prompt fulfillment of its task.

One reason Grant expected Lee to fall back on Richmond in short order, before Sigel had time to get in position on his flank, was that he intended to oblige him to do so by launching a back-door attack on the capital, from across the James, at the same time Meade was effecting a crossing of the Rapidan, sixty-odd miles to the north. The commander of this third force would be Major General Benjamin F. Butler, who had won a reputation for deftness, along with the nickname "Spoons," in the course of his highly profitable occupation of New Orleans, all of last year and most of the year before. Much as Sigel had been commissioned to attract German-born patriots to the colors, Butler had been made a general to prove to Democrats — at whose Charleston convention in 1860 he had voted fifty-seven consecutive times to nominate Jefferson Davis for President of the United States — that the war was not exclusively a Republican affair; Grant did not select, he inherited him, political abilities and all. For the work at hand, the former Bay State senator would have some 35,000 effectives of all arms, about half of them to be brought up from Florida and South Carolina by the commander of the Department of the South, Major General Quincy A. Gillmore, while the other half would be drawn from Butler's own Department of Virginia and North Carolina. He was to have naval support in moving up the James from his initial base at Fortress Monroe, as well as for the landing at City Point. That would put him within easy reach of Petersburg, the southside railroad center only twenty miles from his true objective, Richmond, which he was then to seize by means of a sudden lunge across the river. Or if Lee had managed a quick fall-back in such strength as to prevent a crossing at that point, Butler, having severed the city's rail connections with the granaries to the south, would combine with Meade and Sigel, upstream or down, for the resultant siege of the capital and its eventual surrender.

If all went as intended in the three-way squeeze he had designed to achieve Lee's encompassment, Grant himself would be there to receive the gray commander's sword at the surrender ceremony. For by now he had decided not only that he would return to the East for the duration of the war, so as to be able to interpose between the Washington politicians and the strategy they might attempt to subvert, but also that the most effective position from which to do this would be in close proximity to the headquarters of the Army of the Potomac. There were, indeed — in addition to the most obvious one, that being in the field would remove him from the constricting atmosphere of the District of Columbia and the disconcerting stares of over-curious civilians, in and out of government — several reasons for the decision: not the least of which was that Meade, in command of much the largest of the three armies in Virginia and charged with much the heaviest burden in the fighting, was outranked not only by Butler and Sigel, whose armies were assigned less arduous tasks, but also by Burnside, whose corps would move in his support and had to be more or less subject to his orders if he was to avoid delays that might prove disastrous. Although the problem could be ignored in the easier-going West — there Thomas, for instance, outranked Sherman, and McPherson was junior to several other major generals in all three armies — Easterners were notoriously touchy about such matters, and if a command crisis arose from the striking of personality sparks on the question of rank, Grant wanted to be there to settle it in person, as only he could do. If this resulted in some discomfort for Meade, whose style might be cramped and whose glory would no doubt be dimmed by the presence of a superior constantly peering over his shoulder and nudging his elbow, this was regrettable, but not nearly as much so, certainly, as various other unfortunate things that might happen without Grant there.

Besides, there was still another reason, perhaps of more importance than all the rest combined. For all its bleeding and dying these past three years, on a scale no other single army could approach, the paper-collar Army of the Potomac had precious few real victories to its credit. It had, in fact, in its confrontations with the adversary now awaiting its advance into the thickets on the south bank of the river it was about to cross, a well-founded and long-nurtured tradition of defeat. The correction for this, Grant believed, was the development of self-confidence, which seemed to him an outgrowth of aggressiveness, an eagerness to come to grips with the enemy and a habit of thinking of wounds it would inflict rather than of wounds it was likely to suffer. So far, this outlook had been characteristic not of eastern but of western armies; Grant hoped to effect, in person, a transference of this spirit which he had done so much to create in the past. Twenty months ago, it was true, John Pope had come east "to infuse a little western energy" into the flaccid ranks of the accident-prone divisions that came under his command in the short-lived Army of Virginia. Unfortunately, he had only contrived to lengthen by one (or two or three, if Cedar Mountain and Chantilly were included) the list of spectacular defeats;

his troops had wound up cowering in the Washington defenses — what was left of them after the thrashing Lee had administered, flank and rear. But Grant, despite this lamentable example, had much the same victory formula in mind. The difference was that he backed it up, as Pope had been unable to do, with an over-all plan, on a national scale, that embodied the spirit of the offensive.

Sherman, for one, believed he would succeed, although the severely compressed and beleaguered Confederacy still amounted, as Grant said, to "an empire in extent." He expected victory, not only because of the plan they had developed in part between them in the Cincinnati hotel room, but also because he believed that the struggle had entered a new phase, one that for the first time favored the forces of the Union, which at last had come of age, in a military sense, while those of the South were sliding past their prime. Or so at any rate it seemed to Sherman. "It was not until after both Gettysburg and Vicksburg that the war professionally began," he later declared. "Then our men had learned in the dearest school on earth the simple lesson of war... and it was then that we as professional soldiers could rightly be held to a just responsibility." Heartened by the prospect, he expressed his confidence to Grant before they parted: he to return to Nashville, the headquarters of his new command, and his friend and superior to Washington for a time, riding eastward past crowds that turned out to cheer him at every station along the way.

Nor was there any slackening of the adulation at the end of the line. "General Grant is all the rage," Sherman heard from his senator brother John the following week. "He is subjected to the disgusting but dangerous process of being lionized. He is followed by crowds, and is cheered everywhere." The senator was worried about the effect all this might have on the man at whom it was directed. "While he must despise the fickle fools who run after him, he, like most others, may be spoiled by this excess of flattery. He may be so elated as to forget the uncertain tenure upon which he holds and stakes his really well-earned laurels." Sherman, though he was pleased to note that his brother added: "He is plain and modest, and so far bears himself well," was quick to jump to his friend's defense, wherein he coupled praise with an admonition. "Grant is as good a leader as we can find," he replied. "He has honesty, simplicity of character, singleness of purpose, and no hope or claim to usurp civil power. His character, more than his genius, will reconcile armies and attach the people. Let him alone. Don't disgust him by flattery or importunity. Let him alone."

Let him alone, either then or later, was the one thing almost no one in Washington seemed willing to do; except Lincoln, who assured Grant that he intended to do just that, at least in a military sense. "The

particulars of your plan I neither know nor seek to know," he was to
tell him presently, on the eve of commitment, and even at their first
interview, before the general left for Tennessee, he had told him (according to Grant's recollection of the exchange, years later) "that
he had never professed to be a military man or to know how campaigns
should be conducted . . . but that procrastination on the part of commanders and the pressure from the people at the North and Congress,
which was always with him, forced him to issue his series of 'Military
Orders' — one, two, three, etc. He did not know but they were all
wrong, and did know that some of them were. All he wanted or had
ever wanted was someone who would take the responsibility and act,
and call on him for all the assistance needed."

Welcome though this was to hear, Grant was no doubt aware
that the President had said similar things to previous commanders (John
C. Frémont, for example, whom he told: "I have given you carte
blanche. You must use your own judgment, and do the best you can."
Or McClellan, who quoted his assurances after Antietam: "General,
you have saved the country. You must remain in command and carry
us through to the end. I pledge myself to stand between you and harm")
only to jerk the rug from under their feet a short time later, when their
backs were turned; Lincoln had never been one to keep a promise any
longer than he believed the good of the country was involved. However,
in this case he supplemented his private with public remarks to the
same effect. "Grant is the first *general* I have had," he was reported to
be saying. "I am glad to find a man who can go ahead without me."
To a friend who doubted that Grant should be given so free a rein, he
replied: "Do you hire a man to do your work and then do it yourself?"
To another, who remarked that he was looking well these days, he responded with an analogy. "Oh, yes, I feel better," he laughed, "for now
I'm like the man who was blown up on a steamboat and said, on coming
down, 'It makes no difference to me; I'm only a passenger.' "

Partly Lincoln's ebullience was the result of having learned, if not
the particulars, then at any rate certain features of Grant's plan. Of its
details, an intimate said later that they "were communicated only to
Grant's most important or most trusted subordinates" — Meade, Butler,
and Sigel, of course, along with Sherman and Banks. "To no others,
except to members of his personal staff, did Grant impart a knowledge
of his plans; and, even among these, there were some with whom he was
reticent." The President and the Secretary of War were both excluded,
though he was willing to discuss with them the principle to be applied in
bringing "the greatest number of troops practicable" to bear against
the forces in rebellion; for example, that the units charged with the
occupation of captured territory and the prevention of rebel incursions
into the North "could perform this service just as well by advancing as

by remaining still, and by advancing they would compel the enemy to keep detachments to hold them back, or else lay his own territory open to invasion." Lincoln saw the point at once, having urged it often in the past, although with small success. "Those not skinning can hold a leg," he said. Grant, as the son of a tanner, knew that this had reference to hog-killing time in the West, where all hands were given a share in the work even though there were not enough skinning-knives to go round. He liked the expression so well, in fact, that he passed it along to Sherman the following week in a letter explaining Sigel's share in the Virginia campaign: "If Sigel can't skin himself he can hold a leg while someone else skins."

By that time he was in the field, where he enjoyed greater privacy in working on his plan for the distribution of knives to be used in flaying the South alive. Having returned to Washington on March 23, he established headquarters three days later at Culpeper, six miles beyond Brandy Station on the Orange & Alexandria Railroad, about midway between the Rappahannock and the Rapidan. This was the week of the vernal equinox; tomorrow was Easter Sunday. Yet a fifteen-inch snow had fallen that Tuesday and the land was still locked in the grip of winter, as if to mock the hope expressed to Sherman that the armies could launch their separate but concentric attacks by April 25. To the west, in plain view, the Blue Ridge Mountains bore on their peaks and slopes deep drifts of snow, which Grant had been told by old-timers hereabouts would have to have melted away before he could be sure that bad weather had gone for good and the roads would support his moving trains and guns. Down here on the flat at least its whiteness served to hide the scars inflicted by commanders North and South, who, as one observer remarked, "had led their armies up and down these fields and made the landscape desolate." Roundabout Culpeper, he added, "not a house nor a fence, not a tree was to be seen for miles, where once all had been cultivated farmland or richly wooded country. Here and there, a stack of chimneys or a broken cistern marked the site of a former homestead, but every other landmark had been destroyed. The very hills were stripped of their forest panoply, and a man could hardly recognize the haunts familiar to him in his childhood."

Although at present much of this was mercifully blanketed from sight, the worst of the scars no snow could hide, for they existed in men's minds and signified afflictions of the spirit, afflictions Grant would have to overcome before he could instill into the Army of the Potomac the self-confidence and aggressiveness which he considered prerequisite to the successful prosecution of its offensive against an adversary famed throughout the world as the embodiment of the qualities said to be lacking on the near side of the river that ran between the armies. Discouraging to his hopes for the inculcation of the spirit of the offensive, the very landmarks scattered about this fought-over section of Virginia served as doleful reminders of what such plans had come to in the past. Westward beyond the snow-clad Blue Ridge lay the Shenandoah Valley, where Banks and Frémont had been sorely drubbed and utterly confused, and northeastward, leading down this way, ran the course of the Buckland Races, in which the cavalry had been chased and taunted. Cedar Mountain loomed dead ahead; there Sigel, thrown forward by bristly Pope, had come a cropper, as Pope himself had done only three weeks later, emulating the woeful example of Irvin McDowell on the plains of Manassas, where the rebels feasted on his stores, forty miles back up the railroad. Downriver about half that distance, Burnside had suffered the throbbing pain and numbing indignity of the Fredericksburg blood-bath and the Mud March; while close at hand, just over the Rapidan, brooded the Wilderness, where Hooker had come to grief in a May riot of smoke-choked greenery and Meade had nearly done the same, inching forward through the ice-cramped woods a scant four months ago, except that he pulled back in time to avoid destruction. All these were painful memories to the veterans who had survived them and passed them on to recruits as a tradition of defeat — a tradition which Grant was seeking now, if not to erase (for it could never be erased; it was too much a part of history, kept alive in the pride of the butternut scarecrows over the river) then at any rate to overcome by locking it firmly in the past and replacing it with one of victory.

In working thus at his plans for bringing that tradition into existence, here and elsewhere, he was assisted greatly by a command arrangement allowed for in the War Department order appointing him general-in-chief in place of Halleck, who was relieved "at his own request" and made chief of staff, an office created to provide a channel of communication between Grant and his nineteen department heads, particularly in administrative matters. The work would be heavy for Old Brains, the glory slight; Hooker, who had feuded with him throughout his eastern tenure, sneered that his situation was like that of a man who married with the understanding that he would not sleep with his wife. But Halleck thereby freed Grant from the need for attending to a great many routine distractions. Instead of being snowed under by paperwork, the lieutenant general could give his full attention to strategic planning, and this he did. From time to time he would return to Washington for an overnight stay — primarily, it would seem, to visit Mrs Grant, who had joined him in Cincinnati for the ride back east — but mainly he kept to his desk in the field, poring over maps and blueing the air of his Culpeper headquarters with cigar smoke, much as he had done a year ago in the former ladies' cabin of the *Magnolia*, where he planned the campaign that took Vicksburg.

Of all these several component segments, each designed to contribute to Grant's over-all pattern for victory on a national scale, the first to go awry was the preliminary one — preliminary, that is, in the sense that it would have to be wound up before the more valid thrust at Mobile could begin — involving Banks and Steele in the far-off Transmississippi, hundreds of miles from the two vital centers around which would swirl the fighting that would determine the outcome of the war. It was the first because it had already begun to falter before Grant was in a position to exercise control. Moreover, once he was in such a position, as general-in-chief, his attempts along that line only served to increase the frustration which both subordinates, proceeding as it were against their hearts, had been feeling all along. Not that it mattered all that much, whatever he did or did not do, for the seeds of defeat had been planted in the conception. By then the only cure would have been to abandon the crop entirely; which would not do, since Lincoln himself, with a fretful sidelong glance at France's latter-day Napoleon, had had a hand in the sowing.

Promptly after the midsummer fall of Port Hudson opened the Mississippi to Union trade throughout its length, Halleck had taken the conquest of Texas as his prime concern in the western theater. It seemed to him the logical next step. Besides, he had always liked to keep things tidy in his rear, and every success achieved under his direction had been followed by a pause for just that purpose. After Donelson, after Corinth, after Vicksburg, he had dismembered the victorious blue force, dispersing its parts on various lateral or rearward assignments, with much attendant loss of momentum. Consequently, although it was here that the North had scored all but a handful of its triumphs in the field, the war in the West had consisted largely of starts and stops, with the result that a considerable portion of the Federal effort had been expended in overcoming prime inertia at the start of each campaign. And so it was to be in the present case, if Old Brains had his way. With the President's unquestioning approval — which, as usual, tended to make him rather imperious in manner and altogether intolerant of objections — Halleck had been urging the conquest of Texas on Banks, who had been opposed in the main to such a venture, so far at least as it involved his own participation. A former Massachusetts governor and Speaker of the national House of Representatives, he was, like most political appointees, concerned with building a military reputation on which to base his postwar bid for further political advancement. He had in fact his eye on the White House, and he preferred a more spectacular assignment, one nearer the center of the stage and attended with less risk, or in any case no more risk than seemed commensurate with the prize, which in his opinion this did not; Texas was undeniably vast, but it was also comparatively empty. He favored Mobile as a fitting objective by these standards, and had been saying so ever since the surrender of Port Hudson first gave him the feel of laurels on his brow. Halleck had stuck to Texas, however, and Halleck as general-in-chief had had his way.

Texas it was, although there still was considerable disagreement as to the best approach to the goal, aside from a general conviction that it could not be due west across the Sabine and the barrens, where, as one of Banks's staff remarked, there was "no water in the summer and fall, and plenty of water but no road in the winter and spring." Halleck favored an ascent of Red River, to Shreveport and beyond, which would allow for gunboat support and rapid transportation of supplies; but this had some of the same disadvantages as the direct crosscountry route, the Red being low on water all through fall and winter. While waiting for the spring rise, without which the river was unnavigable above Alexandria, barely one third of the distance up to Shreveport, Banks tried his hand at a third approach, the mounting of amphibious assaults against various points along the Lone Star coast. The first of these, at Sabine Pass in September, was bloodily repulsed; the navy lost two gunboats and their crews before admitting it could put no troops ashore at that point. So Banks revised his plan by reversing it, end for end. He managed an unsuspected landing near the mouth of the Rio Grande, occupied Brownsville unopposed, and began to work his way back east by way of Aransas Pass and Matagorda Bay. There he stopped. So far he had encountered no resistance, but just ahead lay Galveston, with Sabine Pass beyond, both of them scenes of past defeats which he would not risk repeating. All he had got for his pains was a couple of dusty border towns and several bedraggled miles of beach, amounting to little more in fact than a few pinpricks along one leathery flank of the Texas elephant. By now it was nearly spring, however, and time for him to get back onto what Halleck, in rather testy dispatches, had kept assuring him was the true path of conquest: up the Red, which soon was due for the annual rise that would convert it into an artery of invasion.

By now, too, as a result of closer inspection of the prize, Banks had somewhat revised his opinion as to the worth of the proposed campaign. Mobile was still what he ached for, but Mobile would have to wait. Meantime, a successful ascent of the Red, as a means of achieving the subjugation of East Texas, would not only add a feather to his military cap; it would also, by affording him and his army valuable training in the conduct of combined operations, serve as excellent preparation for better and more difficult things to come. Besides, study disclosed immediate advantages he had overlooked before. In addition to providing a bulwark against the machinations of the French in Mexico, the occupation of Shreveport would yield political as well as strategic fruits. First there was Lincoln's so-called Ten Percent plan, whereby a state would be permitted to return to the national fold as soon as ten percent of its voters affirmed their loyalty to the Union and its laws. With Shreveport firmly in Federal hands, Confederate threats would no longer deter the citizens of West Louisiana and South Arkansas from taking the oath required; Louisiana and Arkansas, grateful to the Administration which had granted them readmission, would cast their votes in the November election, thereby winning for the general who had made such action possible the gratitude of the man who, four years later, would exert a powerful influence in the choice of his successor. There, indeed, was a prize worth grasping. Moreover, the aforementioned strategic fruits of such a campaign had been greatly enlarged in the course of the fall and winter, occasioned by Steele's advance on Little Rock in September, which extended the Federal occupation down to the Arkansas River, bisecting the state along a line from Fort Smith to Napoleon, and posed a threat to Confederate installations farther south. Ordnance works at Camden and Arkadelphia had been shifted to Tyler and Marshall, Texas, where they now were back in production, as were others newly established at Houston and San Antonio. Cut off from the industrial East by the fall of Vicksburg, still-insurgent Transmississippians had striven in earnest to develop their own resources. Factories at Tyler, Houston, and Austin, together with one at Washington, Arkansas, were delivering 10,000 pairs of shoes a month to rebel quartermasters, and inmates of the Texas penitentiary at Huntsville were turning out more than a million yards of cotton and woolen cloth every month, to be made into gray or butternut uniforms for distribution to die-hard fighters in all three states of the region. Shreveport itself had become an industrial complex quite beyond anyone's dream a year ago, with foundries, shops, and laboratories for the production of guns and ammunition, without which not even the doughtiest grayback would constitute the semblance of a threat. If Banks could lay hands on Shreveport, then move on into the Lone Star vastness just beyond, the harvest would be heavy, both in matériel and glory. By late January, having considered all this, and more, he was so far in agreement with Halleck that he wired him: "The occupation of Shreveport will be to the country west of the Mississippi what that of Chattanooga is to the east. And as soon as this can be accomplished," he added, his enthusiasm waxing as he wrote, "the country west of Shreveport will be in condition for a movement into Texas."

Another persuasive factor there was, which in time would be reckoned the most influential of them all, though less perhaps on Banks himself than on various others, in and out of the army and navy, about to be involved in the campaign. This was cotton. Banks was intrigued by the notion that the proposed invasion not only could be carried out on a self-supporting basis, financially speaking, but could result in profits that would cover other, less lucrative efforts, such as the ones about to be launched through the ravaged counties of northern Virginia and across the red-clay hills and gullies of North Georgia. What was more, he backed his calculations with experience. On his march up Bayou Teche to Alexandria, in April of the year before, he had seized an estimated $5,000,000 in contraband goods, including lumber, sugar and salt, cattle and livestock, and cotton to the amount of 5000 bales. This last represented nearly half the value of the spoils — and would represent even more today, with the price in Boston soaring rapidly toward two dollars a pound in greenbacks. Yet those 5000 bales collected along the Teche were scarcely more than a dab compared to the number awaiting seizure in plantation sheds along the Red and in the Texas hinterland; Banks predicted that the campaign would produce between 200,000 and 300,000 bales. Even the lower of these two figures, at a conservative estimate of $500 a bale, would bulge the Treasury with no less than a hundred million dollars, which by itself would be enough to run the whole war for two months. Nor was that all. In addition to this direct financial gain, he would also put back into operation the spindles lying idle in the mills of his native state, where he had got his start as a bobbin boy and where the voters would someday turn out in hordes to express their thanks for all he had done for them and the nation in their time of trial. It was no wonder his enthusiasm rose with every closer look at the political, strategic, and financial possibilities of a campaign he formerly had thought not worth his time.

Perhaps the most persuasive factor of all, so far at least as Banks was concerned, was that he secured Halleck's approval of a plan, worked out between them, that assured the coöperation not only of Steele, who would move south from Little Rock to the vicinity of Shreveport with 15,000 troops, but also of Sherman, who was to send 10,000 of his veterans to Alexandria for a combination with the 20,000 Banks himself would bring to that point by repeating last year's profitable march up the Teche. Including a marine brigade and the crews of twenty-odd warships under Rear Admiral David D. Porter, which were to serve as escort for the transports bringing Sherman's men from Vicksburg and thenceforth as an integral part of the command in its ascent of the Red, this would give Banks a total strength of just under 50,000; which he believed was sufficient, in itself, to guarantee success in the campaign. His opponent, General Edmund Kirby Smith, commanding that vast, five-state Transmississippi region already beginning to be known as "Kirby-Smithdom," had not much more than half that many soldiers in all of Arkansas, Louisiana, Texas, and the Indian Territory combined. Such opposition as Smith might be able to offer the veteran 45,000-man blue army and its hard-hitting 210-gun fleet, Banks was not unjustified in believing, would only serve to swell the glory involved in the inevitable outcome.

Sherman himself was inclined to agree with this assessment, though he was aware (as Banks perhaps was not, having had little time for theoretic study) of Napoleon's dictum that the most difficult of all maneuvers was the combination of widely divided columns, regardless of their over-all numerical superiority, on a field of battle already occupied by an enemy who thus would be free, throughout the interim preceding their convergence, to strike at one or another of the approaching columns. His only regret, the red-haired general said when he came down to New Orleans in early March to confer with Banks about his share in the campaign, was that Grant had forbidden him to go along. He stayed two days, working out the arrangements for his troops to be at Alexandria in time for a meeting with Banks's column on the 17th — the same day, as it turned out, that he would meet with Grant in Nashville, though he did not know that yet — then steamed back upriver to Vicksburg, declining his host's invitation to stay over for the inauguration on March 5 of the recently elected Union-loyal governor of Louisiana, one Michael Hahn, a Bavaria-born lawyer and sugar planter who had opposed secession from the start. Despite the delay it would entail, Banks apparently felt obliged to remain for the ceremony — which was quite elaborate, one item on the program being a rendition of the "Anvil Chorus" in Lafayette Square by no less than a thousand singers, accompanied by all the bands of the army, while church bells pealed and cannon were fired in unison by electrical devices — then at last, after managing to get through another two weeks of attending to additional political and administrative matters, got aboard a steamboat for a fast ride up the Mississippi and the Red for the meeting at Alexandria with Sherman's men and his own, whose ascent of the Teche had been delayed by heavy going on roads made nearly bottomless by rain. Before leaving he had written to Halleck of the public reaction to the inaugural celebration, thousand-tongued chorus, electrically fired cannon, and all. "It is impossible to describe it with truth," he wrote. In the future, much the same thing would be said of the campaign he was about to give the benefit of his personal supervision.

It was March 24 by the time he reached Alexandria, one week late. Even so, he got there ahead of the men in his five divisions, who did not complete their slog up the Teche until next day. Plastered with mud and eight days behind schedule, they did not let the hard and tardy march depress their spirits, which were high. "The *soldier* is a queer fellow," a reporter who accompanied them wrote; "he is not at all like other white men. Tired, dusty, cold or hungry — no matter, he is always jolly. I find him, under the most adverse circumstances, shouting, singing, skylarking. There is no care or tire in him." Banks, for all the dignity he was careful to preserve, shared this skylark attitude when he arrived, and with good cause. The time spent waiting for him to show had been put to splendid use by Sherman's veterans, who had arrived on time, with one considerable victory already to their credit and another scored before the Massachusetts general joined them.

Three divisions under Brigadier General A. J. Smith, a Pennsylvania-born West Pointer, they had left Vicksburg on March 10 and gone ashore two days later at Simsport, just up the Atchafalaya from its confluence with the Red. While Porter's twenty-two heavily gunned warships — thirteen of them ironclads, accompanied by some forty transports and quartermaster boats — returned to the Red for a frontal attack on Fort De Russy, a once-abandoned but now reoccupied Confederate strongpoint about halfway up to Alexandria, the infantry crossed a lush, bayou-mazed prairie called Avoyelles to come upon the fortification from the rear. Such few rebels as they saw en route were quick to scamper out of reach, having no apparent stomach for a fight. By late afternoon of March 14 the bluecoats were in position for a mass assault, not only hearing the roar of Porter's guns, which showed that he too was in place on schedule, but also receiving a few of his heavy shells that overshot the fort. Just before sundown, at a cost of only 38 killed and wounded, they stormed and took it, along with its ten guns and its garrison of 300 bitter, shell-dazed men, who, according to a newsman with the attackers, "screamed in demoniac tones, even after our banners flaunted from their bastions and ramparts." This done, the victors got back aboard their transports for the thirty-mile ride to Alexandria: all, that is, but the men of one division, who stayed behind to raze the fort by tearing out and burning its wooden beams and leveling the earthworks, after which they gave it the finishing touch by blowing up the powder magazine.

They had received excellent schooling in such work under Sherman, especially on the recent expedition to Meridian, where, in Sherman's words, they had cut "a swath of desolation fifty miles broad across the State of Mississippi which the present generation will not forget." In such work they used sledges and crowbars more than rifles, and though it involved much vigorous exercise, it was not only a fine way of relaxing from the rigors of the Vicksburg siege, it was also a good deal safer, since their efforts were mainly directed against civilians. Moreover, this particular division had a commander, Brigadier General T. Kilby Smith, whose views along these lines coincided more or less with their own. "The inhabitants hereabouts are pretty tolerably frightened," the thirty-three-year-old former lawyer was presently to write home to his mother in Ohio. "Our western troops are tired of shilly shally, and this year they will deal their blows very heavily. Past kindnesses and forbearance has not been appreciated or understood; frequently ridiculed. The people now will be terribly scourged." Presumably such words had been passed down as well as out, for private residences had begun to burn in Simsport almost as soon as the transports ran out their gangplanks for the troops to go ashore, and their progress across the lovely Avoyelles Prairie was marked by the ruins of burnt-out houses, some with nothing to show they had been there except an unsupported chimney; "Sherman Monuments," these were called. Arcadians of the region, a gentle people with a heritage of freedom, many of whom had been pro-Union up to now, were indeed "terribly scourged." The pattern was set for the campaign, so far at least as the western troops — "Sherman's gorillas," they dubbed themselves — were concerned. Next would come the turn of the inhabitants of the piny uplands beyond Alexandria, although a correspondent of the St Louis *Republican* was already predicting that unless such practices were discouraged there was a danger of "our whole noble army degenerating into a band of cutthroats and robbers."

By way of proving their skill as fighters as well as burners, six regiments of gorilla-guerillas, accompanied by a brigade of Banks's cavalry that rode in ahead of his infantry, pressed on above Alexandria to Henderson's Hill, twenty miles up Bayou Rapides, on a forced reconnaissance which reached a climax on the night of March 21 with a surprise attack, through rain and hail and darkness, that captured a whole regiment of rebel cavalry, some 250 men and mounts, together with all four guns of a battery also caught off guard by the assault. Returning to base three days later, they paraded their captives before Banks, who had just arrived and was delighted to find that they had not wasted the time spent waiting for him and the rest of the five divisions they were supposed to reinforce. When these wound up their march next day, March 25, he had concentrated under his immediate command by far the most impressive display of military strength ever seen in the Transmississippi, on land or water. With ninety pieces of field artillery and considerably better than twice that number of heavier guns afloat, he had 30,000 effectives on hand, practically all of them seasoned campaigners, and was about to move up the Red for a conjunction near Shreveport with half that many more under Steele, who he now learned had left Little Rock two days ago, marching south-southwest toward the same objective. The outlook was auspicious, especially in light of the fact that his troops had already proved their superiority, first at Fort De Russy and again at Henderson's Hill, over such forces of the enemy as they had managed to trick or cower into remaining within their reach. But then next day, as he was about to order a resumption of the march, a high-ranking courier arrived with Grant's eleven-day-old letter of instructions from Nashville, written while waiting for Sherman to join him there.

This could not but give Banks pause, stipulating as it did that if he did not feel certain of taking Shreveport by the end of April he was to return A. J. Smith's command to Sherman by the middle of that month "for movements east of the Mississippi." Discouraging as this was in part — for it not only fixed him with a tighter schedule than he had felt obliged to follow when he set out, it also threatened him with the imminent loss of the three best divisions in his army — Banks took heart at something else the letter said. If the expedition was successful, he was to leave the holding of Shreveport and the line of the Red to Steele, while he himself returned to New Orleans for an advance on Mobile as part of the new general-in-chief's design for a spring offensive in the central theater. This was the assignment he had coveted all along, and though he was aware of the danger of being over-hasty in military matters, this went far toward reconciling him to the step-up in the tempo of his march. With Mobile to follow, more or less as a reward for past successes, he wanted this Red River business over and done with as soon as possible. Accordingly, he put his cavalry in motion that same day and followed it two days later with his infantry, while A. J. Smith's men got back aboard their transports to accompany the fleet. The immediate objective was Grand Ecore, sixty miles upstream or roughly half the total distance. His plan was to move rapidly to that point and to Natchitoches, four miles south of Grand Ecore and the river, after which would come the leap at Shreveport that would wind up the campaign.

Banks himself did not leave Alexandria until after April 1, having remained behind to supervise an election on that date, by such voters as had taken the loyalty oath, of delegates to a state convention whose task it would be to draw up a new constitution tying Louisiana more firmly to the Union. Meanwhile the troops had been making excellent progress, encountering nothing more than scattered resistance that was easily brushed aside. By the time of the April Fool election, both Natchitoches and Grand Ecore had been occupied by leading elements of the respective columns, one advancing by land, the other by water. This meant that the campaign was back on schedule, despite the delay at the start. So far all was well, except perhaps that the lack of opposition had resulted in a dwindling of public concern outside the immediate area of operations. "It is a remarkable fact," the New Orleans correspondent of the New York *Tribune* declared on April 2, "that this Red River expedition is not followed by that anxious interest and solicitude which has heretofore attended similar army movements. The success of our troops is looked upon as a matter of course, and the cotton speculators are the only people I can find who are nicely weighing probabilities and chances in connection with the expedition."

If anxious interest and solicitude were what he was seeking, he could have found them not only in the New Orleans cotton exchange but also up Red River, aboard the flagship of the fleet. Porter had already lost one of his prized vessels, the veteran *Conestoga*, sunk March 8 in a collision on the Mississippi while returning from Vicksburg with a heavy load of ammunition that took her to the bottom in four minutes. She was the eighth major warship the admiral had lost in the past sixteen months, and two of these had been captured and turned against him, at least for a time. What was worse, it had begun to seem to him that if he continued to go along with Banks he would be in danger of losing a great many more, not so much through enemy action — he had never been one to flinch from combat — as through an act of nature; or, rather, a non-act. The annual rise of the Red, which usually began around New Year's, had not thus far materialized. Perhaps it was merely late this year; but twice before, in 1846 and 1855, it had not occurred at all. That was a nine-year interval, and now that another nine years had elapsed, there were indications that if Porter got his boats above the mile-long falls and rapids at Alexandria, he might not be able to get them down again. If the river, instead of rising, took a drop, he would be left with the agonizing choice of blowing them up or having them fall into rebel hands, which would mean nothing less than the undoing of all the navy had accomplished in these past two years of war on the western waters. That was unthinkable, but he had boasted so often that he could take his fleet "wherever the sand was damp," the admiral now found it impossible to renege on his promise to stay with the army to the end of its upstream trek. After three days of tugging and bumping — during which time the river, to his alarm, began to dwindle, then rose slightly — he got his largest ironclad, *Eastport*, over the falls; after which he followed with a dozen lighter-draft gunboats and twenty transports laden with troops. "The water is quite a muddy red and looks anything but inviting," a sailor wrote in his diary as the column began its winding crawl to Grand Ecore. "The transports from the head belch out three bellowing whistles which is caught up by the next, and sometimes two or three vie in a euphonious concert much resembling the bellowing of cattle at the smell of blood."

So far, except for the considerable slaughter of pigs and chickens encountered on the march, the smell of blood had been little more than a figurative expression. Moreover, if Banks could judge by indications, the Confederates were either content to have it remain so, or else they were incapable of having it otherwise, knowing only too well that most of the blood that would be spilled would be their own. In any case, the one thing they had not done was fight, and as he boarded his headquarters boat at Alexandria for an upstream ride on the evening of April 2 — a nattily dressed man in his vigorous prime, two years short of fifty, wearing highly polished boots and chinking spurs, a light-blue overcoat, buckskin gauntlets elbow-high, a bell-crowned hat, and a neatly groomed mustache and brief imperial — he got off a dispatch to

Halleck expressing his confidence in "an immediate and successful issue" of the campaign, the end of which he believed was in plain view.

"Our troops now occupy Natchitoches," he informed Old Brains, "and we hope to be in Shreveport by the 10th of April. I do not fear concentration of the enemy at that point. My fear is that they may not be willing to meet us."

In the course of the past three years Lincoln had read other such dispatches, and all too often they had turned out to be prologues to disaster. Reading this one, when in time it reached Washington, he frowned and shook his head in disapproval.

"I am sorry to see this tone of confidence," he said. "The next news we shall hear from there will be of a defeat."

A defeat was what the Confederates had very much in mind for the invaders: especially Major General Richard Taylor, Kirby Smith's West Louisiana commander, who had crossed swords with Banks before, first in the Shenandoah Valley, two years ago, and then along the Teche the previous year. Tactically, the second of these confrontations had not been as brilliant as the first, in which Taylor, serving as one of Stonewall Jackson's ablest lieutenants, had helped to strip the former Bay State politician of so many well-stocked wagons that he had been nicknamed "Commissary" Banks; but the aptness of this nom-de-guerre had been redemonstrated last summer, west of New Orleans, when Taylor's surprise descent on Banks's forward supply base at Brashear City, yielding an estimated $2,000,000 in ordnance and other stores, helped immeasurably to equip the army he had been raising for the defense of his home state ever since his transfer from Virginia. A son of Zachary Taylor and brother of Jefferson Davis's first wife, now just past his thirty-eighth birthday, he was described by one of his soldiers as "a quiet, unassuming little fellow, but noisy on retreats, with a tendency to cuss mules and wagons which stall on the road."

This tendency had been given a free rein for the past three weeks, in the course of which he had been obliged to fall back nearly two hundred miles before an adversary he was convinced he could whip, if he could only manage to meet him on anything approaching equal terms. But there was the rub. With fewer than 7000 troops in the path of better than four times that number backed by the guns of the Union fleet, he had no choice except to continue his retreat, hard though it was to suffer without retaliation the vandalism of A. J. Smith's gorillas, not to mention such professional indignities as Fort De Russy and the loss of most of his cavalry at Henderson's Hill. His consolation was that he was falling back toward reinforcements, which Kirby Smith kept assuring him were on the way from Arkansas and Texas. However — as might have been expected of a young man who had served his war apprenticeship under the bloody-minded and highly time-conscious Stonewall — he chafed at the delay. On the last day of March, with his troops in motion for a concentration forty miles northwest of Natchitoches and less than half that distance from the Texas border, he sent an irate dispatch informing the department commander that his patience was near the snapping point. "Had I conceived for an instant that such astonishing delay would ensue before reinforcements reached me," he told Smith, "I would have fought a battle even against the heavy odds. It would have been better to lose the state after a defeat than to surrender it without a fight. The fairest and richest portion of the Confederacy is now a waste. Louisiana may well know her destiny. Her children are exiles; her labor system is destroyed. Expecting every hour to receive the promised reinforcements, I did not feel justified in hazarding a general engagement with my little army. I shall never cease to regret my error."

"Hydrocephalus at Shreveport produced atrophy elsewhere," he afterwards protested, complaining acidly that while his superior "displayed much ardor in the establishment of bureaux, and on a scale proportioned rather to the extent of his territory than to the smallness of his force," Smith neglected the more vital task of resisting blue aggression in the field. In thus indulging his fondness for classical allusion, while at the same time venting his spleen, Yale man Taylor was not altogether fair to a West-Point-trained commander who by now had spent a hectic year being responsible for a region the size of western Europe, much of it trackless and practically none of it self-sustaining, at any rate in a military sense, at the time he assumed his manifold duties. Not the least of these was the establishment of those bureaus of supply and communication scorned by Taylor but made altogether necessary by the loss, within four months of Smith's arrival, of all practical connection with the more prosperous half of his country lying east of the Mississippi. In short, he had been involved in a year-long strategic and logistic nightmare. If at times he seemed to vacillate in the face of danger, that was to a large extent because of the scantiness of his resources, both in manpower and equipment, in contrast to those of an adversary whose own were apparently limitless and who could move against him, more or less at will, by land and water. Missouri had been lost before he got there. Then had come the subtraction of the northern half of Arkansas, suffered while pinprick lodgments were being made along the lower coast of Texas. Now it turned out that all this had been by way of preparation for a simultaneous advance by two blue columns under Steele and Banks, converging respectively from the north and east upon his headquarters at Shreveport and containing between them more veteran troops than he had in his entire five-state department, including guerillas and recruits. If he was jumpy it was small wonder, no matter how resentful Richard Taylor might feel at being obliged to backtrack, across the width of his beloved home state, before the menace of a force four times his own.

Warned early of the double-pronged threat to his headquarters and supply base — the fall of which would mean the loss, not only of Louisiana and what remained of Arkansas, but also of much that lay beyond — Smith decided to meet the nearer and larger danger first: meaning Banks. He would hit him with all the strength he could muster, then turn and do the same to Steele when he came up. Accordingly, he alerted his Texas commander, Major General John B. Magruder, to prepare his entire force, garrisons excluded, for a march to support Taylor. In Arkansas, Lieutenant General Theophilus Holmes was given similar instructions, except that he was to retain his cavalry for use against Steele's column, slowing it down as best he could until such time as Taylor had disposed of Banks and was free to come in turn to his assistance. These alerting orders were issued in late February, before either enemy force had been assembled. In early March, though neither Federal column had yet set out, Magruder was told to put his men in motion. They amounted in all to some 2500 horsemen, combined in a division under Brigadier General Thomas Green, and left Magruder with only about the same number for the defense of all of Texas: a situation the Virginian considered not unlike the one he had faced two years ago, on the York-James peninsula, when he found himself standing with one brigade in the path of McClellan's huge blue juggernaut. Meanwhile Holmes, whose deafness was only one of the symptoms of his superannuation, had been relieved at his own request and succeeded by Major General Sterling Price, his second in command; Price was told to put his alerted troops — two small divisions of infantry under Brigadier General T. J. Churchill, with a combined strength of 4500 effectives — on the march for Shreveport. These were the reinforcements Taylor had been expecting all the time he was fading back across the width of Louisiana, protesting hotly at their nonarrival.

Green's progress was necessarily slow across the barrens and the Sabine, but Churchill's was impeded by Smith himself. By now the Transmississippi chieftain had begun to suspect that he had hoisted himself onto the horns of a dilemma: as indeed he had, since he thought he had. Having attended boldly to the threat posed by Banks, he feared that he had erred in leaving Price too little strength to hinder Steele, who might be able to descend on Shreveport before Taylor could dispose of Banks and come to its defense. Taking council of his fears, which were enlarged by information that Steele had set out from Little Rock on March 23, Smith held Churchill for a time at headquarters, so as to be able to use him in either direction, north or south, depending on whether the need was greater in Arkansas or Louisiana, then finally, in response to Taylor's increasingly strident dispatches, ordered Churchill to move south to Keatchie, a hamlet roughly midway between Shreveport and Taylor's latest point of concentration, just southeast of Mansfield. He had known what to do, but he had been so hesitant to do it that he had wound up not knowing what to do after all.

Dick Taylor had not helped with his hard-breathing threats to gamble everything on a single long-odds strike, provoked by desperation and congenital impatience. "When Green joins me, I repeat," he notified headquarters, "I shall fight a battle for Louisiana, be the forces of the enemy what they may." Horrified, Smith urged caution. "A general engagement should not be risked without hopes of success," he warned, reminding his impetuous lieutenant that rashness "would be fatal to the whole cause and to the department. Our role must be a defensive policy." Moreover, such resolution as he had managed so far to maintain, regarding his plan for meeting the two-pronged Federal menace, was grievously shaken by Taylor's expressed opinion that Steele, a "bold, ardent, vigorous" professional, might constitute a graver danger, despite his reported disparity in numbers, than the amateur Banks, who was "cold, timid, [and] easily foiled." Smith continued to waver under the suspicion that he had chosen the wrong man to tackle first. Finally on April 5, alarmed by news that Steele was making rapid progress, and in fact had completed nearly half his southward march by crossing the Little Missouri River the day before, he decided to ride down to Mansfield for a conference with Taylor. His intention was to revise his plan by reversing it. He would concentrate everything first against Steele, rather than in front of Banks, even if this meant standing a siege at Shreveport or retreating into Texas, where — it now occurred to him, as a further persuasive argument for postponing the showdown — a defeat would be more disastrous for the invaders.

Taylor was dismayed by his chief's vacillation. Asked for his advice three days ago he had been quick to give it. "Action, prompt, vigorous action, is required," he replied. "While we are deliberating the enemy is marching. King James lost three kingdoms for a mass. We may lose three states without a battle." He still felt that way about it, and he said so, face to face with Smith at Mansfield on the morning of April 6. Smith heard him out, a mild-mannered Floridian just under forty, outwardly unperturbed by the short-tempered Taylor, but left that afternoon to return to his headquarters, still gripped inwardly by indecision. Taylor, though he had been reinforced that day by Green, whose arrival raised his strength to 9000 effectives, still had been given no definite instructions. Churchill's 4500 were at Keatchie, twenty miles away, but when or whether they would be released to him he did not know. All Smith had said was that he would inform him as soon as he made up his mind — the one thing he seemed incapable of doing. Taylor apparently decided, then and there, that if anything was going to be done in this direction he would have to accomplish it on his own. And that was what he did, beginning the following day, except that he had considerable help from his opponent, who presented him with a tactical opportunity he did not feel he could neglect, with or without the approval of his superior, forty miles away in Shreveport.

Banks came on boldly, still exuding confidence as he prepared at Natchitoches and Grand Écore for the final stage of his ascent of the Red. Alexandria lay sixty miles behind him, Shreveport only sixty miles ahead. The first half of this 120-mile stretch had been covered in five days of easy marching, and he planned to cover the second half in less.

Such frets as he had encountered up to now came not from the rebels, who he was convinced wanted no part of a hand-to-hand encounter, but from internal complications. For one thing, smallpox had broken out in the Marine Brigade, with the result that it was returned to Vicksburg and Kilby Smith's division took over the pleasant duty of "escorting" — that is, riding with — the fleet. The loss of these 3000 marines, who had not been included in his original calculations anyhow, was largely offset by the arrival of the 1500-man Corps d'Afrique, composed of Negro volunteers who had proved their combat worth to doubters at Port Hudson the year before.

Another complication was not so easily dismissed, however, for it had to do with money: meaning cotton. Banks had been getting very little of this because of Porter, who had been getting a great deal of it indeed — all, in fact, that came within his 210-gun reach. Unlike the army, which seized and turned over rebel cotton to the government as contraband of war, the navy defined cotton as subject to seizure more or less as if it was an authentic high-seas prize, the proceeds of which were to be divided among the officers and crew of the vessel that confiscated it, the only stipulation being that the bales had to have been the property of the Confederate government. Very little of it was, of course, but that did not cramp Porter or his sailors. They simply stenciled "C.S.A." on each captured bale, then drew a line through the still-wet letters and stenciled "U.S.N." below. When an army colonel remarked that the result signified "Cotton Stealing Association of the United States Navy," the admiral laughed as loud as anyone, if not louder, in proportion to his lion's share of the proceeds as commander of the fleet. This would not have been so bad, in itself; Banks, though punctiliously honest, had grown more or less accustomed to such practices by others, in the service as in politics. The trouble was that the upriver planters, hearing of Porter's activities below, began to burn their cotton rather than have it fall into his hands. By the time the civilian speculators, who had accompanied the army from New Orleans and were prepared to pay the going backwoods price for the hoarded staple, arrived in the wake of the gunboats, bearing trade permits signed by Chase and even Lincoln, there was nothing left for them to buy, either cheap or dear, for resale to the hungry mills of New England. Moreover, they directed their resentment less at Porter, who after all was doing nothing they would not have done in his place, than at Banks, who they believed had lured them up this winding rust-colored river only to dash their hopes by failing to deliver even a fraction of what he had encouraged them to expect. By the time they reached Alexandria it was evident there was nothing to be gained by going farther; Banks made it official by ordering their return. They had no choice except to obey, but they were bitter as only men could be who had been wounded in their wallets. "When General Banks sent them all back to Alexandria, without their sheaves," a staff officer later wrote, "they returned to New Orleans furious against him and mouthing calumnies."

It was of course no good thing, militarily or politically, for a man to have such enemies in his rear, but at least he was rid of a frock-coated clan who, he complained, had "harassed the soul out of me." And though they would be quick to fix the blame on him in case of a mishap, let alone an outright failure, Banks was more confident than ever that nothing of the kind was going to happen. It was not going to happen because there would be no tactical occasion for it to happen; Taylor simply would not risk a probable defeat. After reviewing his troops at Natchitoches on April 4 — a frequent practice which always brought him pleasure and tended to enlarge his self-respect — the former Bay State governor said as much in a letter to his wife. "The enemy retreats before us," he informed her, "and will not fight a battle this side of Shreveport if then."

When two days later — April 6: the second anniversary of Shiloh — he set out on the final leg of his advance, his route and order of march demonstrated, even more forcefully than his letters to Halleck and Mrs Banks had done, the extent of his conviction that the rebels would not dare to stand and fight before he reached his goal. At Grand Ecore the land and water columns diverged for the first time in the campaign, the former taking an inland road that curved west, then northwest, through the villages of Pleasant Hill and Mansfield, and finally northeast, back toward the Red, for a meeting with the fleet abreast of Springfield Landing, roughly two thirds of the way to Shreveport, which they then would capture by a joint attack. Banks chose this route either because he did not know there was a road along the river (there was, and a good one) or else because he thought the inland road, leading as it did through piny highlands, would make for better progress. If this last was what he had in mind, he was mistaken in that too. According to one of the marchers, a heavy rain soon made the single narrow road "more like a broad, deep, red-colored ditch than anything else." Heavy-footed, sometimes ankle-deep in mire, they cursed him as they slogged: particularly A. J. Smith's Westerners, who by now had acquired a scathing contempt for the former Massachusetts politician and the men of his five divisions, mainly Easterners from New York and New England. Paper-collar dudes, they called them, and referred with grins to the general himself, whose lack of military training and acumen was common gossip around their campfires, as "Napoleon P. Banks" or, even more scornfully, "Mr Banks."

Nor was the poor condition of the road itself the worst of the disadvantages an inland march involved. Beyond Natchitoches, in addition to being deprived of the support of Porter's heavy guns, the westering column would encounter few streams or wells, which would make for thirsty going, and little or nothing in the way of food or feed. One look at the sparsely settled region back from the river convinced a newsman that "such a thing as subsisting an army in a country like this could only be achieved when men and horses can be induced to live on pine trees and resin." Fortunately — at least from the subsistence point of view — Banks had brought along a great many wagons, no fewer in fact than a thousand, which assured that his soldiers would suffer no shortage of bacon or hardtack or coffee while crossing the barrens, although Smith's gorillas, whom Sherman had accustomed to traveling light, were so unappreciative as to sneer that they were loaded with iron bedsteads, feather bolsters, and other such creature comforts for the city-bred dandies under his command. That was of course false, or in any case a gross exaggeration, but it was altogether true that those thousand wagons and their teams did at once decrease the speed and greatly increase the length of the column: the more so because of the way they were distributed along it, with an eye for accessibility rather than for delivering or receiving an attack. Up front was a division of cavalry, followed by its train of 300 wagons. Next came the three remaining infantry divisions (the fourth had been left on guard at Alexandria, charged with unloading and reloading supply boats in order to get them over the low-water falls and rapids) of the two corps that had slogged up the Teche under Major General William B. Franklin, top man in the West Point class of 1843, in which he had finished twenty places above his classmate U. S. Grant, and a veteran of hard fighting in Virginia. Close behind them came their train of 700 wagons, with the Corps d'Afrique as escort. A. J. Smith's two remaining divisions (the third, Kilby Smith's, was taking it easy aboard transports, ascending Red River with the fleet) brought up the rear. However, so slow was the progress, so wretched the road, and so strung-out the column by the accordion action of all those interspersed mules and wagons, it was not until the following morning that Smith's jeering veterans lurched into motion out of Grand Ecore. By then the column measured no less than twenty miles from head to tail: a hard day's march under better conditions, by far, than here prevailed.

That was April 7, and before it was over Banks had cause to

suspect that he had erred in his estimate of the enemy's intention. Three miles beyond Pleasant Hill by midafternoon of this second day out, the cavalry encountered mounted graybacks who, for once, did not scamper at the threat of contact. Instead, to the dismay of the Federal horsemen, they set spur to their mounts, some half a dozen regiments or more, and charged with a wild Texas yell. The bluecoats broke, then rallied on their reserves; whereupon the rebels fell back, as before. That was about all there was to it; but the cavalry commander, Brigadier General Albert Lee, a thirty-year-old former Kansas lawyer, began to reflect intently on the disadvantages of his situation, particularly with regard to those 300 wagons directly in his rear, between him and the nearest infantry support. Several times already he had asked Franklin to let him shift his train back down the column, combining it with the infantry's, but Franklin had declined; let the cavalry look after its own train, he said. Now that the rebs were showing signs of fight, Lee made the same request again, with a further plea for infantry reinforcements, and received the same reply to both requests. In fact, when the young cavalryman tried to make camp near sunset, six miles beyond Pleasant Hill, Franklin sent word for him to push on four miles farther, train and all, so that the infantry would have plenty of room to clear the town next morning. Lee obeyed, though with increased misgivings, and was brought to a halt at nightfall, just short of his objective, Carroll's Mill, where he found gray riders once more drawn up in a strong position directly across his front, midway between Pleasant Hill and Mansfield.

Depressed by the notion of what was likely to result if he was struck by superior numbers on the march next day, he repeated his plea for reinforcements to Colonel John S. Clark, one of Banks's aides, who came forward that night to see how things were going. The colonel, agreeing that things were not going well, or in any case that the danger Lee foresaw was possible, rode back to present the cavalryman's request to Franklin in person, only to have him refuse it as flatly as before. So Clark returned to Pleasant Hill, where headquarters had been established that afternoon, for a conference with the army commander. Banks agreed that caution was in order, overruled Franklin, and directed him to send a brigade of infantry to reinforce the cavalry by daybreak. Franklin did so, though it went against his grain, and when Lee started forward next morning at sunrise he was pleased to find the rebel horsemen once more fading back from contact after each long-range exchange of shots, apparently intimidated by the steely glint of bayonets down the column, which signified that the front-riding cavalry now had close-up infantry support.

This continued for half a dozen miles: quick spatters of small-arms fire, followed by sudden gray withdrawals. It was hard for Lee to tell whether the Johnnies were really afraid of him or only pretending to be, in order to lure him on. Then the head of the column emerged from the dense pine woods to find itself on the rim of a large clearing, half a mile deep and half again as wide, with a broad, low hill in the center, on whose crest he saw a line of butternut skirmishers. He halted, brought his infantry to the front, and sent them forward, textbook style. The gray pickets gave ground before the massed advance, but when Lee rode up to the crest of the hill down whose opposite slope the rebs had scrambled for safety, he found his worst fears realized. There below him, in the woods along the far edge of the clearing, stretched a Confederate line of battle: not merely cavalry now, he saw, but infantry too, in heavy files, with artillery mixed in.

It was Taylor, and it was here, within twenty miles of the Texas border — only that bit short of having retreated across the entire width of his home state, leaving its people to the by no means tender mercy of the self-styled "gorillas" in his wake — that he was determined to make his stand. Last night, on his own initiative, he had sent Churchill word to march at dawn from Keatchie, twenty miles away; after which (but no sooner than the sun was four hours high, lest there be time for his order to be countermanded) he got off a note to Kirby Smith at Shreveport, saying laconically of Banks: "I consider this as favorable a point to engage him at as any other."

Sabine Crossroads, the place was called, three miles short of Mansfield, where four roads forked. One led east, allowing the Federals a chance to effect an early junction with their fleet; another branched northwest to Keatchie, which would place them in the path of the reinforcements moving toward him; while the other two ran generally north along parallel routes, giving the invaders a straight shot at Shreveport. Once they were where those four roads came together, free to choose whichever fit their fancy, Taylor's hope of blocking them would be gone, along with his chance to catch them out from under the umbrella protection of their heavy naval guns, strung out on a narrow, ditchlike road in a single, wagon-choked column. Moreover, in considering the tactical opportunity Banks was thus affording him, he had more in mind than a mere defensive stand, whatever numerical odds he might encounter. Like his old mentor in the Shenandoah Valley, he hoped to inflict what Stonewall had sometimes called "a speedy blow" or, more often, "a terrible wound."

Accordingly, while Tom Green and his Texans continued the harassment they had begun in earnest three miles this side of Pleasant Hill, Taylor chose his field of fight and began to make his preparations, including the summoning of the two infantry divisions then at Keatchie. The two already with him, under Major General J. G. Walker and Brigadier General Alfred Mouton, were ordered to return at first light, from Mansfield back to Sabine Crossroads, where they would take position along the near edge of the clearing, respectively on the right and left of the road that crossed the low hill just ahead. Cavalry under Brigadier Generals Hamilton Bee and James Major would guard the flanks, and a four-gun battery, posted astride the road, would stiffen the center. In Mansfield itself, by way of further preparation, private houses were selected and put in order for use as hospitals, and surplus wagons were sent rearward to clear the streets. Taylor was leaving as little as possible to chance, though he was also prepared to seize upon anything chance offered in the way of tactical opportunities; Green's troopers, for example, the most experienced and dependable body of men in his command, were to be employed wherever they seemed likely to prove most useful in that regard when they arrived. This force of 9000 infantry, cavalry, and artillery would be increased to 13,500 when Churchill got there, and though Taylor would not enjoy a numerical superiority even then — there were 20,000 blue effectives in the twenty-mile-long column toiling toward him — he intended to make up for that with the sheer fury of his attack, which he would design to make the most of his intimate knowledge of the ground, having chosen it with just that aim in mind. Nor was terrain the only advantage on which he based his belief that he would win when it came to shooting. "My confidence of success in the impending engagement was inspired by accurate knowledge of the Federal movements," he later wrote, adding that he was encouraged as well by previous acquaintance with "the character of their commander, General Banks, whose measure had been taken in the Virginia campaigns of 1862 and since."

By midmorning, April 8, he had established the line of battle the blue cavalry commander found confronting him when he topped the hill at midday. Young Lee sent back at once for additional reinforcements, meantime getting his batteries into positions from which to probe the gray defenses. A long-range artillery duel ensued, in the course of which Banks arrived in person for a look at the situation. He was undismayed. In fact, this was precisely what he had said he wanted on the day he set out from Grand Ecore: "The main force of the enemy was at last accounts in the vicinity of Mansfield, on the stage road between Natchitoches and Shreveport, and the major general commanding desires to force him to give battle, if possible, before he can concentrate behind the fortifications of Shreveport or effect a retreat westerly into Texas." Warned now by Lee that, in his opinion, "we must fall back immediately, or we must be heavily reinforced," Banks told him to hold what he had; he himself would "hurry up the infantry." That took time, partly because the cavalry train had two or three miles of the road blocked, but about 3.30 the other brigade of Franklin's lead division arrived to join the first. Hard on its heels came a courier with instructions for Lee to advance immediately on Mansfield. Shocked — for the town was three miles beyond the enemy line of battle, and he estimated that the rebels "must have some 15,000 or 20,000 men there; four or five times as many as I had" — the young cavalryman rode in search of Banks, who confirmed the validity of the order. Paraphrasing his protest, Lee said later: "I told him we could not advance ten minutes without a general engagement, in which we would be most gloriously flogged, and I did not want to do it." Given pause by this, although he was unwilling to abandon the attack, the army commander at any rate agreed to postpone it until another division of Franklin's infantry arrived, and he sent a staffer back to see that it was hurried forward with a minimum of delay.

Dick Taylor had bided his time up to now, but only by the hardest. Though he affected the unbuttoned, rather languid combat style of his father, Old Rough-and-Ready, sitting his horse with one leg thrown across the pommel of his saddle while casually smoking a cigar, he was anxious to force the issue. At one point, around 2 o'clock, when he believed he saw bluecoats massing for an attack on his left, he shifted one of Walker's brigades to Mouton and one of Bee's regiments to Major, but aside from this he did little except watch for an opening that would justify going over to the offensive before Churchill arrived from Keatchie. Meantime the Union buildup continued, although toward no apparent climax; Banks seemed unwilling to throw the punch that would invite the counterblow Taylor was eager to deliver. Finally, just after 4 o'clock, with a scant three hours of daylight still remaining, he decided to wait no longer. Mouton, on the strengthened left, was told to go forward.

He did so, promptly: "like a cyclone," one blue defender later said, while another described the charging graybacks as "infuriated demons." Mouton was among the first to fall, thirty-five years old, a West-Point-trained Shiloh veteran, son of the Creole governor who had helped to vote Louisiana out of the Union. His senior brigadier, Camille Armand Jules Marie, Prince de Polignac — "Polecat" to his Louisianians and Texans, who were unable to pronounce the royal name of the young Crimea veteran with the dapper beard and spike mustache — took over and pressed the uphill charge. His unleashed soldiers struck and broke the Federal right, routing two of the regiments there, and turned three captured guns on the fugitives as they fled. Taylor, observing the success of this while it was still in midcareer, sent word for Walker and Bee to go in, too: which they did, with similar results on the right, while Green threw his Texans into the melee on the left, exploiting on horseback the confusion Mouton and Polignac had begun on foot. All down the line, as the gray chargers emerged from the pine woods into the clearing to strike at both ends of the confused blue line, the high-throated rebel yell rang out.

Some on the opposite side did what they could to stay the rout. "Try to think you're dead and buried," a Massachusetts colonel told his men, "and you will have no fear." Either they did not try it at all, or else they tried and found it did not work; in any case, they ran and kept on running. Apparently it was the abruptness of the assault that made it so demoralizing, and this applied as much to those in the rear as to those up front. "Suddenly," a journalist on Banks's staff would recall, "there was a rush, a shout, the crashing of trees, the breaking down of rails, the rush and scamper of men. It was as sudden as though a thunderbolt had fallen among us, and set the pines on fire. I turned to my companion to inquire the reason of this extraordinary proceeding, but before he had the chance to reply, we found ourselves swallowed up, as it were, in a hissing, seething, bubbling whirlpool of agitated men." Franklin was among them by then, having brought his second division up the hill in time for it to join the rout and add to the lengthening casualty list, which would include some 1500 captives and about half that many killed and wounded. One of these last was Franklin himself, who was struck by a bullet in the shin and lost his horse, then took off rearward on a borrowed mount to brace his third division for the shock about to come. Banks too was intimately involved in the confusion, and like Franklin he did what he could, which was not much. Removing his hat for easy recognition, he shouted to the skulkers running past him on the road: "Form a line here! I know you will not desert me." He knew wrong. "Hoo!" they cried, and kept running. So he drew his sword and waved it about; but that worked no better. By then the fleeing troops had become what one of them afterwards called "a disorganized mob of screaming, sobbing, hysterical, pale, terror-stricken men."

Taylor was intent on completing his triumph by pressing the pursuit. Near sundown there was an interruption by a courier who arrived from Shreveport with a letter Kirby Smith had written that morning, urging caution. "A general engagement now could not be given with our full force," he advised. "Reinforcements are moving up — not very large, it is true. . . . Let me know as soon as you are convinced that a general advance is being made and I will come to the front." Taylor scanned it hastily, then looked up smiling. "Too late, sir," he said. "The battle is won." However, he took time to get off a dispatch announcing the victory to his chief, so far as it had been accomplished up to now. "Will report again at the close of the action," he ended the message. "Churchill's troops were not up in time to take part [but] will be fresh in the morning. I shall push the enemy to the utmost."

He did not wait for morning; Jackson-style, he made full use of the hour of daylight still remaining, though the going was as rough for him as it was for the retreating Federals. Panicky teamsters, unable to turn around on the narrow road, had unhitched their mules for a mounted getaway and left the wagons behind as a barricade against pursuit, their bare tongues extended at all angles to trip the unwary. One result of this was the denial of the road to such guns as had avoided capture up to then; Taylor took no less than twenty of them in all, along with ten times as many wagons, some with and some without their teams, but all loaded. Meantime Franklin was putting his third division, which was as large as the other two combined, into a stout defensive position along a ridge just back from a creek in a ravine about four miles from Sabine Crossroads. The pursuers came up raggedly, attacked piecemeal in the dusk, and were repulsed. Taylor knew it was time to call a halt, but not quite yet if his men were to have water for the night; so he contented himself with driving the blue pickets back to their ridge and taking possession of the creek in the ravine. There he stopped, intending to renew the pressure in the morning, and the firing died away in the darkness, giving place to a silence broken only by the wounded crying for water and by the scavengers, back up the road, reveling on the good things found in the captured Yankee train.

As one of his own generals had predicted at the outset, to his face, Banks had been "most gloriously flogged." Out of 12,000 Federals engaged, 2235 had been killed, wounded, or captured, while Taylor, with 9000, had lost less than half as many. Nor was that the worst of it, by any means. In addition to twenty guns and two hundred wagons, Banks had also lost time — the one thing he could least afford to lose if he was to occupy Shreveport and get Sherman's soldiers back to him on schedule. And to make matters worse, caught as he was without water for his parched troops on the ridge, he must lose still more time by retreating still farther to reach another stream and another stout position in which to defend himself from the blood-thirsty graybacks, whom he could hear feasting on their spoils, back up the road, and who obviously intended to have another go at him tomorrow, probably at daylight. Even if he could stay here all night without water, it was doubtful whether A. J. Smith's two divisions, camped a dozen miles away at Pleasant Hill, could arrive in time for a share in the defense. A council of war advised the obvious, and the withdrawal got under way at 10 o'clock. By midnight all the survivors were on the march in a bedraggled column made up largely of stragglers blown loose from their commands, "men without hats or coats, men without guns or accoutrements, cavalrymen without horses and artillerymen without cannon, wounded men bleeding and crying at every step, men begrimed with smoke and powder, all in a state of fear and frenzy."

One among them saw them so, yet supposed in his extreme distress that Banks was the most dejected man of all. He had left Grand Ecore expecting to be in Shreveport within four days, yet here he was, marching in the opposite direction into the dawn of that fourth day. As he rode among his trudging men it must have begun to occur to him that a great deal more than the van of his army had been wrecked at Sabine Crossroads. Any general who could not capture Shreveport with the odds as much in his favor as these had been was not likely to be given the chance to take Mobile. And without that feather in his cap, his chances of occupying the White House were considerably diminished, if not abolished, especially when he recalled the scapegoat hunt that invariably followed every failure such as the one in which he was now involved. Who that scapegoat was likely to be, he knew only too well; perhaps he even had time to regret the cotton speculators he had sent back to New Orleans "without their sheaves," and who were there now, "mouthing calumnies." He was indeed dejected by the time he drew near Pleasant Hill, having failed to spot a good defensive position anywhere along the road, though it may well have improved his outlook to find A. J. Smith's hard fighters already disposed for battle and looking determined. "If it comes to the worst," an Iowa colonel had told his troops when he called them out at 2 o'clock that morning to give them news of the defeat a dozen miles away, "I ask of you to show yourselves to be men."

They showed that, and more, when Taylor came up eleven hours later, hard on the trail of the dejected bluecoats he had whipped the day before, and after a two-hour rest halt, required by Churchill's road-worn Arkansans and Missourians, flung his reinforced victors forward with orders for them to "rely on the bayonet, as we had neither time nor ammunition to waste."

This was bravely said, but it was far from easily done. Taking heart from the stalwart look of Sherman's veterans, Banks had spent the morning hours preparing to defend the low, open, house-dotted plateau known felicitously as Pleasant Hill. During this time, according to a newsman, the area "had the appearance of a parade ground on a holiday, regiments marching to the right, regiments marching to the left, batteries being moved and shifted." Near the center of all this activity, in the yard of a house affording a panoramic view of the line thus being drawn, the journalist observed "a small cluster of gentlemen to whom all this phantasmagoria had the meaning of life and death, and power, and fame." It was Banks, surrounded by his chief lieutenants. He wore his light blue overcoat buttoned high against the April chill, and he passed the time "strolling up and down, occasionally conversing with a member of his staff or returning the salute of a passing subaltern." Franklin was there, limping on his wounded leg, his manner calm except for an occasional nervous tug at his whiskers, and so were A. J. Smith, sunlight glinting on his spectacles, and Brigadier General Charles P. Stone, who, after six months of confinement in army prisons and nine of unemployment, had been militarily resurrected by Banks as his chief of staff, thus giving the West Pointer a chance to dispel the cloud of suspicion that had gathered about his head and caused his arrest following Ball's Bluff, where he was accused of having treasonably exposed his men to slaughter. Not yet forty, "a quiet, retiring man who is regarded, by the few that know him, as one of the finest soldiers of our time," Stone sat on a rail fence, smoking cigarettes — a modern touch; cigarettes would continue to be rare and exotic until well into the following decade — and seemed to the reporter "more interested in the puffs of smoke that curled around him than in the noise and bustle that filled the air."

Gradually the noise and bustle died away as the various outfits settled down in their assigned positions and the day wore on and grew warmer. The genial cluster of uniformed gentlemen began to seem to the newsman "a rather tedious party," and apparently they themselves were of much the same opinion. Having done all they could in the way of preparation, the gold braid wearers had nothing to do now but wait, and while they did so they milled about rather aimlessly; "group after group formed and melted away," the reporter noted, "and re-formed and discussed the battle of the evening before, and the latest news and gossip of New Orleans, and wondered when another mail would come."

Whatever tedium his lieutenants might be experiencing, Banks had felt his confidence rise steadily with the sun. By noon, when the generals broke for lunch, he had convinced himself there would be no serious fighting today, and afterward, digesting the excellent meal while the sun swung past the overhead and began its long decline, he took such heart that he began to think of recovering the initiative and thereby repairing the damage his reputation had suffered yesterday. Surely Grant and Lincoln would forgive him for being a little behind schedule if he emerged from these piny highlands with a substantial victory in his grasp. He would go back over to the offensive; he would redeem his failure; he would salvage his career. Though his train was already well on its way to Grand Ecore — what was left of it, at any rate — he made up his mind to resume the advance on Shreveport, and he got off a message saying as much to Porter. "I intend to return this evening on the same road with General Franklin's and General A. J. Smith's commands," he informed the admiral. Today was Saturday, and he added that he expected "to be in communication with the transports of General Kilby Smith and the gunboats at Springfield Landing on Sunday evening or Monday forenoon."

Once more he was wrong in a prediction, but this time it was not for lack of a tactical success. Aware that the Federals were braced for an attack from straight ahead, Taylor took his time about deploying for an end-on strike by Churchill, designed to crumple and roll up the Union left while Walker held in front; Green meantime would probe and feint at the enemy right, working his way around it in order to cut off the expected blue retreat to Grand Ecore, and Polignac would be in reserve, since his division had suffered two thirds of the casualties yesterday, though he would of course be committed when the time was ripe. It was close to 5 o'clock before Churchill, having roused his men from their two-hour rest, had marched them into position in the woods due west of the unsuspecting Federal left.

He then went forward with much of the fury Mouton had shown the day before, provoking similar consternation in the Union ranks. To one defender, "the air seemed all alive with the sounds of various projectiles." These ranged, he said, "from the spiteful, cat-like spit of the buckshot, the *pouf* of the old-fashioned musket ball and the *pee-ee-zing* of the minie bullet, to the roar of the ordinary shell and the *whoot-er whoot-er* of the Whitworth 'mortar-pestle'; while the shrieks of wounded men and horses and the yells of the apparently victorious rebels added to the uproar." Back up the Mansfield road, Green and Walker chimed in with their guns, contributing new tones to the concert, and now that the assailed enemy flank had begun to crumble, they put their troops in motion, mounted and dismounted, against the right and center. Churchill kept up the pressure, gathering prisoners by the score as Franklin's unstrung men fled eastward across the open ground of the plateau. Determined to make up for having missed it, the Arkansans and Missourians were intent on restaging yesterday's blue rout, about which they had heard so much since their arrival from Keatchie the night before, in time to share in the pursuit but not the glory.

A. J. Smith's two divisions had not been at Sabine Crossroads either, but they too were very much in the thick of things at Pleasant Hill: as Churchill's elated attackers soon found out. Smith had seen the flank give way, the graybacks whooping in pursuit of Franklin's rattled soldiers, who by now were in flight through the village behind their line, and had sent a reserve brigade in that direction on the double, soon following it with other units which he pulled out of his portion of the line to meet the graver threat. Attempting a wide left wheel, which would enable them to assault the Federal center from the rear and in mass, the cheering rebels at the extremity of the pivot were caught end-on by the advancing blue brigade, freezing the cheers in their throats and bringing them to a huddled, stumbling halt. They wavered, lashed by sheets of fire, and then gave way, not in a single rush but in fragments, as regiment after regiment came unhinged. They made one stand, in a heavy growth of cane along a creekbank they had passed on their way in, but Smith's Westerners came after them with a roar, delivering point-blank volleys and finally closing with clubbed muskets; whereupon the gray withdrawal, already touched with panic, degenerated abruptly into a rout. Now it was the Federals doing the whooping and the crowing, and the Confederates doing the running, as the counterattack grew into a grand right wheel, pivoting irresistibly on the retaken village of Pleasant Hill, so recently overrun by gray attackers.

Taylor saw and tried to forestall the sudden reverse, but Walker had just been carried from the field with a bullet in his groin, Green was intent on maneuvering to cut off the expected blue retreat, and Polignac could not come up through the gathering dusk in time for anything more than a try at discouraging the exultant pursuit. This he managed to do, holding a line two miles from the scene of the break, while the other three divisions fell back another four miles to the nearest water. The battle was over and Taylor had lost it, along with three guns abandoned when his flankers were themselves outflanked and thrown into sudden retreat. With some 12,500 men engaged, the Confederates had suffered a total of 1626 casualties, while the Federals, with about the same number on the field, had lost 1369. Though it was by no means as great as yesterday's, when fortune had smiled on the other side and blood had flowed more freely, Banks knew whom to thank for this disparity, along with much else. When the firing stopped and the rebels had passed out of sight in the pines and darkness, he rode over to A. J. Smith and took him gratefully by the hand. "God bless you, General," he said. "You have saved the army."

Tremendously set up by the sudden conversion of near-certain defeat to absolute victory, he was more anxious than ever to get back on the track to Shreveport, and he not only said as much to Smith while shaking his hand; he also sent a message instructing Albert Lee, who was riding escort, to turn the wagon train around and come back to Pleasant Hill. However, when he returned to headquarters to confer with Franklin and two of his brigadiers, William H. Emory and William Dwight — both had commanded divisions under Banks for more than a year, and both had always given him dependable advice — he found all three West Pointers opposed to resuming the offensive, especially in the precipitous manner he proposed. Franklin and Emory favored an eastward march across Bayou Pierre to Blair's Landing on the Red, there to reunite with Kilby Smith, secure a safe supply line, and regain the protection of the fleet, whereas Dwight urged a return to Grand Ecore for the same purpose. This last was much the safest course, and Banks, his enthusiasm quenched by this dash of cold water from the high-ranking trio of professionals, decided to adopt it. Orders went out for an immediate resumption of the retreat.

When word of this reached A. J. Smith he went at once to protest what seemed to him a loss of backbone. Banks refused to reconsider his decision, citing his lack of supplies, his loss in the past two days of just over 3600 men, and the advice of all his other generals. Smith then asked for time at least to bury his dead and finish gathering up his wounded, but Banks declined that too. Furious, the bespectacled Pennsylvanian, his gray-streaked whiskers bristling with indignation, went to Franklin, whom he found enjoying a cup of coffee, and proposed that, as second in command, he put Banks in arrest and take charge of the army for a rapid advance on Shreveport. Franklin stirred and sipped his coffee, nursed his injured shin, and said quietly: "Smith, don't you know this is mutiny?" That ended the protest, if not the anger. In the small hours after midnight, leaving their non-walking wounded behind — the train had left that morning with all the wagons: including through some mixup, those containing the army's medical supplies — the weary bluecoats formed ranks and slogged away from the scene of their victory, down the road to Grand Ecore.

Ten miles in the opposite direction, up the Mansfield road at Carroll's Mill, Taylor was wakened from his badly needed sleep at 10 o'clock that night by Kirby Smith, who had learned of the Sabine Crossroads fight at 4 o'clock that morning and left Shreveport at once to join his army in the field, only to find at the end of his sixty-mile horseback ride that still a second unauthorized battle had been fought. What was worse, even though this one had been lost, Taylor seemed intent on provoking a third — with any number of others to follow, so long as his blood was up and anything blue remained within his reach. It was more or less clear to Smith by now that if the Louisianian was left to his own devices he would use up the army entirely, leaving him nothing with which to defend his Transmississippi headquarters and supply base from an amphibious assault by Porter, whose gunboats and gorilla-laden transports were at Loggy Bayou, within pouncing distance of Shreveport, and/or an overland attack by Steele, whose troops had crossed the Little Missouri five days ago, brushing Price's horsemen casually aside, and by now might well be closer to their goal than its supposed defenders were at Carroll's Mill. Informed of this, Taylor increased his chief's dismay by proposing to ignore that double threat in order to keep the heat on Banks; both Porter and Steele would withdraw of their own accord, he argued, as soon as they learned that the main Federal column had pulled back. Smith would not hear of taking such a risk, even though Taylor kept insisting that, with Banks on the run and Porter likely to be stranded by low water, "we had but to strike vigorously to capture or destroy both." Finally the department commander ended the discussion with a peremptory order for the infantry to take up the march for Shreveport the following day. If the danger there was as slight as Taylor claimed, he could return and try his hand at the destruction he had in mind downriver.

The result next morning was a rather unusual tactical situation wherein two armies, having met and fought, retreated in opposite directions from the field for which they had presumably been contending. It was made even more unusual, perhaps, by the fact that the victors were unhappier than the losers, and this was especially true of the two commanders. Disgruntled though Taylor was at having been overruled by his superior, Banks was put through the worse ordeal of being sneered at by his military inferiors, all the way down to the privates in the ranks. Taking their cue from Franklin, who avoided such blame as came his way by letting it be known that he would never have recommended a withdrawal if the army had had a competent general at its head, even regimental commanders looked askance at Banks as he rode by them, doubling the column. The men themselves did more than exchange sly glances. Angry because some four hundred of their wounded comrades had been left behind to be nursed and imprisoned by the rebels, they began the march in a mutinous frame of mind, muttering imprecations. But presently the company clowns took over. After the manner of all soldiers everywhere, in all ages, they began to ridicule their plight and mock at the man who had caused it, inventing new words for old songs which they chanted as they slogged. For example, in remembrance of Bull Run:

> In eighteen hundred and sixty-one
> We all skedaddled to Washington.
> In eighteen hundred and sixty-four
> We all skedaddled to Grand Ecore.
> Napoleon P. Banks!

This last — "Napoleon P. Banks!" — was shouted for good measure as the general rode past, and recurred as a refrain in all the parodies they sang. Nor were such high jinks limited, as before, to A. J. Smith's irreverent gorillas. Banks's own men, whom he had commanded at Port Hudson and through the easy-living months in New Orleans, took up the songs and bawled them as he passed along the roadside, trailing a kite tail of smirking officers from his staff.

Fortunately, they had nothing worse to contend with, in the way of opposition on the march, than butternut cavalry which mainly limited its attention to stragglers until near the end of the second day, April 11, when it made a cut-and-slash attack that drove the rear brigade into Grand Ecore on the run. Once there, their prime concern was to protect themselves from the vengeful Taylor, who was reported to be hard on their heels with 25,000 effectives. They themselves would not have that many on hand until Franklin's fourth division came up the Red from Alexandria and A. J. Smith's third division returned from Loggy Bayou with the fleet, whose heavy guns they presently heard booming in the distance, apparently involved in some kind of trouble far upstream. Meantime they kept busy constructing a semicircular line of intrenchments around the landward side of the high-sited village on its bluff. They worked hard and well, incorporating the trunks and tops of large trees which they felled for use as breastworks and abatis. Not only did they require no urging from their officers in this work; they kept at it after they were told that they could stop.

"You don't need any protection. We can whip them easily here," Franklin chided a detail of diggers as he rode on a tour of inspection.

But they remembered Sabine Crossroads and the hilltop they had lost to a savage rebel charge: the result, they now believed, of having trusted their security to generals like this one. They kept digging.

"We have been defeated once," a spokesman replied, leaning on his shovel, "and we think we will look out for ourselves."

In point of fact they were by no means in such danger as they feared. Far from closing on their heels, Taylor's four divisions of infantry were fifty muddy miles away at Mansfield, marched there against his wishes in order to have them within supporting distance of Shreveport. And even when it turned out that the withdrawal had been unnecessary because his prediction was fulfilled — Steele veered from his southwest course on April 12 for an eastward strike at Camden, which would put him as far from Shreveport as he had been when he crossed the Little Missouri a week ago, and Porter not only ventured no farther up the Red, he was even now bumping his way downstream in an effort to rejoin Banks — Taylor constituted no real threat to the Federals intrenched at Grand Ecore, even though he was free at last to move against them, since he had by then a good deal less than one fourth the number of soldiers his adversary believed he was about to use in an all-out assault on the blufftop citadel. Convinced by captured dispatches that Banks would soon be obliged to withdraw if he was to get Sherman's troops across the Mississippi within the little time remaining, Kirby Smith believed there would be small profit in pursuing him through a region exhausted of supplies. Instead, he decided to go in person after Steele, who was still a threat, and for this purpose he took from Taylor not only Churchill's Arkansans and Missourians, who had been lent to help in stopping Banks, but also Walker's Texans, who would now return the favor by helping to stop Steele. That left the Louisiana commander with barely 5000 men in all: Polignac's infantry, bled down to fewer than 2000 effectives, and Green's cavalry, which numbered only a little above 3000, including a small brigade that had just arrived. In any case, however few they were, on April 14 he started them southward for Grand Ecore, where the bluecoats had obligingly penned themselves up, as if in a stockyard, awaiting slaughter.

Taylor himself went up to Shreveport next day, on the outside chance that he could persuade his chief to countermand the orders which he believed would deprive him of a golden opportunity. "Should the remainder of Banks' army escape me I shall deserve to wear a fool's cap for a helmet," he had said the week before, but now that his force had been reduced by more than half he was less confident of the outcome: especially when he learned that Tom Green, while attempting to add to the problems of the Union fleet in its withdrawal down the still-falling Red, had been killed two days ago in an exchange of fire with the gunboats at Blair's Landing, twenty miles above Grand Ecore. A veteran of the Texas war for independence, the Mexican War, the horrendous New Mexico expedition of early 1862, and the retaking of Galveston, the fifty-year-old Hero of Valverde had been Taylor's most dependable lieutenant in last year's fighting on the Teche and the Atchafalaya, as well as in the campaign still in progress down the Red. His loss was nearly as heavy a blow as the loss of the three divisions about to set out for Arkansas, and caused Taylor to redouble his efforts to have them returned while there was still a chance to overtake and destroy the invaders of Louisiana, afloat and ashore. But Kirby Smith was not to be dissuaded; Steele was the major danger now, and he intended to go after him in strength. "Should you move below and Steele's small column push on and accomplish what Banks has failed in, and destroy our shops at Jefferson and Marshall," he told Taylor, "we will not only be disgraced, but irreparably deprived of our means and resources."

Accordingly, he left Shreveport on April 16, taking Walker and Churchill with him. Taylor stayed on for two more days, arranging for the shipment of supplies, and then set out on the 19th to join what he called "my little force near Grand Ecore." He was still hopeful that the Federals could be bagged, despite the disparity in numbers, and he counted on using deception to that end. Compelled, as he said, "to eke out the lion's skin with the fox's hide," he had instructed his unit commanders to keep Banks on edge, and deceived as to their strength, "by sending drummers to beat calls, lighting campfires, blowing bugles, and rolling empty wagons over fence rails."

All this they had done, and more, with such effect that when Taylor dismounted near Grand Ecore on the evening of April 21, ending his ninety-mile ride, he found that the Federals had begun to pull out of the place that afternoon. The head of their column was already beyond Natchitoches, slogging south in an apparent attempt to take up a safer position at Alexandria, if not to get away entirely. Determined not to permit this, Taylor set about planning how to intercept the retiring bluecoats and, if possible, bring them to battle, although they outnumbered him five to one, exclusive of their heavily gunned flotilla. Their march was down the narrow "island" lying between Cane River and the Red, and it was his hope to force them into a strung-out halt that would give him a chance to go to work on them piecemeal. With this in mind, he sent Bee's brigade of cavalry on a fast ride south to Monett's Ferry, forty miles away at the far end of the island, with instructions to block the crossing of the Cane at that point, so that the rest of his troops could be thrown upon some vulnerable segment of the blue column stalled between there and Natchitoches. This was an ambitious undertaking for some 5000 men opposed by 25,000, but Taylor undertook it gladly, anticipating the Cannae he had been seeking all along.

Banks anticipated much the same thing, and moved rapidly to avoid it if he could. He was by now, as a result of the strain of the past ten days, about as edgy as even Taylor could have wished, and this edginess had been provoked by more than the various nerve-jangling ruses those "22,000 to 25,000" graybacks had been practicing in the woods beyond his semicircular line. For one, there was a growing sense of failure. He still had spasms and flickers of hope, during which he planned to go back over to the offensive, but these grew fewer and weaker as the days wore on, until finally they stopped. For another, he had found waiting for him at Grand Ecore a message from Sherman, notifying him that his lease on A. J. Smith's three divisions had expired and ordering their immediate return. This could be ignored or counter-manded because of the exigencies of the situation, which plainly would permit no such detachment; but a few days later, on April 18, he received from Grant a follow-up letter of instructions that had for him, in his present hemmed-in state, a sound of hollow mockery not so easily dismissed. Written at the end of March, it set forth in some detail the procedure he was to follow, once Shreveport had been taken, in moving without delay against Mobile. "You cannot start too soon," the letter ended. "All I would now add is that you commence the concentration of your force at once. Preserve a profound secrecy of what you intend doing, and start at the earliest possible moment."

That was perhaps the cruelest blow; Grant had written as if in fervid haste, lest time be wasted between the fall of Shreveport, apparently expected momentarily, and the arrival of his letter urging Banks to be quick in taking the road to glory, which led from Shreveport to the White House, by way of Mobile, Atlanta, and Richmond. Contrasting what was with what might have been — for the road's only entrance, for him, was Shreveport, and he could not get there to take it — the former Bay State governor was correspondingly depressed. He relieved his spleen to some degree, however, with a pair of summary dismissals. One was of Stone, his chief of staff (Stone took no further part in the war, though afterwards he served the Khedive of Egypt in the same capacity for thirteen years, with the rank of lieutenant general, and then returned to act as chief engineer in the construction of the pedestal for the Statue of Liberty); Banks let him go because he found him "very weak," and the same might have been said of young Albert Lee, whom he relieved of duty as cavalry commander and sent back to New Orleans, although not without regret. He testified later that Lee had been "active, willing, and brave," if not skillful, and had "suffered, more or less unjustly, as all of us did, for being connected with that affair."

Such administrative corrections had little effect on a tactical situation which seemed to be growing increasingly grim as the rebels out in the brush continued to beat drums, build a myriad of campfires, blow bugles, and bring up what sounded like thousands of wagonloads of supplies and ammunition. For what purpose all this was being done Banks could only guess, but with every passing hour he was brought closer to the inevitable conclusion that if he could not go forward, as was obviously the case, then he would do well not to postpone going back. This applied most of all to Porter's gunboats, for the river was still falling: was already down, in fact, to half the seven-foot depth required to float them over the double falls at Alexandria. The thing to do was get back there as soon as possible, before the river took another perverse drop, for a close-up look at what was reported to be an impossible situation. So the admiral advised, although the temptation was strong to remain where he was, under the friendly bluff at Grand Ecore, his recent trip to Loggy Bayou having given him all too graphic a preview of what to expect in the course of his return to the Mississippi, down those more than three hundred winding miles of the Red. "It is easy to die here, and there are many ways of doing it," a sailor diarist had observed en route. In addition to the more or less normal dangers involved in descending a swift and crooked river at the speed required to maintain steerage — staved-in bows, unshipped rudders, broken wheels, and punctured hulls, all brought on by collisions with other boats, with underwater snags, with the iron-hard red clay bottom — there were the rebels to contend with, fast-firing marksmen who shot at passing or stalled vessels from hidden positions along both banks. At Blair's Landing, for example, where Tom Green was killed by a blast of canister, the fleet was exposed to what one veteran skipper called "the heaviest and most concentrated fire of musketry I have ever witnessed." As a result of this and other such nightmare encounters at places with names like Campti and Coushatta Chute, the thirty-boat flotilla got back from its ten-day upstream excursion sadly altered in appearance: especially the vessels loaded with Kilby Smith's gorillas, to which the butternut riflemen and cannoneers had given their particular attention. "The sides of some of the transports are half shot away," a soldier noted in his diary on April 15, after watching them come in, "and their smoke-stacks look like huge pepper boxes."

Porter recommended an immediate return to Alexandria, but Banks was not quite ready to make so frank an admission of defeat. That took him another four days, two of which he used to compose a letter to Grant, explaining that his retrograde movement from Mansfield had been due more to a shortage of water and the nonarrival of Steele than to resistance by the enemy — though he added, rather ingeniously, that the stubborn quality of the latter had proved the campaign to be "of greater importance than was generally anticipated at its commencement," and asked therefore that he be allowed to continue it beyond schedule, but only a bit, since "immediate success, with a concentration of our forces, is within our reach." Knowing Grant's low tolerance for failure, however skillfully disguised, he did not have much hope that his request would be granted, and he had even less hope, in case it was, that he would be continued in command. At the end of the four days (April 19: the day Taylor set out on his ninety-mile ride from Shreveport) Banks issued orders for a withdrawal to Alexandria. It got underway two days later, after A. J. Smith moved out and occupied Natchitoches, from which point he would cover the retreat by protecting the flanks of the column as it passed, then follow to serve as rear guard on the long march down the "island" between the two rivers, Cane and Red.

Whatever shortcomings the invaders had shown in the past forty days, they demonstrated conclusively, in the course of the next two, that their ability to cover ground at a fairly dazzling rate of speed not only had not been impaired, but in fact had been considerably improved by the events of the past two weeks. The march began at 5 o'clock in the afternoon, and by the time the tail of the column left Grand Ecore at 3 o'clock next morning, April 22, the men at the head were twenty miles away, taking their first rest while waiting for the others to close up. Before nightfall, the entire command had cleared Cloutierville, thirty-two miles from the starting point. Not even then was the blistering pace relaxed; Banks had learned that the rebels intended to contest his crossing of the Cane at Monett's Ferry, another dozen miles southeast, and he pressed on, determined to get off this jungly island and past the last natural obstacle between him and Alexandria, where he would recover the protection of the fleet and his army could once more break out its shovels and throw up dirt between itself and the danger of assault.

So far, its performance had been highly commendable from the logistics point of view; nor had it permitted haste to interfere unduly with the exercise of its various other talents. A. J. Smith's irrepressible campaigners, while holding off pursuers with one hand, so to speak, still found time for more than their usual quota of vandalism and destruction with the other. Grand Ecore had gone up in flames at the outset, along with the surplus goods the army left behind; then Natchitoches, whose old-world French and Spanish charm had been admired by many of its blue-clad visitors, was put to the torch as a farewell gesture. Gray cavalry came up in time to turn fire-fighters and save the latter place, as well as Cloutierville the following day, far down the island. But Smith's troops made up for this double disappointment with the amount of damage they inflicted on barns and houses along the road between the two, including even the cabins of the Negroes who turned out to welcome them. "At night the burning buildings mark our pathway," a marcher recorded. "As far as the eye can reach, we see in front new fires breaking out, and in the rear the dying embers tell the tale of war."

Close in their rear with Polignac, while his cavalry harassed their flanks and rode hard to get into position in their front, Taylor was finding it "difficult to restrain one's inclination to punish the ruffians engaged in this work." He meant that the prisoners were a temptation in that regard — blue-clad stragglers picked up along the roadside, blown and blistered or drunk on looted whiskey, unable to hold the pace Banks was setting them in his eagerness to attain the safety Alexandria would afford — but there was also the temptation for the pursuers to strike before the tactical iron was hot. Too quick a blow, delivered before the Federals had been brought to a disjointed halt on unfavorable terrain, would merely hasten their march and inflict only superficial damage, not to mention that it would be likely to disclose the smallness of Taylor's command; whereas if he waited till their path was blocked he might be able to bag the lot by tricking them (much as Bedford Forrest had tricked Abel Streight, about this time last year in Alabama) into surrendering to the "superior force" Banks believed was breathing down his neck. However, the Lousianian soon had cause to regret that he had stayed his hand, forgoing a leaner in hope of a fatter prize. Brigadier General Richard Arnold, Lee's replacement as chief of the Union cavalry — a thirty-six-year-old West Pointer, son of a former governor of Rhode Island and descendant of a distinguished New England family that included the notorious Benedict — had come upon Bee's dismounted brigade in a stout defensive position overlooking, from the opposite bank, the approaches to the Cane at Monett's Ferry. Instead of attempting the suicidal attack Bee expected, head-on down the road, Arnold located an upstream crossing for the infantry to use while he kept up a show of force in front and probed industriously below, as if in search of another crossing a couple of miles downriver, to attract Bee's attention in that direction.

It was neatly done. Emory's division, coming up at the head of the Federal main body on the morning of April 23, crossed the river two miles above the ferry and struck in force at the upstream rebel flank, while a second arriving division added its weight to the frontal demonstration and the downstream feint. This last was so well carried out, indeed, that Bee — a Charleston-born adoptive Texan whose younger brother had given T. J. Jackson his nom-de-guerre at First Manassas, but who himself had been a desk soldier until the present campaign — believed he was swamped on the right as well as the left, though in fact he had managed to inflict rather heavy casualties on the attackers from upstream. "The critical moment had come," he later reported; "the position turned on both flanks and a large force close in front ready to spring on the center." He counted himself fortunate to get away — "in good order at a walk," he noted — with a loss of "about 50 men and 1 artillery wagon . . . while the enemy lost full 400 killed and wounded," and he complained that, with fewer than 2000 men in all, he had been expected to block the path of "an army of 25,000 marching at their leisure on the main road to Alexandria." Yet that was exactly what had been expected of him, and Taylor was no more inclined to be charitable in such cases than was the man Bee's brother had caused to be nicknamed Stonewall. The fact remained that Banks had made his getaway, avoiding the destruction planned for him, and Bee had let the escape hatch be slammed ajar with a loss to himself of only "about 50 men and 1 artillery wagon." Nor was the disparity of losses any mitigation of the offense. "He displayed great personal gallantry, but no generalship," Taylor said of the South Carolinian, and ordered his removal from command.

Into the clear at last, though greatly relieved to be out of a jungle whose gloom seemed made for ambuscades, Banks did not slacken the pace for his foot-sore troops. He was still not half way to his goal, and he covered the last fifty miles with something of the hard-breathing urgency of a long-distance runner entering the stretch and catching sight of the tape drawn taut across the finish line, ready to be breasted. All through what was left of that day and the next, molested by nothing worse than small clusters of Confederate horse taking pot shots at the column from off in the pines, he kept going hard and fast, his over-all casualties now increased to about 4000, more than half of them captured or missing in battle and on the march. On the third day, April 25 — the fifth since he left Grand Ecore — the lead division slogged into Alexandria, followed next day by the others. There they promptly got to work with their shovels, heaving dirt, despite the recovered protection of Porter's fleet: what was left of it, at any rate, after an equally strenuous five days of fighting rebels and the river.

The admiral had suffered woes beyond a landman's comprehension, including the loss of his finest ironclad, the 700-ton *Eastport*. Sunk by a torpedo eight miles below Grand Ecore, she was patched and raised with the help of two pump boats hastily summoned upriver, and continued on her way — only to ground again in the shallow water forty miles below. Porter unshipped her four 9-inch guns, along with her other four 50- and 100-pounder Dahlgren and Parrott rifles, loading them onto a flat behind the light-draft gunboat *Cricket*, and thus got her afloat; at least for a time. She had only gone a few more miles, bumping bottom as she went, when she ran full tilt into a pile of snags, and there she stuck and settled. After three days' work by her crew and skipper, Lieutenant Commander Ledyard Phelps, who could not bear to lose "the pride of the western waters," Porter, having observed that such efforts to haul her off only made her stick the harder, gave orders for her destruction. A ton and a half of powder was distributed about her machinery and hold. When the electrical detonator failed to work, Phelps himself, in accordance with the tradition requiring the captain to be the last to abandon ship, applied a "slow match," then went over the side and into a waiting launch. The match was almost not slow enough, however. When the *Eastport* blew, Phelps was only a short way off and barely avoided being crushed by one of the dory-sized fragments from the 280-foot iron hull that came hurtling down and raised huge red geysers all around the launch.

Porter had a double reason for ordering the ironclad's destruction. One was that further delay seemed likely to cost him not only the *Eastport* — which, in point of fact, had been Confederate at the outset, captured uncompleted up the Tennessee River near the Mississippi town

that gave her her name, just after the fall of Fort Henry in early 1862 —
but his other boats as well. While the attempted salvage work was in
progress, enemy marksmen were gathering on both hostile banks of the
river and adding to his discomfort by sniping at the flotilla. Small-arms
fire, though deadly enough, was only part of the danger; for presently,
emboldened by the absence of the infantry escort now on the march with
Banks, they brought up batteries of horse artillery and opened fire from
masked positions. So intense and accurate was this, Porter lost one of his
unarmored pump boats that afternoon and the other the following morning, together with all but five of about 175 Negroes, mostly fieldhands
taken aboard from surrounding plantations, who were scalded to death
by steam from a punctured boiler. The gunboats *Juliet* and *Fort Hindman*
lost 22 men between them in the course of the downstream run, along
with their stacks and most of their upper works. Hardest hit of all,
though, was the *Cricket*, now serving as the flagship. Rounding a bend,
she came upon a rebel battery cleverly sited atop a bluff, and took 38
hits within the five minutes she was exposed to its plunging fire. Out of
her crew of fifty, 31 were casualties, including a dozen killed. "Every
shot [went] through and through us, clearing all our decks in a moment,"
according to the admiral, who had to take the wheel himself when he
ran up to the pilot house and found the helmsman badly wounded.

This was the firing the soldiers heard at the end of their long
march from Grand Ecore, and when Porter reached Alexandria next
morning, April 27, he saw at close range the validity of his other reason
for having abandoned the deep-draft ironclad far upstream: which was
that, even if he had managed to get her this far down, he would not have
been able to get her one mile farther. The Red had dwindled by now to
a depth of three feet four inches over the falls — two inches less than
half the draft of his heavier gunboats — and there still was no sign that
the river was going to rise at all this spring, if indeed it ever stopped
falling. In fact, it was becoming more evident every day that the fate of
the *Eastport* was likely to be the fate of every warship in the fleet; that
is, if they were to be kept out of enemy hands. And now there was
added to the admiral's woes, as if this last was not enough, the apprehension that he was about to be left on his own by the army. Banks
came aboard the badly shot-up *Cricket* with a ten-day-old letter just
arrived from the general-in-chief, peremptorily ordering him to desist
from any activity that might cause him to be "detained one day after the
1st of May in commencing your movement east of the Mississippi." Today was Wednesday; May Day was Sunday, barely four days off. "No
matter what you may have in contemplation," Grant had added by way
of emphasis, "commence your concentration, to be followed without
delay by your advance on Mobile."

Knowing how eager the Massachusetts general was to engage in
the very campaign Grant's letter not only authorized but *ordered* him

to undertake at once, Porter had a nightmare vision of the fleet — or anyhow the dozen vessels trapped above the falls — being left stranded high and dry, unprotected from heavy-caliber snipers or highly explosive underwater devices, its fate restricted to a choice between capture and self-destruction. If the former was unthinkable, involving as it well might do the loss of all the navy had won in the past two years on western rivers, the latter choice was only a bit less so, since either would mean professional ruin for the admiral himself. Partly his apprehension was based on his contempt for Banks, which encouraged him to think the worst of the one-time politician, especially in regard to his feeling any obligation to a man who he knew despised him, who was of a rival and often high-handed branch of the service, and whom he could protect only by disregarding a direct order from a superior famed for sternness in such matters.

But in this the admiral did the general wrong. Banks quickly made it clear that he had no more intention of abandoning the navy here at Alexandria than he had had at Grand Ecore the week before, and for much the same reasons. One was that it was not his way, no matter what Porter might think of him, to desert an associate in distress. Another was that he still had nearly a hundred downriver miles to go before he would be out of the Red River country, and he wanted naval protection all the way. Still another, which would require the navy's continued support even more, was that he had not completely given up the notion that he could retrieve his reputation in the region where he had lost it. Whether he would get that chance depended on Grant's reply to the letter sent ten days ago from Grand Ecore, suggesting a return to the recently abandoned upriver offensive, provided he could secure "a concentration of our forces." That meant Steele, who was long since overdue, but about whose progress Banks knew little except for a disconcerting rumor that the Arkansas commander had turned aside from his southwest march on Shreveport for an eastward lunge at Camden, 165 air-line miles due north of Alexandria and almost twice that far by the few roads.

Meantime, while waiting to hear again from Grant and finally from Steele, Banks and Porter — despite their mutual distaste for striking, even figuratively, so intimate an attitude — put their heads together in an attempt to solve the apparently insoluble problem of how to get armored gunboats, drawing seven feet of water, down a still-falling river whose rocky bottom was in places only three feet four inches below its russet surface.

★　★　★

Steele had been at Camden, just as Kirby Smith had been informed and Banks had chanced to hear. In fact, he had been there for the past twelve days, penned up like his supposed partner at Grand Ecore, behind intrenchments. But he was there no longer. He had pulled out during the small hours of this same April 27 — headed not for the Red, as Banks expected and Smith intended to prevent, but back toward Little Rock, the headquarters he had left five weeks ago today. In the course of the first three of these he had crossed the Saline, the Ouachita, the Little Missouri, then the Ouachita once more, along with a number of lesser streams in a region as wet as the upper Red was dry; now he was hard on the march for the Saline again, fifty air-line miles to the north, hoping to put that river between him and his pursuers, a superior force dead bent on his destruction, and thus bring an end to what a Saint Louis newsman would presently call "a campaign of forty days in which nothing has been gained but defeat, hard blows, and poor fare."

Although he seemed on the face of it to have done even worse than Banks — who, in all conscience, had done poorly enough by almost any standards, not excluding Pleasant Hill, which amounted to little more than a pause in his flight before inferior numbers — it could at least be said of Steele, by way of extenuation, that he had never had a moment's belief that anything good was going to come of an under-taking he had protested being involved in from the start. Unlike the former Massachusetts governor, whose inveterate optimism was inclined to feed on straws, he had not been lured by cotton or dazzled by stars in a political firmament which for him did not exist. Yet he had certain other disadvantages. For one, while Banks merely believed he was out-numbered, Steele actually was outnumbered, at any rate in the final stage, when Kirby Smith came after him with all but a handful of the infantry Dick Taylor had used to drive the larger Federal column pell-mell down the Red, ironclads and all. The Arkansas commander's losses, though so far only half as great as those in Louisiana, stood a dis-mal chance of being considerably greater in the end. Banks had lost some 4000 men to date, but at least he had found sanctuary within the Alexandria intrenchments: whereas Steele, in northward flight for Little Rock with hordes of exultant graybacks hot on his trail across the hundred miles of intervening hinterland, was in grievous danger of losing about three times that many, the only limit being that that was all he had. Still, for whatever consolation it was worth, the outcome could scarcely be direr than he had predicted in response to Halleck's original suggestion that he move on Shreveport in coöperation with Banks's ascent of the Red. He could only do so, he wired back, "against my own judgment and that of the best-informed people here. The roads are most if not quite impracticable; the country is destitute of provision." Moreover, he added, if he marched south the butternut guerillas were likely to hold carnival in North Arkansas and Southwest Missouri, with predictable results. "If they should form in my rear in considerable force I should be obliged to fall back to save my depots, &c." He thought it best not to go at all, in any case not in earnest. A feint at Arkadelphia or

Little Rock
Left 23 Mar
Returned 3 May
De Vall's Bluff

Hot Springs

STEELE
CAMDEN EXPEDITION

Rockport

Arkadelphia
29 Mar

Jenkins Ferry
30 Apr
Pine Bluff

Arkansas River

Okalona
3 Apr

Princeton

Little Missouri River

Mt. Elba

Washington

Marks Mill
25 Apr

Monticello

Prairie d'Ane
10-13 Apr

Camden
15-28 Apr

Spring Hill

Poison Spring
18 Apr

Saline River

El Dorado

ARKANSAS
LOUISIANA

Ouachita River

Minden

Shreveport

BANKS
RED RIVER CAMPAIGN

to Vicksburg

Monroe

to Marshall

Red River

Keatchie

Loggy Bayou

Mansfield

Blair's Landing

Sabine Crossroads
8 Apr

Grand Ecore
11-21 Apr

Pleasant Hill
9 Apr

Natchitoches
2-6 Apr

Cloutierville

Monett's Ferry
23 Apr

Sabine River

Bailey's Dam:
gunboats complete run,
12 May

Ft. De Russy
14 Mar

Bailey's Bridge:
Banks crosses
Atchafalaya
19-20 May

Mississippi River

Natchez

T E X A S

LOUISIANA

Alexandria
18-27 Mar;
25 Apr-13 May

Marksville

Mansura
16 May

Red River

Yellow Bayou
18 May
Simsport

MISS.
LA.

0   Miles   30

Hot Springs was the most he could recommend as a means of discouraging a rebel concentration against Banks, and having said as much — this was March 12, ten days past the time Old Brains had wanted him to set out southward — he remained at Little Rock, awaiting a reply. It came within three days, but not from Washington and not from Halleck. A brief telegram signed *U. S. Grant Lieutenant General* arrived from Nashville on March 15: "Move your force in full coöperation with General N. P. Banks' attack on Shreveport. A mere demonstration will not be sufficient."

That was that. Grant might or might not approve of this Transmississippi undertaking, conceived before his appointment as director of the nation's military effort, but it was clear he wanted it over and done with in the shortest possible time, and it was equally clear that to achieve this he intended to employ his accustomed method of bringing everything available to bear: including Steele. Accordingly, the Arkansas commander wasted no more energy on appeals which might have influenced Halleck but would obviously — as he knew from past experience, first as a classmate at West Point, then as a division commander in the Vicksburg campaign — do nothing but anger the new general-in-chief and probably bring on his own dismissal. Rather, he spent the next eight days preparing to move (an election of delegates to a constitutional convention, requiring the presence of his troops as poll watchers to protect the reconverted "loyal" ten percent of the state's voters from as many of the irreconcilable ninety percent as were not already in the field with Price, had been held the day before, March 14, with predictably satisfactory results) and then on March 23, midway through Holy Week, he set out.

Originally he had intended to proceed due south down the Ouachita, by way of Monroe, for a meeting with Banks at Alexandria. By now, though, it was too late for that; Alexandria had been taken, and he would scarcely be helping Banks by making him wait for him that far down the Red. So he chose instead to march southwest, through Arkadelphia and Washington to reach the upper Red, which he would then descend for a combination, near Shreveport, with the amphibious column moving northwest up that river toward that goal. An epicure and a sportsman, a breeder and racer of horses, forty-five years old, high-voiced and dandified in dress — "a velvet-collared esthete," one observer called him — Fred Steele was rumored by his enemies to live in the style of an Oriental prince, surrounded by silk-clad servants and pedigreed lapdogs, although this alleged limp-wristed aspect was considerably at odds with a lifetime habit of blasphemy, a full if silky beard, and a combat infantry record going back to the Mexican War, in which he had won two brevets for gallantry as an officer of the line. He had under him, for service in the campaign now beginning, some 14,000 effectives of all arms. Of these, a column including a little more than half — 5000 infantry and artillery, 3000 cavalry — left Little Rock under his immediate supervision, while another containing 4000 — the so-called Frontier Division, in occupation of Indian territory — marched from Fort Smith under Brigadier General John M. Thayer, who had orders to join the main body at Arkadelphia by April 1. A third force of about 2000, mostly cavalry and therefore highly mobile, was based on Pine Bluff, with instructions to divert attention in that direction, away from the column on the march to the southwest, and keep a close watch on the rebel garrison at Camden, one of the places where Sterling Price had had his headquarters since his loss of all the northern portion of the state in the fall of the previous year.

A warm-up march of nine miles on the first day flexed muscles used but scantly during months of easy duty. But next morning — Holy Thursday, and the weather remained clear — the men turned out of their blankets in the chill pre-dawn to find themselves involved in the full panoply of war. "Bugles rang out as we had never heard them before," an Iowa soldier would recall. "If an enemy had been in hearing distance, he must have thought we were at least a hundred thousand men, to raise such a wide-spread din." On the near bank of the Saline River by nightfall, still with no evidence that a single rebel was within earshot, they were informed that they would be on half-rations for the balance of the march. Digesting this as best they could, they woke to find it raining, which made for a hard Good Friday on soft roads. The same was true the next day and the next, Easter Sunday, when they crossed the Ouachita. The going was slow, especially across the frequent bottoms, which had to be corduroyed to get the wagons through. They did not reach Arkadelphia until March 29, having covered only seventy miles in a solid week of marching.

The worst of it, though, was that there was no sign at the rendezvous of the column from Fort Smith, and no word of its whereabouts came back from scouts sent out to find it. A three-day wait, while welcome as a rest, reduced the dwindling supply of food and forage in the trains, and still there was no message from Thayer, whose division was known to have left Fort Smith two days before the main body left Little Rock. The earth might have swallowed him up: or the rebels, none of whom seemed to be lurking in this direction. On April 1, after three days of marking time and further depleting his supplies, Steele decided he could wait no longer. He ordered the southwest march resumed down the old military road that led to Washington, thirty miles beyond the Little Missouri, which lay twenty-five miles ahead. On that day — April Fools' — the marchers encountered their first opposition, in the form of slashing attacks by mounted graybacks who struck them flank and rear.

They encountered only cavalry because that was all Price had to send against them. His two small divisions of infantry, summoned to

Louisiana to help Taylor go for Banks, had reached Kirby Smith at Shreveport on the day Steele set out from Little Rock with the same goal in mind; so that, however much this might benefit him tactically by reducing the type and number of troops he would encounter on his march through Arkansas, the Federal commander had no sooner gotten started than he failed in his main purpose, which was to keep the Transmississippi Confederates from ganging up on Banks. In any case, having accomplished this much without the firing of a shot, Price was left with only five brigades of cavalry, some 5000 effectives in all, badly scattered about the state. Two of these, combined in a division under Brigadier General James Fagan, were stationed east of the Saline to counter a possible Union advance from Pine Bluff, while two of the remaining three were posted at Camden, on the lower Ouachita, and the third was just west of Washington, on the upper Red. These three were under Brigadier General John S. Marmaduke and contained about 3200 troopers, veterans of many fights and raids, particularly those in Brigadier General J. O. Shelby's brigade, hard-bitten Missourians who asked for nothing better than a chance to come to grips with the bluecoats on the march. Two more brigades were said to be on the way from Indian Territory under Brigadier General Samuel B. Maxey, freed by Thayer's withdrawal to Fort Smith for his share in the Arkansas offensive, but Price had no way of knowing when they would arrive. "Retard the enemy's advance," Smith urged him in an Easter dispatch. "Operate on their communications if practicable. Time is everything with us." This aggressiveness was somewhat modified, however, by a warning not unlike the ones that were stretching Taylor's patience thin at the same time: "Do not risk a general action unless with advantage to yourself. You fall back toward reinforcements." Accordingly, Price held Fagan where he was, shielding Camden from attack by the bristly Pine Bluff garrison, and turned Marmaduke loose on Steele with instructions to deal as roughly with him as the disparity in numbers would allow. Marmaduke ordered a concentration of two brigades in the path of the Federal advance, intending to give ground as slowly as conditions would permit, while the third brigade — Jo Shelby's — set out on a circuitous march to get into position to harass the flanks and rear of the enemy slogging through Arkadelphia. Which Shelby did: beginning with the slashing attack he launched on All Fools' Day against just those tender parts of the blue column.

Steele came on, skirmishing front and rear, still not knowing what had become of Thayer or whether his division still existed. Sizeable clashes at Hollywood, a few miles out of Arkadelphia, and then next day at Spoonville and Antoine, along Terre Noir Creek, cost him more in time than they did in men. Time was what he could least afford, however, obliged as he was to balance his consumption of rations against his dwindling supply, already reduced by about three fourths though he was still a good deal short of halfway to his goal. On April 3, while the head of the column moved into the valley of the Little Missouri, diverging from the Washington road to secure a crossing at Elkin's Ferry, off to the south, Marmaduke launched a concerted attack on the main body, back at Okolona. Steele had to call a halt to fight him off, losing still more time and consuming still more rations. At this rate, he perceived, he was never going to make it; Shreveport might as well have been on the Gulf of Mexico or the back side of the moon. Still he pressed on, and next day, having secured a bridgehead at the ferry, he began to cross the river, still under attack from several directions. Then on April 6, with most of his men across, word came from Thayer. He had been delayed by poor roads; he had had to change his route; he would arrive from Hot Springs in a day or two or three. Steele cursed, shrill-voiced and blasphemous, and kept his troops at work corduroying the soggy bottoms for the passage of his and Thayer's trains. Finally, on April 9 — one day short of three weeks on the march — the Frontier Division came up and began to cross the Little Missouri. For Steele and his men, marking time on the south bank, the meeting with the frontiersmen was a let-down. "While we lay here," one recorded in disgust, "the long-looked-for and much-talked-of reinforcement of 'Thayer's command' arrived, from Fort Smith. A nondescript style of reinforcement it was too, numbering almost every kind of soldier, including Indians, and accompanied by multitudinous vehicles, of all descriptions, which had been picked up along the roads."

Worst of all, from Steele's point of view, though the buggies and carriages and buckboards were heavily loaded with plunder, they had little in them in the way of food. What Thayer had mainly brought him was another 4000 mouths to feed, reducing still further any chance Steele had of getting to Shreveport before he starved. There was nothing for it, he decided, but to send back word to department headquarters for a train to be made up and dispatched to him at once, "using, if necessary, every wagon and mule at Little Rock," with a thirty-day supply of "one-half rations of hard bread, one-quarter rations of bacon, and full rations of salt and coffee for 15,000 men." Whether he could survive in the barrens surrounding Elkin's Ferry until the supplies arrived, and whether they had any chance of getting through the rebel-infested region he had just traversed with so much fret, Steele did not know. Nor did he intend to find out, on either count. "Leaving here," he informed his adjutant in Little Rock, thereby giving the destination for the train, "I shall proceed directly to Camden with the whole force."

Nothing Confederate was any longer there to dispute its seizure; Price had evaluated Camden and joined Marmaduke two days ago, bringing Fagan's two brigades along to get in on the action. That raised the total to half a dozen gray brigades, one of Maxey's having ridden in the day before from Indian Territory, so that Price now had about half as many troops as Steele and Thayer, who had 12,000 between them. The Virginia-born former Missouri governor, white-haired in his middle fifties and weighing close to three hundred pounds, mild-mannered despite his imposing bulk and much beloved by his soldiers — although he and they had won no solid victory since Wilson's Creek and Lexington, back in the early days of the war in his home state — had intended to use all six brigades to contest a crossing at Elkin's Ferry; but when he arrived to find the Federals established in their bridgehead he revised his plan to take advantage of a line of shallow earthworks already dug along the near side of the Prairie d'Ane, a gently rolling stretch of meadowland affording his horsemen an excellent field for maneuver, five to ten miles back from the river and about midway between Arkadelphia and Spring Hill. The latter place he now thought was Steele's immediate objective, and the earthworks blocked the way there.

Preliminary skirmishing continued through April 8 and 9 (Banks had left Natchitoches two days before, and while Thayer was crossing the Little Missouri the Louisiana commander was falling back from Sabine Crossroads and Pleasant Hill) and then on April 10 Steele moved against Price across the undulating prairie. All morning and into the late afternoon (while Banks was intrenching feverishly at Grand Ecore and Tom Green was riding toward Blair's Landing, where he would encounter Porter and the naval gun that killed him) the skirmishing continued, gradually building almost to battle proportions — including a noisy exchange of long-range artillery fire which accomplished little except to demoralize a pet bear named Postlewait, the mascot of a rebel battery — until it faded and died away. The following day was much the same, long blue lines of skirmishers moving forward only to recede, and so was the next. On April 13 Maxey's other brigade arrived, Choctaw riders led by Colonel Tandy Walker, eager to use their scalping knives on Thayer's men, who had been despoiling their homes for the past year out in the Territory. But that was not to be: at least not yet. Under cover of these impressive demonstrations, it soon developed, Steele had been preparing, not for a mass assault, but for a withdrawal, a tangential march due east to Camden, forty miles away.

It was neatly done, and in the course of it Steele's soldiers gave a good account of themselves. Left holding the bag on the Prairie d'Ane, Price sent Marmaduke on a cross-country ride to block the road ahead, while Fagan and Maxey set out to overtake the bluecoats who had camped the night before on Terre Rouge Creek, well to the east. Both gray forces were able to get in position for their work, front and rear, but neither had the strength to carry it out. Thayer, whose division served as rear guard, managed to hold off his attackers through a two-day running fight, and German-born Brigadier General Frederich Salomon, commanding the advance division, repulsed Marmaduke in a hotly contested two-hour engagement, fourteen miles from Camden, on the morning of April 15. Just before dark of that same day Steele's lead brigade marched into the town, followed that night and next morning by all the others. While the Federals got to work improving the Confederate-dug intrenchments, semicircular in design and anchored at both ends to the Ouachita, above and below, Price came up and made a leisurely investment of the place. Steele was besieged: besieged by greatly inferior numbers: *self*-besieged, so to speak. Rare as this was in military annals, the situation was not unlike the one that obtained at the same time at Grand Ecore, 125 air-line miles to the south, with the difference that Steele had only a two-to-one advantage, while Banks had better than twice that.

Another difference, far more stringent and constricting, was that the Louisiana Federals had a fleet to bring supplies up the river they were based on, whereas those in Arkansas had to depend on foraging expeditions, highly vulnerable to ambush and assault by the enemy waiting just outside their lines for just such opportunities. Steele had managed to get his wagons through, but there was little in them that was edible. "Our supplies were nearly exhausted, and so was the country," he wrote Halleck on April 17, explaining his perpendicular divergence. "We were obliged to forage from five to fifteen miles on either side of the road to keep our stock alive." The same was true at Camden, however, and next day he received a double shock, half of which provided a graphic demonstration of the risk attendant on venturing outside his fortifications, although the only alternative was starvation. Fifteen miles out the Washington road there was a settlement with an ominous name: Poison Spring. Returning from a successful hunt for food in that direction, a train of 198 heavily loaded wagons, escorted by a mixed command of 1100 infantry, cavalry, and artillery with four guns, was jumped by Marmaduke and Maxey, who had better than 3000 troops between them. The slaughter was heavy, the rebel success almost complete. All four guns were taken, together with 170 of the wagons and their teams, the rest being burned. According to one of the captors, the train was "laden with corn, bacon, stolen bed quilts, women's and children's clothing, hogs, geese, and all the *et ceteras* of unscrupulous plunder." This helped to explain the heavy losses of the escort, nearly one third of whom were killed or captured by the infuriated attackers: particularly by Tandy Walker's Choctaws, who whooped with delight at finding the 1st Kansas (Colored) to their front. This was one of Thayer's outfits, well known for its ransack activities in the past, and the troopers unsheathed their knives for bloody work. According to the regimental commander, the high death rate among his casualties, 117 out of 182, was due to the fact that a number of the wounded were "murdered on the spot" by the vengeful red men. Confederate losses totaled 115, many of them only slightly hurt. The Federals lost 301, mostly killed or missing, plus all their guns and wagons.

By the time the survivors came stumbling back from Poison Spring that afternoon, Steele had been profoundly shaken by the other half of the double shock to his nervous system. It had been given him by a scout sent out the week before to get some news of Banks. Returning with word that the Louisiana commander had been thrown into reverse, first at Sabine Crossroads and then again at Pleasant Hill, the messenger reported that he had left him at Grand Ecore, three days back, though where he might be now he did not know. Steele was quick to perceive the dangers of noncoöperation, now that they were directed at himself. If his supposed partner were to pull out, every rebel in the Transmississippi would be free to concentrate against Camden and its hungry garrison, with results no doubt as grisly as those at Poison Spring this morning. He thought this over for four days, wincing at the prospect — which was in fact more likely than he yet knew; Banks left Grand Ecore on the third of these days, beginning another withdrawal, this time to Alexandria, another ninety miles downriver — and then appealed to his superiors not to allow him to be swamped and slaughtered because an adjoining commander lost his army or his nerve. "Although I believe we can beat Price," he protested, "I do not expect to meet successfully the whole force which Kirby Smith could send against me, if Banks should let him go."

Next day, April 23, he heard at last from Banks himself, who proposed, in a dispatch written a week ago at Grand Ecore, before he decided to withdraw farther down the river, that Steele march south at once to join him on the Red for a resumption of the advance upriver. "If you can join us on this line," Banks told him, "I am confident we can move to Shreveport without material delay, and that we shall have an opportunity of destroying the only organized rebel army west of the Mississippi."

Steele wanted no part of such an operation, and frankly said as much that same day in his reply. "Owing to contingencies," he wrote, "it is impossible for me to say definitely that I will join you at any point on Red River within a given time." Among the contingencies, he was careful to say, was Price's army, which was not only highly "organized," whatever Banks might imply to the contrary, but had recently been "very much encouraged by an order of General E. K. Smith, detailing his success against your command." He wished Banks well in whatever he might undertake of an offensive nature down in Louisiana, but as for himself, he had his hands full where he was; "I desire to coöperate with you in the best manner possible, at the same time covering Arkansas until Shreveport shall be ours." Moreover, he informed the man he held responsible for a large part of the woes he now saw looming, "We have been receiving yesterday and today rumors of reinforcements sent by Kirby Smith to Price at this point, and of a contemplated attack. It is said that 8000 infantry have arrived." Interrupted by the jar of guns, he set his pen aside to look into the cause of the disturbance, then took it up again with something of the perverse satisfaction of a prophet watching his gloomiest fears materialize in fact. "They have just opened upon my outposts with artillery," he continued. "This may be to get as near our lines as possible tonight, preparatory to a general attack tomorrow morning."

He was wrong about the attack next morning. Rather than a prelude to assault, the boom of guns was part of a design to frighten him into retreat. But he was altogether right about the rebel reinforcements and his adversary's intention to make bloody use of them. Kirby Smith had arrived three days ago from Shreveport, accompanied by three divisions of infantry flushed with pride for their recent victory over Banks, and he had it in mind to bag the Camden garrison entirely: in which case, he said later, "the prize would have been the Arkansas Valley and the fortifications of Little Rock," to be used in turn, quite possibly, as a base from which to recover the offensive in Missouri. Before this ambitious program for reversing the tide of war could be placed in execution, however, Steele would have to be disposed of, and Smith had no intention of trying to do so by attacking him in his intrenchments, either at Camden or at Little Rock. He preferred to catch him out in the open, between the two, after frightening or forcing him into attempting a retreat across the intervening barrens, where the blue column could be intercepted and cut to pieces by the now superior gray force. The infantry-artillery demonstration of April 23 having resulted only in causing the Federals to button themselves more tightly in their works, Smith intensified his efforts to smoke them out by disrupting their supply lines, particularly those beyond the Ouachita, which Price had not felt strong enough to threaten up to now. Accordingly, while the Camden demonstration was in progress, Fagan crossed the river at Eldorado Landing, twenty miles downstream, with instructions to use his division, reinforced to a strength of more than 3000 by the addition of Shelby's brigade, to strike at logistical targets along the Saline and the Arkansas, as well as along the roads that ran between and across them, from Little Rock and Pine Bluff, down to Camden. The result was not long in coming, and when it came it was as decisive, on a larger scale, as the rout at Poison Spring.

Crossing the Ouachita on the morning of April 24, Fagan was informed by Shelby's scouts, who had ridden ahead, that a large train, heavily guarded, had left Camden two days ago, sent by Steele to Pine Bluff for supplies. Determined to intercept the Federals before they got across the Saline at Mount Elba, he led his troopers on a forced march of forty-five miles to halt at midnight near Marks Mill, where the road he had taken from Eldorado Landing joined the one connecting Camden and Pine Bluff, five miles short of the river. He was pleased to learn that the blue train, delayed by muddy going on cut-up roads, had made camp at nightfall on the near side of Moro Bottom, a few miles to the west, and he was also pleased to hear that the prize was quite as plump as he had hoped: 240 government wagons, together with a number of other vehicles belonging to "cotton speculators, refugees, sutlers, and other army followers," escorted by three regiments of infantry, one of cavalry, and a six-gun battery — in effect, a reinforced brigade, whose strength of 1440 effectives was less than half his own. Anticipating a larger reward than Marmaduke and Maxey had won at Poison Spring, a week ago tomorrow, Fagan instructed Shelby to use his Missourians to block the road between Marks Mill and Mount Elba, thus to prevent an escape across the Saline, and posted his other brigades near Marks Mill itself, with orders to assail the flank and rear of the slow-grinding column as soon as it came up next morning.

It came up shortly after dawn and the action went as planned, except for a more determined resistance by the Iowa, Ohio, and Indiana infantrymen than had been expected. Alarmed by the sudden attack, they panicked, then rallied and counterattacked. Fagan used his superior numbers with skill, however, and after about four hours of hard fighting, some of it hand to hand — especially when Shelby came back and forced the issue; "I determined to charge them first, last, and all the time," he later reported — the blue regiments surrendered one by one, in different quarters of the field. "Less than 150 of the brigade escaped from the conflict," the Federal commander admitted, "the balance, including the wounded, being made prisoners." Himself among them, these totaled 1300, excluding the civilian hangers-on, whose captured vehicles brought the haul to more than 300 wagons, together with their teams. All were taken, along with the six guns and the four regimental standards, and Fagan, whose own loss of more than 300 killed and wounded testified to the savagery of the fighting, rode off northward, mindful of Kirby Smith's instructions for him to maneuver in the region between Camden and Little Rock, not only in order to continue his depredations, but also in order to be in position to intercept the retreat of Steele, which was expected any day now.

Even so, it came sooner than either side had anticipated before hearing of Fagan's coup. Informed of the disaster that night by the handful of fugitives who made it back to Camden from Marks Mill, Steele called an immediate council of war to ponder what had better be done to meet this latest crisis. The choice seemed limited to starvation, surrender, or flight. Without exception, his chief subordinates — Salomon, Thayer, and Brigadier General Eugene Carr, his cavalry commander — advised the last, and after a day of feverish preparations, including the destruction of such goods as there was no room for in the depleted train, issued what scant rations were left to his alerted troops, which in some cases consisted of two crackers of hardtack and half a pint of cornmeal, together with a warning that this was likely to be all they would get until they had covered a considerable portion of the hundred-mile trek to Little Rock. All day (while Porter was blowing up the *Eastport* and Banks was getting resettled in Alexandria, which the tail of his column had reached that morning) they worked from dawn to dark to complete their preparations for departure, loading wagons, rolling packs, destroying unneeded equipment with a minimum of noise and smoke, lest the rebels in their camps across the way become aware that they were leaving. By way of adding to the deception, and thereby lengthening the head start, drums beat a noisy tattoo at 8 o'clock, followed an hour later by taps, which was sounded on a far-carrying bass drum. Meantime the loaded wagons were rolling slowly across the Ouachita on the pontoon bridge. By midnight all were over and the infantry followed, breaking step to muffle the hollow sound of their crossing. In the small hours of April 27, with Camden lying silent and empty behind them, dark except for a few scattered lamps left burning to encourage the illusion that the army was still there, the engineers silently took up the bridge, knowing that it would be needed when and if they reached the Saline, then hurried after the column, which had been halted several miles beyond the river to give the troops some rest for the ordeal that lay ahead.

Back at Camden, the Confederates did not discover until well after sunrise that they were besieging an empty town. It was midmorning before they marched in, and even then the infantry could not take out after the departed garrison until some way was found for them to cross the bridgeless Ouachita. While Marmaduke's troopers were swimming their mounts across, and Maxey's were preparing for an unexpected return to Indian Territory in response to a report of a threatened invasion from Missouri — Kirby Smith made them a speech of thanks for their Arkansas service before they set out on their long ride home — Price began the construction of a "floating bridge," to be used in ferrying Churchill's and Walker's three divisions over the swollen river. Building and then using the raft, which had a limited capacity, was an all-afternoon, all-night affair; it was daylight, April 28, before the pursuit began in earnest. As a result of the loss of Maxey and the recent detachment of Fagan, who had done excellent work at Marks Mill but now was somewhere off to the north and west, unaware that Camden had been evacuated or that a race to the death was in progress in his rear, Smith was down to about 10,000 effectives. Although this amounted to nothing like the preponderance he might have enjoyed, he pressed them hard in the wake of the fleeing Federals — whose trail was marked by abandoned equipment, including personal effects, foundered mules, and wagons buried axle-deep in mud — knowing only too well that if he did not overtake them before they crossed the Saline he might as well give up hope of coming to grips with them anywhere short of Little Rock; which meant, in effect, that he would not be able to come to grips with them at all, since there they would have the advantage of intrenchments and could summon reinforcements from other departments roundabout.

Steele was down to roughly the same number of troops as Smith, having suffered 2000 casualties in the past month without inflicting half as many. What was worse, his men had been on short rations all this time, which tended to make them trembly in the legs and short on endurance. However, he had not only gained them a full day's head start in the race for the Arkansas capital, he had also managed to coax or prod them into making good time on the way there. Shortly after noon on this second day out of Camden, the head of the column reached the town of Princeton, in whose streets his rear guard bivouacked that night, two thirds of the distance to the Saline, which in turn was halfway to his goal. He had chosen this nearly barren route to Little Rock, rather than the more accustomed one through Pine Bluff, in order to avoid the Moro swamps, where the train that fell to Fagan had been so grievously delayed; but presently, as rain began to patter on the marchers and the road, he began to doubt that he had chosen wisely. The mud deepened, slowing the pace of his soldiers as they slogged along in the ankle-twisting ruts of the wagons up ahead, and the rain came down harder every hour. Before nightfall, rebel troopers — Marmaduke's amphibious horsemen — were shooting and slashing at the bedraggled tail of the column. By that time, though, the van had reached the Saline at Jenkins Ferry, and the engineers were getting their pontoons launched and linked and floored, while other details worked at corduroying the two-mile long approach across the bottoms giving down upon the river, beyond which there stretched another just as long and just as mean. Such labor was too heavy for troops in their condition, faint for sleep as well as food. While they strained at cutting and placing timbers, Steele's chief engineer afterwards reported, "wagons settled to the axles and mules floundered about without a resting place for their feet." After dark, he added, the work continued by the light of fires, and "every exertion [was] made to push the impedimenta across before daylight, it being evident that the enemy was in force in our rear. But we failed. The rain came down in torrents, putting out many of the fires, the men became exhausted, and both they and the animals sank down in the mud and mire, wherever they were, to seek a few hours' repose."

It was here, in this "sea of mud," as the engineer called it, that fleers and pursuers — blue and gray, though both would be dun before the thing was over — fought the Battle of Jenkins Ferry, a miry nightmare of confusion and fatigue. This last applied as much to one side as the other; for if the Confederates had no foundered mules and ship-wrecked wagons to haul along or strain at, they had to make a faster march, with fewer halts, in order to overcome the substantial Union lead. North of Princeton by nightfall, they took a four-hour rest, then moved out again at midnight. By 7.30 next morning, April 30, the lead brigade had come up to where Marmaduke's dismounted troopers were skirmishing with blue infantry posted astride the road leading down to the ferry, two miles in its rear. Price committed his troops as fast as they arrived, first Churchill's own and then its companion division, led by Brigadier General Mosby Parsons. They made little headway, for the Federals were crouched behind stout log breastworks, in a position whose access was restricted on the left and right by Toxie Creek and an impenetrable swamp. Moreover, this narrow, alley-like approach not only afforded the charging infantry no cover, it was for the most part slathered over with a spongy, knee-deep layer of mud and brim-full pools of standing water. Their only protection was a blanket of fog, thickened presently by gunsmoke, which lay so heavily over the field that marksmen had to stoop to take aim under it or else do their shooting blind. In point of fact, however, this was more of an advantage for the defenders, who were already lying low, than it was for the attackers toiling heavy-footed toward them through the mire. Besides, fog stopped no bullets: as the rebels soon found out, encountering fire that was no less murderous for being blind. They fell back, abandoning three guns in the process, and failed to recover them when Price, after giving the blown attackers time to catch their breath, ordered the assault renewed.

Kirby Smith was on the field by then, coming up with Walker, who insisted on remaining with his men despite his unhealed Louisiana wound, suffered three weeks ago today at Pleasant Hill. Committed just after Churchill and Parsons were thrown back the second time, his Texans attacked with such fury and persistence that all three of their brigade commanders were wounded, two of them mortally. But they did no better, in the end, than the Arkansans and Missourians had done before them. The bluecoats were unshaken behind their breastworks, apparently ready to welcome another attempt to budge them, although the Confederates were not disposed to try it, having lost no fewer than 1000 casualties in the effort, as compared to about 700 for the defenders, including stragglers who had fallen by the wayside on the three-day march from Camden. It was past noon; the last Federal wagon had passed over the river an hour ago, escorted by the cavalry, and now the infantry followed, unmolested by the former owners of the three captured guns they took along. Once on the far side of the Saline, they cut the bridge loose from the south bank and set it afire, partly because they had no further use for it, having no more rivers to cross, and partly because their mules were too weary to haul it. Bridgeless, the rebels could do nothing but let them go, even if they had been of a mind to stop them; which they no longer were, having tried.

Fagan came up soon afterward from over near Arkadelphia, where he had gone for supplies after proceeding north, then west and south, from the scene of his coup five days ago at Marks Mill, less than thirty miles downstream from the battle fought today. Though he made good time on his thirty-four-mile ride from the Ouachita to the Saline, which began at dawn when he learned that Steele was on the march for Little Rock by way of Jenkins Ferry, he not only arrived too late for his 3000 troopers to have a share in the fighting, he was also on the wrong side of the river for them to undertake pursuit. Kirby Smith saw in his failure to intercept and impede the Federals one of the might-have-beens of the war, saying later that if Fagan had "thrown himself on the enemy's front on his march from Camden, Steele would have been brought to battle and his command utterly destroyed long before he reached the Saline." Dismissing this, however, as "one of those accidents which are likely to befall the best of officers," the even-tempered Floridian was more inclined to count his gains than to be-moan lost opportunities. He had, after all, frustrated both Union attempts to seize his Shreveport base and drive him from his department, and though Banks at Alexandria was still to be reckoned with as a menace, the Arkansas column was no longer even the semblance of a threat, at least for the present, to the region it had set out forty days ago to conquer. At a cost to himself of about 2000 casualties, a good portion of whom had already returned to his ranks, Smith had in-flicted nearly 3000, two thirds of them killed or captured and there-fore permanent subtractions. Losing three guns he had taken ten, all told, in a campaign that had cost the invaders 635 wagons surrendered or destroyed, according to the Federal quartermaster's own report, along with no less than 2500 mules. The list of captured matériel was long, including weapons of all types, complete with ammunition, not to mention sutler goods, rare medical supplies, and enough horses to mount a brigade of cavalry. But the major gain, as Smith himself declared, was that he had "succeeded in driving Steele from the valley of the Ouachita . . . and left myself free to move my entire force to the support of Taylor."

That was clearly the next order of business. With one prong of the two-pronged Union offensive — Steele — now definitely snapped off, it was time to attend to the other — Banks — already severely bent. After giving the divisions of Churchill, Parsons, and Walker two days of badly needed rest, Smith issued orders on May 3 for them to return at once to Camden and proceed from there "by the most direct route to Louisiana."

Steele's men returned on the same day to Little Rock near exhaustion, having found the going even more arduous on the north side of the Saline than on the south. Partly this was because they were one day hungrier and one battle wearier, but it was also because the mud was deeper and timber scarce. As a result of this shortage of corduroy material, they had a much harder time trying to keep the wagons rolling. When one stuck beyond redemption, as many did, it was burned to keep it from falling into rebel hands, and when teams grew too weak to be led, as many did, they were set free: all of which added greatly to the army's loss of equipment and supplies. From dawn of May Day to 4 a.m. the next, out of the soggy bottoms at last, the infantry slogged in a daze that was intensified that night by the lurid flicker of roadside fires the cavalry had kindled to light their way through the darkness. "A strange, wild time," one marcher was to term it, recalling that hardtack sold for two dollars a cracker, while in one instance two were swapped for a silver watch. Late the second afternoon a shout went up from the head of the column, announcing that a train had come out from the capital with provisions. They made camp for the night, wolfing their rations before turning in, and were off again at sunrise. When the fortifications of Little Rock came into sight, around midmorning of May 3, they halted to dress their tattered ranks and thus present as decent an appearance as they could manage, then proceeded into town, giving a prominent place in the column to the three captured guns that were all they had to show, in the way of trophies, for their forty-two days of campaigning.

"The Camden Expedition," Steele called the unhappy affair, as if Shreveport had never been part of his calculations. But the men themselves, being rather in agreement with the Saint Louis journalist that all they had gained for their pains was "defeat, hard blows, and poor fare," were not deceived. They had failed to reach their assigned objective, whatever their silky-whiskered commander might claim to the contrary, and they knew only too well what the failure had cost them: not to mention what it might cost Banks, who seemed likely to lose a great deal more, now that Steele had left the rebels free to shift their full attention to matters in Louisiana.

★ ★ ★

All would now depend on speed in that direction: speed for the three divisions on the way to Taylor, speed for him in bringing them to bear, and speed for Banks and Porter in solving, before that happened, the problem of how to get ten gunboats, some of which drew seven feet of water, down and past a mile-long stretch of river less than half that deep. It was in that sense a race, with the odds very much in favor of the Confederates. So far at least as the concentration went, they had only to do in Louisiana what they had just finished doing in

Arkansas; whereas the Federals were confronted with a problem that seemed, on the face of it, insoluble. Yet by now, before they even knew that Steele had backtracked and a race was therefore on, the blue commanders had found a way to win it. Or in any case they had found a man who believed he knew a way to win it, if they would only let him try.

On April 29 — while Marmaduke was closing on Steele near Jenkins Ferry and opening the action that would swell to battle proportions tomorrow morning — Lieutenant Colonel Joseph Bailey, Franklin's chief of engineers, came to Banks with a plan for raising the level of the river by installing, above Alexandria, a system of wing dams that would constrict and thereby deepen the channel leading down to and over the falls. A former Northwest lumberman, thirty-nine years old this week, he had used such methods to get logs down sluggish Wisconsin streams, and he was convinced they would work here, too, on a larger scale and for a larger purpose. "I wish I was as sure of heaven as I am that I can save the fleet," he said. Banks needed little persuading, not only because he was desperate enough by now to try almost anything, but also because the young engineer had demonstrated his ability along those lines the previous summer at Port Hudson, where he had salvaged, by damming a shallow creek to float them free, a pair of transports the rebels had left lying on their sides in the mud. The general took him that evening to present his plan to Porter. Contemplating the loss of his gunboats and the wreck of his career, the admiral was in an unaccustomed state of dejection; "This fatal campaign has upset everything," he had recently complained to Wells in a dispatch designed to prepare the Secretary for darker ones to follow. His first reaction to Bailey's proposal was to scoff at it. "If damning would get the fleet off, we would have been afloat long ago," he broke in, brightening a bit at this evidence that his sense of humor, such as it was, was still in working order. When it was explained to him further that the navy would have little to do but stand by and watch the army sweat and strain, he declared that he was willing on those terms. Accordingly, Banks issued orders on the last day of April for the thing to be tried, and Bailey, given 3000 soldiers to use as he saw fit in getting it done, put them to work without delay on May Day morning.

His plan was to construct above the lower falls, where the Red was 758 feet wide, a pair of wing dams, each extending about three hundred feet out into the river, then sink high-sided barges filled with brick across the remaining gap. The north bank dam was to be formed of large trees laid with the current, their branches interlocked and their trunks cross-tied with heavy timbers on the downstream side; while the one on the south bank, where trees were scarce, would consist of huge cribs, pushed out and sunk and anchored in place with rubble of all kinds. Most of the left-bank work was done by a Maine regiment of highly skilled axmen and loggers, the rest being left to three regiments of New Yorkers, experienced in tearing down old buildings — one was the military academy of which Sherman had been superintendent just before the war — for bricks and stone, to be used to hold the sunken cribs and barges in position against the force of the nine-knot current. They worked day and night, under a broiling sun and by the light of bonfires, much of the time up to their necks in the swift, rust-colored water.

At the outset they provoked more jeers than cheers from the sailors and off-duty soldiers looking on, but as the ends of the two dams drew closer together, day by day and hour by hour, interest mounted and skepticism lessened among the spectators on the gunboats and both banks, who now began to tell each other that Bailey's notion might just be practicable, after all. The sailors, especially those aboard the "teakettles," as the ironclads were called, were pleased to be afforded this diversion, now that rising temperatures had added physical discomfort to their boredom. "During the day," an officer recorded, "the iron on the decks would get so hot that the hand could barely rest upon it. At night, sleep was impossible. The decks were kept wetted down, and the men lay on them, getting, toward the morning hours when the hulls had cooled down, such sleep as could be secured." Nor were excursions ashore of much help in this regard, involving, as they sometimes did, another form of torture which southern women, then and later, were adept at inflicting. "Saw quite a number of ladies from Pine Village opposite Alexandria," a sailor wrote in his diary after one such visit. "Two in particular were out on display promenade, one of whom had a beautiful black squirrel which ran all over her, up her dress sleeves and under her lace cape into her bosom, with a familiarity that made me envy the little favorite and sent a thrill that did not feel very bad through all the little veins in my body."

Still, being bored or titillated, painful though they were in their different ways, was better than getting shot at: as a good many soldiers and sailors could testify from experience while the dams were being built. If Taylor lacked the strength to interfere with the work going on behind the Federal intrenchments, he could at least make life hectic for the troops who manned them, and he could do considerably worse to those who ventured outside them, on foot or afloat. On the day Bailey started construction, the transport *Emma* was captured at David's Ferry, thirty miles below Alexandria, her captain and crew looking on as prisoners while the rebels burned her. Three days later another, the *City Belle*, was served in much the same fashion a few miles farther down, this time with a 700-man Ohio regiment aboard. More than a third of the soldiers were captured — 276 by Taylor's count — while the rest went over the side, escaped ashore, and eventually made their way back through the lines. Next day, May 5, saw the gravest loss of all. The transport *Warner*, escorted by the gunboats *Covington* and *Signal* while taking another regiment of Ohioans downriver to begin their reënlistment furloughs, came under fire from a masked battery as she rounded a bend near the mouth of Dunn's Bayou. Disabled by an unlucky shot in her rudder, she spun with the current, absorbing heavy punishment from riflemen posted along the high south bank, and when the two warships tried to come to her assistance by bringing their seventeen guns to bear on the rebel four, they were given the same treatment in short order. *Covington*, hulled repeatedly, went aground and was set afire by her skipper, who got away into the woods with 32 of his crew of 74, leaving the rest to the mercy of the gray marksmen who by then were at work on *Signal*. They cut her up so badly that the captain, prevented from destroying her by the fact that there was no time for removing the wounded, struck his colors and surrendered his 54 survivors, together with some 125 killed and wounded left strewn about the decks of the *Warner* when she and they were abandoned by her crew and their fellow soldiers. That brought the total for the past five days to better than 600 amphibious Federals killed or captured, together with three transports and two gunboats, at a cost to the Confederates of little more than the ammunition they expended. Worst of all, from the point of view of the soldiers and sailors cooped up in Alexandria or marooned above the falls, the Red was emphatically closed to Union shipping. They had to subsist on what they had, which by now was very little, or starve; or leave.

Along with everyone else in blue, Banks preferred the last of these three alternatives, although it appeared about as unlikely as the first. At this stage, the choice seemed narrowed to the second — starvation — which was scarcely a choice at all. As of May Day, he computed that he could subsist his army for three weeks on half-rations out of what he had on hand. That might or might not be enough, depending on whether the work begun on the dams that day could be completed within that span, but there seemed little doubt, at best, that he would lose his train for lack of animals to haul the wagons. Forage was so short already that Taylor was complaining, and exulting, that the horses he captured were little more than skeletons. Pitiable as they were, he intended to be still harder on them in the immediate future, as a means of being harder on the men who rode or drove them. On May 7, after claiming that his downstream successes near Dunn's Bayou had converted the lower Red, formerly a broad Federal highway of invasion, into "a *mare clausum*," he reported to Kirby Smith: "Forage and subsistence of every kind have been removed beyond the enemy's reach. Rigid orders are given to destroy everything useful that can fall into his hands. We will play the game the Russians played in the retreat from Moscow."

So he intended, gazing all the while back over his shoulder for some sign of the approach of the troops from Arkansas, without whom he lacked the strength to come to earnest grips with the beleaguered Unionists. All he could do was pray that they would arrive before the bluecoats started the downstream march that would increase the distance his reinforcements would have to cover before they could be brought to bear.

In point of fact, the race was closer than he knew. Faith had replaced skepticism in the attitude of the watchers at the dam site. "Before God, what won't the Yankees do next!" a gray-haired contraband cried in amazement at his first sight of the week-old work in progress, now rapidly nearing completion. Crews of the largest of the ten warships above the falls, having caught the spirit of the workers in the water, were busy lightening their vessels by stripping off side armor, which they dumped in a five-fathom hole upstream to keep it out of rebel hands, and unloading such heavy materials as commandeered cotton, anchors, chains, ammunition, and most of the guns, which — all but eleven old 32-pounders, spiked and sunk, like the iron plating, to forestall salvage — were to be carted below on wagons for reloading in deep water beyond the falls. By the following day, May 8, the river had risen enough to allow three of the lighter-draft boats, the tinclad *Fort Hindman* and the broad-bottomed monitors *Osage* and *Neosho*, to pass the upper falls and take station just above the dam, awaiting the further rise that would enable them to make their run. That would not take long, apparently, for now that the dam was finished and the rubble-laden barges sunk to plug the gap between the wings, the river was rising so swiftly that it deepened more than a foot between sunset and midnight, increasing the midstream depth to a full six feet. Another foot would do it, the engineers said. As the depth increased, however, so did the speed of the current and the resultant pressure on the dam, which mounted in ratio to both. Banks, for one, began to fear that the whole affair would be swept away in short order. Arriving for an inspection by the light of bonfires late that night, he sent Porter a message expressing hope that the flotilla would be ready to move down at a moment's notice, since it seemed to him unlikely that the dam, already trembling under the weight of all that water, could survive past dawn.

He was wrong by about one hour. It held all night, then blew at 5.30 next morning when two of the barges shifted, first tentatively, then with a rush, and went with the boom and froth of current through the re-created gap.

Porter was on the scene. He had paid Banks's warning no mind last evening, but now that its validity was being demonstrated so cataclysmically, he reacted in a hurry by leaping astride a horse for a fast ride upstream to order the boats above the upper falls to start their run before the water, rushing Niagara-like between the unplugged wings of the dam, fell too low for them to try it. All but *Lexington*, the oldest vessel with the fleet — one of the three original "timberclads," she was a veteran of practically all the river fights since Belmont, where Grant got his start, and had harassed the Confederates trying to get some sleep in the captured Federal camps after the first day's fight at Shiloh — were unready for action of any kind, moored to bank with their steam down and all but their anchor watches taking it easy about the decks. *Lexington* got under way at once, passing scantly over the rocks of the upper falls, and headed straight for the 66-foot opening between the two remaining barges. The admiral, one of the thousands of soldiers and sailors who lined both banks of the Red to watch her go, later reported her progress and the reaction, afloat and ashore: "She entered the gap with a full head of steam on, pitched down the roaring current, made two or three spasmodic rolls, hung for a moment on the rocks below, and then was swept into deep water by the current and rounded to, safely into the bank. Thirty thousand voices rose in one deafening cheer, and universal joy seemed to pervade the face of every man present."

Encouraged by *Lexington*'s example, the skippers of the three boats that had crossed the upper falls the previous day decided to try their hand at completing the run before the mass of water drained away and left them stranded in the shallows of the rapids. *Neosho* led off, advancing bravely under a full head of steam. At the last minute, however, just as she was about to enter the gorge, the pilot lost his nerve and signaled for the engine to be stopped. It was, but not the monitor herself. She went with the sucking rush of the current, out of control; her low hull plunged from sight beneath the spume as she went into the gap, careening through at an angle so steep it was nearly a dive, and struck bottom with an iron clang, loud against the bated silence on both banks; then reappeared at last below, taking cheers from the watchers and water through the hole the stones had punched along her keel. This last was slight and soon repaired — a small price to pay for deliverance from a month's captivity, not to mention the risk of self-destruction or surrender. The other two warships, *Osage* and *Hindman*, made it through in a more conservative style, with less excitement for the troops on shore but also with less damage to themselves. Four boats were now below the double falls, assured of freedom and continuing careers in their old allegiance. But the remaining six were trapped as completely as before, the water having fallen too low for them to cross the upper falls by the time they got up steam enough to risk the run.

Banks was more or less unstrung by the fulfillment of his prediction that the dam was about to go. He foresaw indefinite postponement of the departure which just last night had seemed so near, and he was correspondingly cast down, having seen the effects of starvation only too clearly last summer at Port Hudson when the scarecrow garrison lined up for surrender. "We have exhausted the country," he told Porter that afternoon, "and with the march that is before us it will be perilous to remain more than another day."

The admiral, perhaps because he had put less faith in the dam as a means of deliverance, reacted less despairingly to the mishap. After all, he had saved four of his boats already — four less than he had feared he well might lose — and he believed he could save the other half dozen as well, if the army would only stand fast until the dam could be replugged. But there was the rub. Banks, in his depression, was giving what seemed to Porter signs that he was about to pull out, bag and baggage, workers and all, and leave the stranded warships to the mercy of butternut marksmen who had demonstrated at Dunn's Bayou, four days ago, their skill at naval demolition when there was no army standing by to hold them off. On May 11, when Banks displayed further jumpiness by sending a staff officer to complain that the navy seemed unmindful of the need for utmost haste, Porter did what he could to calm him down. "Now, General," he replied soothingly, "I really see nothing that should make us despond. You have a fine army, and I shall have a strong fleet of gunboats to drive away an inferior force in our front." Up to now, he artfully pointed out, the press had been highly critical of the conduct of the campaign; but think what a glorious finish the salvation of the flotilla would afford the journalists for the stories yet to be filed. And having thus appealed to the former governor's political sensibilities, the admiral closed with an exhortation designed to stiffen his resolution. "I hope, Sir, you will not let anything divert you from the attempt to get these vessels all through safely, even if we have to stay here and eat mule meat."

No blue-clad soldier or sailor had yet been reduced to such a diet; nor would one be here, though Banks was quick to reply that he had no intention of leaving the navy in the lurch. The reason again was Bailey, who once more solved a difficult engineering problem in short order. Instead of attempting to plug the swift-running gap between the still-intact wings of the dam just above the lower falls, he decided instead to construct another at the upper falls, similar to the first, and thus not try any longer to sustain the weight of all that water with one dam. It was done with such dispatch, his thousand-man detail being thoroughly experienced in such work by now, that within three days — that is, before sunset of the day Porter urged Banks to stand by him "even if we have to stay here and eat mule meat" — three more vessels completed their runs down the mile-long rapids and over the two sets of falls. These were the veteran Eads gunboats *Mound City*, *Pittsburg*, and *Carondolet*. Next day, May 12, the remaining three — the armored steamer *Chillicothe*, the fourth Eads gunboat *Louisville*, and finally the third monitor *Ozark*, successor to the *Eastport* as the pride of the river fleet — did the same. The admiral and his precious warships were delivered, thanks to Bailey, to whom he presented, as a personal gift, a $700 sword. The engineer also received, as tokens of appreciation, a $1600 silver vase from the navy, a vote of thanks from Congress, and in time a two-step promotion to brigadier general. None of this was a whit too much, according to Porter, who said of the former Wisconsin logger in his report: "Words are inadequate to express the admiration I feel for the abilities of Lieutenant Colonel Bailey. This is without doubt the best engineering feat ever performed. Under the best circumstances a private company would not have completed this work under one year, and to an ordinary mind the whole thing would have appeared an utter impossibility."

He might have added that his own mind seemed to fit in that category, since he had prejudged the attempt in just that way. But for the present, steaming down the lower Red, where the going was deep and easy because of backwater from the swollen Mississippi, he was altogether occupied with savoring his freedom, his narrow delivery from ruin. "I am clear of my troubles," he wrote home to his mother that week, though he was not so far clear of them that he forgot to add: "I have had a hard and anxious time of it."

So had Banks had a hard and anxious time of it, and so was he still, along with the slogging troops under his command. Leaving Alexandria on May 13, the day after Porter completed his run, they had another sixty hostile miles to cover before they would return to their starting point, Simsport on the Atchafalaya, where Sherman's men had opened the campaign, just one day more than two full months ago. In point of fact, except as a location on the map, the town no longer existed; A. J. Smith's gorillas had burned it at the outset. And now, looking back over their shoulders as they set out, they had a similar satisfaction — similar not only to Simsport, but also to Grand Ecore, three weeks ago, as well as to a number of lesser hamlets in their path, before and since — of seeing Alexandria aflame. It burned briskly under a long, wind-tattered plume of greasy smoke, while over the levee and down by the bank of the river, as one Federal would recall, "thousands of people, mostly women, children, and old men, were wringing their hands as they stood by the little piles of what was left of all their worldly possessions." They had been driven there by the sudden press of heat from a score of fires that quickly merged after starting simultaneously with the help of a mixture of turpentine and camphene, which the soldiers slopped on houses and stores with mops and brooms. Experience had greatly improved their incendiary technique. "Hurrah, boys! This looks like war!" Smith shouted by way of encouragement as he rode through the streets, rounding up his men for departure.

They had their usual assignment as rear guard, the post of honor on retreat, while the Easterners took the lead. Banks rode with the more congenial troops up front, commanded now by Emory; Franklin, after recommending that his chief engineer's proposal for saving the fleet be tried, had left on May Day, still fretted by his shin wound, which seemed to require more skilled attention than the Transmississippi doctors were able to furnish, and by disgust and bitterness at having been prominently connected with still another large-scale defeat. Banks of course had that fret too, without the red-badge distraction of a physical injury, but he felt better, all in all, than he had done at any time in the past horrendous month. For one thing, the salvation of the flotilla had given journalists the upbeat ending Porter had dangled as bait for prolonging the army's stay in Alexandria, and for another his casualties had been replaced, before the end of April, by reinforcements who arrived from Pass Cavallo, Texas, under Major General John A. McClernand, resurrected from his Grant-enforced retirement in Springfield, Illinois, and put in command of the lower Texas coast by his old friend and fellow townsman Abraham Lincoln. That brought the army's total strength to 31,000 effectives up the Red, more than Banks had had directly under him so far in the campaign. Even though there was no compensation for the loss of twenty guns, two hundred wagons, and something over a thousand mules, this added strength brought added confidence; which, aside from military skill, had been the thing most lacking at headquarters since the crossroads confrontation short of Mansfield, five weeks ago today. Moreover, there was the relief of having the end at last in sight, whatever disappointments had occurred along the way, and of discovering that Taylor, for all his bluster in the course of the Alexandria siege, seemed considerably less a menace now that the cooped-up bluecoats were out in the open, inviting the attack he formerly had seemed anxious but now seemed strangely reluctant to deliver.

At any rate that appeared to be the case throughout the first three days of the march downriver. Crossing the Choctaw Bayou swamps on the second day out of smouldering Alexandria, the Federals occupied Marksville on the evening of the third. That was May 15; they had covered forty miles by then, molested by nothing worse than grayback cavalry, which failed in its attempts to get at the wagons drawn by scarecrow mules, and were a good two thirds of their way to the sanctuary a crossing of the Atchafalaya would afford them. Banks tempered his optimism, however, by reminding himself that the tactical situation resembled the one that had obtained, or had seemed to obtain, on the march from Natchitoches to within three miles of Mansfield, where it ended in disarray. The resemblance was altogether too close for comfort, let alone for premature self-congratulation; Taylor might well be planning a repeat of that performance at another crossroads, somewhere up ahead. And sure enough, advancing next morning across the Avoyelles Prairie, five miles south of Marksville, Banks found the Confederates disposed in force athwart his path, much as they had been at Sabine Crossroads, except that here the terrain was open and gave him a sobering view of what he faced. Their line of battle extending east and west of the village of Mansura, they had thirty-odd pieces of artillery — more than half of them had been his own, up to the time of the previous confrontation just short of Mansfield, which this one so uncomfortably resembled — unlimbered and ready to take him under fire as soon as he ventured within range. Their numbers in infantry and cavalry were hard to estimate, masked as their center was by the town, but Banks did not decline the challenge. He shook out his skirmishers, put his own guns in position — as many of the remaining seventy, in any case, as he could find room for on the three-mile width of prairie — formed his infantry for attack with cavalry posted neatly on both flanks, and then went forward, blue flags rippling in the breeze.

The result, as the troops began to move and the guns to growl, was enough to make observers in both armies, each of which had a full view of the other, catch their breath in admiration. Advancing across the lush and level prairie — "smooth as a billiard table," Taylor was to say of it in his report — the Union host was "resplendent in steel and brass," according to one of its members, a Connecticut infantryman who afterward tried his hand at a word sketch of the scene, including "miles of lines and columns; the cavalry gliding over the ground in the distance with a delicate, nimble lightness of innumerable twinkling feet; a few batteries enveloped in smoke and incessantly thundering, others dashing swiftly to salient positions; division and corps commanders with their staff officers clustering about them, watching through their glasses the hostile army; couriers riding swiftly from wing to wing; everywhere the beautiful silken flags; and the scene ever changing with the involutions and evolutions of the vast host." It was, in short, that seldom-encountered thing, picture-book war — which it also resembled, as events developed, in its paucity of bloodshed. Though the armies remained in approximate confrontation for four hours, the action was practically limited to artillery exchanges, since neither commander seemed willing to venture within point-blank range of the other's guns. When at last Banks brought A. J. Smith's Westerners forward for an attack on the rebel left, Taylor withdrew in that direction, south and west, and the Federals resumed their march to the south and east, through Mansura, then on to Bayou de Glaise, on whose banks they stopped for the night. Next day, May 17, after skirmishing warmly with enemy horsemen on both sides of Moreauville, they pushed on to Yellow Bayou, within five miles of Simsport and the Atchafalaya, which would shield them from further pursuit once they were across it.

If Banks had known the extent of the odds in his favor, he not only would have been less surprised at the sidelong rebel withdrawal from Mansura, he would also have been considerably less concerned for the safety of his army, which in fact enjoyed a five-to-one numerical advantage over the force attempting to waylay and impede it. Taylor fairly ached for some sign of the three divisions on the march from Arkansas; to no avail. "Like 'Sister Ann' from her watch tower," he was to write, "day after day we strained our eyes to see the dust of our approaching comrades.... Vain, indeed, were our hopes. The commander of the 'Trans-Mississippi Department' had the power to destroy the last hope of the Confederate cause, and exercised it with all the success of Bazaine at Metz. 'The affairs of mice and men aft gang aglee,' from sheer stupidity and pig-headed obstinacy." And lest his meaning be clouded by his fondness for religious and historical allusions and poetic misquotations, he made the charge specific and identified by name the man he held responsible for his woes: "From first to last, General Kirby Smith seemed determined to throw a protecting shield around the Federal army and fleet."

This bitterness would grow; would in time become obsessive. But for the present the Louisiana general directed most of his attention to a search for some way, despite the odds, to inflict more vengeful damage on the spoilers of his homeland before they fled beyond his reach. The side-step at Mansura, allowing them to press on south and east, had been as necessary as it was painful; for if Taylor was to preserve his little army for future use, he could not afford to take on the blue host without a tactical advantage totally lacking on the open prairie. Then next day he received, as if from Providence, what he believed might be the chance for which he prayed. Pushing on through Moreauville, the Federal main body reached Yellow Bayou only to learn from its scouts, who had ridden ahead, that backwater from the Mississippi had swollen the Atchafalaya to a width too great for spanning by all the pontoons the engineers had on hand. Without a bridge, the crossing would be at best a slow affair, involving the use of transports as ferries. Penned up with its back to the river, as it had been at Grand Ecore and Alexandria, the blue mass would grow more vulnerable as it shrank, regiment by regiment, until at last a gray assault could be launched against the remnant — perhaps with the help, by then, of the slow-moving troops from Arkansas — extracting payment in blood for the vandalism of the past nine weeks. Taylor brightened at the prospect, and next morning, May 18, moved his infantry up to join his cavalry on Yellow Bayou, intending to advance from there and establish a semicircular, close-up line of intrenchments from which to observe the dwindling Union army, held under siege amid the ashes of what had once been Simsport.

Looking out across the unbridgeable 600-yard expanse of the Atchafalaya, a swollen barrier to the safety his army could only attain by reaching the far side, Banks foresaw an outcome all too similar to the one his adversary was moving to effect. Still, his despair was not so deep as to keep him from doing all he could to ward it off. When he was informed, around midmorning, that Taylor had moved up to

Yellow Bayou, close in his rear, he instructed A. J. Smith to counter-march and drive him back. Smith returned to the Bayou, crossed three brigades, and pitched without delay into the rebel skirmish line, throwing it back on the main body, which then attacked and drove him back in turn. It went that way for a couple of hours, first one side gaining ground and then the other — each had about 5000 men engaged — until at last the underbrush caught fire and both withdrew in opposite directions, choked and scorched, from the crackling barricade of smoke and flame. That ended the action. Unresolved and indecisive as it was, Smith's gorillas once more had proved their worth as fighters as well as burners, losing about 350 to inflict a total of 608 casualties on Taylor.

Nothing daunted, the Louisianian prepared to return to the offensive next day, May 19. But that was not to be. The back-and-forth engagement on the west side of Yellow Bayou turned out to be the last of the campaign — for the simple reason that presently no blue-clad troops remained within his reach. Banks by then had bridged the unbridgeable Atchafalaya.

Once more the *deus ex machina* was Joe Bailey. Handed the problem by Banks, the engineering colonel promptly solved it by mooring all the available riverboats and transports side by side across the near-half-mile width of the stream, like oversized pontoons, and bolting them together with timbers which then served as stringers for planks laid crosswise on them to form a roadbed. Soon after midday, though the varying heights of the boats on which it rested gave it something of the crazy, up-and-down aspect of a roller coaster, Banks had the bridge he needed to reach the sanctuary beyond the river. The wagon train began to cross at once, followed that night by the guns and ambulances; next morning, May 20, the troops themselves were marched across and the makeshift bridge dismantled in their rear. Two days later — a solid month past the time when they had been scheduled to rejoin Sherman in far-off Georgia — Smith's three divisions filed back aboard their transports and set out for Vicksburg. Banks meantime was as full of praise for Bailey, here on the Atchafalaya, as Porter had been the week before, back up the Red. "This work was not of the same magnitude, but was as important to the army as the dam at Alexandria was to the navy," he said of the improvised bridge in his final report, and repeated his recommendation that the former logger be promoted to brigadier as a reward for his resourcefulness under pressure.

Another upbeat flourish had been provided, but so had additions been made to the list of casualties — more than fifteen hundred of them, all told, since the return to Alexandria in late April. Army losses for the campaign now stood at 5245 killed, wounded, and missing, and to this were added some three hundred naval casualties, suffered in the course of the subtraction from the flotilla of an ironclad, two tinclads, three transports, a pair of pump boats, and 28 guns of various calibers,

captured or spiked and abandoned up the Red. This Federal total of
about 5500 exceeded by well over a thousand the Confederate total
of 4275. Losses in matériel were of course even more disproportionate,
not only because the rebels had lost much less in battle, but also because
they had had a great deal less to lose: aside, that is, from civilian
property, the destruction of which, if included, would doubtless swing
the balance the other way. But perhaps the greatest contrast lay in
what a member of Banks's official family called "the great and bitter
crop of quarrels" raised in the northern ranks by what he referred to
as "this unhappy campaign." If on the Confederate side there were
arguments in the scramble to divide the glory, on the Union side there
were hotter ones involved in the distribution of the blame. Looking
back over the events of the past seventy days, the staffer noted that
feelings had been severely ruffled and several lofty reputations quite
undone. "Franklin quitted the department in disgust," he recalled;
"Stone was replaced by Dwight as chief of staff, and Lee as chief of
cavalry by Arnold; A. J. Smith departed more in anger than in sorrow;
while between the admiral and the general commanding, recriminations
were exchanged in language well up to the limits of 'parliamentary'
privilege."

Now still another illustrious name was added to the list: Banks's
own. Not that he was relieved outright or shunted into obscurity, as so
many others had been in the doleful course of the past six weeks. This
was an election year, and too much rode on the outcome for the authorities to risk alienating a man with as many votes as the one-time Speaker
of the House controlled. Lincoln and Halleck put their heads together
and came up with the answer. Major General Edward R. S. Canby, a
forty-six-year-old Kentucky-born West Pointer, had come east after
the New Mexico campaign of 1862, in which he had managed to save
the Far West for the Union, and had since been involved in administrative matters, including the reëstablishment of law and order in New
York after the draft riots of 1863. In all these positions his outstanding
characteristic had been his prudence, a rare quality nowadays in the
Transmississippi; Lincoln and Halleck, with Grant's concurrence —
Canby had been another of his classmates at the Point — decided to
send him there to supply it, not as Banks's replacement, but rather as
his superior, by placing him in charge of the newly created "Military
Division of West Mississippi," which stretched from Missouri to the
Gulf and from Florida to Texas. Banks's unquestioned abilities as an
administrator, honest amid corruption, were thus preserved for the
government's use, along with his political support, while his military ineptness was set aside by depriving him of any further independence —
or, as it turned out, service — in the field.

Canby was waiting for him with the necessary papers at Simsport,
and accompanied him on the final leg of the retreat, another hundred

miles downriver to Donaldsonville, where the campaign formally ended on May 26, seventy-five days after its start and more than a month beyond its scheduled finish. An Iowa soldier wrote in his diary that Banks looked "dejected and worn" at that stage, and small wonder. More had ended and more had been lost, for him, than the campaign. The former governor, whose reduction of Port Hudson had opened the Mississippi to northern trade throughout its length, was now the mere desk-bound head of a subdepartment in an organization commanded by a man almost two years his junior in age and three full years behind him in date of rank. That came hard, but that was by no means the worst of it for Banks, who was taunted not only by the thought of what he had lost but also by the thought of what he had failed to gain. Mobile might someday be attacked and taken, but not by him, and along with much else that had gone with the winds of war — including all those hundreds of thousands of bales of cotton, which were to have put the national effort on a pay-as-you-go basis, but which instead had tainted it with scandal — were his hopes for the highest political office. All that had ended up the Red. He not only had been defeated by his enemies up that river, he had been oversloughed by his superiors on his return: "a fit sequel," the Saint Louis *Republican* asserted, "to a scheme conceived in politics and brought forth in iniquity."

If contention was less widespread on the Confederate side, where there was more credit than blame to be divided, such contention as there was only flared the higher on that account. Taylor's distress in reaction to his fear that the Federals were going to escape — the result, he claimed, of "sheer stupidity and pig-headed obstinacy" on the part of the high command at Shreveport — was mild compared to the frustration he felt when the bluecoats did in fact improvise an Atchafalaya crossing before the arrival of the Arkansas reinforcements enabled him to exact the retribution he felt they owed. Though his pride in his outnumbered army was as boundless as his contempt for the invaders ("Long will the accursed race remember the great river of Texas and Louisiana," he said of the latter in a congratulatory order he issued to his troops on May 23. "The characteristic hue of its turbid waters has a darker tinge from the liberal admixture of Yankee blood. The cruel alligator and the ravenous garfish wax fat on rich food, and our native vulture holds high revelry over many a festering corpse") his wrath had mounted with each passing day of the unimpeded blue retreat. Moving up to Yellow Bayou five days ago, he had taken time to communicate his chagrin at having been obliged to step aside, just when he had the vandals within his grasp, for lack of strength to stand his ground at Mansura. "I feel bitterly about this," he protested in a dispatch to Kirby Smith's adjutant, "because my army has been robbed of the just measure of its glory and the country of the most brilliant and complete success of the war."

The further it receded into the past, the more "brilliant and complete" that missed victory became. Indeed, within a week or so, Taylor had come to believe that his superior's military ineptness, which had obliged him to forgo a certain triumph, might well have cost the South its one best chance to win its independence. What was more, he said as much to Kirby Smith himself on June 5, in a letter combining indignation and despair. "In truth," he wrote, quite as if he had a corner on that rare commodity, "the campaign as a whole has been a hideous failure. The fruits of Mansfield have turned to dust and ashes. Louisiana, from Natchitoches to the Gulf, is a howling wilderness and her people are starving. Arkansas is probably as great a sufferer. In both States abolition conventions are sitting to overthrow their system of labor. The remains of Banks' army have already gone to join Grant or Sherman, and may turn the scale against our overmatched brethren in Virginia and Georgia." What made the hot-tempered Louisianian angriest was the contrast between this and the situation that might have obtained if his chief had not rejected his advice on how to go about disposing of the invaders, which he was certain would have led to their destruction and the reversal of the tide of war. "The roads to Saint Louis and New Orleans should now be open to us. Your strategy has riveted the fetters on both." The more he wrote — and he wrote at length, including a full critique of the campaign, with emphasis on the mismanagement of events beyond his reach, both here and in Arkansas — the angrier he grew: until finally, as he drew to a close, his wrath approached incandescence. "The same regard for duty which led me to throw myself between you and popular indignation, and quietly take the blame for your errors," he wound up, "compels me to tell you the truth, however objectionable to you. The grave errors you have committed in the recent campaign may be repeated if the unhappy consequences are not kept before you. After the desire to serve my country, I have none more ardent than to be relieved from longer serving under your command."

Thus Taylor, whose rage had made him as blind to the virtues of others as he was perceptive of their faults. To refer to the just-ended campaign as "a hideous failure," simply because it had not yielded all that he had hoped for, was to overlook its fruits, which in fact were far from slight. Inflicting more than 8000 casualties on Steele and Banks, at a cost to Price and Taylor of 6500, Smith had captured or caused the destruction of 57 pieces of artillery, nearly half of them naval, along with about a thousand wagons, most of them loaded with valuable supplies, and more than 3500 mules and horses. This was a considerable tactical haul, by almost any standards, and yet the strategic gains were even greater. Despite the hot-tempered Louisianian's claim to the contrary, the campaign had cost Sherman the use of 10,000 veterans in North Georgia; which meant that he moved with that many fewer against Joe Johnston, while Johnston's own army was enlarged by nearly twice that number because the upset of Banks' schedule had ruled out an early movement against Mobile, leaving Polk free to shift from Demopolis toward Dalton with some 20,000 troops who otherwise would have been drawn in the opposite direction by the threat to coastal Alabama. The greatest effect of the campaign up Red River thus was felt in northern Georgia, where a net difference of 30,000 men was registered in favor of the defenders of Atlanta. If the South was going to lose the war, then this would no doubt prolong the conflict. On the other hand, this might just narrow the long odds enough for the South to win it.

That of course remained to be seen. In the meantime, there was nothing Kirby Smith could do, despite his disinclination in such matters, but act on Taylor's insubordinate letter. Appointing Walker as his successor, he ordered him to Natchitoches, there to await instructions from their superiors, and forwarded the correspondence to Richmond with a covering letter to his friend the President. The good of the service required that he or Taylor be removed from command, the mild-mannered Floridian declared, adding that if Davis thought it best — as he well might do; Smith freely acknowledged the Louisianian's "merits as a soldier" — "I will willingly, with no feeling of envy or abatement of interest in the service of my country, turn over my arduous duties and responsibilities to a successor."

It made a sorry end, this falling-out by the victors, after all the glory that had been garnered up the Red and on the Saline; Dick Taylor was afterwards far from proud of his conduct in the quarrel, and set it down as the result of overwork and nervous strain. For the present, though, he was not unhappy to be reunited with his wife and children in Natchitoches, the lovely old French-Spanish town he recently had saved from Sherman's burners, there to await the judgment of his presidential brother-in-law.

✗ 3 ✗

Davis had troubles enough by then, and differences enough to attempt to compose, without the added problem of trying to heal this latest split between two of his friends, one of whom was among the nation's ranking field commanders, responsible for the conduct of affairs in the largest of all its military departments, while the other was his first wife's younger brother. Down in Georgia, for example, on March 10 — the day A. J. Smith's gorillas left Vicksburg, beginning the ten-week campaign that would take them up and down Red River, and the day before Grant left Washington for the meeting with Sherman in Nashville, where they would begin to plan the campaign designed to bring Georgia to its knees and the Confederacy to extinction — Governor Joseph E.

Brown addressed the state legislature, which he had called into special session to hear some things he had to say on the subject of the war. What he had to say, in essence, was that the war had been a failure. This was not only because it was now to be waged on his doorstep, so to speak, but also because, as he saw it, the authorities in Richmond had abandoned the principles embodied in the Declaration of Independence, including "all self-government and the sovereignty of the States."

Brown's solution, as set forth in his address, was for the Confederacy to dissolve itself into its components, thus calling a halt to discord and bloodshed: after which, in an atmosphere of peace and fellowship, a convention of northern and southern governors would assemble at Baltimore or Memphis, Montreal or the Bermuda Islands, and each state, North as well as South, would "determine for herself what shall be her future connection, and who her future allies." In other words, he would stop and start anew, this time without taking so many wrong turnings in the pursuit of happiness along the path that led to independence. Brown was careful, in the course of his speech, not to propose that Georgia rejoin the Union. That would have amounted to outright treason. He proposed, rather, that the Union rejoin Georgia, and he favored "negotiation" as the means of achieving this end. "In a crisis like the present," he maintained, "Statesmanship is ever more important than Generalship. Generals can never stop a war, though it may last twenty years till one has been able to conquer the other. Statesmen terminate wars by negotiation."

Praised for its acumen or condemned as disloyal, the address pleased some of its hearers and outraged others, depending largely on their predilections. Politically, an observer remarked, "Georgia was rent asunder." Among the governor's firmest supporters, though he was not in Milledgeville to hear him, was Alexander H. Stephens, Vice President of the Confederacy. Stephens not only gave the speech his full approval — as well he might; "I advised it from stem to stern," he admitted privately — but arrived in person six days later from Liberty Hall, his estate at nearby Crawfordville, to reinforce it with one of his own, twice as long and twice as bitter, in which he lashed out at the national authorities for their betrayal of the secessionist cause by adopting conscription and suspending the writ of habeas corpus. "Better, in my judgment," he declared, "that Richmond should fall and that the enemy's armies should sweep our whole country from the Potomac to the Gulf than that our people should submissively yield to one of these edicts." A small, pale-faced man with burning eyes and a shrill voice, weighing less than a hundred pounds in the voluminous overcoat he wore against the chill he felt in all but the hottest weather, he spoke for three full hours, in the course of which he sustained at several points a critic's charge that his alarm "had long ago vaulted into the hysterical." Where personal freedom was concerned Stephens rejected all arguments as to expediency. "Away with the idea of getting our independence first, and looking after liberty afterward!" he cried. "Our liberties, once lost, may be lost forever." If he had to be ruled by a despot, he said darkly, he preferred that it be a northern one, and he closed on a dramatic note, quite as if he expected to be clapped in arrest by government agents as soon as he came down off the rostrum. "I do not know that I shall ever address you again, or see you again," he told the legislators filling the chamber, row on row, from wall to wall. "As for myself," he added by way of farewell—though he knew, as Patrick Henry had not known before him, that the authority he assailed would not dare call him to account—"give me liberty as secured in the Constitution, amongst which is the sovereignty of Georgia, or give me death!"

He proceeded not to the dungeon he had seemed to predict, but back to Liberty Hall, where he continued to fulminate, in letters and interviews, against the government of which he was nominally a part and the man whose place he would take in case of death or the impeachment he appeared to recommend. Reproached by a constituent for having "allowed your antipathy to Davis to mislead your judgment," Stephens denied that he harbored any such enmity in his bosom. "I have regarded him as a man of good intentions," he replied, "weak and vacillating, petulant, peevish, obstinate but not firm." Having gone so far, however, he then revoked the disclaimer by adding: "Am now beginning to doubt his good intentions." Meantime, back in Milledgeville, Brown's managers were steering through the legislature a double set of resolutions introduced by Little Aleck's younger brother Linton, one condemning the Richmond authorities for having overriden the Constitution, the other defining Georgia's terms for peace as a return, North and South, to the "principles of 1776." This took three days; the governor had to threaten to hold the legislators in special session "indefinitely" in order to ram the resolutions through; then on March 19 they passed them and were permitted to adjourn. Brown had his and the Vice President's addresses printed in full, together with Linton Stephens's resolutions, and distributed copies to all the Georgia soldiers in the armies of Lee and Johnston.

Stephens and Brown were two of the more unpleasant facts of Confederate life that had to be faced in Richmond by officials trying to get on with a long-odds war amid runaway inflation and spreading disaffection. Others were nearer at hand. In North Carolina, for example — that "vale of humility," a native called the state, "nestled between two humps of pride," Virginia and South Carolina — the yearning for peace had grown in ratio to a general disenchantment with "glory," of which the war, according to Governor Zebulon Vance, had afforded the Old North State too meager a share. Less bitter than Joe Brown — of whom a fellow Georgian was saying this spring,

"Wherever you meet a growling, complaining, sore-headed man, hostile to the government and denunciatory of its measures and policy, or a croaking, despondent dyspeptic who sees no hope for the country, but, whipped himself, is trying to make everybody else feel as badly as himself, you will invariably find a friend, admirer, and defender of Governor Brown" — Vance was an unrelenting critic of the ways things were done or left undone at Richmond, and his correspondence was heavy with complaints, made directly to the President, that Carolinians were constantly being slighted in the distribution of promotions and appointments. Late in March, Davis lost patience and sought to break off the exchange, protesting that Vance had "so far infringed the proprieties of official intercourse as to preclude the possibility of reply. In order that I may not again be subjected to the necessity of making so unpleasant a remark, I must beg that a correspondence so unprofitable in its character, and which was not initiated by me, may here end, and that your future communications be restricted to such matters as may require official action." But Vance, a self-made man from old Buncombe County, had long since learned the political value of persistence; he was not so easily restrained. Scarcely a mail arrived from Raleigh that did not include a protest by the governor that some worthy Tarheel had been snubbed or overlooked in the passing out of favors, military as well as civil. Davis could only read and sigh, thankful at least that Vance kept his distance, even though it was not so great as the distance Brown and Stephens kept.

That was by no means the case with Edward A. Pollard, who was not only very much at hand as associate editor of the Richmond *Examiner,* but also took the trouble to let the authorities know it daily. He often seemed to despise the Confederacy to its roots, and seldom relaxed in his efforts to impale its chief executive on what was agreed to be the sharpest pen in the journalistic South. Invective was his specialty, and when he got on his favorite subject — Jefferson Davis — he sometimes raised this specialty to an art. "Serene upon the frigid heights of infallible egotism," the Kentucky-born Mississippian was "affable, kind, and subservient to his enemies" but "haughty, austere, and unbending to his friends," and though he assumed "the superior dignity of a satrap," he was in fact, behind the rigid mask, "an amalgam of malice and mediocrity." Future historians of various persuasions were to take their cue from this carving-up of a man on his wrong side; it was small wonder that Pollard, who spoke with the gadfly rancor of Thersites, found many who nodded in gleeful agreement as they read his jabs and jibes. They read him, in this fourth and gloomiest spring of a war they had begun to believe they could not win, to find relief from a frustration which grew, like his own, in ratio to the dwindling of their hopes.

Thoroughly familiar with the American proclivity for blaming national woes on the national leader, Davis had engaged in the practice too often himself not to expect it to be turned against him. He viewed it as an occupational hazard, one that more or less went with his job, and he spoke of it as a man might speak of any natural phenomenon — gravity, say, or atmospheric pressure — which could not be abolished simply because it bore within it the seeds of possible disaster. "Opposition in any form can only disturb me inasmuch as it may endanger the public welfare," he had said. Moreover, no one could sympathize more with the people who felt this fourth-spring frustration, for no one was in a position to know as well how soundly based the feeling was. Such blame as he attached to men like Stephens and Brown and Pollard was not for entertaining, but rather for giving vent to their defeatist conclusions, since by so doing they betrayed their high positions, converting them to rostrums for the spreading of despair, and did indeed "endanger the public welfare." As for the frustration itself, Davis not only sympathized with, he shared it. However much he might condemn those who gave way under pressure, he knew only too well how great that pressure was: especially for those who saw the problem, as he did, from within. Wherever he looked he perceived that the Confederacy's efforts to "conquer a peace" were doomed to failure. And this applied most obviously to the three most obvious fields for aggressive endeavor, whereby the South might attempt to force its will upon its mortal adversary: 1) by entering upon negotiations with representatives from the North to obtain acceptable peace terms, 2) by mounting and sustaining a military offensive which would end with the imposition of such terms, or 3) by securing the foreign recognition and assistance which would afford the moral and physical strength now lacking to achieve the other two.

As for the first of these, Davis had pointed out the difficulty, if not the impossibility, of pursuing this line of endeavor three months ago in response to a letter from Governor Vance, in which the Carolinian urged that attempts be made to negotiate with the enemy, not only because such an expression of willingness on the part of the South to stop shooting and start talking would "convince the humblest of our citizens . . . that the government is tender of their lives and happiness, and would not prolong their sufferings unnecessarily one moment," but also because the rejection by the North of such an offer would "tend greatly to strengthen and intensify the war feeling [of our people] and will rally all classes to a more cordial support of the government." Davis replied that while such results were highly desirable, "insuperable objections" stood in the way of their being achieved. One was that, by the simple northern device of refusing to confer with "rebel" envoys, all such offers — except to the extent that they were "received as proof that we are ready for submission" — had been rejected out of hand. He himself had seldom neglected an opportunity, in his public addresses and messages to Congress, to inform the enemy and the world that "All we ask is to be let alone." Nothing had come of this, in or out of official channels, and it was becoming increasingly clear that to continue such efforts was "to invite insult and contumely, and to subject ourselves to indignity, without the slightest chance of being listened to."

Suppose, though, that they did somehow manage to break through the barrier of silence. What would that do, Davis asked, but confront them with another barrier, still more "insuperable" than the first? "It is with Lincoln alone that we could confer," he reminded Vance, "and his own partisans at the North avow unequivocally that his purpose in his message and proclamation [of Amnesty and Reconstruction] was to shut out all hope that he would *ever* treat with us, on *any* terms." The northern President himself had made this clear and certain, according to Davis. "Have we not been apprised by that despot that we can only expect his gracious pardon by emancipating all our slaves, swearing obedience to him and his proclamation, and becoming in point of fact the slaves of our own Negroes?" In the light of this, he asked further, "can there be in North Carolina one citizen so fallen beneath the dignity of his ancestors as to accept or enter into conference on the basis of these terms? That there are a few traitors in the state who would be willing to betray their fellow citizens to such a degraded condition, in hope of being rewarded for their treachery by an escape from the common doom, may be true. But I do not believe that the vilest wretch would accept such terms for himself."

Having gone so far — for the letter was a long one, written in the days before he sought to break off corresponding with the Tarheel governor — Davis then proceeded to the inevitable conclusion that peace, if it was to come at all, would have to be won by force of arms. "To obtain the sole terms to which you or I could listen," he told Vance, "this struggle must continue until the enemy is beaten out of his vain confidence in our subjugation. Then and not till then will it be possible to treat of peace."

That brought him to the second, and much the bloodiest, of his three aggressive choices: the launching of an offensive that would not stop short of the table across which peace terms would be dictated to an enemy obliged to accept them as a condition of survival in defeat. Pleasant though this was to contemplate as a fitting end to slaughter and privation, it amounted to little more than an exercise in the realm of fantasy. If three blood-drenched years of war, and three aborted invasions of the North, had taught anything, they had taught that, however the conflict was going to end, it was not going to end this way. Davis, for one, never stopped hoping that it might, and even now was urging a course of action on Joe Johnston, down in Georgia, designed to bring about just such a closing scene. That the general declined to march all-out against the Union center was not surprising; Johnston had always bridled at cut-and-slash urgings or suggestions, and in this case, out-numbered and outgunned as he was, he protested with ample cause. Nor was he the only one to demonstrate reluctance. "Our role must be a defensive policy," Kirby Smith was warning his impetuous lieutenants out in the Transmississippi; while nearer at hand, and weightiest by far in that regard, the nation's ranking field commander was tendering much the same advice to his superior in Richmond. The most aggressive of all the Confederate military chieftains — indeed, one of the most aggressive soldiers of all time, of whom a subordinate had declared, quite accurately, on the occasion of his appointment to head the Virginia army, just under two years ago: "His name might be Audacity. He will take more chances, and take them quicker, than any other general in this country, North or South" — R. E. Lee had taken care, well before the occasion could arise, to forestall even the suggestion that he attempt another large-scale offensive when the present "mud truce" ended in the East. Back in early February, in response to a presidential request for counsel, he said flatly: "We are not in a condi-tion, and never have been, in my opinion, to invade the enemy's country with a prospect of permanent benefit."

There Davis had it. For though Lee added characteristically that he hoped, by a limited show of force, to "alarm and embarrass [the enemy] to some extent, and thus prevent his undertaking anything of magnitude against us," this was no real modification of his implied opinion that past efforts to end the war on northern soil — his own two, which had broken in blood along Sharpsburg ridge and across the stony fields of Gettysburg, as well as Bragg's, which had gone into re-verse at Perryville — had been errors of judgment, serving, if for nothing else, to demonstrate the folly of any attempt at repetition of them. Such a statement, from such a source, was practically irrefutable, especially since it was echoed by the commanders of the other two major theaters, Smith and Johnston. The war, if it was to be won at all by southern arms, would have to be won on southern ground.

Third and last of these choices, the securing of foreign recognition and assistance, had long been the cherished hope of Confederate states-men: especially Davis, who had uttered scarcely a public word through the first twenty months of the war that did not look toward intervention by one or another of the European powers. However, as time wore on it became clearer that nothing was going to come of such efforts and expectations — Russia had been pro-Union from the start, and France, whatever her true desires might be, could not act without England, where the Liberals in power took their cue from voters who were pre-dominantly anti-slavery and therefore, in accordance with Lincoln's persuasions, anti-Confederate — the southern President, smarting under the snubs his unacknowledged envoys suffered, grew increasingly petu-lant and less guarded in his reaction. Fifteen months ago, addressing his home-state legislature on the first of his western journeys to revive confidence and bolster morale, he lost patience for the first time in public. " 'Put not your trust in princes,' " he advised, "and rest not your hopes on foreign nations. This war is ours; we must fight it out ourselves." The applause this drew, plus the growing conviction that nothing any Confederate said or did had any effect whatever on the outcome in Europe, encouraged further remarks along this line. Nor was his reaction limited to remarks. In June of 1863, with Lee on the march for Gettysburg and Vicksburg soon to fall, the exequatur of the British consul at Richmond was revoked. The presence of such consuls had long been irksome, not only because they sought to interfere in such matters as the conscription of British nationals and the collection of British debts, but also because they were accredited to a foreign power, the United States, rather than to the country in which they operated, the Confederate States, whose very existence their government denied except as a "belligerent." The strain increased. In August, James M. Mason, the still unreceived ambassador to England, was told to consider his mission at an end, and before the following month was out he gave up his London residence and removed the diplomatic archives to Paris. In October the final strings were cut. Declaring their continued presence at Charleston, Savannah, and Mobile "an unwarranted assumption of jurisdiction," as well as "an offensive encroachment," Davis expelled all British consular agents from the South.

In Paris, Mason found the position of his fellow ambassador, John Slidell, highly enviable at first glance. Fluent in New Orleans French, the urbane Louisianian had practically free — though, alas, unofficial — access to Napoleon and Eugénie, both of whom were sympathetic to his cause; or so they kept assuring him, although nothing tangible in the way of help had so far proceeded from their concern. In many ways, the situation in Paris was more frustrating than the one in London, where Mason's non-reception at least had not built up hopes that came to nothing every time. By now, as a result of such recurrent disappointments, Slidell had become convinced that he was being led along for some purpose he could not fathom, but which he suspected would be of little benefit, in the end, either to him personally or to the government he represented. Disenchanted with the postcard Emperor, he was turning bitter in his attitude toward his job. "I find it very difficult to keep my temper amidst all this double dealing," he informed his friend and chief, Secretary of State Judah P. Benjamin. In point of fact, his experiences at court seemed to have jaundiced him entirely, for he added, by way of general observation: "This is a rascally world, and it is most hard to say who can be trusted."

What it came down to, in the end as in the beginning, whether Slidell was right or wrong about Napoleon and his motives, was that France could not act without England. And now, as the war moved

into its fourth critical spring, Davis could not resist lodging a protest
which, in effect, burned the last bridge that might have led to a rap-
prochement with that all-important power. The trouble stemmed from
British acceptance of evidence supplied by U.S. Ambassador Charles
Francis Adams that certain warships under construction by the Lairds
of Liverpool, ostensibly for the Viceroy of Egypt, were in fact to be
sold to the Confederacy, which intended to use these powerful steam
rams to shatter the Union blockade. "It would be superfluous in me to
point out to your lordship that this is war," Adams informed Foreign
Secretary Lord John Russell. It was indeed superfluous, since Russell,
already alarmed by Seward's tail-twisting threats along that line, had
previously taken steps to prevent delivery of the vessels by detaining
them. That was in September, six months ago, and as if this was not
enough to placate Seward there arrived in Richmond on April 1 — not
through regular diplomatic channels, but by special courier under a flag
of truce, as between belligerents — a message for Jefferson Davis from
Lord Richard Lyons, the British minister in Washington, containing
an extract from a dispatch lately sent by Russell protesting "against
the efforts of the authorities of the so-called Confederate States to
build war vessels within Her Majesty's dominions to be employed
against the Government of the United States."

Davis bristled. Hard as this governmental decision was to take —
for the matter was still in litigation in the British courts, and he hoped
for a favorable outcome there — the phrase "so-called" cut deeper,
adding insult to injury as it did. Never one to accept a slight, let alone
a snub, the Mississippian summoned his secretary and dictated a third-
person reply. "The President desires me to say to your Lordship, that . . .
it would be inconsistent with the dignity of the position he fills, as
Chief Magistrate of a nation comprising a population of more than twelve
millions, occupying a territory many times larger than the United
Kingdom . . . to allow the attempt of Earl Russell to ignore the actual
existence of the Confederate States, and to contumeliously style them
'so-called,' to pass without a protest and a remonstrance. The President,
therefore, does protest and remonstrate against this studied insult, and
he instructs me to say that in future any document in which it may be
repeated will be returned unanswered and unnoticed." Lyons had not
used diplomatic channels for delivery of his message; Davis, stung in
his national pride, did not use diplomacy at all in his response. Warming
as he dictated, he termed British neutrality "a cover for treacherous,
malignant hostility," and closed with an icy pretense of indifference.
"As for the specious arguments on the subject of the rams . . . while
those questions are still before the highest legal tribune of the kingdom
. . . the President himself will not condescend to notice them." The
signature read, "Burton N. Harrison, Private Secretary."

Such satisfaction as Davis got from thus berating the Foreign

Secretary for his government's "persistent persecution of the Confederate States at the beck and bidding of officers of the United States"
was small recompense for the knowledge that the South, engaged in
what its people liked to think of as the Second American Revolution,
would have no help from Europe in its struggle for independence. And
what made this especially bitter to accept was a general historical agreement that in the original Revolution, with the Colonists in much the
same position the Confederates were in now — unable, on the face of
it, either to enforce or to negotiate a peace — such help had made the
difference between victory and defeat. "This war is ours; we must fight
it out ourselves," Davis had warned, by way of prelude to a year of hard
reverses, and though the words were bravely spoken and loudly applauded at the time, there was sadness in the afterthought of what they
meant in terms of the lengthening odds against success or even survival.
Militarily, the handwriting on the wall was all too clear. In late November, within five months of the staggering midsummer news from
Gettysburg and Vicksburg that Lee's army had been crippled and
Pemberton's abolished, Bragg's army was flung bodily off Lookout
Mountain and Missionary Ridge, impregnable though both positions
had been said to be, and harried southward into Georgia. With these
defeats in mind, it was no wonder that every Sunday at Saint Paul's in
Richmond — the obvious goal of the huge offensive the North was
about to launch as a follow-up of its triumphs, east and west, over the
three main armies on which the Confederacy had depended for existence — the congregation recited the Litany with special fervor when
it reached the words, "From battle and murder, and from sudden death,
good Lord, deliver us."

The good Lord might, at that. For though military logic showed
that the South could not win an offensive war, fought beyond the
Potomac or the Ohio, there was still a chance that it could win a defensive one, fought on its own territory. It could win, in short, because the
North could lose. In his letter to Vance, defining the conditions for
peace under "the sole terms to which you or I could listen," Davis had
not simply declared that the enemy must be beaten, period. He had
said that the enemy must be "beaten out of his vain confidence in our
subjugation," which was quite another thing. What he was saying was
that for the North, committed by necessity to achieving an unconditional
surrender, to settle for anything less than total conquest would amount
to giving the South the victory by default. Lincoln knew this as well as
Davis did, of course, and was not likely to coöperate in the dismemberment
he had pledged himself to prevent. Yet the whole say-so would not be
Lincoln's. Beyond the looming figure of the northern leader were the
northern soldiers, and behind them were the northern people. If either
became discouraged enough, soldiers or civilians, the war would end
on terms not only acceptable but welcome to the South. The problem

was how to get at them, beyond the loom of their leader, in order to influence their outlook and their choice. Davis saw cause for hope in both directions — tactical on one hand, political on the other — if certain requirements could be met.

Paradoxically, the tactical hope resulted from past Confederate defeats. Davis saw in every loss of mere territory — Nashville and Middle Tennessee, New Orleans, even Vicksburg and the Mississippi and the amputation of all that lay beyond — a corresponding gain, not only because what had been lost no longer required a dispersal of the country's limited strength for its protection, but also because the resultant contraction allowed a more compact defense of what remained. What remained now was the heartland, an 800-mile-wide triangle roughly defined by lines connecting Richmond, Savannah, and Mobile. Agriculturally and industrially, as well as geographically, this was the irreducible hard core of the nation, containing within it the resources and facilities to support a war of infinite length and intensity, so long as it and its people's will to fight remained intact. How long that would have to be, not in theory but in fact, depended on the validity of the companion political hope, according to which it would only be until November — specifically, the first Tuesday after the first Monday in that month — or, at worst, until early the following March — specifically, Inauguration Day. For this was a presidential election year in the North. The northern people, restrained by an iron hand these past three years, would finally have the chance to speak their minds on the question of war or peace, and the southern leader did not doubt that if his tactical hope was fulfilled — if no great Union victory, worth the agony to the army and the sorrow on the home front, was scored within that eight-month span by the blue drive on the heartland — his political hope would be fulfilled in turn. Weary of profitless bloodshed, the northern people would vote to end the war by turning Lincoln out of office and replacing him with a man who preferred to see half the nation depart in peace, as the saying went, rather than to continue the aimless destruction the two halves would have been visiting on each other for nearly three years. That was the prospect Davis had referred to, four months ago, when he declared in his State of the Nation address, opening the fourth session of Congress: "We now know that the only reliable hope for peace is in the vigor of our resistance, while the cessation of hostility [on the part of our adversaries] is only to be expected from the pressure of their necessities."

In brief, the problem between now and November was how to add to the North's war weariness, already believed to be substantial in certain regions where Copperheads were rampant, without at the same time increasing the South's disconsolation beyond the point of no return. This might or might not be possible, in light of the long odds, but in any case the prerequisite was that the northern people were to be denied the tonic of a large-scale victory within the triangular confines of the secessionist heartland — especially a tonic of the spirit-lifting kind that had come with the celebration of such victories as Vicksburg and Missionary Ridge, which had seemed to show beyond denial that a blue army could rout or capture a gray one as the result of a confrontation wherein Federal generalship was up to the standard set by the Confederates in the first two years of the war. Moreover, the general who had designed and directed both of those triumphs was now in over-all command of the Union forces, presumably chafing for the mud truce to end so he could get his armies headed south. Given the conditions that obtained in regard to numbers and equipment, plus the lightweight boxer's need for yielding ground in order to stay free to bob and weave and thus avoid a slugging match with his heavyweight opponent, there were bound to be southern losses and northern gains in the months immediately ahead; but that was not in itself a ruinous concession by the South, provided the losses and gains could be kept respectively minor and high-priced. In fact, such losses would serve admirably to drive home to the North the point that the prize was by no means worth the effort. The object was to make each gain so costly in blood and tears that the expense would be clearly disproportionate to the profit — if not in the judgment of the Federal high command, whose political or professional survival depended on continuing the conflict, then at any rate in the minds of those who would be casting their ballots in November, many of whom had an intensely personal interest in the casualty lists, future as well as past, and who might therefore be persuaded that their survival, unlike their leaders', depended on bringing the conflict to a close. Thus the South would be waging war not only on its own terrain (an advantage from which it had profited largely in the past) but also in the minds of northern voters who would be going to the polls, under what Davis termed "the pressure of their necessities" some seven months from now, to register a decision as to whether sustaining Lincoln's resolution that the rebels not be allowed to depart in peace was worth the continuing loss of their blue-clad sons and brothers and nephews and grandsons down in Georgia and Virginia.

Time and time alone would provide the answer to the question of survival; Patrick Henry's "liberty or death" applied quite literally to Confederate hopes and fears, which had between them no middle ground a man could stand on, patriot or traitor. Give or take a week or two, depending on the weather, the six months that would follow the end of large-scale inactivity in Georgia and Virginia, where the major forces lay mud-bound in their camps, would decide the issue, since Lincoln's appeal on that all-important Tuesday in November was likely to be in ratio to the progress of his soldiers in the field. Meantime, though, while the outsized armies on both sides took their ease and prepared as best they could for the shock to come, lesser forces had not been idle, east or west. And for the most part, when the military balance sheet was struck, the result of these out-of-season confrontations was encouraging to the hopes of the South for continuing its resistance to the superior weight the North could bring to bear.

Of these several upbeat Confederate successes — for though it was by far the most remote (Shreveport and Richmond were a thousand air-line miles apart; communication between them was necessarily slow and at best uncertain) it was not only the largest in numbers engaged, it was also achieved against the longest odds — the most encouraging was Kirby Smith's frustration of the double-pronged offensive designed by the Federals for completion of their conquest of the Transmississippi. All through the last half of March and the first half of April, the news from Louisiana and Arkansas had been gloomy; Banks and Steele appeared unstoppable in their respective penetrations, across the width and down the length of those two states, with Texas obviously next on the inexorable blue list. Then came word of Mansfield and Pleasant Hill, of Prairie d'Ane and Poison Spring; Steele and Banks were in full retreat from Price and Taylor, and Porter's dreaded ironclads were in flight from probable capture or destruction, bumping their bottoms as they scurried down the Red. It was incredible, and Camden and Jenkins Ferry, like Mansura and Yellow Bayou, only added to the glory and the uplift when news of them reached Richmond across those thousand embattled air-line miles. Other successes had preceded this, and others were to follow. Down in Florida, for example, an all-out Union effort to return that scantly defended state to its old allegiance, in accordance with Lincoln's recent proclamation, had been thrown into sudden reverse by Brigadier General Joseph Finegan's decisive late-February victory at Olustee, which drove the disarrayed invaders all the way back to the banks of the Saint Johns River. About the same time, westward in Mississippi, Sherman was slogging practically unopposed from Vicksburg to Meridian, where he was to be joined by a heavy cavalry column from Memphis for a hundred-mile extension of the march to Selma, a major industrial center whose destruction would do much to weaken the South's ability to sustain its armies in the field. This went by the board, however, when he learned that no cavalry column was any longer moving toward him; Nathan Bedford Forrest, lately promoted to major general with authority to raise a cavalry force of his own in the region the blue troopers would traverse, had whipped them soundly at Okolona, despite their two-to-one numerical advantage, and sent them staggering back to Memphis, part afoot and the rest on mounts so winded that two thirds of them were presently judged unfit for service. Sherman, left marking time, had to be content with wrecking what he held. "Meridian, with its depots, storehouses, arsenals, hospitals, offices, hotels, and cantonments, no longer exists," he reported as his wreckers, having done their worst, fell in for the march back to Vicksburg. But Selma still existed, together with all that Sherman listed and still more — including its vital cannon foundry, which, thanks to Forrest and his green command, continued to forge the heavy-caliber guns that would tear the ranks of other columns of invasion in other quarters of the South. Similarly the following week, as March came in, a raid by 3500 horsemen under Brigadier General Judson Kilpatrick, intended to achieve the liberation of an equal number of prisoners held in Richmond, was turned back at the city limits by old men and boys, home guardsmen serving worn-out artillery pieces long since replaced by new ones, captured or manufactured, in the batteries with Lee on the Rapidan. Soon regular graybacks arrived from there, overtaking the raiders who had slipped past them two nights ago, and harried the survivors into the Union lines, well down the York-James peninsula. Like March itself, Kilpatrick (called "Kill Cavalry" now) had come in like a lion and gone out like a lamb, and Richmonders were proud of their scratch resistance in the emergency that prevailed until the regulars came up.

Olustee and Okolona, like the improvised action that marked the limit of Kilpatrick's penetration, were primarily defensive victories, counterpunches landed solidly in response to Federal leads. But now, between mid-March and mid-April, there followed two exploits that were even more encouraging to Confederate hopes, though admittedly on a limited scale, because they proved that the South could still defy the lengthening odds by mounting and being successful in offensive operations. One was eastern, necessarily amphibious since it occurred in the region giving down upon the North Carolina sounds, while the other was western, staged throughout the length of the critical geographical corridor that lay between the Tennessee River and the Mississippi and extended all the way north to Kentucky's upper border, the Ohio, whose waters no uniformed Confederate had gazed upon since John Morgan's troopers crossed it, ten months ago, on the ill-fated raid from which the colorful brigadier himself had returned only by breaking out of prison.

Forrest, in command of what he called "the Cavalry Department of West Tennessee and North Mississippi," had never stopped thinking of this river-bound, 100-mile-wide, 200-mile-long stretch of land as belonging to him, particularly as a recruiting area, although all of it lay well beyond the Union lines and had done so in fact for nearly two years now. For him, as for most of his men — North Mississippians, West Tennesseans, and Kentuckians — the region was home, and he and they looked forward to returning there, if only on a visit. Indeed, he had already done so twice since it passed into northern hands, once at the beginning and once at the end of the year just past, and now he was going back for the third time. Accordingly, after disposing of Sherman's troopers by chasing them pell-mell into Memphis, he reorganized his own, grown to a strength of about 5000 and seasoned by their recent victory, into two divisions, commanded by Brigadier Generals Abraham Buford and James R. Chalmers, and set out northward with one of them — Buford's — on March 15 from his headquarters at Columbus, Mississippi. There were, he said, some 3000 recruits still available in West Tennessee, and he intended to have them, along with much else that was there in the way of horses and equipment which now were U.S. Army property.

The alarm went out at once to Federal garrisons in all three states bordering the Mississippi south of the Ohio; Forrest was much feared, his unorthodox methods and slashing attacks, often delivered in utter disregard of the odds and the tactics manuals, having led one blue opponent to protest that he was "constantly doing the unexpected at all times and places." Nor did all the complaints have their origin beyond the enemy lines. Some Southerners had their objections, too, although these were primarily social. A former Memphis alderman and planter, a self-made millionaire before the war, the forty-two-year-old Forrest had not only been "in trade"; the trade had been in slaves. And though some Southerners might fight for the peculiar institution, or send their sons to fight for its preservation, they would not willingly associate with others who made, or once had made, a living from it. "The dog's dead," a young Mississippi aristocrat wrote in his diary this winter. "Finally we are under N. Bedford Forrest. . . . I must express my distaste to being commanded by a man having no pretension to gentility — a negro trader, gambler — an ambitious man, careless of the lives of his men so long as preferment be *en prospectu*. Forrest may be, and no doubt is, the best cavalry officer in the West, but I object to a tyrannical, hot-headed vulgarian's commanding me."

In Jackson, Tennessee, on March 20 — presumably with the disgruntled young grandee in tow — Forrest sent word for Chalmers to take up the march, feinting at Memphis en route to add to the confusion in his rear, and detached a regiment to move against Union City, up in the northwest corner of the state. This was the 7th Tennessee Cavalry, Confederate, and by coincidence the town was garrisoned by the 7th Tennessee Cavalry, Union, whose surrender was accomplished in short order four days later, March 24, by a pretense of overwhelming strength, including the use of wheeled logs in place of guns (actually, there were fewer troops outside than there were inside, while the outer 7th had no guns at all) and a blood-curdling note, sent forward under a flag of truce, which ended: "If you persist in defense, you must take the consequences. N. B. Forrest, Major General, Commanding." The Union colonel decided not to persist. Instead he surrendered his 481 men, together with 300 horses and a quantity of arms and stores — all, as the colonel who had signed the general's name declared, "almost without the loss of blood or the smell of powder." Sending his prisoners south, where Chalmers was bristling as if on the verge of clattering into

Memphis, he rode hard to catch up with the main column, which Forrest had led northward through Trenton two days ago, then across the Kentucky line near Fulton, to descend on Paducah in the early afternoon of the following day, March 25, having covered the final muddy hundred miles in fifty hours.

Paducah, strategically located at the confluence of the Tennessee and the Ohio, was an important Union supply base, and it was supplies the general was after, not the garrison, which retired posthaste into a stoutly fortified earthwork supported by two gunboats patrolling the river in its rear. While sending in his usual demand for an unconditional surrender — "If you surrender you shall be treated as prisoners of war, but if I have to storm your works you may expect no quarter" — Forrest put his troopers to work on the unprotected depot, gleaning what he later reported to be "a large amount of clothing, several hundred horses, and a large lot of medical stores," along with about fifty prisoners who had not made it into the fort before the gates were shut. Inside, the blue commander declined to capitulate despite continued threats and demonstrations, including one all-out attack that was launched by a Kentucky regiment whose colonel, a native of Paducah, disobeyed restraining orders, apparently in an excess of pride and joy at being home again, and led a charge in which he and some two dozen of his men were killed or wounded. These were the only Confederate casualties, although the town itself was badly damaged by shells thrown into it from the gunboats and the fort. At midnight, having gathered up everything portable and destroyed much that was not — a government steamboat found in dry dock, for example, and a number of bales of precious cotton awaiting shipment on the landing — Forrest withdrew in the direction from which he had appeared, eight hours before. At Mayfield, a dozen miles southwest, he halted to give his captives a head start south and to furlough his three Kentucky regiments, with instructions to go to their nearby homes for a week, there to secure new clothes and mounts, at the end of which time they would reassemble at Trenton, fifty miles south of the Tennessee line. This they did, on schedule and to a man, many of them accompanied by recruits, fellow Kentuckians anxious for service under "the Wizard of the Saddle," as Forrest was beginning to be called.

He was by then in Jackson, planning another strike before he ended what was afterward referred to as his "occupation" of West Tennessee. His losses so far, including those of Chalmers, who had been skirmishing much of the time near Memphis, amounted to 15 killed and 42 wounded, as compared to Federal losses of 79 killed, 102 wounded, and 612 captured. This was a clear gain, but there was more. While planning a sudden enlargement of these figures, he did not neglect the normal intelligence-gathering duties of cavalry on the prowl. In fact, from his vantage point well within the enemy lines — even as Grant was

at work on the details in Washington, Cincinnati, Culpeper, and elsewhere — Forrest not only saw through the latest Union "grand design"
for the conquest of the South, he also recommended a method by which
he believed it could be frustrated, if not shattered, at least in the western
theater. "I am of the opinion," he wrote Joe Johnston on April 6, "that
everything available is being concentrated against General Lee and
yourself. Am also of opinion that if all the cavalry in this and your own
department could be moved against Nashville that the enemy's communication could be broken up." What would come of this plea that he
be turned loose on Sherman's life line remained to be seen. For the present, however, he had a lesser blow in mind, one that he had mentioned
two days earlier in a report to Polk, whereby he intended to mount and
equip his growing number of recruits: "There is a Federal force of 500
or 600 at Fort Pillow which I shall attend to in a day or two, as they
have horses and supplies which we need."

Fort Pillow, established originally by the Confederates atop a
bluff overlooking the Mississippi forty miles above Memphis, had been in
enemy hands for nearly two years, ever since the evacuation of Corinth
following Shiloh, and was garrisoned by a force of about 550. Half were
Negroes, former slaves who had volunteered for service in the army
that freed them in the course of its occupation of the plantations they
had worked on, while the other half were Union-loyal whites; "Tennessee Tories" and "Homemade Yankees," their since-departed neighbors,
many of whom now rode with Forrest, contemptuously styled the
latter. This was the place and these were the men Forrest had said he
would "attend to," and accordingly, by way of creating a diversion, he
sent Buford with one brigade to menace Columbus and ride back into
Paducah, where newspapers were boasting that he had overlooked 140
fine government horses kept hidden in an old rolling mill throughout
the recent raid. Buford's instructions were to get those horses and, in
the process, draw the enemy's attention northward, away from Pillow,
which would be attacked by his other brigade and one from Chalmers,
who was told to come along and take command of both — 1500 men in
all — for the march, which got under way on April 10, and the investment, which began at daylight two days later. Northward, on the
Mississippi and the Ohio, Buford carried out his assignment to the letter,
detaching a couple of companies to menace Columbus while he rode
with the main body into Paducah at noon on April 14. There, as before,
the defenders fell back to their fortified position, and the raiders gathered up the horses they had missed three weeks ago. Returning south
across the Tennessee line next day, they found that Chalmers too had
carried out his assignment to the letter: so zealously so, in fact, that he
and his men and Forrest, who was in over-all command, were already
being widely accused of having committed *the* atrocity of the war. "The
Fort Pillow Massacre," it was called, then and thereafter, in the North.

Arriving at dawn of April 12 Chalmers had the fort invested by the time Forrest came up at midmorning and took over. Pillow's original trace, some two miles long and an average 600 yards in depth, had been reduced to about half that by the Confederates before their evacuation, and now the Federals had contracted it still farther into a single earthwork, 125 yards in length, perched on the lip of the bluff and surrounded on three sides by a ditch six feet deep and twelve feet wide. Parapets four feet thick at the top and eight feet tall added greatly to the sense of security when the defenders were driven in from their outer line of rifle pits, although they presently found a drawback to this massiveness which the attackers were quick to exploit. "The width or thickness of the works across the top," a rebel captain afterwards explained, "prevented the garrison from firing down on us, as it could only be done by mounting and exposing themselves to the unerring fire of our sharpshooters, posted behind stumps and logs on all the neighboring hills." Their six guns were similarly disadvantaged, since the cannoneers could not depress them enough to fire at the attackers at close range. "So far as safety was concerned," the captain summed up, "we were as well fortified as they were; the only difference was that they were on one side and we were on the other of the same fortification." In partial compensation, the Federals had a gunboat in support, which flung a total of 282 rounds of shell, shrapnel, and canister at the dodging graybacks in the course of the fight. Also, there was the reassuring thought of what half a dozen double-shotted guns could do in the way of execution if any mass of rebels tried to scale those high dirt walls and poke their heads above that flat-topped parapet.

Forrest was thinking of that too, of course, but he did not let it deter him any more than he did the loss of three horses shot from under him in the course of the five hours he spent maneuvering for a closer hug and waiting for the arrival of his ammunition train to refill the nearly empty cartridge boxes of his rapid-firing troopers. Shortly after 3 o'clock the train arrived, and the general sent forward under a flag of truce his usual grisly ultimatum. "Should my demand be refused," the note closed, "I cannot be responsible for the fate of your command." By way of reply, the Union commander requested "one hour for consultation with my officers and the officers of the gunboat." But Forrest by now had spotted a steamer "apparently crowded with troops" approaching, as well as "the smoke of three other boats ascending the river." Believing that the Federals were stalling for time in which to gain reinforcements and additional naval support, he replied that he would give them twenty minutes and no more; "If at the expiration of that time the fort is not surrendered, I shall assault it." Either because he considered this a bluff, or else because he believed an assault was bound to fail — his soldiers, white and black, apparently were of the same conviction, for they had been taunting the rebels gleefully and profanely from the parapets throughout the cease-fire that attended the exchange — the Union commander replied succinctly, "I will not surrender." Forrest had no sooner read the note than he turned to his bugler and had him sound the charge.

The assault was brief and furious, practically bloodless up to a point, and proceeded according to plan. While the sharpshooters back on the hillsides kept up a harassing fire that skimmed the parapet, the first wave of attackers rushed forward, leaped into the slippery six-foot ditch, and crouched in the mud at the bottom, presenting their backs to the men of the second wave, who thus were able to use them as stepping-blocks to gain the narrow ledge between the ditch and the embankment just beyond, then lean down and hoist their first-wave comrades up beside them. It was as neatly done as if it had been rehearsed for weeks, and in all this time not a shot had been fired except from the hillsides and around on the flanks, where Forrest had other marksmen at work on the gunboat. "Shoot at everything blue betwixt wind and water," he had told them: with the result that the vessel, which had closed to canister range, kept its ports tight shut to protect its gunners and took no part in attempting a repulse. By now the attackers were all on the narrow ledge, holding their unfired weapons at the ready and keeping their heads well down while the hillside snipers continued to kick dirt on the parapet, across whose width, although the graybacks were only a few feet away, flattened against the opposite side of the earthwork, no member of the garrison could fire without exposing two thirds of his body to instant perforation. At a signal, the sharpshooters held their fire and the men on the ledge went up and over the embankment, emptying their pistols and rifles into the blue mass of defenders, who fought briefly against panic, then broke rearward for a race to the landing at the foot of the bluff, where they had been told that the gunboat, in the unlikely event of a rebel breakthrough, would cover their withdrawal by pumping grape and canister into the ranks of their pursuers.

It did not work out that way, not only because the gunboat was shut up turtle-tight and took no part in the action, but also because the graybacks were too close on their heels for the naval gunners to have been able to fire without hitting their own men, even if they had tried. Flailed from the rear by heavy downhill volleys, the running bluecoats next were struck in the flanks by the troopers who had been shooting at the gunboat. Some kept going, right on into the river, where a number drowned and the swimmers became targets for marksmen on the bluff. Others, dropping their guns in terror, ran back toward the Confederates with their hands up, and of these some were spared as prisoners, while others were shot down in the act of surrender. "No quarter! No quarter!" was being shouted at several points, and this was thought by some to be at Forrest's command, since he had predicted and even threatened that what was happening would happen. But the fact was, he had done and was doing all he could to end it, having ordered the firing stopped as soon as he saw his troopers swarm into the fort, even though its flag was still flying and a good part of the garrison was still trying to get away. He and others managed to put an end to the killing and sort out the captives, wounded and unwounded. Out of a total Federal force of 557, no less than 63 percent had been killed or wounded, and of these about two thirds — 221, or forty percent of the whole — had been killed. Forrest himself lost 14 killed and 86 wounded. Before nightfall, having seen to the burial of the dead by the survivors, he gathered up his spoils, including the six pieces of artillery, and moved off with 226 prisoners, twenty of whom were men so lightly wounded they could walk. Next morning he sent his adjutant, accompanied by a captured Union captain, back to signal another gunboat — which had resumed the shelling of the woods around the fort, unaware that there was no longer anything Confederate there to shoot at, only Federals — to put in, under a flag of truce, and take the more seriously wounded aboard for treatment downriver in Memphis. That ended the Fort Pillow operation.

But not the talk, the cultivated reaction which quickly mounted to a pitch of outraged intensity unsurpassed until "the Rape of Belgium" fifty years later, when propaganda methods were much improved by wider and faster means of disseminating "eyewitness" accounts of such "atrocities," true or false. Within six days a congressional committee — strictly speaking, a subcommittee of the feared and ruthless Joint Committee on the Conduct of the War — left Washington for Tennessee, having been appointed to gather "testimony in regard to the massacre at Fort Pillow," and within another three days was taking depositions from survivors, along with other interested parties, which resulted in a voluminous printed report that the rebels had engaged in "indiscriminate slaughter" of men, women, and children, white and black, and afterwards had not only set barracks and tents afire, roasting the wounded in their beds, but had also "buried some of the living with the dead," despite their piteous cries for mercy while dirt was being shoveled on their faces. "Many other instances of equally atrocious cruelty might be enumerated," the report concluded, "but your committee feels compelled to refrain from giving here more of the heart-sickening details." Southerners might protest that the document was "a tissue of lies from end to end," as indeed it largely was, but they could scarcely argue with the casualty figures, which indicated strongly that unnecessary killing had occurred, although it was in fact the opposite of "indiscriminate." For example, of the 262 Negro members of the garrison, only 58 — just over twenty percent — were marched away as prisoners; while of the 295 whites, 168 — just under sixty percent — were taken. The rest were either dead or in no shape for walking. Here was discrimination with a vengeance, as well as support for a Confederate sergeant's testimony, given in a letter written home within a week of the affair, describing how "the poor, deluded negroes would run up to our men, fall upon their knees and with uplifted hands scream for mercy, but were ordered to their feet and then shot down." This was not to say that Forrest himself had not done all he could, first to prevent and then to end the unnecessary bloodshed. He had, and perhaps the strongest evidence of his forbearance came not from his friends but from his enemies of the highest rank. Within three days of the fall of the fort, when news of the "massacre" reached Washington, Lincoln told Stanton to investigate without delay "the alleged butchery of our troops." Stanton passed the word to Grant, who wired Sherman that same day: "If our men have been murdered after capture, retaliation must be resorted to promptly." Sherman undertook the investigation, as ordered, but made no such recommendation: proof in itself that none was justified, since no one doubted that otherwise, with Sherman in charge, retaliation would have been as prompt as even Grant could have desired.

As for Forrest, his mind was soon on other things, including the removal of his spoils and a stepped-up enforcement of the conscription laws throughout West Tennessee. His recruiting methods were as rigorous as they were thorough. "Sweep the country, bringing in every man between the ages of eighteen and forty-five," he told his agents. "Take no excuse, neither allow conscripts to go home for clothes or anything else; their friends can send them." Haste was required, for before he got back to Jackson, two days after Pillow fell, he received a dispatch from Polk directing him to return promptly to Okolona, where his two divisions would combine with those under Major General Stephen D. Lee, Polk's chief of cavalry in the Department of Mississippi, Alabama, and East Louisiana, to meet an anticipated raid-in-force from Middle Tennessee, southward through Decatur, Alabama. Forrest replied that the order would of course be complied with, though in his opinion "no such raid will be made from Decatur or any point west of there." Events were to prove him right in this, but even if such a raid had been intended he believed that the best way to turn it back was by striking deep in its rear. He still had his eye on Sherman's life line. He wanted to hit it, and he wanted to hit it hard. This time, however, he presented his views not only to Polk and Johnston, who seemed unwilling or unable to act on them, but also to Jefferson Davis, addressing him directly. Stephen Lee had about 7000 cavalry, and he himself was approaching that strength by now. "With our forces united," he wrote Davis on April 15, "a move could be made into Middle Tennessee and Kentucky which would create a diversion of the enemy's forces and enable us to break up his plans." It was Sherman he meant — specifically, the long rail supply line reaching down from Louisville on the Ohio, through Nashville on the Cumberland, to Chattanooga on the Tennessee. That was a lot of track, and Forrest had long since shown what he could do to a railroad when he turned his troopers loose on one in earnest. Moreover, he assured the Commander in Chief lest the plan be considered an impractical hare-brained escapade like the one on which John Morgan had come to grief last summer, "such an expedition, managed with prudence and executed with rapidity, can be safely made."

Whatever merit there was in the proposal, for the present at least the authorities in Richmond were more interested in a project closer at hand, involving an attempt to recover the North Carolina coastal region, which got under way in earnest that same week, two days after Forrest wrote his letter. A Tarheel brigade under a native North Carolinian, Brigadier General Robert Hoke, had been detached from the Army of Northern Virginia to undertake the job in coöperation with an ironclad ram that had been under construction for the past year in a cornfield at Edwards Ferry, two thirds of the way up the Roanoke River to Weldon. General Braxton Bragg, assigned as the President's chief military adviser after his removal from command of the Army of Tennessee, had conceived the plan, secured the troops, and worked out the details, beginning with an amphibious assault on Plymouth at the point where the Roanoke flowed into Albemarle Sound. Occupied for more than two years by the Federals, who had fortified it stoutly, the town would have to be attacked by water as well as by land, since otherwise the heavy guns of the Union fleet, on station in support of the place, would drive the attackers out about as soon as they got in. Bragg had much confidence in Hoke, who was given large discretion after a detailed briefing on this opening phase of the campaign — a veteran, though not yet twenty-seven, he had fought with distinction in all the major eastern engagements from Big Bethel through Chancellorsville, where he was severely wounded — as well as in the ironclad successor to the *Virginia* and the *Arkansas*, both of glorious memory.

Christened *Albemarle*, she was launched from the riverside cornfield in which she had been built, mostly by local carpenters and blacksmiths, and set off downstream on the day she was commissioned, April 17, en route to her maiden engagement. Sheathed in two layers of two-inch iron and mounting a pair of 6.4-inch Brooke rifles pivoted fore and aft to fire through alternate portholes, she was just over 150 feet in length, 34 feet in the beam, and drew 9 feet of water. Because of the numerous twists and turns in the river this far up — which, incidentally, had served to protect her from interference by Federal gunboats during her construction — she set out stern-foremost, dragging a heavy chain from her bow to steer by. Fitters were still at work on her armor and machinery, and portable forges were brought along for emergency repairs. They soon were needed, first when the main driveshaft wrenched loose from its coupling, late that night, and next when the rudderhead broke off, early the following morning. Three miles from Plymouth the second night, and ten hours behind schedule because of time-out for repairs, she was stopped by reports that the river ahead was obstructed by hulks which the enemy, hearing rumors that the *Albemarle* was approaching completion, had sunk in the channel to tear out her bottom in case she ventured down. Aboard as a volunteer aide to her skipper, Commander James W. Cooke — another Tarheel and a veteran of more than thirty years in the old navy — was her builder, Gilbert Elliott, a native of nearby Elizabeth City, where he had learned his craft in his grandfather's shipyard. Elliott set out in the darkness in a small boat with a pilot and two men, taking a long pole for soundings, and presently returned to report that, thanks to the unusually high stage of the river this spring, "it was practicable to pass the obstructions provided the boat was kept in the middle of the stream."

Cooke by then had turned the ram around and cleared for action. He had no contact with Hoke ashore, but on being informed that a sporadic attack had been in progress against Plymouth most of the day and up until 9 o'clock that night, when the skirmishers withdrew — presumably because of the nonarrival of the *Albemarle*, without whose help the town could not be held under the frown of a quartet of gunboats just inside the mouth of the river — he weighed anchor and stood down to engage. It was close to 4 o'clock in the morning, April 19, when he passed safely over the sunken hulks, taking a few harmless heavy-caliber shots from the fort as he went by, and came in sight of the four Union warships. Warned of his approach, they were prepared to receive him. The two largest, *Miami* and *Southfield* — big, double-ended side-wheel steamers of a novel design, with rudders fore and aft for quick reversals — were lashed together, but not too tightly, in accordance with a plan to catch the *Albemarle* between them, thus making her useless as a ram, while they tossed explosives down her stack. Cooke avoided this by steering close to the south bank, then turning hard aport as he drew nearly abreast of the shackled gunboats, presenting his long, tapered bow to the nearer of the two. Both opened on him with solids at close range, bringing as many of their dozen guns into play as could be brought to bear, but with no more effect than if the shots had been tennis balls, except that they left spoon-shaped dents in the armor when they bounced. Closing fast, with the force of the current added to her thrust, the ironclad put her snout ten feet into *Southfield*'s flank, penetrating all the way to her fireroom, but then had trouble withdrawing it from so deep a wound. The two hung joined, the ram taking water into her forward port because of the weight of the rapidly sinking gunboat: seeing which, the captain of the *Miami* ran to one of his 9-inch Dahlgrens, depressed it quickly, and fired three explosive shells pointblank at the rebel monster. All three shattered against the iron casement, a scant twenty feet away. Pieces of the third, which was fired with a short fuse, flew back from the target and knocked down most of the gun crew, including the captain, who lay dead with the jagged fragments stuck deep in his chest and face.

Albemarle's captain was backing his engines hard to free the ram of the weight on her bow, but by the time he managed to do so, the *Miami* — called the "Miasma" by her crew, who had found duty aboard her boring up to now — cut loose from the sinking *Southfield* and ran with all her speed for open water. Followed out into Albemarle Sound by the other two gunboats, which had observed the action at long range, she wanted no more of a fight with an adversary impervious to shot and shell alike. Cooke attempted a brief pursuit, then broke off when he saw that it was fruitless, mainly because his engines were getting almost no draft through his badly shot-up smokestack, and turned back to give his full attention to the fort. Now it was the Federals' turn to learn what it was like to try to hold the place while under attack from the river as well as the land.

They found it hard indeed. Delaying only long enough to patch up his riddled stack and get in touch with the Confederates ashore, Cooke steamed back past Plymouth that afternoon and opened on the fort in conjunction with Hoke, whose batteries were skillfully disposed for converging fire and whose infantry returned to within small-arms range of the Federal ramparts. The result was altogether harrowing for the defenders, caught thus as it were between the devil and the deep blue sea, the landward attackers and the *Albemarle*, both of which kept up the pressure until well after sunset and resumed it at daylight with even greater fury. "This terrible fire had to be endured without reply, as no man could live at the guns," the fort's commander was to report. "The breast-height was struck by solid shot on every side, fragments of shell sought almost every interior angle of the work, the whole extent of the parapet was swept by musketry, and men were killed and wounded even on the banquette slope. . . . This condition of affairs could not be long endured without a reckless sacrifice of life; no relief could be expected, and in compliance with the earnest desire of every officer I consented to hoist a white flag, and at 10 a.m. of April 20 I had the mortification of surrendering my post to the enemy with all it contained." This included 2834 soldiers, thirty guns, and a large haul of supplies, all secured at a cost to the attackers of less than 300 casualties, only one of whom was naval, a seaman hit by a pistol ball while the *Albemarle* had her snout in the sinking *Southfield*. "Heaven has crowned our efforts with success," a presidential aide-observer wired Davis, who replied directly to Hoke: "Accept my thanks and congratulations for the brilliant success which has attended your attack and capture of Plymouth. You are promoted to be a major general from that date."

Young Hoke was the hero of the hour, together with Cooke and the *Albemarle*, all down the eastern seaboard, and Bragg — though his basic planning went unnoticed amid the general praise for Hoke and Cooke — was hard at work, now that the ram had reversed the naval advantage, projecting exploits of a similar nature for the immediate future.

It was this the Federals feared. Unable to get an ironclad through any of the shallow inlets into Pamlico Sound, and with no time left in which to build one there, they saw no way to stop the apparently invulnerable, new-hatched monster before it returned the whole region to Confederate control. "The ram will probably come down to Roanoke Island, Washington, and New Bern," the district commander, Major General John J. Peck, informed his department chief, Ben Butler, on the day Plymouth fell. "Unless we are immediately and heavily reinforced, both by the army and navy, North Carolina is inevitably lost." Butler shared the alarm, although belatedly. Two months earlier, when the navy had asked him to send troops up the Roanoke to destroy the rebel vessel on its stocks, he had replied: "I don't believe in the ironclad," and even now, in passing on to Halleck the news that the fort had been reduced in part by the guns of the nonexistent warship, he declined to accept a fraction of the blame, which he declared was all the navy's for having left the garrison's water flank exposed. "Perhaps this is intended as a diversion," he ended blandly. "Any instructions?"

In point of fact, New Bern was next on the *Albemarle*'s list, once she finished off the gunboats skittishly awaiting her emergence into the Sound from which she took her name, and Hoke was told to prepare for this, rather than for an early return to the Army of Northern Virginia, despite that army's commander's pleas that he and his brigade were needed to help meet the attack that was soon to be launched across the Rapidan. Whatever disappointment this might involve for Lee, outnumbered two to one by the bluecoats on the north side of the river, Plymouth made a fine addition to the list of late winter and early spring victories which the President was compiling for inclusion in the message he was preparing for delivery to Congress when it convened next week in Richmond.

"Recent events of the war are highly creditable to our troops," he wrote, "exhibiting energy and vigilance combined with the habitual gallantry which they have taught us to expect on all occasions. We have been cheered by important and valuable successes in Florida, northern Mississippi, western Tennessee and Kentucky, western Louisiana, and eastern North Carolina, reflecting the highest honor on the skill and conduct of our commanders and on the incomparable soldiers whom it is their privilege to lead. . . . The armies in northern Georgia and in northern Virginia," he added, by way of compensation for the fact that there had been no such recent, gloom-dispelling triumphs in either of those regions, "still oppose with unshaken front a formidable barrier to the progress of the invader, and our generals, armies, and people are animated by cheerful confidence."

So he would say, and so Congress would be pleased to hear. But there were things he left unmentioned because to air them — involving, as they did, plans untried and expectations unfulfilled — would serve to deepen, rather than relieve, the nation's gloom regarding one of the two main armies on which it depended for survival. Davis's disappointment was not in Lee, who was fairly immobilized by the fact that a solid third of the Army of Northern Virginia had been detached for the past seven months; it was in Johnston, who had been given command of the Army of Tennessee with the understanding, at least on the part of the Richmond authorities, that he would go over to the offensive in an attempt to recover East and Middle Tennessee, lost by his predecessor in the course of the bloody, erratic, year-long retreat from Murfreesboro to Dalton. "You are desired to have all things in readiness at the earliest practicable moment for the movement indicated," the transplanted Virginian was reminded in early March. "The season is at hand and the time seems propitious."

Plans for such an offensive were quite explicit. Union forces now preparing at Chattanooga and Knoxville for a spring advance were dependent on uninterrupted communication with Nashville; if this supply line could be severed, both would be obliged to abandon what they held, with much attendant disruption of their plans. In line with this, Richmond's proposal was that Johnston be reinforced by Polk for a shift northeast to Kingston, forty miles west of Knoxville, where he would be joined by two divisions under Lieutenant General James Longstreet, detached from Lee and wintering near Greeneville, for an advance across the Tennessee River with a combined strength of more than 70,000 men. By such a move, the authorities assured him, "Knoxville [would be] isolated and Chattanooga threatened, with barely a possibility for the enemy to unite. Should he not then offer you battle outside of his entrenched lines, a rapid move across the mountains from Kingston to Sparta (a very practicable and easy route) would place you with a formidable army in a country full of resources, where it is supposed, with a good supply of ammunition, you may be entirely self-sustaining, and it is confidently believed that such a move would necessitate the withdrawal of the enemy to the line of the Cumberland." Bragg was the author of these suggestions, and he wrote from experience. In essence, they called for a repetition of the movement he himself had made soon after he assumed command of the army in the summer of 1862, whereby the western seat of war was shifted, practically overnight and practically without bloodshed, from Mississippi to North Georgia and from there all the way north to Kentucky. The Federals then had been obliged to give up, at least for a season, their designs on Chattanooga, and Bragg was of the opinion that if Johnston would only profit by his example the same results could be obtained in regard to their designs on Atlanta — provided, of course, that he advanced before his adversaries did. "To accomplish this," he was re-reminded in mid-March, "it is proposed that you move as soon as your means and force can be collected."

Johnston had many objections to the plan. Time had probably run out; he lacked supplies, as well as the mules and wagons needed to haul them; the Federals, in greatly superior numbers, would combine and jump him as soon as he got started, obliging him to fight at a disadvantage and with nothing to do, in case of defeat, but scatter his troops in the mountains. What he preferred, he told Bragg on March 18, was to stand where he was, letting the bluecoats crack their skulls against his works, then follow them up when they retreated. Meantime, he urged, the proffered reinforcements under Longstreet should be sent to him at Dalton for a share in the defensive battle, rather than have them wait in idleness to join him on the march. Bragg's reply, three days later, was curt and stiff: "Your dispatch . . . does not indicate an acceptance of the plan proposed. The troops can only be drawn from other points for an advance. Upon your decision of that point further action must depend." Alarmed at this evidence that he would not be reinforced on his own terms, Johnston was quick to assert that he had been misunderstood. "I expressly accept taking offensive," he wired back. "Only differ with you as to details. I assume that the enemy will be prepared for an advance before we are and will make it to our advantage. Therefore, I propose as necessary both for offensive and defensive to assemble our troops here immediately. Other preparations for advance are going on."

For two weeks there was no reply to this. The answer, when it came on April 7, was in a dispatch addressed not to Johnston but to Longstreet, who was told to prepare his two divisions for an immediate return to Virginia. Johnston was depressed by this lack of confidence, and outraged by reports that he had declined to move against the enemy. "I learn that it is given out," he wrote to a senator friend whose son was on his staff, "that it has been proposed to me to take the offensive with a large army & that I refused. Don't believe any such story." Besides, he said, after outlining his objections to the plan he had rejected, Lee's army, not his, was the one that should have been ordered to advance. "It would have been much easier to take the offensive (excuse such frequent use of that expression) in Va. than here," he wrote, basing his statement on the erroneous double claim that Lee's army was not only larger than his but also had a smaller blue army to its front. However, he was not greatly surprised at the way things had gone. The authorities in Richmond — Davis himself, Secretary of War James A. Seddon, and now Bragg, his erstwhile friend — had about as low an opinion of him, apparently, as he had of them;

which was low indeed. His consolation was in his men. "If this army thought of me and felt toward me as some of our high civil functionaries do," he closed his letter, "it would be necessary for me to leave the military service. But thank heaven, it is my true friend."

It was true the army was his friend; no general on either side, not even R. E. Lee or George McClellan, had more affection from the soldiers he commanded. "He was loved, respected, admired; yea, almost worshipped by his troops," a Tennessee veteran was to say. Richmond had taken this quality into account in sending him to Dalton to repair the shattered morale of an army which had recently been thrown off Missionary Ridge and chased southward into Georgia by the opponent it faced there now. And in this he had succeeded. "He restored the soldier's pride; he brought the manhood back to the private's bosom," the same veteran declared. The drawback, according to those who had advised against his appointment, was that he was too defensive-minded for the tactical part of his assignment. He had only assumed the offensive once in the whole course of the war, and that had been at Seven Pines, which might well seem to him the exception that proved the unwisdom of attacking, since all it had got him was the wound that had cost him the command he most preferred, now held by Lee, and a subsequent transfer to the less congenial West. Those who had opposed his appointment in December, on grounds that he would never go forward as intended, were quick to point out now in April that their prediction had been fulfilled. In fact, they said, if he continued to follow his accustomed pattern of behavior, he would be likely to fall back from Dalton at the first bristly gesture by the Federals in his front. Davis and Seddon, who had favored his appointment — primarily, it was true, because no one could think of another candidate for the job — were obliged to admit the strength of this, as evidence of what to expect, and so was Bragg after his exchanges with the general, by letter and wire, throughout the latter part of February and the first two thirds of March. It was then, on the heels of this admission by Davis and Seddon and Bragg, that the summons went to Longstreet for a quick return to Lee. They had given up on Johnston, who would neither go forward nor refuse to go forward, and who they knew from past experience (in northern Virginia, down on the York-James peninsula, outside beleaguered Vicksburg, and back in the piny woods of Mississippi) would wind up doing exactly as he pleased in any case. He always had. He always would. The only decision left was whether to keep him — and the fact was, they had no one to put in his place. So they kept him. And in keeping him, however regretfully, they committed the Army of Tennessee to the defensive and gave up all hope for a slash at the Union center as a means of disrupting at the outset the latest Grand Design for their subjugation.

Lee was committed to the defensive, too, though not by inclination or from choice. "At present my hands are tied," he confessed in a mid-April letter to Bragg. "If I was able to move . . . the enemy might be driven from the Rappahannock and obliged to look to the safety of his own capital instead of the assault upon ours." As it was, he added, writing from the stripped region about Orange where his infantry was camped, "I cannot even draw to me the cavalry or artillery of the army, and the season has arrived when I may be attacked any day."

It was a question of subsistence for mounts and men. Scarcely a tree in the district wore its bark below the point to which a horse could lift its mouth, and few of the few animals on hand were fit for rigorous service; "Fully one half of them were incapable of getting up a gallop," a cavalry officer complained, "a trembling trot being their fastest gait." Conditions were nearly as bad for the leaned-down soldiers. Though Davis himself had managed to get hold of 90,000 pounds of meat for shipment to the Rapidan during a critical, near-starvation period that winter, this did not go far with troops whose usual daily ration comprised four ounces of bacon or salt pork, often rancid, and a scant pint of rough-ground corn meal. Sprouting grass was a help to the horses this rainy April, but hunger was still a condition of existence for the men. This pained Lee, who did not like to add to other people's troubles by recounting his own, into making a formal complaint to the President, coupled with the strongest warning he had given at any time in the twenty-two months since he assumed command: "My anxiety on the subject of provisions for the army is so great that I cannot refrain from expressing it to Your Excellency. I cannot see how we can operate with our present supplies. Any derangement in their arrival or disaster to the railroad would render it impossible for me to keep the army together, and might force a retreat into North Carolina."

That too was in mid-April — April 12 — one week after he had alerted the army to prepare for a Union crossing, any day now, of the river to its front. On that same April 5, having pored over information received from scouts, northern papers, and citizens beyond the Rapidan, he gave Davis his estimate of the situation. "The movements and reports of the enemy may be intended to mislead us, and should therefore be carefully observed," he wrote. "But all the information that reaches me goes to strengthen the belief that Genl Grant is preparing to move against Richmond." This was as far as he went at the time; he said nothing of his new opponent's probable route (or routes) or schedule. Three days later, however, he wrote of receiving two more reports from reliable scouts, in which "the general impression was that the great battle would take place on the Rapidan, and that the Federal army would advance as soon as the weather is settled." Continuing to study all the evidence he could gather — including much, of course, that was false or merely worthless — he arrived within another week at a considerably more detailed estimate, and he passed this too along to

Davis, saying: "We shall have to glean troops from every quarter to oppose the apparent combination of the enemy."

He expected three attacks, all to be delivered simultaneously from three directions: 1) a main assault across the Rapidan, more or less against his front, 2) a diversionary advance up the Shenandoah Valley, off his western flank, and 3) a rear attack, up the James, to menace Richmond from the east and south. To meet this last, he proposed that General P. G. T. Beauregard be shifted from his present command at Charleston, which Lee believed was no longer on the list of Union objectives, and brought to Petersburg or Weldon to take charge of the defense of southside Richmond. The Valley threat he would leave for the time being to Major General John C. Breckinridge, who had a small command in the Department of Southwest Virginia. As for the main effort, the blue lunge across the Rapidan, he kept that as the continuing exclusive concern of the Army of Northern Virginia. Recent news that Longstreet would soon be coming back with two of his three divisions, after seven months in Georgia and Tennessee, made Lee yearn for a return to the old days and the old method of dealing with such a threat as he faced now. "If Richmond could be held secure against the attack from the east," he told the President on April 15, "I would propose that I draw Longstreet to me and move right against the enemy on the Rappahannock. Should God give us a crowning victory there, all their plans would be dissipated, and their troops now collecting on the waters of the Chesapeake would be recalled to the defense of Washington." Having said as much, however, he returned to such realities as the scarcity of food for his men and horses, then closed on a note of ominous regret: "But to make this move I must have provisions and forage. I am not yet able to call to me the cavalry or artillery. If I am obliged to retire from this line, either by a flank movement of the enemy or the want of supplies, great injury will befall us."

On April 18 he ordered all surplus baggage sent to the rear, a sort of ultimate alert well understood by the troops to mean that fighting might begin at any time. Still Grant did not move. Lee's impatience mounted during the following week — in the course of which Breckinridge was warned to brace for action in the Valley and Beauregard, in compliance with orders from Richmond, reached Weldon to assume command of the region between the James and Cape Fear rivers — though he acknowledged that the gain was worth the strain, if only because the half-starved horses thus were allowed more time to graze in peace on the new-sprung grass. "The advance of the Army of the Potomac seems to be delayed for some reason," he wrote Davis on April 25. "It appears to be prepared for movement, but is probably waiting for its coöperative columns." He closed with an invitation for the President to visit the army, "if the enemy remains quiet and the weather favorable," by way of affording himself a diversion from the daily grind in Richmond. Davis declined, under pressure of business; Congress would convene next week, for one thing. But four days later Lee enjoyed a diversion of his own.

Longstreet's two divisions had arrived at last from Tennessee and were in camp around Gordonsville, nine miles south of army headquarters at Orange. Lee did not know whether Meade would cross the Rapidan on his left or right, taking John Pope's intended route down the Orange & Alexandria Railroad or Joe Hooker's through the Wilderness. He rather thought (and certainly hoped) it would be the latter, but since he lacked solid evidence to that effect he kept Longstreet's hard-hitting veterans off to his left rear, in case the bluecoats came that way. On April 29 he rode down to review them for the first time in nearly eight months, which was how long it had been since they left the Old Dominion to supply Bragg's Sunday punch at Chickamauga. They were turned out in their ragged best, leather patched, metal polished, their shot-torn regimental colors newly stitched with the names of unfamiliar western battles, and when Lee drew rein before them, removing his hat in salute, the color bearers shook their flags like mad and the troops responded with an all-out rebel yell that reverberated from all the surrounding hills, causing the gray-haired general's eyes to brim with tears. "The effect was as of a military sacrament," an artillerist later wrote. Lee wept, another veteran explained, because "he felt that we were again to do his bidding." Deep Southerners or Westerners to a man — South Carolinians and Georgians, Alabamians and Mississippians, Arkansans and Texans — there was not a Virginian among them, and yet it was as if they had come home. A First Corps chaplain riding with the staff turned to a colonel as the yell went up and Lee sat there astride his gray horse Traveller, uncovered in salute, and asked: "Does it not make the general proud to see how these men love him?" The colonel shook his head. "Not proud," he said. "It awes him."

Awed or proud — no doubt with something of both, despite the staffer's protest — Lee felt his impatience mount still faster next day, back at Orange, when he got word that a four-division corps under Ambrose Burnside, formerly encamped at Annapolis and thought to be intended for service down the coast, had passed through Centerville two days ago and had by now reached Rappahannock Station, from which position it could move in direct support of the Army of the Potomac. Perhaps it was for this that Grant had been waiting to put his three-pronged war machine in motion. As for Meade, Lee informed Davis on this final day in April, "Our scouts report that the engineer troops, pontoon trains, and all the cavalry of Meade's army have been advanced south of the Rappahannock. . . . Everything indicates a concentrated attack on this front." His faith was in God and in the "incomparable infantry" of the Army of Northern Virginia, but now as he awaited the onslaught of the blue juggernaut whose numbers were roughly twice his own, he displayed more urgency of manner than those closest to him had ever seen him show on his own ground. Evidence of an early assault continued to accumulate, and still the Federal tents remained unstruck beyond the Rapidan. Lee's aggressive instinct, held in check by hard necessity, broke its bounds at last. "Colonel," he told a member of his staff, "we have got to whip them; we must whip them!" Apparently that was the high point of his impatience, for having said as much he paused, then added with a smile of amused relief: "It has already made me better to think of it."

Lee's confidence was based on past performance, against odds as long and sometimes longer, and Davis too drew reassurance from that source, having just completed his third full year of playing Hezekiah to Lincoln's Sennacherib. Whatever frets he had about developments out in Georgia, here in the Old Dominion at least the Confederacy had won for itself the military admiration of the world. Six blue comanders, in all their majesty and might — Irvin McDowell and George McClellan, John Pope and Ambrose Burnside, Joseph Hooker and George Meade — had mounted half a dozen well-sustained offensives, each designed to achieve the reduction of Richmond in short order, and all six had been turned back in various states of disarray. Now there was Grant, who seemed to many only a seventh name to be added to the list of discomfited eastern opponents. "If I mistake not," a young officer on Lee's staff wrote home on hearing of the elevation of this latest transfer from an inferior western school, "[Grant] will shortly come to grief if he attempts to repeat the tactics in Virginia which proved so successful in Mississippi." There were dissenters: Longstreet, for example, who had been Grant's friend at the Academy and a groomsman at his wedding — and who had fought, moreover, in a theater where Grant was in command. "We must make up our minds to get into line of battle and to stay there," Old Peter had told his visitors at Gordonsville the day before, "for that man will fight us every day and every hour till the end of the war." But for the most part there was general agreement that what had been done six times before (four of them, and the last four at that, more or less on this same Rapidan-Rappahannock line) could be done again by Lee, whose army was a rapier in his hand. If Grant was a fighter, as Longstreet said, there would be nothing unusual in that. One of the worst-defeated of the six had been known as "Fighting Joe," and the one who had been given the soundest drubbing of them all — the "miscreant" Pope — had also arrived with western laurels on his brow and a reputation for coming to savage grips with whatever tried to stand in his path of conquest.

Besides, what was called for now was not necessarily the outright defeat or even repulse of the invaders, east or west. What was called for, Davis could remind himself, was a six-month holding action which

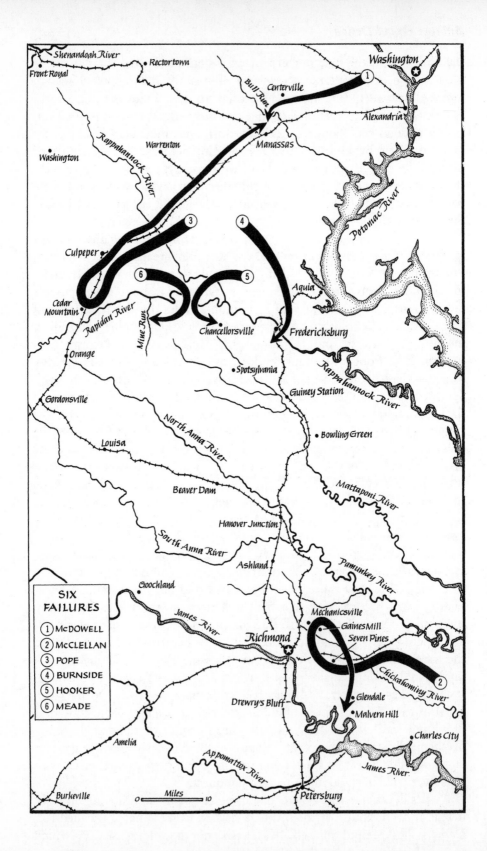

Shenandoah River
Front Royal
Rectortown
Washington
Bull Run
Centerville
① Washington
Alexandria
Warrenton
Manassas
Washington
Rappahannock River
③
④
Culpeper
⑥
⑤
Aquia
Cedar Mountain
Rapidan River
Mine Run
Chancellorsville
Fredericksburg
Orange
Spotsylvania
Rappahannock River
Gordonsville
Guiney Station
North Anna River
Louisa
Bowling Green
Beaver Dam
Mattaponi River
Hanover Junction
South Anna River
Ashland
Pamunkey River
Goochland

SIX
FAILURES
① McDOWELL
② McCLELLAN
③ POPE
④ BURNSIDE
⑤ HOOKER
⑥ MEADE

James River
Richmond
Mechanicsville
Gaines Mill
Seven Pines
Chickahominy River
②
Drewry's Bluff
Glendale
Malvern Hill
Charles City
Amelia
James River
Appomattox River
Burkeville
Miles
0   10
Petersburg

would allow them no appreciable gain except at a price that would be regarded as prohibitive, in money and blood, by voters who would be making their early-November choice between peace and war. In light of this, a head-down fighter like Grant might serve the South's purpose far better than would an over-all commander who was inclined to count his casualties and take counsel of his fears. Not that Davis abandoned all hope for a repetition of what had happened in the past to opponents who had come in roaring and gone out bleating; he hoped for it profoundly, and not without cause. Don Carlos Buell and William S. Rosecrans were western examples to match the six discomfited in Virginia, and Sherman had shown himself to have many of the qualities that made Grant an ideal opponent at this juncture. In some ways, now that the notion of an offensive against the Union center had been abandoned as a gambit, Joe Johnston seemed an excellent choice as a foil for the red-haired Ohioan, whose impulsiveness might expose him to the kind of damage his government could least afford on the eve of its quadrennial election. By way of further encouragement, Davis had only to consider more recent successes, scored east and west by Kirby Smith, Finegan, Forrest, and Hoke, for proof that the South could still stand up to combinations designed for its destruction, and could also carry the war to the enemy when the opportunity came. Just as Banks and Steele had been driven back across the Atchafalaya and the Saline — not only against the numerical odds, but also, as it were, against the tactics manuals — so might Sherman and Grant be driven back across the Tennessee and the Rappahannock. Like many brave men, before and since, Davis had found that when a difficulty amounted to an impossibility, the best course to pursue was one that did not take the impossibility into account. That was what he had meant all along when he said, "I cultivate hope and patience, and trust to the blunders of our enemy and the gallantry of our troops for ultimate success."

For the most part this attitude was shared by the people of Richmond. In fact, among the party-goers and the well-to-do — they had to be that; a dollar in gold was worth more than thirty in Confederate paper, while calico and coffee were $10 a yard and pound, eggs $2 a dozen, and cornfield beans were selling at $60 a bushel — there had never been a social season as lively as the one now drawing to a close. "Starvation parties" were all the rage, along with charades and taffy pulls, although they seemed to one diarist to have a quality of desperation about them, as if the guests were aware that these revels, honoring "Major This, or Colonel That, or Captain T'other," would be the last. In February Lincoln had issued a draft call for 500,000 men — more than the Confederacy could muster in all its camps between the Rappahannock and the Rio Grande — and then in March had upped the ante by calling for "200,000 more." All the South could do, by way of response, was lower and raise the conscription age limits to seventeen and fifty, robbing thus the cradle and the grave, as some complained, or as Davis put it, in regard to the half-grown boys about to be drafted and thrown into the line, "grinding the seed corn of the nation." Meanwhile U. S. Grant, "a bull-headed Suvarov," was poised on the semicircular horizon, about to lurch into motion from three directions, and in Richmond, his known goal, the revelry continued. "There seems to be for the first time," the diarist noted, "a resolute determination to enjoy the brief hour, and never look beyond the day."

Elsewhere about the country it was apparently much the same; a young man just back from Mobile reported that he had attended sixteen weddings and twenty-seven teas within the brief span of his visit. He did not add that he had found the gayety forced in that direction, but to a Richmond belle, looking back a decade later on this fourth and liveliest of the capital's wartime springs, the underlying sense of doom had been altogether inescapable. "In all our parties and pleasurings," she would recall, "there seemed to lurk a foreshadowing, as in the Greek plays where the gloomy end is ever kept in sight."

✗ 4 ✗

Grant was angered throughout April by increasingly glum reports of developments out in the Transmississippi, which in effect snapped off one prong of his spiky offensive before it could even be launched. "Banks, by his failure," he complained to Halleck, "has absorbed 10,000 veteran troops that should now be with Sherman, and 30,000 of his own that should have been moving toward Mobile; and this without accomplishing any good result." Nor was that the worst of it. Even more exasperating, from a somewhat different point of view, was the knowledge that Johnston now would not only have no worries about his rear and his supply lines to the Gulf, but would also be able to summon to the defense of North Georgia reinforcements who otherwise would have been occupied with the defense of South Alabama. Banks and Steele, as co-directors of the Louisiana-Arkansas fiasco, had disarranged the Grand Design at the outset; or as a friend of Grant's, after repeating his complaint that "30,000 men were rendered useless during six of the most important months of the military year," was to put it in a later appraisal of the situation, "The great combination of campaigns was inaugurated with disaster."

By way of insuring against such blunders here in the East, Grant contented himself with sending explicit and detailed instructions to Franz Sigel, who had received a military education in his native Germany, regarding the projected movement up the Shenandoah Valley and down the Virginia Central Railroad. But he went in person, soon after his return from Tennessee, to confer with the altogether nonprofessional Ben Butler, whom he had never met and with whom he had had no correspondence as to his share in the three-pronged convergence on Lee and Richmond. Arriving on April 1 at Fortress Monroe, the Massachusetts general's headquarters at the tip of the York-James peninsula, he decided that a good way to size up the former Bay State politician would be to invite his views on the part he thought he ought to play in the campaign scheduled to open within four weeks. Butler promptly gave them, and Grant was pleased, as he said later, to find that "they were very much such as I intended to direct"; that is, an amphibious movement up James River for a landing at City Point, eight miles northeast of Petersburg, the hub of Virginia's life-sustaining rail connections with the Carolinas and Georgia, and a fast northward march of twenty miles for a knock at the back door of the Confederate capital while Meade, so to speak, was climbing the front steps and Sigel was coming in through the side yard. This augured well. Still, gratifying as it was to find his military judgment confirmed in advance by the man who was charged with carrying out this portion of the plan it had produced, Grant did not neglect to give Butler, before he got back aboard the boat next morning for the return up Chesapeake Bay, written instructions as to what would be expected of him when jump-off time came round. "When you are notified to move," he told him, "take City Point with as much force as possible. Fortify, or rather intrench, at once, and concentrate all your troops for the field there as rapidly as you can." He added that, though "from City Point directions cannot be given at this time for your future movements," Butler was to bear in mind "that Richmond is to be your objective point, and that there is to be coöperation between your force and the Army of the Potomac."

The latter, being charged with the main effort, was of course Grant's main concern, and when he returned to Culpeper next day he found it in the throes of an unwelcome top-to-bottom reorganization. Designed to achieve the double purpose of tightening the chain of command and of weeding out certain generals who had proved themselves incompetent or unlucky, the shakeup involved the consolidation of a number of large units. Indeed, there was no unit above the size of a brigade that was unaffected by the change. Two of the five corps were broken up and distributed among the remaining three, while the same was done with four of the fifteen infantry divisions, leaving eleven. The result was painful to men in outfits which thus were abolished or in any case lost their identity in the shuffle. Cast among strangers they felt rejected, disowned, orphaned. They felt resentful at having been cannibalized, stung in their unit pride that theirs had been the organizations selected for such a fate, and they voiced their resentment to all who would listen. "The enemies of our country have, in times past, assailed [this division] in vain," one dispossessed commander protested, "and now it dissolves by action of our own friends." Although the recommendation had been made by Meade before Grant left Tennessee, the soldiers put the blame on the new general-in-chief, since the order of approval came down from Washington just two weeks after his arrival. By way of registering their complaint, at the first large-scale review Grant held after his return from Fortress Monroe in early April the men of one absorbed outfit wore their old corps badge on the crown of their caps, as usual, and — as he could see as soon as they swung past him — pinned the new one to the seat of their trousers.

He took no apparent offense at this, having other, more pressing matters on his mind. One was numbers. However well the chain of command was tightened, however ruthlessly high-ranking incompetents were purged, the army would be able to do little effective fighting, especially of the steam-roller kind Grant favored, unless its ranks were full and reserves were ample. And there was the rub. As spring advanced, the army moved closer to the time when it might lose the very cream of its membership, the men who had come forward on hearing that Sumter had been fired on, back in the pre-draft spring of 1861, and had learned since then, in what Sherman termed "the dearest school on earth," what it meant and what it took to be a soldier. Such veterans, survivors of many a hard-fought field, were scarcely replaceable. They were in fact not only the backbone, they were the body of the army, constituting roughly half the total combat force. Now their three-year enlistments were about to expire, and if they did not reënlist the army was apt to melt away, like the snow on the crest of the Blue Ridge, along with the volunteer organizations whose rolls they filled. Nor was this true only of the Army of the Potomac. Of the 956 volunteer infantry regiments in all the armies of the Union, 455 — nearly half — were scheduled to leave the service before the end of summer, while of the 158 volunteer batteries of artillery, 81 — more than half — would presently be free to head for home: unless, that is, enough of their members reënlisted to justify continuing their existence. By way of encouraging such commitments, the government offered certain inducements designed to make a combined appeal to greed and pride. These included, in the former category, a $400 bounty (to be increased by the amount his home town and county, or rather the civilians who had remained there for whatever reasons, were willing to put up) and a thirty-day furlough. As for pride, a man who reënlisted was to be classified as a "volunteer veteran" and was authorized to wear on his sleeve a special identifying chevron, a certificate of undeniable cold-blood valor. To these was added, as an appeal to *unit* pride, the guarantee that any regiment in which as many as three fourths of the troops "shipped over" would retain its numerical designation and its organizational status.

This last was perhaps the most effective of the lot: especially when regimental commanders, anxious to hold their outfits together as a prerequisite for holding onto their rank, carried the process down to the company level, where a man's deepest loyalties lay. Any company that attained its quota was encouraged to parade through the regimental camps, fifes shrieking and drums throbbing, while onlookers cheered and tossed their caps. Such enthusiasm was contagious, and the pressure grew heavier on holdouts in ratio to the nearness of the goal, until at last reluctance amounted to disloyalty, not only to comrades already committed, who stood in danger of being scattered among strangers, but also to the regiment, which would die a shameful death without its quota of reënlisted volunteers. "So you see I am sold again," one such wrote home, explaining that he had been swept off his feet by a fervor as strong as the spirit that makes a man be "born again" at a church revival. Not that the bounty and the prospect of a trip home, sporting the just-earned chevron, were not attractive. They were indeed, and especially together; $400, a tempted veteran pointed out, "seemed to be about the right amount for spending-money while on a furlough." Besides, regional supplements often raised the sum to more than a thousand dollars: a respectable nest egg, and enough for the down payment on a farm or a small business, once the fighting ended. Until then, after three years of life in the service, home was likely to be no great fun anyhow, except on a visit — and even that had its limitations, according to some who had been there and found that it fell considerably short of their expectations. "I almost wish myself back in the army," a furloughed soldier, barely a week after his departure, wrote to a comrade still in camp. "Everything seems to be so lonesome here. There is nothing going on that is new." In any case, as a result of these several attractions and persuasions, by mid-April no less that 136,000 veterans had signed on for another three years or the duration of the war.

Most of these were in the West, where the troops expected an early victory and were determined to be in on the kill; "fierce-fighting western men," one of their generals called them, "in for work and in for the war." In the Army of the Potomac the result was less spectacular; 26,767 veterans reënlisted — about half as many as signed up for another three years under Sherman, and also about half as many as were up for discharge. This meant that about the same number would soon be going home, dropped as emphatically from the army roster as if each man had stopped a rebel bullet. They would have to be replaced, and mainly this would be done by the conscripts and substitutes who now were arriving as a result of Lincoln's February call. Whatever they meant to Grant and Meade, for whom they were merely numbers on a fatted strength report, to the men they joined they were a mixed blessing at best. At worst, they were considerably less. "Such another depraved, vice-hardened and desperate set of human beings never before disgraced an army," an outraged New Englander complained. Partly this was the result of rising wages, which made enlistment a greater sacrifice than ever, and partly it was because the outsized bounties had created a new breed of soldier: the bounty jumper. "Thieves, pickpockets, and vagabonds would enlist," a later observer remarked, "take whatever bounty was paid in cash, desert when opportunity offered, change their names, go to another district or state, reënlist, collect another bounty, desert again, and go on playing the same trick until they were caught." One nimble New Yorker confessed to having made thirty-two such "jumps" before he wound up in the Albany penitentiary, while another New England veteran recorded that no less than half the recruits in his regiment received in one large draft had so quickly forgotten their assumed names, on the trip down to the Rappahannock, that they could not answer roll call when they got there. What was more, the delivery system was far from efficient. Out of a shipment of 625 recruits intended for a distinguished New Hampshire regiment, 137 deserted en route and another 118 managed to do the same within a week of their arrival — 36 to the rear, 82 into the Confederate lines — leaving a residue of 370, who were either the most patriotic or else the least resourceful of the lot. Across the way, on the south bank of the Rapidan, rebel pickets put up a placard: "Headquarters, 5th New Hampshire Volunteers. RECRUITS WANTED." In much the same vein, they sent over a mock-formal message inquiring when they could expect to receive the regimental colors.

Something else this latest influx of draftees brought into the Rappahannock camps that was more disturbing than the rising desertion rate. Though few in numbers, compared to the men already there, the newcomers effected a disproportionate influence on certain aspects of soldier life. "They never tired of relating the mysterious uses to which a 'jimmy' could be put by a man of nerve," a startled veteran would recall, "and how easy it was to crack a bank or filch a purse." Such talents did not go unexercised, so far at least as the limited field allowed; nothing anyone owned was safe that was not nailed down, and there were more ways than one to skin a cat or fleece a sheep. With all that crisp new bounty money injected into the economy, gambling increased hugely and so did the stakes. According to one awed observer, "Thousands of dollars would change hands in one day's playing, and there were many ugly fights engaged in, caused by their cheating each other at cards." Outraged by what he called "this business of filling up a decent regiment with the outscourings of humanity," another veteran infantryman recorded that "the more we thought of it, the more discontented we became. We longed for a quiet night, and when day came we longed to be away from these ruffians." The result was a necessary tightening of restrictions, in and out of drill hours and applicable to all. That came hard. "No pleasure or privilege for the boys in camp any more," a volunteer lamented, "for the hard lines and severe military discipline apply with a rigidness never before applied." Old-

timers yearned for a return to the easy-going life they once had
groused about, and they blamed its loss, illogically or not, on Grant,
whom they saw as a newcomer like all those unwelcome others, though
in fact the change had begun before he had any notion, let alone intention, of coming east to assume command of all the armies.

More logically — quite accurately, in fact — they put the blame
on him for another change which was going to have an even more bale-
ful effect on the lives of thousands of men now in his charge. In mid-
April, in a further attempt to lengthen his numerical advantage over
the forces in rebellion, Grant put an official end to the three-year-old
practice of exchanging Federal and Confederate prisoners of war. Whatever its shortcomings from a humanitarian point of view, militarily the
decision was a sound one. Not only did a man-for-man exchange favor
the side on which a man was a larger fraction of the whole, but in this
case there was also the added dividend that, in ending such a dis-
advantageous arrangement, the Union would be burdening its food-poor
adversary with a mounting number of hungry mouths to feed. Just how
much prolonged misery this was likely to cause, Grant's own troops
knew only too well, either from having been captured in the days when
they could be exchanged, or from awareness of what the daily food
allowance consisted in the camps across the river. It was hard enough
on the rebels, whose stomachs had long since shrunk to fit their rations,
but for men accustomed to eating all they could hold ("Our men are
generally overloaded, fed, and clad," their chief quartermaster was protesting even now, "which detracts from their marching capacity and
induces straggling") such deprivation would amount to downright
torture. Moreover, the prospect was further clouded by the knowledge that it had been devised by their own commander, the same man
they accused of having foisted the detested reorganization upon them,
as well as of having polluted their camps with rowdy gangs of thugs.

One further thing Grant did, however, that went far toward
making up for the unpopularity of those other changes that followed
hard on his arrival. This was to reach into the back areas of the war,
especially into the fortifications around the capital, and pluck thousands
of easy-living soldiers from their cushy jobs for reassignment to duty in
the field. Individually and in groups, stripped of their plumes and fire-
gilt buttons, they came down to the Rappahannock in a somewhat
bewildered condition, if not in a state of downright shock, and the
troops already there were glad to welcome them with cheers and jeers.
The warmest welcome went to regiments of heavy artillery, prised out
of their snug barracks, issued Springfields, and converted overnight
into congeries of unblooded rifle companies; "Heavy Infantry," the
veterans called them, or just "Heavies." The shocking thing about such
regiments, aside from their greenness, was their size. Popular with volunteers in search of easy duty and security from wounds, several of them

had as many as 1800 men apiece. "What division is this?" a Massachusetts soldier asked when one of them marched in, his own regiment being down to 207 effectives at the time. Other conversions were applauded about as lustily. Parade-ground cavalry units, for example, were suddenly unhorsed, handed muskets in place of carbines, and told that they would henceforth go afoot. "Where are your horses?" a heavy infantryman inquired of a dismounted cavalry outfit that came slogging into camp soon after his own regiment arrived. "Gone to fetch your heavy guns," one of the former troopers snapped. Teamsters too were subject to such abrupt indignity, and many of them were similarly converted and accoutered, as a result of an order reducing transportation to one wagon per brigade. "You needn't laugh at me," a transmuted teamster called to a braying mule in a passing train. "You may be in the ranks yourself before Grant gets through with the army."

In point of fact, now that they had time to look him over and examine the results of some of the changes he introduced, the men had begun to see that, whatever else he might do, in or out of combat, he clearly meant business, and they found they liked the notion of this. Some high-ranking officers, particularly the starch-collared regulars among them, might have doubts about the new general-in-chief (an old-line colonel of artillery, for instance, wrote home that he found him "stumpy, unmilitary, slouchy and western-looking; very ordinary, in fact") but the troops themselves, according to an enlisted diarist, would "look with awe at Grant's silent figure" whenever he rode out on inspection, which was often. They liked his reticence, his disregard of mere trappings, his eye for the essential. He was seldom cheered, except by greenhorn outfits trying to make points, but he seemed not to care or even notice. "Grant wants soldiers, not yawpers," a veteran observed approvingly. What was more, his success in prising the heavies out of the Washington fortifications was good evidence that he had the confidence of the authorities there — something most of his predecessors had lacked, to their discomfort and the resultant discomfort of the army in their charge. This was seen as an excellent sign, as well as a source of present satisfaction. There was also a solidity about him that was welcome after service under a series of commanders who had shown a tendency, and sometimes more than a tendency, to fly asunder under pressure. A New Englander put it simplest: "We all felt at last that *the boss* had arrived." Grant returned the compliment in kind. "The Army of the Potomac is in splendid condition and evidently feels like whipping somebody," he informed Halleck on April 26, one month after establishing headquarters at Culpeper: adding, "I feel much better with this command than I did before seeing it."

He had good cause to feel so, even though by now he was already one day past the date he had set for the simultaneous jump-off, east and west. Numerically, as a result of those various recruitment stratagems in the army and on the home front, he was in better shape than anyone had dared to hope, particularly on the Rappahannock. After Burnside shifted his corps into position for closeup support of Meade, Grant had 122,146 infantry, cavalry, and artillery effectives on hand for the main-effort crossing of the Rapidan. This figure included only the troops who were "present for duty, equipped"; another 24,602 were on extra duty, sick, or in arrest, bringing the total to just under 147,000. Even at the lower figure, and leaving Butler and Sigel out of account, he had about twice as many effectives as Lee, who had 61,953 of all arms. In Georgia, moreover, the ratio was roughly the same. Sherman had 119,898, including men on reënlistment furloughs, while Johnston had 63,949, including Polk, who would be free to join him once the pressure was on and the Union strategy was disclosed. Just when that would be, east and west, depended in part on the method by which this pressure was to be applied; that is, on the tactical details of the strategy Grant and Sherman had worked out between them, six weeks ago, in the Cincinnati hotel room. Grant was willing to leave the working out of such details to his red-haired friend, as far as they were to be applied in the West. In the East, however, he had made the matter his prime concern ever since he had set up headquarters in the field.

From Culpeper, there in the toppled V of the rivers, and from the peak of nearby Stony Mountain, where an observation post had been established for surveillance of the landscape roundabout, he could give the problem informed attention. South of the V, disposed on a front of nearly twenty miles along the right bank of the river, from Mine Run upstream to Rapidan Station and beyond, Lee and his army lay in wait under cover of intrenchments they had spent the past six months improving. The problem was how to get at him: or, more precisely, how to get around him and then at him, since a frontal assault, across the river and against those earthworks, would amount to downright folly, if not suicide en masse. Once the blue army was on his flank or in his rear, however, with nothing substantial between itself and Richmond, Lee would be obliged to come out of his works for the showdown battle Meade had been told to seek. This being so, the question was reduced to whether to move around his right flank or his left, east or west of that twenty-mile line of intrenchments. Much could be said for the latter course. The country was more open in that direction, affording the attackers plenty of room for bringing all of their superior force to bear, and there was also the prospect of gobbling up what was left of the Orange & Alexandria Railroad, down to Gordonsville, and then moving onto the Virginia Central, converting them into a supply line leading back to the Potomac, while denying their use to the defenders. All this was good, so far as it went, but there were two considerable drawbacks. One was that the rebels would wreck the railroad as they withdrew, requiring the pursuers to rebuild it and then keep it rebuilt despite attempts by regular and irregular grayback cavalry to re-wreck it. To guard against this would require the crippling detachment of fighting men from the front to the rear in ever-increasing numbers, all the way back to the Rappahannock, since even a temporary break might prove disastrous, dependent as the army would be on that single line for everything it needed, including food for 56,500 horses and mules and better than twice that many soldiers. The other drawback was that a movement around Lee's west flank would uncover the direct approach to Washington. In some ways this was a greater disadvantage than the other; Lincoln was notoriously touchy in regard to the safety of his capital, and every commander who had neglected to remember this had found himself in trouble as a result. So far, since the advent of the new general-in-chief, the President had maintained a hands-off attitude toward all things military, for which Grant was altogether thankful, but that attitude might not extend to the point of seeing Washington endangered, even in theory, especially now that the surrounding fortifications had been stripped of their outsized regiments. Between them, these two drawbacks — one having to do with supply difficulties, the other having to do with Lincoln — fairly well ruled out a movement around the Confederate left. Grant shifted his attention to the region beyond Lee's right: more specifically, to the country between Mine Run and the confluence of the rivers, fifteen miles east of Stony Mountain and about ten miles this side of Fredericksburg.

That way, the march would be shorter, Washington would be covered from dead ahead, and the supply problem would be solved by ready access to navigable streams on the outer flank, affording rapid, all-weather connection with well-stocked depots in the rear and requiring no more than minimal protection. Here too there was a drawback, however, one that was personally familiar to every soldier who had served for as long as half a year in the eastern theater. The Wilderness, it was called: a forbidding region, some dozen miles wide and eight miles deep, which the army would enter as soon as it crossed that stretch of the Rapidan immediately east of Lee's right flank, a leafy tangle extending from just beyond Mine Run to just beyond Chancellorsville. Joe Hooker, for one, could testify to the pitfalls hidden in that jungle of stunted oak and pine, and so could the present commander of the army that had come to grief in its depths, chief among them being that the force on the defensive had the advantage of silent concealment — an advantage the butternut veterans had used so well, five months ago, that Meade still considered himself lucky to have got back out of there alive. Conversely, the blue army's main advantage, its preponderance in men and guns, would scarcely matter if it was brought to battle there; numbers counted for little in those thickets, except to increase the claustrophobia and the panic that came from being shot at from close quarters by a foe you could not see, and artillery had to fire blind or not at all. As a drawback, this could hardly be overrated; but Grant believed he saw a way to avoid it. The answer was speed. If the troops moved fast enough, and began their march after nightfall screened the crossing from the rebel lookout station on Clark's Mountain across the way, they could get through the Wilderness and gain the open country just beyond it, where there was plenty of room for maneuver, before Lee had time to interfere. Moreover, this belief was founded on experience. Both Meade and Hooker, who had crossed by the same fords Grant intended to use now — Ely's and Germanna — had spent two full days on the far side of the river before they came to grips with anything substantial, and in both cases, what was more, they had done so as part of their plans: Meade by moving directly against the enemy at Mine Run, Hooker by calling a halt at Chancellorsville and inviting the enemy to attack him. Grant had no intention of doing either of these things. He intended to bull right through, covering those eight vine-choked miles in the shortest possible time — certainly less than two full days — and thus be out in the open, where Lee would have nothing better than a choice between attacking or being attacked. Either would suit Grant's purpose admirably, once he had his troops on ground where their superior numbers and equipment could be brought to bear and thus decide the issue in accordance with the odds.

By way of assuring speed on the projected march, or in any case a touch of the hard-driving ruthlessness that would be needed to obtain it, he had already made one important change in the makeup of the arm of the service that would lead the way across the Rapidan and down the roads beyond. In conference with Lincoln and Halleck, soon after his return from Tennessee and before he established headquarters in the field, he had expressed his dissatisfaction with cavalry operations in the eastern theater. What was needed, he said, was "a thorough leader." Various candidates for the post were mentioned and discarded, until Halleck came up with the answer. "How would Sheridan do?" he asked. This was Major General Philip H. Sheridan, then in command of an infantry division under Thomas near Chattanooga. His only experience with cavalry had been a five-week term as colonel of a Michigan regiment after Shiloh, nearly two years ago, and he had not only never served in Virginia, he had never even been over the ground in peacetime, so great was his dislike of all things southern. But Grant thought he would do just fine in command of the eastern army's three divisions of 13,000 troopers. "The very man I want," he said, and Sheridan was sent for. He arrived in early April, checked into Willard's, and went at once to the White House, much as Grant had done the month before. The interview was marred, however, when the President brought up the familiar jest: "Who ever saw a dead cavalryman?" Sheridan was not amused. If he had his way, there were going to be a great many dead cavalrymen lying around, Union as well as Confederate. Back at Willard's with friends, he said as much, and more. "I'm going to take the cavalry away from the bobtailed brigadier generals," he vowed. "They must do without their escorts. I intend to make the cavalry an arm of the service."

He was different, and he brought something different and hard into the army he now joined. "Smash 'em up, smash 'em up!" he would say as he toured the camps, smacking his palm with his fist for emphasis, and then ride off on his big hard-galloping horse, a bullet-headed little man with close-cropped hair and a black mustache and imperial, bandy-legged, long in the arms, all Irish but with a Mongol look to his face and form, as if something had gone strangely wrong somewhere down the line in Ireland. Just turned thirty-three, he was five feet five inches tall and he weighed 115 pounds with his spurs on; "one of those long-armed fellows with short legs," Lincoln remarked of him, "that can scratch his shins without having to stoop over." Mounted, he looked about as tall and burly as the next man, so that when he got down from his horse his slightness came as a shock. "The officer you brought on from the West is rather a little fellow to handle your cavalry," someone observed at headquarters, soon after Sheridan reported for duty. Grant took a pull at his cigar, perhaps remembering Missionary Ridge. "You'll find him big enough for the purpose before we get through with him," he said. And in point of fact, the undersized, Ohio-raised West Pointer held much the same views on war as his chief, who was Ohio born and had finished West Point ten years earlier, also standing about two thirds of the way down in his class. Those views, complementing Sheridan's even more succinct "Smash 'em up, smash 'em up!" could be stated quite briefly, a staff physician found out about this time. They were sitting around, idle after a hard day's work, and the doctor asked the general-in-chief for a definition of the art of war. Grant turned the matter over in his mind — no doubt preparing to quote Jomini or some other highly regarded authority, his listeners thought — and then replied, as if in confirmation of what his friend Longstreet was telling Lee's staff about now, across the way: "Find out where your enemy is. Get at him as soon as you can, and strike him as hard as you can. And keep moving on."

That was to be the method, and by now he had also arrived at the date on which it would begin to be applied. April 27 — the day after he told Halleck, "I feel much better with this command" — was his forty-second birthday; a year ago today, at Hard Times, Louisiana, he had braced his western army for the crossing of the greatest river of them all, the Mississippi, and the opening of the final stage in the campaign that took Vicksburg. It was therefore a fitting day for fixing the date for what would be the greatest jump-off of them all, east or west, east *and* west. Burnside by now was in motion from Annapolis, charged with replacing Meade's troops on guard along the railroad between Manassas and the Rappahannock, and Meade was free to concentrate his whole force in the V of the two rivers. Today was Wednesday. Allowing a full week for the completion of all this, together with final preparations for crossing the Rapidan at designated fords, Grant set the date for Wednesday next: May 4. Notice of this was sent at once to Meade and Burnside, as well as to Sigel and Butler, at Winchester and Fort Monroe, and to Sherman in North Georgia, who would pass the word to subordinates already poised for the leap at Dalton. This was nine days later than the tentative date Grant had set in early April, but he saw in the delay a double gain. Not only would it afford more time for preparation, which should help to eliminate oversights and confusion; it would also allow the Wilderness roads just that much additional time to dry, an important factor in consideration of the need for speed in getting out of that briery snare in the shortest possible time.

As for getting out of Washington — also a highly desirable thing, from a personal point of view — Grant had done that, for good, the previous Sunday. Except for the chance they gave him to be with his wife, his brief visits there had brought him little pleasure and much strain. The public adulation had increased, and with it the discomfort, including a flood of letters requesting his autograph (he had found a way to cut down on these, however; "I don't get as many as I did when I answered them," he said dryly) and a great deal of staring whenever he ventured out, which he seldom did unless it was unavoidable, as it was for example in getting from the station to Willard's and back. Observing his "peculiar aloofness," a protective garment he wore against the stares, one witness remarked that "he walked through a crowd as though solitary." On his last morning there, having taken breakfast in the hotel dining room before leaving to catch the train for Virginia, he was spotted by a reporter as he came out into the lobby. "He gets over the ground queerly," the journalist informed a friend that night. "He does not march, nor quite walk, but pitches along as if the next step would bring him on his nose. But his face looks firm and hard, and his eye is clear and resolute, and he is certainly natural, and clear of all appearance of self-consciousness." On the theory that this might be his last chance for some time, the reporter presumed to intercept him with a question: "I suppose, General, you don't mean to breakfast again until the war is over?" — "Not here I don't," Grant said, and went on out.

Nothing he had said or written, in conference or in correspondence with Lincoln or Halleck or anyone else, had given any estimate as to how much time the campaign about to open would require before it achieved what he called "the first great object," which was "to get possession of Lee's army." His preliminary instructions to Meade, for instance — "Lee's army will be your objective point.

Wherever Lee goes, there you will go also" — had been dated April 9; but whether the result so much desired would be attained within a year, or more, or considerably less, or not at all, remained to be seen. No one was more concerned with the specific timing than Lincoln, who would face a fight for survival in November, a fight he had good cause to believe he would lose unless the voters' confidence was lifted within the next six months by a substantial military accomplishment, rather than lowered by the lack of one to compensate for the lengthening casualty lists. And yet, despite the anxiety and strain — so well had he learned his lesson in the course of having shared in the planning, and often in the prosecution, of half a dozen failed offensives here in the East in the past three bloody years — he maintained his hands-off attitude, even to the extent of not asking his new general-in-chief for an informal guess at the schedule, east or west. It was as if, having tried interference to the limit of his ability, he now was determined to try abstention to the same extent. He had learned patience, and something more; he had learned submission. "I attempt no compliment to my own sagacity," he recently had told a Kentucky friend in a letter he knew would be published. "I claim not to have controlled events, but confess plainly that events have controlled me."

In line with this, as if to underscore his hands-off intention while at the same time giving assurance of continuing support, he sent Grant a farewell note on the last day of April, four days before the big offensive was to begin.

> Lieutenant General Grant:
>
> Not expecting to see you again before the spring campaign opens, I wish to express in this way my entire satisfaction with what you have done up to this time, so far as I understand it. The particulars of your plan I neither know nor seek to know. You are vigilant and self-reliant; and, pleased with this, I wish not to obtrude any constraints or restraints upon you. While I am very anxious that any great disaster or capture of our men in great numbers shall be avoided, I know these points are less likely to escape your attention than they would be mine. If there is anything wanting which is within my power to give, do not fail to let me know it. And now, with a brave army and a just cause, may God sustain you.
>
> Yours very truly,
> A. Lincoln.

Next day — May Day — Grant "acknowledged with pride" the President's "very kind letter" as soon as it reached him at Culpeper. "It will be my earnest endeavor that you and the country shall not be disappointed," he wrote, and added, by way of returning the compliments paid him: "Since the promotion which placed me in command of all the armies, and in view of the great responsibility and importance of success, I have been astonished at the readiness with which everything asked for has been yielded, without even an explanation being asked. Should my success be less than I desire and expect, the least I can say is, the fault is not with you."

And having said as much he turned his attention back to matters at hand. Two nights from now, in the small hours of Wednesday morning, the army would be moving down to the river for a crossing.

★ ★ ★

Braced as best he could manage for the blow he knew was coming, though he did not know just when or where it would land, Jefferson Davis had cause to be grateful for the apparent delay beyond the final day of April, which arrived without bringing word to Richmond that the Union drive had opened from any direction, east or west. Not only did this afford him time for additional preparations, such as getting a few more soldiers up to Lee or down to Beauregard; it also seemed to mean that he and his country would emerge unscathed from what had been in the past, for them, the cruelest month. Although he was by no means superstitious, the pattern was too plain to be denied. In April of 1861 the war itself had begun when Lincoln maneuvered him into opening fire on Sumter. Next year it had brought the death of his friend and idol, Albert Sidney Johnston, together with defeat in the half-won battle of Shiloh. Last year, in that same unlucky month, Grant and Hooker had launched the two offensives that cost the Confederacy the knee-buckling double loss of Vicksburg and Stonewall Jackson. However, this fourth April seemed about to be proved the exception to the rule. Militarily, so far as actual contact was concerned, the news from all three major theaters — from Louisiana and Arkansas, out in the Transmississippi, from Fort Pillow in the West, and from Plymouth, here in the East — had been nothing but good all month. If Davis, on the last morning in April, having walked the four blocks from the White House to his office adjoining Capitol Square and found no unduly woeful dispatch on his desk, paused to congratulate himself and his country on their delivery from the jinx, it would not have been without apparent justification. Yet he would have been wrong, horribly wrong. Before the day was over he would be struck the heaviest personal blow of the war: just such a blow as his adversary Lincoln had been struck, twenty-six months ago, in that other White House up in Washington.

He worked all morning, partly on administrative matters, which critics saw as consuming a disproportionate share of his time, and partly on intelligence reports — they made for difficult sifting, since different commanders predicted different objectives for the overdue Union offensive, generally in hair-raising proximity to their headquarters — then broke for lunch, which his wife brought on a tray from home to tempt his meager appetite. Before the dishes could be set in front of him, however, a house servant came running with news that Joe, their five-year-old, third of the four children who ranged in age from nine to three, had fallen from a high rear balcony onto the brick-paved court-yard thirty feet below. They hurried there to find him unconscious. Both legs were broken and his skull was fractured, apparently the result of having climbed a plank some carpenters had left resting against the balustrade when they quit for the noonday meal. He died soon after his mother reached him, and the house was filled with the screams of his Irish nurse, hysterical with sorrow and guilt from having let him out of her sight. His brother Jeff, two years older, had been the one to find him lying crumpled on the bricks. "I have said all the prayers I know how," he told a neighbor who came upon him kneeling there beside his dying brother, "but God will not wake Joe."

Under the first shock of her loss, the emotional impact of which was all the greater because she was seven months pregnant, Varina Davis was nearly as bad off as the nurse. But the most heartbreaking sight of all, Burton Harrison thought, was the father's "terrible self-control," which denied him the relief of tears. Little Joe had been his favorite, the child on whom he had "set his hope," according to his wife. Each night the boy had said his prayers at his father's knee, and often he had come in the early morning to be taken up into the big bed. Davis retired to his White House study, determined to go on with his work as an antidote to thinking of these things, and Mrs Davis joined him there as soon as she recovered from her initial shock. Presently a courier arrived with a dispatch from Lee. Davis took it, stared at it for a long minute, then turned to his wife with a stricken expression on his face. "Did you tell me what was in it?" he asked. Grief had paralyzed his mind, she saw, and her husband realized this too when he tried to compose his answer. "I must have this day with my little son," he cried, and moved blindly out of the room and up the stairs. Visitors heard him up there in the bedroom, pacing back and forth and saying over and over as he did so: "Not mine, O Lord, but thine." Meantime the boy was laid out in a casket, also in one of the upper rooms. His nurse lay flat on the floor alongside him, keening, while across the hall the father paced and paced the night away. "Not mine, O Lord, but thine," he kept saying, distracted by his grief.

All night the mourners came and went, cabinet members, high-ranking army and navy officers, dignitaries in town for the convening of Congress two days later, and yet the tall gray stucco house had an aspect of desolation, at once eerie and garish. Every room was brightly lighted, gas jets flaring, and the windows stood open on all three stories, their curtains moving in and out as the night breeze rose and fell. Next afternoon — May Day: Sunday — the funeral procession wound its way up the steep flank of Oregon Hill to Hollywood Cemetery, where many illustrious Confederates lay buried. Although Joe had been too young for school, having just turned five in April, more than a thousand schoolchildren followed the hearse, each bearing a sprig of evergreen or a spray of early flowers which they let fall on the hillside plot as they filed past. Standing by the open grave, Davis and his wife were a study in contrast. Heavy with the child she would bear in June, she wore black, including a veil, and her tall figure drooped beneath the burden of her grief, while her husband, twenty years her senior at fifty-five, yet lithe of form and erect as one of the monuments stark against the sky behind him, wore his accustomed suit of homespun gray. Down below, the swollen James purled and foamed around its rocks and islands, and now for the first time, as they watched him stand uncovered in the sunlight beside the grave of the son on whom he had set his hope, people saw that Davis, acquainted increasingly with sorrow in his private as in his public life, had begun to look his age and more. The words "vibrant" and "boyish," so often used by journalists and others to describe their impression of him, no longer applied. Streaks of gray were in his hair, unnoticed until now, and the blind left eye looked blinder in this light.

There was no evidence of this, however, in his message of greeting to the newly elected Second Congress when it convened the following day on Capitol Hill. Though the words were read by the clerk, in accordance with custom, their tone of quiet reliance and not-so-quiet defiance was altogether characteristic of their author. "When our independence, by the valor and fortitude of our people, shall have been won against all the hostile influences combined against us, and can no longer be ignored by open foes or professed neutrals, this war will have left with its proud memories a record of many wrongs which it may not misbecome us to forgive, [as well as] some for which we may not properly forbear from demanding redress. In the meantime, it is enough for us to know that every avenue of negotiation is closed against us, that our enemy is making renewed and strenuous efforts for our destruction, and that the sole resource for us, as a people secure in the justice of our cause and holding our liberties to be more precious than all other earthly possessions, is to combine and apply every available element of power for their defense and preservation." By way of proof that such a course of action could be effective against the odds, he was pleased to review the triumphs scored in all three major theaters since the previous Congress adjourned: after which he passed at once to the expected peroration, assuring his hearers that, just as they were on God's side, so was God on theirs. "Let us then, while resolute in devoting all our energies to securing the realization of the bright auspices which encourage us, not forget that our humble and most grateful thanks are due to Him without whose guidance and protecting care all human efforts are of no avail, and to whose interposition are due the manifold successes with which we have been cheered."

Just over sixty air-line miles northwest of the chamber in which the clerk droned through the presidential message, Lee was meeting with his chief infantry lieutenants atop Clark's Mountain, immediately north-east of the point where the railroad crossed the Rapidan north of Orange. He had called them together, his three corps and eight division com-manders, to make certain that each had a good inclusive look at the terrain for which they would be fighting as soon as Grant made the move that Lee by now was convinced he had in mind. Not that most of them had not fought there before; they had, except for Longstreet and his two subordinates, who had missed both Chancellorsville and Mine Run; but the panoramic view from here, some six or seven hundred feet above the low-lying country roundabout, presented all the ad-vantages of a living map unrolled at their feet for their inspection and instruction, and as such — lovely, even breath-taking in its sweep and grandeur, a never-ending carpet with all the vivid greens of advancing spring commingled in its texture — would serve, as nothing else could do, to fix the over-all character of the landscape in their minds. For the most part — though their youth was disguised, in all but two heavily mustached cases, by beards in a variety of styles, from full-shovel to Vandyke — they were men in their prime, early-middle-aged at worst. Longstreet was forty-three, and the other two corps com-manders, Lieutenant Generals Richard S. Ewell and A. P. Hill, were respectively four years older and five years younger, while the division commanders averaged barely forty, including one who was forty-eight; "Old Allegheny," he was called, as if he vied in ancientness with the mountains beyond the Blue Ridge. Aside from him, Lee at fifty-seven was ten years older than any other general on the hilltop, and like Davis, despite the vigor of his movements, the quick brown eyes in his high-colored face, and the stalwart resolution of his bearing, he had begun to show his age. His hair, which had gone from brown to iron gray in the first year of the war, was now quite white along his temples, and the same was true of his beard, which he wore clipped somewhat closer now than formerly, as if in preparation for long-term fighting. The past winter had been a hard one for him, racking his body with frequent attacks that were diagnosed as lumbago, and though his health improved with warming weather, the opening months of spring had been even harder to endure, not only because they brought much rain, which tended to oppress him, but also because it galled his aggressive nature to be obliged to wait, as he fretfully complained, "on the time and place of the enemy's choosing" for battle. Just over twenty months ago, after less than three months in command of the newly-assembled army with which he had whipped McClellan back from the outskirts of

Richmond, he had stood on this same mountaintop and watched Pope's blue host file northward out of the trap he had laid for it there in the V of the rivers, and he had said to Longstreet then: "General, we little thought that the enemy would turn his back upon us thus early in the campaign." It was different now. Grant he knew would move, not north across the Rappahannock, but south across the Rapidan, and all Lee could do was prepare to meet him with whatever skill and savagery were required to drive him back: which, in part, was why he had brought his ranking subordinates up here for a detailed look at the terrain on which he planned to do just that. Believing as he did that an outnumbered army should be light on its feet and supple in the hands of its commander, his custom was to give his lieutenants a great deal of latitude in combat, and he wanted to make certain that they were equipped, geographically at least, to exercise with judgment the initiative he encouraged them to seize whenever they were on their own — as, in fact, every unit commander, gray or blue, was likely to be in that tangled country down below, especially in the thickets that lay like pale green smoke over that portion called the Wilderness, stretching eastward beyond Mine Run.

The Rapidan flowed to their right, practically at their feet as they stood looking north toward Culpeper, the hilltop town ten miles away, where A. P. Hill had been born and raised and where Grant now had his headquarters. Another ten miles farther on, hazy in the distance, the dark green line of the Rappahannock crooked southeast to its junction with the nearer river, twenty miles due east of the domed crest of Clark's Mountain, and then on out of sight toward Fredericksburg, still another ten miles beyond the roll of the horizon. All this lay before and below the assembled Confederates, who could also see the conical tents and white-topped wagons clustered and scattered in and about the camps Meade's army had pitched in the arms of the stream-bound V whose open end was crossed by the twin threads of the railroad glinting silver in the sunlight. There was a good deal of activity in those camps today, as indeed there had been the day before, a Sunday, but the generals on the mountain gave their closest attention to the gray-green expanse of the Wilderness, particularly its northern rim, as defined by the meandering Rapidan; Hooker and Meade had both crossed there in launching the two most recent Union offensives, and Lee believed that Grant would do the same, even to the extent of using the same fords, Ely's and Germanna, four and ten miles respectively from the junction of the rivers. He not only believed it, he said it. Apparently that was another reason he had brought his lieutenants up here: to say it and to show them as he spoke. Suddenly, without preamble or explanation, he raised one gauntleted hand and pointed specifically at the six-mile stretch of the Rapidan that flowed between the two points where the Federals twice had thrown their pontoon bridges in preparation for all-out assaults on the Army of Northern Virginia. "Grant will cross by one of these fords," he said.

Deliberately spoken, the words had the sound of a divination, now and even more so in the future, when they were fulfilled and his hearers passed them down as an instance of Lee's ability to read an opponent's mind. However, though this faculty was real enough on the face of it, having been demonstrated repeatedly in most of his campaigns, it was based on nothing occult or extrasensory, as many of his admirers liked to claim, but rather on a careful analysis of such information as came to hand in the normal course of events — from enemy newspapers closely scanned, from scouts and spies and friendly civilians who made it through the Yankee lines, from loquacious deserters and tight-mouthed prisoners tripped by skillful interrogation — plus a highly developed intelligence procedure, by which he was able not only to put himself in the other man's position, but also to *become* that man, so to speak, in making a choice among the opportunities the situation seemed to afford him for accomplishing the destruction of the Army of Northern Virginia. Like other artists in other lines of endeavor, Lee produced by hard labor, midnight oil, and infinite pains what seemed possible only by uncluttered inspiration. Quite the opposite of uncanny, his method was in fact so canny that it frequently produced results which only an apparent wizard could achieve. The Clark's Mountain prediction was a case in point. Lee had spent a major part of his time for the past two months — ever since Grant's arrival and elevation, in early March — at work on the problem of just what his new adversary was going to do, and for the past two weeks — ever since April 18, when he ordered all surplus baggage sent to the rear — he had given the matter his practically undivided attention: with the result that, after a process of selection and rejection much like Grant's across the way, he had come up with what he believed was the answer. Grant would cross the Rapidan by Ely's Ford or Germanna Ford, and having done so he either would turn west for an attack on the Confederate right flank, as Meade had done in November, or else he would do as Hooker had intended to do, a year ago this week, and maneuver for a battle in the open, where he could bring his superior numbers to bear. Which of these two courses the Federal commander meant to adopt once he was across the river did not really matter to Lee, since he did not intend to give him a chance to do either. Lee's plan was to let him cross, then hit him there in the Wilderness with everything he had, taking advantage of every equalizing impediment the terrain afforded, in order to whip him as thoroughly as possible in the shortest possible time, and thus drive him, badly cut up, back across the Rapidan. He did not say all this today, however. He merely said that Grant would cross by one of those fords on the rim of the Wilderness, and then he mounted Traveller and led the way back down the mountain.

Nor did he act, just yet, on the contingent decision he had reached. Only today, in fact, he had instructed Longstreet to shift one of his two divisions northwest of Gordonsville, in order to have it in a better position to meet the challenge Grant would pose if he attempted a move around the Confederate left, in the opposite direction from the one predicted. Lacking definite confirmation of what was after all no more than a theoretical opinion, an educated guess, Lee could not commit his army to a large-scale counteraction of a movement which there was even an outside chance the enemy might not make; he had to leave a sizeable margin for error, including total error. That night, however, the signal station on Clark's Mountain reported observing moving lights in the Federal camps, and next morning — May 3: Tuesday — there were reports of heavy clouds of dust, stirred up by columns marching here and there, and smoke in unusual volume, as if the bluecoats were engaged in the last-minute destruction of camp equipment and personal belongings for which they would have no use when they moved out.

All day this heightened activity continued, past sundown and into the night. Presently the signalmen blinked a message to army headquarters that long columns of troops were passing in front of campfires down there on the far bank of the Rapidan. Headquarters responded with a question: Was the movement west or east, upstream in Hill's direction on the left or downstream in Ewell's direction on the right? The signal station was in visual communication with both corps commanders, as well as with Lee, but it could find no answer to the question. All that could be seen across the way was the winking of campfires as files of men passed in front of them. There was no way of telling, from this, whether the troops were moving upstream or down, to the left or to the right. By now it was close to midnight; May 4 would be dawning within five hours. Lee decided to act at last on yesterday's prediction, and sent word accordingly for the signalmen to flash a message to the corps on the right, down toward Mine Run: "General Ewell, have your command ready to move at daylight."

CHAPTER

2

The Forty Days

★ ✗ ☆

GRANT CAME AS LEE HAD SAID HE WOULD, only more so, crossing the Rapidan not merely by "one of those fords," Ely's or Germanna, but by both — and, presently, by still another for good measure. Sheridan's new-shod cavalry led the way, splashing across the shallows in the darkness soon after midnight, May 4, and while the engineers got to work in the waist-deep water, throwing a pair of wood and canvas pontoon bridges at each of the two fords, the troopers established bridgeheads on the enemy side of the river at both points and sent out patrols to explore the narrow, jungle-flanked, moonless roads tunneling southward through the Wilderness. Near the head of one column the horsemen got to talking as they felt their way toward Chancellorsville, a name depressing to the spirits of any Federal who had been there with Joe Hooker just a year ago this week. One of the group, anticipating a quick pink-yellow stab of flame and a humming, bone-thwacking bullet from every shadow up ahead, remarked uneasily that he had never supposed "the army went hunting around in the night for Johnnies in this way."

"We're stealing a march on old man Lee," a veteran explained.

They thought this over, remembering the loom of Clark's Mountain and the rebel lookout station on its peak, and before long someone put the thought into words. "Lee will miss us in the morning."

"Yes, and then watch out," another veteran declared. "He'll come tearing down this way ready for a fight."

Though all agreed that this would certainly be in character, Lee did no such thing: at least not yet. Morning came and the crossing progressed smoothly in their rear, including the installation of still a fifth bridge at Culpeper Mine Ford, two miles above Ely's, to speed the passage of the army train, the laggard, highly vulnerable element to which all the others, mounted or afoot, had to conform for its protection on the march. Slow-creaking and heavily loaded with ten days' subsistence for nearly 150,000 men and ten days' grain for better than 56,000 mules and horses (strung out along a single road, if any such had been available, this monster train would have covered the sixty-odd miles from the Rapidan to Richmond without a break from head to tail) the wagons passed over the two lower fords in the wake of Major General Winfield S. Hancock's II Corps, the largest of Meade's three, which crossed at Ely's in the darkness and began to make camp at Chancellorsville, five miles from the river, before noon. The brevity of the march was necessary if the combat units were to provide continuous protection for the road-jammed train, but the men, slogging along under packs about as heavy-laden as the wagons in their rear, were thankful for the early halt; they carried, as directed in the carefully worded order, "50 rounds of ammunition upon the person, three days' full rations in their haversacks, [and] three days' bread and short rations in their knapsacks." At Germanna, meantime, Major General Gouverneur K. Warren's V Corps crossed and marched six miles southeast to Wilderness Tavern, near the intersection of the Germanna Plank Road and the Orange-Fredericksburg Turnpike, where it made camp in the early afternoon, five miles west of Hancock, leaving room behind for Major General John Sedgwick's VI Corps to bed down beside the road, between the tavern and the river, well before sundown. Grant was pleased, when he reached the upper ford about midday and clattered over with his staff, to note that the passage of the Rapidan was being accomplished in excellent order, strictly according to schedule, and without a suggestion of enemy interference. "This I regarded as a great success," he later reported, because "it removed from my mind the most serious apprehensions I had entertained, that of crossing the river in the face of an active, large, well-appointed, and ably-commanded army."

Gratified by the evidence that he had indeed stolen a march on old man Lee, he got off a wire at 1.15 to Burnside at Rappahannock Station, instructing him to bring his IX Corps down to Germanna without delay. Another went to Halleck, back in Washington: "The crossing of the Rapidan effected. Forty-eight hours now will demonstrate whether the enemy intends giving battle this side of Richmond. Telegraph Butler that we have crossed." This done, he rode on a short distance and established headquarters beside the road, near a deserted house whose front porch afforded him and his military family a shaded, airy position from which to observe his soldiers on the march. He was dressed uncharacteristically in full regimentals, including his sword and sash and even a pair of brown cotton-thread gloves, three stars glinting impressively on each shoulder of his best frock coat. What was more, his manner was as expansive as his trappings — a reaction, apparently, to his sudden release from concern that he might be attacked with his army astride the river. As he sat there smoking and swapping remarks with his associates, a newspaper correspondent approached and asked the question not even

Lincoln had put to him in the past two months. How long was it going to take him to reach Richmond?

Grant not only expressed no resentment at the reporter's inquisitive presumption; he even answered him. "I will agree to be there in about four days," he said, to the astonishment of the newsman and his staff. Then he added: "That is, if General Lee becomes a party to the agreement. But if he objects, the trip will undoubtedly be prolonged."

Laughter increased the pervasive feeling of well-being and relief, and orders soon were distributed for tomorrow's march, which had been prepared beforehand for release if all went well: as, indeed, all had. One change there was, however, occasioned by a report that Sheridan received that afternoon. Chagrined at encountering none of Major General J. E. B. Stuart's highly touted butternut troopers in the course of his probe of the Wilderness south of the two fords, he learned that this was because they were assembled near Fredericksburg for a grand review next day at Hamilton's Crossing, a dozen miles to the east, and he asked permission to take two of his three divisions in that direction at first light in order to get among them, smash them up, and thus abolish at the outset of the campaign one of the problems that would have to be solved before its finish. Grant was willing, and so was Meade, though more reluctantly, being hidebound in his notion as to the primary duty of cavalry on a march through enemy country. In any case, the army would still have one of its mounted divisions for such work, and that seemed ample, especially if tomorrow's advance required no more of the blue outriders than today's had done. For one thing, since the train would not complete its crossing of the Rapidan before late tomorrow afternoon, and would thus require that the three infantry corps hold back and keep well closed up for its protection, the marches were to be about as brief. Hancock would move south and west, first to Todd's Tavern and then to Shady Grove Church, down on the Catharpin Road, extending his right toward Parker's Store on the Orange Plank Road, which was to be Warren's stopping point. Warren in turn would extend his right toward Wilderness Tavern, his present position astride the Orange Turnpike, which Sedgwick would occupy tomorrow, leaving one division on guard at Germanna Ford until Burnside's lead division arrived. Despite their brevity (Hancock had nine miles to cover, Warren and Sedgwick barely half that) all marches were to begin at 5 o'clock promptly, which was sunup. Upon reaching their designated objectives, Wilderness Tavern, Parker's Store, and Shady Grove Church — each commanding a major road coming in from the west, where Lee presumably still was unless he had already taken alarm and fallen back southward — all units were to prepare at once for getting under way as promptly the following day, Friday the 6th, which would take them out of the Wilderness and into the open country beyond, in position for coming to grips with the Confederates on terrain that would favor the army superior in numbers.

Forty-eight hours would tell the story, Grant had informed Halleck early that afternoon, and all the indications were that the story would have an ending that was happy from the Federal point of view. Careful planning seemed to have paid off handsomely. Not only were his "most serious apprehensions" — that he would be jumped while astride the Rapidan — behind him, but his second greatest worry — that he would have to fight in the blind tangle of the Wilderness — was all but behind him, too. "Enemy moving infantry and trains toward Verdiersville," the signal station on Stony Mountain informed him at 3 p.m. "Two brigades gone from this front. Camps on Clark's Mountain breaking up. Battery still in position behind Dr Morton's house, and infantry pickets on the river." That had far more the sound of preparations for a withdrawal than for an attack, and there seemed to be little of urgency in the Confederate reaction, such as it was. Grant could turn in for a good night's sleep in a much less fretful state of mind than the one in which he had lain down the night before, while poised for the crossing which now was complete except for a couple of thousand more wagons and Burnside's corps, whose arrival would give him a combat strength of 122,000 effectives on the rebel side of the river: an army which, arrayed for battle, two ranks deep, with one third of its units held rearward in reserve, would extend for twenty-five miles from flank to flank. That was roughly twice as many troops as Lee could muster of all arms. Grant was not only willing, he was altogether anxious to take him on at the earliest possible moment, preferably out in the open, where he could bring his superior ordnance to bear, or if not there then here in this green maze of vines and briers and stunted oaks and pines, if the opportunity offered and that was what it came to. He turned in early and apparently slept well.

That was not the case with a good many of the men who were bivouacked in this haunted woodland by his orders. Unlike him, they had been here before, and the memory was painful. In the fields around Wilderness Tavern, it was afterwards recalled — including the one just east of the deserted, ramshackle tavern itself, where Stonewall Jackson's maimed left arm was buried — there was little or no singing round the campfires, the usual pastime after a not-too-hard day's march, and there was even a tendency to avoid the accustomed small talk. This was due, one soldier declared, to "a sense of ominous dread which many of us found it almost impossible to shake off." There was, in fact, much about the present situation that was remindful of the one a year ago, when all ranks had engaged in a carnival of self-congratulation on the results of careful planning and stout marching; "The rebel army is now the legitimate property of the Army of the Potomac," Hooker had announced on that other May Day, just before he came to grief, suffering better than 17,000 casualties before he managed to scurry out of this scrub oak jungle and back across the Rappahannock, beyond the reach of a gray army barely one third the size of his own. Grant, they knew, was no such spouter, but they remembered Fighting Joe and other even more unpleasant things, such as brush fires set by bursting shells, in which men with broken backs and bullet-shattered legs had been roasted alive before the stretcher bearers could get at them. Even recruits could see the danger. "These woods will surely be burned if we fight here," one said when they first called a halt that afternoon.

Over near Chancellorsville, where the whippoorwills began calling plaintively soon after sunset, now as then, the mood was much the same. The fighting had been heaviest around here last year, and there still were many signs of it, including skeletons in rotted blue, washed partly out of their shallow graves by the rains of the past winter. No one but the devil himself would choose such ground for a field of battle, veterans said; the devil and old man Lee. In an artillery park near the ruin of the Chancellor mansion, which had burned to its brick foundations on the second day of conflict, a visiting infantryman looked glumly at a weathered skull that stared back with empty sockets, grinning a lipless grin. He prodded it with his boot, then turned to his comrades — saying "you" and "you," not "we" and "us," for every soldier is superstitious about foretelling his own death, having seen such words come true too many times — and delivered himself of a prediction. "This is what you are all coming to," he told them, "and some of you will start toward it tomorrow."

In point of fact, the conversion of the blue invaders into skeletons was just the kind of grisly work Lee had in mind, and he was moving toward it, even now, with everything he had. Grant had taken care, in his assignment of objectives for the following day, to see that each of the three main roads coming in from the west would be covered by a corps of infantry; for though logic and the evidence, such as it was, tended to indicate that his adversary was in the process of falling back to a strong defensive position athwart his path — probably on the banks of the North Anna, twenty miles to the south — there was a chance that the old fox might mass his troops for an attack, down one or another of those roads, in an attempt to strike while the Union army was strung out in the Wilderness. The truth was, Lee was coming by all three, a corps on each.

Ewell, alerted the night before, would march eastward on the Orange Turnpike, nearest the river, while Hill took the Orange Plank Road, which paralleled the turnpike at a distance that varied from one to three miles until the two converged, just short of Chancellorsville, twenty-five miles away; Longstreet, down around Gordonsville, had a greater distance to travel and would make a later start, having to call in his troops from the far-left positions they had been obliged to hold until Grant was committed to the upstream movement with all his force. Ewell, with three divisions, began his march at 9 o'clock. Hill reached Orange before noon, left one division there to guard the nearby Rapidan crossings, and had his other two in motion on the plank road shortly afterwards, the army commander riding with him near the head of the column. Since the troops on the turnpike had a three-hour head start and a straighter route, Ewell was told to regulate his speed by that of Hill. Longstreet then was notified by courier to set out with his two divisions, crossing the North Anna by Brock's Bridge, due east of Gordonsville, then turning north to strike the Catharpin Road at Richard's Shop, from which point his march would parallel those of the other two corps, on his left between him and the Rapidan. Lee's plan, though he announced no details yet, was to get within reach of the Federals as soon as possible, bring them to a Wilderness-hampered halt with Hill and Ewell, then launch an all-out hip-and-thigh assault with all three corps, as soon as Longstreet came up on the right.

Ewell stopped for the night at Locust Grove, a couple of miles into the Wilderness beyond Mine Run. Clustered about their skillet wagons for supper, the men of his three divisions had no such reaction to their surroundings as the men of Warren's four divisions were experiencing around Wilderness Tavern, five miles up the pike, or those of Hancock's four at Chancellorsville, another five miles east. Outnumbered as usual on the eve of contact, and having fought here against odds as long and longer, the butternut veterans understood that the cramped, leaf-screened terrain would work to their advantage, now as before, and their bivouacs hummed with banter and small talk as they bedded down, after ravening their rations, to rest for the shock they knew was likely to come tomorrow. Five miles southwest on the plank road, and still five miles short of the western limits of the Wilderness, it was much the same with the men of Hill's two divisions, rolled in their blankets and sleeping under the stars. At sundown he had called a halt at Verdiersville, eleven miles beyond Orange and nine from Parker's Store; "My Dearsville," Hill's troops dubbed the hamlet. Here Lee had had his headquarters during the Mine Run confrontation last November, and his tent was pitched, tonight as then, in a field beside the road. Soon there began to come to its flap a series of couriers bearing dispatches from all quarters of Virginia — dispatches which in turn bore out, to the letter, predictions he had been making for the past month as to the nature of the offensive the Federals now had launched.

Of these, the most alarming came from the President himself. A blue force, estimated at 30,000 of all arms and said to be commanded by Ben Butler, was unloading from transports at City Point and Bermuda Hundred, on the south bank of the James less than twenty miles from

Richmond, in position to break its vital rail connections with Petersburg and points south, if not indeed to come swarming across its bridges and into its streets in a matter of hours, since the capital had scarcely one tenth that many troops for its defense. "With these facts and your previous knowledge," Davis wired, demonstrating his accustomed calmness under pressure, as well as his abiding trust in Lee, "you can estimate the condition of things here, and decide how far your own movements should be influenced thereby." Lee's decision was not to allow his movements to be influenced at all by this development. He would continue to concentrate on meeting the threat to his immediate front, he informed Davis, and leave Butler to Beauregard, who had been ordered to proceed at once from Weldon to confront the southside invaders with such troops as he could muster in his newly formed department. Lee's reaction to a second grievous danger, reported from out in the Shendandoah Valley, was much the same. Warned that a force of undetermined strength under Sigel had begun an advance up the Valley in conjunction with another movement west of the Alleghenies, he replied with a wire instructing Breckinridge to assume "general direction of affairs" beyond the Blue Ridge. "I trust you will drive the enemy back," he told him. This done, he put both dangers — one to his rear, the other to his flank, and both to his lines of supply and communication — out of his mind, at least for the present, in order to give his undivided attention to the problem at hand: specifically, how best to deal with Meade's blue host, which had crossed the Rapidan bent on his destruction, but which was camped for the present across his front in the green toils of the Wilderness.

That the Federals had called at least a temporary halt, instead of pressing ahead on a night march to escape those toils and oblige him to race southward for a meeting in the open, was welcome news indeed, received in a series of messages Jeb Stuart kept sending to Verdiersville from shortly after dark until near midnight, when he apparently decided that the time had come to give his short-winded animals some rest. Abandoning his plans for the Hamilton's Crossing review next day, the cavalry leader was bringing his spruced-up troopers westward along the southern fringes of the Wilderness in order to get in position by morning on the right front of the army, there to protect its open flank and reconnoiter the enemy advance when it resumed. That too was welcome news, ensuring a continuous stream of intelligence, such as only cavalry could gather, and providing a resilient cushion against shock. Welcome, too, was a late-evening dispatch from Longstreet informing headquarters that he had crossed Brock's Bridge and would camp there tonight, on the near bank of the North Anna; he expected to reach Richard's Shop by noon tomorrow, nine miles from Shady Grove Church and twelve from Todd's Tavern. This meant that he most likely would be able to move into his assigned position, up the Catharpin Road, by nightfall, in plenty of time for launching the all-hands attack at first light Friday, after

Ewell and Hill made contact tomorrow and set the bluecoats up for the assault designed to drive them back across the river they had crossed today. Accordingly, Lee had his adjutant notify Ewell that he was to move out early in the morning, continuing his march up the turnpike in order to menace the Union flank if Grant kept heading south. If he veered east, toward Fredericksburg, Ewell was to pursue him and fall upon his rear; or if he turned this way, Ewell was to take up a strong defensive position and hold him there in the tangled brush until Hill and Longstreet came up on the right, at which point they would all three go over to the offensive in accordance with Lee's plan. In any case, the adjutant added, "the General's desire is to bring him to battle as soon now as possible."

At breakfast next morning between dawn and sunup Lee was in excellent spirits, refreshed by four or five hours of sleep and encouraged by a follow-up message, just in from Stuart, that the three Federal corps had in fact spent the whole night in their Wilderness camps. He expressed his satisfaction at this evidence that all was working as he hoped, as well as at information that a brigade of Ewell's, detached for guard duty at Hanover Junction, would be rejoining no later than tomorrow. Together with last-minute piecemeal reinforcements sent from Richmond during the past week, this would give him an over-all strength of nearly 65,000 men in his eight divisions of infantry and three of cavalry. Four brigades were still detached (Hoke's, in North Carolina, and three with Major General George E. Pickett, comprising Longstreet's third division, still convalescing in southside Virginia from its brief, horrific experience on the third day at Gettysburg, ten months back) but Lee regretted this less than he might have done except for a miscalculation that contributed to the boldness of his plan for the annihilation or quick repulse of the enemy in the thickets up ahead. He estimated the combined strength of Meade and Burnside at not more than 75,000 men, and therefore assumed — quite erroneously, since the Federals, with considerably better than half again that many troops, had in fact almost twice the number Lee could muster — that he was about to fight against the shortest odds he had faced at any time since he assumed command of the Army of Northern Virginia, two victory-crowded years ago next month. Rising from breakfast he mounted Traveller and gave A. P. Hill the word to resume his march up the plank road, first across the "Poison Fields," as the leached-out mining region west of the Wilderness was called, and then into the briery hug of the jungle where he intended to come to grips with the invaders who, Stuart reported, seemed unaware of his presence on their flank.

Beyond the moldering six-months-old intrenchments around the headwaters of Mine Run, a couple of miles out of Verdiersville, this unawareness ended with a spatter of fire from a detachment of Union cavalry armed with seven-shot carbines. They were few in number,

apparently, and easily driven back (Stuart had arrived by now, resplendent in his red-lined cape, to attend to this by fanning his horsemen
out on the right and front) but word was certainly on the way to Grant
that graybacks were approaching Parker's Store in strength. Moreover,
a staff officer arrived from Ewell about this time to report that he had
sighted heavy columns of bluecoats crossing the Wilderness Tavern
intersection, two miles ahead on the Germanna Plank Road, perpendicular to the turnpike. It stood to reason that if Ewell could see the enemy,
so could the enemy see him; Grant would be forewarned in that direction, too. Lee repeated his instructions that the Second Corps, continuing to regulate its march by that of the Third, was to move on and make
contact, but added that he preferred not to "bring on a general engagement" until Longstreet came up. Hill was deep in the Wilderness
by then, out of touch with Ewell as a result of a widening divergence,
beyond Verdiersville, of the plank road from the turnpike, which was

almost three miles away by the time he reached Parker's Store at noon. At
this point, still riding near the head of Hill's two-division column, Lee
heard a rising clatter of rifle fire from the left front. Obviously there was
fighting on the turnpike, and from the sound of it, filtered through three
miles of brush and branches, the engagement was indeed "general,"
mounting to a quick crescendo like the rapid tearing of canvas, though
it lacked the deeper, rumbling tones artillery gave a battle at that distance.
     Mindful of Lee's admonition not to "bring on a general engage-
ment," Ewell had deployed his lead division when he got within a couple
of miles of the Union-held crossroad, then brought up the second for
close support on both sides of the pike, warning the two commanders —
Major Generals Edward Johnson and Robert Rodes, who at forty-eight
and thirty-five were the oldest and youngest infantry division command-

ers in the army — "not to allow themselves to become involved, but to
fall back slowly if pressed." So he later reported, but the words had little
application when the time came, as it did all too soon: especially for the
men of Johnson's lead brigade, Virginians under Brigadier General John
M. Jones, who caught the initial and overwhelming impact of a whole
blue division that came hurtling at them, as if out of nowhere, through
brush and vines that limited vision to less than sixty feet in any direction.
Caught thus, they found it as impossible to "fall back slowly" as they had
to avoid becoming "involved." Losing Jones, who was killed by an early
volley from the dense wave of attackers, they broke and fled, spreading
panic through the ranks of an Alabama brigade Rodes had posted in their
rear. Ewell, so close to the front that the attack exploded practically in
his face, whirled his horse and raced back to bring help from his third
division, Major General Jubal Early's, which had kept to the road in
order to come up fast in an emergency such as the one that was now at
hand. In the lead was Brigadier General John B. Gordon's brigade,
Georgians who had a reputation for aggressiveness on short notice.

"General Gordon!" Ewell cried, his dragoon mustache bristling and
his prominent eyes bulging as he checked his mount with a hard pull on
the reins, "the day depends on you!"

"These men will save it, sir," Gordon replied, partly for the benefit of the troops themselves, who had come crowding up, as was their
custom at such times, to hear what the brass had to say.

Going at once from march to attack formation, he advanced one
regiment unsupported in a countercharge straight up the pike, while the
rest deployed to go in on the right. On the left, two of Johnson's three
intact brigades reacted by clawing their way through the brush toward
the sound of firing, and Rodes's four did likewise, including the Alabamians who had been rattled by the flight of the Virginians through their
ranks. As suddenly as it had risen, the tide of battle turned, and for the
former attackers, overlapped on both flanks and savagely assailed from
dead ahead by the screaming Georgians, the outcome was even more
disastrous. Now it was their turn to backtrack, losing heavily in the
process — though not as heavily as two other blue divisions, coming up in
sequence on the left and groping blindly for the flank they had been told
to support but could not find. Struck before they could form for attack or
defense, they were driven eastward in confusion, suffering grievously in
killed and wounded and losing several hundred prisoners, many of whom
fled unknowingly into the rebel lines, bereft of all sense of direction in
that maze of vines and brambles. It was, as one veteran said, a conflict "no
man saw or could see"; "A battle of invisibles with invisibles," another
called it. "As for fighting," a third declared, "it was simply bushwhacking
on a grand scale, in brush where all formation beyond that of regiments or
companies was soon lost and where such a thing as a consistent line of
battle on either side was impossible."

The pattern of Wilderness fighting had been set, and one of its principal elements was panic, which came easily and spread rapidly on terrain that had all the claustral qualities of a landscape in a nightmare, with a variety of background sounds that ranged from a foreboding silence, so dense that a man was likely to jump six feet at the snap of a twig, to a veritable cataract of noise, referred to by a participant as "the most terrific musketry firing ever heard on the American continent."

Ewell, still mindful of Lee's admonition, did not pursue beyond the point at which the fight had opened, just under two miles west of the crossroad. It was 3 o'clock by now, and he could tell himself, quite truthfully, that he had done all that was asked of him and more, inflicting much heavier casualties than he suffered and fixing the enemy there in the tangled depths of the Wilderness. He put his men to work intrenching a line that extended about a mile to the left and a mile to the right of the turnpike, and after hauling off two guns he had captured in the course of his counterattack, he settled down to wait for tomorrow, when Longstreet would be up and the army would go over to the offensive. Fighting continued on a lesser scale all afternoon and into the evening, and though he lost two more brigade commanders — Brigadier Generals Leroy Stafford of Louisiana and John Pegram of Virginia, the former mortally wounded and the latter shot in the leg — Ewell had no doubt that he would be able to hold his newly fortified position, no matter what the Yankees sent against him.

There was no such assurance down on the plank road, three miles south, where a separate battle swelled to a sudden and furious climax at about the time the disjointed contest on the pike began to wane. For Hill, whose two divisions were struck by a much heavier and far better coördinated attack than the one that had been launched against Ewell's three, there was no waning; there was hard, stand-up fighting from the moment of earnest contact, around 4 o'clock, until darkness and exhaustion persuaded the troops of both sides to rest on their arms, where they then were, for a resumption at first light tomorrow of a struggle that had been touch-and-go for the past four hours. His two divisions, commanded by Major Generals Henry Heth and Cadmus Wilcox, had continued their march beyond Parker's Store to within a mile of the Brock Road, on which the Union infantry was known to be moving south, when stiffened resistance brought the head of the gray column to a halt. Heth formed for battle astride the road, and Lee — taking over for Hill, who was sick today, as he had been at Gettysburg — set up headquarters in a roadside clearing near the farmhouse of a widow named Tapp. He had no sooner dismounted to confer with Stuart and Hill, who had stayed with his men despite his disability, than a platoon of blue-clad skirmishers walked into the clearing from behind a stand of pines in its northeast corner, rifles at the ready. Apparently as startled as the high-ranking Confederates were by the sudden confrontation, the Federals faded back into the pines instead of opening fire or advancing to make the capture that would have changed the course of the war. However thankful Lee was for this deliverance from the hands of the bluecoats, their presence served to emphasize the dangerous possibility of an enemy plunge, whether on purpose or by accident, into the heavily wooded gap which the divergence of the two routes had created between Hill, down here on the plank road, and Ewell, whose battle was still in full swing on the turnpike. Accordingly, Lee sent word for Wilcox to extend Hill's left by moving his division northward into the brush beyond the clearing, thus to forestall a penetration of the gap, while Heth resumed his eastward advance to develop the strength of the blue force in his front. Though he still intended to withhold delivery of his main effort until Longstreet was on hand, the southern commander's hope was that Heth would be able to carry the Brock Road intersection, less than a mile away, as an effective means of bringing the Union army to a severed, panicky halt in the very depths of the Wilderness, half a dozen miles from open ground in any direction.

It was now past 3 o'clock. A note went at once to Heth asking whether, in his judgment, he could seize the intersection without bringing on a "general engagement." Heth replied that the enemy seemed to be there in strength; he could not tell how much an attack would spread the action, but he was willing to give the thing a try if that was what was wanted. While Lee was turning this over in his mind, back at the Widow Tapp's, a sudden uproar from the immediate front — louder, even, than the one that had exploded in Ewell's face, four hours ago — informed him that the decision had been taken out of his hands. Unsupported by Wilcox, who had moved off to the left, Heth was under heavy, all-out assault from dead ahead.

Both attacks — the one against Ewell, up on the turnpike, and the present one down the plank road against Hill — were the result of a deliberate decision by Grant, whose self-confidence and natural combativeness had not been lessened by the enlargement of his responsibilities and who was determined, moreover, not to yield the tactical initiative to an opponent with a reputation for making the most of it on all occasions. If this meant the abandonment of his original intention to get into, through, and out of the Wilderness in the shortest possible time, then that just had to be. His primary talent had always been instinctive, highly improvisatorial at its best, and though there was little about him that could be described as Napoleonic, he trusted, like Napoleon, in his star. The overriding fact, as Grant saw it, was that the rebels were there in the tangled brush, somewhere off to the west, and he was determined to hit them. He was determined, in Sheridan's phrase, to smash them up at every opportunity.

Meade began it, quite on his own. Shortly after 7 o'clock that morning, by which time the leading elements of all three corps had been two hours on the march, he was notified by Warren that the commander of his rear division, preparing to head south from Wilderness Tavern, had sighted a heavy butternut column moving toward him on the turnpike, two or three miles west of the Germanna Plank Road intersection. Reacting fast, Meade ordered Warren to bring his other three divisions back to their starting point and advance his whole corps down the pike, in order to confront and, if possible, destroy the rebel force. He believed that it amounted to no more than a division, "left here to fool us," he told Warren, "while they concentrate and prepare a position toward the North Anna," and he saw in the situation an opportunity to effect a considerable subtraction from Lee's army before coming to earnest grips with the rest of it in the open country to the south. With time to spare and the train still grinding slowly down the crowded roads to the east, he could afford a brief delay, especially one that held the promise of so rich a prize. In any case, with his exterior flank so threatened by a force of undetermined strength, he believed the decision was tactically sound; for, as he told Grant in a note informing him of the order for Warren to countermarch and attack, "until this movement of the enemy is developed, the march of the corps must be suspended."

Arriving shortly afterward for a meeting near the tavern, in whose yard Meade was conferring with Warren, Grant not only indorsed his chief lieutenant's aggressive reaction to the news that there were rebels on his flank; he also enlarged upon it, in a characteristic manner, with words that applied not only here but elsewhere. "If any opportunity presents itself for pitching into a part of Lee's army," he told him, "do so without giving time for disposition." In accordance with this policy — which might be described as: "Hit now. Worry later" — when word was brought that another gray force had been spotted marching eastward on the plank road, down around Parker's Store, Hancock too was given orders to backtrack. Instead of continuing down the Catharpin Road to Shady Grove Church, his previous objective, he would turn right when he reached Todd's Tavern and take the Brock Road north to its intersection with the road on which this second rebel column was advancing. Similarly, now that the plot had thickened, Sedgwick was told to send one division to join Warren's turnpike attack and another down the Brock Road to the intersection Hancock had been assigned to cover. His third division would remain on guard at Germanna Ford until Burnside's arrival, expected by midday, when it too would come down and get in on the action — whichever, if either, fight was still in progress by that time — leaving Burnside's four divisions as an available reserve, to be on call if they were needed. Thus Grant, though he still had no specific information as to the size or composition of either rebel column approaching his open flank, was determined to strike them both with everything he had.

While couriers went pounding off to deliver these several messages, Grant and Meade rode a short way down the pike, a bit under half a mile beyond a boggy little stream called Wilderness Run, and turned off into the southwest quadrant of the Germanna Plank Road intersection, where there was a meadow adjoined by a farmhouse belonging to a family named Lacy. Headquarters tents were being pitched there, in accordance with the change in plans, and the two generals dismounted and climbed a knoll on the far side of the field. Grant took a seat on a convenient stump, lighted another of the twenty cigars he distributed among the various pockets of his uniform at the start of every day, and sat calmly, an imperturbable figure wreathed in tobacco smoke, waiting for the attack to be launched beyond the heavy screen of brush at the rim of the clearing. Time dragged, the sun edging slowly toward meridian, and presently he took a penknife out of his trouser pocket, picked up a stick, and started to whittle. Snagged by the blade, the fingertips of his thread gloves began to fray, until at last they were ruined. He took them off, unbuttoned his coat because of the increasing heat, and resumed his whittling. At noon, or a little after, a sudden clatter of stepped-up rifle fire announced that the action had finally opened about one mile down the turnpike.

At first it was difficult to tell how the thing was going. The clatter moved westward, diminished briefly, as if it had paused for breath, then swelled louder than ever and rolled back east for another pause: after which a similar uproar came from the left front, subsided, and then was repeated. Along the limited horizon, west and southwest, the trees began leaking smoke along a line that seemed to conform in general to the one from which the initial attack had been launched an hour ago. All that was clear, so far, was that little or nothing had been gained, although it was fairly certain by now that there were a good many more graybacks out there in the brush than Meade had supposed at the outset. Grant kept whittling.

Presently details filtered rearward, brought to the Lacy meadow by dispatch bearers on lathered horses. Complying with Grant's instructions, relayed by Meade, that he was to give no "time for disposition," Warren had told Brigadier General Charles Griffin, the commander of what had been his rear but now was his lead division, not to wait for word from the heads of the three divisions assigned to support him on the flanks — Brigadier General Horatio G. Wright of Sedgwick's corps, on the march down from Germanna to go in on his right, and Brigadier Generals James S. Wadsworth and Samuel W. Crawford of his own corps, who were countermarching to come up on his left — but to pitch right into the Confederates, hard and fast, as soon as he got his troops in line astride the pike, trusting that the others would be there in time to furnish whatever assistance he might need. That was what he did; but he did so, as it turned out, unsupported in the crisis that resulted. Wright did not arrive for a full two hours, having gotten lost in the woods about as soon as he left the road, and Wadsworth and Crawford only came up in time to get badly mauled themselves, floundering around in the brush as if they were involved in a gigantic and altogether murderous game of blindman's bluff: as indeed they were — particularly Wadsworth, a Hudson River grandee who, at fifty-six, was nine years older than any other division commander in the army. Just now he was feeling the weight of all those years. Trying to navigate by compass in that leafy sea of green, he got badly turned around and drifted northward so that his naked left was exposed to a sudden descent by Gordon's screaming Georgians, who tore into it so savagely that the whole division fell back in disorder, the men crying "Flanked! We're flanked!" as they ran. Crawford caught it even worse from the rallied Alabamians when he came up, groping blind after he lost touch with the navigating Wadsworth. A former army surgeon who had been on duty at Fort Sumter when it fell, he was thirty-four, the next-to-youngest of Meade's division commanders, but he looked considerably older after three years of combat, including a bad wound taken at Antietam. "A tall, chesty, glowering man, with heavy eyes, a big nose, and bushy whiskers," he habitually wore what one of his soldiers described as "a turn-out-the-guard expression." His expression just now, however, was one of outrage. His division had once been Meade's own, made up entirely of Pennsylvanians, and Crawford was outraged at the heavy and useless losses he had suffered, including one veteran regiment captured practically intact when it fled in the wrong direction and found itself surrounded by grinning rebel scarecrows when it stumbled to a halt.

Unquestionably though, to judge by individual reaction, the most outraged man on the field today was Griffin. A hard-case West Pointer and a veteran of the Mexican War at thirty-eight, he was much admired by his men, including a brigade of regulars who had followed him through a lot of fighting over the past two years. An old line artilleryman, he was especially furious at the loss of a section of guns which had to be abandoned down the turnpike when his flanks were overlapped and his troops fell back to avoid being swamped by no less than seven Confederate brigades. The blame, as he saw it, lay with the commanders who had failed to come up on his left and right, and as soon as he managed to stabilize the line his three brigades had fallen back to, he got on his horse and galloped off to protest to Meade in person. Crossing the headquarters meadow, he dismounted and stalked up the knoll at the far side, fuming and cursing as he came. Meade heard him out and did what he could to soothe him, although with small success.

The air was full of God-damns. Finally, relieved by at least having vented his spleen, Griffin went back down the knoll, remounted his horse, and rode off to rejoin his division on the firing line. Grant, who had stopped whittling for the first time while the tirade was in progress, got up from his stump and walked over to Meade. He had not quite caught Griffin's name, but he had never been one to put up with out-of-channels insubordination, even in the easier-going West. "Who is this General Gregg?" he asked. "You ought to put him under arrest." Meade, whose extreme irascibility was masked today by an unaccustomed calm, turned to Grant with the same gentleness he had shown the angry brigadier. "His name's Griffin, not Gregg," he said, "and that's only his way of talking." In grizzled contrast to his younger chief, and towering a full head above him, Meade leaned forward as he spoke and buttoned up Grant's coat for him, as if in concern that he might catch cold after being overheated. Grant went back to his stump and his whittling.

By then it was close to 3 o'clock. Off to the south, although the sound of it did not get through until Warren's had died down, the second battle had been shaping up for the past hour. All that was there at the start was Brigadier General George W. Getty's division of Sedgwick's corps, which had come down from Germanna before midday to take over from a hard-pressed regiment of cavalry the task of delaying the progress of the second Confederate force, in position astride the plank road about half a mile from the Brock Road intersection, while Hancock came up from Todd's Tavern on a march that was much impeded by V Corps artillery, which had halted to await developments. Hancock arrived at 2 o'clock, riding at the head of his four-division column, and when Getty informed him that the graybacks to his front were commanded by the ever-aggressive A. P. Hill and that he might have to fall back at any moment under increasing pressure from such a savage fighter, thus uncovering the crossroad whose loss would cut the army in two and expose its train to capture or destruction, Hancock ignored Grant's instructions to forgo time-consuming preparations and instead put his troops to work improvising crude log breastworks along the road in rear of the position, north and south of the plank road intersection, thus to provide them with something on which to rally in case they were repulsed. Peremptory orders for an immediate advance put an end to this at about 3.30. Leaving Brigadier Generals Francis Barlow's and John Gibbon's divisions posted well down the Brock Road to guard against an attack from the southwest — he had been warned that Longstreet's corps was on the march, somewhere off in that direction, though it was not expected to arrive until tomorrow — Hancock put Major General David Birney's and Brigadier General Gershom Mott's divisions in line on the right and left of Getty's and sent them forward with orders to drive the enemy back on

Parker's Store, three miles from the vital crossroad in their rear, and thus abolish, for once and for all, this threat to the safe passage of the army through the Wilderness, together with its train. It was just past 4 o'clock by then, and on second thought, by way of giving more weight to the blow, he had Gibbon send two of his three brigades to stiffen the center of the attack which had now begun to roll.

It did not roll far, even though at this stage all that blocked the path of these 25,000 attackers was a single gray division with fewer than 7500 in its ranks. Advancing through the tangled brush, the Federals delivered blind volleys of musketry that lopped the saplings at breast height, all across their front, and made it nearly impossible, so heavy and continuous was the fire, for any standing defender to survive. The trouble was that scarcely a Confederate was standing.

While waiting for a reply to his offer to go forward, if that was what Lee wanted, Heth — like Hancock, who was similarly engaged at the same time, half a mile away on the Brock Road — had had his men dig in and lie low along the slight, densely wooded ridge on which they had halted when the blue resistance stiffened. Prone beneath solid-seeming sheets of lead that slashed the leaves and clipped the breast-high branches, the troops along the ridge replied with volleys of their own. Not only were these as heavy as the ones the front-rank Federals were throwing; they were also a good deal more deadly. Caught thus, erect and unprotected by anything more substantial than smoke and foliage, the attackers suffered cruelly from a foe they could not see. Mott's division, bogged shoetop-deep in a swamp on the left, directly in front of the ridge, broke and ran from that first decimating fire, as did other outfits all along the line. Whole companies, whole regiments fell back in shock and panic, some of them all the way to the log defenses they had built an hour ago. There they were met, individually and collectively, with a curt demand from provost guards with leveled bayonets: "Show blood!" Those who could not show it were hoicked back into line alongside the troops who had not bolted, who were still in position, up there in

the bullet-whipped brush, firing blind — "by earsight," it was called —
in the general direction of the rebels lying prone in comparative safety
on their ridge, pumping volley after horrendous volley into the blue
mass down in the boggy swale to their immediate front.

Hancock, a hard hitter, never hit harder than he did here in the
Wilderness today, despite confounding difficulties of terrain far better
suited for defense (once the shock of surprise had been dispelled) than
for attack. A second assault was mounted and delivered, then a third
and a fourth, all with the disadvantage of trying to maintain alignment, as well as a precarious sense of direction, while attacking veterans
who had only to lie low and fire as rapidly as they could load their overheated rifles. Up at army headquarters, where there was full awareness
of the importance of keeping the Brock Road clear for travel, Meade had
Warren send Wadsworth's division south, across the mile-wide gap
between him and Hancock, with instructions to strike the left flank
of the rebels, fixed in position by headlong pressure from the front.
Hancock meantime was doing all he could to increase that pressure,
having added two of Barlow's four brigades to the struggle. This gave
him close to 30,000 men in his attack force, even after the deduction
of casualties, which were heavy and getting heavier by the minute,
including Brigadier General Alexander Hays, a lifelong friend of
Grant's and one of the heroes of Gettysburg, killed at the head of his
brigade in Birney's division. However, Lee by then had recalled Wilcox
from his attempt to link up with Ewell and close the gap across the
center. He came back fast and went in hard, supporting Heth just as
his flank was about to crumble. This doubled the number of defenders and reduced the odds from three- to two-to-one. Even so, the
issue could not have remained much longer in doubt, except that gathering darkness finally ended the contest. It dwindled by common consent,
then flared up momentarily as Wadsworth finally arrived in the twilight after thrashing around in the brush on a three-hour search for the
battle raging furiously one mile to the south. When he came up, in
position at last to wreck the interior rebel flank, Lee had no reserves
to throw in his path except a single Alabama battalion of 125 men, de-
dailed to guard the host of prisoners who had been streaming rearward
ever since the fight began. The Alabamians formed a widespread
skirmish line, leaving the prisoners to the care of a handful of wounded,
and went in yelling for all they were worth, quite as if they had an army
at their backs. Wadsworth stumbled to a halt, apparently convinced
that his jungle-foundered soldiers were about to be swamped by superior
numbers, and hastily took up a stout defensive position on Hancock's
right as night came down.

While both sides turned to attend to such of their wounded as
they could reach — lucky ones, these, compared to others caught between the lines, calling for help that could not come because the slight-

est movement drew instant volleys from troops made panicky by fear of a night attack at such close quarters, or trapped by fires that sprang up and spread rapidly when the night breeze rose and fanned the sparks in the dry leaves to flames — Grant went to his headquarters tent in the Lacy meadow to study reports of what had happened today and to make plans for what he wanted to happen tomorrow. He would, of course, continue the offensive on both fronts, though his best chance for a breakthrough seemed to lie with Hancock, who reported that he would have made one today if darkness had not ended the battle an hour too soon. Sedgwick, joined late in the day by his third division under Brigadier General James B. Ricketts, would remain in position on the right of the northern sector, with Warren, minus Wadsworth, on the left. These five divisions had attacked again near sunset, but with no greater success than before; Ewell, buttoned up tight in his intrenchments, would not budge. Tomorrow's attack in this sector would be made primarily to prevent him from sending reinforcements down to Hill, who was to be hit with everything Hancock could lay hands on: his own four divisions, plus one from each of the other three corps, including Burnside's, which had been arriving all afternoon, too late for today's fight but in plenty of time for tomorrow's. In addition to sending one division to Hancock, Burnside would leave another on guard at Germanna Ford and march the other two down the Germanna Plank Road tonight, turning off, south of the turnpike intersection, to move west through the woods for a plunge into the gap between Warren's left and Hancock's right and a drive against Hill's interior flank, which he would assail by turning south again, as soon as he was well into the gap between the two Confederate corps. Such was Grant's victory formula, compounded tonight for application tomorrow.

Jump-off time, he said, would be at first light, 4 o'clock. Sedgwick and Warren, with five divisions, would attack and pin down Ewell, while Hancock and Burnside, with nine divisions, were overrunning Hill — and Longstreet too, if he arrived by then and was put into that portion of the line. All that was known just now was that he was on the march, somewhere off to the south and west; Hancock was warned to be on the lookout for him on the far left, in case Lee tried something foxy in that direction, though Grant was as usual a good deal more intent on what he had in mind to do to the enemy than he was on what the enemy might or might not do to him. Meade was in full agreement with these orders, as indeed he had been with all orders from the start, except that he suggested that the jump-off be advanced an hour to sunrise, 5 o'clock, so that the troops commanders would have a little daylight time in which to get their men in line for the assault. Grant considered this briefly, then agreed, and the two turned in, along with their staffs, to get some sleep for the hard day coming up.

.   .   .

Lee too was planning an offensive for tomorrow, and he intended, moreover, to launch it in the same region Grant had chosen as the scene of his main effort: in the vicinity of the plank road intersection. This involved a revision, not of purpose — the Virginian had counted, all along, on going over to the offensive as soon as his whole army was at hand — but of method. Formerly Longstreet had been told to proceed up the Catharpin Road to Todd's Tavern, a position from which he could turn the Union left, but the daylong need for closing the tactically dangerous gap between Hill and Ewell now provoked a change of plans, whereby Old Peter would shift from the Catharpin to the Plank Road and come up, not on Hill's right, but in his rear; Little Powell then could sidle northward to connect with Ewell, thus abolishing the gap, while Longstreet took over his position and prepared to launch, with his own two divisions and Hill's third, a dawn attack designed to crumple Grant's left flank, roll it up, and in conjunction with Hill and Ewell, who would advance in turn against the Federals to their front, fling the blue invaders back across the Rapidan. Accordingly, around 7 o'clock, while Hill's battle was still raging and the outcome was in doubt, Lee sent Longstreet word of the change in objectives, together with a guide to insure against going astray on the cross-country night march he would have to make in order to get from one road to the other. A message went at the same time to Major General Richard Anderson, commander of Hill's third division, which had moved from Orange to Verdiersville today, instructing him to continue his march up the plank road beyond Parker's Store tonight, in order to be with Longstreet in plenty of time for the attack at first light tomorrow.

Heth and Wilcox — who could testify to the all-too-probable truth of Hancock's claim, across the way, that another hour of daylight would have given him the breakthrough he had been seeking — were pleased to learn from Hill that Longstreet and Anderson would be up tonight to relieve their fought-out men. Whether Lee had revised his previous estimate of the enemy strength or not, Little Powell was convinced that his 15,000 veterans had taken on upwards of 40,000 bluecoats in the Wilderness today, and he had little patience with the concern of his two division commanders about the tangled condition of their lines, which had come so close to buckling under repeated assaults that, in the words of one witness, "they were like a worm fence, at every angle." Heth went to Hill and told him flatly: "A skirmish line could drive my division and Wilcox's, situated as we now are." He proposed that a new line be drawn, just in rear of their present disordered position, for them to fall back on before morning, when, as he predicted, "we shall certainly be attacked." Little Powell would not hear of this, partly because such a move would have meant abandoning many of the wounded and also because it would rob his soldiers of their hard-earned rest. "Longstreet will be up in a few hours," he said. "He will form in your front. . . . The men have been marching and fighting all day and are tired. I don't wish them disturbed." Heth went back to his troops, but soon returned with Wilcox, who joined him in the proposal that both divisions be withdrawn to a new line. Hill repeated that he wanted the men to get their sleep between now and midnight, when Longstreet was expected. They went away, but Heth, whose heart was heavy with foreboding, came back for still a third time to renew the argument. This vexed Hill, whose own sleep was being interrupted now. "Damn it, Heth," he said angrily, "I don't want to hear any more about it. The men shall not be disturbed." Heth retired for good this time, though it was already after midnight and Longstreet was obviously behind schedule. 1 o'clock, 2 o'clock, 3 o'clock passed, and still there was no news that Old Peter was approaching. Not long before dawn, the two division commanders sent for a battalion of corps engineers to come forward with picks and shovels in a belated attempt to complete the neglected intrenchments before they were overrun by the blue attackers Heth was convinced would come with the sun, if not sooner.

Back at the Tapp farm, Lee had known since 10 o'clock that the First Corps would not be up till daylight at the earliest. The young cavalry officer who had ridden down to the Catharpin Road with instructions for the change in routes, Major Henry McClellan of Stuart's staff, had also been charged with giving Longstreet's lead division verbal orders to press on without delay, thereby assuring an early arrival in Hill's rear. He left about 7 and returned three hours later, highly indignant, to report to Lee that the commander of that division, Major General Charles W. Field, a West Pointer and a stickler for regulations — he had lately been promoted and appointed to his post, having served in Richmond as superintendent of the Bureau of Conscription since the loss of a leg at Second Manassas, twenty months ago — flatly declined to accept from a stray cavalryman possibly garbled verbal orders that were in contradiction to the ones he had received from his corps commander, which were that he was to rest his men at Richard's Shop until 1 o'clock in the morning. Then and not until then, he said stiffly, would the march be resumed. This meant that Old Peter's leading elements could scarcely arrive before sunup, since the distance from Richard's Shop was about a dozen miles, two or three of them over rugged terrain, across fields, through woods, and by roundabout lanes connecting the two main roads; but Lee seemed oddly unperturbed. When McClellan offered to ride back with written orders which Field would have no choice except to obey, the Virginian declined with a shake of his gray head. "No, Major," he said calmly. "It is now past 10 o'clock, and by the time you could return to General Field and he could put his division in motion, it would be 1 o'clock. At that hour he will move."

Lee returned to his tent for more paper work, including an 11 o'clock dispatch informing the Secretary of War of what had occurred since Grant's crossing of the Rapidan the day before — "By the blessing of God," he wrote of today's hard fight, "we maintained our position against every effort until night, when the contest closed" — then turned in for another four or five hours of sleep before rising to face what might well be disaster.

He did not mention the possibility of disaster or its cause, either to Seddon in Richmond or to Hill, whose troops were sleeping helter-skelter in the brush, in whatever random positions they had occupied when darkness ended the fighting and they fell asleep on their arms, many of them too weary to eat the scant rations sent up later in the evening. Perhaps, like Little Powell, Lee reasoned that rest would do more for them than would fretting about a situation they could do but little to repair in the few hours of darkness that remained. In any case, he left them and their commander undisturbed until dawn began to filter through the thickets and a popping of rifles, like individual handclaps, warned that another day of battle had begun: May 6. Exposed by daylight to this picket fire, the engineers dropped their picks and shovels, which they had had small chance to use, and scuttled rearward. Within an hour, sharply at 5 o'clock as the sun was rising, this intermittent racket merged and grew in abrupt intensity to a steady clatter, described by one observer as "the noise of a boy running with a stick pressed against a paling fence, faster and faster until it swelled into a continuous rattling roar." The Federals were attacking in greater strength than yesterday, along and down both sides of the plank road, and after a brief resistance the two Confederate divisions did just what Heth had said they would do. They broke. Though they did not scatter in panic or drop their rifles, still they made for the rear, more or less in a body, some among them firing as they went. "The men seemed to fall back upon a deliberate conviction that it was impossible to hold the ground and, of course, foolish to attempt it," one among them later wrote by way of explanation, adding rather philosophically: "It was mortifying, but it was only what every veteran has experienced."

Up on Ewell's front the dug-in troops held firm under assault, but Sedgwick and Warren were accomplishing all that was asked of them by keeping him from sending reinforcements down to the far end of the line. Such flaw as there was in the execution of Grant's plan was in the center. Burnside, ordered to penetrate the rebel gap and descend on Hill's interior flank, had gotten himself and his two divisions lost as soon as he left the road last night and struck out through the brush; he was somewhere rearward now, behind the space between Warren and Hancock, disoriented and wandering in circles while the conflict raged, first to his right, then his left, sometimes front and sometimes rear. Hancock was furious at this dereliction. Shouting to be heard above the din on the plank road, he told one of Meade's staff officers that if those missing 10,000 men could be added to the pressure being exerted, "we could smash A. P. Hill all to pieces!" In point of fact, he seemed well on the way to doing it anyhow. Except for the troops with Barlow, whose division had been reunited down the Brock Road to guard against a possible flank attack, he had all the men assigned to the main effort massed and in motion, flushing graybacks as they went. Forty years old, "a tall, soldierly man with light brown hair and a military jaw," he had what the staffer described as "the massive features and the heavy folds round the eye that often mark a man of ability." Elated by the propitious opening of that portion of the battle in his charge, he made a handsome figure on horseback, and his elation grew as the attack continued. Just ahead was the Tapp clearing, and beyond it the white tops of wagons parked in the Confederate rear. "We are driving them, sir!" Hancock called proudly to the staff man. "Tell General Meade we are driving them most beautifully."

Lee was there in the clearing, doing all he could to stiffen what little was left of Hill's resistance, and so had Longstreet himself been there, momentarily at least, when the blue assault was launched. He came riding up just before sunrise, a mile or two in advance of his column, the head of which had reached Parker's Store by then, and Hill's chief of staff crossed the Tapp farmyard to welcome him as he turned off the road. "Ah, General, we have been looking for you since 12 o'clock last night. We expect to be attacked at any moment, and are not in any shape to resist." Unaccustomed to being reproached by unstrung colonels, however valid their anxiety, Old Peter looked sternly down at him. "My troops are not up," he said. "I've ridden ahead — " At this point the sudden clatter of Hancock's attack erupted out in the brush, and Longstreet, without waiting to learn more of what had happened, whirled his horse and galloped back to hurry his two divisions forward. So Lee at least knew that the First Corps would soon be up. His problem, after sending his adjutant to order the wagon train prepared for withdrawal, was to hang on till these reinforcements got there, probably within the hour, to shore up Hill's fast-crumbling line. Presently, though, this began to look like more than he could manage; Wilcox and Heth, overlapped on both flanks, gave ground rapidly before a solid mass of attackers, and skulkers began to drift rearward across the clearing, singly and in groups, some of them turning to fire from time to time at their pursuers, while others seemed only intent on escape. Their number increased, until finally Lee saw a whole brigade in full retreat. Moreover, this was not just any brigade; it was Brigadier General Samuel McGowan's brigade of South Carolinians, Wilcox's best and one of the finest in the army.

"My God, General McGowan!" Lee exclaimed from horseback,

breasting the flood of fugitives. "Is this splendid brigade of yours running like a flock of geese?"

"General, these men are not whipped," McGowan answered, stung in his pride by this public rebuke. "They only want a place to form and they will fight as well as they ever did."

But there was the rub. All that was left by now for them to form on was a battalion of Third Corps artillery, four batteries under twenty-eight-year-old Lieutenant Colonel William Poague, lined up along the west side of the clearing which afforded one of the Wilderness's few real fields of fire. The cannoneers stood to their loaded pieces, waiting for Hill's infantry to fall back far enough to give them a chance to shoot at the bluecoats in pursuit. However, there was no time for this; Poague, with Lee's approval, had his guns open at what was already point-blank range, shaving the heads of the Confederate retreaters in order to throw their anti-personnel rounds into the enemy ranks. This took quick effect, particularly near the road, where the Federals tended to bunch up. Flailed by double-shotted grape and canister, they paused and began to look for cover: seeing which, the cannoneers stepped up their rate of fire. Lee remained mounted alongside Poague, who kept his men at their work — "getting the starch out of our shirts," they called it — without infantry support. This could not continue long before they would be overrun, but meantime they were making the most of it. Smoke from the guns drifted back, sparkling in the early-morning sunlight, and presently Lee saw through its rearward swirls a cluster of men running toward him, carrying their rifles at the ready and shouldering Hill's fugitives aside.

"Who are you, my boys?" he cried as they came up in rear of the line of bucking guns.

"Texas boys!" they yelled, gathering now in larger numbers, and Lee knew them: Hood's Texans, his old-time shock troops, now under Brigadier General John Gregg — the lead brigade of Field's division. Longstreet was up at last.

"Hurrah for Texas!" Lee shouted. He took off his wide-brimmed hat and waved it. "Hurrah for Texas!"

No one had ever seen him act this way before, either on or off the field of battle. And presently, when the guns ceased their fuming and the Texans started forward, they saw something else they had never seen: something that froze the cheers in their throats and brought them to a halt. When Gregg gave the order, "Attention, Texas Brigade! The eyes of General Lee are upon you. Forward . . . march!" Lee rose in his stirrups and lifted his hat. "Texans always move them," he declared. They cheered as they stepped out between the guns. "I would charge hell itself for that old man," a veteran said fervently. Then they saw the one thing that could stop them. Lee had spurred Traveller forward on their heels; he intended to go in with them, across the field and after the bluecoats in the brush. They slacked their pace and left off cheering. "Lee to the rear!" began to be heard along the line, and some of them addressed him directly: "Go back, General Lee, go back. We won't go unless you go back." He was among them now, flushed with excitement, his eyes fixed on the woods ahead. They stopped, and when an attempt by Gregg to head him off had no effect, a sergeant reached out and took hold of Traveller's rein, bringing the animal to a halt. "Lee to the rear! Lee to the rear!" the men were shouting. But his blood was up; he did not seem to hear them, or even to know that he and they were no longer in motion. At this point a staff colonel intervened. "General, you've been looking for General Longstreet. There he is, over yonder." Lee looked and saw, at the far end of the field, the man he called his war horse. For the first time since he cleared the line of guns he seemed to become aware that he was involved in something larger than a charge. Responding to the colonel's suggestion, he turned Traveller's head and rode in that direction. On the way he passed in rear of Brigadier General Evander Law's Alabama brigade, about to move out on the left. "What troops are these?" he asked, and on being told he called to them: "God bless the Alabamians!" They went forward with a whoop, alongside the Texans, who were whooping too. "I thought him at that moment the grandest specimen of manhood I ever beheld," one among them later wrote. "He looked as though he ought to have been, and was, the monarch of the world."

Longstreet yielded to no man in his admiration for Lee, yet his admiration never amounted to idolatry, especially if idolatry included a willingness to put up with tactical interference. Seeing him thus "off his balance," he later wrote, he informed him with jocular bluntness, as soon as he came up, "that his line would be recovered in an hour if he would permit me to handle the troops, but if my services were not needed I would like to ride to some place of safety, as it was not quite comfortable where we were." Lee complied by retiring westward a short distance with his staff officers, who no doubt were glad to get him out of there, and Old Peter kept his word, here and on the opposite side of the plank road as well.

There his other division had been put in line by its commander, Brigadier General Joseph Kershaw, whose Georgians, South Carolinians, and Mississippians hooted cruelly when Heth's badly shaken troops fell back through their ranks. "Do you belong to Lee's army?" they jeered, seeing their old comrades thus for the first time in eight months. "You don't look like the men we left here. You're worse than Bragg's men!" Taking over, they stalled Hancock's advance on this side of the road, while Field was doing the same across the way. Then the two divisions went forward together against the Federals, who were wearier and a good deal more disorganized than they had known until they were brought to a halt, first by Poague's four rapid-firing batteries and then by 10,000 newly committed rebels whose appearance was as sudden as if they had dropped out of the sky. Still, the going was rough for the First Corps, most of whose members had never fought in the region west of Fredericksburg before. Some brigades lost heavily, including the Texans, who went in boasting that they had "put General Lee under arrest and sent him to the rear." A captured private from the brigade expressed its collective opinion when his captors asked him what he thought of this Battle of the Wilderness. "Battle be damned," he said hotly. "It aint no battle, it's a worse riot than Chickamauga! At Chickamauga there was at least a rear, but here there aint neither front nor rear. It's all a damned mess! And our two armies aint nothing but howling mobs."

Before 10 o'clock, despite the various impediments of terrain and the refusal by most of Hancock's men to panic under pressure, Longstreet fulfilled his promise to recover the line that had begun to be lost at sunrise. Halting there, within half a mile of the Brock Road, he proceeded to consolidate the position, reinforced presently by Anderson, whose division arrived while the First Corps was advancing and moved up in its support. Hill meantime had rallied his other two divisions and swung them northward, in accordance with Lee's orders, to plug the gap that had yawned since yesterday between him and Ewell. Finding it unexploited by the Federals, whose own gap had been enlarged by Longstreet — Law's whooping Alabamians had struck and scattered Wadsworth's ill-starred division on Hancock's right, driving the remnant west and north, all the way to the Lacy meadow, and Burnside was still on his circuitous tour of the brush — Hill's men, willingly and hurriedly, did what they had failed to do the night before. They intrenched. Lee's line was now a continuous one, reasonably compact, and he had all his troops on hand at last, including Ewell's detached brigade, which arrived at midmorning from Hanover. The time had come for him to go over to the all-out offensive he had planned to launch as soon as he managed to bring Grant to a standstill in the thickets — as he now had done.

"There was a lull all along the line," a regimental commander later said of this period during which reconnaissance parties went out and came back and last-minute instructions were delivered: adding, "It was the ominous silence that precedes the tornado."

Tactically, Grant was in far worse shape than he or anyone else in the Lacy meadow seemed to know. In addition to the unmanned gap across his center, he had both flanks in the air. No blue army had ever remained long in any such attitude, here in Virginia, without suffering grievously at the hands of Lee for having been so neglectful or inept; Hooker, for example, had left only one flank open, but his discomfiture had been complete. Now the same treatment might well be in store for Grant, on practically that same ground just one year later.

Headquarters had been more or less in a turmoil for the past two hours, ever since Hancock's attack went into reverse. First, there was the matter of Burnside's nonarrival, which not only reduced the intended strength of the main effort but also left it unsupported on the right, exposing Wadsworth to the catastrophe that ensued. In point of fact, after all that had happened yesterday, the aging New Yorker — a brigadier since shortly after First Bull Run, military governor of the District of Columbia during the tenure of McClellan, whom he had helped to frustrate, and an unsuccessful candidate for governor of his home state on the Republican ticket in '62, the year of the Democratic sweep — had seemed to suspect from the start that today would be no better. He was feeling his years, and he told an aide he thought perhaps he ought to turn the command of his division over to someone else and go to the rear. As it was, however, he stayed and managed, today as yesterday, to lose his sense of direction in the course of the attack and came crowding down on the units to his left, creating a jam on the near side of the plank road and thereby adding to the effectiveness of Poague's fire from the Tapp farmyard, as well as to the confusion that prevailed when Law assailed his unprotected right. One of his three brigades disintegrated without more ado, and Wadsworth, in an attempt to keep the other two from doing likewise, appealed to them from horseback to stand firm; whereupon he was hit in the back of the head and fell to the ground with a bullet in his brain. His troops ran off and left him, pursued by the rebels, who gathered him up and took him back to one of their aid stations. (He died there two days later, having been stared at by a great many of his enemies, who came for a look at a man reputed to possess "more wealth than the treasury of the Confederate government." Rich men were not unusual in the armies of the South, where the West Point tradition was strong in leading families and no $300 commutation fee could secure exemption from conscription, but were rarely encountered on the other side, particularly on the firing line.) Meantime the fallen general's troops continued their flight all the way to the Lacy meadow, as if they expected to find sanctuary there with Grant, who sat on his accustomed stump atop the knoll, still whittling, still wreathed in cigar smoke. Headquarters was alarmed by their sudden appearance, even though they did not seem to be pursued, and presently, when long-range shots began to fall in the vicinity, an anxious staffer, fearful that the meadow was about to be overrun, suggested that it would be prudent to shift the command post rearward. Grant stopped whittling. "It strikes me it would be better to order up some artillery and defend the present location," he said quietly. This was done, although there was nothing the gunners could see in the way of targets, and Hancock bolstered what remained of Wadsworth's division by sending reinforcements over from the left.

On the right, Sedgwick and Warren had suffered heavy losses in carrying out their instructions to keep attacking Ewell's intrenchments and thus prevent his sending reinforcements down to Hill. This they had done, and in doing it they had kept him on the defensive. But if they assumed from this that he would remain so, or that Sedgwick's outer flank was secure because it was covered by Flat Creek, they would be disabused before nightfall; Gordon, whose brigade was on the left, was trying even now to get permission from his superiors to turn the Federal flank, which he insisted was wide open to such a maneuver, having scouted it himself. So far, Ewell and Early had declined to let him try it, being convinced that Burnside's corps was posted rearward in support. Obviously, Sedgwick's immunity from attack, based as it was on this misconception by Gordon's superiors, was going to last no longer than Burnside remained unaccounted for in the Union order of battle. Once he found his way up to the firing line and was identified, Ewell and Early would have to abandon their objection to Gordon's proposal and unleash him, with results that were likely to be spectacular if Sedgwick's dispositions were as faulty as the Georgian claimed to have seen with his own eyes.

Just now, however — for Burnside, having spent the past five hours out of pocket, was to spend another three in the same fashion, lost to friend and foe alike, before he managed to get where he belonged — the gravest danger was on the opposite flank, which was also exposed to being turned or struck end-on. This was due to a combination of misconceptions, based on erroneous information from headquarters. Hancock had kept Barlow in position down the Brock Road all this time, yesterday and today, in expectation that Longstreet would arrive from that direction. Instead he had come up the plank road, converting Hill's near rout into a counteroffensive; but Hancock still held Barlow where he was, outside the action, because only two of Old Peter's divisions, Field's and Kershaw's, had so far been identified. The third, Pickett's — reported to have been with Longstreet at Gordonsville, though in fact it was south of Richmond — might be maneuvering for an attack up the Brock Road, perhaps in conjunction with Anderson's division of Hill's corps, which had also not yet been accounted for. So Barlow was kept where he was, a mile and a half from the plank road intersection, to guard against a tangential strike by these 10,000 missing rebels. Meantime, evidence had accumulated to support the belief that they were already at hand, including one frantic eyewitness report that they were advancing in mass up the Brock Road. This was a case of mistaken identity; the advancing mass turned out to be a herd of Federal convalescents, marching from

Chancellorsville to rejoin the army by Hancock's roundabout route. No sooner was this mistake discovered, however, than heavy firing was heard from down around Todd's Tavern, where the Brock and Catharpin roads intersected, less than three miles from Barlow's outpost on the Union left. The assumption was that the cavalry must have encountered Pickett's column, coming up from the Catharpin Road, and was doing what it could to hold him off while Barlow got ready to receive him. This was partly correct and partly wrong. It was cavalry, right enough, but that was all it was. The blue troopers were shooting, not at Pickett (who was perhaps of greater service to his country here today, though he was not within sixty miles of the battle, than he had been ten months ago at Gettysburg, leading the charge that would be known forever after by his name) but at Stuart. Sheridan had served Grant poorly yesterday by plunging eastward, with two thirds of the army's cavalry, into the vacuum Stuart had left around Fredericksburg when he moved westward to take position on Lee's right. Still intent on closing with the graybacks, more for the purpose of destroying them than of finding out what was happening in their rear, Sheridan's horsemen made such a racket with their rapid-firing carbines that Barlow thought a large-scale action was in progress, though in fact it was nothing more than an unprofitable skirmish, which did not result in the slightest penetration of the cavalry screen Stuart kept tightly drawn to prevent his adversary from catching even a glimpse of the preparations now being made for attack, four miles northwest. As it was, Barlow was so impressed by the uproar down around Todd's Tavern that he called urgently for reinforcements to help him meet what he was convinced was coming, and Hancock obliged by sending him two brigades from the main body, which by then was back on the line it had left at sunrise.

Hancock had his hands full where he was, holding Longstreet west of the Brock Road, immediately north and south of the plank road intersection. For better than five hours now, advancing and retreating, the fighting had been as heavy as any he had ever seen, and so too had his casualties and the expenditure of ammunition. Drummer boys were pressed into unfamiliar service as stretcher bearers, and when they got to the rear with their anguished burdens, the stretchers were loaded with boxes of cartridges for the return to the firing line, so that, as one reporter wrote, "the struggle shall not cease for want of ball and powder." Involved as he was in the direction of all this, blinded by thickets and appealed to simultaneously from the left and right — Barlow was convinced that he was about to be hit by Pickett, and Wadsworth's division, adjacent to the unmanned gap across the army's center, had just come apart at the seams — Hancock was apparently too busy to notice that the contraction of his front in the vicinity of the crossroad, resulting from his losses and the withdrawal of four brigades to meet the reported dangers on the far left and the right, had widened to about a mile the brush-choked interval between the main body and Barlow's outpost position down the road. Consequently, though he was reasonably well protected against a flank attack by Pickett, who wasn't there, he was not protected at all from one by Longstreet, who was. His immediate left — as Gordon was saying of Sedgwick's right, four miles away — was wide open to either a turning movement or an end-on strike.

Then came the lull, a half-hour breathing space. Hancock spent it shoring up his line against an expected renewal of Longstreet's frontal effort to drive him back from the vital crossroad. Atop the knoll in the Lacy meadow, Grant, with a hole in his center and both flanks in the air, continued to whittle. Then, around 11 o'clock, the storm broke. Within minutes of the opening shots, according to Meade's chief of staff, the uproar of the rebel attack "approached the sublime."

"Longstreet, always grand in battle, never shone as he did here," a First Corps artillerist said of the general in his conduct of this morning's fighting on the right. Within three hours of his arrival he introduced tactics into a battle which, up to then, had been little more than a twenty-hour slugging match, with first one side then the other surging forward through the brush, only to fall back when momentum was lost and the enemy took his turn at going over to the offensive. All attacks had been frontal except for chance encounters, when some confused unit — a regiment or a brigade or, as in Wadsworth's case, a division — got turned around, usually in the course of an advance through blinding thickets, and exposed a naked flank to being torn. Now Old Peter, who was always at his calmest when the conflict roared its loudest, undertook to serve a Federal corps, reinforced to a strength of seven divisions, in that same tearing fashion.

Lee had ordered the army's chief engineer, Major General Martin L. Smith, to report to Longstreet at about the time the Federals began to yield the ground they had won from Hill. Sent out to reconnoiter the Union left, Smith — a forty-four-year-old New-York-born West Pointer whose most distinguished service to his adopted country up to now had been at Vicksburg, where he not only laid out and supervised the construction of its hilly defenses, but also commanded one of the divisions that manned them under siege — returned at 10 o'clock to report that he had found Hancock's flank wide open to attack from within the mile-wide gap that yawned between his main body and Barlow's outpost. Moreover, an unfinished and unmapped railroad, work on which had been abandoned when the war began, afforded an ideal covered approach to that vulnerable point; troops could be massed in the brush-screened cut, just where the roadbed made a turn southeast, perpendicular to the unguarded flank a briery quarter mile away.

Old Peter's eyes lighted up at the news, but he was no more inclined to be precipitate here than he had been at Second Manassas when a similar opportunity arose. He summoned his young chief of staff, Lieutenant Colonel G. Moxley Sorrel, instructed him to take charge of a force made up of three brigades, one from each of the three divisions at hand, and conduct them to the designated point for the attack. Knowing how likely such maneuvers were to become disorganized under the influence of exuberance, he stressed the need for careful preparation. "Form a good line," he told him, "and then move, your right pushed forward and turning as much as possible to the left." Characteristically, before sending him on his way, he added in true First Corps style: "Hit hard when you start, but don't start until you have everything ready."

Sorrel assembled the three brigades, headed by Brigadier Generals William Wofford, G. T. Anderson, and William Mahone, respectively from Kershaw's, Field's, and Richard Anderson's divisions, and just as he was about to move out, Colonel John M. Stone of Heth's division, in position on Longstreet's left, requested permission to add the weight of his Mississippi brigade to the blow about to be struck. Hill and Heth were willing, and that made four brigades from as many divisions, a pair each from two corps, not one of them under a professional soldier and all in charge of a young staff officer who never before had commanded troops in action. Sorrel was a former bank clerk, twenty-six years old, intensely ambitious and strikingly handsome, a Georgian like his chief, though of French not Dutch extraction. As he set out, leading this force of about 5000 into the railway cut, then eastward through its leafy tunnel to the bend where they would mass for the attack, he knew that his great hour had come and he was determined to make the most of it, for his own and his country's sake. Old Peter, who had a great affection for him dating back to First Manassas, watched him disappear in the woods, then settled back to wait for the uproar that would signal the launching of the flank assault. He kept his remaining eleven brigades in position astride the plank road, maintaining frontal contact and preparing to increase the pressure when the time came. Already he was planning a larger turning movement to follow the one about to start. Once Hancock's line had been rolled up, the fronts of the other two Confederate corps would be uncovered in rapid sequence; Hill's two divisions would join the grand left wheel, and Ewell's three would drive straight ahead, cutting the Federals off from the fords by which they had crossed the Rapidan. Obliged to fall back on Fredericksburg, Grant's army would be cut to pieces, train and all, as it jammed the narrow Wilderness trails and scattered in the brush. Anticipation made the wait seem long, though in fact it was quite brief. At 11 o'clock, within half an hour of his setting out, Sorrel's attack exploded on the Union left and began to roll northward, clattering across the right front of the Confederate position. Longstreet ordered his main body forward simultaneously to exploit and enlarge the panic already evident in the enemy ranks.

The end-on blow was as successful as even Sorrel had dared to hope it would be. Struck without preamble by a horde of rapid-firing rebels who came screaming through what up to then had been a curtain of peaceful green, the first blue unit — a brigade that had just been withdrawn from the line to catch its breath while the lull was on — disintegrated on contact, its members taking off in all directions to escape the sudden onslaught, and though others reacted differently, having at least had a semblance of warning that something horrendous was headed in their direction from the left, the result was much the same in the end, as unit after unit, finding itself under simultaneous fire from the front and flank, sought to achieve a similar deliverance from fury. Consternation in such cases was followed by a strangely deliberate acceptance of the military facts of life, the difference being that they reacted, not as individuals, but as a group seeking safety in numbers. A man from one of Gibbon's brigades reported that the first he knew of a flank attack was when he saw troops from Mott's division, on his left, trudging rearward in a body. At first, so deliberate was their step, so oddly sullen their expression, he could not make out what was happening. "[They] did not seem to me demoralized in manner," he declared, "nor did they present the appearance of soldiers moving under orders, but rather of a throng of armed men returning dissatisfied from a muster." The best explanation another observer could give was that "a large number of troops were about to leave the service," and apparently they were doing all they could to leave it alive. One thing at least was clear to a staff officer who watched them slogging rearward, oblivious to pleas and threats alike. "They had fought all they meant to fight for the present," he said, "and there was an end to it." Hancock himself put it simplest, in a statement years later to Longstreet: "You rolled me up like a wet blanket."

Elation on the Confederate side was correspondingly great, and it too was a sort of mass reaction. Here, the cheering troops perceived as soon as the flank attack began to roll, was another Chancellorsville in the making. Moreover, they were aware of the highly encouraging difference that, instead of launching their turning movement with a scant two hours of daylight left for its exploitation, as Jackson's men had done, they now had a substantial eight or nine such hours: enough, surely, to complete the destruction already under way. Not that they wasted time, simply because so much of it was available; Sorrel had carried out his orders with speed and precision. Wofford and Mahone were abreast in front, respectively on the left and right, supported by G. T. Anderson and Stone, whose added pressure shattered what little resistance was encountered or by-passed in the course of the advance.

Within less than an hour they had driven northward all the way to the plank road; some of Wofford's Georgians, in fact, plunged eagerly across it, intent on the chase, though Mahone's Virginians called a halt at that point, in accordance with instructions. When Sorrel rode up he found the plank road unobstructed all the way to its intersection with the Brock Road, where the displaced and rattled Federals were taking shelter behind the breastworks Hancock had had them build the day before. From the opposite direction he saw Longstreet and his staff riding toward him on the plank road, accompanied by several unit commanders to whom the burly lieutenant general was apparently giving directions for the follow-up assault. They made up a sizeable cavalcade, and Sorrel could see from their manner, their gestures and expressions as they rode, that they shared the exuberance he was feeling at the success of his first experience as a leader of men in battle.

Their high spirits were voiced by Brigadier General Micah Jenkins, the twenty-eight-year-old commander of a brigade in Field's division, who had just been informed that his troops would play a major role in the follow-up attack. "I am happy," the young South Carolina aristocrat told Longstreet, excited by the prospect of enlarging the gains already made. "I have felt despair for the cause for some months, but now I am relieved, and feel assured that we will put the enemy back across the Rapidan before night." When Sorrel came up Jenkins embraced and congratulated him warmly. "We will smash them now," he said.

Old Peter thought so, too. Engineer Smith had returned from a second reconnaissance of the Union left to report that a second turning movement, designed to flank the rallying bluecoats out of their breastworks along the Brock Road, was altogether as feasible as the first. Just then, however, as the cavalcade continued its ride east to within musket range of the Brock Road intersection, there was a sudden spatter of fire from the woods to the right front; some of Mahone's men were shooting at some of Wofford's, having mistaken them for Federals when they came hurrying back across the plank road to take their proper place in line. Aggressive as always, Longstreet whirled his horse in that direction, apparently intending to stop the undisciplined firing. Others followed his example — including Joe Kershaw, who had ridden forward to confer with Wofford on the condition of his detached brigade — and were met by a heavier volley from the Virginians in the woods. Four men were hit: a courier and a staff captain, both of whom were killed instantly, Micah Jenkins, who died a few hours later with a bullet in his brain, and Longstreet. "Friends! They are *friends!*" Kershaw shouted in a voice that rang above the clatter and the groans, and almost at once Mahone's veterans ceased firing and hurried out of the woods to express their regret for what had happened.

By then solicitous hands were helping the wounded lieutenant general to dismount. Hit solidly by a bullet that passed through the base of his neck and lodged in his right shoulder, he had been lifted straight up by the impact and had come down hard, his right arm hanging useless, though he managed to stay in the saddle, bleeding heavily, until his companions were there to ease him to the ground, the upper part of his body propped against the trunk of a roadside tree. Exultation turned to dismay as word spread rapidly through the Wilderness that Old Peter had been hit. All down the line, men's thoughts were more than ever of Chancellorsville, but with the bitter irony of remembering that Jackson too had been shot by his own soldiers, less than four miles up the road through these same woods, at the climax of a successful flank attack. As for Longstreet, his thoughts were neither on the past nor on the present, despite his pain. His concern was for the immediate future, the follow-up assault that would complete his victory. Field being the ranking division commander present in the corps, Longstreet blew the bloody foam from his mouth to say to Sorrel: "Tell General Field to take command, and move forward with the whole force and gain the Brock Road." Soon his staff physician was there to tend his wounds, and when Lee arrived he told him, in such detail as his shaken vocal cords allowed, of his plan for turning the Federals out of their new position. By now a stretcher had been brought. He was lifted onto it, his hat placed over his face to shield his eyes, and carried back down the plank road to a waiting ambulance. On the way, when he heard troops by the roadside saying, "He is dead. They are only telling us he is wounded," he raised his hat from his face with his usable hand. The answering cheers, he declared long afterward, served to ease his pain somewhat on the jolting rearward journey.

A wandering artillery major, on a fruitless search for a decent gun position, came up just as the ambulance moved off. Later he wrote of what he saw and felt. Members of the general's staff, "literally bowed down with grief," were all around the vehicle; "One, I remember, stood upon the rear step of the ambulance, seeming to desire to be as near him as possible. All of them were in tears." The doctor had said that Longstreet's wounds were not necessarily fatal, but they recalled that the prognosis had been even more favorable in Jackson's case right up to the day he died, a year ago next week. Though he had never really liked Old Peter, the artillerist wanted to see for himself what his condition was. For one thing, the procession's resemblance to a funeral cortege lent credence to a rumor that the general was dead. "I rode up to the ambulance and looked in. They had taken off Longstreet's hat and coat and boots. The blood had paled out of his face and its somewhat gross aspect was gone. I noticed how white and dome-like his great forehead looked and, with scarcely less reverent

admiration, how spotless white his socks and his fine gauze undervest,
save where the black red gore from his breast and shoulder had stained
it. While I gazed at his massive frame, lying so still except when it
rocked inertly with the lurch of the vehicle, his eyelids frayed apart
till I could see a delicate line of blue between them, and then he very
quietly moved his unwounded arm and, with his thumb and two
fingers, carefully lifted the saturated undershirt from his chest, holding
it up a moment, and heaved a deep sigh. He is not dead, I said to myself, and he is calm and entirely master of the situation. He is both
greater and more attractive than I have heretofore thought him.''

Back up the road, at the scene of the wounding, Field was doing
what he could to carry out his orders to "take command, and move
forward." But this was by no means as easy a task as Longstreet seemed
to think. Other disruptive accidents, like the one that had just cost
the corps its chief, were apt to follow if the main body, still in line
astride the plank road, and Sorrel's flankers, drawn up facing it, were
left to fight with their fronts at right angles. Lee ordered a postponement of the follow-up assault until the lines were readjusted. This was
done, although the process was a slow one. Not only was the confusion
greater than had been thought, it had also been increased by the loss
of Jenkins and Old Peter. Four mortal hours, from noon to 4 o'clock,
were required to get the troops untangled and into satisfactory positions
for attack, and when they went forward at 4.15 they found that
Hancock, too, had made good use of the time afforded for adjustments.
He had strengthened his breastworks, brought up reinforcements, and
posted a secondary line in support of the first. Worst of all (or best,
depending on the point of view) he had shored up and realigned

his outer flank, which the attackers found no longer dangling in the air. At a couple of
points the Confederates achieved
a penetration — one, where the
log breastworks caught fire,
forcing the defenders to abandon them, and Jenkins's Carolinians came leaping through the
flames, intent on avenging the
fall of their young brigadier —
but in both cases supporting
troops came up and restored the
line by driving them out again:
proof, if any such was needed,
that seven divisions, snug behind breastworks and with both flanks secure
(Burnside had come up at last, midway through the four-hour lull, and
gone into position on Hancock's right) were not to be driven, or even

budged, by three divisions attacking head-on through bullet-flailed brush. An hour of such fighting was quite enough to show that nothing more was going to be accomplished here. It was time — indeed, almost past time — to look elsewhere: meaning in Ewell's direction, up on the opposite flank.

All day, though he had had no chance to go in person, Lee had been sending messages to the Second Corps, urging an offensive in that quarter to relieve the pressure on the First or, if that was impracticable, the detachment of reinforcements to strengthen the offensive on the right. Invariably Ewell had replied that he could do neither. There was no fit opening for an attack; he needed all his troops to maintain his position astride the turnpike. When Lee arrived at 5.30 asking, "Cannot something be done on this flank?" Ewell said again that he believed it would be unwise to assault the Federals in their intrenchments, and he was supported in this by Early, who was at corps headquarters when Lee rode up. Gordon was also there, intending to renew his daylong plea that he be unleashed, and when his two superiors finished protesting that there was nothing to be done, he presumed to appeal to the army commander himself for permission to strike at the enemy flank, which he insisted had been wide open to attack for more than eight hours now. Ewell and Early repeated their objections, based on the conviction that Burnside was posted in Sedgwick's rear to forestall such a move. Lee, who knew that Burnside was in front of Hill, wasted no more time on reproaches, although, as Gordon later wrote, "his silence and grim looks . . . revealed his thoughts almost as plainly as words could have done." He simply ordered the attack to be made at once.

It was launched at straight-up 6 o'clock, and within the limitations of the little daylight time remaining — sunset came at 6.50 and darkness followed quickly in the thickets of the Wilderness — it was altogether as successful as Gordon, for the past nine hours, had been telling Ewell and Early it would be. With the support of the brigade that had arrived that morning from Hanover, North Carolinians under twenty-seven-year-old Brigadier General Robert D. Johnston, the Georgians struck and scattered Ricketts's unwary flank brigade and captured its commander, Brigadier General Truman Seymour. Seymour had led a division in the ill-starred Florida campaign, and after being whipped at Olustee had returned to Virginia to head a brigade whose members were known in both armies as "Milroy's weary boys," a description applied two years ago, after Stonewall Jackson gave them the run-around in the Shenandoah Valley, and confirmed last year when Ewell encountered them near Winchester on his way to Gettysburg. Weary or not, they broke badly again today and spread panic through the rest of the division, as well as through part of Wright's division, which was next in line and which also had a brigade commander scooped up by the rebels in the confusion. This was Brigadier General Alexander Shaler, a Connecticut-born New Yorker whose capture was especially welcome because he had recently been in charge of the prison for Confederate officers on Johnson's Island in Sandusky Bay, where winters were cold and blankets few; now he would get a taste of prison life from the inside, looking out, instead of from the outside, looking in. Seymour and Shaler, for all their lofty rank, were only two among some 600 Federals taken captive in the attack, while about as many more were killed or wounded, bringing Sedgwick's total loss to well over a thousand in one hour. Gordon himself lost only about fifty in the course of what his men referred to, ever afterwards, as their "finest frolic." The blue right flank was "rolled up" for more than a mile before dusk put an end to the advance and obliged the Georgians and Carolinians, who by then had plungèd all the way to the Germanna Plank Road, to pull back with their prisoners, their booty from the over-run camps, and their conviction that an earlier attack, in Gordon's word's, "would have resulted in a decided disaster to the whole right wing of General Grant's army, if not in its entire disorganization."

Lee was inclined to think so, too, especially if the attack on this flank, against Sedgwick, had been delivered at the same time as Longstreet's against Hancock, on the other; in which case the indications were that Grant would have been overwhelmed and routed, not merely discomfited and bled down another one percent. An earlier visit to the left by the army commander would no doubt have resulted in an earlier attack, but Lee had come as soon as he felt he could leave the critical right, where the contest had been touch-and-go since sunrise. The trouble was that he could not be everywhere at once, despite the need for him to do just that. Although this impossible need had grown more pressing ever since the death of Stonewall Jackson, today it had become downright acute. Longstreet's departure left his corps in the hands of a newly promoted major general who had been with it less than three months, none of the time in combat, and whose deskbound year in Richmond seemed to have made him utterly inflexible at a time when flexibility was among the highest virtues. Hill's failing health, worse today than yesterday, and likely to be still worse tomorrow, obviously required him to take a sick leave that would deprive the army, however briefly, of the most aggressive of its corps commanders. It was harder, even, to think of Lee without A. P. Hill than it was to think of him without Longstreet, for Hill had never been detached. As for Ewell, although by ordinary standards he had done well today and yesterday, holding his own against the odds, he seemed incapable of doing one whit more than was required by specific orders; Ewell in the Wilderness, unable to bring himself to unleash Gordon despite repeated pleas from headquarters that *something* be attempted in that direction, was disturbingly like Ewell at Gettysburg, where his indecisiveness had cost the army its one best chance for a quick victory in what, instead, turned out to be a bloody three-day battle that ended in retreat.... All this might well have been heavy on Lee's mind as he rode southward, three miles through the twilight, to the Tapp farm. He was faced, at this most critical juncture, with a crisis of command: a crisis that would have to be resolved if the Army of Northern Virginia — at the close of only the second day of fighting, in what promised to be the longest and grimmest of its campaigns — was to survive the continuing confrontation, here in the depths of the Wilderness, with an enemy force roughly twice its size, superbly equipped, and still in possession of the main artery leading southeast, through the thickets and beyond into open country, where the tactical odds would lengthen and the capital itself would be in danger of being taken, either by sudden assault or inexorable maneuver.

All around him, as he dismounted in front of his tent in the Tapp farmyard, was confusion. East and north, out in the jungle where the battle had raged for two incredibly savage days, the moans of the wounded, blue and gray, were heightened to screams of terror when a brisk wind sprang up, shortly after dark, and fanned random smouldering embers into flames that spread faster through the underbrush than an injured man could crawl. Dead pines, their sap long dried to rosin, burned like twenty-foot torches, and the low clouds took on an eerie yellow cast, as if they reflected the glow from molten sulphur on the floor of hell. The roar of wind-whipped flames through crackling brush was punctuated from time to time by a clatter resembling the sudden clash of pickets, as groups of disabled men from both sides, huddled together against a common danger, were engulfed by the inferno and the paper-wrapped charges in their pockets or cartridge boxes caught fire and exploded. While stretcher bearers and volunteers did what they could to rescue all the wounded they could reach, others along the Confederate line of battle — including those Third Corps veterans who had thought they were too tired for such exertion the night before — worked hard to strengthen their defenses for a renewal of the contest at first light tomorrow. They expected it, and so did their commander. Less soundly beaten, tactically, and with no greater losses, Hooker had pulled back across the river. But neither Lee nor his soldiers thought it likely that Grant would do what Fighting Joe had done; at least not yet. Judging their new opponent by his western reputation, as well as by his aggressive performance over the past two days, they believed he would stay and fight.

Next to a retreat, which he did not expect, Lee preferred a Federal attack, and that was what he had his men prepare for. If Grant was to be beaten further, to and beyond the point at which he would have no choice except to pull back across the river, it would have to come as the result of a bloody, morale-shattering repulse. In any case, the next move was up to the invader. Today's abortive follow-up assault by the First Corps, launched after the long delay occasioned in part by the fall of its commander, had shown only too clearly that the Confederates, whatever their successes when they caught the enemy off balance, lacked the strength to drive an opponent who was not only twice their size but was also braced for the shock in well-prepared intrenchments — and there could be no doubt that the Federals were as hard at work on their defenses, left and right and center, as the gray-backs were on their side of the line. Obliged as he was, now that all chances for surprise had been exhausted, to rule out a resumption of the offensive by his badly outnumbered army, Lee's decision not to attack amounted to a surrender of the initiative. This was a dangerous procedure against an adversary as nimble as Grant had shown himself to be in the campaign that brought Vicksburg under siege, but Lee had no choice. His hope, as he turned in for the night, was that Grant, despite his freedom to maneuver, would continue to forget his Vicksburg method and hold instead to the pattern of headlong assault he had followed so far in Virginia. That might lead to his repulse, and another repulse, if decisive enough, might lead to his destruction. The alternative for Lee, who had no such freedom to maneuver, was stalemate and defeat.

This second day of battle in the Wilderness had been Grant's hardest since the opening day at Shiloh, where his army and his reputation had also been threatened with destruction. Here as there, however — so long, at least, as the fighting was in progress — he bore the strain unruffled and "gave his orders calmly and coherently," one witness noted, "without any external sign of undue tension or agitation." Internally, a brief sequel was to show, he was a good deal more upset than he appeared, but outwardly, as he continued to sit on his stump atop the knoll in the Lacy meadow, smoking and whittling the critical hours away, he seemed altogether imperturbable. When word came, shortly before noon, that Hancock's flank had been turned and the left half of his army was in imminent danger of being routed, his reaction was to send more troops in that direction, together with additional supplies of ammunition, followed at 3 o'clock by orders for a counterattack to be launched at 6 to recover the lost ground and assure the holding of the Brock Road leading south. As it turned out, Hancock was himself assaulted a second time, nearly two hours before that, and had to use up so much of the ammunition in repelling the attack that not enough was left for compliance with the order. Besides, Grant by then was faced with an even graver crisis on his right. Sedgwick too had been flanked and was being routed, he was told, by a rebel force that had penetrated all the way to the Germanna Plank Road, cutting the army off from its nearest escape hatch back across the Rapidan.

Meade was a steadying influence, in this case as in others. "Nonsense," he snorted when a pair of flustered staffers came riding in from the crumpled flank after sundown to report that all was lost in that direction, including all hope of deliverance from the trap the rebels had sprung on Sedgwick and were about to enlarge in order to snap up everything in blue. "Nonsense! If they have broken our lines they can do nothing more tonight." He had confidence in John Sedgwick, the least excitable of his corps commanders, and he showed it by sending reinforcements from the center to help shore up the tottered right. Grant approved, of course, and had an even stronger reaction to an officer of higher rank who came crying that this second flank assault meant the end of the northern army unless it found some way to get out from under the blow about to fall. "This is a crisis that cannot be looked upon too seriously," he declared. "I know Lee's methods well by past experience. He will throw his whole army between us and the Rapidan, and cut us off completely from our communications." Grant was not a curser, but his patience had run out. He got up from the stump, took the cigar out of his mouth, and turned on this latest in the series of prophets of doom and idolators of his opponent. "Oh, I am heartily tired of hearing about what *Lee* is going to do," he said testily. "Some of you always seem to think he is suddenly going to turn a double somersault and land in our rear and on both our flanks at the same time. Go back to your command and try to think what we are going to do ourselves, instead of what *Lee* is going to do."

Further reports of havoc on the right were received with the same firmness, the same quick rejection of all notions of defeat, although — as Rawlins told a friend who rode over to headquarters to see him later that evening — "the coming of officer after officer with additional details soon made it apparent that the general was confronted by the greatest crisis in his life." By nightfall, however, Meade's assessment was confirmed; Sedgwick established a new and stronger line, half a mile south and east of the one he had lost to Gordon's flankers, who withdrew in the twilight from their position astride the road leading back to Germanna Ford. Then, and not until then, did the general-in-chief show the full effect of the strain he had been under, all this day and most of the day before. He broke. Yet even this was done with a degree of circumspection and detachment highly characteristic of the man. Not only was his personal collapse resisted until after the damage to both flanks had been repaired and the tactical danger had passed; it also occurred in the privacy of his quarters, rather than in the presence of his staff or gossip-hungry visitors. "When all proper measures had been taken," Rawlins confided, "Grant went into his tent, threw himself face downward on his cot, and gave way to the greatest emotion." He wept, and though the chief of staff, who followed him into the tent, declared that he had "never before seen him so deeply moved" and that "nothing could be more certain than that he was stirred to the very depths of his soul," he also observed that Grant gave way to the strain "without uttering any word of doubt or discouragement." Another witness, a captain attached to Meade's headquarters — Charles F. Adams, Jr, son and namesake of the ambassador — put it stronger. "I never saw a man so agitated in my life," he said.

However violent the breakdown, the giving way to hysteria at this point, it appeared that Grant wept more from the relief of tension (after all, both flanks were well shored up by then) than out of continuing desperation. In any case it was soon over. When Rawlins's friend, Brigadier General James H. Wilson — a friend of Grant's as well, formerly a member of his military family and recently appointed by him to command one of Sheridan's cavalry divisions — reached headquarters about 9 o'clock, less than an hour after the collapse Rawlins presently described, he found the general "surrounded by his staff in a state of perfect composure," as if nothing at all had happened. And in fact nothing had: nothing that mattered, anyhow. Unlike Hooker, who broke inside as a result of similar frustrations, Grant broke outside, and then only in the privacy of his tent. He cracked, but the crack healed so quickly that it had no effect whatever on the military situation, then or later. Whereas Hooker had reacted by falling back across the river, such a course was no more in Grant's mind now than it had been that morning, before sunup, when he was accosted by a journalist who was about to leave for Washington to file a story on the first day's fighting. Asked if he had any message for the authorities there, Grant, whose usual procedure was to hold off sending word of his progress in battle until the news was good, thought it over briefly, then replied: "If you see the President, tell him, from me, that, whatever happens, there will be no turning back."

Late that evening another journalist, New York *Herald* correspondent Sylvanus Cadwallader, was reassured to find that Grant still felt that way about the matter, despite the tactical disappointments of the day just past. Seated on opposite sides of a smouldering headquarters campfire, these two — the reporter because he was too depressed for sleep, and the general, he presumed, for the same reason — were the last to turn in for the night. Formerly of the Chicago *Times*, Cadwallader had been with Grant for nearly two years now, through the greatest of his triumphs, as well as through a two-day drunk up the Yazoo last summer, and for the first time, here in the Wilderness tonight, he began, as he said afterward, "to question the grounds of my faith in him. . . . We had waged two days of murderous battle, and had but little to show for it. Judged by comparative losses, it had been disastrous to the Union cause. We had been compelled by General Lee to fight him on a field of his own choosing, with the certainty of losing at least two men to his one, until he could be dislodged and driven from his vantage ground. [Yet] we had gained scarcely a rod of the battle-field at the close of the two days' contest." He wondered, as a result of this disconsolate review of the situation, whether he had followed Grant all this long way, through the conquest of Vicksburg and the deliverance of Chattanooga, only "to record his defeat and overthrow" when he came up against Lee in the Virginia thickets. Musing thus beside the dying embers of the campfire, he looked across its low glow at the lieutenant general, who seemed to be musing too. "His hat was drawn down over his face, the high collar of an old blue army overcoat turned up above his ears, one leg crossed over the other knee, eyes on the ashes in front." Only the fitful crossing and recrossing of his legs indicated that he was not asleep, and Cadwallader supposed that the general's thoughts were as gloomy as his own — until at last Grant spoke and disabused him of the notion. He began what the reporter termed "a pleasant chatty conversation upon indifferent subjects," none of which had anything to do with the fighting today or yesterday. As he got up from his chair to go to bed, however, he spoke briefly of "the sharp work General Lee had been giving us for a couple of days," then turned and went into his tent to get some sleep. That was all. But now that Cadwallader realized that the general had not been sharing them, he found that all his gloomy thoughts were gone. Grant opposed by Lee in Virginia, he perceived, was the same Grant he had known in Mississippi and Tennessee, where Pemberton and Bragg had been defeated. "It was the grandest mental sunburst of my life," he declared years later, looking back on the effect this abrupt realization had had on his state of mind from that time forward. "I had suddenly emerged from the slough of despond, to the solid bedrock of unwavering faith."

In the course of the next twenty hours or so — May 7 now, a Saturday — the whole army experienced a like sequence of reactions, from utter doubt to mental sunburst. Reconnaissance parties, working their way along and across the charred, smoky corridors last night's fires had left, found the rebels "fidgety and quick to shoot" but content, it seemed, to stay tightly buttoned up in the breastworks they had built or improved since yesterday. Lee preferred receiving to delivering an attack, and Grant apparently felt the same, since he issued no orders directing that one be made. For this the troops were duly thankful, especially those who had had a close-up look at the enemy lines, but they were also puzzled. The Federal choice seemed limited to attack or retreat, and they had not thought that Grant, despite the drubbing he had received these past two days, would give up quite this early. Still, word soon came that the pontoon bridges had been taken up at Germanna and relaid at Ely's Ford to hasten the passage of the ambulance train with the wounded, who were to be sent by rail to Washington. This meant that a withdrawal of the army, whether by that route or through Fredericksburg, would have to proceed by way of Chancellorsville, the hub where roads from the south and west converged to continue north and east. Swiftly now the conviction grew that everything blue would be headed in that direction after sundown. Sure enough, such guns as had found positions for direct support of the infantry — including those on the knoll in the Lacy meadow — were limbered and started rearward that afternoon, obviously to avoid jamming the roads that night, and in this the men saw confirmation of their worst judgments and suspicions. Grant, for all his western bulldog reputation, was merely another Pope, another Hooker, at best another Meade. They had been through this before; they recognized the signs. "Most of us thought it was another Chancellorsville," a Massachusetts infantryman would remember, while a Pennsylvania cavalryman recorded that his comrades used a homlier term to describe the predicted movement. They called it "another skedaddle."

If the Chancellorsville parallel was obvious — both battles had been waged in the same thicket, so to speak, between the same two armies, at the same time of year, and against the same Confederate commander — it was also, at this stage, disturbingly apt. By every tactical standard, although the earlier contest was often held up as a model of Federal ineptitude, the second was even worse-fought than the first. Hooker had had one flank turned; Grant had both. Hooker had achieved at least a measure of surprise in the opening stage of his campaign; Grant achieved none. Indeed, the latter had been surprised himself, while on a march designed to avoid battle on the very ground where this one raged for two horrendous days, not only without profit to the invaders, but also at a cost so disproportionate that it emphasized the wisdom of his original intention to avoid a confrontation on this terrain. Moreover, it was in the three-way assessment of casualties, Hooker's and Lee's, along with his own, that the comparison became least flattering. Grant lost 17,666 killed and wounded, captured and missing — about four hundred more than Hooker — while Lee, whose victory a year ago had cost him nearly 13,000 casualties, was losing a scant 7800, considerably fewer than half the number he inflicted. Here the comparison tended to break down, however, because for anything like comparable losses, North and South, it was necessary to go back to Fredericksburg, the most one-sided of all the large-scale Confederate triumphs. In plain fact, up to the point of obliging Grant to throw in the sponge and pull back across the river, Lee had never beaten an adversary so soundly as he had beaten this one in the course of the past two days.

What it all boiled down to was that Grant was whipped, and soundly whipped, if he would only admit it by retreating: which in turn was only a way of saying that he had not been whipped at all. "Whatever happens, there will be no turning back," he had said, and he would hold to that. The midafternoon displacement of the guns deployed along the Union line of battle was in preparation for a march, just as the troops assumed, but not in the direction they supposed. No more willing to accept a stalemate than he was to accept defeat, he would shift his ground, and in doing so he would hold to the offensive; he would move, not north toward Washington, but south toward Richmond, obliging Lee to conform if he was to protect the capital in his rear. Grant thus clung to the initiative Lee surrendered when he had exhausted all his chances for surprise. Now it was Grant's turn to try again for a surprise, and he planned accordingly.

The objective was Spotsylvania Courthouse, less than a dozen miles down the Brock Road from the turnpike intersection. With an early start, to be made as soon as darkness screened the movement from the rebels in their works across the way, it was not too much to expect that the leading elements would be in position there by dawn, plying shovels and swinging axes in the construction of fortifications which Lee, when he caught up at last, would be obliged to storm, even if the storming meant the destruction of his army, because they would stand between him and the capital whose protection was his prime concern. Warren would have the lead and would go all the way tonight, marching down the Brock Road across the rear of Hancock, who would fall in behind, once Warren had passed, and stop at Todd's Tavern, where he would guard the rear and slow the progress of the rebels if they attempted to follow by this route. Sedgwick would move east on the turnpike to Chancellorsville, then south by the road past Piney Branch Church to its junction with the Brock Road at Alsop, between Todd's Tavern and Spotsylvania, close in Warren's rear and also within supporting distance of Hancock. Burnside would follow Sedgwick after taking the plank road to Chancellorsville, but would call a halt at Piney Branch Church to protect the trains and the reserve artillery, which were to assemble at that point. Sheridan's troopers would probe the darkness in advance of both columns, and he was directed to patrol the western flank in strength, in order "to keep the corps commanders advised in time of the approach of the enemy." Warren and Sedgwick would move out at 8.30, Hancock and Burnside as soon thereafter as the roads were clear. The emphasis was on silence and speed, both highly desirable factors in a maneuver designed to outfox old man Lee.

Meade issued the march order at 3 o'clock, in compliance with earlier instructions from Grant, and when the guns pulled out soon afterward, taking a five-hour lead to clear the roads for the infantry that night, the troops along the line of battle drew their conclusions and went on exchanging occasional long-range shots with the graybacks while awaiting their turn to join what they were convinced was a retreat. Soon after dark the expected orders came; Warren's and Sedgwick's veterans slung their packs, fell in quietly on the Brock Road and the turnpike, and set out. To the surprise of the V Corps men, the march was south, in rear of Hancock's portion of the line. At first they thought that this was done to get them onto the plank road, leading east to Chancellorsville, but when they slogged past the intersection they knew that what they were headed for was not the Rapidan or the Rappahannock, but another battle somewhere south, beyond the un-suspecting rebel flank. Formerly glum, the column now began to buzz with talk. Packs were lighter; the step quickened; spirits rose with the growing realization that they were stealing another march on old man Lee. Then came cheers, as a group on horseback — "Give way, give way to the right," one of the riders kept calling to the soldiers on the road — doubled the column at a fast walk, equipment jingling. In the lead was Grant, a vague, stoop-shouldered figure, undersized-looking on Cincinnati, the largest of his mounts; the other horsemen were his staff. Cincinnati pranced and sidled, tossing his head at the sudden cheering, and the general, who had his hands full getting the big animal quieted down, told his companions to pass the word for the cheers to stop, lest they give the movement away to the Confederates sleeping behind their breastworks in the woods half a mile to the west. The cheering stopped, but not the buzz of excitement, the elation men felt at seeing their commander take the lead in an advance they had supposed was a retreat. They stepped out smartly; Todd's Tavern was just ahead, a little beyond the midway point on the march to Spotsyl-vania.

Up on the turnpike, where Sedgwick's troops were marching, the glad reaction was delayed until the head of the column had covered the gloomy half dozen miles to Chancellorsville. "The men seemed aged," a cannoneer noted as he watched them slog past a roadside artillery park. Weary from two days of savage fighting and two nights of practically no sleep, dejected by the notion that they were adding still another to the long list of retreats the army had made in the past three years, they plodded heavy-footed and heavy-hearted, scuffing their shoes in the dust on the pike leading eastward. Beyond Chancellors-ville, just ahead, the road forked. A turn to the left, which they ex-pected, meant recrossing the river at Ely's Ford, probably to undergo another reorganization under another new commander who would lead them, in the fullness of time, into another battle that would end in another retreat; that was the all-too-familiar pattern, so endless in repetition that at times it seemed a full account of the army's activities in the Old Dominion could be spanned in four short words, "Bull Run: da capo." But now a murmur, swelling rapidly to a chatter, began to move back down the column from its head, and presently each man could see for himself that the turn, beyond the ruins of the Chancellor mansion, had been to the right. They were headed south, not north; they were advancing, not retreating; Grant was giving them another go at Lee. And though on sober second thought a man might be of at least two minds about this, as a welcome or a dread thing to be facing, the immediate reaction was elation. There were cheers and even a few tossed caps, and long afterwards men were to say that, for them, this had been the high point of the war.

"Our spirits rose," one among them would recall. "We marched free. The men begin to sing. . . . That night we were happy."

✗ 2 ✗

Lee was marching too, by then, having divined once more his adversary's intention. That morning, after riding the length of his Wilderness line and finding it strangely quiet — in contrast, that is, to the fury of the past two days, when better than 25,000 men had been shot or captured, blue and gray, along that four-mile stretch of tangled woodland — he drew rein on the far left to talk with Gordon, who supposed from Grant's lack of aggressiveness that he was about to retreat. "Grant is not going to retreat," Lee told him. "He will move his army to Spotsylvania." Surprised, the Georgian asked if there was any evidence that the Federals were moving in that direction. "Not at all, not at all," Lee said as he turned Traveller's head to ride back down the line. "But that is the next point at which the armies will meet. Spotsylvania is now General Grant's best strategic point."

There was, as he said, no indication that Grant was moving, but there was at least negative evidence that when he did move — as obviously he would have to do, in lieu of assaulting the Wilderness intrenchments, before he used up the supplies in his train — it would not be back across the Rapidan; Ewell had sent word, shortly after sunup, that the Federals were dismantling their pontoon bridges at Germanna, and though Ely's Ford was still available it seemed unlikely that they would give up either if they intended to retire to the north bank. That left Fredericksburg as a possible escape route, and in fact there were reports from cavalry scouts that wagon traffic was heavy in that direction. But there was also a report from Stuart, waiting for Lee when he got back to the Widow Tapp's, that the Union cavalry had returned to Todd's Tavern this morning, in strength enough to drive the Confederate horsemen out and hold the place against all efforts to retake it. Todd's Tavern was down the Brock Road, midway between Grant's present position and Spotsylvania, which lay in the angle between the Richmond, Fredericksburg & Potomac and the Virginia Central railroads and offered an excellent approach to Hanover Junction, where the two lines crossed en route to Richmond from the north and west, both of them vital to the subsistence of Lee's army. Spotsylvania then, as Lee told Gordon, was his adversary's "best strategic point," if what he wanted was either to steal the lead in a race for Richmond or to take up a stout defensive position which Lee would be obliged to attack, whatever the tactical disadvantages, not only because it would sever his lines of supply, but also because it lay between him and the capital whose protection was his primary concern.

As evidence, this was far from conclusive, but it was persuasive enough to cause him to summon Brigadier General William N. Pendleton, the fifty-four-year-old former Episcopal rector who served as his chief of artillery, and instruct him to begin at once the cutting of a road through the woods, due south from the army's right flank on the Orange Plank Road, down to Shady Grove Church on the Catharpin Road — the midpoint for Lee, as Todd's Tavern, which was also on the Catharpin Road, was for Grant — to be used as soon as the first hard evidence reached headquarters that his opponent had taken, or was about to take, the first step in the race for Spotsylvania. The new road, if it was finished in time, would shorten the march by doing away with the need to backtrack down the plank road to Parker's Store before turning south; but this was small comfort alongside the knowledge that Grant even then would have a shorter route, a better road to travel all the way, and the advantage of deciding when the race would begin or whether, indeed, it would be run at all.

Another, and possibly greater, disadvantage lay in the fact that the lead corps on the march would be the First, since its position was on the right and therefore closest to the objective. Normally — as in the case of the movement into the Wilderness earlier this week — one or both of the other two corps, composed for the most part of Jackson's famed "foot cavalry," sought out the foe or rounded his flank to set him up for the Sunday punch methodical Old Peter would deliver when he came up in turn. Moreover, the corps was now to be commanded by a general, forty-two-year-old Richard Anderson, whose reputation had never been one for dash or fire and whose performance over the past year under Hill had been undistinguished at best, while at worst it had been a good deal less than that. At Gettysburg, for example, the kindest thing that could be said of the easy-going South Carolinian's lack of aggressiveness was that it had been due to sloth. His earlier record, made in the days when he commanded first a brigade and then a division under Longstreet, had been better, and this was Lee's main reason, together with the consideration that he was the senior major general with the army, for giving the post to him instead of Early, whom Lee otherwise preferred. A former member of the corps, which Early was not — Field was of recent appointment and Kershaw was still a brigadier — Anderson would be welcomed back by the officers and men of the two divisions he would command, while his Third Corps division would pass into the capable hands of Mahone, the army's senior brigadier. Yet this was perhaps the greatest of all gambles, the appointment of genial, uninspired Dick Anderson to replace his most dependable lieutenant at a time when dash and fire, both of which were conspicuous by their absence from his record, seemed likely to be the decisive factors in a contest that would begin at any moment and had Richmond for the prize. The fact that Lee was more or less obliged to take that gamble was one measure of the extent to which attrition was wearing down the army in his charge.

That afternoon he saw that still another such change was in the offing. Riding his line for the second time that day, he stopped off at Third Corps headquarters, which had been set up in a deserted house about midway between the plank road and the turnpike, and found A. P. Hill looking paler and sicker than ever. Though red-bearded Little Powell was unwilling to relinquish command at this critical juncture, it was evident that he soon would be obliged to do so. This meant that, once more — with Anderson transferred and Heth and Wilcox insufficiently seasoned — a temporary successor would have to be found outside a corps whose regular chief was incapacitated. In this case, however, the problem was simplified by having been faced beforehand, although in another connection; Jubal Early, runner-up as a candidate for command of the First Corps, would be brought in from the Second to lead the Third, at least until Hill recovered from the ailment he would not yet admit was grave enough to require him to step down. One dividend of this arrangement, similar to the one that had given Anderson's division to Mahone, was that Early's division could pass to Gordon, for whom Lee felt a growing admiration because of his performance yesterday. Lee's conversation with Little Powell was interrupted about 4 o'clock by a staff colonel who came down from the attic of the house, where he had established an observation post by ripping some shingles from the roof, to report on something he had seen with the aid of a powerful marine glass trained on what he believed was Grant's headquarters, a bit under two miles across the way. A number of heavy guns, held in reserve there all through the fighting, had just pulled out and headed south down the Brock Road, toward the Confederate right.

Though Grant's dead were still thickly strewn in the woods in front of his line, along with a few surviving wounded, and though none of the blue infantry had yet shown any sign of preparing for a shift, Lee took this limited artillery displacement as the first step in the race for Spotsylvania, which lay in the direction the guns had gone. Accordingly, he returned at once to the Tapp farm and issued orders for Anderson to march that night, taking Pendleton's just-cut southward trace through the woods to Shady Grove Church, then eastward across the Po River to Spotsylvania, which he was to hold against all comers: provided, of course, that he got there first. The new corps commander's instructions were for him to withdraw his two divisions from their present lines as soon as darkness masked the movement from the enemy, then give the troops a few hours' rest and sleep before setting out, at 3 o'clock in the morning, on the race for the objective a dozen miles away. Ewell and Hill were told to follow, in that order, as soon as they judged that the situation in their front would justify withdrawal.

In accordance with these instructions, Anderson pulled back about 9 o'clock, but finding no suitable rest area in the immediate rear — fires had sprung up again in the smouldering brush, fanned alive, as on the past two nights, by the early evening breeze — he set out at once, down Pendleton's trace, with the intention of making a bivouac farther south, outside the smoky battle zone, in which the men could get some rest between then and 3 a.m., the designated hour for the start of the march. He had not gone far, however, before he abandoned the notion of making any considerable halt at all. For one thing, there simply was no usable stopping place this side of Shady Grove, down along the fringes of the Wilderness, and for another the condition of the newly built "road," stump-pocked and cluttered with fallen trunks and limbs, was so miserable that the rate of march along it in the dark could scarcely be much better than a mile-an-hour crawl. He perceived that if he was to win the race for Spotsylvania he would need every minute of the four or five hours he would gain by keeping moving instead of halting in accordance with Lee's order; so he kept moving. Eager to do well on his first assignment as a corps commander, Anderson here rendered Lee and the Confederacy the greatest service of his career.

Jeb Stuart too had one of his great days, perhaps his finest, although the action promised little of the glory he had chased in former times. His three cavalry divisions, under Major Generals Wade Hampton, Fitzhugh Lee, and W. H. F. Lee — the first was a wealthy South Carolina planter-sportsman, fifteen years older at forty-six than his cinnamon-bearded chief, while the second and third, Virginians both, were respectively the commanding general's twenty-eight-year-old nephew and twenty-seven-year-old son — were scattered about the landscape to undertake the double task of protecting the Confederate march and impeding that of the Federals. There were six brigades, two in each division. Stuart assigned half of these to accompany the gray column, shielding its flank and clearing its front, while the other three moved out ahead to block and bedevil the bluecoats who were slogging southeast on a parallel route, a couple of densely wooded miles away. Brigadier General Thomas Rosser, detached from Hampton, led his brigade directly to Spotsylvania, under instructions to hold the place, if possible, until Anderson arrived. Fitz Lee meantime turned northwest, up the Brock Road, to give his full attention to the Federals moving down it: two brigades of mounted men opposing a four-division corps of infantry preceded by a cavalry division half again larger than his own. Near Todd's Tavern he put his troopers to work in the darkness, felling trees to obstruct the road as they withdrew. This gave the blue marchers almost as hard a time as their opponents were having on the crude trace across the way, and presently they had an added problem the Confederates did not have. When daylight began to filter through the thickets, the graybacks began to take potshots at the head and flanks of the Federal column, bringing it to a stumbling halt from time to time while details moved cautiously forward to flush the rebel marksmen out of their ambuscades. This continued, down past Alsop, to within two miles of Spotsylvania. There at last, beyond the fringes of the Wilderness and on comparatively open ground where he could bring his horse artillery into play, Fitz Lee had his dismounted men pile fence rails for a barricade and get down behind it, there in the dust of the road and the grass of the adjoining fields, for a last-ditch fight while couriers set out to bring Anderson cross-country to join in the defense. So far it had been cavalry against cavalry, and Fitz had managed to hold his own, despite the Union advantage of numbers and rapid-fire weapons. Sooner or later, however, the blue troopers would be replaced by infantry, brought forward Grant-style in a solid mass to overlap and overrun his flimsy breastwork. Unless Anderson came up fast and first, there would be nothing substantial between the Federals and Spotsylvania; Grant would have won the race whose prize was Richmond.

The sun by then was an hour high, and Anderson's two divisions, having covered nine miles on their all-night march out of the Wilderness, were ending an hour-long breakfast halt in the open fields, half a mile short of the Po and within about three miles of their objective. Sustained and heartened by the meal, such as it was — a frizzled chunk of fatty bacon, a piece of hardtack warmed and softened in the grease, and a cup of "coffee" boiled from roasted peanuts: poor fare, by any ordinary standards, but quite as much as they were accustomed to (and considerably more, in any case, than Warren's road-worn men received across the way) — the troops resumed their eastward march across the Po. Kershaw's division had the lead. About halfway to Spotsylvania, as he drew near a peculiar roadside dwelling built of squared logs and referred to locally as the Block House, he was met by a cavalry courier urging speed in the final heat of the race; Fitz Lee needed help, and he needed it quick. Fortified by the meager Sunday breakfast, the two front brigades quickened their step and hurried a mile northward, across the fields, to where the dismounted troopers were making their last-ditch stand on the Brock Road. "Run for our rail piles!" a cavalryman shouted as the men of the leading regiment came up. "The Federal infantry will reach them first if you don't run!"

They did run, and barely made it. Crouching behind the hastily improvised works, they opened fire on the advancing bluecoats at a range of sixty yards and blasted them back, at least for the moment. Thanks to Lee and Anderson, as well as to Stuart and Fitzhugh Lee — not to mention their own stout legs — they had won the race, although by a margin of less than a minute.

Whether it would stay won was another matter. Apparently not; for while the Federal infantry, recovering from the shock of having encountered more than cavalry in defense of the stacked rails, was massing for a heavier assault, Stuart sent word that Rosser's brigade had been driven out of Spotsylvania by a division of blue troopers who came surging down the road from Fredericksburg. Calm despite this evidence that the race had been lost after all, Anderson rerouted Kershaw's other two brigades, instructing them to proceed at once to the courthouse and fling the Federals out before they had time to intrench or bring in reinforcements. Field's division was coming up by now, and Anderson got the men into line on Kershaw's left, just in time to repulse a second and much heavier attack, which otherwise would have turned his western flank. No sooner had this been done than word came from the south that the blue horsemen had withdrawn from Spotsylvania of their own accord, apparently in the belief that they were escaping from a trap. Anderson at once summoned Kershaw's two detached brigades to rejoin him, leaving the defense of the town to Stuart, who by now had brought Fitz Lee down to help Rosser prevent a return by the rapid-firing Federals, in case they got their nerve back. Kershaw's men came hurrying up the Brock Road in time to extend his right and share in the repulse of a still heavier third assault by the Union infantry. This time, though they were punished even more cruelly in the course of their advance across the open fields and down the road, the bluecoats did not scatter or fall back as far as they had done before; they took up a semicircular position, just beyond easy rifle range of the defenders, and began to intrench.

This last was something the Confederates had been doing all along. Familiar enough with Grant's method by now to expect that at least one more all-out attack would be made on their line before the Union commander would be satisfied that it could not be shattered, they worked with picks and shovels and axes, bayonets and frying pans, tin cups and anything else that came to hand, improving and extending the fence-rail "works" they had inherited from Fitz Lee. By the time the sun swung past the overhead and the third assault had been repulsed, the artillery-studded defenses, extending about one mile west and half a mile east of the Brock Road, roughly a mile and a half from Spotsylvania, had grown as formidable as if they had been occupied for days. Across the way, however, in the woods and fields beyond the line the Federals were at work on, more blue troops were coming up and massing south of Alsop, obviously in preparation for a fourth assault, to be launched with greater numbers and on a broader front. Anderson's two divisions had fought Warren's four to a standstill, but now that Sedgwick's three were being added to the weight that Grant could bring to bear, the odds seemed overwhelming. About 2.30 the commanding general arrived, having ridden across the Po ahead of Ewell, whose corps by now was passing Shady Grove Church, a good two hours from the field of fight. Informed of the situation, Lee sent word for Ewell to hasten his march. This was no easy thing to ask of men who were trudging wearily through heat that was more like June than May, but fortunately the weather seemed to be having an even more lethargic effect on the Federals, who, unlike Ewell, had been marching all the previous night. It was 5 o'clock before they completed their leaden-legged dispositions and started forward. By then, Ewell's lead division had arrived and gone into position on Anderson's right, in time to block the attack on that flank and assist in driving the bluecoats back upon their works. It was smartly done, and that ended the fighting for the day.

Lee turned in early, rounding out a busy, fateful Sunday. Rising at 3 o'clock next morning — May 9; just one week ago today, although it seemed a great deal longer, he had stood on Clark's Mountain, extended a gauntleted hand, and told his assembled generals: "Grant will cross by one of those fords" — he wired the President of his success in frustrating the designs of the Army of the Potomac by winning the race for Spotsylvania: "We have succeeded so far in keeping on the front flank of that army, and impeding its progress, without a general engagement, which I will not bring on unless a favorable opportunity offers, or as a last resort. Every attack made upon us has been repelled and considerable damage done to the enemy." He expected the attacks to be renewed today, but he had little doubt of being able to withstand them, so long as the Federals held to the headlong methods they had favored on three of the past four days. A. P. Hill's corps, under Early — Hill had broken down at last, too sick to mount a horse, though he insisted on riding along in an ambulance in order to be with his men — was on the march even now, under instructions to come up on Ewell's right. With his army united and intrenched, dispositions complete and both flanks snug, Lee feared nothing the blue force could do, at least on this front, and he said as much in the telegram this morning. "With the blessing of God," he told Davis, "I trust we shall be able to prevent General Grant from reaching Richmond."

On the Union side, the trouble the leading elements had encountered in losing the race for Spotsylvania was compounded, in about equal parts, of weariness and Sheridan. Or perhaps it just came down to a prevalent loss of temper; weariness made tempers short, and Sheridan's was short enough already. In any case, after the elation that came with finding they were advancing, not retreating, the troops settled down to an ill-regulated march — stop and go, but mostly stop — that soon became what one of Sedgwick's men described as "a medley of phantasmagoria." Down on the Brock Road, tunneling southeast through the blackness, Warren's dust-choked marchers had it worse, for though the total distance was less, their progress was jerkier, mainly because of the cavalry up front, which seemed not only to have no definite notion of where it was going, but also to be in no hurry whatever to get there. One delay of about an hour, for example, was occasioned by an all-out fistfight between two cavalry regiments, one composed of veterans who effected a forcible exchange of their run-down horses for the well-groomed mounts of the other, made up of recruits who were not so green as to take such treatment without protest, even though the protest accomplished nothing except a prolongation of the delay. All this was short of Todd's Tavern, the midpoint of the march, where the real jam-up began.

Sheridan, like Stuart except that he began the campaign with 13,000 sabers, as compared to the Confederate 8500, had three divisions in his charge. One of these, James Wilson's, he ordered to move roundabout by the Fredericksburg road to Spotsylvania, while the other two, under Brigadier Generals Alfred Torbert and David Gregg, moved out in front of Warren's infantry to block the crossings of the Po before the rebels got there. So he intended. As all too often happened, however, someone failed to get the word — in this case, two someones: Gregg and Torbert. Reaching Todd's Tavern around midnight, Meade and his escort found the infantry column stalled and the crossroad jammed with Gregg's troopers, held up in turn by Torbert's, who were waiting for orders on the road beyond. Neither had been told what to do, and neither was doing anything at all. Meade got them moving by telling Gregg to proceed down the Catharpin Road toward Corbin's Bridge, where he would cover the wooded approaches from Parker's Store, and Torbert (or rather his senior brigadier, Wesley Merritt; Torbert was sick tonight) to remain on the Brock Road, clearing the way to Spotsylvania for the infantry and sending one brigade to the Block House, where it would stand in the path of any rebels on the march from Shady Grove. After issuing these instructions Meade sent word of them to Sheridan, wherever he might be, and rode back to get Warren on the move again. By now it was past 1 a.m. and the going was even slower than before. Up ahead, in the woods beyond the tavern, Merritt's troopers found the narrow road obstructed and enemy horsemen taking shots at them, out of the darkness, when they dismounted by lantern light to drag the just-felled timber from their path. This got worse as the march continued, especially for the infantry, with sudden starts and stops, races to close the resultant gaps, and long waits for the column to lurch into motion, segment by jangled segment. The first glimmers of daylight, so fervently hoped for in the gloom, only made things worse by improving the marksmanship of the snipers in the brush. Just before sunup Sheridan himself came pounding onto the scene on his big black horse. Fuming at Meade's highhanded "interference," which seemed to him to have exposed the cavalry to piecemeal destruction by scattering it about the countryside, he sent word for Wilson to withdraw at once from Spotsylvania, lest he be trapped there without adequate support when the rebel infantry arrived. Meantime the dismounted graybacks continued to snipe at the head of the column, toppling riders from their saddles. Beyond Alsop, within two miles of the courthouse — where, for all he knew, Wilson was being cut to pieces by superior numbers before he could pull out — Sheridan was galled even more by having to call on Warren's infantry to come forward with their bayonets and pry Fitz Lee's stubborn troopers out of their fence-rail barricade, which had proved too formidable for Merritt's frazzled cavalry to storm.

Chafed by the delays and aggravations, Warren was determined, now that Sheridan had his horsemen out of the way, to settle the issue before the defenders had time to strengthen their position on the low ridge just ahead, barely a mile and a half from the objective of his disjointed nightlong march. He told Brigadier General John C. Robinson, whose division had the lead, to attack as fast as his men could make it down the road. Weary, outdone, and unfed as they were, wobbly on their legs for lack of sleep, this wasn't very fast; but it was fast enough, as the thing developed, to accomplish their destruction in short order.

Robinson, a large, hairy New Yorker with an outsized beard and shaggy brows, a crusty manner, and a solid reputation earned in practically all of the major eastern battles, was at forty-seven Wadsworth's successor as the oldest division commander in the army. He studied the terrain, peering briefly out across a shallow valley, scarped along its bottom and lightly timbered, then up the gentle slope on its far side to where the graybacks crouched behind the fence rails they had stacked along the thickly wooded crest, about a quarter mile away. The scene had a certain bucolic charm, particularly by contrast with the smothering hug of the Wilderness, but Robinson found the situation tactically unpromising and he said as much to Warren, asking for time to bring up his three strung-out brigades and mass them before launching the assault. Warren said no, there was nothing across the way but dismounted cavalry; go in now, with the brigade at hand, and go in hard. This Robinson did, as hard at least as his winded men could manage after crossing the gullied valley and wheezing up the incline, only to have the rebel line explode in their faces, a scant sixty yards away. In quality and volume — a sudden, heavy bank of flame-stabbed smoke, jetting up and out, and a rattling clatter much too loud for carbines — the fire left no doubt that the line was occupied, not by cavalry, as the attackers had been informed when they set out, but by infantry who met them with massed volleys and blasted them back down the slope, a good deal faster than they had climbed it on their way to the explosion.

Nor was that the worst of the affair. By now the second brigade, four regiments of Maryland troops whose enlistments were to expire before the month was out, had come up and begun its descent into the valley, coincident with the arrival of Anderson's corps artillery on the ridge ahead. Startled to find the first wave of attackers in retreat from momentary contact with the rebels, the second was caught and churned up fearfully by a deluge of projectiles. The Marylanders broke, scrambling rearward in a race with the comrades they had intended to support. Dismayed and angered, Robinson hurried forward to rally them in person, but went down with a bullet through one knee. His third brigade fared no better, being struck in the flank and scattered by a savage counterattack, launched about as soon as it came up. This brought the casualty total to just under 1200 killed and wounded in less than an hour, while as many more were fugitives and stragglers, captured or otherwise unaccounted for. Robinson's knee wound cost him his leg, which was taken off that night. He was out of the war for keeps. And so, as another result of this brief engagement, was his division. It was disbanded next day, the remnants of its three cut-up brigades being distributed among the other divisions of the corps. Demoralized or not, these reinforcements were badly needed by all three, for they had suffered cruelly in the wake of Robinson's fiasco; Anderson's second division had arrived by then to strengthen the rebel line against the Federals, who were committed division by division, as fast as they came up, and division by division were repulsed. By the time Meade arrived, around midday, Warren had done his worst. He had to admit that he could not get over or around the Confederate intrenchments with what was left of his corps. Meade told him to hold what he had, then summoned Sedgwick from his reserve position, north of Alsop, to add the weight of his three divisions to the attack.

This took time — five hours, in all; Sedgwick's men were weary too — but the interim was livened, at any rate for the gossip-hungry clerks and staff, by a personality clash. Sheridan dropped by army headquarters, still fuming about last night's "interference," and Meade, losing his famous temper at last, retorted hotly that the cavalry had been doing less than had been expected of it ever since the campaign opened. That the charge was true did not make it any more acceptable to Sheridan, who replied, bristling, that he considered the remark a calculated insult. Meade recovered his balance for a moment. "I didn't mean that," he said earnestly, placing one hand on the cavalryman's shoulder in a conciliatory gesture. Sheridan stepped back out of reach ("All the Hotspur in his nature was aroused," a staff observer later wrote) and continued his protest. If the cavalry had done less than had been hoped for, he declared, it was not his fault, but Meade's; Meade had countermanded his orders, interfered with his tactical dispositions, and worst of all had kept his troopers hobbled by assigning them such unprofitable and distractive tasks as guarding the slow-plodding trains and providing escorts for the brass. If results were what Meade wanted, he should let the cavalry function as it was meant to function — on its own, as a compact hard-hitting body. Give him a free rein, Sheridan said, and he would tackle Jeb Stuart on his own ground, deep in the Confederate rear, and whip him out of his boots. The argument continued, both men getting madder by the minute, until Meade at last decided there was only one way to resolve their differences. He went to Grant.

Three days ago, the general-in-chief's reaction to a similar confrontation had been decisive. "You ought to put him under arrest," he had said of the riled-up Griffin. Today though, having heard Meade out, he seemed more amused than angered: especially by the bandy-legged cavalryman's reported claim that he would whip Jeb Stuart out of his boots if Meade would only turn him loose. "Did Sheridan say that?" he asked. Meade nodded. "Well," Grant said, "he generally knows what he's talking about. Let him start right out and do it."

Meade, having thus been taught the difference between eastern and western insubordination, returned to his own headquarters and issued the order; Sheridan would take off next morning, with all three of his divisions, on a maneuver designed to provoke Stuart into hand-to-hand combat by threatening the capital in his rear. Meantime Sedgwick was coming up. By 5 o'clock he had his three divisions in line alongside what was left of Warren's four, and all seven went forward, more or less together, in a final attempt to turn the day's disjointed fighting into a Union victory by taking possession of Spotsylvania, a mile and a half beyond the rebel works. It failed, as the earlier attacks had failed, because Lee again managed to get enough of his veterans — in this case, Ewell's lead division — up to the critical point in time to prevent a breakthrough. His losses had been light today, while Meade's had been comparatively heavy. "The ground was new to everyone, and the troops were tired," Meade's chief of staff explained.

For Grant, who smoked as he watched the sunset repulse, the day had been a grievous disappointment. Not only had he failed to pass Lee's front, but the resultant tactical situation in which he now found himself seemed to favor the defensive at least as much as had been the case in the one he abandoned, just last night, in the belief that it offered him little or no chance to achieve the Cannae he was seeking. Moreover, though he said that he left the Wilderness because he saw no profit in assaulting the works Lee's men had thrown up in the brush, the fortifications here were even more formidable, laid out on dominant ground between unfordable rivers, and getting stronger by the hour. Still smoking, he looked out across the shallow valley where so many of Warren's men had fallen — tousled rag-doll shapes becoming indistinguishable as the daylight faded into dusk — then turned, as imperturbable as ever, and rode back to his tent, there to make a study of the situation, based on such information as had been gathered.

Today's reconnaissance (for that was all it came to, in the end) had been costly, and next morning it grew more so, although nothing so patently wasteful as a repetition of yesterday's headlong approach to the problem was attempted. While Hancock and Burnside were on the march, summoned to come up on the right and left, Warren and Sedgwick limited their activities to improving their intrenchments and making a cautious investigation of the Confederate position. Restricted in scope by the absence of the cavalry, which had taken off soon after sunrise to challenge Stuart, this last was a gingerly business at best. Rebel marksmen, equipped with imported Whitworth rifles mounting telescopic sights, were quick to draw a bead on anything blue that moved, especially if it had a glint of brass about the shoulders. Moreover, in addition to this lack of respect for rank, they seemed to have none for the supposed reduction of accuracy by distance, with the result that there was a good deal of ducking and dodging on the Union side, even though the range was sometimes as great as half a mile. This not only interfered with work, it was also thought to be detrimental to discipline and morale. John Sedgwick looked at it that way, for one, and reproved his troops for flinching from a danger so remote. "What? Men dodging this way for single bullets?" he exclaimed when he saw one outfit react in such a manner to a far-off sniper. "What will you do when they open fire along the whole line? I am ashamed of you. They couldn't hit an elephant at this distance." The soldiers wanted to believe him, partly because they admired him so — "Uncle John," they called him with affection — but the flesh, being thus exposed, was weak; they continued to flinch at the crack of the sharpshooter's rifle, even though it was a good 800 yards away, and at the quick, unnerving whiplash of near misses, which seemed to part the hair of every man at once. "I'm ashamed of you, dodging that way," Sedgwick said again, laughing, and repeated: "They couldn't hit an elephant at this distance." Next time the glass-sighted Whitworth cracked, a couple of minutes later, Sedgwick's chief of staff was startled to see the fifty-year-old general stiffen, as if in profound surprise, and slowly turn his head to show blood spurting from a half-inch hole just under his left eye. He pitched forward, taking the unbraced colonel down with him, and though the doctors did what they could to help, they could not staunch or even slow the steady spurt of blood from the neat new hole beside his cheekbone. He smiled strangely, as if to acknowledge the dark humor of what had turned out to be his last remark, and did not speak again. Within a few minutes he was dead.

Sudden as it was, his death was a knee-buckling shock to the men of his corps, who had made him the best-loved general in the army. Besides, when corps commanders started toppling, alive one minute and dead the next, struck down as if by a bolt of blue-sky lightning, who was safe? All down the line, from brigadiers to privates, spirits were heavy with intimations of mortality. Sorrowfully, the staff carried his body back to army headquarters and laid it in a bower of evergreens beside the road, there to receive the salute of passing troops till nightfall, when he began the journey north to Cornwall Hollow, his home in the Connecticut Berkshires. Nor was the grieving limited to those who had served under him, or even under the same flag today; R. E. Lee, across the way, was saddened by this final news of his old friend. Meade wept, and Grant himself was stunned when he heard that Sedgwick had been hit. "Is he really dead?" he asked. Later, after characterizing the fallen general as one who "was never at fault when serious work was to be done," he told his staff that Sedgwick's loss was worse for him than the loss of a whole division. For the present, though, he found it hard to accept the fact that he was gone. "Is he really dead?" he asked again.

One fact was clear, in any case, and this was that a great many men of various ranks, now alive, were likely to be dead before long if they were ordered to overrun the intrenchments to their front. Formidable as these works had seemed at sundown, they were downright awesome this morning after an unmolested night of labor by the troops who manned them. Studded with guns at critical points throughout its convex three-mile length, Lee's Spotsylvania line was constructed, Meade's chief of staff declared, "in a manner unknown to European warfare, and, indeed, in a manner new to warfare in this country." Actually, it was not so much the novelty of the individual engineering techniques that made this log-and-dirt barrier so forbidding; it was the combination of them into a single construction of interlocking parts, the canny use of natural features of the terrain, and the speed with which the butternut veterans, familiar by now with the fury of Grant's assaults, had accomplished their intricate task. Traverses zigzagged to provide cover against enfilade fire from artillery, and head logs, chocked a few inches above the hard-packed spoil on the enemy side of the trench, afforded riflemen a protected slit through which they could take unruffled aim at whatever came their way. Where there were woods in front of the line, the trees were slashed to deny concealment for two hundred yards or more, and wherever the ground was open or insufficiently obstructed, timber barricades called abatis were installed within easy rifle range, bristling with sharpened sticks to entangle or slow the attackers while the defenders, more or less at their leisure, picked them off. For Grant, the prospect was altogether grim. To assault seemed suicidal, and yet to do nothing was militarily unsound, since a stalemate under such circumstances might well allow Lee to detach troops for operations against Butler or Sigel, back near Richmond or out in the Shenandoah Valley. On the other hand, to maneuver him out of position again by swinging wide around one of his flanks would amount to nothing more than a postponement of the inevitable showdown, which in that case would occur in closer proximity to his capital and would probably result in his being reinforced by units from the garrison charged with its ultimate defense. Grant pondered these three alternatives, unwelcome as they were, until about midday, when Burnside, coming up on the left, provided information which suggested a fourth alternative, more acceptable than the others. While making his far-out eastern swing across Ni River, the ruff-whiskered general reported, he had encountered Confederate infantry, and though he had not had much trouble driving them off, it seemed to him that they might be the leading element of a detached force of considerable strength, engaged in a deep penetration of the Federal left rear for a strike at the army's Fredericksburg supply base.

Burnside could scarcely be classed as a skilled assessor of enemy intentions, but in the absence of Sheridan's cavalry, which might otherwise have been sent out to confirm or refute the validity of the report, Grant accepted the information at face value, partly on grounds that such a move would be altogether in character for Lee. By now, after the buffeting he had taken in the course of the past five days, the old fox must be groping rather desperately in his bag of tricks for some such table-turning maneuver as the one he had devised, under similar circumstances, when he sent Jackson wide around Pope's flank for a strike at the supply base in his rear, compelling that hapless commander to abandon his position in short order. Grant's reaction was equally characteristic, and quite different. Instead of allowing concern for his base to deflect him from his purpose, he saw in this supposed development a chance to strike from an unexpected direction while his opponent's attention was distracted and his army was divided. Hancock, who had come up on the right, was instructed to detach one division, as a possible reinforcement for Burnside, and proceed westward with the other three for an upstream crossing of the Po. A fast march down the opposite bank — first south, to reach the road from Shady Grove, then eastward along it to the bridge one mile west of the Block House — would put him in position for a second crossing, well below the point where the rebel flank was anchored, and a sudden descent on Lee's left rear. At worst, this should bring the Confederates out of their intrenchments by obliging them to turn and meet the unexpected threat; while at best, assailed as they would be from two directions, north and south, it would result in their destruction. In any case that was the plan, devised in reaction to Burnside's report, and Grant considered it well worth a try, especially since the ablest of his surviving corps commanders was charged with its execution.

Hancock crossed upstream that afternoon, putting in three pontoon bridges, and encountered only sporadic opposition from butternut horsemen on the prowl. Even so, he had not reached the Shady Grove Road, leading eastward to the downstream point where he was to make the crossing that would land him in Lee's rear, before darkness obliged all three divisions to call a halt in the woods on the south bank. An early start next morning — Tuesday, May 10 — brought the head of the column within easy reach of Blockhouse Bridge by sunup. To Hancock's surprise, there on the opposite bank, fortifications had been thrown up overnight and were occupied in considerable strength, bristling with guns trained expectantly on the bridge and its approaches. Once more, with the help of his hard-working cavalry, Lee had forestalled a maneuver designed to discomfit or destroy him; Hancock could only regret that he had not waited until this morning to make his upstream crossing, in which case he would not have afforded the rebels a full night to work on their plans for his reception. Not much given to spilt-milk thinking, he devised an alternate crossing, half a mile downriver, and got one division in motion at once, intending to follow with the other two, when a courier arrived from Meade with instructions for a quick return by two of his divisions to their former position in line on the right of Warren. He himself was to come back with

them, the message directed, to take charge of his and Warren's corps
for an all-out frontal attack on the Confederate intrenchments at 5
o'clock that afternoon.... Hancock scarcely knew what to make of
this sudden change of plans. By now, one brigade of the advance
division was across the river; he had only to follow with the other
two divisions and Lee's flank would be turned; instead of which,
apparently, Meade intended to revert to a direct assault, Fredericksburg style, on fortifications that were admittedly the most formidable
ever constructed by an army in the field. Still, orders were orders, com-
prehensible or not. Recalling the crossed brigade, lest it be gobbled
up in the bridgehead it was holding, he left his lead division behind,
with instructions to continue what had now become no more than a
demonstration, and set out at once with the other two to recross the
Po by the three bridges they had installed with such high hopes the
day before.

Back on the main front, to which Hancock was returning, Grant
had ordered the change in plans as a result of Lee's failure to sustain
Burnside's assessment that he had detached a major portion of his army
for a strike at the Union supply base. In point of fact, what the IX
Corps had encountered on its approach march, down across the Ni the
day before, had not been infantry at all, but more of Stuart's
ubiquitous cavalry, dismounted as skirmishers to delay the Federal
concentration; Burnside had simply been mistaken, here as elsewhere
in his career, and Grant decided that if Lee had not divided his army,
it would be unwise for him to divide his own, particularly if this
involved detaching Hancock, his most dependable lieutenant, who
would be needed to help meet whatever crisis Lee had it in mind to
precipitate, not in theory but in fact. Accordingly, he had had Meade
summon Hancock back to his former position alongside Warren, who
had also contributed to the decision by informing his superiors that,
despite his failure yesterday, he believed he could score a breakthrough
today if he was properly supported. It was true, the attack would be
made against what seemed to be the most impregnable part of the rebel
line, but when Warren declared that he had examined it carefully and
believed it could be broken, Grant was altogether willing to give him
the chance to prove his claim. Hancock would come up on his right,
and Sedgwick's corps was already posted on his left; at 5 o'clock they
would all go forward together, and if Warren's judgment proved
sound, Lee's defenses would be pierced, his position overrun, and his
army shattered. Richmond then would be Grant's for the taking,
which in turn would mean that the war was approximately over, all
but the incidental task of picking up the pieces.

It did not work out that way for a variety of reasons. Like
Sheridan two days ago, Warren was anxious to accomplish something
solid that would cancel his poor showing up to now, and this apparently

made him oversanguine in his assessment of the chances for a break-through, as well as overeager to get started. Faulty judgment thus laid the groundwork for a failure which impatience served to enlarge. Around 3.30, with Sedgwick's corps alerted on his left and one of Hancock's divisions back in position on his right, he decided that to wait another hour and a half for jump-off time, as scheduled, would be to risk losing the opportunity he believed he saw. Or perhaps he acted out of knowledge that Hancock, when he came up on the right, would take command by virtue of his rank. In any case he appealed to Grant, through Meade, for permission to attack at once. Always ready to encourage aggressiveness, Grant was willing, and Warren — who had put on his dress uniform that morning, evidently for the purpose of making a good appearance on what he hoped would be his finest day since Gettysburg — went forward, around 4 o'clock; into chaos. Exposed in the slashings and snagged by the abatis, his troops were badly cut up, their ranks thrown into disorder by artillery and rifle fire from the flanks and dead ahead. Some among the bravest pressed on to within point-blank range of the rebel works, and a few even made it to the crest of the parapet. But that was all; there was no penetration anywhere along the line. Warren kept trying, only to have the process repeated. He was deeply discouraged at seeing his hopes break in blood on the rim of the intrenchments, even though Grant and Meade were not: not so deeply, at any rate, that it caused them to discontinue the effort to score a breakthrough here today. When Hancock arrived soon after 5 o'clock with his other division, back at last from his overnight excursion on the far side of the Po, he was ordered to resume the attack at 6.30, taking charge of all the troops on the right, his own and Warren's.

Elsewhere along the concave Union line, north and northwest of Spotsylvania, results had been no better up to now. Posted astride the Fredericksburg Road to block the movement Lee failed to make, Burnside had scarcely been engaged; his only consequential loss today was the commander of his lead division, Brigadier General T. G. Stevenson, a young Bostonian of high promise, who was killed instantly, much as Sedgwick had been the day before, by a long-range sniper. Sedgwick's corps, headed now by Horatio Wright, who was also a Connecticut-born professional, had made no more of a dent in the enemy defenses than Warren's corps had done, but a close-up look at the rebel works had given one brigade commander a notion of how to go about making a good deal more than a dent.

This was Colonel Emory Upton, a twenty-four-year-old New Yorker who had graduated from West Point less than a month after Sumter and since then, aside from a brief, unhappy period as a drill instructor of volunteers, had served with distinction in all the army's battles, winning five promotions along the way. Strong on theory, as

well as action, Upton returned from a personal examination of the
Confederate fortifications to report to his division chief, Wright's
successor Brigadier General David Russell, that he believed he knew a
way to score a breakthrough in short order. His notion was that the
troops should attack on a narrow front, four lines deep, without pausing
to fire until a limited penetration had been achieved; whereupon the
first line would fan out left and right to widen the breach and the
second would plunge straight ahead to deepen it, supported by the
third and fourth, which would form the reserve and be called upon,
as needed, in any or all of the three directions. Russell liked the plan
and took Upton to see the corps commander, who liked it too. In
fact, Wright liked it so well that he not only gave the young colonel
twelve regiments to use in the attack, but also arranged to have a full
division standing by to exploit whatever success was gained. Speed and
precision being the main elements, together with a clear distribution of
duties, Upton took the dozen unit commanders forward to the line of
departure, along the edge of a dense belt of pines 200 yards from the
rebel works, and indicated to each of them just what was expected of
him. The point selected for assault was about midway down the
western face of a salient which Ewell's corps had occupied to deny the
Federals possession of some high ground where they might otherwise
have posted batteries to enfilade this central portion of Lee's line, the
two wings of which slanted sharply back from the salient or "angle,"
as it was called. Rebel guns were thick in there, thicker than anywhere
else along the line, but it was Upton's plan to get among them fast and
overwhelm the crews before they had much chance to use them. Having
explained all this to the individual leaders, and shown them their
objectives on the map and on the ground, he told them to bring their
regiments forward, one at a time to avoid attracting attention to the
buildup, and post them under cover for the assault, which was set for
6 o'clock, one hour before sunset and two before dark.

At ten minutes past the appointed time, having waited for the prearranged bombardment to die down, Upton gave the signal and the
column started forward with a cheer, three regiments in each of its
four lines. Almost at once the rebel guns took up the challenge, blasting
away at the mass of bluecoats running toward them across the field, but
despite the delay involved in breaking through the tangled abatis, set
up about midway between the woods and the intrenchments, men of
all three leading regiments were mounting the parapet within five
minutes of the jump-off. These first arrivers were shot or bayonetted or
clubbed back — Upton later reported that at this stage the defenders
"absolutely refused to yield the ground" — but as others came up, the
weight of numbers began to tell. Presently there was hand-to-hand
fighting in the trenches, which broke off when the second wave of
attackers arrived and the badly outweighed Confederates turned and

ran for their secondary defenses, just under 200 yards in their rear. Many did not make it, being captured or shot down. Meantime the first Federal line had fanned out left and right, widening the gap, and the reserves were surging forward to support the second in its continued penetration. So far, everything had worked precisely as Upton had planned; the rebel line was broken. Whether the break would be extended, or even remain — Confederate reinforcements were coming in fast by then from other parts of the salient — depended now on the division Wright had given the assignment of exploiting just such a success as had been gained.

This was not one of his own divisions, but the one that had been detached from Hancock when he crossed the Po the day before. Originally intended for support of the IX Corps, it had been attached to Wright when the threat to Burnside turned out to be nonexistent, and Wright had given its commander, Gershom Mott, instructions to support Upton by advancing simultaneously on the apex of the "angle," thus to divert the attention of the defenders away from the main effort, midway down the western face of the salient; after which he was to move fast to consolidate, and if possible enlarge, whatever gains had been scored in that direction. As it turned out, he was only too successful, both for his own sake and for Upton's, in carrying out the first half of this assignment. Forming his two brigades in full view of the objective, half a mile away, Mott did such a thorough job of attracting the attention of the rebels (particularly the gunners, who had crowded into that narrow space no fewer than 22 pieces of artillery with which to take him under fire across half a mile of open ground) that his division was knocked to pieces within minutes. Already badly shaken by their Wilderness experience, the troops milled about briefly under this pounding, some of them attempting ineffectively to return the fire with their outranged rifles, then scuttled backward in confusion, seeking cover and concealment. Staff officers, sent out to search for them that evening, found them deep in the rearward woods, huddled in groups about their regimental flags and boiling coffee to help them recover from the shock. Like Robinson's division, which had gone out of existence as a result of its misadventure two days ago, Mott's too would presently be abolished, the remnant of its two brigades being assigned three days afterward to another division in Hancock's corps.

But that was later. A more immediate consequence of the rout was that Upton's breakthrough went for nothing, not only because he was left without support, but also because the defenders now were free to concentrate all their attention and strength on healing the breach. This they were quick to do, obliging Upton to fight his way out of the rebel lines with much of the fervor and urgency he had displayed while fighting his way in. Darkness, gathering fast after sundown, was a help in the disengagement; all twelve regiments made it

back to their own lines, having suffered about one thousand casualties.
That was also about the number they inflicted, mostly in the form of
prisoners taken in the initial rush and escorted into the Federal lines
before the counterattack obliged their captors to follow in their wake.
Far on the right, Hancock's attack, deferred till sunset, was repulsed at
about the same time, as decisively as Warren's had been earlier, and
Burnside continued his pointless vigil on the left. Night came down as
the fighting ended. Men sat around campfires and discussed the events
of the day, which provoked much blame of Mott and praise for Upton.
Across the way, notes faint in the distance and filtered through the
trees, a Confederate band lent an eerie touch to the scene by playing
"Nearer, My God, to Thee," but this was offset to some extent, or
anyhow balanced, when a Union band responded with the "Dead
March" from *Saul*.

     One of Upton's warmest admirers was the general-in-chief, who
rewarded him with a battlefield promotion — subject, of course, to
Washington approval — "for gallant and meritorious services." Much
encouraged by the young colonel's tactical contribution, which he saw
as the key to Lee's undoing if the maneuver could be repeated on a
larger scale and properly supported, Grant was in high spirits. A headquarters orderly saw him talking to Meade about the prospect that
night with unaccustomed animation, puffing rapidly on a cigar. "A
brigade today," he was saying; "we'll try a corps tomorrow."

     Thinking it over he realized however that tomorrow would be
too soon. One trouble with today's attack was that it had been launched
with not enough daylight left for its full exploitation; dawn would be
a much better time in that regard, and the preceding darkness would
help to conceal the massing of large bodies of troops within charging
distance of the rebel works. So Grant, having ruled out tomorrow, decided that the assault would be delivered at first light on the following
day, May 12 — which would also give him plenty of time for briefing
all commanders, high and low, and an unhurried movement of units,
large and small, into their designated jump-off areas. Given the method,
the tactical execution was fairly obvious. Hancock would be shifted
from the far right to the center, where he would be in charge of the
main effort, and he would make it with his whole corps, against the
very point that Mott had failed to hit today, the apex of the "angle,"
the military theory being that the tip of a salient was hard to defend
because fire from the lines slanting back from that forward point
could not converge on a force advancing from dead ahead. It was true,
this theory had not applied too well on that same ground today; Mott
had been wrecked before he got within reach of the objective. But
Hancock's assault would be delivered Upton-style, without pauses for
alignment or for firing, and if it worked as well for him as it had
worked for Upton, his men would be up to the enemy works, and

maybe over them, before the defenders had time to offer much resistance. Moreover this attack, unlike the one today, would be heavily supported. Burnside, off on the left, would move up close tomorrow night and launch a simultaneous assault next morning against the salient's eastern face, while Wright and Warren kept up the pressure on the right and the far right. Further details could be worked out next day, when the formal order was drawn up. In any case, after Upton's demonstration late today, a Tuesday, Grant had little doubt that Lee's defenses would be breached on Thursday and that careful planning would see to it that the breach was enlarged to victory proportions. He went to bed in a better frame of mind than he had done on any of the other five nights since May 4, when his army completed its crossing of the Rapidan unopposed.

That his mood was still the same on Wednesday, hopeful and determined, was demonstrated shortly after breakfast by his response to a request from a distinguished visitor, U. S. Representative Elihu B. Washburne of Illinois, that he give him some word of encouragement to take back to Washington with him. Grant's congressional guardian angel from the outset of the war, Washburne had spent the past week at headquarters, where, incongruous in somber civilian broadcloth amid the panoply of the staff, he had been something of a puzzle to the troops; they could not figure who or what he was, until a wit explained that the general, with his usual concern for the eventualities, had brought his private undertaker along on the campaign. Now that he was returning to his duties at the capital, the congressman told Grant as they stood outside the latter's tent to say goodbye, it might be a good idea to relieve the anxiety of the President and the Secretary of War by sending them some word on the progress of the fighting here in Virginia. "I know they would be greatly gratified," Washburne said, "if I could carry a message from you giving what encouragement you can as to the situation." Grant looked doubtful. He was aware that anything of the kind would be released to the public, and he did not want to be hurt, as others before him had been hurt, by the boomerang effect of overoptimistic statements. Pleased though he was with his progress so far, he replied, he knew that the road ahead was a long one and he was therefore "anxious not to say anything just now that might hold out false hopes to the people." He hesitated, then added: "However, I will write a letter to Halleck, as I generally communicate through him, giving the general situation, and you can take it with you." He stepped inside the tent, sat down at his field desk, and after heading a sheet of paper, "Near Spottsylvania C. H., May 11, 1864 — 8.30 a.m.," scribbled a couple of hundred words, puffing away at his cigar as he wrote. "We have now ended our sixth day of very hard fighting," he informed Halleck. "The result up to this time is much in our favor. But our losses have been heavy, as well as those of the enemy. . . . I am now sending back to Belle Plain all my wagons for a fresh supply of provisions and ammunition, and purpose to fight it out on this line if it takes all summer.... I am satisfied the enemy are very shaky, and are only kept up to the mark by the greatest exertions on the part of their officers and by keeping them intrenched in every position they take."

When he finished he had a clerk make a fair copy, which he then signed and folded and gave to Washburne, along with a farewell handshake, before returning to work on his plans for tomorrow's dawn assault. Staff officers read the retained draft of the letter, one afterwards recalled, without finding in it anything unusual or "epigrammatic" until a few days later, when the New York papers reached camp with excerpts from it splashed across their front pages in large headlines — particularly a phrase or sentence which someone, either the copyist here or another at the far end, polished up a bit: "I propose to fight it out on this line if it takes all summer." That caught the attention of the editors, and through them the public, with a force unequaled by anything Grant had said or written since the Unconditional Surrender note at Donelson, more than two years ago. "I propose to move immediately upon your works" had passed into history as a watchword signifying Federal determination to press for total victory over the forces in rebellion, and so too, now, did "I propose to fight it out on this line if it takes all summer."

Grant's assessment of the Confederates as "very shaky" indicated that he had not really believed it would take "all summer" to settle the issue at hand that Wednesday morning, north of Spotsylvania. By mid-afternoon — coincident with a sudden change in the weather, brought on by a light drizzle of rain that dropped the temperature from the unseasonable high it had been holding for the past few days — the field order for tomorrow's attack was being distributed to the commanders of all four corps. Already in close proximity to the enemy along their respective portions of the line, Warren and Wright would remain more or less where they were, and Burnside had only a limited adjustment to make. It was otherwise with Hancock, who had to shift three of his divisions into position with the fourth, Mott's, which by now, although considerably diminished and dejected, had been reassembled just in rear of the area where it had begun its ill-fated advance the day before. The division he had left beyond the Po when he returned with the other two, in accordance with orders from Meade, had also recrossed the river after a clash with a rebel force Lee sent over from his right, and in this rear-guard action the division had had to leave behind a gun that, in the haste of the withdrawal, got wedged so tightly between two trees that it could not be freed. Hancock took this hard, the more so because it was the only piece of artillery the II Corps had ever lost in battle, and he was determined to get full revenge tomorrow.

Just now, though, he had his hands full getting his troops into position for the attack at first light, which the almanac said would come at 4 a.m. The march began at dusk, along a narrow road soon churned to mud by a pelting rain that seemed to be getting harder by the hour. It was midnight before the head of the column reached the jump-off area and the four divisions, three of them wet and cold from their rainy march, started forming in the dripping woods. This too was a difficult business, for more reasons than the unpleasantness of the weather or the loss of sleep and lack of food. Here on reconnaissance earlier that day, unable to see far or clearly through the steely curtain of rain, Hancock had tried to get Mott's disheartened men to drive the enemy pickets back so he could get a look at the objective; but little or nothing came of the attempt — they had too vivid a memory of what those 22 guns up there had done to them the day before — with the result that his examination of the apex of the "angle," along with most of the intervening ground across which he would charge, had practically been limited to what he could learn from the map. And so it was to-night, in the rain and darkness. The best Hancock could do was give his division commanders a compass bearing, derived from the map by drawing a line connecting a house in their rear with a house in the approximate center of the rebel salient, and tell them to move in that direction when they received his order to advance.

Four o'clock came, but not daylight; the almanac had not taken the rain or fog into account. Finally at 4.30, though there still was scarcely a glimmer of light from what the compass showed to be the east, word came for the lead division to go forward, followed closely by the other three.

Fearing the worst as they stumbled forward through fog so dense that it held back the dawn, Hancock and his soldiers were in better luck than they had any way of knowing. For one thing, those 22 guns assigned to defend the apex of the salient up ahead, which they expected to start roaring at any moment, tearing their close-packed ranks with shot and shell within seconds of hearing a picket give the alarm, were by no means the threat they had been two days ago, when they all but demolished one of these four divisions attempting this same thing on this same ground. They were in fact no threat at all. They were not there. They had been withdrawn the night before, as the result of an overdue error by Lee, whose intelligence machinery, after a week of smooth if not uncanny functioning, had finally slipped a cog.

Reports of activity beyond the Union lines had been coming in from various sources all the previous afternoon. A lookout perched in the belfry of a Spotsylvania church, which commanded a view of the roads in rear of the enemy left, informed headquarters of what seemed to be a large-scale withdrawal in that direction, and this was confirmed between 4 and 5 o'clock by two messages from Lee's cavalryman son, whose division — left behind by Stuart when he took out after Sheridan, two days ago, with three of his six brigades — was probing for information in that direction. Heavy trains were in motion for Fredericksburg, young Lee declared, and Federal wounded were being taken across the Rappahannock in large numbers to Belle Plain, eight miles beyond on the Potomac. "There is evidently a general move going on," he notified his father. Here as in the Wilderness, the southern commander was alert to the danger of having his opponent steal a march on him, and here as there he was prepared to react on the basis of information less than conclusive or even substantial. Such activity in Grant's left rear could mean that, having found the Spotsylvania confrontation unprofitable and restrictive, he had one of two strategic shifts in mind: 1) a limited retreat to Fredericksburg, where he would consolidate his forces and better cover his supply line for a subsequent advance by land or water, or 2) another swing around the Confederate right, to interpose his army between Lee and Richmond. From Lee's point of view, though a similar endeavor had failed four days ago, the latter was the more dangerous maneuver, one that he simply could not afford to have succeed. In this case, however, he believed from the evidence that what Grant was about to attempt was a withdrawal to the Rappahannock line, and he wanted to prevent this — or, more strictly speaking, take advantage of it — almost as much as he did the other. In conversation with two of his generals about an hour before sundown he told why.

It began as a discussion of Grant's worth as a tactician. Lee was visiting Harry Heth's headquarters, on the far right near the courthouse, as was A. P. Hill, up and about but still not well enough to return to duty, when a staff officer happened to remark that, in slaughtering his troops by assaulting earthworks, the Union commander was little better than a butcher. Lee did not agree. "I think General Grant has managed his affairs remarkably well up to the present time," he said quietly. Then he turned to Heth and told him what he had come for. "My opinion is the enemy are preparing to retreat tonight to Fredericksburg. I wish you to have everything in readiness to pull out at a moment's notice, but do not disturb your artillery till you commence moving. We must attack those people if they retreat."

Hill spoke up, pale but impetuous as always. "General Lee, let them continue to attack our breastworks. We can stand that very well."

The talk was then of casualties, and though no one knew the actual number of the fallen on either side (Grant in fact had lost about 7000 men by now in front of Spotsylvania, while Lee was losing barely one third that many) all expressed their satisfaction with the present position, which they were convinced they could maintain longer than the Federals could afford to keep assaulting it. Lee rose to go; "We must attack those people if they retreat," he had declared, and in parting he explained what he meant by that. "This army cannot stand a siege," he said. "We must end this business on the battlefield, not in a fortified place."

From there he rode in the rain to the center, where Ewell had disposed his three divisions to defend the salient, one along its eastern face and the apex, another along its western face, where Upton had scored an abortive breakthrough yesterday, and the third in reserve, posted rearward under instructions to move quickly in support of any stricken point along the inverted U of the intrenched perimeter. Dubbed the "Mule Shoe" by its defenders in description of its shape, the position was a little under a mile in depth and about two thirds as wide, heavily wooded for the most part and crisscrossed by a few narrow, winding roads. Because of this last, which would make removal of the guns a difficult business in the dark and the deepening mud, Lee told Ewell to get the batteries that were posted in the forward portion of the salient withdrawn before nightfall, in order to avoid delaying pursuit of the Federals when word arrived that their retreat was under way. It was close to sunset now, and while Ewell got to work on this Lee rode to First Corps headquarters on the left. After giving Anderson the instructions he had earlier given Heth — to be ready to pull out at a moment's notice, but to leave his artillery in position until then — the gray commander returned to his tent to get what sleep he could between then and 3.30, his usual rising time at this critical stage of the campaign.

Within the salient, as night wore on and the rain came down harder, a feeling of uneasiness, which began with the departure of the guns, pervaded the bivouacs and trenches. At first it was vague — "a nameless something in the air," one soldier was to call it, looking back — but after midnight it grew less so, particularly for the men who held the "toe" of the shoe-shaped line and were closest to the enemy position. A sort of rumble, slow but steady, came from the saturated darkness out in front; some likened it to the muffled thunder of a waterfall, others to the grinding of a powerful machine. Veterans who heard it, over and under the pelting of the rain, identified it as the sound of troops in motion by the thousands. Either a retreat was under way, as Lee had said, or else a heavy attack was in the making. If it was the latter, there was difficulty in telling whether the enemy was moving to the left or right, for a strike at Anderson or Early, or massing for another assault on the Mule Shoe. One of Edward Johnson's brigade commanders, Brigadier General George H. Steuart, a Maryland-born West Pointer, went out to his picket line for a closer investigation. He had not listened long before he decided that the Federals not only were preparing an attack, but were aiming it at him. His next thought was of the gun pits standing empty along his portion of the works, and he went at once to Johnson to urge the prompt return of his artillery, parked since sundown back near Spotsylvania. Old Allegheny passed the request to

Ewell, who approved it. All 22 of the withdrawn guns would be back in position by 2 o'clock, he said.

When the appointed time had come, but not the guns, Steuart's anxiety mounted. After waiting another hour he went again to Johnson, who had a staff officer make the round of the brigades with orders for the troops to turn out and check the condition of their rifles, while another rode back to inform Ewell that the artillery had not arrived as promised. All this time, that muffled grinding sound continued in the outer darkness. Shortly before 4.30, just as the fog began to lift a bit, Johnson was relieved to learn that the missing guns were returning up the road from the base of the salient. Before they came in sight, however, the sound out front in the paling darkness rose in volume and intensity, drawing nearer, until it became the unmistakable tramp of a marching host. From a distance of about 300 yards a mighty cheer went up — the deep-chested roar of charging Federals, as distinguished from the high-throated scream that was known as the rebel yell — and heavy masses of blue infantry, close-packed and a-bristle with bayonets glinting steely in the dawn, broke through the fog directly in front of the apex of the salient. Alerted, the Confederates rose and gave the attackers point-blank volleys. In some cases the fire was effective, while in others it was not, depending on whether unit commanders had acted on the warning to have their men draw the dampened charges from their rifles and reload. Not that it mattered tactically; for whether their losses were high or low, the various elements of the dense blue mass surged up and over the parapet, into the trenches. Johnson, who was sometimes called "Old Clubby" because of the stout hickory stick he used as a cane to favor the leg he had been shot in, two years back, limped about amid the confusion and implored his troops to keep fighting, despite the odds; the guns would soon be up to settle the issue, he told them, and for a moment it seemed to be true. The lead battery unlimbered, there in the toe of the Mule Shoe, and managed to get off one round each from two of the pieces. But that was all. "Stop firing that gun!" the cannoneers heard someone shout as they prepared to reload, and looked around to find scores of rifles leveled at them by hard-eyed Federals who had broken the gray line. They raised their hands. Others were less fortunate, taking fire from all directions before they knew the place had been overrun. "Where shall I point the gun?" a rattled corporal asked a badly wounded lieutenant. "At the Yankees," he replied with his last breath. But the two rounds already gotten off were all that were fired before all but two of the 22 guns were surrendered, most of them still in limber on the road.

Lee was breakfasting by lantern light when the rapid-fire clatter erupted in the Mule Shoe to inform him that the enemy, far from retreating, was launching an assault upon his center, which he had stripped of guns the night before. From the volume of sound he knew the attack was a heavy one, and presently, when he mounted Traveller to ride in that direction, he saw at first hand that, so far at least, it had also been successful. Fugitives fled past him, streaming rearward, with and without their weapons. "Hold on!" he cried, removing his hat so they would know him. "Your comrades need your services. Stop, men!" Some stopped and some kept running past him with a wild look in their eyes. "Shame on you men; shame on you!" he called after them in his deep voice. "Go back to your regiments." As he drew near the base of the salient he met an officer from Edward Johnson's staff riding to bring him word of what had happened up ahead. Pouring in through a quick break just east of the apex, which was held by Stonewall Jackson's old Manassas brigade, the Federals had fanned out rapidly, left and right, to come upon the adjoining brigades from the flank and rear. Johnson himself had been taken, after being surrounded and very nearly shot because he would not stop hobbling about, brandishing his hickory club and calling for his troops to rally, even though a whole company of bluecoats had their rifles trained on him. Steuart too was a prisoner, along with a number of his soldiers, and the Stonewall Brigade had surrendered practically en masse when the enemy came up in its rear and blocked the possibility of escape. In all, no less than half of Johnson's 5000-man division had been shot or captured in the first half hour of fighting, along with twenty guns and well over half of the regimental flags.

That was the worst of it. On the credit side, Lee was presently to learn, Rodes's division, by "refusing" its flank adjoining the break at the apex, was holding fast to the western face of the salient, and Wilcox had managed to do the same on the right, where Early's line joined Ewell's, even though an attack of nearly equal strength had been made against that point by Burnside at about the same time Hancock struck. This meant that, up to now at any rate, the breakthrough was laterally contained. Whether it could also be contained in depth was another matter, and it was to this that Lee gave his immediate attention. "Ride with me to General Gordon," he told the orphaned staff man, and continued to spur Traveller toward the open end of the Mule Shoe, where Gordon's division had been posted with instructions to support Rodes or Johnson in such a crisis as the one at hand.

Gordon had already begun to meet the situation by sending one of his three brigades forward on a wide front, the men deployed as skirmishers to blunt the Federal penetration, and was preparing to counterattack with the other two, his own Georgians and Pegram's Virginians, when Lee rode up. "What do you want me to do, General?" Gordon asked. Lee wanted him to do just what he was doing, and said so, knowing only too well that unless the Union drive was stopped his army would be cut in half. Gordon saluted and returned to the work at hand. However, as he was about to give the signal to go forward he looked back and saw that Lee, faced with a crisis as grave as the one six days ago in the Wilderness, was responding in the same fashion here at Spotsylvania. Still with his hat off, he had ridden to a position near the center of the line, between the two brigades, with the obvious intention of taking part in the charge. Horrified — for he knew how great the danger was, even here near the base of the salient, having just had his coat twitched by a stray bullet out of the woods he was about to enter — the young brigadier wheeled his horse and rode back to confront his gray-haired chief. "General Lee, this is no place for you," he told him. "Go back, General; we will drive them back." Soldiers from both brigades began to gather about the two horsemen for a better view, and Gordon spoke louder, wanting them to reinforce his plea. "These men are Virginians and Georgians. They have never failed you. They never will. Will you, boys?" The answer was prompt and vociferous. "No! No!" "General Lee to the rear; Lee to the rear!" "We'll drive them back for you, General!" Lee kept looking straight ahead, apparently determined not to be put off, until a tall Virginia sergeant took the matter into his own hands by grabbing Traveller's rein, jerking his head around, and leading him rearward through the cheering ranks.

Behind him Lee heard Gordon's voice ring out above the roar of battle, which grew louder as the breakthrough deepened: "Forward! Guide right!" And while the Virginians and Georgians crashed into the woods to come to grips with the attackers, as they had promised they would do, the southern commander resumed his higher duties. Of these, the most immediate was to find some means of strengthening the counterattack now being launched, and in this connection his first thought was of the fugitives, the troops blown loose from their units when the forward part of the salient went. "Collect together the men of Johnson's division and report to General Gordon," he told the orphaned staffer. That would help, though probably not enough. He thought then of Mahone's division, detached from Early two days ago to meet the threat from across the Po at Blockhouse Bridge, and sent word for Mahone to leave one brigade in the newly dug intrenchments there, protecting his flank, and move at once with the other three to reinforce Gordon's effort to restore the integrity of his broken center.

In point of fact Gordon was already doing remarkably well on his own, first by stemming, then by reversing the flow of the blue flood down the salient. His success in this unequal contest — in effect, a matching of three brigades against four divisions — was due in part to the fury of his assault, inspired by Lee, and in part to the assistance given by the hard-core remnant of Johnson's division, as well as by the troops from the adjoining divisions of Rodes and Wilcox, whose interior flanks hooked onto the wings of his line as he advanced. All this helped; but perhaps the greatest help came from the Federals themselves, who by then were in no condition, tactically or otherwise, to offer sustained resistance to what Gordon threw at them. Boiling over the works and onto unfamiliar ground, a maze of trenches and traverses, thickly wooded in spots and cluttered with prisoners and debris, they scarcely knew which way to turn in order to make the most of the breakthrough they had scored with such comparative ease and speed. The impetus at this point came mainly from the rear, as more and more of Hancock's men continued to pour into the salient; eventually there were close to 20,000 of them in an area less than half a mile square, with such resultant jumbling of their ranks that what had been meant to be a smoothly functioning military formation quickly degenerated into a close-packed mob, some of whose members were so tightly wedged against their fellows that, like muscle-bound athletes, they could not lift their arms to use their weapons. It was at this discordant stage that Gordon struck, and the effect of his fire on the men in that hampered mass of blue was appalling. A bullet could scarcely miss its mark, or if it did it struck another quite as vital. Turning to breast the pressure from the rear, where there was little knowledge of what was going on up front, they broke as best they could, a stumbling herd, and fled back up the salient to gain the protection of the intrenchments they had crossed on their way in. Gordon's troops came after them, screaming and firing as they ran.

Down the eastern face of the salient, the critical point being near its base, where Ewell's line joined Early's, Burnside had attacked at about the same time Hancock did; but there was less confusion here, on both sides, for the simple reason that there had been no penetration. Recoiling, the three blue divisions — made up of greener, less determined men than the veterans under Meade — found what cover they could, within range of the rebel works, and contented themselves with firing at whatever showed above the parapet. This gave Wilcox so little trouble that he was free to assist in Gordon's counterattack, thus helping to keep Hancock off his flank. Across the way, down the western face of the salient, Rodes was able to do the same, for the even simpler reason that he had not been hit at all; not yet. But then at 6 o'clock, with Hancock's attackers tamped firmly back into the toe of the Mule Shoe, Wright struck. He came up hard, with everything he

had, against that portion of Rodes's front where Upton had scored
the original breakthrough, two days back. Rodes managed to prevent
a repetition of that archetypical success, though only by the hardest.
Much of the fighting was hand-to-hand, across the works, but Wright's
attack, like Hancock's, was muscle-bound, hampered by its bulk; he too
had close to 20,000 men and he was mindful of Grant's concern that
he bring the weight of every one of them to bear. Rodes kept his
badly outnumbered division in position, but he knew that the line
might go with a rush at any moment under all that pressure. Accordingly, he sent word to Lee that if he was to prevent a second breakthrough — potentially even more dangerous than the first, since it
would put the attackers in rear of practically every Confederate in the
salient — he must have reinforcements, and have them quick.

They were already on the way from Blockhouse Bridge. Sent for
earlier to strengthen Gordon's counterattack, the three brigades from
Mahone's division could be used instead to shore up Rodes; provided
of course that they came up in time. Impatient at their nonarrival, Lee
rode westward in rear of Anderson's position — which had not been
attacked, so far, but was under fire from Warren's long-range artillery
— to meet them and save time by redirecting their march to the hard-
pressed west face of the salient, where the Federals were hammering at
the works. Presently he came upon the lead brigade, Carnot Posey's
Mississippians, now under Brigadier General Nathaniel Harris, a thirty-
year-old former Vicksburg lawyer. Lee rode alongside Harris, giving
instructions, and the Union gunners, spotting the column in brisk motion
across the way, lengthened their ranges to bring it under fire. They
concentrated mainly on the horsemen at its head, with the result that
Lee had to give all his attention to Traveller, who began to rear wildly
amid a flurry of plunging shot and bursting shell. Lee kept his seat,
doing what he could to calm the animal, but Traveller kept rearing. It
was well he did; for as he went back on his hind legs, boxing the air
with his forehoofs, a solid shot, which otherwise would have killed
or maimed both horse and rider, passed directly under his belly.
Horrified, the Mississippians began to yell: "Go back, General! Go
back! For God's sake, go back!" They tried to get between him and the
exploding shells, urging him to hurry out of range, but Lee was in no
more of a mind to retire from this fourth Lee-to-the-rear tableau than
he had been to quit the other three. His blood was up, now as before;
anxiety was on him. At last he said, "If you will promise me to drive
those people from our works, I will go back." The soldiers cheered
and, while Lee watched admiringly, took up the march at a faster rate,
joining Rodes in time to prevent a breakthrough which one of his
brigadiers had just warned him was only minutes away.

Now, however, this second phase of the contest, which ended
with the approximate restoration of Lee's line, merged into the third,

a struggle even fiercer than the two that had gone before. Tamped back into the toe of the Mule Shoe, Hancock's troops found cover by recrossing the log parapet and taking shelter behind it. There they stayed and there they fought, sometimes at arm's length, much as Wright's men were doing on their right, down the western face of the salient, where the region of Upton's abortive penetration acquired a new name: The Bloody Angle. The term had been used before, in other battles elsewhere in the war, but there was no doubt forever after, at least on the part of those who fought there, that here was where the appellation best applied. It soon became apparent to both sides that what they were involved in now was not only fiercer than what had gone before, today, but was in fact more horrendous than what had gone before, ever. This was grimmer than the Wilderness — a way of saying that it was worse than anything at all — not so much in bloodshed, although blood was shed in plenty, as in concentrated terror. These were the red hours of the conflict, hours no man who survived them would forget, even in his sleep, forever after. Fighting thus at arm's length across that parapet, they were caught up in a waking nightmare, although they were mercifully spared the knowledge, at the outset, that it was to last for another sixteen unrelenting hours. "All day long it was one continuous assault," a Pennsylvanian would recall. But in truth it was as much a defense as it was an attack, on either side, and the two were simultaneous. Neither victory nor defeat was any longer a factor in the struggle. Men simply fought to keep on fighting, and not so much on instinct as on pure adrenalin. Slaughter became an end in itself, unrelated to issues or objectives, as if it had nothing whatever to do with the war. Troops were killed by thrusts and stabs through chinks in the log barricade, while others were harpooned by bayonetted rifles flung javelin-style across it. Sometimes in this extremity even the instinct for self-preservation went by the board. From point to point, some wrought-up soldier would leap up on the parapet and fire down into the opposite mass of blue or gray, then continue this with loaded rifles passed up by comrades until he was shot down and another wrought-up soldier took his place. Rain fell, slacked, fell again in sheets, drenching the fighters and turning the floor of their slaughter pen to slime. Down in the trenches, dead and wounded men were trampled out of sight in the blood-splotched mud by those who staggered up to take their posts along the works, until they too were dropped or forced to retire because their weapons became so powder-fouled from rapid firing that they could not be loaded to fire again. High though the casualties were along this portion of the line, they would have been much higher if there had been time or room for taking aim. As it was, the largely unaimed fire — particularly heavy from the Federal side, where men were stacked up twenty deep in places — passed over the heads of the Confederates to destroy a whole grove of trees within the salient;

some, including an oak nearly two feet in diameter, were actually felled by the chipping bullets, which, to the amazement of a Vermont brigadier, continued their work until the fallen trunks and limbs "were cut to pieces and whipped into basket-stuff." One of Wright's officers, fighting in the Bloody Angle, tried afterwards to sum up what he had lived through. "I never expect to be believed when I tell of what I saw of the horrors of Spotsylvania," he wrote, "because I should be loath to believe it myself were the cases reversed."

Warren's infantry moved out at last, shortly after 9 o'clock, in a full-scale assault on the Confederate left, but this was broken up so effectively by Anderson's artillery and massed small-arms fire that not a Federal reached the works along this portion of the line. Severely hurt, the attackers recoiled and did not venture out again, permitting Lee to detach a brigade from each of the two First Corps divisions as reinforcements for Ewell in the Mule Shoe. They were sorely needed. It was noon by then and men were falling there from nervous exhaustion as well as from wounds. Veterans who had survived the worst this war afforded, up to now, went through the motions of combat after the manner of blank-faced automatons, as if what they were involved in had driven them beyond madness into imbecility; they fought by the numbers, unrecognizant of comrades in the ultimate loneliness of a horror as profoundly isolating in its effect as bone pain, nausea, or prolonged orgasm, their vacant eyes unlighted by anger or even dulled by fear. There were exceptions. One man, for example, stopped fighting to plunder an abandoned knapsack, and finding clean clothes in it, stripped off his butternut rags to exchange them for the laundered finery, underwear and all, then returned cheerfully to the grisly work at hand, apparently refreshed. But for the most part they had that look, well known to experienced officers of the line, of troops whose numbness under pressure might give way at any moment to utter panic, an abrupt collapse of all resistance. Unit commanders began to send word to superiors that the men were near their limits of endurance, but the answer was always the same: Hold on longer, a little longer, until a new line of intrenchments, under construction across the base of the salient by Martin Smith's engineers, could be completed to provide shelter for the troops when they withdrew. So they kept fighting, albeit mechanically, up in the blood-drenched toe of the Mule Shoe and down its western shank, and Hancock and Wright kept battering, although they too had most of the same problems with regard to keeping their larger masses of men involved in the meat-grinder action along those two portions of the line.

Sunset, twilight, and the following darkness brought no slackening of the struggle; 9 o'clock came, then 10, and then 11; "Not yet" was still the answer to urgent requests for permission to retire to the line being drawn across the gorge of the salient, half a mile in rear of the apex which had been under bloody contention for the past eighteen hours. Finally, at midnight, word arrived and was passed along the zigzag curve of trenches — defined against the moonless blackness by the wink and glare of muzzle flashes, fitful stabs of pinkish yellow stitching their pattern back and forth across the parapet — for a piecemeal disengagement to begin. Unit by unit, so stealthily that they were not detected, the weary graybacks stumbled rearward through the bullet-tattered woods to where the new line had been dug. It was close to dawn before the last of them completed their somnambulistic withdrawal and took up their position in the works near the Brock Road. Daybreak showed the abandoned salient held only by corpses, the sodden trenches yawning empty save for these and other shattered remnants of the all-day battle. Still hugging the outward face of the log barricade, the Federals did not cross it even now that the defenders had departed, and the Confederates were glad that this was so. Exhausted, out of contact at last, blue and gray alike slept on their arms in the mud where they lay, oblivious to the pelting rain. Lee had preserved the integrity of his position, but at a cruel cost, having had nearly 3000 of his hard-core veterans captured and a somewhat larger number killed or wounded. Grant had lost as many, if not more; 6820 was the subsequent Federal count for this one day, a figure almost as great as the total for the three preceding days, when the Confederates lost fewer than one third as many. The gray army, fighting for the most part behind intrenchments, had managed to maintain its one-for-two ratio of casualties suffered and inflicted since the start of the campaign. But that was by no means the whole story of comparable attrition, which, as it applied to the men of highest rank on the two rosters, was just the other way around. Eight days of combat had cost the Army of Northern Virginia better than one third of its corps, division, and brigade commanders — 20 out of 57, killed or captured or severely wounded — while its adversary was losing barely half as many, 10 out of 69. And presently word arrived that still another Confederate general was to be added to the doleful list, one whose loss might prove the hardest to bear of them all, since his absence in the past had left the army and its famed commander groping blind.

Soon after the blue assault was launched, on the morning of May 12, Lee received a telegram informing him of the mishap, which had occurred within ten miles of Richmond the afternoon before. "Gentlemen, we have very bad news," he announced to a group around him; "General Stuart has been mortally wounded. A most valuable and able officer — " He paused, as if in search of further words for a formal statement, but then gave up and merely added in a shaken voice: "He never brought me a piece of false information." His sorrow was commensurate with his personal affection for, and his military debt to, the stricken horseman. Still, throughout the long day's fight at Spotsylvania, he kept hoping that somehow Jeb would pull through this crisis, as he had escaped so many other dangers over the past three years. Late that night, however, shortly before the withdrawal to the line still under construction across the base of the embattled salient, a second message came; Stuart was gone. Lee put his hands over his face to conceal his emotion. Presently he retired to his tent to master his grief, and when one of the dead cavalryman's staff officers arrived to tell him of Jeb's last minutes, back in Richmond, he remarked: "I can scarcely think of him without weeping."

★   ★   ★

Directed by Grant, through Meade, to "cut loose from the Army of the Potomac, pass around Lee's army, and attack his cavalry and communications," Sheridan was determined not only to make the most of the opportunity, which came his way as a result of the high-tempered clash at headquarters earlier that same Sunday, May 8, but also to do so in a style that was in keeping with his claim that, left to the devices he had been urging all along, he could whip Jeb Stuart out of his boots. "We are going out to fight Stuart's cavalry in consequence of a suggestion from me," he told his three division commanders that evening, and he added, by way of emphasizing the highly personal nature of the challenge as he saw it: "In view of my recent representations to General Meade I shall expect nothing but success."

His method of assuring this was demonstrated at first light next morning, back near Fredericksburg, when the march began down the Telegraph Road, the main-traveled artery to Richmond. Riding four abreast, accompanied by all 32 of their guns and such forage and ordnance wagons as were needed, the 12,000 blue troopers comprised a column thirteen miles in length. They moved not at a run or trot, and not by separate, converging routes — both of which had been standard procedure on raids in the past — but at a walk and in a single inspissated column, compact as a fist clenched for striking on short notice. Not much concerned with deception, and even less with speed, Sheridan's dependence was on power, the ability of his three combined divisions to ride through or over whatever got in their path. Previous raiders had sought to avoid the fast-moving rebel horsemen, lest they be delayed or thwarted in their attempt to reach their assigned objectives; but Sheridan's objective, so to speak, was just such a confrontation. He defined the raid as "a challenge to Stuart for a cavalry duel behind Lee's lines, in his own country," and the more there were of the gray riders when the showdown was at hand, the better he would like it, since that would mean there were more to be "smashed up." His confidence was in numbers and the superiority of his horses and equipment: as was shown within an hour of the outset, when the head of the column ran into brisk fire from an enemy outpost line and stopped to ponder the situation. Little Phil, as his troopers had taken to calling him, came riding up and asked what was the matter. Skirmishers, he was told — apparently in strength. "Cavalry or infantry?" he demanded, and on being informed that they were cavalry, barked impatiently: "Keep moving, boys. We're going on through. There isn't cavalry enough in all the Southern Confederacy to stop us."

Southward the march led down across the Ni, the Po, the Ta, and around the mazy sources of the Mat — four streams that combined to contribute their waters and their names to the Mattaponi — until, well in the rear of Lee's far right, the column turned off the Telegraph Road and headed southwest for Chilesburg and the North Anna, three miles beyond which lay Beaver Dam Station, Lee's advance supply base on the Virginia Central Railroad. Stores of all kinds were collected there, drawn from the Carolinas and the Shenandoah Valley; Sheridan planned to "go through" them in the course of his move on Stuart and the Confederate capital itself, which he would approach by the front door, if it came within his reach, while Ben Butler's infantry was knocking at the back. Torbert's division, still under Wesley Merritt, had the lead, followed by Gregg and Wilson. Progress was steady all day long, mainly because Sheridan refused to be distracted, whether by threats or the rumor of threats, which were frequent, front and rear. When a rebel brigade launched an attack on his rear guard south of the Ta, for example, he simply detached one of Gregg's brigades as a reinforcement and kept the main body moving at the deliberate pace he had set at the start, on the far side of the Ni. Just before dusk the North Anna came in sight; Merritt crossed with his three brigades while the other two divisions went into camp on the near bank. Before long, the sky was aglow in the direction Merritt had moved and the night breeze was fragrant with the aroma of burning bacon, wafted northward all the way from Beaver Dam.

Much of the burning — close to a million rations of meat and better than half a million of bread, along with Lee's entire reserve of medical stores — had been done by the depot guards themselves, who fired the sheds to keep their contents out of the hands of the raiders. First on the scene was the brigade of twenty-four-year-old Brigadier General George A. Custer, Michiganders as skilled in wrecking as they were in fighting. They added more than a hundred railway cars to the conflagration, as well as two locomotives — one fourth of all the Virginia Central had in operation at the time — and for lagniappe freed 378 Union soldiers, captured in the Wilderness and en route to prison camps. After the excitement of all this, the horsemen bedded down for a few hours' sleep by the fitful light of the fading embers of the station, and were roused before dawn to get to work on the railroad track. Ten miles in all were torn up, together with the telegraph wires and poles that ran beside it, before the whooping troopers fell back into column to resume their march. Like their comrades on the north bank, they were well rested despite their overnight carnival of destruction, having slept in one large bivouac that required few sentinels, rather than in scattered groups requiring many. Reconsolidated, the three divisions proceeded again at an energy-saving walk, a road-wide dusty blue serpent more than a dozen miles long and crawling inexorably south. So leisurely, so unperturbed was this horseback saunter through the springtime greenness of Virginia — except of course for those engaged in the rear-guard fret of fending off the rebels snapping persistently at their heels — that the raiders had to remind themselves from time to time that they were deep in enemy country, out for blood.

By late afternoon (Tuesday, May 10: Upton was massing for his abortive penetration of Ewell's works, thirty air-line miles due north) the head of the column reached Ground Squirrel Bridge on the South Anna, and there in the grassy fields beside the river, well over halfway to Richmond, Sheridan called a halt for the night. He might have kept on; today's march had been a good deal shorter than yesterday's and there were still a couple of daylight hours left; but this was an excellent place to feed and water his mounts and rest his men. Besides, he not only was in no hurry, he also reasoned that Stuart by now, as he said later, was "urging his horses to the death so as to get in between Richmond and our column," and he preferred it so.

He wanted Jeb to win the race, since only in that way would it end in the confrontation he was seeking.

Stuart had accepted the gambit and was proceeding much as Sheridan supposed: with one exception. Unlike his opponent, who had stripped the Federal army of practically every horseman he could lay hands on, the southern cavalry commander had resisted the temptation to jump this latest adversary with everything he had, and instead of leaving Lee to grope as blind as Grant was going to be for the next week or two, had taken up the pursuit with only three of his six brigades, some 4500 sabers opposing 12,000 engaged in what might turn out to be an attempt to seize the scantly defended capital already menaced by Butler's army from the far side of the James. One factor in this decision to forgo a better chance at personal laurels was that he could not know, until the Yankees cleared Beaver Dam on the morning of the second day, whether their intention was to keep on riding south for Richmond or turn north for a strike at Spotslyvania from the rear, in which case Lee of course would need all the help he could get, especially from his cavalry. As a result of this limiting decision, made at the outset, Stuart knew as well as Sheridan did that, in light of the numerical odds prevailing, the confrontation could have only one result if it was head-on; Sheridan — whose three well-mounted divisions were equipped with rapid-fire carbines, whereas the three gray brigades were armed with single-shot muzzle loaders and mounted on crowbait horses — would ride right over him. Stuart's solution, in considering this dilemma, was not to avoid the confrontation, despite the likelihood that it would be disastrous on those terms, but rather to arrange for it to be something other than head-on and to get what assistance he could from the Richmond garrison, scant as it was, when the march of the two columns intersected in the vicinity of the threatened capital.

Whatever he lacked in comparative strength — even at the outset of the raid, before his underfed, short-winded horses started breaking down from the strain of the chase — there was at least no diminution of his accustomed vigilance and vigor. Pressing close in rear of the outsized blue formation with one of Fitz Lee's brigades, he sent for Fitz and his other brigade, as well as Brigadier General James B. Gordon's brigade of W. H. F. Lee's division, and with these three took up the pursuit in earnest, first down the Telegraph Road, then southeast to the North Anna, beyond which, as night came down, he saw to his distress the spreading reflection of the flames at Beaver Dam, where a three-week supply of food went up in smoke while the men for whom it had been intended went hungry in the Spotsylvania woods. In just one day, by this one blow, Sheridan had accomplished more than any of his predecessors had managed to do in the past three years. What was worse, with Richmond not much farther south than he had come already, he seemed likely to accomplish a great deal more, unless Stuart found some way to check or divert him. Up to now, the grayjackets had been limited to attacks on the Union rear, since to have doubled the blue column for a strike at its head would have left the raiders free to turn for an unmolested dash against the rear of Lee's intrenchments. By next morning, though, with all the enemy horsemen over the North Anna, proceeding south past the charred base they had destroyed the night before, Stuart was free at least of that restriction; he could give his full attention to covering Richmond, since that now seemed without much doubt to be the Federal objective. Accordingly, he told Gordon to keep his brigade of North Carolinians close on the tail of the blue column, impeding it all he could, while Fitz Lee and his two Virginia brigades, under Brigadier Generals Lunsford Lomax and Williams Wickham, rode east along the Virginia Central to regain the Telegraph Road, just this side of Hanover Junction, and hurry down it to take up a position in which to intercept the raiders before they got to Richmond. A message went to Braxton Bragg, informing him of the danger to the capital in his charge. Stuart hoped to be reinforced from the city's garrison in time for the confrontation on its outskirts, but if Sheridan brushed past him, he told Bragg, "I will certainly move in his rear and do what I can."

So much for intention; execution, he knew, would be a larger order. However, before setting out to catch up with Fitz, Jeb took advantage of an opportunity Sheridan had unwittingly given him to call on his wife Flora and their two children, who were visiting on a plantation near Beaver Dam Station, thought until yesterday to be a place of safety from the Yankees. She came out to meet him on the front steps of the house, and though he did not take the time to dismount, he at least had the satisfaction of leaning down from the saddle to kiss her hello and goodbye before continuing on his way. The parting had a somber effect on the normally jovial cavalier. So many goodbyes by so many soldiers had turned out to be last goodbyes in the course of the past three years, and today was the anniversary, moreover, of the death of his great and good friend Stonewall Jackson. Stuart rode in silence for a time before he spoke to his only companion, a staff major, on a theme he seldom touched. He did not expect to survive the war, he said, and he did not want to live anyhow if the South went down in defeat.

Sheridan's calculation that his adversary would be "urging his horses to the death so as to get in between Richmond and our column" was nearly confirmed quite literally that night. Tireless himself, Jeb was not inclined to have much patience with tiredness in others. "We must substitute *esprit* for numbers," he had declared in the early days of the war, adding in partial explanation, not only of his exuberant fox-hunt manner, but also for the gaudy uniform — red-lined cape, bright yellow sash, black ostrich plume, and golden spurs — he wore with such flamboyance, on and off the field of battle: "I strive to inculcate in my men the spirit of the chase." Overtaking Fitz Lee soon after dark near Hanover Junction, he learned from Gordon, who sent a courier cross country, that the Federals had made an early halt that afternoon at Ground Squirrel Bridge on the South Anna. This was within twenty miles of Richmond, five miles closer than Stuart himself was at the time;

Jeb was all for pushing ahead on an all-night march, until Fitz persuaded him that unless he stopped to feed and rest his weary mounts he would arrive with no more than a handful of troopers, the remainder having been left behind to clutter the road with broken-down horses. Stuart relented, on condition that Fitz would have his men back in the saddle by 1 a.m., but rode on himself for another few miles before he lay down by the roadside to get a little sleep. Up and off again before the dawn of May 11 — unaware, of course, that this was to be his last day in the field — he crossed the South Anna at sunrise and passed the farm where he had bivouacked, one month less than two years ago tomorrow night, on the eve of his first "ride around McClellan," the exploit that had made his name a household word. Nearing Ashland, four miles south on the Richmond, Fredericksburg & Potomac, he found that a brigade of raiders, detached from the main column, had struck the place the night before, burning a locomotive and a train of cars, along with several government warehouses, while tearing up six miles of track. Stuart quickened his pace at this evidence of what might be in store for Richmond, fifteen miles away, unless he managed to head the marauders off or force them into retreat by pitching into their rear while they were attacking the works that ringed the city. Today as yesterday, however, a staff officer who rode with him found him inclined to speak of personal rather than of military matters. "He was more quiet than usual, softer and more communicative," the staffer observed, believing, as he later wrote, that Jeb somehow felt "the shadow of the near future already upon him."

Informed by another courier from Gordon that the Federal main body had resumed its march from Ground Squirrel Bridge this morning on the Mountain Road from Louisa, Jeb found his problem as to the choice of an interceptive position more or less solved before he got there. Less than half a mile below the junction of the Mountain and Telegraph roads, which came together to form Brook Turnpike, a macadamized thoroughfare running the last six miles into Richmond, was an abandoned stagecoach inn called Yellow Tavern, paintless now, made derelict by progress, and set amid rolling, sparsely wooded fields of grass and grain. Stuart arrived at 8 o'clock, ahead of his troops, and after sending word to Bragg that he had won the race, proceeded at once to plan his dispositions. Sporadic firing up the Mountain Road confirmed that Gordon still was snapping terrierlike at the heels of the Union column, as instructed, and gave warning that Fitz Lee not only had no time to spare in getting ready to receive it, but also could expect no reinforcements from Bragg on such brief notice. Stuart's decision was to compromise between taking up a frontal and a flank position, since the former would invite the powerful enemy force to run right over him, while the latter would afford him little more than a chance to pepper the blue troopers as they galloped past him, bound for Richmond. He had Fitz put Wickham on the right, one mile north of Yellow Tavern, facing south into the V of the converging roads, and Lomax on the left, his left advanced so that the two brigades came together at an angle, presenting a concave front which allowed a concentration of fire upon whatever moved against them down the western arm of the V. By 10 o'clock these dispositions were completed; Stuart had his men in line, dismounted except for a single regiment, the 1st Virginia, which he held in reserve to be hurried wherever it was needed most. Within another hour the enemy too had come up and was massing for attack.

This was approximately what Sheridan had been wanting all along, and now that he had it he took care to make the most of it. Richmond lay just ahead, the prize of prizes, but he was in no hurry; Richmond would still be there tonight and tomorrow, whereas Stuart, with his reputation for hairbreadth extractions, might skedaddle. From noon until about 2 o'clock he reconnoitered the Confederate position, probing here and there to test its strength, then settled down in earnest, using one brigade to hold off Gordon in his rear, two more to block the turnpike escape route, and the remaining four against Fitz Lee, whom he outnumbered two-to-one in men and three-to-one in guns. For another two hours the fight was hot, sometimes hand to hand at critical points. By 4 o'clock Sheridan had found what he believed was the key to Lee's undoing, and orders went for Merritt to press the issue on the right, crumpling Lomax to fling him back on Wickham, after which the whole line would move forward to exploit the resultant confusion. Merritt passed the order on to Custer, who promptly attacked with two regiments mounted and the other two on foot as skirmishers, striking hard for the left of the rebel line just north of Yellow Tavern.

Stuart was there, having sensed the point of greatest danger from his command post near the center. A conspicuous target in his silk-lined cape and nodding plume, he laughed at an aide's protest that he was exposing himself unnecessarily. "I don't reckon there is any danger," he replied. For three years this had apparently been true for him, although his clothes had been slit repeatedly by twittering bullets and he once had half of his mustache clipped off by a stray round. Moreover, he was encouraged by a dispatch from Bragg expressing the opinion that he could hold the Richmond works with his 4000 local defense troops and the help of three brigades of regulars he had ordered to join him from the far side of the James, provided the raiders could be delayed long enough for these reinforcements to make it across the river. Jeb figured there had been time for that already, and once again was proudly conscious of having carried out a difficult assignment, though he was determined to gain still more by way of allowing a margin for error. Arriving on the far left as the two Michigan regiments thundered past in a charge on a section of guns just up the line, he drew his big nine-shot LeMatt revolver and fired at the blue horsemen going by. They took the guns, scattering the cannoneers, but soon came tumbling back, some mounted and some unhorsed by a counterattack from the 1st Virginia, which Fitz Lee threw at them. Stuart had ridden forward to a fence, putting his horse's head across it between two of his butternut soldiers in order to get as close as possible to the bluecoats coming back. "Steady, men, steady!" he shouted, still firing his silver-chased pistol at the enemy beyond the fence. "Give it to them!" Instead, it was they who gave it to him: one of them anyhow. A dismounted private, trotting past with his revolver drawn — John A. Huff of the 5th Michigan, who had served a two-year hitch in a sharpshooter outfit, winning a prize as the best marksman in his regiment, then returned home and reënlisted under Custer, apparently out of boredom, though at forty-five he was old for that branch of the service — took time to fire, almost casually in passing, at the red-bearded officer thirty feet away. Jeb's head dropped suddenly forward, so that his plumed hat fell off, and he clapped one hand to his right side. "General, are you hit?" one of the men alongside him cried as the blue trooper ran off down the fence line, pistol smoking from the fire of that one unlucky shot. "I'm afraid I am," Stuart replied calmly when the question was asked again. "But don't worry, boys," he told the distressed soldiers gathering rapidly around him; "Fitz will do as well for you as I have done."

They got him off his horse and did what they could to make him comfortable while waiting for an ambulance. Fitz Lee came riding fast when he heard of the wound, but Jeb sent him back at once to take charge of the field. "Go ahead, Fitz, old fellow," he said. "I know you'll do what is right." Then the ambulance came and they lifted him into it, obviously in pain. Just as it started rearward a portion of the line gave way and a number of flustered gray troopers made off across the field. "Go back!" Stuart called after them, sitting up in his indignation despite the wrench to his hurt side. "Go back and do your duty, as I have done mine, and our country will be safe. Go back, go back!" Then he added, though in different words, what he had told the staff major yesterday about not wanting to survive the South's defeat: "I'd rather die than be whipped!" Presently a surgeon and other members of his staff overtook the mule-drawn ambulance and stopped it, out of range of the Federals, for an examination of the wound. While his blood-stained sash was being removed and his bullet-torn jacket opened, Stuart turned to Lieutenant Walter Hullihen, a staff favorite, and addressed him by his nickname: "Honeybun, how do I look in the face?" Hullihen lied — for his chief was clearly in shock and getting weaker by the minute. "You are looking all right, General," he replied. "You will be all right." Jeb mused on the words, as if in doubt, knowing only too well what lay in store for a gut-shot man. "Well, I don't know how this will turn out," he said at last, "but if it is God's will that I shall die I am ready."

By now the doctor had completed his examination and ordered the ambulance to move on. He believed there was little chance for the general's survival, but he wanted to get him to Richmond, and expert medical attention, as soon as possible. An eighteen-year-old private followed the vehicle for a time on horseback, looking in under the hood at the anguished Stuart until it picked up speed and pulled away. "The last thing I saw of him," the boy trooper later wrote, "he was lying flat on his back in the ambulance, the mules running at a terrific pace, and he was being jolted most unmercifully. He opened his eyes and looked at me, and shook his head from side to side as much as to say, 'It's all over with me.' He had folded arms and a look of resignation."

Fitz Lee by then had restored his line, and Sheridan, after prodding it here and there for another hour, decided the time had come to move on after all. Shadows were lengthening fast; moreover he had intercepted a rebel dispatch urging Bragg to send substantial reinforcements. So he broke off what he called "this obstinate contest" north of Yellow Tavern, and pushed on down Brook Turnpike, through the outer works of Richmond, to within earshot of the alarm bells tolling frantically in the gathering darkness. This was the route Kilpatrick had taken ten weeks ago, only to call a halt when he came under fire from the fortifications, and Little Phil had a similar reaction when he drew near the intermediate line of defense, three miles from Capitol Square. "It is possible that I might have captured the city of Richmond by assault," he would report to Meade, "but the want of knowledge of your operations and those of General Butler, and the facility with which the enemy could throw in troops, made me abandon the attempt." His personal inclination was to plunge on down the pike, over the earthworks and into the streets of the town, though he knew he lacked the strength to stay there long; "the greatest temptation of my life," he later called the prospect, looking back. "I should have been the hero of the hour. I could have gone in and burned and killed right and left. But I had learned this thing: that our men knew what they were about. . . . They would have followed me, but they would have known as well as I that the sacrifice was for no permanent advantage."

Forbearance came hard, but he soon had other matters on his mind. Withdrawal, under present circumstances, called for perhaps more daring, and certainly more skill, then did staying where he was or going in. Gordon was still clawing at his rear on Brook Turnpike, and Fitz Lee was somewhere off in the darkness, hovering on his flank; Bragg, for all he knew, had summoned any number of reinforcements from beyond the James, and presently the confusion was compounded by a howling wind- and rainstorm (the one that was giving Hancock so much trouble, out on its fringes, on the night march into position for his dawn assault on the toe of Ewell's Mule Shoe) so severe that the steeple of old St John's Church, on the opposite side of Richmond, was blown away. Sheridan turned eastward, headed for Meadow Bridge on the Chickahominy, which he intended to cross at that point, putting the river between him and his pursuers, and then recross, well downstream, to find sanctuary within Butler's lines, as had been prearranged, at Haxall's Landing on the James. In addition to the rain-lashed darkness, which made any sense of direction hard to maintain, the march was complicated by the presence of land mines in his path; "torpedoes," they were called, buried artillery projectiles equipped with trip wires, and the first one encountered killed a number of horses and wounded several men. Sheridan had an answer to that, however. Bringing a couple of dozen prisoners forward to the head of the column, he made them "get down on their knees, feel for the wires in the darkness, follow them up and unearth the shells." Despite the delay he reached Meadow Bridge at daylight: only to find that the rebels had set it afire the night before to prevent his getaway. At the same time he discovered this, Bragg's infantry came up in his rear and Fitz Lee's vengeance-minded troopers descended whooping on his flank.

He faced Wilson and Gregg about to meet the double challenge, and gave Merritt the task of repairing the bridge for a crossing. Fortunately, last night's rain had put the fire out before the stringers and ties burned through; a new floor could be improvised from fence rails. While these were being collected and put in place, the two divisions fighting rearward gave a good account of themselves, having acquired by now some of the foxhunt jauntiness formerly limited to their gray-clad adversaries. For example, when instructed by Sheridan to "hold your position at all hazards while I arrange to withdraw the corps to the north side of the river," James Wilson made a jocular reply. "Our hair is badly entangled in [the enemy's] fingers and our nose firmly inserted in his mouth. We shall, therefore, hold on here till something breaks." Nothing broke; not in the blue ranks anyhow, though James Gordon was mortally wounded on the other side, shot from his horse while leading a charge by his brigade. Merritt finished his repair work in short order and the three divisions withdrew, without heavy losses, to camp for the night down the left bank of the Chickahominy, near the old Gaines Mill battlefield. Proceeding by easy marches they rode past other scenes from the Seven Days, including Malvern Hill, to Haxall's Landing, which they reached on May 14. The raid was over, all but the return, and Sheridan was greatly pleased with the results, not only because of the specific damage accomplished at Beaver Dam and Ashland, but also because of other damage, no less grave for being more difficult to assess. At a cost of 625 killed and wounded and missing, he had freed nearly 400 Union prisoners and brought them with him into Butler's lines, along with some 300 captive rebels. How many of the enemy he had killed or wounded in the course of the raid he could not say, but he knew at least of one whose loss to Lee and the Confederacy was well-nigh immeasurable. The killing of Jeb Stuart at Yellow Tavern, he declared, "inflicted a blow from which entire recovery was impossible."

After three days' rest with Butler he was off to rejoin Grant. The northward march was uneventful except for a rather spectacular demonstration, staged while crossing the high railroad bridge over Pamunkey River, of the indestructibility of the army pack mule. Falling from a height of thirty feet, one of these creatures — watched in amazement by a regiment of troopers whose colonel recorded the incident in his memoirs — "turned a somersault, struck an abutment, disappeared under water, came up, and swam ashore without disturbing his pack." On May 24 the three divisions rejoined the army they had left, two weeks and one day ago, near Spotsylvania.

Stuart by then had been eleven days in his grave, not far from the church that lost its steeple in the windstorm on the night he arrived from Yellow Tavern. After six mortal hours of being jounced on rutted country roads because the ambulance had to take a roundabout route to avoid the raiders on the turnpike, he reached his wife's sister's house on Grace Street at 11 o'clock that evening, and there, attended by four of Richmond's leading physicians through another twenty hours of suffering, he made what was called "a good death" — a matter of considerable importance in those days, from the historical as well as the religious point of view. After sending word of his condition to his wife at Beaver Dam, in hope that she and the children would reach him before the end, he gave instructions for the disposition of his few belongings, including his spurs and various horses. "My sword I leave to my son," the impromptu will concluded. The night was a hard one, with stretches of delirium, but toward morning he seemed to improve; an aide reported him "calm and composed, in the full possession of his mind." Shortly after sunrise on May 12, when the rumble of guns was heard from the north, he asked what it meant, and on being told that part of the capital garrison had gone out to work with the cavalry in an attempt to trap the raiders at Meadow Bridge: "God grant that they may be successful," he said fervently, then turned his head aside and returned with a sigh to the matter at hand: "But I must be prepared for another world." Later that morning the President arrived to sit briefly at his bedside. "General, how do you feel?" he asked, taking the cavalryman's hand. "Easy; but willing to die," Jeb said, "if God and my country think I have fulfilled my destiny and done my duty."

Davis could scarcely believe the thirty-one-year-old Virginian was near death; he seemed, he said afterward, "so calm, and physically so strong." But one of the doctors, seeing the Chief Executive out, told him there was no chance for Stuart's recovery. The bullet had pierced his abdomen, causing heavy internal bleeding, and probably his liver and stomach as well; "mortification" — peritonitis — had set in, and he was not likely to see another dawn. That afternoon Jeb himself was told as much. "Can I last the night?" he asked, realizing that his wife might not arrive before tomorrow because of the damage to the railroad north of Richmond, and received the doctor's answer: "I'm afraid the end is near." Stuart nodded. "I am resigned, if it be God's will," he said. "I would like to see my wife. But God's will be done." Near sunset he asked a clergyman to lead in the singing of "Rock of Ages," and it was painful to see the effort he made to join the slow chorus of the hymn. "I am going fast now, I am resigned; God's will be done," he murmured. That was shortly after 7 o'clock, and within another half hour he was dead.

Flora Stuart and the children did not arrive until four hours later, but were with him in plenty of time for the funeral next day at St James Church and the burial in Hollywood Cemetery. There was no military escort; the home guard was in the field and Lee could spare no soldiers from the Spotsylvania line. Davis and Bragg were there, along with other government dignitaries, but Fitz Lee's troopers were still out after Sheridan, down the Peninsula. Such were the last rites for the man John Sedgwick, dead himself for four days now, had called "the greatest cavalry officer ever foaled in America."

★   ★   ★

"His achievements form a conspicuous part of the history of this army, with which his name and services will be forever associated," Lee was presently to declare in a general order mourning the fallen Jeb. This was the hardest loss he had had to bear since the death of Jackson, and coupled as it was with the disablement of Longstreet, the indisposition of A. P. Hill, and the increasing evidence that one-legged Ewell would never fulfill the expectations which had attended his appointment as Stonewall's successor, there was cause for despair in the Confederate army, near exhaustion from its twenty-hour struggle for the Mule Shoe. Fortunately, as if in respectful observation of Stuart's funeral fifty miles away in Richmond, the following day was one of rest. For the next two days, and into a third, rain fell steadily — "as if Heaven were trying to wash up the blood as fast as the civilized barbarians were spilling it," a South Carolina sergeant of artillery observed. Such killing as there was was mostly done at long range, by cannoneers and snipers on both sides. There was little actual fighting, only a lumbering shift by the Union army, east and south. Lee conformed to cover Spotsylvania, extending his right southward, beyond the courthouse, to the crossing of the Po. The blue maneuver seemed quite purposeless, not at all like Grant; Lee was puzzled. Unable to make out what the Federals were up to, if anything, he remarked sadly to a companion: "Ah, Major, if my poor friend Stuart were here I should know all about what those people are doing."

Grant was not as quiescent as he seemed; anyhow he hadn't meant to be. During the day of rest from his exertions of May 12 he considered what to do to break the stalemate his headlong efforts had produced. A move around Lee's left would draw the old fox into open country, but in the absence of Sheridan's troopers Grant would be at a disadvantage, maneuvering blind against a foe who still had half his cavalry on hand. His decision, then, was to strike the enemy right by shifting Warren from his own right to his left on a night march that would end in a surprise attack at first light, May 14; Wright would follow to extend the envelopment which, if successful, would turn Lee out of his Spotsylvania works and expose him to destruction when he retreated. Orders to effect this were issued before the day of rest was over; but all that came of them was lumbering confusion and the loss of many tempers. Floundering through roadless mud, rain-whipped underbrush, and swollen creeks, the V Corps did not reach its jump-off position on the Fredericksburg Road until 6 a.m., two hours behind schedule, and had to spend the rest of the day collecting the thousands of mud-caked stragglers left exhausted in its wake. The attack had to be called off, and instead there followed another day of rest.

This time it was Wright who had a notion. The Confederates having conformed to the Union movement by shifting Anderson to their right, Wright suggested that a sudden reversal of last night's march — left to right, instead of right to left — would provide a capital opportunity for a breakthrough on the rebel left, which had been thinned to furnish troops for the extension of the line down to Snell's Bridge on the Po. Grant liked and enlarged the plan to include Hancock, setting dawn of May 18 as the time of attack. Reoccupying the abandoned Mule Shoe in the darkness of the preceding night, Hancock and Wright were to assault the new works across its base, while Burnside made a diversionary effort on their left and Warren stood by to join them once the fortifications were overrun. That gave two full days for getting ready; Grant wanted the thing done right, despite the mud. Moreover, on the first of these two days the rain left off, letting the roads begin to dry, and the second — May 17 — hastened the drying process with a sun as hot as summer. Everything went smoothly and on schedule: up to the point at which the six divisions moved into the Mule Shoe in the darkness, under instructions to take up positions for the 4 a.m. assault. So much time was spent occupying and moving through the first and second lines of the original intrenchments, undefended though they were, that it was 8 o'clock before the troops were in position to make the surprise attack that should have been launched four hours ago, at the first blush of dawn.

It would not have been a surprise in any case, even if the attackers had stayed on schedule. Rebel cavalry scouts, undistracted by the blue troopers taking their rest at Haxall's Landing, and lookouts in the Spotsylvania belfry, surveying the Union rear with glasses, had reported the countermovement yesterday. That left only the question of just where on the left the blow was going to land, and this in turn was answered by Ewell's outpost pickets, who came back in the night to announce that the assault would be delivered from the Mule Shoe. At first the defenders could not credit their luck; this must be a feint, designed to cover the main effort elsewhere. An artillery major, whose battalion had lost eight of its twelve guns in the dawn assault six days ago, reported later that he and his cannoneers "could not believe a serious attempt would be made to assail such a line as Ewell had, in open day, at such a distance," but he added that "when it was found that a real assault was to be made, it was welcomed by the Confederates as a chance to pay off old scores." Pay them off they did, and with a vengeance, from the muzzles of 29 guns commanding the gorge of the abandoned salient and the shell-ripped woods beyond, first with round shot, then with case and canister as the Federals pressed forward "in successive lines, apparently several brigades deep, well aligned and steady, without bands, but with flags flying, a most magnificent and thrilling sight, covering Ewell's whole front as far as could be seen." The conclusion was foregone, but the gunners made the most of their opportunity while it lasted. Double-timing over the mangled corpses of the fallen, the attackers managed to reach the abatis at scattered points, only to find the fire unendurable at that range. They fell back with heavy losses and the worst wounds of the campaign, and when they reëntered the woods they had emerged from such a short time back, the guns fell silent, not out of mercy, but simply to save ammunition in case the attack was resumed. It was not. "We found the enemy so strongly intrenched," Meade admitted in a letter to his wife, "that even Grant thought it useless to knock our heads against a brick wall, and directed a suspension." By 10 o'clock the one-sided carnage was over, and nowhere along the line had the opposing infantry come to grips. "This attack fairly illustrates the immense power of artillery well handled," Ewell's chief of artillery said proudly.

Perhaps by now, if not earlier, Grant had learned the error of his statement to Halleck, a week ago today: "I am satisfied the enemy are very shaky." By now perhaps he also had discovered the basis for what had seemed to him the overexaltation of Lee by many high-ranking Federals, who had not agreed with their new general-in-chief that the Virginian would be likely to fall back in haste from the Rapidan when he found the blue army on his flank. "Lee is not retreating," Colonel Theodore Lyman of Meade's staff wrote home that night. "He is a brave and skillful soldier and will fight while he has a division or a day's rations left." As for the troops who served the gray commander, wretchedly fed and clad though they were, Lyman considered them anything but shaky. "These rebels are not half starved," he added. "A more sinewy, tawny, formidable-looking set of men could not be. In education they

are certainly inferior to our native-born people, but they are usually
very quick-witted, and they know enough to handle weapons with
terrible effect. Their great characteristic is their stoical manliness. They
never beg or whimper or complain, but look you straight in the face
with as little animosity as if they had never heard a gun fired." Indeed,
at this stage of the contest, there was a good deal more disaffection in the
Union than there was in the Confederate ranks. "We fought here. We
charged there. We accomplished nothing," a blue artillerist complained,
while a disgruntled infantryman protested specifically, in the wake of
this second Mule Shoe fiasco, that the army was being mishandled from
the top. The Wilderness had been "a soldier's battle," he said, in which
no one could see what he was doing anyhow. "The enlisted men did not
expect much generalship to be shown. All they expected was to have
battle-torn portions of the line fed with fresh troops. There was no
chance for a display of military talent." But that was not the case at
Spotsylvania, he went on. "Here the Confederates are strongly intrenched, and it was the duty of our generals to know the strength of the
works before they launched the army against them." He was bitter, and
the bitterness was spreading: not without cause. There was a saying in
the army, "A man likes to get the worth of his life if he gives it," and
the survivors here could not see that their fallen comrades, shot down in
close-packed masses flung off-schedule against impregnable intrenchments, had gotten the smallest fraction of the worth of theirs.

Whatever else he saw (or failed to see; he was admittedly not
much given to engaging in hindsighted introspection) Grant saw clearly
enough that something else he had said in the week-old letter to Halleck
was going to have to be revised, despite the wide publicity it had received in the newspaper version: "I propose to fight it out on this
line if it takes all summer." Stalemate was little better than defeat, in his
opinion, and yet — having assaulted headlong twice, without appreciable
success, and tried in vain to turn both enemy flanks — that seemed the
best he could do in this location. Ten May days were a long way short
of "all summer," yet they sufficed to show that he had nothing to gain
from continuing the contest on "this line." So he decided, quite simply,
to abandon it: not, of course, by retreating (retreat never entered his
mind) but by shifting his weight once more with a wide swing around
Lee's right, in the hope once more that he would catch him napping.
Still without his cavalry to serve as a screen for the movement and keep
him informed of his adversary's reaction — although it was true Sheridan had failed him in both offices before — he decided to try a different
method of achieving Lee's destruction. He would mousetrap him.

Hancock was to be the bait. Grant's plan, as set forth in orders
issued next morning, May 19, was for the II Corps to march that night
to the Richmond, Fredericksburg & Potomac Railroad, six miles east,
then down it on the far side of the Mattaponi River to Milford Station,

well beyond Lee's flank and deep in his right rear. Lee could be expected to try to overtake and destroy Hancock, and this would mean that he would be exposed to the same treatment by Grant, who would give Hancock about a twenty-mile head start before moving out with the other three corps for a leap at the gray army whose attention would be fixed on the bright lure dangling off its flank, beyond the Mattaponi. That was the plan, and there was about it a certain poetic justice, since it was a fairly faithful reproduction of what Lee himself had done to Pope on the plains of Manassas — except that he had lacked the strength to follow it through to the Cannae he was seeking, whereas Grant did not, having just received about half of the more than 30,000 reinforcements sent from Washington over a ten-day period starting four days ago. By way of preparation for the move, he shifted Burnside around to the far left on May 18, returned Wright to his former position alongside Warren, and placed Hancock in reserve beyond the Ni, ready to take off promptly the following night on the march designed to lure Lee out of his Spotsylvania intrenchments and into open country, where he would be exposed to slaughter.

First, though, there was a delay involving bloodshed. On the day whose close was scheduled to see Hancock set out eastward, Lee lashed out at the denuded Federal right.

Alert to the possibility that Grant might steal a march on him, the Confederate commander, on receiving word that morning that the Federals had resumed their ponderous sidle to his right, ordered Ewell, who held the left, to test the validity of the report by making a demonstration to his front. Though he was down to about 6000 effectives — considerably less than half his infantry strength two weeks ago, when he opened the fight in the Wilderness — Ewell, feeling perky as a result of his easy repulse of yesterday's assault, asked if he might avoid the risk of a costly frontal attack, in case the Yankees were still there, by conducting a flank operation. Lee was willing, and Ewell took off shortly after noon on a reconnaissance in force around the end of the empty-looking — and, as it turned out, empty — Union works. Accompanied by Hampton's two brigades of cavalry, he carried only six of his guns along because of the spongy condition of the roads, and even these he sent back when he reached the Ni, about 3 o'clock, and found the mud too deep for them to make it over, although Hampton managed to get his four lighter pieces across by doubling the teams. So far, Old Bald Head had encountered nothing blue; but presently, he reported, less than a mile beyond the river, on his own in what had been the Federal right rear, "I came upon the enemy prepared to meet me."

What he "came upon" was Warren's flank division, posted beyond the Ni as a covering force for Hancock, whose corps was getting ready to take off eastward after sundown. Responding to orders from headquarters to reinforce Warren instead, Hancock sent his largest division first — a new one, just arrived the day before from Washington, under Brigadier General Robert Tyler — and followed with Birney's three bled-down brigades. Tyler had been a heavy artilleryman until recently, and so had all his men, except that, unlike him, they had seen no combat up to now. Their reception by the Army of the Potomac was unkind, to say the least. In addition to the usual taunts — "Why, dearest, did you leave your earthworks behind you?" — they were greeted by the veterans, who were returning from their botched and bloody assault down the Mule Shoe, with a gruesome demonstration of what was likely to happen to infantry in battle. "This is what you'll catch up yonder," the wounded told them, displaying shattered arms and other injuries Ewell's batteries had inflicted at close range. One roadside group had a mangled corpse which they kept covered with a blanket until one of the oversized greenhorn regiments drew abreast, and then they would uncover it with a flourish. The heavies had been singing as they marched, perhaps to keep their courage up, but they fell silent under the impact of this confrontation with what was left of a man who had been where they were headed. As it happened, the attack was suspended before they were committed. That was yesterday, however. This was today, and they were about to discover at first hand what combat meant.

Ewell, having found what he came looking for — or, to put the case more critically, having blundered into what he had been in search of — would have been glad to withdraw without bloodshed, but the bluecoats gave him no choice except to fight, not only at a numerical disadvantage, but also without guns to take up the challenge from the many turned against him. The resultant two-hour struggle, which began about 5.30, might well have completed the destruction of Lee's Second Corps if Wade Hampton had not managed to post his rapid-firing battery of horse artillery where it could hold the enemy off while Ewell fell back across the Ni and returned under cover of darkness to his intrenchments, minus another 900 of his men. The Federals lost a good deal more — 1535 killed or wounded or missing, most of them Tyler's — but at least they could claim a victory, having remained in control of the field and taken no less than 472 prisoners. A larger gain was the admission of the heavies to full membership in the army that had greeted them with jeers the day before. They had made up in staunchness, even veterans agreed, for what they lacked in skill. "Well, they got a little mixed and didn't fight very tactically," one of their officers replied to a question from a correspondent, "but they fought confounded plucky."

This last was good news for Grant, who was going to have to depend increasingly on such replacements in the weeks ahead. Three days ago, on May 16, with 12,000 of his cavalry away, his strength was down to 56,124 effectives — less than half the number he had mustered when he crossed the Rapidan, twelve days before. About 35,000 of the absent were battle casualties, lost in the Wilderness and here at Spotsylvania. Another 4000-odd had fallen sick and been sent to Washington hospitals to recover or to die. The rest, a substantial 14,000, were deserters or men whose enlistments had expired, members of the first of the thirty-six regiments scheduled for discharge when their time was up in May and June. There was, therefore, much encouragement for Grant in this May 19 evidence that he could count on the heavies, as well as on the newly drafted troops among them, for staunchness during the critical period in which they learned their bloody trade and became, in their turn, veterans more or less like the men who had jeered at them on their arrival but now would jeer no more. In any case, he depended on them to lend their weight to whatever blows he decided to throw, and he did not let his heavy losses for the past two weeks, on and off the field of battle, deter him from his purpose, which was to whip the rebel army in the process of maneuvering it back on Richmond. Today's affair amounted to no more than an interruption, a twenty-four-hour delay. He would move out tomorrow night, as planned: with one exception, one revision prompted by Ewell's sortie across the Ni that afternoon, which apparently served to remind Grant just how bloody-minded Bobby Lee could be. Instead of sending Hancock well in advance of the other three corps, to be dangled as bait on the east bank of the Mattaponi, he decided to move at a much closer interval, lest the bait be gobbled before the rest of the army came up in support. Accordingly, orders were sent, not only to Hancock, but also to Warren, Wright, and Burnside, that the march to Milford Station would begin tomorrow night, May 20, and would be conducted with all possible secrecy — in the hope, once more, of stealing a march on old man Lee.

But no amount of secrecy could hide what Lee already knew as a result of Ewell's rather heavy-handed investigation of the Union dispositions in his front. Grant had stripped his right for another shift in the opposite direction, and Lee prepared for another interception, alerting all three of his corps commanders to be ready to march at the tap of a drum. Despite such precaution, the enemy would of course move first; yet Lee had little fear that he would lose the pending race, whenever it began. He had chosen Hanover Junction as his point of concentration just beyond the North Anna, at the crossing of the two critical rail lines back to Richmond. From there he believed he would be able to parry any thrust the Federals were likely to attempt, and this time — unlike the last, in the sprint for Spotsylvania — he would have the advantage of the interior route of march, traveling the chord of the arc his adversary's movement would necessarily describe. His confidence, in this as in much else, was based on the events of the past two weeks; especially on a comparison of losses. Though he did not know the precise figures, even for his own army, let alone Grant's — the latter had suffered a total of 36,065 casualties (17,666 in the Wilderness, 18,399 at Spotsylvania) while Lee was losing barely half as many (just under 8000 in the Wilderness, just over 10,000 at Spotsylvania) — he knew that Grant's were disproportionately heavy. No opponent, so far, had been able to sustain such losses without removal from command or frustration of his plans by Washington; nor, he hoped, would this one, despite his known tenacity and his reported unconcern for costs. Lee's confidence was in himself and in his men. "With the blessing of God, I trust we shall be able to prevent General Grant from reaching Richmond," he had told the President ten days ago, and that trust had been confirmed. Moreover, though it was true the contemplated shift to Hanover Junction would mean giving up half the region between his present position and the capital in his rear, the line of the North Anna was one of great natural strength, highly dangerous for an army attempting to cross it, as Grant's would do, in the face of determined resistance. Besides, he was presently to remind Davis, "[Grant's] difficulties will be increased as he advances, and ours diminished."

One reason for this — in addition, that is, to the advantageous lengthening and shortening of their respective lines of supply and communication, vulnerable to attack by raiders and tedious to maintain — was that Lee would be moving toward the first reinforcements he had been able to count on, or even contemplate with any real degree of hope, since the opening of Grant's triple-pronged offensive. The reason he could count on them now was that two of the Federal prongs had, in effect, been snapped off short in the course of the past week. Breckinridge, out in the Shenandoah Valley, and Beauregard, on the far side of the James, had scored tactical successes which served not only to neutralize or abolish the separate threats from those directions by Franz Sigel and Ben Butler, but also to convert at least a part of each of those two outnumbered and hard-pressed Confederate forces into reserves, available for rapid shipment by rail to the Army of Northern Virginia from the south and west; which, incidentally, was still another reason for Lee's choice of Hanover Junction, where the two lines met and crossed from Richmond and the Valley, as his point of concentration after leaving Spotsylvania. By May 20, with the evidence getting heavier by the hour that the Federals in his immediate front were about to begin their march around his right, Lee called on both victorious commanders — Breckinridge by orders wired directly, since he was already under his command, and Beauregard by means of an urgent request to the War Department — to hasten the departure for Hanover Junction of every soldier they could spare from those two fronts.

It was well that he specified haste, for the signs of Grant's imminent departure continued to multiply all day. By nightfall Lee was so convinced that the Federals were about to march that he decided to begin his own next morning. Accordingly, he sent instructions for Ewell, whose corps would peel off from the left in order to lead the movement south, to start at daylight unless he saw an opening for a strike at the enemy rear. Old Bald Head, finding no such opportunity, stepped off at 4 a.m. May 21 — a scant six hours, events would show, after Hancock started out across the way.

✕ 3 ✕

Sigel's offensive, like his chief's, was subdivided into three columns of penetration, each with a different preliminary objective to be attained before all three combined for a linkup with Grant's main body in front of Richmond. His own main body, consisting of about 8000 of all arms, would march the length of the Shenandoah Valley, from Winchester to Staunton, where he would strike the Virginia Central Railroad. Crook meantime, with roughly the same number, would move west of the Valley, southward in two columns, one of about 6000 infantry under his personal direction, the other of about 2000 cavalry under Brigadier General W. W. Averell, against the Virginia & Tennessee. Crook's objective was Dublin Station and the nearby railway bridge across New River, Averell's the salt works and lead mines at Saltville and Wytheville, a day's ride west of Dublin: from which point the two would proceed east along the Virginia & Tennessee to Salem, tearing up track as they went, and then turn north, through Lexington, for a hookup with Sigel at Staunton and, subsequently, with Meade somewhere east or southeast along the Virginia Central, which was to be given the same hardhanded treatment as the reunited 16,000 moved along it to be in on the kill when Lee was brought to bay.

Crook's being the more lucrative assignment, at least in the opening stage of the campaign — salt and lead were rare necessities in the Confederacy, and the intended double blow at Saltville and Wytheville would go far toward making them rarer — Sigel started first, on April 30, hoping to draw attention and troops away from the region beyond the Alleghenies. It worked. By the time Crook's infantry set out from Gauley Bridge on May 2, beginning the rugged trek from the Kanawha, southward up the left bank of New River to Dublin Station, a roundabout distance of more than a hundred miles, the rebel department commander was busy stripping Southwest Virginia of its few defenders in order to get them aboard trains for rapid shipment to Staunton and a fast march northward, down the turnpike, to challenge Sigel's bid for control of the wheat-rich Shenandoah Valley. Within another three days, when Averell's mounted column began its parallel march on May 5 from Logan Courthouse, fifty miles southwest of Gauley Bridge, the Confederate shift was well under way. Crook made good time, considering the nature of the terrain. At Shannon's Bridge by sunset of May 8, only seven miles from Dublin, he learned that a rebel force was lying in wait for him two miles ahead on a wooded spur of Cloyd's Mountain.

A fork-bearded West Pointer, Ohio born and thirty-five years old, a veteran of Antietam and Chickamauga, he rode ahead next morning to look the position over — and found it strong. "They may whip us," he said as he lowered his binoculars, "but I guess not."

He guessed right. The Confederate force of about 3000, part militia and home guards, commanded by Brigadier General Albert Jenkins, a former Charleston lawyer in what was now called West Virginia, was routed by a charge in which one of Crook's brigade commanders, Colonel Rutherford B. Hayes, made a showing that stood him in good stead when he ran for President twelve years later. Jenkins was wounded and taken, along with two of his three guns and many rifles dropped by his green troops when they fled; Union surgeons removed his mangled arm and gave him such care as they had time for, but he died the following week, thirty-three years old and still a captive. His losses at Cloyd's Mountain numbered 538, the Federals' 643. Crook, overcome by excitement and exhaustion — he had hurried about the contested field with his waterproof boots full of water from crossing a creek — fell to the ground in a faint as soon as he saw that the battle was won, but revived in time, attended by his staff, to order an immediate advance on Dublin and the Virginia & Tennessee Railroad, five miles ahead. Arriving before dark, he put his men to work firing and wrecking the depot installations, along with a large accumulation of military stores, and set out at first light next morning, May 10, to destroy the 400-foot wooden railway bridge across New River, eight miles east. By midday it was burning briskly, and soon afterwards it collapsed with a great hiss of steam into the river. "A fine scene it was," Hayes noted in his diary.

Having thus carried out his preliminary assignment — marching and fighting and wrecking, all three boldly and with skill — Crook now had only to wait for Averell to join him and continue the movement as planned, east along the railroad to Salem, then north through Lexington for the meeting with Sigel at Staunton. Yet he did neither. He not only declined to wait for the cavalry column, he also declined to press on eastward in accordance with his orders. Instead he decided to return at once to West Virginia: specifically to Meadow Bluff, on the Greenbrier River near Lewisburg, where he could draw supplies from Gauley Bridge, his starting point some fifty miles northwest. His reason, as he gave it two weeks later in his report, was that "I saw [at the Dublin telegraph office] dispatches from Richmond stating that General Grant had been repulsed and was retreating, which determined me to move to Lewisburg as rapidly as possible." Isolated as he was, and accepting the rebel claim at face value, he feared that Lee would send troops west by rail from Orange to cut him off and up, and under pressure of this fear he bolted for the fastness of the mountains. Not even the arrival of outriders from Averell, bringing word that the troopers had found

Saltville too well guarded for attack but that the column was moving on Wytheville even now, deterred Crook from making as quick a getaway as he could manage. He simply replied that Averell was to do his best to carry out the instructions he himself had just discarded, and took off northward, well beyond New River, which he crossed upstream and down. He made good time. It was five days later, May 15, before the cavalry overtook him at Union, eight miles beyond the West Virginia line.

Averell had a harrowing tale to tell: one that was unrelieved, moreover, by any such tactical victory as Cloyd's Mountain or any such gaudy feat as the demolition of New River Bridge. He had raided in this direction before, with conspicuous success, including the burning of Salem in December, but that had been done against next to no opposition. This time there was not only a considerable force in opposition — as he was told when he reached Tazewell on May 8, just this side of the state line — it was also commanded by John Morgan, who was known to be hungry for revenge for the indignities he had suffered in the Ohio Penitentiary during the four months preceding his year-end breakout. Now he was back in the field at last, having been rejoined by about 750 of his "terrible men," survivors of the disastrous July raid through Indiana and Ohio, and was posted at Abingdon to work with local units in defense of a department including portions of Southwest

Virginia and East Tennessee. At Tazewell Averell learned that the famed Kentuckian had shifted his headquarters and his troops to Saltville when he got word that a blue column was headed that way. What his strength was Averell did not know; he estimated it at 4500, better than twice his own. Consequently, he decided to forgo the scheduled destruction of the salt works, vital though they were to the Confederacy's efforts to feed its armies, and to strike instead directly at Wytheville and the lead mines, leaving Morgan holding the bag at Saltville. He feinted in that direction on May 9, then swung east, riding hard to give the rebels the slip. He thought he had succeeded until, approaching Wytheville the following afternoon, he found Morgan drawn up to meet him at a place called Crockett's Cove.

The position was admirably suited for defense, but that was not what Morgan had in mind. Fuming because the approach of the enemy column had delayed a projected return to his native Bluegrass, he charged and struck and kept on charging and striking the rattled Federals, who thus were afforded no chance to discover that they were not outnumbered. "My men fought magnificently, driving them from hill to hill," he wrote his wife that night. "It was certainly the greatest sight I ever witnessed to see a handful of men driving such masses before them. Averell fought his men elegantly, tried time and time again to get them to charge, but our boys gave them no time to form." This was Morgan's first engagement since the late-November jailbreak and he made the most of it until darkness ended the running fight, four miles east of Wytheville. He turned back then for Abingdon, to resume his plans for another "ride" into Kentucky, and Averell, minus 114 of his troopers, limped eastward to Dublin and beyond, where the railroad bridge had toppled hissing into New River that afternoon. Informed by his outriders that Crook had shied off into the mountains, he forded the river and tore up another ten miles of track and culverts before turning north to overtake his chief at Union on May 15. Hungry because supplies were low, and lashed by heavy rains, the reunited column spent two days getting over the swollen Greenbrier, then trudged upstream to Meadow Bluff, May 19, on the verge of exhaustion.

Crook's infantry had been seventeen days on the march from Gauley Bridge, the last eight without a regular issue of rations, and had crossed seventeen mountain ranges, each a bit steeper, it seemed, than the one before. They had accomplished little, aside from incidental damage to the railroad and the destruction of the New River bridge, but Crook was reassured to learn at Meadow Bluff that his superior, the major general commanding the department, had accomplished even less in the Shenandoah Valley. In fact, it now developed, the wide-swinging western column had been quite right not to press on east and north to Staunton, as instructed, since Sigel had covered barely half the distance from Winchester to that point, marching deliberately up the Valley

Pike, before he was obliged to turn and flee back down it, pursued by the victors of the battle that had defined the limit of his penetration.

It was Breckinridge's doing, and he did it on his own. Hearing from Lee in early May, while the Army of Northern Virginia was on its way to the confrontation with Grant in the thickets south of the Rapidan, that he was to assume "general direction of affairs" beyond the Blue Ridge, the former U.S. Vice President, electoral runner-up to Lincoln in the presidential race of 1860, continued his efforts to collect all movable troops in Southwest Virginia for a meeting with Sigel in the Valley. "I trust you will drive the enemy back," Lee had told him, and the tall, handsome Kentuckian, forty-three years old, with lustrous eyes, a ponderous brow, and the drooped mustache of a Sicilian brigand, was determined to do just that. Accordingly, he left the defense of the western reaches of his department to Jenkins and Morgan, scant though their resources would be in event of an attack, and set out for Staunton at once, by rail, with two veteran brigades of infantry totaling just under 2500 men. North of there, and hard at work observing and impeding Federal progress south of Winchester, was Brigadier General John D. Imboden, whose 1500 cavalry were all that would stand in Sigel's path until Breckinridge arrived. The Kentuckian reached Staunton on May 12 and set off promptly down the turnpike for New Market, forty miles away, where Imboden was skirmishing with advance elements of the blue main body, still a dozen miles to the north. Including these butternut troopers, Breckinridge would go into battle with close to 5000 of all arms: a figure he attained by mustering all the militia round-about — 750 at the most — and by summoning from Lexington the cadet corps of the Virginia Military Institute, 247 strong, all under conscription age and commanded by one of their professors, who later recalled that although Breckinridge said he hoped to keep these fifteen-, sixteen-, and seventeen-year-olds in reserve through the bloodiest part of the fighting (thus to avoid what Jefferson Davis had referred to as "grinding the seed corn of the nation") he added in all honesty that, "should occasion require it, he would use them very freely."

Occasion was likely to require it. Pleased that he had succeeded in drawing the rebels north and east, away from the now vulnerable installations in Southwest Virginia, Sigel was intent on completing his preliminary assignment by winning control of the Shenandoah Valley before the wheat in its fields was ripe for grinding into flour to feed Lee's army. This would entail whipping the gray force gathering to meet him, and he marched south with that welcome task in mind, anticipating his first victory since Pea Ridge, out in Arkansas more than two years ago, for which he had been made a major general. All the battles he had been involved in since that time, however slightly, had been defeats — Second Bull Run and Fredericksburg were examples — with the result that his demonstrations of military competence had been limited to the conduct of retreats. A book soldier, academy-trained in his native Germany, which he had fled in his mid-twenties after serving as Minister of War in the revolution of 1848, he was anxious to win the glory he had prepared for, though he did not let ambition make him rash. Advancing from Winchester, up the turnpike that led ninety miles to Staunton, he moved with skill and proper deliberation. There were mishaps, such as the loss of 464 men in a cavalry regiment surprised and captured by Imboden while on outpost duty beyond Front Royal, May 11, but Sigel knew how to accept such incidental reverses without distraction, even though this one, combined with the need for detaching troops to guard his lengthening supply line, reduced his combat strength to roughly 6500 of all arms. Past Strasburg by then, he kept his mind on the job ahead and continued his march up the pike to Mount Jackson, terminus of the Manassas Gap Railroad, on May 14. This was only seven miles from New Market, occupation of which would give him control of the single road across Massanutton Mountain and thus secure his left flank practically all the rest of the way to Staunton. He had sent his cavalry ahead to seize the crossing of the north fork of the Shenandoah River, two miles south of Mount Jackson, and when they arrived that afternoon they were taken under fire by a rebel battery posted on a height just over a mile beyond the bridge. They settled down to a brisk artillery exchange, preparing to force a crossing, but Sigel — perhaps recalling what had happened three days ago, when nearly 500 other troopers had been gobbled up near Front Royal — sent word that he preferred to wait until the infantry came up next morning, when all arms would combine to do the thing in style.

Breckinridge was within earshot of the cannonade. Just arrived from Staunton with his two brigades, plus the VMI cadets, he was taking a late afternoon dinner with Imboden at Lacy Springs, a dozen miles to the south, and when he heard the guns begin to rumble he told the cavalryman to return at once to New Market, hold the crossing of the North Fork till dark if possible, then fall back to a position just this side of the town, where he would join him before daybreak. Imboden, with Sigel's coöperation, carried out these instructions to the letter. Awakened at dawn by the arrival of the infantry — Sunday, May 15 — he assisted in getting the troops in line for what was intended to be a defensive battle. But when sunrise gave a clear view of the field, Breckinridge studied it carefully through his glasses and changed his mind. Sigel's men had crossed the river at first light to take up a position astride the turnpike north of town, and the Kentuckian apparently liked the looks of what he saw. "We can attack and whip them here," he said. "I'll do it."

And did. While the Confederates were adjusting their dispositions for attack, the guns on both sides — 28 of them Union, opposed by half as many firing north — began exchanging long-range shots across the rooftops of the town. This continued for an hour, at the end of which the gray line started forward, one brigade on the right, the other on the left, with a regiment of dismounted cavalry between them on the pike, supported by the cadets whose spruce uniforms had resulted in their being greeted with cat-calls by veterans on the march; "Katydids," they called them. Imboden struck first with a horseback charge through some woods on the right, and the infantry went forward through the town, cheered by citizens who came running out to meet them. On the far side, they scattered the blue pickets, then went for the main line. Sigel disengaged skillfully and fell back half a mile, disposing his troops on high ground to the left and right of a hillock on which a six-gun battery was slamming rapid-fire shots into the ranks of the advancing rebels. Spotting this as the key to the position, Breckinridge ordered the dismounted troopers to charge and take it, supported by the cadets; which they did, though only by the hardest, not only because of heavy fire from the well-served artillery, but also because of a gully to their front, less than two hundred yards from the fuming line of guns and floored with what turned out to be calf-deep mud. Moreover, as the movement progressed, it was the troopers who were in support. Lighter, more agile, and above all more ardent, the cadets made better time across the soft-bottomed depression, and though they were hit repeatedly with point-blank canister, they soon were among the cannoneers, having suffered better than twenty percent casualties in the charge: 8 killed and 46 wounded. Slathered with clay and stained by smoke, many of them barefoot, having lost their shoes and socks in the mud of the gully, the survivors were scarcely recognizable as yesterday's dapper Katydids. But they carried the position. "A wild yell went up," Imboden would remember, "when a cadet mounted a caisson and waved the Institute flag in triumph over it."

Sigel was in his element. Lean-faced and eager, not yet forty, his lank hair brushed dramatically back to bring out his sharp features and brief chin beard, he maintained an icy, steel-eyed posture under fire, but betrayed his inner excitement by snapping his fingers disdainfully at shellbursts as he rode about, barking orders at his staff. Unfortunately, he barked them in German, which resulted in some confusion: as, for example, when he directed that two companies of a West Virginia regiment move up to protect the six-gun battery under attack by the cadets. "To my surprise," he later protested, "there was no disposition to advance. In fact, in spite of entreaties and reproaches, the men could not be moved an inch!" And when the rest of the gray line surged forward to take advantage of the respite gained by the boy soldiers, there was nothing Sigel could do but attempt another displacement, and this he did, as skillfully as he had performed the first, though at a considerably higher cost. By now he was back on the knoll from which the rebel horse artillery had challenged his crossing of the river yesterday, four miles north of town. He held on there, through a lull occasioned by the need for refilling the cartridge boxes of the attackers, and when they came on again he fell back across the North Fork, burning the bridge behind him. Secure from pursuit, at least for the present, he intended to stand his ground despite heavy losses (831 killed and wounded and missing, as compared to the enemy's 577) but decided a better course would be to retire to Mount Jackson, where he could rest and refit before resuming his interrupted southward march. He got there around 7 o'clock that evening, took up a stout position, and remained in it about two hours before concluding that the wisest course, after all, would be to return to Strasburg, another twenty miles back down the pike. A night march got him there the following afternoon, and after one more trifling readjustment — rearward across Cedar Creek next morning, May 17, to make camp on the heights he had left a week ago — he finished his long withdrawal from the unfortunate field of New Market and began making incisive preparations for a return.

But that was not to be; not for Sigel at any rate. Stymied at Spotsylvania, Grant was growing impatient at having heard nothing of or from his director of operations beyond the Blue Ridge. "Cannot General Sigel go up Shenandoah Valley to Staunton?" he wired Halleck, who replied that, far from advancing, Sigel was "already in full retreat. ... If you expect anything from him you will be mistaken," Halleck added. "He will do nothing but run. He never did anything else." Grant was furious: about as much so as he was with Banks, whose Red River fiasco came to an end that same week. Four days later, on May 21, Franz Sigel was relieved of his over-all command.

Lee on the other hand was delighted with his lieutenant's conduct of affairs in that direction, and was quick to express his gratitude. "I offer you the thanks of this army for the victory over General Sigel," he wired Breckinridge on the morning after the battle. "Press him down the Valley, and if practicable follow him into Maryland." This last was in line with the suggestion he had made to Stonewall Jackson, two years ago today, at the outset of the campaign that had frightened the Washington authorities into withholding troops from McClellan's drive on Richmond, and he hoped that it might have the same effect on Grant's more energetic effort. In any event, New Market had saved the wheat crop in what was called "the bread basket of Virginia," and even if Breckinridge lacked the strength to undertake a crossing of the Potomac, it at least freed a portion of his command to reinforce the army north of Richmond. Lee, in a follow-up telegram that same day, left the decision to the general on the scene. "If you can follow Sigel into Maryland, you will do more good than by joining us," he wired. "[But] if you cannot, and your command is not otherwise needed in the Valley or in your department, I desire you to prepare to join me."

Breckinridge answered next morning that he preferred the latter course. He would move, he said, with 2500 men. Anticipating the shift from Spotsylvania, Lee replied: "Proceed with infantry to Hanover Junction by railroad. Cavalry, if available, can march."

★　★　★

That was on May 17, the day when news of a greater victory, together with the promise of much heavier reinforcements, was relayed to Lee from Beauregard, twelve days into a campaign that began with every prospect of a Union triumph, south of the James, and ended quite the other way around. Indeed, nothing could better illustrate the abruptness with which fortune's frown and smile were interchangeable than the contrast between the elation of Richmond's citizens on that date and the gloom that had descended on May 5, when they learned from downstream lookouts that an amphibious column ten miles long, containing no less than two hundred enemy vessels, was steaming up the river that laved the city's doorstep. Loaded at Yorktown the day before — while Grant was crossing the Rapidan — the armada had rounded the tip of the York-James peninsula in the night, and now, with the morning sun glinting brilliant on the water — and Grant and Lee locked in savage combat, eighty miles to the north — it was proceeding up the broad, shining reaches of the James.

Five ironclads led the way and other warships were interspersed along the line of transports, a motley array of converted ferries, tugs and coasters, barges and canal boats, whose decks were blue with 30,000 soldiers, all proud to be playing a role in what seemed to one of them "some grand national pageant." What was more, they had a commander who knew how to supply the epitomizing gesture. Riding in the lead, Ben Butler brought his headquarters boat about, struck a pose on the hurricane deck, and steamed back down the line. As he sped past each transport, past the soldiers gaping from its rail, he swung his hat in a wide vertical arc toward the west and lurched his bulky torso in that direction, indicating their upstream goal and emphasizing his belief that nothing could stop them from reaching it in short order. Unaware that within two weeks he and they were to wind up caged — or, as his superior was to put it, "corked" — they cheered him wildly from ship after ship as he went by, then cheered again, even more wildly, as he turned and churned back up the line, still waving his hat and lunging his body toward Richmond.

After dropping one division off at City Point, within nine miles of Petersburg, the flotilla proceeded north, past the adjoining mouth of the Appomattox River, and debarked the other five divisions at Bermuda Hundred, a plantation landing eighteen crow-flight miles from the rebel capital. Ashore, as afloat, the gesticulating Butler rode with the van, and close up he was even stranger-looking than he had been when viewed across the water; "the strangest sight on a horse you ever saw," one witness thought, attempting a word portrait of the former Massachusetts senator who shared with Banks, though he was more than a year his junior at forty-five, the distinction of being the U.S. Army's ranking active major general. "With his head set immediately on a stout, shapeless body, his very squinting eyes, and a set of legs and arms that look as if made for somebody else and hastily glued to him by mistake, he presents a combination of Victor Emmanuel, Aesop, and Richard III, which is very confusing to the mind. Add to this a horse with a kind of rapid, ambling trot that shakes about the arms, legs, etc. till you don't feel quite sure whether it is a centaur or what it is, and you have a picture of this celebrated General."

Despite the neckless, bloated look, the oddly assorted members, and the disconcerting squint of his mismatched eyes, Butler was all business here today. Mindful of Grant's injunction that he was to "use every exertion to secure footing as far up the south side of the river as you can, and as soon as you can," he landed the bulk of his army just short of the first of the half dozen looping bends or "curls" of the James,

where the Confederates had heavy-caliber guns sited high on the steep bluffs to discourage efforts to approach the city by water, and next morning he began to comply with another item in his instructions: "Fortify, or rather intrench, at once, and concentrate all your troops for the field there as rapidly as you can." Five miles west of Bermuda Hundred, between Farrar's Island and Port Walthall, the James and the Appomattox were less than four miles apart. By intrenching this line he would be safe from a frontal attack, while the rivers secured his flanks and rear. It was true, the Bermuda debarkation required a crossing of the Appomattox to reach either City Point or Petersburg, but this was better, Butler reasoned — bearing in mind Grant's double-barreled admonition "that Richmond is to be your objective point, and that there is to be coöperation between your force and the Army of the Potomac" — than having to cross it in order to reach the fattest and probably best-defended prize of all. By sundown of May 6, his first full day ashore, he not only had completed the preliminary intrenchment of the line connecting the bends of the two rivers, he also had sent a brigade of infantry another two or three miles west to look into the possibility of cutting the railroad between Petersburg and Richmond, which in turn afforded the rebel defenders their only rail connection with the Carolinas and the reinforcements they no doubt were calling for, even now, in their distress at his appearance on their doorstep.

Encouraged by a report from the brigadier who conducted the reconnaissance (he had run into spirited resistance on the turnpike, half a mile short of the railroad, but nothing that could not be brushed aside, he thought, by a more substantial force) Butler decided next morning to go for the railroad in strength, then turn southward down it to knock out Petersburg and thus assure that his rear would be unmolested when he swung north to deal with Richmond. While the others kept busy with axes and spades, improving the earthworks protecting their base from attack, four of the fourteen brigades in the two corps, each of which had three divisions, moved out to attend to this preamble to the main effort: three from Gillmore and one from Major General W. F. Smith, whose third division had debarked at City Point and was still there, despite his protest that it "might as well have been back in Fort Monroe." The march was along the spur track from Port Walthall, and their initial objective was its junction with the trunk line, three miles west. As they approached it around midday, a spatter of fire from the skirmishers out front informed them that the junction — grandly styled Port Walthall Junction, though all it contained was a run-down depot and a couple of dilapidated shacks — was defended. The four brigades came up in turn to add their weight to the pressure being exerted, but the rebels either were there in heavy numbers or else they were determined not to yield, whatever the odds. This continued for two hours, in the course of which the Federals managed to overlap one gray flank and tear up about a quarter mile of track on the main line. But that was all. At 4 o'clock, having suffered 289 casualties, Butler decided to pull back behind his fortifications and return in greater strength tomorrow; or, as it turned out, the day after.

Both good and bad news awaited him, back on Bermuda Neck. The bad was from the navy, which had sent a squadron out the day before to investigate an account by a runaway slave that the Confederates had torpedoes planted thickly in the James, especially in the vicinity of Deep Bottom, a dozen miles up the winding river from Bermuda Hundred. It was all too true: as the crew of the big double-ender *Commodore Jones* found out, about 2 o'clock that afternoon. A 2000-pound torpedo, sunk there some months ago and connected by wires to galvanic batteries on the bank, "exploded directly under the ship with terrible effect, causing her destruction instantly." So her captain later reported from a bed in the Norfolk Naval Hospital. Another witness, less disconcerted because he was less involved, being aboard another gunboat, went into more detail. "It seemed as if the bottom of the river was torn up and blown through the vessel itself," he wrote. "The *Jones* was lifted almost entirely clear of the water, and she burst in the air like an exploding firecracker. She was in small pieces when she struck the water again." For days, bodies and parts of bodies floated up' and were fished out of the James; the death toll was finally put at 69. Just now, though, the problem of how to keep the same thing from happening over and over again was solved by the capture of two men caught lurking in the brush where the batteries were cached. They had triggered the explosion, and what was more they had helped to plant other such charges up ahead. They refused to talk, however, until one of them was placed in the bow of the lead vessel and the squadron continued its upstream probe: whereupon, in the words of an interrogator, he "signified his willingness to tell all."

That more or less solved the problem of torpedoes (in any case, of the ones already planted; future sowings were of course another matter) but next day, about the time the four brigades began their skirmish down the spur track from Port Walthall, the navy was given a violent reminder that older dangers, familiar to sailors long before anyone thought of exploding powder under water, still threatened the existence of the fleet. U.S.S. *Shawneen,* a 180-ton sidewheel gunboat on patrol at Turkey Bend, dropped anchor under the loom of Malvern Hill to give her crew time out for the midday meal, only to have it interrupted when a masked battery and four companies of Confederate infantry opened fire from the north bank, peppering the decks with bullets and puncturing the steam drum. While most of the crew went over the side to keep from being scalded, *Shawneen*'s captain ordered her colors struck to save the lives of the injured still aboard. Ceasing fire, the rebel colonel in command sent out a boat to remove survivors and blow the vessel up; "which was effectively done," he reported, "consigning all to the wind and waves."

Such was the bad news — bad for Butler because it meant that the navy, having lost two ships in as many days, was likely to be reluctant to give him the slam-bang close support he would want when he moved against or beyond the high-sited batteries on Chaffin's and Drewry's bluffs, fortified works flanking the last tortuous upstream bend of the river below Richmond, both of them integral parts of the hard-shell outer defenses he would have to pierce if he was to put the hug on the rebel capital. The good news came from his cavalry, two brigades combined in a 3000-man division under Brigadier General August Kautz, a thirty-six-year-old German-born West Pointer. Off on his own while the rest of the army was steaming up the James, Kautz rode due west out of Suffolk on May 5 for a strike at the Petersburg & Weldon Railroad, damage to which would go far toward delaying the arrival of enemy reinforcements from the Carolinas. Encountering little opposition he did his work in a slashing style: first at Stony Creek on May 7, where he burned the hundred-foot railway bridge twenty miles south of Petersburg, and then next day at the Nottoway River, another five miles down the line, where he put the torch to a second bridge, twice as long, before turning north to rejoin the army two days later at City Point. Encouraged by news of the first of these two burnings, which reached him on May 8, Butler spent that day in camp, secure behind his Bermuda Neck intrenchments, putting the final touches to his plans for a movement against Petersburg next morning, much heavier than the one that had taken him only as far as Port Walthall Junction the day before.

This time he got a solid half of his infantry in motion, 14,000 in all. Smith, on the left, again ran into fire as he approached the Junction and called on Gillmore, who had advanced by then to Chester Station unopposed, to come down and join the fight. Gillmore did, although regretfully, having just begun to rip up track and tear down telegraph wire along the turnpike. But when the two corps began to maneuver in accordance with a scheme for bagging the force at the Junction, the graybacks slipped from between them and scuttled south. Pursuing, the Federals found the Confederate main body dug in behind unfordable Swift Creek, three miles north of Petersburg, which in turn lay beyond the unfordable Appomattox. When Butler came up to observe their fruitless exchange of long-range shots with the enemy on the far side of the creek, Gillmore and Smith informed him that Petersburg couldn't be taken from this direction. The thing to do, they said, was return at once to Bermuda Neck and lay a pontoon bridge across the Appomattox at Point of Rocks, which would permit an attack on Petersburg from the east. Fuming at this after-the-fact advice from the two professionals, Butler replied testily that he had no intention of building a bridge for West Pointers to retreat across as soon as things got sticky, and Smith later declared that he found this remark "of such a character as to check voluntary advice during the remainder of the campaign."

Tempers got no better overnight. Contemplating the situation next morning, with the uncrossable creek still before him, Butler decided that Petersburg was of little importance anyhow, now that Kautz had burned two bridges on the railroad in its rear. Accordingly, he ordered everyone back to Bermuda Neck, there to regroup for an advance to be made on Richmond as soon as he got his plans worked out. They returned the following day, May 11, filing in through gaps in the intrenchments around noon, and Butler retired to his tent to think things over for a while.

If he was bitter, so were his lieutenants, contrasting what had been so boldly projected with what had been so timidly and erratically performed. In Smith's opinion, based on what he had seen in the past six unprofitable days, the army commander was "as helpless as a child on the field of battle and as visionary as an opium eater in council." Butler returned the compliment in kind, including Gillmore in the indictment. Both generals, he said, "agreed upon but one thing and that was how they could thwart and interfere with me," while, to make matters worse, neither of them "really desired that the other should succeed." Feeling his reputation threatened (in the North, that is; in the South he was already known as "Beast" Butler, hanger of patriots, insulter of women) he had written to Stanton two nights ago, from the near bank of Swift Creek, reviewing his progress to date and placing it in the best possible light, even though this involved a rather ingenuous reinterpretation of his share in Grant's over-all design for the crushing of Lee and the taking of Richmond.

"We can hold out against the whole of Lee's army," he informed the Secretary, and he added for good measure: "General Grant will not be troubled with any further reinforcements to Lee from Beauregard's force."

Lee of course had no intention of attacking Butler, who was not even in his department, and though it was true he wanted reinforcements from any source whatever, he certainly expected none from the general opposing the southside threat, since, at the outset at least, that unfortunate commander — George Pickett, of Gettysburg fame — had practically no troops to fight with, let alone detach. He had, in all, fewer than 750 of all arms to stand in the path of the 30,000 Federals debarking at Bermuda Hundred and City Point, nine miles respectively from Drewry's Bluff and his district headquarters at Petersburg, whose garrisons were included in the total that showed him facing odds of forty-to-one or longer. Beauregard, sixty-five miles to the south at Weldon, which he had reached two weeks ago to assume command of the newly created Department of North Carolina and Southern Virginia, replied to an urgent summons from Richmond on May 5 that he was "indisposed," too ill to take the field. Three brigades were en route from his old command at Charleston; he would do his utmost to speed them northward, so long at least as the railroad stayed in operation, and would come up in person as soon as he felt well enough to travel. In the meantime, though, he left it to Pickett to improvise as best he could a defense against the host ascending the James.

Pickett himself was not even supposed to be there, having received orders the day before to proceed by rail to Hanover Junction and there await the arrival of his four brigades — two of which were now with Hoke in the movement against New Bern, down the coast, while the other two were with Major General Robert Ransom, charged with defending Richmond north of the James — for a reunion with Lee's army, then on its way eastward into the Wilderness to challenge Grant's advance. The long-haired Virginian looked forward to returning to duty under Longstreet, whose guidance he had missed these past eight months on detached service. Warned of the landings downriver today, however, he stayed to meet the threat to the near vacuum between the James and the Appomattox, although he was to regret profoundly, in the course of the next five days, that he had not caught an earlier northbound train. Those five days, May 5–10, were an unrelenting nightmare, illuminated from time to time by flashes of incredible luck which then were seen to have served perversely, not to resolve, but rather to prolong the strain on his jangled nerves. Fortunately, two regiments from the first of the three promised brigades from Charleston reached Petersburg on the morning of May 6, and Pickett got these 600 Carolinians up the turnpike in time to delay the advance of the brigade Butler sent probing for the railroad. They managed this, though only by the hardest, and just as they were about to be overrun they were reinforced by a brigade sent down from Richmond: Tennesseans who had arrived that morning under Brigadier General Bushrod Johnson, the first of two western outfits summoned east to replace Pickett's two brigades in the capital defenses. Johnson was a heavy hitter, as he had shown by spearheading the Chickamauga breakthrough, and his attack drove the reconnoitering Federals back on the line of intrenchments constructed that day across Bermuda Neck. Pickett told Johnson to dig in along the pike, and then — reinforced by the rest of the Charleston brigade, which came up after midnight to lift his strength to about 3000 — settled down to wait, as best his tormented nerves would permit, for what tomorrow was going to bring.

What tomorrow brought was Butler's four-brigade attack, 6000 strong, and news that Kautz had burned the bridge over Stony Creek, cutting off hope for the early arrival of more troops from the south. One reinforcement Pickett did receive, however, and this was Major General D. H. Hill, famed for a ferocity in battle rivaling that of his late brother-in-law Stonewall Jackson. His caustic tongue having cost him lofty posts in both of the Confederacy's main armies — together with a promotion to lieutenant general, withdrawn when he fell out with Bragg after Chickamauga — Hill had offered his services to Beauregard as an aide-de-camp, and Beauregard sent him at once to Petersburg to see if Pickett thought he could be of any help. Pickett did indeed think so, and put the rank-waiving North Carolinian in charge of the two brigades in position up the turnpike. Hill handled them so skillfully in the action today around Port Walthall Junction, losing 184 to inflict 289 casualties on a force twice the size of his own, that Butler pulled back, more or less baffled, and spent what was left of that day and all of the next, May 8, brooding behind his Bermuda Neck intrenchments.

Greatly relieved by this turn of events, Pickett experienced a mixed reaction to news that Hoke's projected attack on New Bern had been a failure, due to the nonarrival of the *Albemarle*, which had retired up the Roanoke River on May 5 after a three-hour fight with seven Union gunboats in the Sound from which the ironclad took her name. She had inflicted severe damage on her challengers and suffered little herself, except to her riddled stack, but the engagement had proved her so unwieldy that her skipper decided there was no hope of steaming down into Pamlico Sound to repeat at New Bern the victory she had helped to win two weeks ago at Plymouth. This meant that, without the support of the ram, Hoke's scheduled attack had to be called off: which in turn freed him and his five brigades, including the two from Pickett, for use elsewhere. Nowhere were they needed worse than at Petersburg, and Pickett was pleased to learn that they were to join him there by rail from Goldsboro — though when they would arrive was even more doubtful now than it had been the day before, word having just come in that Kautz had burned a second railway bridge, this one across the Nottoway, twice the length of the first and therefore likely to require about twice the time to replace.

Offsetting this last, there was good news from above. While Hill was making his fight for the Junction, the second western brigade reached Richmond — Alabamians under Brigadier General Archibald Gracie, another Chickamauga hero — and was sent across the James by Ransom, who not only followed in person but also brought along Pickett's other pair of brigades and posted all three in the works around Drewry's Bluff, bracing them for a stand in case the Federals turned in that direction. This addition of 4500 troops, combined with Pickett's remnant and the two brigades with Hill, increased the strength of the southside force to about 8000, roughly one third the number Butler had on Bermuda Neck. Pickett was greatly encouraged by this reduction of the odds — and so, apparently, was Beauregard, who wired from Weldon on May 8: "The water has improved my health." Whether the cause was the water or the buildup (not to mention the strangely hesitant performance by Pickett's opponent, who seemed to be groping his way piecemeal toward eventual destruction) the Louisiana general announced that he soon would be well enough to come to Petersburg and lift the awesome burden of responsibility from the district commander's shoulders.

By then Butler had ended his spell of brooding, and next morning he came on again, this time with half his army, only to pull up short on the north bank of Swift Creek, whose presence he seemed not to have suspected until now. Beauregard arrived the following day, May 10, in time to watch the baffled Army of the James — so Butler styled it — fade back once more from approximate contact and set out rearward to find sanctuary within its fortifications. Coming fast behind him on the railroad were seven veteran brigades of infantry, Hoke's five from Goldsboro and two more from Charleston. All reached Petersburg by nightfall, having marched across the five-mile gap between the Nottoway and Stony Creek, where they got aboard waiting cars for the last twenty miles of their ride. Pickett's five days were up at last, and rather as if the strain had been what kept him rigid, after all, he collapsed and took to his bed with a nervous exhaustion vaguely diagnosed as "fever." To replace him, Beauregard summoned Major General W. H. C. Whiting from Wilmington, and turned at once to the task of organizing the twelve brigades now south of the James into four divisions. Their combined strength was just under 20,000: enough, he thought, to deal with Ben Butler for once and for all by going over to the offensive, provided of course that the Beast could be lured from behind his intrenchments and out from between the two rivers protecting his flanks.

Butler complied, two days later, by moving northward against the works around Drewry's Bluff, apparently having decided to go for Richmond after all. Beauregard had anticipated this by sending Hoke with seven brigades to join Ransom, and now he prepared to follow and take command in person, leaving Whiting to hold Petersburg with the other two brigades of infantry, plus one of cavalry just come up from North Carolina. Arriving at 3 a.m. May 14, after taking a roundabout route to avoid capture, he found that the Federals had driven the defenders from some of the outworks, south and west of Drewry's, and now were consolidating their gains, obviously in preparation for an all-out assault that would open the way to Richmond. The high-spirited Creole, with his big sad bloodhound eyes and his hair brushed forward in lovelocks over his temples, did not quail before this menace; he welcomed it as a chance to catch Butler off balance and drop him with a counterpunch.

Though it came at a rather awkward time, Ransom having detached two brigades two days ago to help fend off Sheridan, whose troopers had broken through the outer defenses north of the capital, Beauregard had a plan involving Grand Strategy which he hoped would provide him with all the soldiers needed to dispose of the threat to Richmond, not only from the south, but from the north as well: not only of Butler, that is, but also of Grant. For three years now the Hero of Sumter had specialized in providing on short notice various blueprints for total victory, simple in concept, large in scale, and characterized by daring. This one was no exception. In essence, the plan was for Lee to fall back on the capital, avoiding all but rear-guard actions in the process, then send Beauregard 10,000 of his veterans, together with Ransom's two detached brigades, as reinforcements to be used in cutting Butler off from his base and accomplishing his destruction; after which, Old Bory subsequently explained, "I would then move to attack Grant on his left flank and rear, while Lee attacked him in front." He added that he not only "felt sure of defeating Grant," but was convinced that such a stroke would "probably open the way to Washington, where we might dictate *Peace! !*"

Thus Beauregard — at 3 o'clock in the morning. Wasting no time by putting the plan on paper, he outlined it verbally for a colonel on his staff and sent him at once to Richmond with instructions to pass it on without delay to the Commander in Chief. Davis was unavailable at that hour, but Bragg was not. Having heard the proposal, he dressed and rode to Drewry's for a conference with its author. Old Bory was waiting, and launched into a fervent plea for action. "Bragg," he said, "circumstances have thrown the fate of the Confederacy in your hands and mine. Let us play our parts boldly and fearlessly. Issue those orders and I'll carry them out to the best of my ability. I'll guarantee success!" Though noncommittal, the grim-faced military adviser listened to further details of the plan and returned to the capital, having promised to lay the facts before the President as soon as possible. This he did: along with his objections, which were stringent.

Not only did the scheme ignore the loss of the Shenandoah Valley and the Virginia Central Railroad, he declared, but "the retreat of General Lee, a distance of sixty miles, from the immediate front of a superior force with no less than 8000 of the enemy's cavalry between him and the Chickahominy . . . at least endangered the safety of his army if it did not involve its destruction." Moreover, he said, such a concentration of troops beyond the James was quite unnecessary; Beauregard already had a force "ample for the purpose of crushing that under Butler, if promptly and vigorously used." Davis agreed that the plan was neither practical not requisite, and in courtesy to the Louisiana general, as well as out of concern for his touchy pride, he rode to Drewry's Bluff to tell him so in person, in the gentlest possible terms.

Beauregard's spirits drooped; but only momentarily. They rebounded at the President's assurance that Ransom's two brigades, having wound up their pursuit of Sheridan, would be ordered back across the James for a share in the attack, and Old Bory, savoring the prospect of belaboring the Beast who had tyrannized New Orleans, set to work devising a plan for assailing him, first frontally, to put him in a state of shock, and then on the flanks and rear, so that, being "thus environed by three walls of fire, [Butler] could have no resource against substantial capture or destruction, except in an attempt at partial and hazardous escape westward, away from his base, trains, or supplies." To accomplish this consummation, his first intention was to assemble all twelve infantry brigades at Drewry's for the assault, but then he decided that, instead of waiting for the troops to arrive from Petersburg by a roundabout march to avoid the Federals on the turnpike, he would have Whiting move up to Port Walthall Junction and pitch into their rear when he heard the guns announce the opening of the attack on their front by the other ten brigades, four each under Hoke and Ransom and two in a reserve division under Brigadier General Alfred Colquitt, who commanded one of the three brigades from Charleston. Notifying

Whiting by messenger and the other three division chiefs in person, he set dawn of May 16 as the jump-off hour.

That gave them a full day to get ready, if Butler would only coöperate by remaining where he was. He did just that, though more from ineptness than by design; an attack planned for that day had to be called off when it turned out that he had provided so well for the defense of his newly won position that there were no troops left for the offensive. Butler was not greatly disturbed by this development, apparently having become inured to the fact that fumbling brought delay. For one thing, he had done well these past three days — especially by contrast with the preceding seven — and had encountered only token opposition in occupying the outworks around Drewry's. So had his cavalry, which he unleashed again when he left Bermuda Neck; Kautz had struck the Richmond & Danville two days ago, wrecking switches and culverts, and by now was astride the Southside line, tearing up sections of track. Back on the James, moreover, though the river was too shallow for the ironclads to proceed beyond City Point, the navy had been persuaded to lend a hand by pushing a few lighter-draft gunboats up to Chaffin's for a duel with the batteries on that bluff. All this should give the rebels plenty to fret about for the next day or two, Butler reasoned; by which time he would be ready to hit them in earnest.

His two corps commanders, while considering themselves honor-barred from tendering any more "voluntary advice," were by no means as confident that the Confederates would be willing to abide a waiting game. Smith, in fact — called "Baldy" from his cadet days when his hair began to thin, though he protested unavailingly nowadays that he still had more of it than did many who addressed him by this unwanted sobriquet — was so disturbed by what he took to be signs of a pending assault on his position that he spent a good part of May 15, a Sunday, scavenging rebel telegraph wire along the turnpike and stringing it from stumps and bushes across his front, low to the ground to trip the unwary; "a devilish contrivance none but a Yankee could devise," Richmond papers were presently to say of this innovation which Burnside had found useful in his defense of Knoxville six months before. Smith hoped it would serve as well here on Butler's right, though he ran out of wire before he reached his flank brigade, nearest the James. He and Gillmore each had two divisions on line; his third was still at City Point, completely out of things, and one of Gillmore's was posted in reserve, back down the pike. The night was dark, soggy with intermittent rain and a heavy fog that seemed to thicken with Monday's dawn, providing a curtain through which — true to Baldy's uncommunicated prediction — the graybacks came screaming and shooting and, as it turned out, tripping over the low-strung wire across much of the Federal right front, where the blow first fell.

Along those hampered portions of the line, Smith was to say, the attackers were "slaughtered like partridges." But unfortunately, as the next phase of the fight would show, there was no wire in front of Gillmore's two divisions on the left; nor was there any in front of the brigade on the far right, where Beauregard was intent on unhinging the Union line, severing its connection with the river, and setting it up for the envelopment designed, as he said, "to separate Butler from his base and capture his whole army, if possible." Struck and scattered, the flank brigade lost five stands of colors and more than 400 prisoners, including its commander, and though the adjoining brigades and Smith's other division stood fast behind their wire, inflicting heavy casualties on Ransom, Gillmore's divisions gave ground rapidly before an advance by Hoke, also losing one of their brigade commanders, along with a good many lesser captives and five guns. Confusion followed on both sides, due to the fog and the disjointed condition of the lines. Beauregard threw Colquitt in to plug the gap that developed between Hoke and Ransom, and Gillmore got his reserve division up in time to stiffen the resistance his troops were able to offer after falling back. By 10 o'clock, after five hours of fighting, the battle had reached the pendulous climax Old Bory intended for Whiting to resolve when he came up in the Union rear, as scheduled, to administer with his two brigades the rap that would shatter the blue mass into westward-fleeing fragments, ready to be gathered up by the brigade of saber-swinging troopers he was bringing with him, up the railroad from the Junction. Two hours ago, a lull in the fighting had allowed the sound of firing to come through from the south. It grew, then died away, which was taken to mean that Whiting had met with slight resistance and would soon be up. Since then, nothing had been heard from him, though Beauregard sent out couriers to find him somewhere down the pike, all bearing the same message: "Press on and press over everything in your front, and the day will be complete."

None of the couriers found him, for the simple yet scarcely credible reason that he was not there to be found. Not only was he not advancing, as ordered, from Port Walthall Junction; he had fallen back in a state of near collapse at the first threat of opposition, despite the protests of subordinates and Harvey Hill, who had reverted to his role of volunteer aide. A brilliant engineer, whose talent had made Wilmington's Fort Fisher the Confederacy's stoutest bastion and who had attained at West Point the highest scholastic average any cadet had ever scored, the forty-year-old Mississippian was cursed with an imagination that conjured up lurid pictures of all the bloody consequences incaution might bring on. Intelligence could be a liability when it took this form in a military man, and Chase Whiting was a case in point for the argument that a touch of stolidity, even stupidity, might be a useful component in the makeup of a field commander. In any event, wrought-up as he was from the strain of the past two lonely days at Petersburg, which he was convinced was about to be attacked by the superior blue force at City Point, he went into something resembling a trance when he encountered sporadic resistance on the turnpike beyond Swift Creek, and ordered a precipitate return to the south bank. Dismayed, the two brigade chiefs had no choice except to obey, and Hill, though he retired from Whiting's presence in disgust, later defended him from rumors that he had been drunk or under the influence of narcotics. Whiting himself had a simpler explanation, which he gave after the return to Petersburg that evening. Berated by the two brigadiers, who could not restrain their anger at having been denied a share in the battle today, he turned the command over to Hill, "deeming that harmony of action was to be preferred to any personal consideration, and feeling at the time — as, indeed, I had felt for twenty-four hours — physically unfit for action."

Up at Drewry's, the truth as to what was happening below lay well outside the realm of speculation. Expecting Whiting to appear at any moment on the far side of the field, Beauregard abstained from attempting a costly frontal assault, which might or might not be successful, to accomplish what he believed could be done at next to no cost by pressure from the rear. Jefferson Davis, who could seldom resist attending a battle whose guns were roaring within earshot, rode down from Richmond to share in the mystery and the waiting. "Ah, at last!" he said with a smile, shortly before 2 o'clock, when a burst of firing was heard from the direction of Whiting's supposed advance. It died away and did not recur, however, and Beauregard regretfully concluded that it had been produced by a cavalry skirmish, not by an infantry attack. After another two hours of fruitless waiting and increased resistance, the Creole general would report, "I reluctantly abandoned so much of my plan as contemplated more than a vigorous pursuit of Butler and driving him to his fortified base.... I therefore put the army in position for the night, and sent instructions to Whiting to join our right at the railroad in the morning."

As it turned out, no "driving" was needed; Butler drove himself. Badly confused by the events of the day — he had lost 4160 killed, wounded, or missing, including two brigade commanders and 1386 other prisoners, as compared to Beauregard's total of 2506 in those three categories — he ordered a nighttime withdrawal to Bermuda Neck. "The troops having been on incessant duty for five days, three of which were in a rainstorm," he informed Washington, quite as if no battle had been fought, "I retired at leisure to within my own lines." Once back there, within the sheltering arms of the two rivers, he busied himself with strengthening his three-mile line of intrenchments, followed by the victorious Confederates, who came up next morning and began digging a three-mile line of their own, studded with guns confronting those in the Union works. Thus, after two weeks of fitful confusion, in the course of which the Federals suffered just under 6000 casualties to inflict about half as many, a stalemate was achieved; Beauregard could not get onto Bermuda Neck, but neither could Butler get off it. The Beast was caged.

Richmonders exulted in the thought of cock-eyed Butler snarling behind bars, but Grant employed a different simile to describe the outcome of his well-laid plan for obliging Lee to fall back, in haste and probable disarray, to protect the threatened capital in his rear. Angered by the news from Bermuda Hundred, which reached him hard on the heels of equally woeful accounts of what had happened to Banks and Sigel, up the Red and at New Market, he borrowed a phrase from a staff engineer whom he sent to look into the tactical situation beyond the James. Butler's army, he presently reported, "was as completely shut off from further operations directly against Richmond as if it had been in a bottle strongly corked."

As for Beauregard the corker, though he was proud of his victory and its outcome, he was by no means content. "We could and should have done more," he said. "We could and should have captured Butler's entire army." Believing that this could still be done, he returned to his former proposal that he and Lee collaborate in disposing of the enemies before them, except that this time he reversed the order of their destruction. "The crisis demands prompt and decisive action," he notified Bragg on the night of May 18, outlining a plan whereby he would detach 15,000 troops for a flank attack on Grant while Lee pulled back to the Chickahominy. Once Grant was whipped, then Lee would reinforce Beauregard for attending to Butler in much the same fashion. Admittedly the odds were long, but Old Bory considered the prize well worth the gamble, especially by contrast with what was likely to result from not trying at all. "Without such concentration," he declared, "nothing decisive can be effected, and the picture presented is one of ultimate starvation."

Davis agreed that the future seemed bleak, but he could not see that Beauregard's plan, which reached his desk the following morning, was one that would make it rosy. All the previous objections still obtained, particularly the danger to Lee in falling back before a superior blue army reported to be receiving heavy reinforcements almost daily, while he himself got none, and it was to this problem that Davis gave his attention in returning the rejected plan to Bragg. "If 15,000 men can be spared for the flank movement," he noted, "certainly 10,000 may be sent to reinforce General Lee." This was not at all what Old Bory had had in mind, since it denied him anything more than a subservient role in Richmond's further deliverance from peril. He protested for all he was worth, and not entirely without success. Not 10,000, but 6000 were ordered detached that day, May 20, from the force that manned the intrenchments confronting and corking the bluecoats on Bermuda Neck. Pickett's four brigades, plus one of the three sent up from Charleston in the course of the past week — all five had been scheduled to do so anyhow, before Butler's appearance up the James — left next day to join or rejoin the Army of Northern Virginia.

❌ 4 ❌

Lee never liked the notion of abandoning any part of the Old Dominion to its foes, but in this case, setting out from Spotsylvania on May 21 to intercept another crablike Union sidle around his right, he not only was moving toward 8500 reinforcements, he also believed he was about to avail himself of his best chance, so far, to "end this business on the battlefield, not in a fortified place." With the two armies in motion, on more or less parallel routes, almost anything could happen, and he was exhilarated, as always, by the prospect. Best of all, though, he looked forward to the confrontation likely to follow on the line of the North Anna, a couple of miles this side of Hanover Junction, where the troops from Breckinridge and Beauregard had been told to join him in time to strengthen the attack he hoped to launch while Grant was astride the deep-banked river. Moreover, with his army holding the inside track, there was little of the strain there had been two weeks ago in the breakneck race for Spotsylvania; Ewell, whose corps had been with-drawn across the Po at dawn, had barely 25 miles to go on the main-traveled Telegraph Road, while Hancock, whose starting point was the north bank of the Ni, had 34 roundabout miles to cover, by inferior roads and without the customary mass of rapid-firing blue troopers to clear and screen his front. This meant that Lee could avoid exhausting his men on the march and still have plenty of time, at its end, for pre-paring the ground on which he would stand to deliver the blow he had in mind.

Ewell set off down the Telegraph Road at noon, Anderson four hours later. While Lee waited beside the Po, preparing to follow, A. P. Hill reported himself fit for duty. Despite his pallor, which seemed to deny his claim of recovery, Lee at once restored him to command, with instructions to hold his corps in position till well after nightfall unless the last of the departing Federals pulled out before that time, and sent Early ahead to resume charge of his division under Ewell. He himself left at 8 o'clock that evening. "Come, gentlemen," he told his staff, and turned Traveller's head southward in the twilight.

Two thirds of the way to Hanover Junction, having ridden past Anderson's marchers under the flooding light of a full moon, he took a two-hour rest beside Polecat Creek — which contributed its waters, but fortunately not its name, to the Mattaponi — and reached the North Anna soon after 8 o'clock next morning, about the same time the head of Ewell's column passed over and began filing into position along the south bank, covering Chesterfield Bridge, by which it had crossed, and the railroad span half a mile below, both of which were also protected by bridgeheads set up on the other side. When Anderson arrived at noon, his two divisions extended the line a mile and a half upstream to Ox Ford, the only point along this stretch of river where the right bank was higher than the left. Army headquarters was established in the southwest quadrant of the crossing of the Virginia Central and the Richmond, Fredericksburg & Potomac; Grant was reported to be marching down the latter. Breckinridge was waiting at Hanover Junction with his two brigades, as ordered, and was given a position in line between Anderson and Ewell. Pickett's division was also there (but not its ringleted commander, who was still convalescing from the strain he had been under, south of the James); Lee assigned it temporarily to Hill, who would arrive tomorrow to extend the line a couple of miles beyond Ox Ford, in case the bluecoats tried a flanking movement from that direction when they came up. For the present, Lee required no digging to be done, partly because he did not know for sure that Grant would attempt a crossing here when he found the graybacks once more in his path, intrenched or not, and also because he wanted to give his

soldiers the leisure to enjoy their first full day out of contact with the enemy since the meeting engagement in the Wilderness, seventeen bloody days ago.

Hill arrived the following morning, May 23, coming in from the west shortly before the midday appearance of the Federals from the north. His approach was by the Virginia Central, since he had crossed the North Anna near Beaver Dam by a longer westerly route to guard the wagon train, and Lee had him rest his three divisions, with Pickett's as a fourth, under cover of some woods around Anderson Station, three miles short of Hanover Junction. While the last of his men were filing in to drop their packs in the shade of the trees, the first enemy columns came into sight beyond the river, heavy blue streams flowing sluggishly down the Telegraph Road and the tracks of the R.F.&P. Greeted by guns emplaced on high ground overlooking Ox Ford, they paused, then resumed their flow as the Union batteries took up the challenge. Short of the ford and the two bridgeheads, they stopped again and engaged the outpost rebels in the kind of long-range firefight known to veterans as a "squabble." Lee was watching with suppressed excitement, foreseeing his chance at another Fredericksburg if Grant would only continue to do as he so much hoped he would, when news arrived from the far left that another Union column was about to force a crossing beyond Jericho Mills, three or four miles above. Hill was available to counter such an upstream threat, but Lee decided to look into it in person before disturbing Little Powell's road-worn troops. Still weary from his all-night ride two nights ago, and feeling the first twinges of an intestinal disorder, he went in a borrowed carriage to the point that was said to be menaced and studied carefully with his binoculars some bluecoats in a skirt of woods across the river. He took his time, then turned at last to a courier he had brought along. "Go back and tell A. P. Hill to leave his men in camp," he said. "This is nothing but a feint. The enemy is preparing to cross below."

He was both right and wrong in this assessment: right in a lesser, wrong in a larger sense: as he discovered when he got back to headquarters, late that afternoon, and heard the uproar of a sizeable engagement on the far left, in the upstream region he had just returned from. Warren had his whole corps there and by 4.30 had completed a crossing of the river, not at the point where Lee had reconnoitered, but at nearby Jericho Mills — which was in fact "below," as Lee had predicted, but a good deal less so than he apparently had expected. Learning that the Federals had crossed and were advancing southward through the woods in unknown strength, Hill sent Wilcox up to meet them and Heth to follow in support if needed. The action opened briskly, on a promising note. Wilcox, by the luck of the draw, struck Wadsworth's depleted division, now under Brigadier General Lysander Cutler, and drove it back in panic on the other two divisions. At this point, however, things began to go badly for the attackers, who seemed to have forgotten, in the course of more than two weeks of defensive combat, how to function on the offensive. Confused by their quick success, they fought disjointedly when they moved forward to complete the Union rout. Struck in turn, they backpedaled and fell into confusion, glad to make their escape under cover of the woods and a furious rainstorm that broke over them at sundown to end the fighting before Heth arrived to join it. They had lost 642 men in the engagement, veterans who would be sorely missed in battles still to come, and had gained nothing more than the infliction of an equal number of casualties on an enemy who could far better afford the loss.

In any case, here was the first definite indication that Grant intended to attack Lee where he was, rather than continue his march downriver in search of an uncontested crossing, and presently there was another such indication, quite as definite, near the opposite end of the line. Under cover of the rainstorm that ended the Jericho Mills affair at sunset, Hancock launched a sudden two-brigade assault on the Chesterfield bridgehead, which was taken so quickly that the defenders not only had no time to fire the wooden structure in their rear, but also lost more than a hundred of their number killed or captured before they could scramble back across.

This was a small price to pay for the disclosure that the Federals were preparing to attack both Confederate wings tomorrow, above and below Ox Ford. On the off chance that it might be a ruse, employed by Grant to screen another sidle, Lee alerted Anderson to be ready for a downstream march next morning. At the same time, though — before turning in for such badly needed sleep as his cramped bowels would permit — he began devising a trap, the design for which was based on personal reconnaissance of the ground and careful study of the map, for Grant's reception if that general acted on the larger probability that he would hold to the plan whose beginnings had just been disclosed, upstream and down, for a widespread double attack on the gray army fanned out along the south bank of the river to his front.

That was just what the northern commander had in mind, and his confidence that he could bring it off, following up the double attack with a double envelopment, was shared by all around and under him, from major generals down to drummer boys and teamsters. Leaving Spotsylvania on May 21, however, after sixteen unrelenting, unavailing days of combat (waged at an average cost of 2300 casualties a day, as compared to Lee's 1100) the blue marchers had been discouraged by this second tacit admission that, despite their advantage in numbers and equipment and supplies, whenever the tactical situation was reduced to a direct confrontation, face to face, it was they and not their ragged, underfed adversaries who broke off the contest and shifted ground for another try, with the same disheartening result.

"Now what is the reason that we cannot walk straight through them with our far superior numbers?" a Michigan soldier asked, and after ruling out individual skill as a factor in the equation — "We fight as good as they" — came up with two possible answers: "They must understand the country better, or there is a screw loose somewhere in the machinery of our army."

Presently though, moving southeast, then south, and then south-southwest through a region so far untouched by war, with well-tended crops along the road and plenty of fence rails available for campfires at the end of each day's march, they perceived once more that the shift was not only sideways but forward. It was Lee, not Grant, who was yielding ground, and sooner or later — sooner, at this rate, for the march to the North Anna was better than twice the length of the one two weeks ago, out of the Wilderness — the southern commander would have none left to yield. Then would come the showdown, the last battle: which, after all, was the only one that counted in the long run, the only one they really had to win to win the war. And steadily, as this conviction grew, so did their confidence in themselves and the man who led them. A Massachusetts regiment, having crossed the Mattaponi on the morning of May 23, was slogging down the railroad, past a siding, and saw Grant, in his now tarnished uniform, perched on a flatcar gnawing a ham bone. When the New Englanders gave him a cheer he responded with a casual wave of the bone, which he then went back to. They liked that in him. It seemed to them that this singleness of purpose, this refusal to be distracted, was as characteristic of his way of fighting as it was of his way of eating. He was giving Lee the kind of attention he gave the ham bone, and it seemed to them that the result might be the same, just ahead on the North Anna — or if not there, then somewhere else this side of Richmond, where Lee would finally run out of space for backing up.

Grant believed the showdown would come here; anyhow he acted on that premise when he came within sight of the river around midday. Warren having taken the lead by turning south at Guiney Station, eight miles short of Milford, he sent him upstream to Jericho Mills and kept Hancock, who followed close behind, marching straight ahead to confront the rebels defending Chesterfield Bridge and the railroad span below. He had hoped that Lee would venture after him for an all-out scrap in the open country south and east of the Mattaponi, but since the old fox had declined the challenge there was nothing for Grant to do, as he saw it, but go for Lee where he now was. As for turning back, he had just finished making this practically impossible by closing down his Belle Plain base on the Potomac, severing all connection with that river except by sea, and opening another at nearby Port Royal on the Rappahannock. If Lee eluded him here on the North Anna he was prepared to leapfrog his base southward again when he took up the pursuit, thus keeping his supply line short and easily defended. But he did not intend to be eluded; he intended to fix the rebel army where it was by striking both of its flanks at once and moving around them to gain its rear; in which case, disadvantaged though the defenders would be, as to position as well as numbers, Lee would have no choice except to fight the showdown battle his adversary was seeking.

Soon after sunset Grant was pleased to learn that all was going well upstream and down. Warren, having crossed unmolested at

Jericho Mills, had repulsed a savage attempt by A. P. Hill to drive him back across the river. He was intrenching now, as a precaution, and would press on south and east tomorrow, to strike and turn the rebel left. Hancock too was ready for full offensive action, having seized the approaches to Chesterfield Bridge by driving off or capturing the hundred or so graybacks attempting to hold it. He would cross at first light, under instructions to serve the enemy right in much the same fashion. Burnside and Wright would be up by then, and they too would have a share in the attack, Burnside by crossing at Ox Ford to exert pressure against the center, thereby helping to fix the defenders in position, and Wright by crossing in Warren's wake to extend his right and make certain that rebel flank was overlapped and overwhelmed.

Such were the orders, and Grant turned in for a good night's sleep, with high hopes for tomorrow. These were encouraged, first thing next morning, May 24, by reports from the left and right. Hancock crossed dry-shod, unopposed, as did Wright upstream at Jericho Mills, following Warren, who encountered only token opposition when he proceeded southeast down the Virginia Central Railroad and the south bank of the river. While Burnside moved into position for a lunge across Ox Ford, good news came from Sheridan that he would be rejoining today, winding up his fifteen-day excursion down to Richmond and the James; Grant was pleased to have him back, along with his 11,000-odd troopers, presumably to undertake the welcome task of gathering up Lee's fugitives at the climax of the movement now in progress. Meantime, awaiting developments across the way, the general-in-chief attended to certain administrative and strategic details, the first of which was the incorporation of the IX Corps into the Army of the Potomac, thus ending the arrangement whereby Burnside, out of deference to his rank, had been kept awkwardly independent of Meade so far in the campaign.

Two other matters he also attended to in the course of the day, both having to do with rectifying, as best he could, the recent setbacks his diversionary efforts had suffered out in the Shenandoah Valley and down on Bermuda Neck. Sigel's successor, Major General David Hunter, was given specific instructions to accomplish all that Sigel had failed to do, and more; that is, to march up the Valley to Staunton, proceed across the Blue Ridge to Charlottesville, and continue from there southwest to Lynchburg, living off the country all the way. As for Butler, though there was no serious thought of removing him from command despite his ineptness, Grant now viewed his bottled army as a reservoir from which idle soldiers could be drawn for active service with the army still in motion under Meade. Accordingly, he was ordered to load a solid half of his infantry aboard transports — under Baldy Smith, whom Grant admired — for immediate shipment, down the James and up the York, to the Army of the Potomac. These 15,000 added reinforcements might or might not be useful, depending on what came of the maneuver now in progress across the North Anna.

Reports from there were beginning to be mixed and somewhat puzzling, not so much because of what was happening, but rather because of so much that was not. First off, finding Ox Ford covered by massed batteries frowning down from the high ground just across the way, Burnside felt obliged to state that any attempt to force a crossing at that point would result in nothing better than a bloodying of the water. Grant saw for himself that this was all too true, and accordingly changed the ruff-whiskered general's orders to avoid a profitless repulse. Leaving one division to keep up a demonstration against the ford, which in fact would serve his purpose about as well, Burnside was told to send his other two divisions — his fourth was still detached, guarding supply trains — upstream and down, to strengthen the attacks on the rebel left and right. But there was where the puzzlement came in. Neither Hancock nor Warren, who by now had been joined by Wright, had met with even a fraction of the resistance they had expected to encounter in the course of their advance. Enemy pickets did little more than fire and fall back at the slightest pressure, they reported. Except for the presence of these few graybacks, together with those in plain view on the high ground opposite Ox Ford, Lee's army might have vanished into quicksand. They found this strange, and proceeded with caution, scarcely knowing what to expect.

All Grant could do, under the circumstances, was approve the caution and advise a continuation of the advance, southeast from the right and southwest from the left. Sooner or later, he felt certain, Hancock and Warren would come upon the rebels lurking somewhere between them, over there, and grind them up as if between two millstones.

Lee rose early, despite a difficult night, and rode again in the borrowed carriage to visit A. P. Hill near Anderson Station. There he learned the details of yesterday's botched attack on Warren, made piecemeal by a single gray division, when a concerted blow by all the available four would have taken full advantage of the original blue confusion to wreck a solid quarter of Grant's army. Contrasting what might have been with what now was — Warren smashed, with Warren advancing southeast through the woods — Lee turned on Little Powell. "Why did you not do as Jackson would have done," he fumed: "thrown your whole force upon those people and driven them back?"

Red-bearded Little Powell had fallen out rather spectacularly, at one time or another, with every other superior he had ever had, including Longstreet and the general whose spirit was being invoked; but he held onto his temper now, rebuked though he was in the presence of his staff, and accepted from Lee, without protest, what he would never have taken from any other man. For one thing, he was aware of the justice of the charge, and for another he could see that Lee was not himself. Unaccustomed to illness, the gray commander had lost his balance under pressure of his intestinal complaint, and lashed out at Little Powell in an attempt to relieve the strain.

None of this was evident, however, when he moved on to the question of how to deal with the advancing Federals. This had to do with the preparation of the topographical trap he had devised the night before; Ewell and Anderson were already at work on their share of it on the right and in the center, down the railroad east of Hanover Junction and along the river in the vicinity of Ox Ford.

The North Anna was no more defensible here at close range than the Rappahannock had been at Fredericksburg, for the same reason that the opposite bank, being higher, permitted the superior Union batteries to dominate the position — all, that is, but a brief stretch of the south bank overlooking Ox Ford and extending about half a mile below. Here the Confederate batteries had the advantage, and here Lee found the answer to his problem: not of how to prevent a crossing, which was practically impossible anywhere else along the line, but of how to deal with the Federals once they were on his side of the river. He would hold this stretch of high ground with half of Anderson's corps, strongly supported by artillery, and pull the other half, along with all of Ewell's, back on a line running southeast to Hanover Junction, just east of which there was swampy ground to cover this new right flank. Similarly, Hill would occupy a line extending southwest from Ox Ford to a convenient northward loop of Little River, just west of Anderson Station. Intrenched throughout its five-mile length, this inverted V, its apex to the north and both flanks securely anchored, would provide compact protection for Lee's army, either wing of which could be reinforced at a moment's notice from the other. Best of all, though, it not only afforded superb facilities for defense; it also gave him an excellent springboard for attack. By stripping one arm of the V to a minimum needed for holding off the enemy on that side, he could mass his troops along the other arm for an attack on that isolated wing of the blue army: *which* wing did not matter, since either would have to cross the river twice in order to reinforce the other, and would therefore not be likely to arrive in time to do anything more than share in the disaster. Here was something for Grant to ponder, when and if he saw it. But the hope was that he wouldn't see it until it blew up in his face.

Leaving Hill to get started on the intrenchment of the western arm, Lee rode back to his headquarters to await developments that would determine which Union wing he would assault. Ewell and Anderson, with Breckinridge still between them, were hard at work, the former having been reinforced by the fifth of the five brigades sent up from Richmond. So skillful were the men by now at this labor, which they formerly had despised as unfit for a white man to perform, that by midday formidable earthworks, complete with slashings and abatis, had risen where none had been six hours before. This augured well for the springing of the trap, once the bluecoats came within snapping distance of its jaws. While Lee waited, however, his intestinal complaint grew worse, and though he tried to attend to administrative matters as a distraction, they only served to heighten his irascibility. The result was fairly predictable. "I have just told the old man he is not fit to command this army!" a flustered aide protested as he emerged from the tent where he had been given a dressing-down by Lee.

Before long it was obvious that the charge, though highly irreverent, was true. Even the general himself had to admit it by taking to his cot, betrayed by his entrails on the verge of the crisis he hoped to resolve by defeating, with a single well-planned attack, the foe who had maneuvered him rearward across forty miles of his beloved Virginia in the past twenty days. If Lee could not deliver the blow, then no one could. It was too late to send for Beauregard, and none of his three ranking lieutenants — one-legged Ewell, who was also nearing physical collapse, or sickly Hill, who had shown only the day before that he was in no condition for larger duties, or lackluster Anderson, who had been less than three weeks in command of anything more than a division — seemed capable of exploiting the present opportunity, which would vanish as soon as the Federals spotted the danger and reacted, either by intrenching or by pulling back across the river for a crossing farther down, beyond reach of the trap that had been installed for their undoing. Time was passing all too fast, and the chance, once gone, might never recur. Lee on his cot broke out vehemently against this deprivation of the victory he felt slipping from his grasp.

"We must strike them a blow," he kept saying. "We must never let them pass us again. We must strike them a blow!"

Betrayed from within, he raged against fate — and rightly; for before the day was over his worst fears were realized. Hancock, nudging down from his crossing at Chesterfield Bridge, and Warren and Wright, skirmishing fitfully all the way from Jericho Mills, came at last upon what the old gray fox had devised for their destruction. Not only were the works about as formidable as the ones they had assaulted with little success at Spotsylvania, but the rebels were still at work with picks and shovels, adding traverses at critical points to avoid exposure to enfilade fire. Moreover, the blue generals were not long in perceiving that such fortifications might have an offensive as well as a defensive use. They took a good hard look and went into a frenzy of digging, east and west, throwing up intrenchments of their own against the attack they believed might come at any moment from either arm of Lee's inverted V. And while they dug they sent headquarters word of the situation, best described years later by Evander Law, commander of one of the three Alabama brigades in the works ahead: "Grant found himself in what may be called a military dilemma. He had cut his army in two by running it upon the point of a wedge. He could not break the point, which rested upon the river, and the attempt to force it out of place by striking on its sides must of necessity be made without much concert of action between the two wings of his army, neither of which could reinforce the other without crossing the river twice; while his opponent could readily transfer his troops, as needed, from one wing to the other, across the narrow space between them."

This was no more apparent to Law, then or later, than it presently was to Grant, who quickly sent down orders canceling the attack. It was apparent, too, that as soon as a withdrawal could be effected without heavy losses, the thing to do was get back out of there. Meantime, the digging progressed and dirt continued to fly. Fortunately the graybacks seemed content with such long-range killing as their snipers and artillery could manage, but this did little to relieve the feeling on the Union side that they had once more been outgeneraled. This was their twentieth day of contact, and the showdown was no closer within their reach than at the outset. Dejection was taking its toll, along with the profitless wear and tear of the past three weeks. "The men in the ranks did not look as they did when they entered the Wilderness," one among them would recall. "Their uniforms were now torn, ragged, and stained with mud; the men had grown thin and haggard. The experience of those twenty days seemed to have added twenty years to their age."

All night they stayed there, and all next day and the following night, still digging, while Grant pondered the situation. He had never liked the notion of backing away from any predicament, most of which he had found would resolve themselves if he held on long enough for the enemy's troubles, whether he knew what they were or not, to be enlarged by time and idleness to unbearable proportions; in which case, he had also found, it was his adversary who got jumpy and pulled back, leaving the field to him. That was not likely to happen here, although Lee's headquarters had been shifted three miles down the R.F.& P. from Hanover Junction, on his doctor's orders to provide a more restful atmosphere for the still ailing general. Fretful and regretful though he was that his well-laid trap had gone unsprung, Lee looked now to the future and the chance to devise another that would not fail. "If I can get one more pull at him," he said of Grant this morning, "I will defeat him."

But that was not likely to happen here either. On May 26, their second day of confronting the Confederates with a divided army, the Federals put on the kind of show that generally preceded a withdrawal and a shift. There were demonstrations along the river and both arms of the fortified V, together with an upstream probe by a full division of cavalry, as if for a crossing in that direction: a likely course for Grant to follow, Lee believed, since it would keep him on the direct route to Richmond and at the same time deprive Lee of the use of the Virginia Central, his only rail connection with the Shenandoah Valley, which not only provided most of the food his army ate but was also his classic route for a counteroffensive designed to frighten the Washington authorities out of their military wits, as he had done twice already to bring about the calling-off or the recall of invasions by Hooker and McClellan, last year and the year before. Though he preferred a downstream Union sidle, which he hoped would eventually put Grant in much the same position as the one that had brought Little Mac to grief two years ago, astride "the confounded Chickahominy," Lee followed his usual intelligence procedure of assuming that his adversary would do what he himself would have done in his place. For that reason, as well as the evidence of the cavalry demonstration, he thought the shift would be upstream, for a crossing beyond his left.

He was wrong: as he found out next morning, in plenty of time to rectify his error with a rapid southward march, still on the chord of the arc the Federals were traveling. Grant had pulled back under cover of darkness and set off down — not up — the North Anna, which combined with the South Anna, five miles southeast of Hanover Junction, to become the Pamunkey. The Pamunkey in turn combined with the Mattaponi to become the York, another forty miles below, but Grant marched only about one third of this distance down the left bank for a crossing at Hanovertown, which put him within fifteen miles of Richmond, ten miles closer than he had been on the North Anna. That was not his only reason for preferring to repeat his accustomed sidle to the left, around Lee's right; he would also be keeping in close touch with his supply base, leapfrogging it south once more as he moved in that direction. As for leaving the Virginia Central in Confederate control, he counted on Hunter to conquer the Valley, now that Breckinridge had departed, and thereby deny its use to Lee even as a source of supplies, let alone as a possible avenue of invasion. Besides, he saw the outcome of this latest confrontation not as a repulse — which in fact it was, with far-reaching effects, despite its comparative bloodlessness (he had suffered only 1973 casualties, and Lee less than half that number) — but rather as conclusive proof that the opposing army had lost its fabled sting. If the rebels would not fight him there on the North Anna, with all the advantage they had secured through Lee's admitted engineering skill, they apparently were in no condition to fight him anywhere at all. Knowing nothing of Lee's debility, he assigned its results to the deterioration of the force his adversary commanded.

"Lee's army is really whipped," he informed Halleck on the day he set out down the Pamunkey. "The prisoners we now take show it, and the action of his army shows it unmistakably. A battle with them outside of intrenchments cannot be had. Our men feel that they have gained the *morale* over the enemy, and attack him with confidence. I may be mistaken," he summed up, "but I feel that our success over Lee's army is already assured."

★ ★ ★

Grant's march was in two columns, of two corps each, along the left bank of the Pamunkey; Warren and Burnside crossed at Hanovertown, Wright and Hancock four miles short of there. Preceded by Sheridan's troopers, who had little to do on the way down but brush off prowling scouts, all four corps passed over on pontoon bridges between noon and midnight, May 28, and though they were delayed by a rackety seven-hour cavalry fight near Haw's Shop, three miles beyond the river, by nightfall of the following day the whole army had pushed south and west to Totopotomoy Creek, which had its beginnings above Atlee, a station on the Virginia Central about midway between the James and the South Anna, and flowed sluggishly eastward a dozen miles to join the Pamunkey just below Hanovertown. Weary from better than forty miles of marching — southeast for two days, then southwest for another — the Federals approached the marsh-fringed creek at last, within ten miles of Richmond, only to find Lee drawn up to meet them on the opposite bank, guns emplaced and all three corps arrayed for battle.

He had been there two days waiting for Grant to make a commitment. Before sundown of May 27, whose dawn showed the enemy gone from the North Anna, he had covered the eighteen miles from Hanover Junction to Atlee, where he took up a position from which he could block a variety of approaches by the wide-ranging bluecoats, either around the headwaters of the Totopotomoy, which would put them back astride the vital railroad north of Richmond, or down across the creek for a five-mile sprint to the Chickahominy and a quick descent on the capital only four miles beyond. Still obliged by his intestinal disorder to continue using the borrowed carriage, he rode in the lead with Ewell's corps — but not with its com-

mander, who made the trip in an ambulance, racked by the same malady that afflicted Lee. Ewell was so much worse next day that he had to yield his place to Early and accept a sick leave of indefinite length; which meant that the army now had two of its three corps, four of its nine infantry divisions, and sixteen of its thirty-five original brigades under men who had not led them at the start of the campaign. Warned that elements of the Union host were across the Pamunkey at Hanovertown, Lee sent Hampton and Fitzhugh Lee to Haw's Shop to discover whether the crossing included infantry — and, if so, where it was headed. Unless he knew that, he could not move out to meet the invaders, lest they slip around one of his flanks for a lunge at Richmond from the north or the northeast.

The result was the largest cavalry engagement since Brandy Station, just under a year ago. After seven hours of savage combat, mounted and dismounted, with heavy losses on both sides — especially in a green South Carolina brigade whose troopers arrived in time for a share in a fight that converted the survivors into veterans overnight — Fitz and Hampton were obliged to give ground, but not before they had driven Sheridan's horsemen back on their supports and taken prisoners from both the V and VI Corps, which gave Lee at least half the information he was seeking. Grant's infantry was indeed over the

Pamunkey, already beyond Haw's Shop, and next day it began working its way south and west along the north bank of the Totopotomoy, still without disclosing whether it intended to cross or round the creek.

Fixed in position east of Atlee until he knew the answer, the southern commander by now had received 10,000 reinforcements. This amounted to about half his losses so far in the campaign: whereas Grant had received some 40,000, roughly the number he had lost in battle. Such disproportionate attrition could have but one result, and Lee implied as much that afternoon to Jefferson Davis, who rode out from the capital to see him for the first time since the opening of the Federal offensive. Further reinforcements would have to come from south of the James, of course, and the President was doubtful that any could be spared from there; Beauregard had been protesting all week that his force — which he had regrouped into two divisions, under Robert Hoke and Bushrod Johnson, and which he kept reminding the Commander in Chief was all that kept Butler's still-bottled army from making a sudden breakout and a dash for the back door of Richmond — had been bled down to, maybe past, the danger point. Davis made it fairly clear, before he left, that the question of detaching more troops from beyond the James would depend to a large extent on the judgment of the commander of that department. That evening Beauregard himself appeared at Atlee for a conference, the upshot of which was that, while he sympathized with Lee in all his troubles, he could not see that they were any larger than his own. As for evidence advanced by Lee that Butler was sending men to Grant, the dapper Creole admitted that perhaps 4000 had left Bermuda Hundred aboard transports in the past few days, but he stressed the claim that a substantial 24,000 still remained to pop the cork he was trying to hold in place with only half as many troops. "My force is so small at present," he had told Davis earlier today, "that to divide it for the purpose of reinforcing Lee would jeopardize the safety of the part left to guard my lines, and would greatly endanger Richmond itself." The most he would agree to was a further study of the situation on his front, and with that he departed to return there, leaving Lee no better off, even in prospect, than he had been when the rather baffling conference began.

Next morning, May 30, Grant pressed down closer along the Totopotomoy, massing opposite Anderson in the center and overlapping Early on the right; Hill, on the left, had only cavalry in his front. That seemed to rule out the Virginia Central as the enemy objective, and presently this view was strengthened by reports that two of the four blue corps had crossed downstream and were taking up a position on the near bank, facing west. Lee believed he saw now what the Federals were up to, and also how to head them off: "After fortifying this line they will probably make another move by their left flank over toward the Chickahominy. This is just a repetition of their former movements. It can only be arrested by striking at once at that part of their force which has crossed the Totopotomoy."

These words were included in a message instructing Anderson to support Early, whose corps, being on that flank, would lead the attack designed to discourage this latest sidle around the Confederate right to gain the Old Church Road, which led down across Beaver Dam Creek to Mechanicsville, where the Seven Days had opened in flame and blood. But even if he was successful in dealing with the immediate threat to Richmond from this line, Lee saw a larger danger looming. Beyond the Chickahominy lay the James, where McClellan had found sanctuary after the holocaust of Malvern Hill. Fortunately, the Washington authorities had not seen fit to sustain him in his position on the north bank of that river, nor to approve his proposal that he cross it for a movement against Richmond from the south, astride its lines of supply from Georgia and the Carolinas. Grant was no Little Mac, however, and the high command might well have learned a lesson from what had followed its failure to sustain his predecessor. In speaking to Early, who was preparing to attack at midday, Lee did not say, as he had said to Anderson, that the Federal threat must be "arrested"; he said, rather, that the Federals themselves must be destroyed. Otherwise the contest would come down to what he wanted to avoid, the loss of all freedom to maneuver.

"We must destroy this army of Grant's before he gets to James River," he told Early. "If he gets there it will become a siege, and then it will be a mere question of time."

Unfortunately, Early came closer to wrecking his newly inherited corps than he did to destroying even a portion of Grant's army. Repeating Hill's error at Jericho Mills, he attacked with one division and failed to bring the other two up promptly to exploit the initial success. Counterattacked from Bethesda Church, his objective on the Old Church Road, he barely managed to hold his ground, and Anderson only arrived in time for a share in the defensive action. Lee rebuked neither of them for the botched performance, in part because they were busy intrenching their new line, which at least forestalled an advance down the ridge between Beaver Dam and Totopotomoy creeks, and in part because of a report that reached him about the time it became apparent that the attack had failed — a report so alarming in its implications that it took precedence over his other dire concerns. Grant's new supply base was at White House Landing, fifteen miles down the Pamunkey from Hanovertown; Lee now received word that substantial reinforcements, identified as Smith's whole corps from Butler's army, were unloading there from transports which had left Bermuda

Hundred yesterday for an overnight trip down the James and up the York.

Grievous though it was to learn that he soon would be facing still a fifth blue corps with his embattled three, the danger here was more than numerical. From his debarkation point at White House, Smith was free to march due west, unhindered, to a position beyond Grant's left (to Cold Harbor, for example, a vital crossroads three miles southeast of Bethesda Church, where the Union line was anchored south of the Totopotomoy after standing firm against Early's mismanaged assault) and thus extend it beyond the reach of Lee's already thin-stretched right for a rapid swing around that flank and a leap across the Chickahominy. Convinced that this was what Grant had in mind, because it was what he would have attempted in his place, Lee first did what he could to meet the threat with what he had on hand in that direction: meaning cavalry. He sent Fitz Lee instructions to take up a position at Cold Harbor and hang on there until he was reinforced, hopefully by morning.

As things now stood, such reinforcements could not come from Hill or Anderson or Early, whose withdrawal from any part of the line would open the way for Grant to move on Atlee or Mechanicsville. They could come from only one source, beyond the James, and Lee had no time to spare for going through regular channels to procure them. Abandoning protocol he telegraphed an urgent request directly to Beauregard for every man he could spare, and when the Creole replied at sunset that the War Department would have to decide "when and what troops to order from here," Lee appealed by wire to the President in Richmond: "General Beauregard says the Department must determine what troops to send.... The result of this delay will be disaster. Butler's troops (Smith's corps) will be with Grant tomorrow. Hoke's division, at least, should be with me by light tomorrow."

It was unlike Lee to use the unequivocal word "disaster," and because it was unlike him it got immediate results. Davis promptly instructed Bragg to send Beauregard a peremptory order detaching Hoke's division for shipment by rail to Lee without delay, and before midnight Lee was informed that every effort was being made to get Hoke and his four brigades north of the Chickahominy by morning.

Once more it was as if Lee had sat in on his adversary's councils or even paid him a visit inside his head. Dissatisfied with the Totopotomoy confrontation (as well he might be; it had cost him another 2013 killed and wounded and missing, first at Haw's Shop and then along the mazy fringes of the creek, with no gain except the infliction of about an equal number of casualties) Grant by now had decided to try another sidle: a brief one, this time, aimed at just the crossroad Lee predicted he would head for.

The choice of Cold Harbor was natural enough. It was there — well clear of the toils of the Totopotomoy, but not quite into those of the treacherous Chickahominy — that the roads from Bethesda Church and White House Landing came together, enabling him to extend his left for a meeting with Baldy Smith, whose corps was debarking fifteen miles due east. Depending more on celerity than surprise, which seemed to be unobtainable here in Virginia anyhow, Grant counted on a rapid concentration at that point for a concerted drive up the left bank of the Chickahominy, one that would strike the assembling rebels before they got set to resist it and would pen them up for capture or destruction with their backs to Powhite Creek, less than two miles west, or Beaver Dam Creek, another three miles upstream; after which he would cross the river with all five corps, either below Mechanicsville or beyond at Meadow Bridge, for a quick descent on Richmond. Accordingly, while Lee was instructing his nephew Fitz to hold Cold Harbor against all comers, Grant sent word for Sheridan to seize and hang onto that vital hub until Wright, crossing in rear of Hancock on the Totopotomoy and then in rear of Burnside and Warren at Bethesda Church, arrived for a meeting with Smith at the end of his march from White House. The result next day, May 31, was another all-out cavalry engagement.

This too was a nearly all-day fight, with no infantry involved on either side till after sunset. Beauregard's bridling reaction to Lee's request for troops had delayed Hoke's departure so effectively that his lead brigade did not unload at Meadow Bridge until near midday, and consequently did not complete its eight-mile hike down the north bank of the Chickahominy until dusk was gathering on the scene of Fitz Lee's long-drawn-out defense of the crossroad his uncle had asked him to hold. As for the Federals, there was no infantry in the attacking columns even then. Concerned with keeping his withdrawal secret in order to give him a decent head start in the shift to the southeast, Grant instructed Wright to wait for nightfall before he set out on a march that was necessarily roundabout, through Haw's Shop, since there was no direct road available down across the Totopotomoy; he would arrive tomorrow morning at the soonest. Smith's delay was for other reasons, mostly involving slip-ups on Grant's staff. His original orders, issued when he embarked two days ago at Bermuda Hundred, called for a march from White House, up the south bank of the Pamunkey to New Castle, and from there to a position supporting the main effort on the Totopotomoy. Since then, Grant's plans had changed, but not Smith's orders, which were forgotten in all the flurry of preparation for the latest sidle. Completing his White House debarkation by mid-afternoon, May 31, Smith struck out northwestward, at a tangent to his intended route due west. Though he called a halt that night near Old Church, two miles short of his assigned objective, to send a wire requesting clarification from headquarters — it seemed to him he was moving into a military vacuum — the reply came back, after some delay, that his orders stood: he was to continue his march to New Castle. This he did, getting farther and farther at every step from the scene of the daylong engagement, now six miles in his left rear, which Sheridan had had to fight alone.

Little Phil frequently preferred it thus, so long at least as what opposed him was cavalry on its own. That was the case here, but he found it difficult to budge or even get at the graybacks, who declined to fight him in the smash-up style he favored. Instead, when he came within a mile of the crossroads about midday, with Torbert's three brigades — Torbert himself, up from his sickbed, had returned to duty the week before — he discovered Fitz Lee's two brigades dismounted and crouched behind fence-rail breastworks, which gave them the advantage of taking aim from an unjogged platform, with little exposure to the rapid-firing weapons of the horsemen galloping toward them. In their rear was Cold Harbor, a name of British derivation signifying an inn that afforded overnight lodging without hot food, adopted here because of the settlement's main feature, a frame tavern set in a triangular grove of trees at the intersection of five roads coming in from all round the compass. Charges by Merritt and Custer were repulsed before they could be pressed home, and as the afternoon wore on it became evident that standard cavalry tactics would not serve; Sheridan had Torbert dismount his men and work them forward, troop by troop, while their fellows provided covering fire to make the defenders keep their heads down. Swarming over the dusty fields and through the brush, pumping lead from their stubby carbines, the blue troopers in their tight-fitting trousers, bobtail jackets, and short-billed kepis looked to one observer "as though they had been especially equipped for crawling through knotholes."

It was a slow and costly business, involving much risk and a good many wounds. Giving up on Baldy Smith after a patrol returned from a fruitless eastward search for some sign of his 15,000-man corps, Sheridan sent for Gregg to come down from Bethesda Church and add his two brigades to the effort being exerted, but the sun was down behind the trees along Powhite Creek by the time the courier rode off with the summons. As it turned out, such reinforcements as reached the field before full dark were Confederate, and infantry at that.

Hard-pressed by the agile blue troopers, who were about within range for a mass charge through the gathering dusk, Fitz Lee's men looked over their shoulders and, seeing Hoke's lead brigade moving toward them up the road past the triangular grove of trees, decided the time had come to fall back on these overdue supports. They did so, only to find that the startled foot soldiers fell back too. Hot and tired from their dusty trek down the Chickahominy, and softened by two weeks of inactivity in the southside trenches, they joined what they took to be

— and what now became — a general retreat, to and through Cold Harbor; which their pursuers seized and occupied, rounding up some fifty laggard graybacks in the process. Sheridan's elation over his sudden victory was modified considerably, however, when he learned from these captives that three more brigades of infantry would soon be up to join the one he had scattered. He decided, despite the arrival of Gregg's division hard on the heels of the rout, that his wisest course would be to pull back from the tavern crossroads before he was over-run. "I do not feel able to hold this place," he notified Meade as the withdrawal got under way. "With the heavy odds against me here, I do not think it prudent to hold on."

Meade thought otherwise, and so did Grant, in view of the sidle now in progress and the intended concentration there; Cold Harbor was to be reoccupied and "held at all hazards," they replied. Little Phil reversed his march, disposed his two divisions about the southwest quadrant of the crossroads, and had the dismounted troopers get to work in the darkness, throwing up temporary breastworks to provide them with cover for meeting the attack he expected would come with the dawn, if not sooner.

It would come with the dawn, and the odds would be even heavier than Sheridan had feared when he pulled back, saying, "I do not think it prudent to hold on." Lee was about to go over to the offensive. What was more, in preparation for bloodier work to follow, he intended to begin with the retaking of the ground the troopers stood on.

Far from being discouraged by his nephew's report that the cross-roads had been seized by Sheridan, he saw in this development confirmation of his suspicion that Grant had another sidle in progress, that Cold Harbor was his intended point of concentration, and that so far he had nothing there but cavalry; which meant that his infantry was still in motion in that direction, strung out on roads converging from the north and east, and might therefore be defeated in detail as it came up — provided, of course, that Lee could get there first with a force substantial enough to inflict the damage he had in mind. He thought he could. Hoke's division was assembling there already, and this was only a fraction of what had become available now that Grant had tipped his hand. Formerly fixed in position east of Atlee by the danger that the Federals would round the headwaters of the Totopotomoy to turn his left, Lee was now free to draw troops from there for use on the opposite flank. His choice was Anderson, whose strength was up to three divisions for the first time in the campaign, Pickett having rejoined him on the march from Hanover Junction. Both the Third and the Second corps had had their turns at offensive action, Hill eight days ago on the North Anna and Early here at Bethesda Church the day before, and both had failed. Now the First — Old Peter's dependables, who had rolled up the blue flank in the Wilderness and won the hairbreadth race for Spotsylvania — would have its turn. Anderson was told to pull back from his position on the Totopotomoy, leaving Little Powell to fill the gap, and make a night march down below Cold Harbor to join Hoke, who was placed under his command for the attack, first on Sheridan, to get possession of the crossroads shortly after dawn, and then on the other Union columns as they arrived from the east and north.

Though he still had not recovered sufficiently from his illness to resume direction of tactical operations, Lee advanced his headquarters to Shady Grove Church, a couple of miles southeast of Atlee Station, to be at least that much nearer the scene of tomorrow's action. Two years ago this evening, riding back from the confused field of Seven Pines — less than ten miles from where he would camp tonight — he had been informed by the President that he would replace the fallen Johnston, and next day he had assumed command of the Army of Northern Virginia. As he retired to his tent in the churchyard tonight to sleep out the final hours of this bloodiest May in American history, he had cause for hope that he would celebrate tomorrow's anniversary with an offensive victory as glorious as the one he had begun to plan on that night two years ago, when McClellan's vast blue host hovered within even easier reach of Richmond than Grant's did now.

There was no occasion for any such celebration on the hot first day of June, only a sorry repetition of the ineptness which had led Grant to believe that the fight had gone out of Lee's army. Anderson moved promptly enough, pulling Kershaw's division out of line in plenty of time for the march across Early's rear and into position on Hoke's left before daylight. His notion was to knock Sheridan back from the crossroads with a dawn attack by these two divisions, then continue the operation when the other two arrived. But a notion was all it remained. Kershaw went forward on schedule, giving his old brigade the lead, and that was when the trouble began and the offensive ended. Colonel Lawrence Keitt, a forty-year-old former congressman, had brought his green but handsomely uniformed regiment up from South Carolina the week before, and by virtue of his seniority over the other colonels took command of the brigade. Long on rank but short on combat experience, he went into his first attack in the gallant style of 1861, leading the way on a spirited gray charger; only to be killed by the first rattling clatter of semiautomatic fire from the two divisions of cavalry in the breastworks just ahead.

That was what had been expected by seasoned observers, who saw in Keitt's display only "inexperience and want of self control," but the reaction among his troops, recently uprooted from two years of languid garrison life in their home state, was something else. When they saw the colonel get toppled from his saddle — transformed, in the wink of an eye, from a saber-waving cynosure into a mangled corpse — they broke for the rear in what a dismayed artillerist called "the most abject rout ever committed by men in Confederate uniform." Nor was that the worst of the shame. "Some were so scared they could not run, but groveled on the ground trying to burrow into the earth." Veteran regiments on their flanks were obliged to give way too; the advance dissolved in panic, unredeemed by Hoke, who had not moved at all. First the brigade and then the division as a whole pulled out of range of the fast-firing Union carbines. Kershaw got the fallback stopped and even attempted to mount another attack, but it went no better. By the time Pickett and Field came up to form on Kershaw's left, around mid-morning, so had Wright arrived with his three divisions in relief of Sheridan, who retired with pride from the defense of what he called "our little works."

They did not stay little long; Wright's men got busy with picks and shovels, deepening and extending them north and south to cover the western approaches to Cold Harbor. Smith's wandering corps slogged wearily into position alongside Wright that afternoon, reaching up to connect with Warren, whose four divisions occupied two miles of line below the Old Church Road, beyond which Burnside anchored the northern flank to the south bank of the Totopotomoy. That left only Hancock's corps and Sheridan's third division north of the creek; Grant sent word for Hancock to withdraw at nightfall for a march to the far left, where Torbert and Gregg were patrolling a boggy two-mile extension of the line down to the Chickahominy. He was instructed to come up in time to take part in a dawn assault that would be launched by all five corps.

Grant's decision to make such an attack was arrived at by a process of elimination. This was coffin corner; another sidle would involve him in the toils of the Chickahominy, and even if he cleared them intact he would find himself confronted, when he swung back west, by Richmond's permanent defenses. He would, in short, be mounting a siege, which at this stage he wanted as little as Lee did, since it represented the stalemate he had avoided from the start. His decision, then, despite the shocks and throes of the past four weeks — the stunning repulse in the green riot of the Wilderness and the unrelieved horror of Spotsylvania, which together had cost him a solid third of the infantry that crossed the Rapidan, and the close call on the North Anna, where incaution had nearly cost him the other two thirds, along with his reinforcements — was to attack the old fox where he was, or anyhow where he would be tomorrow morning. If this was coffin corner for Grant, it was something worse for Lee, whose back was to the wall of his capital and who would have neither time nor space for recovery if even a limited breakthrough could be scored. Grant kept his mind on that agreeable possibility, and when Meade suggested that something might be done with what was left of today, by way of improving tomorrow's chances, he was altogether willing.

Meade proposed a preliminary effort, restricted to the southern half of his present line, to give Wright and Smith a closer hug on the rebel works along their front and better jump-off positions from which to launch their share of the all-out dawn assault. That was how it came about that Anderson, whose four divisions were busy intrenching three miles of line, north and south of a road leading due east to Cold Harbor, was struck by a six-division attack, shortly after 5 o'clock, which not only disposed of any vestigial intention to resume his boggled offensive, but also came close to driving him from his uncompleted works. Pickett and Field held firm under pressure, but a break quickly developed between Hoke's left, where a brigade gave way in panic, and Kershaw's right. Anderson detached a brigade from Pickett to heal the breach, and by sunset the line was approximately restored. Yet the fact remained that, at a moderate price in casualties — moderate, that is, as such things went in this campaign: about 1000 for Smith, 1200 for Wright — Meade had secured the jump-off positions he wanted for tomorrow. Anderson's losses had been light, consisting mainly of stragglers captured when Hoke's left gave way, but he saw only too clearly what might come of this. "Reinforcements are necessary to enable us to hold this position," he notified Lee that night.

This message, conveying Anderson's doubts that he could hold the ground he had been ordered to advance from, put a dispiriting end to an anniversary which had dawned with high hopes that it would close with the celebration of an offensive victory. For the third time in nine days, a corps commander had shown himself incapable of mounting a sustained attack, even under favorable circumstances.

One thing common to all three attempts, in addition to failure, was that neither Lee nor his "poor Stuart" had taken part in them first hand. Jeb of course was gone for good, three weeks in his grave, and Lee was still in no condition for personal conduct of operations in the field; but that did not mean that the ailing general would not keep to his task of devising plans for the frustration of the invaders of his country and his state. Foiled in his efforts to go over to the offensive, he would continue to improvise a defensive in which, so far, he had managed to inflict casualties in ratio to the odds he faced at the opening of the campaign. In this connection he had already moved to meet Anderson's needs before they were expressed, ordering Breckinridge to take up a position on Hoke's right tonight, and now he followed through with instructions that would add Hill's three divisions to the line tomorrow, one on the left of Early and two on the right beyond Breckinridge, tying those flanks respectively to the Totopotomoy and the Chickahominy. All this would take time, however — first for marching, then for digging — and Grant was bristling aggressively all along

the seven miles of Confederate front when the sun came up on the
second day of June.

Fortunately, despite the flurry, there was no attack; Lee had
plenty of time to look to the extension and improvement of his line.
Mounting Traveller for the first time in ten days, he rode down to
Mechanicsville, where he found Breckinridge and his two brigades
enjoying a leisurely breakfast, midway through their march to the far
right. He got the distinguished Kentuckian back on the road again and
then resumed his ride, eastward past Walnut Grove Church to his new
headquarters beyond Gaines Mill, a mile and a half due west of Union-
held Cold Harbor and about the same distance northwest of the scene
of his first victory, scored two years ago this month, when Hood and
Law broke Fitz-John Porter's line on Turkey Hill, now also Union-
held. Mindful of the importance of that feature of the terrain, Lee had
Breckinridge go forward, about 3 o'clock that afternoon, and with the
assistance of one of Hill's divisions, which had just come up, drive a
brigade of bluecoats off its slopes, thus affording his artillery a position
from which to dominate the Chickahominy bottoms on the right.
Simultaneously on the left, Early's corps and Hill's remaining division
felt out the Federal installations above Old Church Road, on toward
the Totopotomoy, and after brushing aside a sizeable body of skirmishers, who yielded stubbornly, confronted the main enemy works
northwest and north of Bethesda Church.

While these two adjustments were being made at opposite ends
of the long line, a heavy rain began to fall, first in big individual drops,
pocking the dust like buckshot scattered broadcast, and then in a steady
downpour that turned the dust to mud. The discomfort was minor on
both sides, compared to the relief from heat and glare and the distraction from waiting to receive or deliver the attack both knew was
soon to be made, if not today then certainly tomorrow.

Rain often had a depressing effect on Lee, perhaps because it
reminded him of the drenched fiasco his first campaign had been, out in
western Virginia in the fall of 1861; but not now; now he valued it as
a factor that would make for muddy going when the Federals moved
against him. Back at his headquarters, near the ruins of Dr William
Gaines's once imposing four-story gristmill on Powhite Creek — Sheridan's troopers had burned it when they passed this way two weeks
ago, returning from the raid that killed Jeb Stuart — the southern commander kept to his tent, still queasy from his ten-day illness, reading
the day's reports while rain drummed on the canvas overhead. He had
done all he could to get all the troops he could muster into line. "Send
to the field hospitals," he had told his chief lieutenants in a circular
issued the last day of May, "and have every man capable of performing
the duties of a soldier returned to his command." Such efforts, combined
with those of Davis, who had summoned reinforcements from as far

away as Florida in the course of the past two weeks, had brought his strength back up to nearly 60,000. Grant had about 110,000 across the way, but Lee feared the odds no more here than he had done elsewhere. In fact he feared them less; for, thanks to Grant's forbearance today — whatever its cause — he had had plenty of time to dispose his army as he chose. Having done so, he was content to leave the rest to God and the steady valor of his troops, whose defensive skill had by now become instinctive.

This last applied in particular to the use they made of terrain within their interlocking sectors. Whether the ground was flat or hilly, bare or wooded, firm or boggy — and it was all those things from point to various point along the line from Pole Green Church to Grapevine Bridge — they never used it more skillfully than here. Occupying their assigned positions with a view to affording themselves only so much protection as would not interfere with the delivery of a maximum of firepower, they flowed onto and into the landscape as if in response to a natural law, like water seeking its own level. The result, once they were settled in, was by no means as imposing as the fortifications they had thrown up three weeks ago at Spotsylvania or last week on the North Anna. But that too was part of the design. No such works were needed here and they knew it, having installed them with concern that they not appear so formidable as to discourage all hope of success in the minds of the Federal planners across the way. Crouched in the dripping blackness after sundown, with both flanks securely anchored on rising streams and Richmond scarcely ten miles in their rear, the defenders asked for nothing better, in the way of reward for their craftsmanship and labor, than that their adversaries would advance into the meshed and overlapping fields of fire they had established, unit by unit, along their seven miles of front.

They were about to get their wish. Indeed, they would have gotten it at dawn today — ten hours before they completed their concentration and were in any condition to receive it — except that Hancock's three divisions had not arrived on the Union left until about 6.30, two hours late and in no shape for fighting, tired and hungry as they were from their grueling all-night march. Grant accepted the delay as unavoidable, and rescheduled the attack for 5 o'clock that afternoon. That would do about as well, he seemed to think. But then, as the jump-off hour drew near, the rebs went into action on both flanks, seizing Turkey Hill and driving the outpost skirmishers back on their works above Bethesda Church. This called for some changes in the stand-by orders, and Grant, still unruffled, postponed the attack once more until 4.30 next morning. After all, all he wanted was a breakthrough, almost anywhere along those six or seven miles of enemy line; he could see that a hot supper and a good night's rest would add to the strength and steadiness of the men when they went forward.

Aside from a general directive that the main effort would be made by the three corps on the left, where the opposing works were close together as a result of yesterday's preliminary effort, tactics seemed to have gone by the board, at least on the upper levels of command. Neither Grant nor Meade, or for that matter any member of their two staffs, had reconnoitered any part of the Confederate position; nor had either of them organized the attack itself in any considerable detail, including the establishment of such lateral communications as might be needed to assure coöperation between units. Apparently they assumed that all such incidental problems had been covered by a sentence in Meade's circular postponing the late-afternoon attack till dawn: "Corps commanders will employ the interim in making examinations of the ground on their front and perfecting the arrangements for the assault." New as he was to procedure in the Army of the Potomac, Baldy Smith — "aghast," he later wrote, "at the reception of such an order, which proved conclusively the utter absence of any military plan" — sent a note to Wright, who was on his left, "asking him to let me know what was to be his plan of attack, that I might conform to it, and thus have two corps acting in unison." Wright's reply was simply that he was "going to pitch in": which left Smith as much in the dark as before, and even more aghast. Grant, in short, was proceeding here at Cold Harbor as if he subscribed quite literally to the words he had written Halleck from the North Anna, a week ago today: "I feel that our success over Lee's army is already assured."

Up on the line, that was by no means the feeling prevalent among the troops who were charged with carrying out the orders contrived to bring about the result expected at headquarters. Unlike their rearward superiors, they had been uncomfortably close to the rebel works all day and knew only too well what was likely to come of any effort to assault them, let alone such a slipshod one as this. Their reaction was observed by Lieutenant Colonel Horace Porter, a young West Pointer, formerly an aide to McClellan and now serving Grant in the same capacity. Passing through the camps that rainy evening, he later wrote, "I noticed that many of the soldiers had taken off their coats and seemed to be engaged in sewing up rents in them." He thought this strange, at such a time, but when he looked closer he "found that the men were calmly writing their names and home addresses on slips of paper and pinning them on the backs of their coats, so that their bodies might be recognized and their fate made known to their families at home."

Some went even further in their gloom. A blood-stained diary, salvaged from the pocket of a dead man later picked up on the field, had this grisly final entry: "June 3. Cold Harbor. I was killed."

They came with the dawn and they came pounding, three blue corps with better than 60,000 effectives, striking for three points along the center and right center of the rebel line, which had fewer men defending its whole length than now were assaulting half of it. Advancing with a deep-throated roar — "Huzzah! Huzzah!" a Confederate thought they were yelling — the attackers saw black slouch hats sprout abruptly from the empty-looking trenches up ahead, and then the works broke into flame. A heavy bank of smoke rolled out, alive with muzzle flashes, and the air was suddenly full of screaming lead. "It seemed more like a volcanic blast than a battle," one Federal later said, "and was just about as destructive."

Dire as their expectations had been the night before, they perceived now for the first time the profoundly intricate nature of the deadfall Lee had devised for their undoing. Never before, in this or perhaps in any other war, had so large a body of troops been exposed to such a concentration of firepower; "It had the fury of the Wilderness musketry, with the thunders of the Gettysburg artillery superadded," an awed cannoneer observed from his point of vantage in the Union rear. And now, too, the committed victims saw the inadequacy of Grant's preparation in calling for a three-pronged assault, directed against three vague and widely spaced objectives. Smith on the right was enfiladed from his outer flank, as was Hancock on the left, and Wright, advancing between them with a gap on either side, found both of his flanks exposed at once to an even crueler flailing. What was worse, the closer the attackers got to the concave rebel line, the more this crossfire was intensified and the more likely an individual was to be chosen as a simultaneous target by several marksmen in the works ahead. "I could see the dust fog out of a man's clothing in two or three places where as many balls would strike him at the same moment," a defender was to say.

Under such conditions, losses tended to occur in ratio to the success of various units in closing the range. Barlow's division for example, leading Hancock's charge against Lee's right, struck a lightly defended stretch of boggy ground in Breckinridge's front and plunged on through to the main line, which buckled under sudden pressure from the cheering bluecoats. Barlow, not yet thirty — "attired in a flannel checked shirt, a threadbare pair of trousers, and an old blue kepi," he looked to a staff observer "like a highly independent mounted newsboy" — was elated to think he had scored the breakthrough Grant had called for. But his elation was short-lived. Attached to one of Hill's divisions on the adjoining slope of Turkey Hill, Joseph Finegan, who had arrived that week with two Florida battalions and been put in charge of a scratch brigade, counterattacked without waiting to be prompted and quickly restored the line, demonstrating here in Virginia the savagery he had shown at Olustee, three months ago in his home state. Barlow's men were ousted, losing heavily in the process, and it was much the same with others up the line. Though nowhere else was there a penetration, even a temporary one, wherever the range became pointblank the attack dissolved in horror; the attackers huddled together, like sheep caught in a hailstorm, and milled about distractedly in search of what little cover the terrain afforded. "They halted and began to dodge, lie down, and recoil," a watching grayback would remember, while another noted that "the dead and dying lay in front of the Confederate line in triangles, of which the apexes were the bravest men who came nearest to the breastworks under that withering, deadly fire."

The attack, now broken, had lasted just eight minutes. So brief was its duration, and so abrupt its finish, that some among the defenders had trouble crediting the fact that it had ended, while others could scarcely believe it had begun; not in earnest, at any rate. One of Hoke's brigadiers, whose troops were holding a portion of the objective assigned to Wright, square in the center of the three-corps Federal effort, afterwards testified that he "was not aware at any time of any serious assault having been given."

Part of the reason for this was the lightness of Confederate losses, especially as compared to those inflicted, although these last were not known to have been anything like as heavy as they were until the smoke began to clear. An Alabama colonel, whose regiment had three men killed and five wounded, peered out through rifts in the drifting smoke along his front, where Smith had attacked with close-packed ranks, and saw to his amazement that "the dead covered more than five acres of ground about as thickly as they could be laid." Eventually the doleful tally showed that while Lee was losing something under 1500, killed and wounded in the course of the day, Grant lost better than 7000, most of them in the course of those first eight minutes.

The attack had ended, but neither by Grant's intention nor with his consent. No sooner had the Union effort slackened than orders came for it to be renewed, and when Wright protested that he could accomplish nothing unless Hancock and Smith moved forward to protect his flanks, he was informed that they had filed the same complaint about his lack of progress in the center, which left them equally exposed. Faced with this dilemma, headquarters instructed each of the corps commanders to go forward on his own, without regard for what the others might be doing.

Up on the line, such instructions had a quality of madness, and a colonel on Wright's staff did not hesitate to say so. "To move that army farther, except by regular approaches," he declared, "was a simple and absolute impossibility, known to be such by every officer and man of the three corps engaged." Here too was a dilemma, and here too a simple answer was forthcoming. When the order to resume the attack was repeated, unit commanders responded in the same fashion by having their troops step up their rate of fire from the positions where they lay.

It went on like that all morning. Dodging shells and bullets, which continued to fall abundantly, dispatch bearers crept forward with instructions for the assault to be renewed. The firing, most of it skyward, would swell up and then subside, until another messenger arrived with another order and the process was repeated, the men lying prone and digging in, as best they could in such cramped positions, to provide themselves with a little cover between blind volleys. Finally, an order headed 1.30 came down to all three corps, eight minutes less than nine hours after it had been placed in execution: "For the present all further offensive operations will be suspended."

Over near Gaines Mill, with occasional long-range Federal projectiles landing in the clearing where his headquarters tent was pitched, Lee had spent an anxious half hour awaiting the return of couriers sent to bring him word of the outcome of the rackety assault, which opened full-voiced on the right, down near the Chickahominy, and roared quickly to a sustained climax, northward to the Totopotomoy. For all he knew, the Union infantry might get there first to announce a breakthrough half a mile east of the shell-pocked meadow overlooking the ruined mill. Mercifully, though, the wait was brief. Shortly after sunrise the couriers began returning on lathered horses, and their reports varied only in degrees of exultation. "Tell General Lee it is the same all along my front," A. P. Hill had said, pointing to where the limits of the enemy advance were marked by windrows of the dead and dying. Confederate losses were low; incredibly low, it seemed. Hoke, as an extreme example, reported that so far, though the ground directly in front of his intrench- ments was literally blue with fallen attackers, he had not lost a single man in his division. In Anderson's corps, Law was hit in the head by a stray bullet that was to take him away from his brigade for good, and Breckinridge, after ending Barlow's costly short-term penetration, was badly shaken up when his horse, struck by a solid shot, collapsed be- tween his knees. No other high-ranking defender received so much as a scratch or a bruise throughout the length of the gray line. By mid- morning, with the close-up Union effort reduced to blind volleys of musketry fired prone in response to orders for a resumption of the attack, it was clear that Lee had won what a staff colonel was to call "perhaps the easiest victory ever granted to Confederate arms by the folly of Federal commanders."

Back in Richmond, although fighting had raged even closer to the city throughout five of the Seven Days, two years ago, citizens had been jolted awake that morning by the loudest firing they had ever heard. Windows rattled with the coming of dawn and kept on rattling past midday, one apprehensive listener declared, "as if whole divisions were firing at a word of command."

No one could say, at that range, who was getting the worst and who the best of it. Before noon, as a result, distinguished visitors began arriving at Lee's headquarters in search of firsthand information. Among them was Postmaster General John H. Reagan, who brought two lawyer friends along to help find out how the battle was going. Lee told them it was going well, up to now at least, and when they wondered if the artillery wasn't unusually active here today, the general said it was, but he added, with a gesture toward the contending lines, where the drumfire of a hundred thousand rifles sounded to Reagan like the tearing of a sheet: "It is that that kills men."

What reserves did he have on hand, they asked, in case Grant managed a breakthrough at some point along his front?

"Not a regiment," Lee replied, "and that has been my condition ever since the fighting commenced on the Rappahannock. If I shorten my lines to provide a reserve, he will turn me. If I weaken my lines to provide a reserve, he will break them."

Thinking this over, the three civilians decided it was time to leave, and in the course of their ride back to the capital they met the President coming out. Today was his fifty-sixth birthday. He had spent the morn- ing, despite the magnetic clatter of the batteries at Cold Harbor, with his three children and his wife, who was soon to be delivered of their sixth; but after lunch, unable any longer to resist the pull of guns that had been roaring for nine hours, he called for his horse and set out on the nine-mile ride to army headquarters. There he found the situation much as it had been described in a 1 o'clock dispatch ("So far every attack has been repulsed," Lee wired) except that by now the Federals had abandoned all pretense of resuming the assault. The staff atmosphere, there in the clearing above Gaines Mill, was one of elation over a victory in the making, if not in fact over one already achieved. Returning to Richmond soon after dark, Davis was pleased to read a message Seddon had just received from Lee in summary of the daylong battle, which now had ended with his army intact and Grant's considerably diminished. "Our loss today has been small," the general wrote, "and our success, under the blessing of God, all that we could expect."

Beyond the lines where Lee's men rested from their exertions, and beyond the intervening space where the dead had begun to spoil in the heat and the wounded cried for help that did not come, the repulsed survivors brooded on the outcome of a solid month of fighting. This was the thirtieth day since the two armies first made contact in the Wilderness, and Union losses were swelling toward an average of 2000 men a day. Some days it was less, some days more, and some days — this one, for example — it was far more, usually as the result of a high-level miscalculation or downright blunder. Even Grant was infected by the gloom into which his troops were plunged by today's addition to the list of headlong tactical failures. "I regret this assault more than any one I ever ordered," he told his staff that evening. Uncharacteristic as it was, the remark made for a certain awkwardness in the group, as if he had sought to relieve his anguish with a scream. "Subsequently the matter was seldom referred to in a conversation," a junior staffer was to state.

Others were less reticent. "I think Grant has had his eyes opened," Meade wrote home, not without a measure of grim satisfaction, "and is willing to admit now that Virginia and Lee's army is not Tennessee and Bragg's army."

According to some observers, such an admission was a necessity if the campaign was to continue. James Wilson, riding over for a visit, found that several members of Grant's official family, including Rawlins, "feared that the policy of direct and continuous attack, if persisted in, would ultimately so decimate and discourage the rank and file that they could not be induced to face the enemy at all. Certain it is," the cavalryman added, "that the 'smash-'em-up' policy was abandoned about that time and was never again favored at headquarters." This would indeed be welcome news, if it was true, but just now the army was in no shape to take much note of anything except its weariness and depletion. A line colonel, stunned and grimy from not having had a full night's sleep or a change of clothes since May 5, found himself in no condition to write more than a few bleak lines in a family letter. "I can only tell my wife I am alive and well," he said; "I am too stupid for any use."

In the past month the Army of the Potomac, under Grant, had lost no less than half as many men as it had lost in the previous three years under McDowell, McClellan, Pope, Burnside, Hooker, and Meade on his own. Death had become a commonplace, though learning to live with it produced a cumulative strain. High-strung Gouverneur Warren, whose four bled-down divisions had fewer troops in them by now than Wright's or Hancock's three, broke out tonight in sudden expostulation to a friend: "For thirty days it has been one funeral procession past me, and it has been too much!" Criticism was mounting, not only against Grant, who had planned — or, strictly speaking, failed to plan — today's attack, but also against those immediately below him on the military ladder. "I am disgusted with the generalship displayed," young Emory Upton wrote his sister on the morning after the battle. "Our men have, in many cases, been foolishly and wantonly slaughtered." Next day, continuing the letter, he went further in fixing the blame. "Our loss was very heavy, and to no purpose. . . . Some of our corps commanders are not fit to be corporals. Lazy and indolent, they will not even ride along their lines; yet, without hesitancy, they will order us to attack the enemy, no matter what their position or numbers. Twenty thousand of our killed and wounded should today be in our ranks."

Horror was added to bitterness by the suffering of the wounded, still trapped between the lines, and the pervasive stench of the dead, still unburied after two sultry nights and the better part of a third day under the fierce June sun. "A deserter says Grant intends to *stink* Lee out of his position, if nothing else will suffice," a Richmond diarist noted, but a Federal staff colonel had a different explanation: "An impression prevails in the popular mind, and with some reason perhaps, that a commander who sends a flag of truce asking permission to bury his dead and bring in his wounded has lost the field of battle. Hence the resistance upon our part to ask a flag of truce."

No more willing to give that impression here in Virginia than he had been a year ago in Mississippi, following the repulse of his two assaults on the Vicksburg fortifications, the Union general held off doing anything to relieve either the stench or the drawn-out agony of his fallen soldiers until the afternoon of June 5, and even then he could not bring himself to make a forthright request for the necessary Confederate acquiescence. "It is reported to me," he then wrote Lee, "that there are wounded men, probably of both armies, now lying exposed and suffering between the lines." His suggestion was that each side be permitted to send out unarmed litter bearers to take up its casualties when no action was in progress, and he closed by saying that "any other method equally fair to both parties you may propose for meeting the end desired will be accepted by me." But Lee, who had no wounded out there, was not letting his adversary off that easy. "I fear that such an arrangement will lead to misunderstanding and difficulty," he replied. "I propose therefore, instead, that when either party desires to remove their dead or wounded a flag of truce be sent, as is customary. It will always afford me pleasure to comply with such a request as far as circumstances will permit."

Thus admonished, Grant took another night to think the matter over — a night in which the cries of the injured, who now had been three days without water or relief from pain, sank to a mewling — and tried a somewhat different tack, as if he were yielding, not without magnanimity, to an urgent plea from a disadvantaged opponent. "Your communication of yesterday is received," he wrote. "I will send immediately, as you propose, to collect the dead and wounded between the lines of the two armies, and will also instruct that you be allowed to do the same." Not so, Lee answered for a second time, and after expressing "regret to find that I did not make myself understood in my communication," proceeded to make it clear that if what Grant wanted was a cease-fire he would have to come right out and ask for it, not informally, as between two men with a common problem, but "by a flag of truce in the usual way." Grant put on as good a face as he could manage in winding up this curious exchange. "The knowledge that wounded men are now suffering from want of attention," he responded, "compels me to ask a suspension of hostilities for sufficient time to collect them in; say two hours."

By the time Lee's formal consent came back across the lines, however, the sun was down on the fourth day of exposure for the wounded and even the mewling had reached an end. Going out next morning, June 7, search parties found only two men alive out of all the Federal thousands who had fallen in the June 3 assault; the rest had either died or made it back under fire, alone or retrieved by comrades in the darkness. At the end of the truce — which had to be extended to give the burial details time to roll up the long blue carpet of festering corpses — Grant fired a parting verbal shot in concluding his white-flag skirmish with Lee: "Regretting that all my efforts for alleviating the sufferings of wounded men left upon the battlefield have been rendered nugatory, I remain, &c., U. S. Grant, Lieutenant General."

Lee made no reply to this, no doubt feeling that none was called for, and not even the northern commander's own troops were taken in by a blame-shifting pretense which did little more than show their chief at his worst. They could discount the Copperhead charge that he was a butcher, "a bull-headed Suvarov," since his methods so far had at least kept the rebels on the defensive while his own army moved forward more than sixty air-line miles. But this was something else, this sacrifice of brave men for no apparent purpose except to salve his rankled pride. Worst of all, they saw in the agony of their comrades, left to die amid the corpses on a field already lost, a preview of much agony to come, when they themselves would be left to whimper through days of pain while their leader composed notes in defense of conduct which, so far as they could see, had been indefensible from the start.

There was that, and there was the heat and thirst, the burning sun, the crowded trenches, and always the snipers, deadly at close range. "I hated sharpshooters, both Confederate and Union," a blue artillerist would recall, "and I was always glad to see them killed." Because of them, rations and ammunition had to be lugged forward along shallow parallels that followed a roundabout zigzag course and wore a man down to feeling like some unholy cross between a pack mule and a snake. "In some instances," another observer wrote, "where regiments whose terms of service had expired were ordered home, they had to leave the field crawling on hands and knees through trenches to the rear." That was a crowning indignity, that a man had to crouch to leave the war, at a time when he wanted to crow and shout, and that even then he might be killed on his way out. Devoured by lice and redbugs, which held carnival in the filthy rags they wore for clothes and burrowed into flesh that had not been washed for more than a month, the men turned snappish, not only among themselves but toward their officers as well. Tempers flared as the conviction grew that they were doing no earthly good in their present position, yet they saw no way to change it without abandoning their drive on Richmond, a scant ten miles away. At a cost of more than 50,000 casualties, Grant had landed them in coffin corner — and it did not help to recall, as a few surviving veterans could do, that McClellan had attained more or less the same position, two years ago, at practically no cost at all.

One who could remember that was Meade, the "damned old goggle-eyed snapping turtle" who had contributed a minor miracle to the campaign by holding onto his famous hair-trigger temper through a month of tribulations and frustrations. But now, in the wake of Cold Harbor, he lost it: lost it, moreover, in much the spectacular manner which those who knew him best had been expecting all along.

Baldy Smith was the first to see it coming. Two days after the triple-pronged assault was shattered, and with thousands of his soldiers lying dead or dying in front of his works, Meade paid Smith a routine visit, in the course of which the Vermonter asked him bluntly how he "came to give such an order for battle as that of the 2d." According to Baldy, Meade's reply was "that he had worked out every plan for every move from the crossing of the Rapidan onward, that the papers were full of the doings of *Grant's* army, and that he was tired of it and was determined to let General Grant plan his own battles." The result, once Grant had been left to his own devices, was the compounded misery out there between the lines. Smith saw from this reaction what was coming of the buildup of resentment, and two days later it came.

While the burial details were at work out front at last, Meade glanced through a hometown newspaper, a five-day-old copy of the

Philadelphia *Inquirer*, and his eye was caught by a paragraph that referred to him as being "entitled to great credit for the magnificent movements of the army since we left Brandy, for they have been directed by him. In battle he puts troops in action and controls their movements; in a word, he commands the army. General Grant is here only because he deems the present campaign the vital one of the war, and wishes to decide on the spot all questions that would be referred to him as general-in-chief." This was gratifying enough, but then the Pennsylvanian moved on to the following paragraph, the one that brought on the foreseen explosion. "History will record, but newspapers cannot, that on one eventful night during the present campaign Grant's presence saved the army, and the nation too; not that General Meade was on the point of committing a blunder unwittingly, but his devotion to his country made him loth to risk her last army on what he deemed a chance. Grant assumed the responsibility, and we are still on to Richmond."

Meade reacted fast. Though the piece was unsigned, he had the *Inquirer* correspondent — one Edward Crapsey — brought to his tent, confronted him with the article, and when the reporter admitted that he had written it, demanded to know the source of his remarks. Crapsey rather lamely cited "the talk of the camp," to the effect that after the second day of battle in the Wilderness, with both flanks turned and his center battered, only Grant had wanted to keep moving south. Enraged by the repetition of this "base and wicked lie," Meade placed the offender in arrest and had his adjutant draw up a general order directing that he "be put without the lines [of the army] and not permitted to return." The provost marshal was charged with the execution of the order next morning, June 8, and he carried it out in style. Wearing on his breast and back large placards lettered LIBELER OF THE PRESS, Crapsey was mounted face-rearward on a mule and paraded through the camps to the accompaniment of the "Rogue's March," after which he was less ceremoniously expelled. "The commanding general trusts that this example will deter others from committing like offenses," Meade's order read, "and he takes this occasion to notify the representatives of the public press that . . . he will not hesitate to punish with the utmost rigor all [such] instances."

Whatever he might have "trusted," the outcome was that Meade now had two wars on his hands, one with the rebels in his front, the other with "the representatives of the public press" in his immediate rear. Making his way to Washington, Crapsey recounted his woes to newspaper friends, who were unanimous in condemning the general for thus "wreaking his personal vengeance on an obscure friendless civilian." What was more, their publishers backed them up; Meade, one said, was "as leprous with moral cowardice as the brute that kicks a helpless cripple on the street, or beats his wife at home." By way of retaliation for what they called "this elaborate insult," they agreed that his name would never be mentioned in dispatches except in connection with a defeat, and they held to this for the next six months or more, with the result that another casualty was added to the long Cold Harbor list, a victim of journalistic strangulation.

Eleven months ago, the Gettysburg victor had been seen as a sure winner in some future presidential election; but not now. Now and for the rest of the year, a reporter noted privately, "Meade was quite as much unknown, by any correspondence from the army, as any dead hero of antiquity."

★ ★ ★

Meade had his woes, but so it seemed did everyone around him, high or low, in the wake of a battle whose decisive action was over in eight holocaustic minutes. Not only had it been lost, and quickly lost; it had been lost, the losers now perceived, before it began. Despite the distraction of wounds that smarted all the more from having been self-inflicted, so to speak, this made for a certain amount of bitter intro-spection at all levels, including the top. A colonel on Lee's staff, coupling quotes from Grant and Hamlet — admittedly an improbable combina-tion — remarked that the Union commander's resolution "to fight it out on this line if it takes all summer" seemed, at this stage, to be "sicklied o'er with the pale cast of thought."

It was in fact, all quips aside, a time for taking stock. Beyond the knowledge that attrition was a knife that cut both ways, Grant had accepted from the outset, as a condition of the tournament, the proba-bility that the knife would slice deeper into the ranks of the attacker; but how much deeper he hadn't known, till now. For twenty-nine days he had been losing about two men to Lee's one, and if this was hard, it was at any rate in proportion to the size of the two armies. Then came the thirtieth day, Cold Harbor, and his loss was five to one, a figure made even more doleful by the prospect that future losses were likely to be as painfully disproportionate if he tried the same thing again in this same region. Lodged as he was in coffin corner, it was no wonder if the cast of his thought was sicklied o'er, along with the thoughts of those around him, staff or line; Rawlins and Upton, for example. Moreover, the effect of that month of losses was cumulative, like the expenses of a spender on a spree, and during the lull which now ensued the bill came due. Halleck sent him what amounted to a declaration of bankruptcy, or in any case a warning that his credit was about to be cut off. On June 7, while the burial details were at work and Meade was berating Crapsey in his tent, Old Brains served notice from Washington that the bottom of the manpower barrel was in sight: "I inclose a list of troops forwarded from this department to the Army of the Potomac since the campaign opened — 48,265 men. I shall send you a few regiments more, when all resources will be exhausted till another draft is made."

These were hard lines, coming as they did at this disappointing juncture in the campaign. Just as the addition of Smith's 15,000 from the Army of the James had not made up for the number who departed from Meade's army because their enlistments had expired or they had broken down physically under the thirty-day strain, so too was Halleck's figure, even with the inclusion of those "few regiments more," considerably short of the number who had been shot or captured in the course of the month-long drive from the Rapidan to the Chickahominy. This would make for restrictions, which in turn seemed likely to require a change in style. Up to the present, Grant had been living as it were on interest, replacing his fallen veterans with conscripts, but from now until another of Lincoln's "calls" had been responded to, and the drafted troops approximately trained for use in the field, he would be living on principal. Formerly replaceable on short notice, a man hit now would be simply one man less, a flat subtraction from the dwindling mass. The law of diminishing utility thus obtained, and though Grant no doubt would find it cramping, if not prohibitive in its effect on his previous method of sailing headlong into whatever got in his path, it afforded in any case a gleam of hope for those around and under him. Some members of his staff had expressed the fear that any attempt to repeat the army's latest effort, here between the Totopotomoy and the Chickahominy, would render it unfit for future use. Now they could stop worrying; at least about that. Grant had no intention of provoking another Cold Harbor and they knew it, not only because they had heard him express regret that he had tried such a thing in the first place, but also because they knew that he could no longer afford it, even if he changed his mind.

One possible source of reinforcements was the remnant of Butler's army, still tightly corked in its bottle on the far side of the James and doing no earthly good except for keeping Beauregard's even smaller remnant from joining Lee. However, as a result of his casualties during the corking operation and the subsequent detachment of Smith, the cock-eyed general was down to about 10,000 men, scarcely enough to warrant the trouble of getting them on and off transports and certainly not enough to make any significant change in the situation north of the Chickahominy. Besides, Grant's mind was turning now toward a use for them in the region where they were. He still thought his plan for a diversionary effort south of the James had been a good one; aside, that is, from the designation of Butler as the man to carry it out. If a real soldier, a professional rather than an all-thumbs amateur, had been in over-all command — Baldy Smith, for example — Richmond might not have fallen by now, but at least it would have been cut off from Georgia and the Carolinas by the occupation of the Petersburg rail hub, and its citizens would be tightening their belts another notch or two to relieve far greater pangs of hunger than they were feeling with their supply lines open to the south. Grant's notion was to reinforce Butler for a breakout from Bermuda Neck, due west to Walthall Junction, or a sidle across the Appomattox for a quick descent on Petersburg. Smith's corps would go, he and his men being familiar with the southside terrain, and possibly a corps or two from Meade. In fact, the more Grant thought about it, there in the stench and dust around Cold Harbor, the more he was persuaded that the thing to do was send Meade's whole army, not only to assure the success of the operation beyond the James, but also to resolve what was fast becoming a stalemate, here on the north bank of the Chickahominy, and remove the troops from the scene of their most disheartening repulse.

Halleck was against it before he even learned the details. He preferred the slower but less risky investment of the Confederate capital from the north, which would not expose the army to the danger of being caught astride the James and would have the added virtue of covering Washington if Lee reverted to his practice of disrupting Union strategy with a strike across the Potomac. But Grant had had quite enough of maneuvering in that region.

"My idea from the start has been to beat Lee's army, if possible, north of Richmond," he admitted in a letter to the chief of staff on June 5, the day he opened negotiations for the burial of his dead, but he saw now that "without a greater sacrifice of human life than I am willing to make, all cannot be accomplished that I had designed." Then he told just what it was he had in mind. "I will continue to hold substantially to the ground now occupied by the Army of the Potomac, taking advantage of any favorable circumstance that may present itself, until the cavalry can be sent to destroy the Virginia Central Railroad from about Beaver Dam for some 25 or 30 miles west. When this is effected, I will move the army to the south side of James River." Cut off from supplies from the north and south, Lee would have no choice except to stay inside his capital and starve, abandon it to his foe, or come out and fight for it in the open. Grant had no doubt about the outcome if his adversary, as seemed likely from past usage, chose the third of these alternatives and tried to stage another Seven Days. "The feeling of the two armies now seems to be that the rebels can protect themselves only by strong intrenchments," he closed his letter, "while our army is not only confident of protecting itself without intrenchments, but can beat and drive the enemy whenever and wherever he can be found without this protection."

Then suddenly things began to happen fast. He learned that night that while he had been writing to Halleck, outlining his plan without committing himself to a schedule, Sigel's successor David Hunter had scored a victory out in the Shenandoah Valley that would shorten considerably the time Grant had thought he would have to devote to smashing Richmond's northwestern supply line. Disdaining the combinations his predecessor had favored — and which, it could be seen now, had contributed to the failure of that segment of the grand design for Lee's defeat — Hunter had simply notified Crook and Averell that he was heading south, up the Valley pike, and that they were to join him as soon as they could make it across the Alleghenies from their camp on the Greenbrier River. He set out from Cedar Creek on May 26, five days after taking command of the troops whipped at New Market the week before, and at the end of a ten-day hike up the turnpike, which he interrupted from time to time to demolish a gristmill, burn a barn, or drive off butternut horsemen trying to scout the column at long range, he reached the village of Piedmont, eleven miles short of Staunton, and found the rebels drawn up in his path, guns booming. Attacking forthwith he wrecked and scattered what turned out to be three scratch brigades, all that were left to defend the region after Breckinridge departed. His reward, gained at a cost of less than 500 killed and wounded, included more than 1000 prisoners, a solid fifth of the force that had opposed him; the body of Brigadier General William E. Jones, abandoned on the field by the fugitives he had commanded until he was shot; and Staunton. Hunter occupied the town next day, his two divisions marching unopposed down streets no blue-clad troops had trod before. Two days later, on June 8, having torn up the railroad west of town as they approached, Crook and Averell arrived from West Virginia to assist in the consumption and destruction of commissary and ordnance stores collected at Staunton for shipment to Lee's army. With his strength thus doubled to 18,000, Hunter promptly took up the march for Lynchburg, another important depot of supplies, located where the Virginia & Tennessee Railroad branched east to form the Southside and the Orange & Alexandria; after which he intended to strike northeast for Charlottesville, where he would get back astride the Virginia Central and move down it to join Grant near Richmond, twisting rails and burning crossties as he went.

Again he was moving toward reinforcements, this time of the doughtiest kind. Grant had no sooner learned of Hunter's coup at Piedmont than he decided to proceed at once with the opening phase of the plan he had outlined that day for Halleck. He sent for Sheridan and gave him orders to take off at dawn of June 7, westward around Lee's north flank, for a link-up with Hunter near Charlottesville; he was to lend the help of his hard-handed troopers in wrecking the Virginia Central on his way back and, if necessary, fight off any graybacks, mounted or dismounted, who might try to interfere. In this connection Grant conferred next day with Meade, explaining the ticklish necessity of keeping enough pressure on Lee to discourage him from sending any part of his army against Sheridan or Hunter, yet not so much pressure that Lee would fall back to the permanent fortifications in his rear, whose strength might also permit such a detachment of troops for the protection of the vital rail supply route from the Shenandoah Valley. (This was also why Grant, in addition to his habitual disinclination in such matters, had not wanted to risk encouraging his opponent by making a forthright request for permission to bury his dead and bring in the wounded suffering in his front.) At the same time, Meade was instructed to start work on a second line of intrenchments, just in rear of his present works, stout enough to be held by a skeleton force if Lee attacked while the army was in the early stages of its withdrawal across the Chickahominy, down beyond White Oak Swamp, to and across the James.

One thing more Grant did while Sheridan was preparing to take off next morning, and that was to call in two of his aides, Horace Porter and another young lieutenant colonel, Cyrus Comstock, who was also a West Pointer and a trained engineer. Both were familiar with the region to be traversed, having served under McClellan in the course of that general's "change of base" two years ago, and Grant had a double mission for them: one as carriers of instructions for Butler at Bermuda Hundred, the other as selectors of a site for what promised to be the longest pontoon bridge in American military history. "Explain the contemplated movement fully to General Butler," he told them, "and see that the necessary precautions are made by him to render his position secure against any attack from Lee's forces while the Army of the Potomac is making its movement." That was their first assignment, and the second, involving engineering skill, followed close behind. "You will then select the best point on the river for the crossing."

They left, and the following day — with Sheridan's troopers gone before dawn, the burial squads at their grisly task out front, and Meade in a snit over Crapsey's piece in the *Inquirer* — Grant got to work, while awaiting the outcome of his preliminary arrangements, on logistic details of the projected shift. He did so, however, over the continuing objections of the chief of staff. Halleck had been against a southside campaign two years ago, when McClellan pled so fervently for permission to undertake what Grant was about to do, and he still was as much opposed as ever, believing that such a maneuver was practically an invitation for Lee to cross the Potomac. The old fox had already crossed it twice without success, it was true, but the third time might prove to be the charm that won him Washington, especially now that Grant, having stripped its forts of soldiers, proposed to leave it strategically uncovered.

Old Brains continued thus to take counsel of his fears; but not Grant, whose mind was quite made up. "We can defend Washington best," he informed Halleck, putting an end to discussion of the matter, "by keeping Lee so occupied that he cannot detach enough troops to capture it. I shall prepare at once to move across James River."

Grant being Grant, and Halleck having long since lost the veto, that was that. The Union commander was soon to find, however, that his effort to keep Lee so occupied with the close-up defense of Richmond that he would not feel able to send any considerable part of his outnumbered force against Hunter or Sheridan had failed. Learning on June 6 of Jones's defeat at Piedmont and Hunter's rapid occupation of Staunton, Lee sent at once for Breckinridge and informed him that he and his two brigades would be leaving next morning for Lynchburg to prevent the capture of that important railroad junction by the bluecoats they had whipped three weeks ago under Sigel, a hundred miles to the north. Instructed to combine his 2100 veterans with the Piedmont fugitives for this purpose, the Kentuckian left on schedule, determined to repeat his New Market triumph, although he would be facing longer odds and was personally in a near-invalid condition as a result of having his horse collapse on him four days ago.

With Grant likely to resume his hammering at any moment, here at Cold Harbor or elsewhere along a semicircular arc from Atlee Station down to Chaffin's Bluff — all within ten miles of Capitol Square — even so minor a reduction in strength as this detachment of two brigades was a risky business for Lee, no matter how urgent the need. Yet before the day was over he was warned of another threat which called for a second detachment, larger and more critical than the first. Sheridan, he learned from outpost scouts, had taken off before dawn with two of his divisions, about the same time Breckinridge left Richmond, headed west by rail for Lynchburg. The bandy-legged cavalryman's march was north, across the Pamunkey; he made camp that night on the near bank of the Mattaponi, and next morning — June 8 — he was reported moving west. Lee reasoned that the blue horsemen intended to effect a junction with Hunter on this or the far side of the Blue Ridge, somewhere along the Virginia Central, which they would obstruct while waiting for him to join them for the return march. If Sheridan was to be thwarted it would have to be done by a force as mobile as his own, and though Lee found it hard to deprive himself of a single trooper at a time when his adversary was no doubt contemplating another sidle, he sent Hampton orders to set out next morning, with his own and Fitzhugh Lee's divisions, to intercept the raiders before they reached either Hunter or the railroad.

Yet this too, as it turned out, was a day that brought unwelcome news of the need for still another reduction of the outnumbered army in its trenches near Cold Harbor. Crook and Averell, Lee was informed, had joined Hunter that morning in Staunton, doubling his strength beyond anything Breckinridge, with less than a third as many troops — including the Piedmont fugitives, once he managed to round them up — could be expected to confront, much less defeat. Obviously he would have to be reinforced; but how? Then came the notion Halleck was even now warning Grant that his proposed maneuver would invite from Lee, who had a way of making a virtue of necessity. Hunter's strength was put at 20,000, and it was clear that if he was to be stopped it would have to be done by two or three divisions, available only — if at all — from the Confederate main body. Such a decrease in the force confronting Grant, merely for the sake of blocking Hunter, seemed little short of suicidal. But how would it be if a sizeable detachment could be used offensively, as a means not only of reclaiming the Shenandoah Valley and covering the supply lines leading to it, but also of threatening Washington by crossing the Potomac? Twice before, a dispersion of force, made in the face of odds as long or longer, had relieved the pressure on Richmond by playing on the fears of the Union high command. McClellan and Hooker had been recalled to protect the menaced capital in their rear; so might Grant be summoned back to meet a similar threat. Impossible though it seemed at this fitful juncture, such a maneuver was never really out of Lee's mind, and it was especially attractive now that rumors had begun to fly that Grant was designing a shift to the James, perhaps for a link-up with Butler on the other side. "If he gets there it will become a siege," Lee had told Early the week before, "and then it will be a mere question of time."

Hampton had no sooner taken off next morning, riding the chord of Sheridan's arc to intercept him, than an alarm from beyond the James lent credence to the rumor that the Federals were preparing a new effort in that direction, or in any case an improved resumption of the old one. Butler, crossing a portion of his command from Bermuda Neck by a pontoon bridge he had thrown across the Appomattox near Port Walthall, launched a dawn attack on the Petersburg intrenchments, four miles south. Beauregard, down to fewer than 8000 troops by now, managed to contain and repulse this cavalry-infantry assault because of the strength of the works and the valiance of the men who occupied them, mostly under- and over-aged members of a militia battalion, reinforced for the crisis by volunteers from the city hospital and the county jail. In the resultant "Battle of the Patients and the Penitents," as it came to be called, these inexperienced defenders — inspired by a local Negro band whose vigorous playing gave the attackers the impression that the works were heavily manned — held their own long enough for gray-jacket cavalry to arrive from the main line, beyond the Appomattox, and drive the bluecoats off. It was over by midafternoon, a near thing at best, and Beauregard, though proud of what had been achieved, warned that he could not be expected to repeat the performance unless the troops he had sent Lee were restored to him. Moreover, he told the War Department, they had better be returned at once, since in his opinion today's attack presaged a much larger one soon to come.

"This movement must be a reconnaissance connected with Grant's future operations," he wired Bragg while the fight was still in progress, and presently he added, by way of emphasizing the risk: "Without the troops sent to General Lee I will have to elect between abandoning lines on Bermuda Neck and those of Petersburg. Please give me the views of the Government on the subject."

Presented thus with a choice between losing Richmond to assault or by starvation, Bragg could only reply that the mercurial Creole was to do what he could to hold both positions, while he himself conferred with Davis, who authorized the return of Gracie's brigade from the capital defenses, and with Lee, who agreed to alert Hoke's division for a crossing at Drewry's in case another southside attack developed. Mainly, though, the Virginian saw this abortive maneuver of Butler's as a feint, designed to distract his attention from more serious threats presented by more dependable Union commanders on the north side of the James: by Meade, who might even now be bracing his army for another all-out lunge, here at Cold Harbor or elsewhere along the Richmond-hugging arc: by Hunter, who was evidently about to resume his march from Staunton, with either Lynchburg or Charlottesville as his intermediate goal, preparatory to a combination with Meade: or by Sheridan, who was in motion between the other two, probably with the intention of descending on the Virginia Central before linking up with Hunter for a return march that would complete the destruction of that vital supply line. Despite a rather superfluous warning from the President, who added his voice to Bragg's — "The indications are that Grant, despairing of a direct attack, is now seeking to embarrass you by flank movements" — Lee could not see that the thing to do, at this critical juncture, was weaken his army below the present danger point for the sake of relieving Beauregard's fears as to what Butler might or might not be up to, down on the far side of the James. Until Grant's intentions became clearer, and until he could see what came of the two detachments already made — Breckinridge, two days ago, and Hampton just this morning — Lee preferred to hold what he had, and hope that others, elsewhere, would measure up to his expectations.

Wade Hampton, whose assignment to lead the two-division column in pursuit of Sheridan was the nearest Lee had come to designating a successor to the fallen Stuart, was intent on fulfilling his share of the army commander's hopes, not so much because of a desire for fame or an ache for glory — "I pray for peace," he would presently say in a letter to his sister, having won the coveted post by demonstrating his fitness for it in the current operation; "I would not give peace for all the military glory of Bonaparte" — as because of a habitual determination to accomplish what was required of him, in this as in other phases of a life of privileged responsibility. He wore no plume, no red-lined cape, and a minimum of braid, preferring a flat-brimmed brown felt hat and a plain gray jacket of civilian cut. His manner, while friendly, was grave, and though he was perhaps the richest man in the South, his spurs were brass, not gold. A Virginia trooper noted another difference between the Carolinian and his predecessor as chief of cavalry, which was that, whereas Jeb had "sometimes seemed to have a delight in trying to discharge his mission with the smallest possible number of men, Hampton believed in superiority of force and exerted himself to concentrate all the men he could at the point of contact."

Superiority of force would not be possible short of the point of contact in this case; for though both mounted columns were composed of two divisions containing a total of five brigades, Sheridan had 8000 troopers, compared to Hampton's 5000, and four batteries of horse artillery opposing three. One advantage the gray riders had, however, and this was that they traveled lighter, with fewer impediments to slow them down. The Federals had a train of 125 supply wagons and ambulances, as well as a herd of beef to butcher on the march, while all the Confederates had was an issue of three-day rations, consisting of half a pound of bacon and a pound and a half of hardtack, carried on the person, along with a sack of horse corn slung from the pommel of each saddle. Another advantage, although no one could be sure of it beforehand, was that Lee had been right about Sheridan's objective; Hampton had a much shorter distance to travel, northwest from Atlee, across the South Anna, in order to get there first. This he did, despite the blue column's two-day head start in setting out on its roundabout route from Cold Harbor, first north across the Pamunkey, then west through Chilesburg, up the left bank of the North Anna for a crossing short of Gordonsville and a quick descent, as ordered, on the Virginia Central between that place and Louisa Courthouse, a dozen miles down the track. Shortly after sunrise, June 11, within about three miles of his objective at the outset of his fifth day on the go, Sheridan ran into fire from rebel skirmishers, who, he now found, had arrived the previous evening and had rested from their two-day ride within earshot of the bugles that called his troopers to horse this morning.

Hampton was not only there, he was attacking in accordance with plans made the night before, after learning that he had won the race for the stretch of railroad Sheridan had in mind to wreck. His own division, with three brigades, was to advance northeast from Trevilian Station, eight miles short of Gordonsville and half that distance above Louisa, where Fitz Lee, having bivouacked his two brigades nearby, was to set out north at daybreak for a convergence upon Sheridan's camp, five miles away. Each division had a convenient road to move on, and Hampton at least was unhindered on the approach march. Hearing firing off to the east, which he took to be Fitz brushing pickets from his path, he sent his lead brigade forward, dismounted, and made contact with the Federals, driving them rapidly back on their supports, who resisted stubbornly even when hit by a second brigade. Hampton withheld full commitment, waiting for Lee to come up and strike the defenders flank and rear. At this point, however, a sudden clatter from the south informed him that his own rear had been struck. By what, and how, he did not wait to learn. Disengaging with all possible speed, and pursued now by the enemy he had driven, he withdrew to find a host of blue marauders laying claim to his headquarters and the 800 horses left behind when he dismounted his lead brigade for the sunrise attack. He attacked again, this time rearward, and what had been a battle became a melee.

The marauders were members of Custer's brigade, one of Torbert's three. While the other two were holding fast under pressure from Hampton, Gregg's division had got the jump on Fitz and driven him back toward Louisa, enabling the Michiganders to slip between the converging gray columns for a penetration deep into Hampton's rear, near Trevilian. Yet they had no sooner begun to gather the fruits of their boldness — the 800 riderless horses, several ordnance wagons, and a couple of guns being held there in reserve — than they were hit, simultaneously from the north and east, by three hornet-mad rebel brigades, two of them Hampton's and one Lee's. Custer not only had to abandon what he had won; he also lost much that he brought with him, including a considerable number of troopers shot or captured, his headquarters wagon containing all his records and spare clothes, and his Negro cook Eliza, known to the soldiers as "the Queen of Sheba" because she usually rode in a dilapidated family carriage the yellow-haired general had commandeered for her professional use and comfort. Shaken, he fell back to the station and held on grimly against the odds, while Torbert fought his way down with the other two brigades and Gregg continued to slug it out with Fitz. The result was about as bewildering to one side as to the other, and was to be even more confusing to future students attempting to reconcile conflicting reports of the action. The Confederates at last pulled back, Hampton toward Gordonsville and Lee in the opposite direction. Sheridan did not pursue, west or east, but contented himself with holding the four miles of track between Trevilian and Louisa. It was a gloomy night for the Federals, especially those in Custer's brigade, which had lost heavily today; but their dejection was relieved, just before sunup, by the reappearance of the Queen of Sheba, grinning broadly and lugging along the gaudy young general's personal valise, which she had managed to bring with her when she stole out of the rebel lines and into her own.

Sheridan was far from pleased with the development of events. After a night of fitful sleep, with graybacks hovering east and west — about to be joined, for all he knew, by reinforcements from both directions, infantry by rail and cavalry on horseback — he put Gregg to work with sledges and crowbars on the four-mile stretch of track and prepared to enlarge his present limits of destruction, first by driving Hampton back on Gordonsville, eight miles northwest, and then by thrusting him aside to clear the way for the scheduled meeting with

Hunter, another twenty miles up the line at Charlottesville. It was past noon, however, before he got Torbert deployed for action; by which time Fitz Lee had joined Hampton, coming roundabout from Louisa, and the two divisions were dug in just above Trevilian, blocking both the Virginia Central and the turnpike leading west. Repeated and costly dismounted assaults failed to budge the rebels, snug in their works, and after nightfall, Gregg having done all the damage he could to the railroad within the cramped limits of the Federal occupation, Sheridan decided to abandon both his position and his mission.

Under cover of darkness he withdrew across the North Anna and took up the return march, retracing the route that had brought him to the unhappy confrontation at Trevilian. He pulled back, he said, because his supplies and munitions were low and there was no word from Hunter, either at Charlottesville or elsewhere, as to their intended combination. In any case, having spent four days on the march out, he took nine to make it back to White House Landing, his ambulances overloaded with wounded and his horses distressed at being reduced to a diet of bearded wheat. Meantime, the limited damage Gregg had done the railroad was repaired so promptly by work gangs that Virginia Central trains were back on schedule before Sheridan reached the Pamunkey and recrossed it under the protection of gunboats whose heavy-caliber frown kept the still-hovering butternut cavalry at bay. Hampton had lost nearly 1100 men in the course of the raid; Sheridan reckoned his own loss at about 800, though a more accurate revision put the figure at 1516, considerably better than twice the number he had lost on the Richmond raid the month before.

R. E. Lee of course was pleased to learn that Little Phil had been disposed of as a threat to his main supply route from the Shenandoah Valley: so pleased, indeed, that he at last named Hampton, rather than his nephew Fitz, as his new chief of cavalry. But word of Sheridan's repulse came in the wake of news of a fateful development, out beyond the Blue Ridge, which not only presented a more substantial menace to the newly delivered supply line, but also served notice that, even if the railroad escaped seizure, there would be little in the way of supplies available for shipment from the region, either to Richmond or to any other point in the shrinking Confederacy. The news was that David Hunter, his strength doubled by the arrival of Crook two days before, had resumed his march up the Valley on June 10. Leaving Breckinridge holding the bag at Rockfish Gap, where the Virginia Central passed through the mountains east of Staunton — the Kentuckian had shifted there from Lynchburg to block the western approach to Charlottesville, which he thought was next on the Union list — Hunter struck out south, not east, and by noon of the day the cavalry battle opened near Trevilian Station, eighty air-line miles away, reached Lexington and took under fire, from across North River, the crenelated turrets and ramparts of V.M.I., whose cadets had shared in the defeat of his predecessor four weeks ago. Marching in, flags flying, he completed his work of destruction, next day and the day after, by putting the torch to what was left of the Institute and turning his soldiers loose on the town to plunder a number of private homes and the library of Washington College. For good measure, after a visit to Stonewall Jackson's grave — perhaps to make certain the famed rebel had not come bursting out of it in his wrath — Hunter ordered the residence of Former Governor John Letcher burned, as he later reported, in retaliation for its absent owner's having issued "a violent and inflammatory proclamation . . . inciting the population of the country to rise and wage guerrilla warfare on my troops."

Such hard-handedness toward civilians was remindful of John Pope, of whom Lee had said: "He ought to be suppressed," and then had proceeded to do just that by dividing his army, confronted near Richmond by a superior force, and sending part of it north and west, under the one-time V.M.I. professor now buried in outraged Lexington, against the fire-breathing secondary invader attempting a descent on his left flank and rear. Close though the resemblance was between the situations then and now, there were also differences, none of them advantageous from the Confederate point of view. One was that Jackson, Lee's right arm, was no longer available to carry out the suppression, and another was the present depleted condition of the Army of Northern Virginia, which had lost in the past forty days a solid forty percent of the strength it had enjoyed at the beginning of the campaign. Its casualties totaled about 27,000, and though it had inflicted a precisely tabulated 54,929 — a number greater than all its original infantry and artillery combined — the forty percent figure, unlike Grant's forty-five percent, applied at the higher levels of rank as well as at the lower. Of the 58 general officers in command of troops on the eve of conflict, back in early May, no less than 23 had fallen in battle, eight of them killed, thirteen gravely wounded, and two captured. Nor was the distribution of these casualties, high and low, by any means even throughout the three corps. Hardest hit of all was the Second: just the one Lee had in mind to detach, since it contained, as a nucleus, the survivors of Jackson's old Army of the Valley and was therefore more familiar than the others with the region Hunter was laying waste. Not only had the corps commander been replaced, but so had the leaders of two of the three divisions, while of the twelve original brigade commanders only one remained at his post, two having been promoted and the other nine shot or captured. At Spotsylvania the corps had lost the equivalent of a full division, and this contributed largely to the reduction, by half, of its outset strength of just over 17,000. There now were barely 8000 infantry in its ranks, distributed through three divisions with only three brigades in each, all but one under leaders new to their responsibilities.

These were drawbacks not to be ignored in reaching a decision; but neither was the need for dealing promptly with Hunter to be passed over. From his current position at Lexington he would no doubt cross the Blue Ridge, marching southeast against Lynchburg or northeast against Charlottesville. One would be about as bad as the other, so far as Richmond was concerned, and there was also the possibility that the wide-ranging Hunter might move against them both, in that order. At Lynchburg, just under a hundred miles due west of the captial, he would be in a position to wreck not only the Southside Railroad but also the James River Canal, both vital to the subsistence of Richmond's citizens and its armies, while at Charlottesville he would be back astride the Virginia Central, which he would destroy, with or without Sheridan's help, on the march to join Grant or come down on Lee's flank. Reduced to those terms, the problem solved itself, insofar at least as they applied to reaching a decision. Like Pope, Hunter would have to be "suppressed," or anyhow stopped and, if possible, driven back. Lee's mind was quite made up. Moreover, there was the persuasive chance that in moving against the despoilers of Lexington he would be killing two birds with one stone. If, after disposing of the bluecoats out in the Valley, the gray column then moved down it, to and across the Potomac to threaten Washington from the rear, still larger benefits might accrue. There was small chance, at this late stage, that Grant's whole force would be recalled — as McClellan's had been — from the gates of Richmond, but it was altogether possible that he would be required to detach part of it for the closeup defense of his capital; or else, in desperation to avoid that, he might be provoked into launching another ill-considered Cold Harbor assault, there or elsewhere, in an attempt to settle the issue overnight. In either event, Lee reasoned, his adversary would be reduced enough for the Army of Northern Virginia to launch an all-out assault of its own: hopefully one that would be as productive as the Seven Days offensive, but in any case one that would be conducted with all the fighting skill his soldiers had acquired in their many victories since that grim beginning under his command.

His decision reached — June 12, a Sunday; the horseback fight was into its second day at Trevilian Station, and Hunter was putting the torch to Governor Letcher's house in Lexington — Lee sent for Jubal Early to talk over with him the nature of his mission. Tall despite an arthritic stoop, a bachelor at forty-seven, dour of face, with a scraggly beard and a habit of profanity, this fellow Virginian and West Pointer was admittedly no Stonewall; but who was? No other corps commander since the fall of Longstreet had done any better on the offensive, and though this was surely the faintest of praise — since, conversely, it could also be said that none had done any worse — the only really black mark against him was his failure, in conjunction with Ewell on the second day in the Wilderness, to take prompt advantage of Gordon's report that Sedgwick's flank was open to attack. No such opportunities must be missed if he was to succeed against the odds that lay before him, first in the Valley and then beyond the Potomac. Tactful as always, Lee made this clear in giving Early verbal instructions for setting out next morning, before daylight, with all three of his divisions and two battalions of artillery. Following as it did the detachment of Breckinridge, with whom he would combine to cover Charlottesville and Lynchburg, Early's departure would deprive Lee of nearly a fourth of his infantry; yet, even with the inclusion of the Piedmont fugitives, the gray force would not be up to Hunter's present strength. Victory would have to be won by superior generalship, by celerity, stealth, and an absolute dedication to the offensive: in short, by the application of principles dear to the commander of the erstwhile Army of the Valley, which was now to be resurrected under Early.

In written orders, sent that night while the Second Corps veterans were preparing feverishly and happily to be gone with the dawn, these hopes were repeated, together with specific instructions for the march. It would be northwest, like Hampton's four days earlier, for a link-up with Breckinridge near Rockfish Gap and a quick descent on Hunter before he reached Lynchburg. After that, if all went well, would come the northward march against a new old adversary, Abraham Lincoln — and, through Lincoln and his fears, against U. S. Grant, who presumably would still be knocking at the gates of Richmond, a hundred miles away.

Grant might still be knocking when the time came, but if so it would be at the back gate, not the front. Under cover of the darkness that would obscure Early's departure, north and west, the Army of the Potomac had begun its withdrawal, east and south, from its works around Cold Harbor for the crossing of the James. Moreover, if all went as intended, here and elsewhere, the issue would have been settled — so far, as least, as Richmond was concerned — well before any rebel detachment, of whatever size, had time to reach the Potomac, much less cross it to threaten Washington. With Sheridan astride the Virginia Central and Hunter about to wreck both the Southside Railroad and the James River Canal at Lynchburg (Grant did not know that Sheridan was being driven off that evening, any more than he knew that Lee was sending Early next morning to do the same to Hunter) Federal seizure of the Petersburg rail hub would cut all but one of the gray capital's major supply lines, the Richmond & Danville, which had only been extended down to Greensboro, North Carolina, the month before. No single route, let alone one as limited as this, could supply the city's needs, including subsistence for its defenders; Lee, more than ever, would be obliged to evacuate his capital or come out from behind his intrenchments for a fight in the open, and Grant did not believe that the Confederacy could survive what would follow the adoption of either course.

He had bided his time, anticipating solutions, and when they came he moved swiftly. When the two aides, Porter and Comstock, returned from their reconnaissance that Sunday morning to report that they had found a good site for the pontoon bridge across the James, ten miles downriver from City Point and just beyond Charles City Courthouse, he evidenced some measure of the strain he had been under this past week. "While listening to our report," Porter would recall, "Grant showed the only nervousness he ever manifested in my presence. After smoking his cigar vigorously for some minutes, he removed it from his mouth, put it on the table, and allowed it to go out; then relighted it, gave a few puffs, and laid it aside again. We could hardly get the words out of our mouths fast enough to suit him, and the numerous questions he asked were uttered with much greater rapidity than usual." This was a different Grant from the stolid, twig-whittling commander of the past six weeks. It was, as the next few days would show, the Grant of the Vicksburg campaign, fast on the march, sudden in striking, and above all quick to improvise amid rapidly developing events. "At the close of the interview," Porter wrote, still amazed years later at the transformation in his chief, "he informed us that he would begin the movement that night."

It began, in point of fact, that afternoon, when Grant and Meade and their two staffs proceeded down the north bank of the Chickahominy, past Dispatch Station on the defunct York River Railroad, to make camp for the night beside a clump of catalpa trees in the yard of a farmhouse near Long Bridge, where two of the five corps were to cross the river, ten miles downstream from the present Union left. The bridge was out, but Wilson's cavalry splashed across the shallows, just after sundown, and got to work throwing a pontoon span to be used by Warren, who began his march in the twilight and was over the river by midnight. Hancock and Wright meantime fell back to the newly dug second line, under orders to hold it at all costs, in case Lee got wind of the withdrawal and launched a night attack. Smith and Burnside simultaneously marched rearward from their positions on the right, the latter turning south beyond the railroad for a crossing of the Chickahominy at Jones Bridge, five miles below Long Bridge, and Smith continuing east to White House Landing, where transports were waiting to give his troops a fast, restful trip down the York and up the James to Bermuda Hundred. Satisfied that Lee had no overnight interference in mind, Hancock and Wright pulled out after midnight to follow Warren and Burnside, respectively, over Long and Jones bridges. Once across, three of the four corps would march hard for Charles City and the James, but Warren was instructed to turn west and take up a defensive position near Riddell's Shop in support of Wilson's troopers, who would patrol the region between White Oak Swamp and Malvern Hill in case Lee, having missed his chance tonight, tried to strike tomorrow at the blue army in motion across his front. Like Wright and Hancock earlier, once he was convinced that Lee had been outfoxed, Warren would take up the march for Charles City and the crossing of the James.

Intricate as these various interdependent movements were, they had been worked out in accordance with the required logistics of allotted time and road space. All went smoothly. Despite the heat of the night and the choking dust stirred up by more than a hundred thousand pairs of shoes, the men stepped out smartly in the darkness, glad to be leaving a dismal field where they had buried so many comrades after so much purposeless suffering. Occupied as they had been with improving their intrenchments, right up to the hour they got orders to withdraw, they took it as an excellent sign that their departure had been preceded by no rumor that a shift was being considered, since what came as a surprise to them was likely to be even more of one to the johnnies across the way, including Old Man Lee. "It was not now the custom," one veteran observed approvingly, "to inform the rank and file, and the newspapers and the enemy, of intended movements." He and others like him in those several widespread dusty columns could remember another nighttime withdrawal from that same field, just two weeks short of two full years ago, and though Cold Harbor was in itself an even more horrendous experience than Gaines Mill, the feeling now was different, and altogether better. Now as then the march was south, away from the scene of a defeat; but they felt now — as they had not done then, while trudging some of these same James-bound roads — that they were moving toward a victory, even Victory itself.

Grant thought so, too, and on sounder ground, knowing, as they did not, what he had devised for the undoing of the rebels on the far side of the river. Smith, whose corps was familiar with the terrain down there, would arrive first, being steam-propelled, and after going ashore at Bermuda Hundred would repeat the maneuver Butler had rehearsed four days ago, across the Appomattox, when his Petersburg reconnaissance-in-strength was stalled by green militia, convicts, convalescents, and Negro bandsmen. That was not likely to happen this time, for three reasons. One was that Baldy would be in charge of the advance, not the nonprofessional Butler, and Grant had already explained to his fellow West Pointer the importance of striking hard and fast. Another was that this attack would not only be made in much greater strength than the other, but would also be launched with the advantage of knowing the layout of the Petersburg defenses. The third reason was that, if there was any delay in the quick reduction of the place, Hancock — whose three divisions, in the lead on the march from Cold Harbor, would be ferried across the James to save time while the 2100-foot pontoon bridge was being assembled — would soon be down to add the weight of the hardest-hitting corps in Meade's army to the pressure Smith was exerting. As for the others, Burnside, Warren, and Wright would be arriving in that order behind Hancock and could be used as then seemed best: probably for a breakout westward from Bermuda Neck, dislodging Beauregard's cork, and a turning movement against Drewry's Bluff, which would block the path of any reinforcements Lee might try to send to Petersburg when he found what Grant had been up to all this time.

Members of the two staffs — Grant's and Meade's — shared the sanguine expectations of their chiefs, at least to the extent that they were privy to the plan, and their confidence grew as the day wore on and they rode south, doubling the columns of guns and men on the dusty roads. All the signs were that the army had indeed stolen a march on Lee, whose cavalry, unable to penetrate Wilson's screen below the Chickahominy, could give him no inkling of what was in progress east of Riddell's Shop, near which Warren's four divisions remained in position without firing a shot all afternoon, so effectively did the blue troopers perform, and then resumed their roundabout hike for the James. By that time the head of Hancock's column had come within sight of the broad, shining river, its choppy little waves as bright as polished hatchets in the sunlight.

Transports and gunboats were riding at anchor, all with steam up for the crossing, and army engineers were at work assembling their pontoons for the nearly half-mile span by which the other three corps would cross, tomorrow and the next day. An officer on Meade's staff observed Hancock's troops slogging down to Wilcox Landing just before sunset, hot and tired from their thirty-mile overnight march, their faded, sweat-splotched uniforms in tatters from forty days of combat, and was struck by the thought that, so far as these hard-bitten veterans were concerned, "the more they serve, the less they look like soldiers and the more they resemble day laborers who have bought second-hand military clothes." Then he watched them react with suspicion and puzzled dislike, much as he himself had done earlier, to their first sight of the neatly turned-out sailors and the engineers in uniforms of dark unweathered blue, until at last they saw, as he had seen, what it was that was so wrong about these strangers. They were clean — clean as visitors from some dirtless planet — and Grant's men, after six weeks on the go, shooting and being shot at, with neither the water nor the time for bathing, had become mistrustful of anyone not as grimy as themselves.

Yet despite the grime and the suspicion that went with it, despite the added weariness and the fret that over the past six weeks they had suffered three separate 18,000-man subtractions from their ranks — first in the Wilderness, then at Spotsylvania, and last on the North Anna, Totopotomoy Creek, and the Chickahominy — their spirits were even higher near the end of the Jamesward trek than at the outset: not only from being on the move again, away from the stench and snipers at Cold Harbor, but also because they could see what had begun to come of this latest sidle. Though they knew nothing of what lay ahead, on the far side of the shining river, they trusted Grant to make the most of the fact that they had given Lee the slip the night before and stolen a march on him today.

They had indeed done both those things, and were now in a position to do more. The first Lee had known of their departure was at sunup — two hours after Early withdrew his three divisions and set out for the Shenandoah Valley — when messengers reached head-quarters, back near Gaines Mill, with reports that the Yankees were gone from their works around Cold Harbor. Advancing scouts un-covered a second line of intrenchments, newly dug and intricately fashioned as if for permanent occupation, but these too were deserted, as were the woods and fields a mile and more beyond. June 13, which was to have been the fortieth day of contact for the two armies, turned out to be a day of practically no contact at all; Grant was gone, vanished with his blue-clad throng, perhaps toward the lower stretches of the Chickahominy, more likely to a new base on the James from which to mount a new advance on Richmond, either by crossing the river for a back-door attack or else by moving up its near bank for an all-out assault on the capital fortifications.

Whichever it was, Lee warned the government of this latest threat and moved to meet it, shifting south to put what was left of his army in position below White Oak Swamp, where he would block the eastern approaches to the city and also be closer to Drewry's for a crossing in case the blow was aimed at Beauregard. While his son's two thin-spread cavalry brigades — all that were left since Hampton and Fitz Lee took out after Sheridan four days ago — probed unsuccessfully at rapid-firing masses of Federal horsemen coming down the Long Bridge Road toward Riddell's Shop, he posted Hill's corps in their support, athwart the field of the Seven Days fight at Glendale, and Anderson's off to the right, reaching down to Malvern Hill, which the cavalry then occupied as a post of observation, although nothing of much interest could be seen from there except a good deal of apparently purposeless activity by Union gunboats at Deep Bottom, down below. Lee's ranks were so gravely thinned by Early's departure that he might have been expected to recall him while there still was time; but when the President inquired that afternoon whether this might not be the wisest course, Lee replied, rather laconically, that he did not think so. At the end of the Forty Days, as at the beginning, he remained the gambler he had always been, the believer that the weaker force must take the longer chances.

"I do not know that the necessity for his presence today is greater than it was yesterday," he said of Early. "His troops would make us more secure here, but success in the Valley would relieve our difficulties that at present press heavily upon us."

Those first four words, "I do not know," were the crux of the matter. All the prisoners taken so far today had been cavalry, which left him with nothing but guesses as to the whereabouts of the Union infantry and artillery, all hundred thousand of them. Most likely they were in motion for the James, but whether Grant intended for them to cross it or advance up the north bank Lee could not tell; nor could he act, for fear of being decoyed out of position, until he secured more or less definite information as to which course his adversary had taken or would take. Either way, the defense of Richmond had come down to a siege, the thing he had tried hardest to avoid. "This army cannot stand a siege," he had told Little Powell a month ago, just as Beauregard, one week later, had warned Bragg: "The picture presented is one of ultimate starvation."

Red Clay Minuet

★ ✗ ☆

AIR-LINE, THE HUNDRED-MILE DISTANCE
from Chattanooga to Atlanta was the same as that from Washington to
Richmond, and so were the respective sizes of the armies, which in each
paired case gave the Union commander a roughly two-to-one numerical
advantage. But there for the most part the resemblance stopped. Meade
and Sherman (or for that matter Grant and Sherman, since that was what
it came to) were as different from each other as were Lee and Johnston,
two very different men indeed, and so too — despite the fact that down
in Georgia, as in Virginia, the rivers mainly ran athwart the projected
lines of advance and retreat — was the terrain, flat or gently rolling in
the East, but mountainous in the West and therefore eminently defensible, at any rate in theory, although few of the place-names strewn
about the map had been connected with much bloodshed since the era
when settlers ousted the aborigines. In point of fact, harking back to
those massacre days, Sherman had something similar in mind for the
Confederates to his front, military and civilian. "If the North design
to conquer the South," he had written home two years ago, "we must
begin at Kentucky and reconquer the country from there as we did
from the Indians."

Now that he faced completion of that massive undertaking, he
was in what he liked to call "high feather." Instructed by Grant "to
move against Johnston's army, break it up, and get into the interior of
the enemy's country as far as you can, inflicting all the damage you can
against their war resources," the red-haired Ohioan, by way of showing
how well he understood his task, replied in paraphrase: "I am to knock
Jos. Johnston, and to do as much damage to the resources of the enemy
as possible."

By way of help in carrying out this project he would have an
advantage, a man-made facility available neither to his flintlock-carrying
predecessors nor to his cohorts in the East: namely, a rapid-transit all-

weather supply line in the form of a railroad, the Western & Atlantic, running all the way to Atlanta — provided, of course, he could put and keep it in shape while nudging Johnston backward; for the rebels would surely wreck it in their wake, and almost as surely would strike at it with cavalry in his rear as he advanced. With this in mind, he made the training of rail repair gangs an integral part of his preparations, including daily workouts as rigorous and precise as the drill required of gun crews, and elevated gandy dancers to a combat status as high as that of riflemen or cannoneers. The same precaution was taken with regard to the much longer line extending rearward from Chattanooga, up through Middle Tennessee and across Kentucky to Louisville, his main supply base on the Ohio. Practically all of this more than three hundred miles of highly frangible track was subject to strikes by grayback troopers from adjoining departments, hard-handed horsemen schooled in destruction by John Morgan and Bedford Forrest, and though Sherman planned to keep these slashers occupied by making adjunctive trouble for them in their own back yards, he also hoped to forestall or reduce the delays that were likely to attend such depredations, in case the raiders broke out anyhow, by turning Nashville into what an amazed staff brigadier presently described as "one vast storehouse — warehouses covering city blocks, one a quarter of a mile long; stables by the ten and twenty acres, repair shops by the fieldful." Also of help in reducing the supply problem would be a certain amount of belt-tightening by the troops, whose divisional trains, in accordance with Sherman's orders, would carry only "five days' bacon, twenty days' bread, and thirty days' salt, sugar, and coffee; nothing else but arms and ammunition." The main thing, as the commanding general saw it, was to keep moving: and this applied as much to rearward personnel as it did to the men up front. "I'm going to move on Joe Johnston the day Grant telegraphs me he is going to hit Bobby Lee," he told a quartermaster officer. "And if you don't have my army supplied, and keep it supplied, we'll eat your mules up, sir; eat your mules up!" Having passed before through un-fought-over regions of the South — recently, for example, on a march across the midriff of Mississippi, from Vicksburg to Meridian and back — he was aware of another resource which he did not intend to neglect. "Georgia has a million of inhabitants," he wrote Grant. "If they can live, we should not starve."

Thus Sherman; a violent-talking man whose bite at times measured up to his bark, and whose commitment was to total war. "I believe in fighting in a double sense," he said this spring, "first to gain physical results and next to inspire respect on which to build up our nation's power." Tecumseh or "Cump" to his family, he was Uncle Billy to his soldiers, one of whom called him "the most American-looking man I ever saw; tall and lank, not very erect, with hair like thatch, which he rubs up with his hands, a rusty beard trimmed close, a wrinkled face, sharp, prominent red nose, small, bright eyes, coarse red hands; black felt hat slouched over the eyes, dirty dickey with the points wilted down, black old-fashioned stock, brown field officer's coat with high collar and no shoulder straps, muddy trowsers and one spur. He carries his hands in his pockets, is very awkward in his gait and motions, talks continually and with immense rapidity." Such intensity often brought on a reaction in observers, including this one. "At his departure I felt it a relief, and experienced almost an exhaustion after the excitement of his vigorous presence."

All this, moreover, was by way of diversion, a spare-time release of superabundant energy from an organism described by another associate as "boiling over with ideas, crammed full of feeling, discussing every subject and pronouncing on all." His main concern for the past two months, as Grant's western heir, had been how to get at or around Johnston's army, posted thirty miles southeast of Chattanooga for the past five months, in occupation of Dalton and the wide, hilly valley of the Oostanaula, which extended southward forty-odd miles to the Etowah and southwestward about the same distance to Rome, where the two rivers combined to form the Coosa. The immediate tactical problem was Rocky Face Ridge, a steep, knife-edge bastion twenty miles long, rimming the upper valley on the west to cover Dalton and the railroad, which after piercing the ridge at Mill Creek Gap, one third of the way down, ran south and east for another hundred miles, through Resaca and Kingston, Allatoona and Marietta, on across the Chattahoochee to Atlanta, Johnston's base and Sherman's goal in the campaign about to open, here in North Georgia, in conjunction with Meade's plunge across the Rapidan, six hundred crow-flight miles to the northeast. Unlike Meade — thanks to Banks, holed up by now in Alexandria after his defeat at Sabine Crossroads — Sherman would not have the supposed advantage of diversionary attacks on the enemy flank or rear by troops from other departments, such as Sigel and Butler had been told to make. Whatever was going to be accomplished in the way of driving or maneuvering Johnston from his position along that ridge would have to be done by the men on hand. And though it was true that at present the Federals enjoyed a better than two-to-one numerical advantage (Johnston had just under 45,000 of all arms, with 138 guns, while Sherman had just over 110,000, with 254) the prospect was anything but pleasing. For one thing — thanks again to Banks, who was in no position to discourage, let alone interfere with, anything the Confederates might take it in mind to do on this side of the Mississippi River — Johnston had another 19,000 effectives and 50 guns, down in Alabama under Polk, presumably ready to join him at the first sign of danger, whereas Sherman could only look forward to receiving about 10,000 due back next month from reenlistment furloughs. That still would leave him roughly a two-to-one advantage, but this by no means assured victory in assailing a position such as the one the rebels occupied, just ahead on Rocky Face Ridge.

Johnston, while successfully resisting Richmond's efforts to nudge him forward across the Tennessee, had spent the past four months preparing to resist the pending Union effort to prod him backward across the Chattahoochee. His two infantry corps, commanded by Lieutenant Generals William J. Hardee and John Bell Hood, each with about 20,000 men, were disposed along the northern half of the ridge, charged with giving particular attention to defending Mill Creek Gap, four miles northwest of Dalton, and Dug Gap, a second notch in the knife edge, five miles south. From the north end of this fortified position, Major General Joseph Wheeler's 5000 cavalry extended the line eastward to give warning in case the Federals tried to descend on Dalton by rounding the upper end of the ridge for a southward strike down the Oostanaula valley, where the ground was far less rugged and less easy to defend.

Sherman had no intention of moving in that direction, however, since to do so would uncover his base at Chattanooga: which brought him, regrettably, back to the dilemma of having to challenge the rebs in their apparently unassailable position, dead ahead on Rocky Face Ridge, securely intrenched and with high-sited guns ready-laid to blast the life out of whatever moved against them, in whatever strength. Moreover, as if nature had not done enough for him already, Johnston's engineers had lengthened the odds against the attackers by clogging the culverts of the railway ramp on the near side of the ridge, thus converting Mill Creek into an artificial lake across the rear of the gap that bore its name. Natives had a grislier designation; Buzzard Roost, they called the desolate notch through which the railroad wound its way. But Sherman, when at last he got a look at the rocky, high-walled gorge, catching glints of sunlight on the guns emplaced for its defense, pronounced it nothing less than "the terrible door of death," a term which would apply about as well to Dug Gap, just below.

George Thomas, who had felt out the gray defenses back in February, as a diversion intended to discourage Johnston from sending reinforcements to Polk while Sherman marched on Meridian, came up with the suggestion that, while McPherson and Schofield took over the position he now held in front of Ringgold, confronting the Rocky Face intrenchments, he take his four-corps Army of the Cumberland down the west side of the ridge to its far end, then press on eastward through unguarded Snake Creek Gap for a descent on the railroad near Resaca, fifteen miles in Johnston's rear. At best, this would expose the Confederates to a mauling when they fell back to protect their life line, as they would be obliged to do; while at worst, even if they somehow managed to avoid encirclement, it would turn them out of their all-but-impregnable position between Chattanooga and Dalton and thus convert the present stalemate, which favored the defenders, into a war of maneuver, which would favor the side with the greater number of troops and guns. Sherman, though the result his lieutenant promised was all he hoped for, rejected the proposal for two reasons. Thomas's command, twice the size of McPherson's and Schofield's combined, comprised a solid two thirds of the Federal total; secrecy would surely be lost in withdrawing so large a force and moving it such a distance, first across the enemy's front, then round his flank — and without secrecy, Sherman was convinced, it would be dangerous in the extreme to divide his army in the presence of so wily an adversary as the distinguished Virginian he faced. That was the first reason. The second was Thomas himself, the plodding, imperturbable Rock of Chickamauga. His specialty was staunchness, not celerity, the quality most needed in the movement he proposed.

But then, having dismissed the project as impractical when examined from that angle, Sherman shifted his point of view and experienced a surge of joy not unlike that of a poet revising the rejected draft of a poem he now perceives will become the jewel of his collection. Celerity, presumed to be lacking in Thomas, was McPherson's hallmark, and the size of his command — just under 25,000, as compared to Thomas's more than 70,000 — seemed about right for the job. Moreover, there would be no need for a withdrawal from the immediate presence of a vigilant opponent; McPherson's two corps, not yet on line, could march south from Chattanooga, under cover of Taylor's Ridge, then swing east through Ship's Gap and Villanow to make a sudden descent on Resaca, by way of Snake Creek Gap, for the cutting of Johnston's life line before the Virginian even knew he was threatened from that direction, his attention having been focused all the while on Thomas, active in his front, and on Schofield, who would feint with his 13,000-man Army of the Ohio against the opposite flank, which lay in the path of his march down the railroad from Knoxville. Thus Sherman set the pattern for the campaign about to open in North Georgia, a pattern that would utilize Thomas's outsized command — which contained more infantry and cavalry than all of Johnston's army, including the troops in Alabama under Polk — as the holding force, fixing the enemy in place, while McPherson and Schofield probed or rounded his flank or flanks to prise or chevy him out of position and expose him to being assailed on the march, or in any case to being struck before he had time to do much digging, anywhere between Dalton and Atlanta.

Sherman was delighted at the prospect, now that it loomed, and he also took a chauvinistic pleasure in the fact that such an arrangement gave the stellar role to McPherson, his favorite as well as Grant's, and the Army of the Tennessee, which had been his own and, up till Vicksburg, Grant's. Grant would approve, he knew when he wrote him of the plan, and as soon as that approval came down he passed the word to his three lieutenants. They would be in position no later than May 3, troops alerted for the jump-off next day, coincidental with Meade's crossing of the Rapidan.

And so it was. Detraining on schedule at Cleveland, where the East Tennessee & Georgia, coming down from Knoxville, branched to connect with Chattanooga and Dalton, both just under thirty miles away, Schofield prepared to march his army — in reality a corps, with three divisions of infantry and one of cavalry — southward along the left fork of the railroad to Red Clay, the state-line hamlet from which he was to launch his disconcerting strike at Johnston's right, down the valley east of Rocky Face. Thomas was poised beyond Ringgold, prepared to confront the defenders on the ridge and hold them in position there by pressing hard against Buzzard Roost and Dug Gap, threatening a breakthrough at both places. McPherson meantime had moved down to Lee & Gordon's Mill, at the south end of Chickamauga battlefield, which gave him a twelve-mile leg on the roundabout march to Resaca and the Oostanaula crossing. On May 4, in accordance with orders, all three began their separate movements designed to "knock Jos. Johnston." Sherman rode with Thomas in the center, but his hopes were with McPherson; "my whiplash," he called the Army of the Tennessee.

Despite the setbacks the rebels had suffered East and West in the past year, hard fighting lay ahead and Sherman knew it. "No amount of poverty or adversity seems to shake their faith," he marveled; "niggers gone, wealth and luxury gone, money worthless, starvation in view . . . yet I see no sign of let up — some few deserters, plenty tired of war, but the masses determined to fight it out." What they needed was more violent persuasion, he believed, and he was prepared to give it in full measure. "All that has gone before is mere skirmishing," he wrote his wife on setting forth.

Mere skirmishing was all it came to in the course of the next two days — the horrendous span of the Wilderness conflict, up in Virginia, where Lee and Meade lost better than 25,000 men between them — while Thomas felt his way forward along the Western & Atlantic and Schofield trudged down the other railroad to Red Clay, which took its name from the salmon-colored soil, powdery in dry weather and a torment to the nostrils of men on the march, but quick to turn as slippery as grease, newcomers would soon discover, under the influence of even the briefest shower.

There was no hurry at this stage of the game, both commanders having been told to give McPherson plenty of time on his roundabout march. On the third day out, the Cumberlanders ran into their first substantial opposition at Tunnel Hill, where the railroad went underground before emerging for its plunge through the gap in the ridge, two miles beyond. The rebs had set up a fortified outpost here, and

Thomas had to attack with a whole corps next day, May 7, in order to drive them back on their main line, dug in along the steep west slope of Rocky Face Ridge, above Buzzard Roost and below it down to Dug Gap, five miles south. While this success — so complete, indeed, that the Confederate rear guard had no time to damage the tunnel before retreating — was being followed up, preparatory to coming to grips in earnest with the defenders on their ridge, Schofield crossed the Georgia line and pressed on for Varnell Station, his initial objective, a little less than midway between Red Clay and Dalton. Harassed by small bodies of gray horsemen, he moved slowly, that day and the next, and then on May 9 detached a brigade of cavalry to brush these gadflies from his path. It was a mistake. Wheeler's troopers, fading back, drew the blue riders out of contact with the main body, then turned and, with a sudden, unexpected slash, killed or captured some 150 of them, including the colonel in command, and drove the remainder head-long from the field.

Sherman was no more upset by this than he was by Thomas's lack of progress on the near side of the intervening ridge. Three full-scale assaults the day before, and another five today — mainly against Mill Creek Gap, but also against Dug Gap, down the line — had met with failure in varying degrees. Two of the uphill attacks, in fact, had managed to put blue troops on the actual crest, within clear sight of Dalton, but they stayed there no longer than it took the defenders to counterattack and drive them back downhill. If anything, this was better than he had expected them to do: especially after his first hard look at what he described as "the terrible door of death that Johnston had prepared for them in the Buzzard Roost." Thomas and Schofield were charged with attracting and holding the attention of the rebels in their respective fronts, and this they had surely done. Sherman's main concern and hopes were still with McPherson, far off beyond the mountains to the south. What one observer called his "electric alertness," while following the progress of the fighting down the railroad below Ringgold, was probably due more to anxiety about his protégé, from whom he had heard nothing in the past three days, than it was to any expectation of victory in Thomas's contest on Rocky Face or Schofield's around Varnell Station, half a dozen miles across the way. Believing strongly in McPherson's military judgment and acumen, he had given him full discretion in conducting the movement designed to outfox Johnston; but he knew only too well that in war few things were certain, least of all the safety of a column deep in the enemy rear, no matter how capably led.

Then all, or nearly all, his worries vanished, giving way to jubilation and high feather. Taking an early supper near Tunnel Hill late that afternoon, May 9, he was delighted to receive a courier bearing McPherson's first dispatch, written that morning when he emerged from Snake Creek Gap after rounding the far end of Rocky Face Ridge. He was within five miles of Resaca, he reported, and pressing on, with nothing to contest his progress but a scattered handful of butternut horsemen, flushed out of the brush on the west side of the gap. Sherman boiled over with elation at the news, for it meant that by now McPherson's guns most likely had destroyed the bridges across the Oostanaula, thereby cutting the Confederates at Dalton off from all supplies and reinforcements south of that critical point; in which case they would have no choice except to turn and flee, and when they did he would come down hard and heavy on their rear, while McPherson stood firm in their front, astride the railroad.

Exultant, he banged the table so emphatically with his fist that the supper dishes did a rattling dance. "I've got Joe Johnston dead!" he cried.

He very nearly did; very nearly; except that Johnston, taking alarm at the first sign of his advance, had moved to forestall him without even suspecting what he was up to, out there beyond the screening

ridges to the west and south. The bluecoats had no sooner stirred
from their camps, May 4, than the southern commander renewed his
plea to Richmond for reinforcements from Polk, even if they amounted
to no more than a single division. "I urge you to send [these troops]
at once to Rome, and put them at my disposal till the enemy can be
met," he wired Bragg. Bragg replied, promptly for once, with orders
for Polk to do as Johnston asked. Moreover, Jefferson Davis (in still
another instance of that "presidential interference" with which his
critics often charged him) enlarged the order by telegraphing instructions for his friend the bishop-general to go along in person and
take with him not only the one requested division, but also "any other
available force at your command." Polk had three divisions of infantry
and one of cavalry, a total of 19,000 men. His decision was to hold
none of them back except a garrison of about 2000 for Selma. After
getting the first division on the road to Rome, where boxcars were being collected to speed this advance contingent down the branch line,
east to Kingston, then northward up the Western & Atlantic to join
Johnston around Dalton, he prepared to follow with the rest next day
for a share in the task of keeping the Yankees out of Atlanta and the
heartland.

That was how it came about that Sherman's "whiplash" lost its
sting. For while Polk was en route from Demopolis — first by rail,
through Selma and Talladega, to Blue Mountain, the end of the line,
and then on foot the rest of the way, seventy rugged miles cross-
country to Rome — a brigade of about 2000 men under Brigadier
General James Cantey was summoned from Mobile to join him there
and thus complete what would constitute a third corps for the Army
of Tennessee, roughly equal in strength to each of the other two. Traveling all the way by rail, through Montgomery and Atlanta, Cantey
reached Rome on May 5, but was shifted two days later to Resaca,
clearing the way for Polk's arrival, placing him closer to Dalton in case
he was needed sooner, and incidentally doubling the strength of the
small garrison in the intrenchments Johnston had had constructed
there to cover the critical Oostanaula crossing. Two mornings later,
on May 9, after pausing only long enough to send the message that
would cause Sherman to set the supper dishes dancing, McPherson
pressed on across Sugar Valley, still driving the handful of butternut
cavalry before him, and at midday, within a mile of Resaca, came
under heavy infantry fire from a line of intrenchments, anchored on
the south to the Oostanaula and curving west and north of the town.

There were only about 4000 Confederates in the works; but Mc-
Pherson did not know that, and in any case this was about 4000 more
than he expected. He felt out the defenses, found them stout, and
decided that under the circumstances, unsupported as he was, deep in
the rear of an enemy twice his size, his wisest course was to exercise

the discretion his orders afforded him and return to Snake Creek Gap, where his 25,000 would be safe from attack by whatever forces Johnston had sent or was sending to meet this no-longer-secret threat to the rebel life line. He was back in the gap by nightfall, and there, with both flanks covered, his front intrenched, and his rear out of reach of the enemy east of the ridge, he lay coiled in compact security — like a snake, ready to strike, or a whip laid away in a cubbyhole, unused.

When Johnston learned that evening of the sudden appearance of bluecoats in his rear he reacted by ordering Hood to move at once with three divisions, one from his own and two from Hardee's corps, to help Cantey meet any renewal of the threat. Hood did so, but when he reconnoitered west of Resaca next afternoon and reported McPherson still immured in Snake Creek Gap, Johnston interpreted the movement as a feint designed to draw his attention away from the main Union effort to turn or overrun the northern half of Rocky Face Ridge. Accordingly, he told Hood to come back to his former position but to drop Hardee's two divisions off at Tilton, a station on the railroad between Dalton and Resaca, from which they could move swiftly to meet a crisis in either direction. Meantime Hardee, stripped of half his corps, had been puzzled by the relative inactivity of Thomas, who, after three days of obstinate hammering, had finally slackened his effort to break through the two gaps. "I am only uneasy about my right," the Georgia-born West Pointer said, "and won't be uneasy about that when Hood returns." All the same, finding himself "unable to decide what the Yankees are endeavoring to accomplish," he began to suspect that they were up to something not in Johnston's calculations.

And so, by now, did Johnston himself. Polk had reached Rome today with his lead division and was sending it on to Resaca ahead of the others, which were close behind. This gave Johnston considerably more security at both places, but still he wondered at the easing of the pressure against one end of the ridge while McPherson took up a position off the other end. He began to suspect that Sherman might be moving more than McPherson, perhaps in the same direction and even farther, for a crossing of the river deep in his rear. Next morning, May 11, he gave Wheeler orders to send some horsemen around the north end of Rocky Face, if possible, for a probe at the flank of the Federals in position there. "Try to ascertain where their left rests," he told him, "and whether they are in motion toward the Oostanaula."

Altogether aware of Sherman's advantage, that with close to twice the number of troops he could apply immobilizing pressure in front while rounding or striking one or both Confederate flanks, Johnston had to count on luck as well as skill in maneuvering his opponent into committing some tactical gaffe that would expose the superior blue army, or anyhow some vital portion of it, to destruction. Such an opportunity, if it came, could scarcely occur except while that army was in motion, and for this reason — plus the fact that it had always been his style, his inclination, even back in the Old Dominion, around Manassas or down on the York-James peninsula — the Virginian was prepared from the outset to relinquish almost any position, no matter how strong, if by so doing he could encourage his adversary, on taking up the pursuit, to commit the blunder that might lead to his undoing. The odds against this were long, he knew, but so were the odds he faced. Moreover, he would be falling back toward reinforcements, even if they amounted to no more than Governor Brown's kid-glove militia, and would be shortening his supply line while the enemy's grew longer and more vulnerable. He also took encouragement from the belief that Sherman —who, after all, had been relieved of duty, back in the first year of the war, under suspicion of insanity — was high-strung, erratic in the extreme, and reported to be enamored of long-chance experiments, both tactical and strategic. These were qualities much to be desired in an opponent at this juncture. The trouble was that Johnston himself, with far less margin for error, had to rely on subordinates quite as erratic and a good deal more temperamental. "If I were President," he confided to a friend soon after taking over the faction-riddled Army of Tennessee, which had just been driven from Missionary Ridge after eighteen months under Braxton Bragg, "I'd distribute the generals of this army over the Confederacy."

In point of fact, that was precisely what R. E. Lee had been doing with some of those subordinates who failed or displeased or failed to please him in the course of the past two years; but Johnston, less in harmony with the authorities in Richmond, mainly had to make do with what he had. Fortunately, this wholesale condemnation did not include the leaders immediately below him on the military ladder. Highly dependable if not brilliant in the discharge of their duties, Polk and Hardee had been corps commanders ever since Shiloh, and Hood, though young and new to both his post and the army — he was thirty-two and had been made a lieutenant general at the time of his transfer from Longstreet, just three months ago, whereas Polk and Hardee, fifty-eight and thirty-eight respectively, had held that rank ever since it was created in the fall of '62 — was a fighter any chief would be glad to have at his disposal when victory swung in the balance and an extra measure of savagery was called for.

While he thus was counting his blessings and woes — and incidentally, such was the diminution of blue pressure against the gaps, admonishing some impetuous artillerists on Rocky Face Ridge for firing at targets not worth their ammunition — he sent word for Polk to proceed at once from Rome to Resaca, where he would assume command "and make the proper dispositions to defend the passage of the river and our communications." Johnston also took the occasion to suggest "the immediate movement of Forrest [who had been left behind for the defense of North Mississippi] into Middle Tennessee." Quite as desirous of cutting Sherman's life line as Sherman was of cutting his, he added that he was "fully persuaded" that Forrest, rested by now from his raid on Paducah and the reduction of Fort Pillow, "would meet no force there that could resist him." What might come of this he did not know; such a decision, involving the abandonment of a portion of the President's home state to Yankee depredations, was up to Richmond. But as evidence accumulated in Dalton that some kind of movement was in progress on the other side of Rocky Face, Johnston took the precaution of shifting another of Hardee's divisions south of Dug Gap, to a position with a road in its rear leading down into Sugar Valley. Late in the day Wheeler returned from his probe of the Union left with confirmation of the wisdom of such precautions. Beyond the ridge, the Federals were "moving everything" to their right, though whether they were massing near Dug Gap for a renewal of their try for a breakthrough there, or were heading for Snake Creek Gap to join McPherson for an attack on Resaca, or had it in mind to slog on past both gateways for a crossing of the Oostanaula farther down, no one could say. In any case Johnston saw that if it turned out to be either of the last two choices he could not long remain where he now was; he would certainly have to fall back no later than tomorrow. The question was whether he would end his withdrawal on this or the far side of the river fifteen miles in his rear.

That evening he was encouraged by a visit and some welcome news from Polk, who had encountered Hood at Resaca and returned with him to Dalton for a conference with their chief. The good news was that his second division had reached Rome today, was already on its way by rail to join the first in the Resaca intrenchments, and would soon be followed by the other two, expected at Rome tomorrow. Johnston shook his old friend warmly by the hand; they had been cadets together at West Point thirty-five years ago. "How can I thank you?" he said with feeling. "I asked for a division, but you have come yourself and brought me your army."

Polk flushed with pleasure at the praise, and after the council of war had ended, around midnight, took part in another exchange which gave him even greater pleasure than the first. On the train ride up to Dalton, Hood had confided that he wished to be baptized and received into the Church, and now that army business was out of the way the churchman was glad to oblige. Episcopal Bishop of Louisiana for twenty years before the war, he often remarked that he looked forward to returning to his priestly calling as soon as the fighting was over and independence had been won. Meantime he seldom neglected a chance, such as this, to work for the salvation of any soul. The two repaired to the young general's quarters, accompanied by members of their staffs, and there by candlelight Polk performed the baptismal rites, using a tin washpan for a font. Then came the confirmation. Because of the mutilations Hood had suffered at Chickamauga and Gettysburg, where he had lost a leg and the use of one arm, the bishop absolved the candidate from kneeling, as was customary, suggesting instead that he remain seated for the ceremony. But Hood would have none of this. If he could not kneel, and he could not, he would stand. And thus it was that, leaning on his crutches, the big tawny-bearded Kentuckian was received into the fold. "Defend, O Lord, this thy child with thy heavenly grace," the bishop intoned, his hand upon the bowed head before him, "that he may continue thine forever, and daily increase in thy Holy Spirit more and more, until he come unto thy everlasting kingdom."

Despite the lateness of the hour, Polk returned that night to Resaca, charged with holding the place on his own until such time as the rest of the now three-corps army joined him. He was unlikely to be alone for long, however; Johnston's mind was about made up. Next morning, as evidence of a full-scale Union sidle continued to mount, he decided to evacuate Dalton — or, more accurately, to complete the evacuation, since nearly half of his army, exclusive of Polk, was already south of the town in any case — as soon as the night was dark enough to mask his withdrawal from the covering ridge.

He would do so, what was more, with small regret. "The position had little to recommend it," he afterwards explained. "At Dalton the Federal army, even if beaten, would have had a secure place of refuge at Chattanooga, while our only place of safety was Atlanta, a hundred miles off with three rivers intervening. . . . I therefore decided to remain on the defensive." His mind, it would seem from this subsequent outline of his strategic intentions, was already on the third of those three rivers. "Fighting under cover," he went on, "we would have trifling losses compared with those inflicted. Moreover, due to its lengthening lines the numerical superiority of the Federal army would be reduced daily so that we might hope to cope with it on equal terms beyond the Chattahoochee, where defeat would be its destruction."

This did not mean that he did not hope to inflict a defeat on the enemy in the course of his hundred-mile withdrawal. He did hope for it, despite the odds, either as the result of breaking the railroad deep in Sherman's rear, which would oblige the blue host to retire, or else as the result of catching his adversary in a tactical blunder that would expose him to piecemeal destruction somewhere down the line: maybe even within the next couple of days near Resaca, Johnston's intended first stop, on the near bank of the Oostanaula, first of the three rivers in his rear.

That was his destination now, and by sunrise next morning — Friday the 13th — not a Confederate was left on the northern half of Rocky Face Ridge or in Dalton itself. Johnston was off on what an opposing general called "one of his clean retreats."

★ ★ ★

Sherman by now was on the verge of completing the movement that prompted Johnston's pull-out. Vexed by the news that his protégé had flinched from pressing the attack that was to have crowned his roundabout march to the outskirts of Resaca — news that hit all the harder by arriving close on the heels of the first report that the objective was practically within McPherson's grasp — the northern commander felt terribly let down. "Such an opportunity does not occur twice in a single life," he lamented, although he was quick to admit that his fellow Ohioan had been "perfectly justified" by his discretionary orders. "I regret beyond measure that you did not break the railroad, however little," he replied next morning, "but I suppose it was impossible."

He rather suspected that he should have used a larger force on the flanking operation, as Thomas originally suggested, and he planned to follow through by doing so now, all out. Leaving one corps of infantry and a cavalry division to continue the demonstration in front of "the terrible door of death," thereby covering Chattanooga and holding the Confederate main body in position around Dalton, he would march the rest of Thomas's army and all of Schofield's down the valley west of Rocky Face Ridge, on around its lower end, to join McPherson for a massive lunge at Resaca, the railroad that ran through it, and the vital river crossing in its rear. Johnston then would be cut off from his base, with no choice except to scatter or give battle: which in either case, as Sherman saw it, would result in his defeat. There was of course an outside chance that Johnston, who would have the advantage of moving a shorter distance over superior roads, might fall rapidly back on Resaca, while the rest of the blue army was en route, and turn on the force holed up in Snake Creek Gap; but that had been considered and taken care of, more or less, beforehand. "Should he attack you," Sherman told McPherson at the close of the dispatch informing him of his measureless regret and his new plan, "fight him to the last and I will get to you."

This was a good deal easier said, and planned, than done. Close to 70,000 troops had to be disengaged from contact with an enemy mainly on high ground, which made secrecy all the more difficult to maintain, and put in motion on narrow, meandering roads. A day was needed to get ready, then better than two more for the march. It was late afternoon of the fourth day, Friday the 13th, before the three commands were consolidated and put into attack formations, west of Resaca, for the contemplated lunge. By then the sun was too far down for anything more than a bit of preliminary skirmishing, including a crossroads cavalry clash in which Judson Kilpatrick and Joe Wheeler — West Pointers both, the former four months into and the latter four months short of his twenty-eighth year — took each other's measure. Kilpatrick was unhorsed by a stray bullet on this unlucky day, and though friendly troopers managed to lug him off the field before the graybacks could get at him, he would be out of action for some weeks.

Regrettable as this was, the loss of time on the cramped approach march down the valley was even more so. McPherson, Thomas, and Schofield were on hand and in line of battle by sundown, within gun range of the rebel works, but Johnston was there ahead of them with all three of his corps, Hood and Hardee having completed their retrograde movement from Dalton before noon. Increased in strength by nearly one third with the addition of Polk's corps to their army, they occupied skillfully laid-out intrenchments that ran in a long convex line from the Oostanaula, downstream from Resaca on their left, to the near bank of a tributary river, the Connasauga, on their right beyond the railroad north of town.

Sherman was neither daunted nor discouraged by his loss of the race for Resaca; Johnston was there, inviting attack with his back to the river, and the redhead planned to oblige him. "I will press him all that is possible," he wired Halleck. "Weather fine and troops in fine order. All is working well." Informed that Grant had emerged from the Wilderness and now was mauling Lee at Spotsylvania, he added, still in the pep-talk vein: "Let us keep the ball rolling."

It rolled, but only a short distance in the course of the daylong fight; Johnston's engineers had given him all he asked in the way of protection for his men. McPherson, on the right — goaded no doubt by Sherman's reproach when they met in Snake Creek Gap the day before: "Well, Mac, you missed the opportunity of your life" — scored what little gain there was by driving Polk's forward elements from some high ground west of the town. Elsewhere along the four-mile curve of the rebel works, the ball either stopped or rebounded. Thomas made no headway in the center, and Schofield took a beating on the left, beyond the railroad, when the Confederates in his front launched a sudden attack that drove him back nearly half a mile as the day ended. This came about as the result of Johnston's calculation that McPherson's success against his left, down near the Oostanaula, must mean that Sherman was concentrating most of his strength in that direction. Accordingly, while Bishop Polk, informally clad in an old hunting shirt and a slouch hat, stiffened his resistance to limit the enemy gains in his front, and Hardee continued to stand fast in the center, wearing by contrast a new dove-gray uniform with fire-gilt buttons and a white cravat, Johnston sent word for Hood to test the Union left for the weakness he suspected. This Hood did, with good results which might have been much better if darkness had not put an end to his pursuit.

Johnston, highly pleased, ordered a renewal of the attack at first light next morning.

He had been in excellent spirits all that day, riding from point to point along the line, at his jaunty best "in a light or mole colored hat, with a black feather in it." A Tennessee private, seeing him thus, recalled the scene years later. A small man, neatly turned out and genial in manner, fluffy white side-whiskers framing the wedge-shaped face with its trim mustache and grizzled chin beard — "like the pictures you see hung upon the walls," the veteran was to write — Johnston sat his horse, head cocked to catch the swell of gunfire, left and right and center, where Polk and Hood and Hardee were defending the works his foresight had provided. Scattered whoops of recognition prompted the rest of the troops in the passing column of Tennesseans, "and the very ground seems to shake with cheers. Old Joe smiles as blandly as a modest maid, raises his hat in acknowledgement, makes a polite bow, and rides toward the firing."

This brightened outlook persisted into the night, but darkened progressively in reaction to the arrival, in all too rapid sequence, of three unwelcome intelligence reports. While visiting Hood on the right he learned that the Union corps left at Dalton had completed its march down the railroad this evening to reinforce Schofield, and riding westward to confer with Polk he found McPherson had brought artillery onto the high ground lost today, with the result that long-range shells were able to reach both the railway and turnpike bridges close in his rear. Endangering as it did his line of retreat, this gave him pause indeed. He instructed his staff engineer to throw a pontoon bridge a mile above the permanent spans, beyond reach of the Yankee guns, and start at once to build a road leading down to it on the near bank and away from it on the other. Sensitive as always to such threats to his flanks or rear, he countermanded Hood's instructions for tomorrow and told him to return instead to the position from which he had launched his attack this afternoon. Presently, with the arrival of the third unwelcome bit of news, he had cause for greater alarm and even greater caution. Cavalry scouts reported that enemy units of considerable strength had crossed the Oostanaula several miles downstream, where a deep eastward bend of the river brought them within easy reach of the Western & Atlantic. Johnston reacted swiftly to this threat to the railroad and his line of retreat by ordering the immediate detachment of Major General W. H. T. Walker's division from Hardee for a night march to the reported point of crossing, there to contest any further advance by the Federals while the rest of the army prepared for a quick withdrawal across the river, either to reinforce Walker or outstrip the blue column which by then might have overwhelmed him.

Morning brought a renewal of Federal pressure all along the line, quite as if there had been no reduction for a sidle. Johnston held his ground, awaiting developments, and shortly after noon received a dispatch from Walker informing him that the report of a downstream crossing was untrue. By then the pressure against Resaca had somewhat diminished, and Johnston decided to go back to his plan for a renewal of the attack by Hood, who promptly returned to the position he had won the day before. A battery, pushed well to the front to support the jump-off, opened prematurely and was replied to so effectively, by infantry and counterbattery fire, that the cannoneers had to abandon all four guns, left mute and unattended between the lines. This did not augur well for the success of Hood's assault, but as he was about to go forward in all-out earnest, a message came from the army commander, once more canceling the attack and instructing the three lieutenant generals to attend a council of war that evening at his headquarters.

There they learned the reason for this second change of plans. A follow-up dispatch from Walker reported the bluecoats over the downstream Oostanaula after all, and Johnston had decided to give up Resaca. The council had not been called for a discussion of his decision, but rather for the assignment of routes on the march to meet this threat to the army's life line; Polk and Hardee would use the turnpike and railway spans, despite the danger of long-range interdictory fire, and Hood the new-laid pontoon bridge.

All went as planned, or nearly so, including heavy volleys of musketry by front-line units at midnight to cover the withdrawal of iron-tired artillery and supply vehicles. Rear guards took up the pontoons and loaded them onto wagons for use in crossing other rivers, farther south, and the railroad bridge was set afire to burn till it fell hissing into the Oostanaula. Through some administrative oversight — not unlike the one at Tunnel Hill a week ago, which left the railway tunnel unobstructed — in the last-minute confusion, as dawn was breaking, the turnpike bridge was overlooked and left standing, fit for use by the pursuers. All that was really lost in the way of army property, however, was the four-gun Confederate battery abandoned between Hood's and Schofield's lines that afternoon. This came hard for the young Kentucky-born West Pointer, who had a great deal of pride in such matters (in time he would take it even harder, since they turned out to be the only guns Johnston lost in the whole course of the campaign) but who consoled himself, as best he could, by pointing out "that they were four old iron pieces, not worth the sacrifice of the life of even one man."

Sherman pressed on after the retiring Confederates, hoping to catch up with them before they had time to develop still another stout position in which to receive him, and continued simultaneously two flanking operations he had set in motion two days ago, both involving only cavalry at the outset. Kilpatrick's division, minus its wounded leader, had been sent five miles downriver on May 14 to install a pair of pontoon bridges at Lay's Ferry, and Sherman had followed this up yesterday by detaching Brigadier General Thomas Sweeny's infantry division from McPherson to march down and cross the river at that point, along with Kilpatrick's troopers, in order to menace Johnston's rear; which Sweeny had done with such success that the graybacks were now in full retreat. At the same time, a wider, deeper, and potentially even more profitable thrust was launched by sending another of Thomas's mounted divisions, under Brigadier General Kenner Garrard, far down the right bank of the Oostanaula to threaten and if possible enter Rome, wrecking its factories and iron works and taking over the branch-line railroad leading east along the north bank of the Etowah to Kingston, on the Western & Atlantic, better than twenty miles below Resaca. Now that Johnston was falling back, Sherman decided to beef up this deeper probe by sending Brigadier General Jefferson C. Davis's division of Cumberlanders to follow the cavalry and take part in the raid on Rome and the eastward strike at Kingston.

The red-haired commander was leaving no card unplayed in his eagerness to come to grips with his skittish opponent, and he scoffed at the notion, advanced by several members of his staff, that Johnston was falling back quite willingly, in accordance with a plan to draw his pursuers southward to their destruction. "Had he remained in Dalton another hour, it would have been his total defeat," Sherman insisted, "and he only evacuated Resaca because his safety demanded it." As for the disappointment some critics expressed at his failure, so far, to bring the wily Virginian to all-or-nothing battle — particularly before Polk arrived from Alabama, in the interim between Dalton and Resaca, to shorten the long numerical odds — he countered that, while he shared the regret that he had not managed to do this, he also saw a clear advantage in the way the campaign had developed up to now. "Of course I was disappointed not to have crippled his army more at that particular stage of the game," he later wrote; "but, as it resulted, these rapid successes gave us the initiative, and the usual impulse of a conquering army."

Determined to make the most of that conquering impulse, he devised a pursuit combining speed with other tactical advantages. While Thomas struck out down the railroad, hard in the wake of the fleeing enemy, McPherson was instructed to proceed at once to Lay's Ferry for a crossing that would place him well to the right on the march south, in position to make another rapid flanking movement as soon as the rebels called a halt or were brought to one by pressure against their rear, and Schofield was told to do the same in the opposite direction, crossing upstream from Resaca at Field's Ferry for a march well to the east, in case it developed that the enemy right was the

flank that should be turned. This not only increased the celerity of
the pursuit by not funneling all the Federal troops down one crowded
road; it also assured that when the time came for fighting, all three
component armies would be ready for action in their accustomed
roles, Thomas's as the holding force and McPherson's and Schofield's
as flankers. Moreover, to bring all three into better numerical balance
and lessen the traffic on the turnpike, Sherman detached Hooker's
three divisions from Thomas and sent them off to the left with Scho-

field, whose strength thus was raised to more than 30,000 while Thomas's
was reduced to about 40,000, three other divisions, including two of
cavalry, having already been detached for the raid on Rome, still in
progress down the Oostanaula, and the preliminary crossing at Lay's
Ferry, where Sweeny's division rejoined McPherson, together with

Kilpatrick's troopers, who fanned out frontward to provide a screen for the column west of the railroad.

The first day's march, May 16, ended at Calhoun, where Sherman thought it likely that Johnston would make a stand, six miles down the track from Resaca, but before he could call in either of the lateral columns, which were also over the river by then, the Confederate rear guard pulled out southward in the darkness, headed apparently for Adairsville, ten miles down the line. There was heavier skirmishing there next day near sundown, but dawn of May 18 showed the graybacks gone again. Schofield by now was in the vicinity of Sallacoa and Mc-Pherson at McGuire, hamlets respectively half a dozen miles east and west of Adairsville; Sherman, riding with Thomas in the center, held to this spread-eagle formation as he took up the march for Kingston, another ten miles down the Western & Atlantic. He felt certain that Johnston would dig in there, on the near bank of the Etowah, and he wanted to get at him before he had much chance to get set for the shock.

Spirits were high in all three columns of pursuit, not only because the rebs were on the run, having been turned out of two practically impregnable positions in less than two weeks, but also because well-drilled rail repair gangs — helped considerably, it was true, by the enemy's rattled negligence in failing to obstruct the tunnel short of Buzzard Roost — had functioned with such efficiency that even the troops out front, in the process of covering better than half the distance from Chattanooga to Atlanta, had scarcely missed a meal along the way. "The rapidity with which the badly broken railroad was repaired seemed miraculous," Major General O. O. Howard, one of Thomas's corps commanders, later noted. "We had hardly left Dalton before trains with ammunition and other supplies arrived. While our skirmishing was going on at Calhoun, the locomotive whistle sounded in Resaca. The telegraphers were nearly as rapid: the lines were in order to Adairsville on the morning of the 18th. While we were breaking up the state arsenal at Adairsville, caring for the wounded, and bringing in Confederate prisoners, word was telegraphed from Resaca that bacon, hard bread, and coffee were already there at our service."

All this had been accomplished, moreover, at a cost of fewer than 4000 casualties, and not only was this figure much lower than had been anticipated, it was also — despite the supposed high price entailed in attacking prepared defenses — not much larger than the enemy total, which included a number of lightly wounded men who had to be left behind and thus became permanent losses, as captives, whereas a Union soldier, left behind under similar circumstances, could be patched up and returned to duty, sometimes overnight. It was no wonder then, with success achieved at so low a cost and without the sacrifice of creature comforts, that spirits were high and the outcome of the expected Kingston confrontation seemed foregone. What was more, as the three main widespread columns prepared for a convergence at that point — forty air-line miles from Tunnel Hill, scene of the opening clash eleven days ago — word came that a prize even more valuable than the state arsenal at Adairsville had fallen into the hands of the invaders. That same morning, May 18, Rome fell undefended to Davis and Garrard, who soon would be working their way east along the branch-line railroad to rejoin the Army of the Cumberland.

Rome with its factories and iron works, so important to the rebel cause, was a strategic plum worth giving thanks for, but tactically the railroad was a prize worth even more, since practically all of Johnston's reinforcements had reached him by that route. Now it was closed, except to Federal use, and Sherman — still with Thomas, who was engaged in what Howard called "a running skirmish" down the Western & Atlantic with troops from Hardee's corps, which apparently had been given the rear-guard post of honor on the Confederate retreat — had 100,000 effectives converging as fast as their legs could carry them toward Kingston, where reports indicated that Johnston had at last been brought to bay with his back to the Etowah River.

For once, by dint of hard marching on rural roads and steady pressure on the rebel rear, execution matched conception; the convergence would be effected by midday tomorrow, May 19, on schedule and with each of the three component armies in its assigned position for the final thrust, Schofield left, McPherson right, and Thomas center. The trouble was that Sherman, for all the speed and precision of his approach, was converging on a vacuum. Johnston was not at Kingston; he was at Cassville, five miles east, preparing to spring an ambush that would eliminate, or at any rate badly mangle, a solid third of the blue force whose commander had at last afforded him the opportunity he had been awaiting ever since the campaign opened, two weeks and better than forty miles ago.

Leaving Resaca, two days back, he had intended to make a stand at Calhoun, provided he could find a suitable position — athwart a rather narrow valley, say, which would afford protection for his flanks and thus oblige the Federals to come at him head-on, their numerical advantage canceled by the limited width of front — but when reconnaissance revealed none he moved on that night, hoping to find what he was seeking near Adairsville the following day, May 17. He did not. He did, however, receive a telegraphic dispatch and some cavalry reports which together had the double effect of lifting his spirits and enabling him to arrive at a plan for stopping the blue army in its tracks. Stephen Lee, left in charge of the adjoining department when Polk departed for Georgia, responded to Johnston's week-old request by announcing that Forrest, with 3500 picked horsemen and two batteries of artillery, would set out within three days for an attack on Sherman's lines of supply and communication up in Middle Tennessee. This was welcome news, indeed, and Johnston called a council of war that evening to pass it on to his corps commanders, along with their respective assignments for carrying out his table-turning plan.

Intelligence reports from Wheeler made it clear that Sherman's pursuit was in three columns, widely spaced, and now that Johnston had decided to continue his march toward the Etowah, he saw in this a rare opportunity to deal with one of those isolated segments before it could call on either of the other two for help. From Adairsville, railroad and turnpike ran due south to Kingston; Hardee would continue on that route, skirmishing as he went, to draw Thomas after him and encourage the impression that he was guarding the rear of the other two corps as they moved ahead of him, down the tracks and pike, for a stand at Kingston. But that was by no means to be the case. Polk and Hood would march instead by a road leading east of south to Cassville, a village about two miles on this side of the Western & Atlantic, which swung due east at Kingston, five miles west. The advantage was that Schofield, reinforced to 30,000, would pass near there on his way to the convergence Sherman would surely order when he became convinced that the graybacks intended to call a halt at Kingston. With Thomas five miles off, McPherson perhaps ten, and Hardee in position to delay their eastward advance along the railroad, Hood and Polk should have ample time to dispose of Schofield before the other two could reach him. With any luck, all three gray corps could then combine to take on Thomas and strike at McPherson when he came up in turn. Dealt with piecemeal, all three Union armies might be destroyed in short order, or anyhow crippled and brought to a stumbling halt; which would serve about as well, since they soon would get the news that Forrest had severed their life line, up in Tennessee. That would leave them no choice except starvation or retreat. Either way, the campaign would be over and the world once more would stand amazed at still another Confederate triumph against overwhelming odds.

Eager though they were to take up their divergent marches, which were to end with a long-deferred return to the offensive, all three corps commanders went with their chief to his tent, where Polk donned his surplice and stood in front of an improvised altar, preparing to fulfill a request Mrs Johnston had made in a letter written two days ago. She wanted the bishop to do for her husband what he had done for Hood the week before; "lead my soldier nearer to God. General Johnston has never been baptised. It is the dearest wish of my heart that he should be, and that you should perform the ceremony." Once more with candlelight glinting on the brass and gold lace of the uniforms of candidate and witnesses, the rite of baptism was performed, after which the group dispersed to prepare for the execution of the plan designed to reverse the tide of war in North Georgia.

Hardee took up his march, southward down the railroad, and with the dawn resumed his "running skirmish" with Thomas, who continued to press hard upon his rear. Meantime the other two corps set out on the road for Cassville, Hood in front with orders to occupy a position tonight from which to strike at the left of Schofield's column next morning, while Polk attacked the front; Hardee would join them from Kingston, later in the day, so that all three could then turn on Thomas and McPherson, simultaneously or in sequence, when they came up in response to Schofield's cries for help. Unwelcome news from Stephen Lee reached Johnston in the course of the approach march, to the effect that a heavy enemy movement out of Memphis had obliged him to postpone Forrest's raid on Sherman's life line. Offsetting this somewhat, however, there was a report from Richmond that the Federals had acknowledged the so-far loss of 45,000 men in Virginia, thirty-one of them generals, and this gave rise to the airing of a theory by some members of Johnston's staff that Sherman's intention was to maneuver his adversary south of the Etowah, then call a halt and hurry reinforcements to the bled-down Army of the Potomac. Johnston put no stock in such talk; he remained intent on the prospect of giving Sherman so much trouble, on this side of the Etowah, that he soon would be seeking assistance, not sending it either to Meade or to Banks, whose fight at Yellow Bayou today was the last on his costly, disheartened retreat down Red River.

Nightfall found the divided Confederate army in position: Hardee at Kingston, prepared to turn east, and Hood and Polk at Cassville, their ambush laid. Johnston's spirits were as high as Sherman's across the way, and on far sounder grounds. Some measure of the Virginian's confidence and martial elation came through in a general order he composed that night and had read at the head of each regiment next morning, May 19:

> Soldiers of the Army of Tennessee:
>   You have displayed the highest qualities of the soldier—firmness in combat, patience under toil. By your courage and skill you have repulsed every assault of the enemy. By marches by day and marches by night you have defeated every attempt upon your communications. Your communications are secured. You will now turn and march to meet his advancing columns. Fully confiding in the conduct of the officers, the courage of the soldiers, I lead you to battle. We may confidently trust that the Almighty Father will still reward the patriots' toils and the patriots' banners. Cheered by the success of our brothers in Virginia and beyond the Mississippi, our efforts

will equal theirs. Strengthened by His support, these efforts will be
crowned with the like glories.

J. E. JOHNSTON,
General.

Despite the weariness resulting from three days and four nights of
marches broken only by rearward skirmishes and fitful snatches of roadside sleep — not to mention the cumulative depression that went with
having abandoned better than forty miles of highly defensible terrain
without so much as a single fight that attained the dignity of a full-
scale battle — the reaction on all levels to the reading of this order, from
regimental commanders down to drummer boys, was quite as ecstatic
as even its author could have wished.

Among those officers who were better informed on current
events, mainly through having read such newspapers as were available
in camp and on the march, there lately had been growing an anxiety
that the good effect of the news from Louisiana and Virginia, which had
raised the price of gold on the New York market to 210, would be impaired by the apparently irreversible retreat of the Confederates in
North Georgia. Now though, with the word that they were going
over to the offensive, their anxiety was relieved and their hope soared,
anticipating a still greater drop in the pocketbook barometer that best
measured northern greed and fears. As for the men in the ranks, though
their faith in Old Joe had never wavered, their spirits took an even
higher bounce as they stood and heard the order read to them this
morning. "I never saw troops happier or more certain of success," one
private would recall. "A sort of grand halo illuminated every soldier's
face.... We were going to whip and rout the Yankees."

Johnston apparently shared this conviction that the Yankees would
be whipped and routed: especially as it applied to Schofield, who was
reported to be advancing heedlessly into the trap about to be sprung
northwest of Cassville. At 10.20, hearing from Hardee that Thomas
was moving in strength on Kingston and soon would be too heavily committed to effect a rapid disengagement, he sent his chief of staff, Brigadier
General W. W. Mackall — who had served Bragg, his West Point classmate, in the same capacity — to tell Polk and Hood "to make quick
work" of their combined lunge at Schofield, so that they would be ready
to turn without delay on Thomas, when he came up in Hardee's wake,
for the second phase of the Confederate offensive. With accustomed
caution, Johnston added to Hood's instructions a warning that, in
launching his flank attack, he was not to undertake "too wide a movement," lest he lose contact with Polk on his left, which not only might
leave Schofield an escape hatch, but also would delay the consolidation
of all three corps for the follow-up strike at Thomas and McPherson.

Such a warning was altogether superfluous, the staffer found when he encountered Hood near Cassville. Not only had the Kentuckian moved out before Mackall got there; by now he was moving back again, feverishly preparing to take up a defensive position in which to resist attack by a blue column reported to be advancing on a road in his right rear, skirmishers deployed and guns booming.

Mackall sent word of this surprise development to Johnston, who flatly declined to credit the report. "It can't be," he said. He did not believe the Federals were there because none of Polk's cavalry had encountered them this morning while reconnoitering in that direction. (In point of fact, they had not been there earlier this morning, and it was entirely accidental that they were there at all. A nomadic fragment from Major General Daniel Butterfield's division, Hooker's corps, they had missed a turning, lost their way, and wound up deep in Hood's right rear, some five miles east of their comrades trudging south on the far side of Cassville.) All the same, though Johnston did not believe in their existence — then, any more than he did ten years later, when he declared: "The report upon which General Hood acted was manifestly untrue" — he took no chances. Having rejected the evidence, he proceeded to act upon it. "If that's so," he said, examining the situation on a map, "General Hood will have to fall back at once."

Accordingly, when Mackall presently returned, he sent him riding again to Polk and Hood with orders canceling their attack. Once more, as had been its custom for the past two weeks, the army would take up a stout defensive position and there await developments: meaning Sherman.

Johnston quickly found what he was seeking along a wooded ridge immediately southeast of Cassville, overlooking the town and the "broad, open, elevated valley" in which it lay. Hood and Polk fell back to there, followed prudently by Schofield, who by now had notified Sherman of the snare he had so narrowly avoided, and Hardee came up that afternoon to take position on their left, closely pursued by Thomas and McPherson, the latter having closed the gap between him and the Cumberlanders in the course of the daylong skirmish, first north, then east of Kingston. Before sundown the guns of both armies were banging away at each other, arching their shots above the hill-cradled streets and rooftops of the village. Despite the dismay of the townspeople at this harrowing turn of events ("Consternation of citizens," a staff lieutenant jotted in his diary; "many flee, leaving all; some take away few effects, some remain between hostile fires") Johnston was greatly pleased with his new position, later referring to it as "the best I saw occupied during the war."

Polk and Hood did not agree with this assessment, and they said as much that evening when they came to headquarters for the council of war to which they had been summoned. Protesting that Union batteries enfiladed that portion of the ridge where their lines joined, they liked the position so little, in fact, that both wanted to leave it at the earliest possible moment. The army had no choice, they said, except to schedule a dawn attack, on the chance of beating Sherman to the punch, or else to fall back tonight across the Etowah. Johnston did not want to do either: certainly not attack the reunited Federals with no better promise of success than the tactical situation seemed to him to afford. Hardee, who arrived at this point in the discussion, sided altogether with his chief, hoping like him that Sherman would oblige them tomorrow by exposing his superior numbers to severe and sudden curtailment by advancing them head-on across that broad, open valley to challenge the defenders on the wooded ridge.

Johnston ended by deciding to retreat. He did so, he explained later, not because he agreed with Hood and Polk that the position had its drawbacks, but "in the belief that the confidence of the commanders of two of the three corps of the army, of their inability to resist the enemy, would inevitably be communicated to their troops, and produce that inability."

The fall-back to the Etowah that night, though Sherman made no attempt to interfere, was by far the most disruptive of the campaign. "All hurried off without regard to order," the young staff diarist recorded. "Reach Cartersville before day, troops come in after day. General Johnston comes up — all hurried over bridges; great confusion caused by mixing trains and by trains which crossed first parking at river's edge and others winding around wrong roads."

Much of the mixup was a manifestation of the army's chagrin at the two-step disappointment it had suffered, first in the cancellation of the attack, which came hard on the heels of the reading of Old Joe's "I lead you to battle" address — "I could not restrain my tears when I found we could not strike," Mackall confessed in a home letter — and then in the directive, which came down that night, for a resumption of the southward march. "Change of line not understood but thought all right," the diarist put it, "but night retreat after issuing general order impaired confidence; great alarm in country round. Troops think no stand to be made north of Chattahoochee, where supply train is sent." Civilians north and immediately south of the Etowah reacted to their abandonment much as the people of Cassville had done the day before, milling about like ants in an upset ant hill. Johnston put the blame, or anyhow most of it, on Hood, and so did members of his staff, including the diarist, who wrote: "One lieutenant general talks about attack and not giving ground, publicly, and quietly urges retreat."

By way of consolation for its woes, the disgruntled army could see for itself the strength of its new position near Allatoona, four miles down the Western & Atlantic from the river. Here, beginning the day of their arrival, May 20, Johnston had his soldiers throw up breastworks commanding the deep, narrow gorge through which the railroad snaked its way, his flanks protected, left and right, by Pumpkin Vine and Allatoona creeks. Fifteen miles to the south, his new supply base was Marietta, just beyond Kennesaw Mountain, about midway between the Etowah and the Chattahoochee, last of the three main rivers between Chattanooga and Atlanta.

Allatoona Pass, as the gorge through this spur of the Appalachians was called, was a still more "terrible door of death" than Buzzard Roost had been, some sixty miles to the north. Paradoxically, though, it was precisely in this abundance of natural strength that the strategic weakness of the position lay. Sherman would be even less apt to call for a main effort here than he had been at Rocky Face Ridge. His solution, now as then, would most likely be to try another sidle — and there was always the danger that, sooner or later, one or another of these complicated flank maneuvers would succeed in accomplishing its purpose of placing the superior blue army squarely between the Confederates and Atlanta; in which case Johnston would have no choice except to attack the Federals where they were, intrenched and waiting, or scatter into the surrounding hills. Either course would mean the loss not only of the campaign (meaning Atlanta) but also of the army, whether by destruction or disintegration, the difference being that one would be somewhat less sudden than the other. All Johnston could do, in the way of attempting to forestall such a calamity, was alert Wheeler to be on the lookout for the first sign of another sidle, up or down the Etowah. He felt sure that one was pending, but he could not move to thwart it until he knew its direction, right or left.

One other thing he could attempt, however, and that was to protect himself from his detractors, in some measure at least, by putting his performance in the best possible light for his Richmond superiors, with emphasis on his desire for coming to grips with his pursuer. Since this latest retreat had no doubt set his critics' teeth on edge, he no sooner crossed the Etowah than he got off a wire to the President explaining the cancellation of the "general attack" he had ordered yesterday: "While the officer charged with the lead was advancing he was deceived by a false report that a heavy column of the enemy had turned our right and was close upon him, and took a defensive position. When the mistake was discovered it was too late to resume the movement." Despite this disappointment, which had obliged him to continue the withdrawal, he pointed out that he had "kept near [Sherman] to prevent his detaching to Virginia, as you directed, and have repulsed every attack he has made."

Next day, May 21, the army having spent the night improving its position near Allatoona, still with no sign of what the Federals were up to, he followed through with another message along similar lines. "In the last six days the enemy has pressed us back to this point, thirty-two miles," he conceded, but he assured Davis that, all this time, "I have earnestly sought an opportunity to strike." The trouble was that Sherman, by constantly extending his right as he moved down the railroad, had obliged the defenders to give ground no less constantly, and then, "by fortifying the moment he halted," had also "made an assault upon his superior forces too hazardous." Without committing himself to anything specific — as, indeed, he could scarcely be expected to do, under the circumstances outlined here — Johnston wanted the Commander in Chief to know that he was in full agreement as to the need for going over to the offensive at the earliest possible moment. Meantime, despite the discouragements generally involved in making a lengthy retrograde movement, he was pleased to report that the slightness of his losses from straggling or desertion showed that the army was in good shape for such exertions as he might presently require.

The answer came not from Davis — not just yet — but from Bragg, who combined good news with bad and wound up with a flourish that seemed to indicate that the Georgia commander perhaps had oversold his case. Another brigade of infantry from Mobile and a regiment of South Carolina cavalry were on their way to join him, but these were the last the government would be sending.

"From the high condition in which your army is reported," the message ended, "we confidently rely on a brilliant success."

★ ★ ★

Johnston's concern, lest the very strength of his Allatoona position deprive him of the quick defensive victory he felt certain he would score if his adversary could only be persuaded to attack him there, was better founded than he knew. Two decades back, as a young artillery lieutenant on detached duty at Marietta with the inspector general, Sherman "rode or walked, exploring creeks, valleys, hills" in the surrounding region, while his less energetic comrades "spent their leisure Sundays reading novels, card-playing, or sleeping." Now this seemingly useless pastime stood him in good stead. "Twenty years later the thing that helped me to win battles in Georgia was my perfect knowledge of the country. I knew more of Georgia than the rebels did." In the course of his rambles, sketch pad in hand, he had spent several days investigating some Indian mounds on the south bank of the Etowah, just north of the gorge where Johnston was intrenched, and "I therefore knew that the Allatoona Pass was very strong, would be hard to force, and resolved not even to attempt it, but to turn the position."

First, though, he would call a halt, a brief time-out from war; the combat troops would take a welcome three-day rest ("to replenish and fit up," he explained to Halleck) while Colonel W. W. Wright and his 2000 nimble rail repairmen, having rebuilt the Resaca bridge in jig time, put the Western & Atlantic back in operation down to Kingston.

"The dead were buried, the sick and wounded were made more comfortable, and everybody got his mail and wrote letters," one appreciative officer would recall. Then on May 23, with twenty days' rations in his wagons, Sherman was ready to cut loose from the railroad and strike out cross-country with everything he had.

His preliminary objective on this all-out flanking operation was Dallas, a road-hub settlement just under twenty miles west of Marietta and about the same distance southwest of Allatoona, where Johnston would be left holding the bag unless he pulled back in time to meet this massive threat to his new supply base, fifteen miles down the track in his rear. As usual, Thomas would take the direct central route, south from Kingston through Euharlee and Stilesboro, while Schofield marched on his left, by way of Burnt Hickory, and McPherson swung well to the right, through Van Wert, to approach Dallas from the west. The march would be a rigorous one, Sherman knew from previous exploration, "as the country was very obscure, mostly in a state of nature, densely wooded and with few roads." It might take longer than he planned: in which case, he told Halleck, his twenty-day rations could be stretched to thirty. But he was not inclined to worry much as he set out from Kingston, riding with Thomas across the Etowah; "the Rubicon of Georgia," he called that river in a dispatch sent just after he gave the jump-off signal. "We are now all in motion like a vast hive of bees," he declared, fairly buzzing with pleasure at being once more on the go, "and expect to swarm along the Chattahoochee in five days."

So he said. But when Schofield captured a lone gray rider at Burnt Hickory next day and found on him a dispatch which showed Johnston already reacting to this latest turning movement, Sherman not only knew that secrecy had gone by the board, along with all hope for a substantial head start in the projected five-day sprint for the Chattahoochee; he also perceived that "it accordingly became necessary to use great caution, lest some of the minor columns should fall into ambush," as Schofield had so nearly done, four days ago, near Cassville.

Caution was indeed called for, he found out the following morning, May 25, when Thomas pressed down in advance of the other two armies for a crossing of Pumpkin Vine Creek. Hooker had the lead, driving butternut cavalry pickets over a bridge which they set on fire just as the first of his three divisions came in sight. He doused the flames, double-timed across, and continued his pursuit of the skittery horsemen. Four miles northeast of Dallas, near a Methodist meeting-house called New Hope Church, he came under fire from a mass of rebel infantry whose march he had apparently interrupted. With soldierly instinct, and as if determined to justify his nom de guerre, Fighting Joe shook out a line of skirmishers and attacked with his lead division, commanded by Brigadier General John W. Geary, a six-foot six-inch Pennsylvanian who had been San Francisco's first mayor and a territorial governor of Kansas. A colonel in the Mexican War before he was thirty, he now was forty-four and had seen much fighting, East and West, including Chancellorsville and Gettysburg, Wauhatchie and Chattanooga, but in none of these had he and his men found harder work than was required of them in the next three hours around New Hope Church, which the attackers ever afterwards referred to as the "Hell Hole."

What Geary struck, and promptly rebounded from, was Hood. His corps had been last of the three to leave Allatoona the day before, when Johnston, warned by Wheeler that Sherman was off on another sidle, marched southwest up the near bank of Pumpkin Vine Creek to intercept him around Dallas. Hardee was there now, with Polk in position on his right to connect with Hood near New Hope Church; so that what Hooker had encountered was not a mere segment of Johnston's army on the march, as he first thought, but the entire right wing of that army, already beginning to scratch out intrenchments in expectation of his arrival hard on the heels of the cavalry pickets fading back before him through what Sherman called "the obscurity of the ambushed country." Undaunted by the truth, which he began to suspect as soon as Geary was flung back, Hooker brought up his other two divisions, led by Butterfield and Brigadier General Alpheus Williams, massed them on a front no wider than Geary had spanned alone, and sent them forward, closely packed, against the rebel center. As a result, Major General Alexander P. Stewart's division caught the brunt of the all-out blue attack, some 20,000 strong. Known to his soldiers as "Old Straight," the nickname he had acquired while teaching mathematics at West Point and at Cumberland University in his home state of Tennessee, Stewart was forty-two and a veteran of all the army's battles, a strict disciplinarian much admired by his men, who gave him today all he asked of them, and more: especially the artillerists, whose guns were advantageously sited to exact a heavy toll from the charging bluecoats. Hooker's three divisions could make no headway against this one, despite two hours of trying without pause. Hood's other two divisions, under Major Generals Thomas Hindman and Carter Stevenson, had little to do on the left and right of the sector being assaulted, but when Johnston himself, alarmed by the desperate nature of the struggle, sent to ask Stewart if he needed reinforcements, the Tennessean replied calmly: "My own troops will hold the position."

Still another hour of such fighting remained, and it was this third hour, even more than the previous two, that prompted the Hell Hole description of the scene. Thunder rumbled and lightning crackled from a huge black cloud that gathered above the crossroad, dwarfing the boom of guns and the flicker of muzzle flashes, then loosed its torrential burden with all the abruptness of a water-filled bag split open, drenching men already wet with sweat from heat and exertion, whether prone behind log barricades or scrambling through bullet- and rain-whipped brush. "No more persistent attack or determined resistance was anywhere made," Stewart was to report with impartial praise. Thunderstorm and fighting came to a simultaneous end as the cloud blew off and the sun went down in a glory of red and purple beyond Dallas and the mountains to the west. Hooker put his casualties at 1665 killed or wounded, but the Confederates, knowing his reputation for understating his own losses while overestimating those of his opponent, were convinced the figure was much too low, since they themselves, fighting mostly behind cover, had lost nearly half that many in the course of the three-hour contest.

Darkness made the going hard for the rest of Thomas's army, coming up in the center, as well as for the other two, closing in on the left and right. "All was hurry and confusion," a Kentucky Federal recorded in his diary, "nearly everyone swearing at the top of his voice." Sherman would later recall that he "slept on the ground, without cover, alongside of a log, [and] got little sleep," but Schofield had worse luck. Swept off his horse by a low-hanging branch while combing the moonless woods in search of Sherman's bivouac, he was hurt by the fall and would be out of action for several days; leadership of his Army of the Ohio passed temporarily to Brigadier General Jacob Cox, the senior division commander. McPherson made it nearly to Dallas by daylight, coming in from the west to find Hardee securely intrenched there, as were Polk and Hood to the northeast.

Sherman probed cautiously at the five-mile rebel line, all that day and part of the next, but found no weakness he considered would justify attack. Accordingly, by midmorning of the second day of unproductive probing, May 27, he decided to turn Johnston's right with a strike at Pickett's Mill, two miles beyond the Hell Hole Hooker had failed to take two days ago. This time Howard drew the assignment, and presently all three of his divisions were in position, massed for assault in case there was serious opposition.

There was indeed, and "serious" was by no means too strong a description of what he was about to encounter in the way of resistance. Suspecting that the Federals would attempt some such maneuver, Johnston the day before had instructed Hardee to shift one of his divisions from the far left to a position beyond Hood's right: specifically, to Pickett's Mill. It was Howard's ill fortune — as it had been Sherman's, on Missionary Ridge six months ago, and Hooker's, two days later at Ringgold Gap — that the division posted in his path was Major General Patrick Cleburne's, by common agreement the best in Johnston's army. Before emigrating to become a lawyer in Helena, Arkansas, Irish-born Cleburne had done a three-year hitch in Her Majesty's 41st Regiment of Foot, an experience that stood the former corporal in good stead when it came to training his division of Arkansans, Texans, Mississippians, and Tennesseans. Except under specific orders, which sometimes had to be repeated, he and his men had never given up a piece of ground assigned to their defense; nor did they do so here today at Pickett's Mill. One-armed Howard gave the lead to his fellow West Pointer, Brigadier General Thomas Wood — whose abrupt, inadvertent withdrawal under orders at Chickamauga had created the "chasm" through which Longstreet plunged to defeat Rosecrans. Wood had his division in place by early afternoon, formed six ranks deep for an end-on strike at the rebel flank, wherever it might be. He moved out, floundered about for a couple of hours in the heavy brush, then paused for some badly needed rest, having sighted the newly turned earth of fresh intrenchments through the trees. It was 4.30 by the time he got his three brigades in motion again, still in a compact formation of two lines each, and what turned out to be a three-hour fight, with an equally horrendous night-time epilogue added for good measure, began almost at once.

His repulse was as complete as it was sudden. Ahead through the trees, as the close-packed blue infantry came on, the head-logs of the newly dug rebel intrenchments seemed to burst into flame, and a long, low cloud of smoke boiled up and out, billowing as it grew, lighted from within by the pinkish yellow blink and stab of muzzle flashes; Cleburne's emphasis on rapid-fire marksmanship in training produced a clatter as continuous as the uproar in a 5000-man boiler factory and an incidence of casualties that matched the stepped-up rate of fire. Wood's division fell apart, transformed abruptly from a compact mass into huddled clusters groping for cover in such low ground as the field afforded. "Under these circumstances," Howard reported, "it became evident that the assault had failed." He brought up reinforcements from Major General John M. Palmer's adjoining corps, as well as from Schofield's army, which was posted in reserve here on the Union left, and did what he could "to bring off the wounded and to prevent a successful sally of the enemy from his works." Darkness helped in both these efforts, but not much. At 10 o'clock, in a rare night action, Cleburne threw Brigadier General Hiram Granbury's Texas brigade into a charge that swept through a ravine where a number of fugitives from the attack had taken refuge, capturing all that were left alive when it was over. Howard's losses in Wood's division alone were 1457 killed, wounded, or captured. Cleburne's were 448, although Howard thought them higher in advancing a claim that "the enemy suffered immensely in the action, and regarded it as the severest attack made during this eventful campaign."

Now it was Johnston's turn to try his hand at what Sherman had been attempting all along. Reasoning that if his adversary was thus extending his left he might also have weakened his right, the Virginian told Hardee to test the Federal defenses around Dallas next morning. Hardee did, passing the word for Major General William Bate to make a probing attack with his division. Bate's repulse, though not as bloody, was as complete as Wood's had been the day before, at the far end of the line. He lost close to 400 men, half of them from the dwindling "Orphan" brigade of Kentuckians under Brigadier General Joseph Lewis, successor to Mrs Lincoln's brother-in-law, Ben Hardin Helm, who had fallen at Chickamauga.

All Bate got for his pains was the knowledge that McPherson was still around Dallas, apparently in undiminished strength — although the fact was he had been under orders to pull out for a march beyond New Hope Church and was about to leave when the rebel attack exploded against his works. Having fought it off, with fewer than half the casualties he inflicted, he notified Sherman and held his ground, awaiting instructions.

Meantime Johnston convened a council of war, at which Hood proposed that his corps be shifted eastward, beyond Cleburne, for an attack on the Union left, to be taken up in sequence by the other two corps with strikes at the right and center. Johnston liked the plan and issued the necessary orders, stipulating that Polk and Hardee would go forward when they heard Hood's artillery begin to roar. They waited past dawn and through sunup, May 29, poised for assault, heads cocked to catch the boom of guns that did not come. What came instead, around midmorning, was a note from Hood informing Johnston that he had found a newly arrived blue division intrenched in his path, perpendicular to the line he had scouted the day before. Finding it "inexpedient" to advance under these conditions, he had halted and now awaited new instructions. Johnston promptly canceled the offensive, directing instead that the army give all its attention to improving its defenses.

McPherson, Thomas, and Schofield were doing the same across the way, each on his own initiative, with the result that both lines grew more formidable than any seen so far in the campaign. Quick to improvise intrenchments — "The rebs must carry their breastworks with them," Federals were saying, marveling at the speed with which their adversaries could establish field fortifications, while the Confederates returned the compliment by remarking that "Sherman's men march with a rifle in one hand and a spade in the other" — blue and gray alike had become adept at the art of making any position well-nigh impregnable within a couple of days. While some troops hastily scratched and scooped out a ditch with bayonets and wooden shovels, canteen halves and fingers, others felled trees to provide timber for the dirt-and-log revetment, atop which a head log would rest on poles extending rearward across the trench to keep it from falling on the defenders in case it was struck by a shell while they were firing through the slit along its bottom between the skid poles. Other trees out front were cut so that their tops fell toward the enemy, their interlaced branches providing an entanglement to discourage assault, and if there was time for more methodical work, sharpened stakes were set in holes bored in logs and these too were placed to delay or impale attackers; *chevaux-de-frise* was the engineers' term for these spiky devices, which Westerners on both sides called "sheep racks." Whatever their name, they were cruelly effective and contributed largely to the invulnerability of the occupants of the trenches, taking it easy under the shade of blankets laid over the works to shield them from the sun. Taking it easy, that is, in a relative sense; for the snipers were sharp-eyed, quick to shoot from dawn to dusk, and the pickets on both sides were fearfully trigger-happy from dusk to dawn; Thomas alone was expending 200,000 rounds of small-arms ammunition daily.

May now ended, and as June came in, two days after Bate's repulse by McPherson helped to offset the subtractions Hooker and Howard had undergone in their assaults on Stewart and Cleburne, both commanders could take a backward look at what the four-week "running skirmish," uninterrupted by anything approaching either the dignity or the carnage of a full-scale battle, had cost them. Sherman's loss throughout the month of May was 9299, including nearly two thousand killed and missing; Johnston's, less precisely tabulated, was about 8500, three thousand of them captured or otherwise missing, left behind on his retrograde movement from Dalton to Dallas. Not even the larger of the two was a shudder-provoking figure at this stage of the war — particularly in comparison with the one being registered simultaneously in Virginia, where Meade was losing men at the rate of 2000 a day and would lose three times that many tomorrow, within less than twenty minutes, at Cold Harbor — but Sherman was getting edgy, all the same, over his inability to come to grips with his opponent on any terms except those that would clearly involve self-slaughter.

This he declined, around New Hope Church, as he had done before, wherever the Confederates called a halt to invite attack on their intrenchments. Instead, he continued to extend his left flank eastward toward the Western & Atlantic, obliging Johnston to conform by extending his right to keep him from slipping past it.

He was eager to get back astride the railroad, since two of his mounted divisions — Garrard's, which had rejoined from Rome, and another led by Major General George Stoneman, former chief of cavalry in the Army of the Potomac, under Hooker, now filling that position in Schofield's Army of the Ohio — had seized lightly held Allatoona Pass that morning, June 1, clearing the way for Sherman's rail repair gangs to extend his all-weather supply line across the Etowah, down to Acworth and beyond. Though Acworth was within ten miles of New Hope Church, the going would be rough, not only because of the rugged nature of the terrain and the probable interference of the rebels, but also because on the day Allatoona fell the rain began to fall as well: no brief tumultuous spring thunderstorm, such as had drenched the Hell Hole fighters, stopping about as abruptly as it started, but rather the slow, steady, apparently endless downpour of a dripping Georgia June. "Rain! Rain!! Rain!!!" an entry in a soggy diary read a few days later. This was as much of a strain on the spirits of men as it was on the backs and legs of mules who lugged ration and ammunition wagons through soupy troughs of wet red clay that once had passed for roads. "These were the hardest times the army experienced," Howard was to say, looking back. "It rained continuously for seventeen days; the roads, becoming as broad as the fields, were a series of quagmires." Mosquitoes stung and thrived, along with something new that bit and burrowed: redbugs, *Eutrombicula alfreddugesi* — chiggers. "Chigres are big, and red as blood," an Illinois private wrote. "They will crawl through any cloth and bite worse than fleas, and poison the flesh very badly. Many of the boys anoint their bodies with bacon rines which chigres can't go. Salt water bathing would cure them but salt is too scarce to use on human flesh."

Salt was not the only scarcity. Cut loose from their bountiful rail supply line, and with little chance to forage on their own, the troops had to live mainly on hardtack and bacon. Men began to come down with the symptoms of scurvy, "black-mouthed, loose-toothed fellows" who went on the roam in search of wild onions or anything green and fit to eat, though with small success in this barren, up-and-down backwoods region, miles off the main track. It was, as Howard said, a difficult time for everyone concerned, including Sherman.

Then on the night of June 4, the sounds of withdrawal muffled by the drumming of the rain, Johnston gave him the slip again. Morning showed the Confederates gone, and though some of his soldiers cheered "the nocturnal departure of the rebellious gentlemen," Sherman himself was far from pleased: especially when he received reports of their new position, which seemed, on the face of it, about as strong as any they had occupied in the past four weeks. Hardee held the left, on Lost Mountain and at Gilgal Church, Polk the center, from Pine Mountain to the Western & Atlantic, six miles below Acworth, and Hood the right, across the railroad, along the base of Brush Mountain. Cavalry covered and extended the flanks, Wheeler eastward, beyond Hood, and Brigadier General William H. Jackson's division, which had come with Polk from Alabama, westward beyond Hardee. Kennesaw Mountain, a commanding height, was two miles in the rear, handy in case another fallback was required, and Marietta about the same distance beyond its crest, which was less than twenty air-line miles from the heart of Atlanta.

By the following day, June 6, the three Union armies were again in confrontation with their foe, Thomas in the center, Schofield on the right, and McPherson on the left, astride the railroad at Big Shanty, a little more than midway between Allatoona and Marietta. Three days later Major General Francis P. Blair, Junior — brother of Lincoln's Postmaster General and a close friend of Sherman's — rejoined McPherson, bringing the 10,000 men of his corps back from their reënlistment furloughs and, incidentally, more than making up for the combat losses in all three armies up to now. By June 11 the hard-working railroad crews had the track repaired all the way to Big Shanty, and the troops, back on full rations and fairly well rested from their recent excursion through the wilds, felt much better.

"If we get to Atlanta in a week, all right," one veteran wrote home. "If it takes two months you won't hear this army grumbling."

Sherman was inclined to be less patient at this point. Though he was pleased that his latest sidle had accomplished its main purpose by obliging the rebels to give up impregnable Allatoona Pass, he was disappointed that it had not taken him all the way to the Chattahoochee (as he had predicted it would do, within five days) instead of fifteen rugged miles short of that river, with Johnston dug in across his front and able to look down his throat, so to speak, from the high ground up ahead. Obviously, if the graybacks were to be dislodged at something less than an altogether grievous price in casualties, this called for another sidle. Yet Sherman did not much like the notion of setting out on still another roundabout march away from the railroad: mainly, no doubt, because the last one had cost him more than he had planned for, both in morale and blood. In fact, before he crossed the Etowah and started his swing around Dallas, his losses had actually been lower than his adversary's, but now, as a result of the repulses he had suffered at New Hope Church and Pickett's Mill, they were nearly a thousand higher. Moreover, it seemed to him that his practice of avoiding pitched battle, wherever the terrain appeared unfavorable, had tended to make his soldiers unaggressive, timid in the face of possible ambush, and flinchy when confronted by intrenchments. Schofield, recovered by now from his horseback fall the week before, accounted for the reaction somewhat differently, seeing the nonprofessional volunteers and draftees as men who brought to army life, and to war itself, the practicality they had learned as civilians with the need for earning a living in the peacetime world outside. "The veteran American soldier fights very much as he has been accustomed to work his farm or run his sawmill," the young West Pointer declared. "He wants to see a fair prospect that it is going to pay."

That might be; Sherman yielded to no man in his admiration for and his understanding of the western volunteer. Still it seemed to him that all three armies were in danger of losing their fighting edge, if indeed they had not already lost it, and he put most of the blame on their commanders. Even McPherson, protégé or not, had begun to receive tart messages complaining of his slowness on the march. As for Schofield, he had come a long way from measuring up to expectations, and Sherman did not hesitate to say so. But Thomas, who had direct charge of two thirds of all the Federals in North Georgia, was the main object of the redhead's impatience and downright scorn.

"My chief source of trouble is with the Army of the Cumberland," Sherman informed Grant by telegraph this week. "A fresh furrow in a plowed field will stop the whole column and all begin to intrench. I have again and again tried to impress on Thomas that we must assail and not defend; we are on the offensive, and yet it seems that the whole Army of the Cumberland is so habituated to be[ing] on the defensive that from its commander down to its lowest private I cannot get it out of their heads."

He turned snappish in reaction to the delays and disadvantages involved in fighting what he called "a big Indian war" against an opponent whose army remained elusively intact and who, as Sherman complained in a letter to his brother in Washington, could "fight or fall back, as he pleases. The future is uncertain," he wound up gloomily, "but I will do all that is possible."

Aside from another unwanted sidle on muddy roads, not much seemed possible just now except to keep up the pressure, dead ahead, in hope that something would give. Nothing did. Johnston had contracted, somewhat retired, and thereby strengthened his line of defense, pulling Hardee in around Gilgal Church and Hood behind Noonday Creek, astride the railroad; Lost and Brush mountains were left to the protection of the cavalry, and Polk reinforced the center, on call to help cover not only the Western & Atlantic but also the wagon roads between Acworth and Marietta.

For outpost and observation purposes, a brigade from Bate's division remained on Pine Mountain, occupying what had become a salient when the line was readjusted in its rear. Called Pine Top by the natives, it was not so much a mountain as it was an overgrown hill, detached from the others roundabout and bristled atop with pine trees. Steepest on its northern face, it afforded a fine view of all three Federal armies and thus was well worth holding onto; Johnston had posted two batteries on its crest to help defend it, including one from South Carolina commanded by Lieutenant René Beauregard, the Creole general's son. Hardee was apprehensive, however, that both troops and guns were too far in advance of the main position for support to reach them before they were gobbled up by a sudden blue assault, and he asked his chief to go with him next morning, June 14, to judge in person the risk to which the salient was exposed.

Johnston agreed and the two set out on horseback as arranged, accompanied by their staffs and also by Polk, who wanted to come along for a look at the country from the hilltop. The rain had slackened and a cool breeze made the ride and the climb up the south slope a pleasant interlude, although Johnston had not gone far before he agreed that Hardee's fears were well founded; he told him to withdraw Bate's brigade and the two batteries after nightfall. Reaching the crest, however, he decided to avail himself of this last chance to study the enemy position from Pine Top, despite a warning that a battery of rifled Parrott guns, about half a mile in front, had been firing with deadly accuracy all morning at anyone who exposed himself to view. Sure enough, the three generals had no sooner mounted the parapet and begun adjusting their binoculars than they were greeted by a bursting shell.

Sherman himself, riding out on a line inspection down below, had seen them, although without personal recognition at that range, and had taken offense at their presumption. "How saucy they are," he said, and he turned to Howard, who held this portion of the front, and told him to have one of his batteries throw a few shots in their direction to "make 'em take cover." He rode on, and Howard passed the word to Battery I, 1st Ohio Light Artillery, whose commander, Captain Hubert Dilger, had already acted on the order before it reached him.

Dilger was something of a character, well known throughout the army, partly because of the way he dressed, immaculate in a white shirt with rolled sleeves, highly polished top boots, and doeskin trousers — hence the nickname "Leatherbreeches" — and partly because of his habit of taking his guns so close to the front in battle that one general had proposed to equip them with bayonets. On leave from the Prussian army, in which he was also an artillerist, he had been visiting New York in 1861 and had joined the Army of the Potomac, fighting in all its battles through Gettysburg before coming west with Hooker to join the Army of the Cumberland. Perhaps because he spoke with a heavy German accent, he trained his crews to respond to hand claps, rather than voice commands, and had won such admiration as an expert, famed for the rapidity and precision of his fire, that he was allowed to function largely on his own, roving about as a sort of free lance and posting his battery wherever he judged it could do the most good. Today he was within half a mile of Pine Top, and when he saw the cluster of saucy Confederates mount the parapet on its crest he ran forward to one of his rifled Parrotts, sighted it carefully, then stepped back. "Shust teeckle them fellers," he told the cannoneer on the lanyard, and clapped his hands.

That was the first shot, a near miss. Johnston gave the order to disperse, and all three generals and their staffs had begun to do so when a second projectile landed even closer.

Hardee and Johnston moved briskly, heading for shelter behind the crest of the hill, but Polk, a portly figure apparently mindful of his dignity, walked off slowly by himself, hands clasped behind his back as if in deep thought. Just then the third shell came shrieking; Dilger had been quick to find the range. It struck the churchly warrior squarely in the side, passing through his left arm and his body and his right arm before emerging to explode against a tree. Johnston and Hardee turned and hurried back through other shell-bursts to kneel beside the quivering corpse of the bishop general. "My dear, dear friend," Hardee groaned, tears falling. Johnston too was weeping as he laid his hand upon the dead man's head. "We have lost much," he said, and presently added: "I would rather anything but this."

An ambulance, summoned by wigwag from the Pine Top signal station, brought Polk's mangled remains down off the mountain that afternoon, followed that night, in accordance with Johnston's evacuation order, by the men of the two batteries and the infantry brigade, who filed down in a long column not unlike a funeral cortege. Indeed, the whole army mourned the fifty-eight-year-old bishop's passing; he had been with it from the outset, before Shiloh, and at one time or another had commanded nearly every soldier in its ranks. There were, of course, those who doubted that his clerical qualities justified his elevation to the leadership of a corps. "Thus died a gentleman and a high Church dignitary," one of his division commanders wrote. "As a soldier he was more theoretical than practical." Though there was

truth in this, it overlooked the contribution he made to the army's
moral tone, which was one of the factors that enabled it to survive
hardships, defeats, retreats, and Bragg. Northerners might express outrage that a man of the cloth, West Point graduate or not, should take
up the sword of rebellion; Southerners took his action as strong evidence
that the Lord was on their side, and they on His. That was part of
what Jefferson Davis meant when he later referred to his old friend's
death as "an irrepairable loss" and said that the country had sustained
no heavier blow since the fall of Sidney Johnston and Stonewall
Jackson.

One service Polk's maiming performed, at any rate, and that
was to break up the pattern of Sherman's incipient depression. He had
small use for the clergy anyhow, as a class, let alone this one who had
joined in the current unholy attempt to dissolve the finest government
the world had ever known, and when the news reached his headquarters
at Big Shanty that afternoon — Federal signalmen decoded a wigwag
appeal from atop Pine Mountain: "Send an ambulance for General
Polk's body" — he took it as a sign that things were going better than
he had thought. Sure enough, morning showed the enemy gone from
the troublesome salient opposite his center. The rain had resumed its
drumming on his tent, still further increasing the depth of the mud on
all the roads, but Sherman did not let that keep his rising spirits from
taking another mercurial jump. Ordering Thomas to close the gap in
front while McPherson and Schofield stepped up the pressure on the
flanks, he rode out to see it done and returned much pleased with
the events of the past two days. Though he was careful, then and down
the years, to deny the rumor that it was he, not Leatherbreeches Dilger,
who had laid with his own hands the gun that sniped the militant
churchman off of Pine Top, he was delighted with the result produced
on this fortieth day of his campaign to "knock Jos. Johnston."

"We killed Bishop Polk yesterday," he wired Halleck, once more
in high feather, "and made good progress today."

✘   2   ✘

Not that, in his revived ebullience, he had dismissed all fear for what
he called "that single stem of railroad 473 miles long," back through
Nashville and Bowling Green, hurdling rivers and burrowing under
mountains to reach his base on the Ohio; "Taxed [as it was] to its
utmost to supply our daily wants," Sherman said flatly that without it
"the Atlanta campaign was an impossibility." It was as much on his
mind as ever, along with the two famed raiders who threatened its
unbroken operation. "Thus far we have been well supplied, and I hope
it will continue," he wrote his wife this week from Big Shanty, "though

I expect to hear every day of Forrest breaking into Tennessee from some quarter. John Morgan is in Kentucky, but I attach little importance to him or his raid. Forrest is a more dangerous man."

Even as he wrote, events were proving him right in both assessments. Morgan, after his victory at Crockett's Cove in the second week of May, reverted to his plan for a return to his homeland, which had been interrupted by the need for keeping Averell away from the salt works and lead mines in the Department of Southwest Virginia. His application for permission to make the raid had been turned down by the Richmond authorities, on the grounds that he was needed where he was, but he did not let that stop him now any more than he had done ten months ago, when he set out on the "ride" that landed him in the Ohio Penitentiary. Besides, having just learned that Brigadier General Stephen Burbridge, Union commander of the District of Kentucky, and a subordinate, Brigadier General Edward Hobson, were even then assembling troops in separate camps for a march across the Cumberlands to visit on Saltville and Wytheville the destruction Averell had failed to accomplish, Morgan believed he now had a more persuasive argument in favor of a quick return to the Bluegrass. Their combined forces were better than twice the size of his own, which amounted to fewer than 3000 men, and he was convinced that the only way to stop them was to distract them before they got started. "This information has determined me to move at once into the State of Kentucky," he informed the War Department on the last day of the month, "and thus divert the plans of the enemy by initiating a movement within his lines."

Forestalling another refusal, he set out that same day. By the time the message reached Richmond, two days later — "A most unfortunate withdrawal of forces from an important position at a very critical moment," Bragg indorsed it, and Seddon added: "Unfortunately, I see no remedy for this movement now" — Morgan was through Pound Gap and back on the soil of his native state.

That was June 2. It took him another five days to complete the rugged 150-mile trek across the mountains to within sight of the Bluegrass, and then on the morning of June 8 he approached the town of Mount Sterling, a day's ride west of Lexington. His strength was 2700 men, less than a third of them veterans from his old command, while another third were unmounted recruits for whom he hoped to find horses and equipment in the stock-rich country up ahead. A beginning was made at Mount Sterling, which he surrounded and captured, along with 380 Federals posted there to guard a large accumulation of supplies, including some badly needed boots.

While the prisoners were being paroled and Morgan was preparing to move on, looters began to break into shops, plunder homes, and even rough up citizens to relieve them of watches and wallets. "It was a general robbery," one merchant later protested, and though officers did what they could to stop the pillage, the undisciplined recruits, many of whom had spent the past two years avoiding conscription and stealing to make a living while on the run, were so far beyond control that some even drew pistols on women to rob them of their jewelry — an outrage the blood-thirstiest guerilla in Missouri had not perpetrated up to now. Confederates had mostly been greeted joyously on previous raids through this section of Kentucky, of which Morgan himself was a boasted product, but they were not likely to be welcome in the future, if indeed there was to be a future for them. A sort of climax was reached when a group of townspeople called indignantly on Morgan to show him an order, issued over the name of one of his brigade commanders, demanding immediate delivery of all the money in the local bank, under penalty of having "every house in the place" put to the torch; $72,000 in gold and greenbacks had been handed over. Morgan paled and turned to the colonel in question, who pronounced the signature a forgery and asked who had presented it. A light-haired officer with a blond beard and a German accent, he was told. Surgeon R. R. Goode answered that description, but when he was sent for he did not appear. He was missing — and remained so, though afterwards he was rumored to be living high in his native Germany.

Morgan could afford no time for an investigation, however desirable one was to clear his name, and set out without further delay for Lexington, his home town just over thirty miles away, leaving the foot-sore, horseless troopers behind to complete the distribution and destruction of the captured stores before taking up the march to join him.

Only about half of them ever did, the rest being killed or captured as the result of a miscalculation. "There will be nothing in the state to retard our progress except a few scattered provost guards," Morgan had predicted on setting out, and this opinion had been bolstered by reports from scouts that the heavy Union column under Burbridge, unaware of what was in progress across the way, had begun its eastward march toward the Cumberlands just before the Confederates emerged from them, headed west. Morgan's announced purpose was to oblige the blue invaders to turn back, but he had not thought they would react with anything like the speed they did. When Burbridge learned at Prestonburg that his adversary had passed him en route, by way of Pound Gap to the south, he not only countermarched promptly; he did so with such celerity that he was on the outskirts of Mount Sterling before daylight, June 9, and launched a dawn attack that caught the scantly picketed gray recruits so completely by surprise that many of them, still groggy from their excesses of the previous day and night, were shot before they could struggle out of their blankets. The survivors — about 450 of the original 800 — managed to fall back through the town and down the road to the west, thankful that the Federals were too worn by their hard return march to pursue.

Morgan was halfway to Lexington when he found out what had happened, and though his first reaction was to turn back and counter-attack with his whole command, on second thought (Burbridge had about twice as many men, well supported by artillery, and Morgan had been able to bring no guns across the mountains) he decided to wait for what was left of the horseless brigade to join him, then continue on to his home town. He approached it that night, made camp astride the pike, and rode in next morning to find, along with much else in the way of supplies and equipment, enough horses in its several government stables to mount all of his still-dismounted men and replace the animals broken down by the long march from Virginia.

Despite this valid military gain, June 10 was another stain on the reputation the raid had been designed, in part, to burnish. "Though the stay of Morgan's command in Lexington was brief, embracing but a few hours," the local paper reported next day, "he made good use of his time — as many empty shelves and pockets will testify." Once more looters took over, and this time veterans joined the pillage. Another bank was robbed, though more forthrightly than the one two days ago; the celebrants simply put a pistol to the cashier's head and made him open the vault, from which they took $10,000. Several buildings were set afire and whiskey stores were stripped, with the result that a good many troopers, too drunk to stay on a horse, had to be loaded into wagons for the ride to Cynthiana, thirty miles north-east. Morgan had learned there were supplies and a 500-man garrison there, and he was determined to have or destroy them both.

He marched by way of Georgetown to arrive next day, demand-ing surrender. This was declined, at first, but then accepted after a house-to-house fight in which, Morgan informed Richmond, "I was forced to burn a large portion of the town." Before he could enjoy the fruits of victory, lookouts spotted a blue column, 1200 strong, approaching from the east. It was Hobson; he too had turned back, well short of the Virginia line, on hearing from Burbridge that the raiders were in his rear. Headed for Lexington, he marched hard for Cynthiana when he saw the smoke and heard the firing. As it turned out, he was marching to join the surrender. Morgan threw two brigades directly at him and circled around to gain his rear with the other. This being done, Hobson was left with no choice except to be slaughtered or lay down his arms. He chose the latter course; which was doubly sweet for Morgan, Hobson having been widely praised for his share in the capture, near Buffington on the north bank of the Ohio River last July, of about half of Morgan's "terrible men," including the raider's second in command and two of his brothers, whom he later joined in prison as a felon. Now with Hobson himself a captive the tables were turned.

Proud of this latest exploit — as well he might be; he now had more prisoners than troopers — Morgan refused to be alarmed when scouts rode in at nightfall to report that Burbridge, having learned of his appearance at Cynthiana, was on the way from Mount Sterling with close to 5000 men. That was three times the strength of the Confederates, who were down to about 1400, half their original force, as a result of casualties, stragglers, and detachments sent out to mislead the numerous Union garrisons roundabout. Even more serious, perhaps, was a shortage of cartridges for the Enfield rifles his raiders favored so much that they declined to exchange them for captured Springfields, even though there was plenty of ammunition for the latter. But Morgan's mind was quite made up. Determined to give his weary men a good night's rest, he announced to his brigade commanders that he would meet the bluecoats next morning on ground of his own choosing, two miles south of town, and whip them as he had whipped Hobson today, whatever the odds. When one colonel protested that Burbridge was too strong to be fought without full cartridge boxes, the Alabama-born Kentuckian replied curtly: "It is my order that you hold your position at all hazard. We can whip him with empty guns."

Preceding another victory, the words would have had a defiant, martial ring, fit for the books and altogether in keeping with his earlier career; but followed as they were by a defeat, they took on the sound not of bravery, but of bravado. Burbridge attacked at dawn, June 12, and though Morgan was prevented from employing his accustomed flanking tactics by the need for putting all his men in line, he managed to stem the assault successfully until the shout, "Out of ammunition!" came from the right and was taken up next by the center, then the left. "Our whole command was soon forced back into the streets of the town, routed and demoralized," one raider would recall. "The confusion was indescribable. . . . There was much shooting, swearing, and yelling. Some from sheer mortification were crying."

Morgan did what he could to accomplish an orderly withdrawal, but what was left of his force by now had been split in two, with the halves presently blasted into fragments, some men fleeing southwest across the Sinking River to Leesburg, others northeast to Augusta. Many, caught on foot, surrendered; others were shot down. Not over half escaped, including their leader. "While falling back on the town," the same trooper wrote, "I saw General Morgan, on his step-trotting roan, going toward the Augusta road. He was skimming along at an easy pace, looking up at our broken lines and — softly whistling. I was glad to see him getting away, for had he been captured he would doubtless have fared badly."

He fared badly enough as it was. Back in Virginia before the month was out — minus half his troopers, even after all the stragglers had come in by various routes across the mountains, and considerably better than half his reputation — he put the raid in the best light he could manage in composing his report, stressing the frustration of Burbridge's expedition against the salt works and lead mines, the capture and parole of almost as many soldiers as he took with him, the procurement of nearly a thousand horses for men afoot and the exchange of roughly the same number of broken-down mounts for fresh ones, the destruction of "about 2,000,000$ worth of U.S. Govt. property," and the disruption of Federal recruitment in central and eastern Kentucky. All this was much; but it was not enough, in the minds of his Richmond superiors, to offset his unauthorized departure in the first place, the misbehavior of his raiders wherever they went, and his second-day defeats at Mount Sterling and Cynthiana. Moreover, he now faced all his old problems, with only about half as many troops, and the confirmed displeasure, if not the downright enmity, of the Confederate War Department. It was fairly clear, in any case, that John Morgan had taken his last "ride," that his beloved home state had seen its last of him and his terrible men.

Sherman was pleased, but hardly surprised, by Morgan's failure. Indeed, aside from having work crews standing by to make quick repairs in case the Kentuckian broke through to damage the railroad below Louisville, he feared him so little that he had scarcely planned for his coming beyond warning local commanders to be on the lookout. The other raider was another matter. After telling his wife, "Forrest is a more dangerous man," the red-haired Ohioan added: "I am in hopes that an expedition sent out from Memphis about the first of June will give him full employment."

It certainly should have done at least that, preceded as it was by a top-to-bottom shakeup of department personnel, beginning with Major General Stephen Hurlbut, commander of the District of West Tennessee. A Shiloh veteran and prewar Republican politician, Hurlbut had high-placed friends — Lincoln himself had made him a brigadier within a month of Sumter — but Sherman, far from satisfied with the "marked timidity" of his attempts to keep Forrest out of the region this past year, replaced him, less than a week after the fall of Fort Pillow, with Major General Cadwallader C. Washburn, who also had lofty Washington connections, including his brother Elihu, Grant's congressional guardian angel. Washburn had shown aggressiveness at Vicksburg, and Sherman chose him for that quality, which he encouraged by sending him a new chief of cavalry who shared it, Brigadier General Samuel D. Sturgis.

Seasoned by combat in Missouri as well as in Virginia (where he had contributed at least one famous quotation to the annals of this war: "I don't care for John Pope one pinch of owl dung") Sturgis had graduated from West Point alongside Stonewall Jackson and George McClellan. That he was more akin militarily to the former than to the latter was demonstrated by the manner in which he took hold on arrival in late April. Forrest by then was returning to North Mississippi from his raid to the Ohio; Sturgis pursued him as far as Ripley, seventy-five miles southeast of Memphis, before turning back for lack of subsistence for his 6400-man column. "I regret very much that I could not have the pleasure of bringing you his hair," he wrote Sherman on his return to Tennessee, "but he is too great a plunderer to fight anything like an equal force, and we have to be satisfied with driving him from the state. He may turn on your communications . . . I rather think he will, but see no way to prevent it from this point and with this force."

In part — the remark about Forrest's hair, for example — this had a true aggressive ring, confirming the choice of Sturgis for the post he filled, but Sherman did not enjoy being told there was no way to keep the raider off his life line. His Georgia campaign had opened by then, and the farther he got from his starting point (Dalton to Resaca; across the Oostanaula to Kingston; then finally over the Etowah for the roundhouse swing through Dallas) the more vital that supply line became, and the more exposed it was to depredation. Concerned lest Forrest give Washburn the slip, he wired orders for the West Tennessee commander to launch "a threatening movement from Memphis," southeast into Mississippi, to prevent Forrest "from swinging over against my communications" in North Georgia or Middle Tennessee. Sturgis was to have charge of the expedition, but Washburn himself saw to the preparations, taking two full weeks to make certain nothing was omitted that might be needed, either in men or supplies or equipment. "The force sent out was in complete order," he later reported, "and consisted of some of our best troops. They were ordered to go in the lightest possible marching order, and to take only wagons for commissary stores and ammunition. They had a supply for twenty days. I saw to it personally that they lacked nothing to insure a successful campaign. The number of troops deemed necessary by General Sherman, as he telegraphed me, was 6000, but I sent 8000."

He sent in fact 8300: three brigades of infantry, totaling 5000, under Colonel William L. McMillen, the senior field officer in the district, and two of cavalry, totaling 3300, led by Brigadier General Benjamin Grierson, who had come into prominence a year ago with the 600-mile raid that distracted Vicksburg's defenders while Grant was beginning the final phase of the campaign that accomplished its surrender. In over-all charge of the two divisions, Sturgis also had 22 guns, of various calibers, and 250 wagons loaded with the twenty-day supply of food and ammunition. Grierson's troopers were equipped with repeating carbines of the latest model, which would give them a big advantage in firepower over their butternut opponents, and part at least of McMillen's command was armed with a zeal beyond the normal, one of his brigades being made up of Negro soldiers who had taken an oath to avenge Fort Pillow by showing Forrest's troops no quarter. "In case of an action in which they are successful," Hurlbut had stated on the eve of his departure, "it will be nearly impracticable to restrain them from retaliation." Now they and their white comrades, mounted and afoot, were on the march toward a confrontation with the man from whom they had sworn to exact vengeance.

They left Memphis on June 1, and as they set out from Collierville next day the rain began to fall, drenching men and horses and drowning fields and roads, much as it was doing 300 miles away in Georgia. Here, as there, the result was slow going, especially for the wagons lurching hub-deep through the mud. Five days of slogging about seven miles a day brought the marchers as far as Salem, a North Mississippi hamlet whose only historical distinction was that it had been Bedford Forrest's boyhood home. A disencumbered flying column of 400 troopers was detached there for a forty-mile ride due east to strike the Mobile & Ohio at Rienzi, a dozen miles below Corinth, in hopes that breaking the railroad at that point would delay the concentration, somewhere down the line, of the Confederates who no doubt by now had begun to gather in the path of the main column. Another three days of heavy-footed plodding, through June 8, covered another twenty miles of the nearly bottomless road to Ripley, where Sturgis had turned back from his pursuit of the plunderer a month ago.

Discouraged by the slowness of his march, as well as by the thought of all those graybacks probably gathering up ahead, he was inclined toward doing the same thing tomorrow, and that night he held a conference with his division commanders to get their views on the matter. Grierson felt much as his chief did. Delay had most likely enabled the rebs "to concentrate an overwhelming force against us," and he was impressed as well by "the utter hopelessness of saving our train or artillery in case of defeat." McMillen, on the other hand, declared that he "would rather go on and meet the enemy, even if we should be whipped, than to return again to Memphis without having met them." The key word here was *again*, Sturgis having turned back at this same point the month before. He thought it over and decided, on balance, that "it would be ruinous on all sides" — not least, it would seem, to the aggressive reputation that had won him his present post — "to return again without first meeting the enemy."

"Under these circumstances, and with a sad foreboding of the consequences," he afterwards summed up, "I determined to move forward, keeping my force as compact as possible and ready for action at all times."

His fears were better founded than he knew, although he was completely wrong about the odds he thought he faced. The Confederates were indeed preparing to oppose him, but it could scarcely be with an "overwhelming force," since the number of men available to the defenders was barely more than half as many as were in the blue column toiling toward them through the rain. On the day Sturgis left Memphis, June 1, Forrest had left Tupelo with 2200 troopers and six guns, bound at last for Middle Tennessee and a descent on Sherman's life line below Nashville. He was in North Alabama on June 3, preparing to cross the Tennessee River, when an urgent message from Stephen Lee summoned him back to meet Sturgis's newly developed threat to the department Lee had inherited from Polk. Forrest returned to Tupelo on June 5, the day the Federals reached his boyhood home fifty miles northwest. Uncertain whether they were headed for Corinth or Tupelo — the 400-man flying column, detached that day for the strike at Rienzi, contributed to the confusion — Lee told Forrest to dispose his men along the M. & O. between those two towns, ready to move in either direction, while he himself did what he could to get hold of more troops to help ward off the 8300-man blow, wherever it might land. His notion was that, if the enemy moved southward, the cavalry should retire toward Okolona, about twenty miles below Tupelo, in order to protect the Black Prairie region just beyond, where most of the subsistence for his department was grown and processed, and also to draw Sturgis as far as possible from his base of supplies and place of refuge in Memphis before giving him battle with whatever reinforcements had been rounded up by then. Lee made it clear before they parted, however, that Forrest was left to his own devices as to what should be done in the meantime, and Forrest took full advantage of the discretion thus allowed him.

He had at the time some 4300 troopers within reach: 2800 in Colonel Tyree Bell's brigade, which was part of Abraham Buford's division, and about 750 in each of two small brigades under Colonels Hylan Lyon and Edmund Rucker. While waiting for Sturgis to show his hand, Forrest spent the next two days posting these commands in accordance with Lee's instructions to cover both Tupelo and Corinth. Bell, with considerably better than half the available force, was sent to Rienzi, which he reached in time to drive off the 400 detached bluecoats before they did any serious damage to the railroad. Rucker and Lyon, with 1500 between them, moved to Booneville, nine miles south of Rienzi, accompanied by Captain John Morton's two four-gun batteries, all the artillery on hand. Forrest was there on June 8 when he received word that Sturgis was at Ripley, twenty miles away, and when he learned next morning that the mud-slathered Union column was continuing southeast, there was no longer any doubt that it was headed not for Corinth but for Tupelo, twelve miles below Guntown, a station on the M. & O. at the end of the road down which Sturgis was marching. A brigade remnant of 500 men under Colonel William A. Johnson arrived that day from Alabama, raising Forrest's strength to 4800. That was all he was likely to have for several days, but he figured it was enough for what he had in mind. He told Johnson to rest his troopers near Baldwyn, twenty miles down the track from Booneville, having decided to hit Sturgis, and hit him hard, before he got to Guntown.

In fact, he had already chosen his field of fight, twenty miles from Ripley and six miles short of the railroad — a timber-laced low plateau where the Ripley-Guntown road, on which the Federals were moving southeast, was intersected at nearly right angles by one from Booneville that ran southwest to Pontotoc — and when he learned that evening that Sturgis had called an overnight halt at Stubbs Farm, nine miles from the intended point of contact, his plan was complete. Orders went out to all units that night, June 9, and the march began before dawn next morning. Forrest led the way with his hundred-man escort company and Lyon's small Kentucky brigade; Rucker and Bell were to follow, along with Morton's guns, and Johnson would come in from the east. The result, that day, was the battle variously celebrated as Guntown, Tishomingo Creek, or Brice's Crossroads.

The enemy had close to a two-to-one advantage in men, as well as nearly three times as many guns, but Forrest believed that boldness and the nature of the terrain, which he knew well, would make up for the numerical odds he faced. "I know they greatly outnumber the troops I have at hand," he told Rucker, who rode with him in advance of his brigade, "but the road along which they will march is narrow and muddy; they will make slow progress. The country is densely wooded and the undergrowth so heavy that when we strike them they will not know how few men we have."

His companion might have pointed out, but did not, that the road they themselves were on — called the Wire Road because in early days, before the railroad, the telegraph line to New Orleans had run along it — was as muddy and as narrow as the one across the way. Moreover, all the Federals were within nine miles of the objective, while aside from Johnson's 500 Alabamians, seven miles away at Baldwyn, all the Confederates had twice as far to go or farther; Lyon, Rucker, and Morton had eighteen miles to cover, and Bell just over twenty-five. Forrest had thought of that as well, however, and here too he saw compensating factors, not only in the marching ability of his troopers, but also in the contrasting effect of the weather on their blue-clad adversaries. The rain had stopped and the rising sun gave promise that the day would be a scorcher.

"Their cavalry will move out ahead of their infantry," he explained, "and should reach the crossroads three hours in advance. We can whip their cavalry in that time. As soon as the fight opens they will send back to have the infantry hurried in. It is going to be hot as hell, and coming on the run for five or six miles, their infantry will be so tired out we will ride right over them."

Aside from the temperature estimate, which was open to question in the absence of any thermometer readings from hell, Rucker was to discover that this was practically a blow-by-blow account of what would follow; but the general quickly returned to present matters. "I want everything to move up as soon as possible," he said. "I will go ahead with Lyon and the escort and open the fight."

Sturgis rose at Stubbs Farm in a better frame of mind, encouraged by the letup of the rain and the prospect that a couple of days of mid-June heat would bake the roads dry, down through Tupelo and beyond. The flying column had returned from Rienzi the night before, and though their mounts were badly jaded the 400 troopers were doubly welcome as replacements for about the same number of "sick and worn-out men" he started back toward Memphis this morning in forty of the wagons his two divisions had eaten empty in the past nine days. These ailing bluecoats would miss a signal experience this hot June 10 at Brice's Crossroads, nine miles down the Guntown road, but their commander — round-faced and rather plump, Pennsylvania-born and a former Indian fighter, with a thick shock of curly hair, a trim mustache, and an abbreviated chin beard, he would be forty-two years old tomorrow: Forrest's age — did not know that, yet. All he knew, for the present, was "that it was impossible to gain any accurate or reliable information of the enemy and that it behooved us to move and act constantly as though in his presence."

This last, however, was precisely what he failed to do. Despite his previous resolution "to move forward, keeping my force as compact as possible and ready for action at all times," compassion for his weary foot soldiers led him to give them an extra couple of hours in camp to dry their clothes and get themselves in order for another hard day's march. Grierson and his troopers rode off for Guntown at 5.30 but McMillen's lead brigade did not set out till 7 o'clock, thus giving Forrest a full measure of the time he estimated he would need to "whip their cavalry" before the infantry "hurried up."

His plan, whose execution today would advance his growing reputation as "the Wizard of the Saddle," was for a battle in three stages: 1) holding attack, 2) main effort, and 3) pursuit. But Sturgis, riding with McMillen at the head of the infantry column, knew nothing of this — not even that Forrest was nearby — until shortly after 10 o'clock, when a courier from Grierson came pounding back with news that the cavalry was hotly engaged, some five miles down the road, with a superior hostile force; he had, he said, "an advantageous position," and could hold it "if the infantry was brought up promptly." Leaving orders for McMillen to proceed "as rapidly as possible without distressing the troops," Sturgis galloped ahead to examine the situation at first hand.

It did not look at all good from the rear, where a nearly mile-long causeway across a stretch of flooded bottomland led to and from a narrow bridge over Tishomingo Creek; "artillery and ambulances and led horses jammed the road," he observed, and when he reached Brice's about noon, another mile and a half toward Guntown, he found the cavalry hard pressed, fighting dismounted amid "considerable confusion." One brigade commander declared flatly that he "would have to fall back unless he received some support," while the other, according to Sturgis, was "almost demanding to be relieved." Grierson was more stalwart. Though the rebels were there "in large numbers, with double lines of skirmishers and heavy supports," he was proud to report that he and his rapid-firing troopers had "succeeded in holding our own and repulsing with great slaughter three distinct and desperate charges." The sun by now was past the overhead. How much longer he could hang on he did not say, but it could scarcely be for long unless he was reinforced, heavily and soon, by men from the infantry column toiling toward him through the mud and heat. Sturgis reacted promptly. With no further mention of concern about "distressing the troops," he sent word for McMillen to hurry his three brigades forward and save the day. "Make all haste," he told him, and followed this with a second urgent message: "Lose no time in coming up."

Grierson was wrong in almost everything he said, and Sturgis was fatally wrong in accepting his estimate of the situation. Those three "desperate charges," for example, had simply been feints, made by Forrest — a great believer in what he called "bulge" — to disguise the fact that his troopers, dismounted and fed piecemeal into the brush-screened line as soon as they came up, were badly outnumbered by those in the two blue brigades, who overlapped him on both flanks and had six pieces of horse artillery in action, unopposed, and four more in reserve. He opened the fight, as he had said he would do, by attacking with Lyon astride the Wire Road, then put Rucker and Johnson in on the left and right, when they arrived, for a second and a third attack to keep the Federals off balance while waiting for Morton's guns and the rest of his command to complete their marches from Booneville and Rienzi. "Tell Bell to move up fast and fetch all he's got," he told a staff major, who rode back to deliver the message.

It was just past 1 o'clock when this last and largest of his brigades came onto the field, close behind Morton; by which time, true to his schedule, Forrest had the enemy cavalry whipped.

Convinced, as he said then and later, that he had been "overwhelmed by numbers," Grierson was asking to have his division taken out of line, "as it was exhausted and well-nigh out of ammunition" for its rapid-firing carbines. McMillen rode up to the crossroads at that point, in advance of his lead brigade, and was dismayed to find that "everything was going to the devil as fast as it possibly could." Like Sturgis earlier, he threw caution to the winds. Though many of his troops had already collapsed from heat exhaustion on the hurried approach march, and though all were blown and in great distress from the savage midday, mid-June Mississippi sun, he sent peremptory orders for his two front brigades to come up on the double quick and restore the crumbling cavalry line before the rebels overran it.

They were hurrying to destruction, and hurrying needlessly at that; for just as they came into position, every bit as "tired out" as Forrest had predicted, a lull fell over the crossroad. It was brief, however, and lasted only long enough for the Confederate commander, now that all his troops were on the field, to mount and launch his first real assault of the day. Giving direction of the three brigades on the right to Buford, a Kentucky-born West Pointer two years his senior in age, he went in person to confer with Bell, whose newly arrived brigade comprised the left. This done, he came back to the right, checking his line along the way. In shirtsleeves because of the heat, with his coat laid over the pommel of his saddle, he "looked the very God of War," one soldier would remember, and as he rode among them on his big sorrel horse, saber in hand, he spoke to the dismounted troopers lying about for some rest in the blackjack thickets. "Get up, men," he told them. "I have ordered Bell to charge on the left. When you hear his guns, and the bugle sounds, every man must charge, and we will give them hell." Other things he said, then and later, went unrecorded. "I notice some writers on Forrest say he seldom cursed," one watcher was to recall. "Well, the fellow who writes that way was not where the 7th Tennessee was that day.... He would curse, then praise and then threaten to shoot us himself, if we were so afraid the Yankees might hit us."

Drawing rein at Morton's position, Forrest told him to double-shot four of his guns with canister and join the charge when the bugle sounded, then keep pace with the front rank as it advanced. Afterwards, the young artillerist, who had celebrated his twenty-first birthday on the field of Chickamauga, told his chief: "You scared me pretty badly when you pushed me up so close to their infantry and left me without protection. I was afraid they might take my guns." Forrest laughed. "Well, artillery is made to be captured," he said, "and I wanted to see them take yours."

But that was after the third stage ended, two days later; now the second, the main effort, was just beginning, and there was a grim struggle, much of it hand to hand, before the contest reached the climactic point at which Forrest judged the time had come to go all-out. Returning to the left, where he believed the resistance would be stiffest, he put an end to the thirty-minute lull by starting Bell's advance up the Guntown road. McMillen's second brigade was posted there, sturdy men from Indiana, Illinois, and Minnesota who, winded though they were from their sprint to reach the field, not only broke the gray attack but launched one of their own, throwing the Tennesseans into such confusion that Forrest had to dismount his escort troopers and lead them into the breach, firing pistols, to stop what had the makings of disaster. Over on the right, Buford too was finding the enemy stubborn, and had all he could do to keep up the pressure along his front. Finally, though, the pressure told. Orders came from Forrest — who fought this, as he did all his battles, "by ear" — that the time had come to "hit 'em on the ee-end." It was past 4 o'clock by now, and simultaneous attacks, around the flanks and into the rear of the Union left and right, made the whole blue line waver and cave in, first slowly, then with a rush.

"The retreat or rout began," in Forrest's words, or as Sturgis put it: "Order gave way to confusion and confusion to panic. . . . Everywhere the army now drifted toward the rear, and was soon altogether beyond control."

Fleeing past the two-story Brice house at the crossroads, the fugitives sought shelter back up the road they had run down, four hours ago, to reach the battle that now was lost. But conditions there were in some ways worse than those in what had been the front: especially along the causeway through the Tishomingo bottoms and on the railless bridge across the creek, the narrow spout of the funnel-shaped host of panicked men, who, as Sturgis said, "came crowding in like an avalanche from the battlefield." Morton's batteries had the range, and their execution was increased by the addition of four Federal guns, captured with their ammunition. Presently a wagon overturned on the high bridge and others quickly piled up behind it, creating what a retreating colonel described as "one indiscriminate mass of artillery, caissons, ambulances, and broken, disordered troops." Some escaped by leaping into the creek, swollen neck-deep by the rains, and wading to the opposite bank. But there was no safety there either. Though Sturgis had hoped to form a new line on the far side of the stream, the rebels were crossing so close in his rear that every attempt to make a stand only brought on a new stampede. The only thing that slowed the whooping graybacks was the sight of abandoned wagons, loaded with what one hungry pursuer called "fresh, crisp hardtack and nice, thin side bacon." They would pause for plunder, wolf it down, and then come on for more.

This continued, well past sundown, to within three miles of last night's bivouac, where there was another and still worse stretch of miry road across one of the headwater prongs of the Hatchie River. It was night now and the going was hard, one officer noted, "in consequence of abandoned vehicles, drowned and dying horses and mules, and the depth of the mud." Despairing of getting what was left of his shipwrecked train through this morass, Sturgis went on to Stubbs Farm, where he was approached before midnight by Colonel Edward Bouton, whose Negro brigade had served as train guard during the battle and had therefore suffered less than the other two infantry commands had done.

"General, for God's sake don't let us give up so," he exclaimed.

But Sturgis, quite unstrung, was at his wit's end. "What can we do?" he said, not really asking.

Bouton wanted ammunition with which to hold Forrest in check, on the far side of the bottoms, while the remaining guns and wagons were being snaked across to more solid ground beyond. Sturgis was too far in despair, however, to consider this or any other proposal involving resistance. Besides, he had no ammunition to give.

"For God's sake," he broke out, distraught by the events of this longest day in his life and the prospect of a sad birthday tomorrow, "if Mr Forrest will let me alone, I will let him alone! You have done all you could, and more than was expected. . . . Now all you can do is to save yourselves."

Mr Forrest, as Sturgis so respectfully styled the man he had said a month ago was "too great a plunderer to fight anything like an equal force," had no intention of letting him alone so long as there was profit to be gained from pressing the chase. Heaving the wreckage off the Tishomingo bridge and into the creek, along with the dead and dying animals, he continued to crowd the rear of the retreating bluecoats. "Keep the skeer on 'em," he told his troopers, remounted now, and they did just that, past sunset and on into twilight and full night. "[Sturgis] attempted the destruction of his wagons, loaded with ammunition and bacon," Forrest would report, "but so closely was he pursued that many of them were saved without injury, although the road was lighted for some distance." Furious at this incendiary treatment of property he considered his already, he came upon a group of his soldiers who had paused, still mounted, to watch the flames. "Don't you see the damned Yankees are burning my wagons?" he roared. "Get off your horses and throw the burning beds off." Much toasted hard-tack and broiled bacon was saved that way, until finally, some time after 8 o'clock, "It being dark and my men and horses requiring rest" — they did indeed, having been on the go, marching and fighting, for better than sixteen hours — "I threw out an advance to follow slowly and cautiously after the enemy, and ordered the command to halt, feed, and rest."

By 1 a.m. he had his troopers back in the saddle and hard on the equipment-littered trail. Within two hours they reached the Hatchie bottoms, where they came upon the richest haul of all. Despite Bouton's plea, Sturgis had ordered everything movable to proceed that night to Stubbs Farm and beyond, abandoning what was left of his train, all his non-walking wounded, and another 14 guns, all that remained of the original 22 except for four small mountain howitzers that had seen no action anyhow. This brought Forrest's total acquisition to 18 guns, 176 wagons, 1500 rifles, 300,000 rounds of small-arms ammunition, and much else. He himself lost nothing, and though he had 492 killed and wounded in the battle — a figure larger in proportion than the 617 casualties he inflicted — his capture of more than 1600 men on the retreat brought the Federal loss to 2240, nearly five times his own. Many of the enemy, especially from Bouton's brigade, which had the misfortune to bring up the rear and suffered heavily in the process, were picked up here in the Hatchie bottoms. A Tennessee sergeant later recalled the scene. "Somewhere between midnight and day, we came to a wide slough or creek bottom; it was miry and truly the slough of despair and despond to the Yanks. Their artillery and wagons which had heretofore escaped capture were now bogged down and had to be abandoned. This slough was near kneedeep in mud and water, with logs lying here and there. On top of every log were Yanks perched as close as they could be, for there were more Yanks than logs." They put him in mind "of chickens at roost," he said, but added: "We who were in front were ordered to pay no attention to prisoners. Those in the rear would look after that."

Four miles short of Ripley at dawn, the pursuers came upon a rear-guard remnant, which Forrest said "made only a feeble and in-effectual resistance." He drove its members back on the town, where they were reinforced and rallied briefly, only to scatter when attacked. "From this place," Forrest's report continued, "the enemy offered no organized resistance, but retreated in the most complete disorder, throwing away guns, clothing, and everything calculated to impede his flight." Beyond Ripley he left the direct pursuit to Buford and swung onto a roundabout adjoining road with Bell's brigade, intending to cut the Federals off at Salem. But that was a miscalculation. Buford pressed them so hard the interception failed; the blue column cleared the hamlet before Forrest got there around sundown. He called off the chase at that point and turned back to scour the woods and brush for fugitives, gather up his spoils, and give his men and mounts some rest from their famous victory, which would be studied down the years, in war colleges here and abroad, as an example of what a numerically inferior force could accomplish once it got what its commander called "the bulge" on an opponent, even one twice its size.

There was no rest, though, for Sturgis and his men, who continued to flee in their ignorance that they were no longer pursued except by rumors of graybacks hovering on their flank. "On we went, and ever on," a weary colonel was to write, "marching all that day and all that interminable [second] night. Until half past ten the next morning, when we reached Collierville and the railroad, reinforcements and supplies, we marched, marched, marched, without rest, without sleep, without food." At any rate they made excellent time. The march down had taken more than a week, but the one back took only a night and a day and a night. In Collierville that morning (June 12; Morgan's troopers were scattering from Cynthiana, 300 miles northeastward in Kentucky) the wait for the train that would take them on to the outskirts of Memphis, seventeen miles away, was in some ways even harder than the 90-mile forced march had been. Relieved of a measure of their fright, they now knew in their bones how tired they were and how thoroughly they had been whipped. An Ohio regimental commander reported that, in the course of their wait beside the railroad track, his troops "became so stiffened as to require assistance to enable them to walk. Some of them, too foot-sore to stand upon their feet, crawled upon their hands and knees to the cars."

Sturgis's hurts were mainly professional, being inflicted on his career. Back in Memphis, amid rumors that he had been drunk on the field — a conclusion apparently reached by way of the premise that no sober man could be so roundly trounced — he put the disaster in the best light he could manage. Winding up his official report with "regret that I find myself called upon to record a defeat," he added: "Yet there is some consolation in knowing that the army fought nobly while it did fight, and only yielded to overwhelming numbers." Just over 8000 troops had been thrown into a rout and driven headlong for nearly a hundred miles by just under 5000, but he persisted in claiming (and even believing, so persuasive were Forrest's tactics) that the odds had been the other way around, and longer. "The strength of the enemy is variously estimated by my most intelligent officers at from 15,000 to 20,000 men."

So he said; but vainly, so far as concerned the salvation of his career. For him, the war ended at Brice's Crossroads. Despite the board's finding no substance in the charge that he had been drunk, either in battle or on the birthday retreat, Sturgis spent the rest of the conflict on the sidelines, awaiting orders that did not come. Disconsolate as he was, he only shared what those who had served under him were feeling. Though in time their aching muscles would find relief and their wounds would heal, the inward scars of their drubbing would remain. "It is the fate of war that one or the other side should suffer defeat," a cavalry major who survived the battle was to write, more than twenty years later. "But here there was more. The men were cowed, and there pressed upon them a sense of bitter humiliation, which rankles after nearly a quarter of a century has passed."

Sherman was disappointed, of course, but he was also inclined to give Sturgis credit for having achieved his "chief object," which had been "to hold Forrest there [in Mississippi] and keep him off our [rail] road." There was truth in a participating colonel's observation that the expedition had been "sent out as a tub to Forrest's whale," and though the price turned out to be high, both in men and equipment, it was by no means exorbitant, considering the alternative. Learning that the raider had been in North Alabama, poised for a strike across the Tennessee River before Sturgis lured him back, the red-haired Ohioan wired the district commander instructions designed to discourage a return: "You may send notice to Florence that if Forrest invades Tennessee from that direction, the town will be burned, and if it occurs you will remove the inhabitants north of the Ohio River, and burn the town" — adding, as if by afterthought: "and Tuscumbia also."

He would send both places up in smoke, along with much else, if it would help to keep "that devil Forrest" off his life line. But that was only an interim deterrent. He had it in mind to follow through, as soon as possible, with a second expedition into northern Mississippi, stronger and better led, to profit by the shortcomings of the first. "Forrest is the very devil," he declared, "and I think has got some of our troops under cower." He proposed to correct this in short order. A. J. Smith's three divisions were on their way back from service up Red River with Banks, hard-handed veterans whose commanders had been closely observed by Sherman in the course of the fighting last year around Vicksburg. He had intended either to bring them to Georgia as reinforcements or else to send them against Mobile; but now, he notified Washington, he had what he considered a better, or in any case a more urgent, use for them. "I will order them to make up a force and go out and follow Forrest to the death, if it costs 10,000 lives and breaks the Treasury. There will never be peace in Tennessee till Forrest is dead."

★ ★ ★

Up in Washington, news of Morgan's defeat was about as welcome as that of Forrest's victory was irksome, although neither of these side shows of the main event provided much more than a brief diversion from the prevalent fret over Grant and Sherman — what their progress against Lee and Johnston meant, if anything, and above all what it was costing them in casualties per mile. These two, between them, would win or lose, if not the war, then in any event the election in November; which perhaps was the same thing. The Democrats would convene in August to nominate a candidate who would run on the issue of ending the conflict by declaring peace, whatever accommodations might be required by their late fellow countrymen down South, and it was generally agreed that the Republicans could not survive a prolongation of the bloody three-year stalemate through the five months between now and the election.

Lincoln had declared himself "only a passenger" on the juggernaut of war, but his hand was still on the tiller of the ship of state and he intended to keep it there if he could. Public attention was mainly fixed on the fighting in Virginia, where the casualties had been awesome from the start, and he tried to offset the civilian reaction by stressing his admiration for Grant's refusal to be distracted by the bloodshed and by recommending that his listeners do likewise. "I think, without knowing the particulars of the plans of General Grant, that what has been accomplished is of more importance than at first appears," he told a crowd that came to serenade him on hearing that the Army of the Potomac had resumed its southward march after two days of cataclysmic battle in the Wilderness. "I believe I know — and am especially grateful to know — that General Grant has not been jostled in his purposes, that he has made all his points, and today he is on his line as he purposed before he moved. . . . I commend you to keep yourselves in the same tranquil mood that is characteristic of that brave and loyal man."

Tranquillity was easier to prescribe than to attain. Hemmed in as he was by cares from all directions, including the importunities of incessant office seekers — "Too many pigs for the tits," he said wryly — Lincoln found the sight of the wounded, returning in their thousands from where he had sent them to get hit, a heavy burden on his spirit. "Look yonder at those poor fellows," he said one day when a long line of ambulances creaked past his halted carriage. "I cannot bear it. This suffering, this loss of life is dreadful." It was during this dark time that a White House visitor watched him pace the dawn-gray corridors in his nightshirt and long wrapper, hands clasped behind his back, head bent low, and with black rings under his eyes from loss of sleep.

By no means all the strain was of a purely military nature. While it was true that some events which normally would have awakened a sharp sense of national loss were muted by the uproar of the guns — the death of Nathaniel Hawthorne, for example, was barely noted amid the excitement over Grant's shift from Spotsylvania to the North Anna — others were so closely tied to the conflict that they stood out in stark relief against its glare. One was the so-called Gold Hoax, perpetrated on May 18, the day before Hawthorne died, by Joseph Howard, the journalist who three years ago had written of Lincoln's furtive passage through Baltimore in a "Scotch cap and long military cloak" to avoid assassination on the way to his inauguration. At 4 a.m. that morning Howard distributed anonymously to all the New York papers a bogus proclamation, complete with the forged signature of the President, fixing May 26 "as a day of fasting, humiliation and prayer," and calling for an additional draft of 400,000 men required by "the situation in Virginia, the disaster at Red River, the delay at Charleston, and the general state of the country."

Defeat, it seemed from the doleful tone of the document, was just around the corner. Only two papers, the *New York World* and the *Journal of Commerce*, were on the street with the story before the forgery was detected; bulletins of denial promptly quashed its effect on the gold market, defeating the scheme. With Lincoln's approval, Stanton moved swiftly in reprisal, padlocking the offices of both papers and clapping their editors into military arrest, along with Howard, who was soon sniffed out. Within three days the editors were released and their papers resumed publication; even Howard was freed within about three months, on the plea that he was "the only spotted child of a large family" and had been guilty of nothing worse than "the hope of making some *money*." No real harm was done, except to increase the public's impression of Stanton — and, inferentially, his chief — as a tyrant, an enemy of free speech and the press. One witness declared, however, that the affair "angered Lincoln more than almost any other occurrence of the war period." His ire was aroused in part by the fact that the country's reaction to the bogus proclamation obliged him to defer issuing an order he had prepared only the day before, calling, in far less doleful words, for the draft of 300,000 additional troops.

They were likely to be needed sooner, not later, at the rate men were falling in Grant's attempt to overrun Lee and Sherman's to outflank Johnston. And on top of these losses, before the month was out, there occurred a hemispheric provocation that seemed likely to bring on a second war, this one with a foreign power: France. Following up his occupation of Mexico City a year ago, purportedly to collect a national debt, Napoleon III landed his puppet Maximilian, whom he had persuaded to assume the title of Emperor of Mexico, at Vera Cruz, May 28; the Austrian archduke and his wife Charlotte were on their way to the capital, where they would reign over an empire designed to stand, with the help of still more French soldiers than the 35,000 already sent, as a bulwark against Anglo-Saxon expansion in Central and South America. This continued defiance of the Monroe Doctrine was hard for Lincoln to abide, but not so hard that he did not manage to do so, deferring action until he could afford to give it his full attention, preferably with a reunited country at his back; "One war at a time" was as much his policy now as it had been on the occasion of his near confrontation with England over the *Trent* affair, more than two years ago.

Besides, a domestic concern of a far more urgent nature than any posed by the latter day Napoleon — specifically, the double-barreled problem of getting renominated and reëlected — was hard upon him at the time. Three days after Maximilian stepped ashore at Vera Cruz, the radicals of Lincoln's own party, aware that they lacked the strength to dominate the regular Republican convention at Baltimore on June 7, called a convention of their own in Cleveland on May 31, one week earlier, and by acclamation nominated John C. Frémont as their candidate for President in the November election.

For some time Jacobinic disaffection had been growing, especially among New England abolitionists and German-born extremists in Missouri, who resented Lincoln's "manifest tendency toward temporary expedients," and complained bitterly that he had *"words* for the ultras and *acts* for the more conservative." Now their opposition had taken this form; they were out in the open, determined to bring him down. Frémont, the party's first presidential candidate in 1856 — he had polled a respectable 1,300,000 votes, as compared to James Buchanan's 1,800,000 — accepted the nomination "with a view to prevent the misfortune of [Lincoln's] reëlection," which he said "would be fatal to the country." Glad to be back in the public eye, after nearly two years of promoting railroads in New York State, the Pathfinder looked forward to a vigorous campaign. The trouble was that his most influential backers had to avoid giving him open support, for fear of committing political suicide, and this had been evident at the convention in Ohio, which one critic described as a "magnificent fizzle," attended mainly by "disappointed contractors, sore-head governors, and Copperheads."

Thousands had been expected, but only about four hundred showed up. Informed of this, Lincoln reached for the Bible on his desk, thumbed briefly through I Samuel until he found what he was seeking, then read it out: *And every one that was in distress, and every one that was in debt, and every one that was discontented, gathered themselves unto him; and he became a captain over them: and there were with him about four hundred men.*

A joke had its uses, particularly as therapy for a spirit as gloomy by nature as this one, but the million-odd votes Frémont might poll in November were no laughing matter. Before then, there would probably be ways to lure the Jacobins back into the fold. Some piece of radical legislation hanging fire in Congress for lack of Executive pressure, say, could be put through; or the scalp of some Administration stalwart they had singled out as an enemy could be yielded up. Meantime, however, the thing to do, if possible, was to solidify what was left of the party and broaden its base to attract outsiders, meaning those hard-war Democrats who would be repelled by the peace plank their leaders were sure to include in the platform at their Chicago convention in late August, nearly three months after the Republicans gathered next week in Baltimore.

Lincoln of course did not attend, despite the proximity to Washington; nor did David Davis, his manager at the convention four years ago and now a Supreme Court justice. Not since Andrew Jackson's reëlection, thirty-two years ago, had any man been chosen to serve a second term as President, although several had tried and failed to get renominated and Van Buren had even succeeded, only to be defeated at the polls. But Davis foresaw no difficulty requiring his considerable talent for maneuver, so far as the place at the top of the ticket was concerned, and he was right; there was no real opposition, only some wistful talk about "the salutary one-term principle," and no trouble. On the first ballot, Missouri's delegates rocked the boat a bit by casting their 22 votes for Grant, but switched when all the other 484 went to Lincoln, whose nomination thus was made unanimous. This done, the convention was free to turn to the business of solidification and broadening; which could be done, at least in part — so it was hoped — by the selection of the right man to replace Vice President Hannibal Hamlin, who not only lacked luster but also had sided with the radicals on most of the whipsaw issues before Congress.

A beginning had been made in this regard, first by changing the name of the party to National Union, which helped to reduce the onus of sectionalism, and then by adopting a platform that had, as one observer put it, "a radical flavor but no Radical planks." Appealing for unity in continuing the national effort to put down the rebellion, it called for the extirpation of slavery as the root cause of the war, promised to visit upon all rebels and traitors "the punishment due to their crimes," thanked soldiers and civilians alike for their sacrifices over the past three years, and wound up by favoring the encouragement of immigration and the construction of a transcontinental railroad. Now came the vice-presidential nomination, and though Lincoln kept aloof from the contest, not wanting to anger the friends of disappointed candidates — "Convention must judge for itself," he indorsed a letter requesting a statement of his wishes as to the contest for second place on the ticket — he had confidants on the scene, including his secretary Nicolay and Henry J. Raymond, editor of the friendly *New York Times* and chairman of the platform committee. When Raymond saw to it that the name of Andrew Johnson, former senator and now military governor of Tennessee, was presented at a critical juncture, scarcely anyone failed to see that here was the best possible way of strengthening the ticket by giving simultaneous recognition to the claims of loyal men from the South, especially the border states, as well as to War Democrats all across the land. Johnson was both, and with an outburst of enthusiasm so vociferous that one delegate later testified that he "involuntarily looked up to see if the roof were lifted," his nomination too was made unanimous.

Lincoln learned informally of the outcome that afternoon, when he happened to walk over to the War Department and was congratulated as he entered the telegraph office. "What! Am I renominated?" he exclaimed, smiling, and when the operator showed him a confirming telegram his first thought was of his wife: "Send it over to the Madam. She will be more interested than I am."

He perhaps wanted to brace her for things to come, and they were not long in coming. Next day the *New York World,* back on the streets after being shut down for its unwitting share in the Gold Hoax three weeks ago, served notice that this was to be the bitterest of campaigns. Commenting on the nominations of Lincoln and Johnson — who like his running mate was a self-made man, having started out as a tailor before he studied law and entered politics — the *World* clucked its tongue over the come-down the national tone had suffered with the selection by the opposition party of this ungracious pair of candidates for the two most honored posts in all the land. "The age of statesmen is gone," the lead editorial lamented; "the age of rail-splitters and tailors, of buffoons, boors, and fanatics, has succeeded. . . . In a crisis of the most appalling magnitude, requiring statesmanship of the highest order, the country is asked to consider the claims of two ignorant, boorish, third-rate backwoods lawyers, for the highest situations in the government. Such nominations, in such a conjecture, are an insult to the common-sense of the people. God save the Republic!"

Lincoln hoped God would, but he was modest in his judgment of why he had been chosen to compete again for the task of serving as God's chief helper in the search for that salvation. "I do not allow myself to suppose that [the delegates] have concluded to decide that I am either the greatest or best man in America," he replied to formal congratulations which presently followed, "but rather they have concluded it is not best to swap horses while crossing the river, and have further concluded that I am not so poor a horse that they might not make a botch of it in trying to swap."

Renomination was only the first, and much the lower, of the two formal hurdles to be cleared if he was to retain his post. The second was reëlection, and that would be a far more difficult matter, requiring not only a great deal of skill in maneuvering his way along the thorny path of politics — skill, that is, such as he had just shown while skimming the first hurdle — but also a great deal of ability on the part of his hand-picked commanders in the field. In short, they would have to convince the public that he and they could win the war; otherwise, neither he nor the war would continue. Up to now, whatever admiration he might express for their refusal to be "jostled," their progress had been made at a price the voters were likely to find excessive, particularly if they were obliged to continue paying it over the course of the next five months. Even as the delegates converged on Baltimore, Grant was engaged in the grisly and belated task of burying his dead at Cold Harbor — a position McClellan had reached two years ago, the opposition press was pointing out, with the loss of less than a tenth as many soldiers — and Sherman, after his fruitless roundhouse swing through Dallas, was just getting back astride the railroad at Big Shanty, having also suffered checks about as abrupt, though not as bloody, along the way at New Hope Church and Pickett's Mill. As a result, in his continuing attempt to bolster national morale, Lincoln was reduced to the necessity of making what he could of such minor victories as Cynthiana, which at least disposed of John Morgan for a season, more or less.

That was on the Sunday ending the week of the Republican convention, and one week later there occurred another side-show triumph which more or less disposed of another Confederate raider; one even more famous, or infamous, than Morgan.

★ ★ ★

Sunday, June 12; U.S.S. *Kearsarge*, a thousand-ton sloop named for one of New Hampshire's rugged mountains, was anchored off the Dutch coast, in the mouth of the River Scheldt near Flushing, when her skipper, Captain John A. Winslow, received word from his government's minister in Paris that the Confederate cruiser *Alabama*, which had eluded him throughout a year-long search of European waters, had steamed into Cherbourg the day before to discharge prisoners, take on coal, and perhaps refit. If he hurried, the telegram said, she might still be there when he arrived.

Winslow hurried. Firing a gun to recall his men on shore, he had the *Kearsarge* under weigh within two hours. Two days later he entered Cherbourg harbor, three hundred miles to the west, and there "lying at anchor in the roads" was the rebel vessel, just as he had prayed she would be. He stopped engines and lay to, looking her over and being in turn looked over; which done, he left to assume a position in the English Channel, beyond the three-mile limit required by international law, for intercepting her when she ventured out. He took precautions against a sudden night attack, knowing the enemy to be tricky, but his principal fear was that the raider might slip past him in the dark and thus avoid the fate he had in mind for her.

He need not have worried on that score, he discovered next day when the American vice consul sent him a message just received from the skipper of the *Alabama:* "My intention is to fight the *Kearsarge* as soon as I can make the necessary arrangements. I hope these will not detain me more than until tomorrow evening, or after the morrow morning at furthest. I beg she will not depart before I am ready to go out. . . . I have the honor to be, respectfully, your obedient servant, *R. Semmes*, Captain."

Winslow made no reply to this except to maintain station beyond the breakwater; which, after all, was answer enough, and spared him moreover the loss of dignity involved in exchanging cards, as it were, with a "pirate" who by now had captured, burned, or ransomed 83 U.S. merchant vessels, worth more than five million dollars, and sunk the heavier gunboat *Hatteras* in short order. Raphael Semmes, for his part, gave all his attention to trimming ship, drilling his gun crews, and otherwise preparing to meet the challenge extended by the *Kearsarge* when she steamed into the harbor, looked him over from stem to stern, then turned with the same cool insolence and steamed back out again to await his response, if any, to the insult. "The combat will no doubt be contested and obstinate," he wrote in his journal that night, "but the two ships are so evenly matched that I do not feel at liberty to decline it. God defend the right, and have mercy upon the souls of those who fall, as many of us must."

Fame aside — for Winslow had none whatever, and the *Kearsarge* had never been within gunshot of a foe; whereas Semmes and the *Alabama* were better known around the world than any other sailor or vessel afloat — the two warships and their captains were indeed quite evenly matched. Messmates for a time in the Mexican War, both men were southern-born, the Confederate in Maryland, Winslow farther south in North Carolina; Semmes was fifty-five, his opponent less than two years younger, and both had close to forty years of naval service, having received appointments as midshipmen in their middle teens. Alike as they were in their histories up to the outbreak of the current war, they were altogether different in looks. Winslow, going blind in his right eye, was rather heavy-set and balding, with a compensating ruff of gray-shot whiskers round his jaw, while Semmes was tall and slender, with a full head of hair, a tuft of beard at his lower lip, and a fantastical mustache twisted to needle points beyond the outline of his face; "Old Beeswax," his men called him.

Conversely, it was not in their histories, which were about as mutually different as could be, but in their physical attributes that the two ships were alike. Both were three-masted and steam-propelled, just over two hundred feet in length and a thousand tons in weight. *Kearsarge* had a complement of 163, *Alabama* about a dozen less. The Federal carried seven guns, the Confederate eight — though this implied advantage was deceptive, mainly because of a pair of 11-inch Dahlgrens mounted on pivots along the center line of the *Kearsarge*, which, combined with the 32-pounders on each flank, enabled her to throw a 365-pound broadside, port or starboard. *Alabama*'s heaviest guns were an 8-inch smoothbore and a 7-inch Blakely rifle, also pivot-mounted, so that, in combination with three 32-pounders on each flank, her broadside came to 264 pounds, a hundred less than her adversary's. Two other disadvantages she had, both possibly dire. One was the state of her ammunition, which had not been replenished since she was commissioned, nearly two years ago; percussion caps had lately been failing to explode the shells, whose powder had been weakened by exposure to various climates on most of the seven seas. The other disadvantage had to do with the vessel's maneuverability and speed. Entering Cherbourg harbor, Semmes declared, she was like "the weary foxhound, limping back after a long chase, footsore and longing for quiet and repose." He had intended to put her in dry dock and give all aboard a two-month holiday; her bottom, badly fouled, needed scraping and recoppering, and her boilers had begun to leak at the seams. *Kearsarge,* on the other hand, though nine months older, had been refitted only three months ago and was in trim shape for the contest. Semmes, however, had confidence in his crew, which he affectionately referred to as "a precious set of rascals," his Blakely rifle, which not only had more range but also provided greater accuracy than did Winslow's outsized Dahlgrens, and his luck, which had never failed him yet.

Concern for this last but by no means least of the things in which he put his trust caused him to defer the promised action three days beyond the "morrow morning at furthest" he had fixed in his Wednesday note begging Winslow not to depart. He wanted to fight on Sunday, considering that his lucky day. It was a Sunday when he ran the *Sumter,* his first raider, past the Union gauntlet below New Orleans, out of the mouth of the Mississippi and into the Gulf of Mexico to begin his career as the scourge of Yankee commerce; a Sunday off the Azores, back in August '62, when he christened the *Alabama,* and a Sunday when he sank the *Hatteras,* as well as many of the other prizes he had taken in the course of the past three years.

His crew found the waiting hard, being anxious for the duel and the shore leave that would follow, but Semmes and his officers kept them busy. They cleaned and oiled the guns and other weapons, including cutlasses and pikes, sorted powder and shot from the magazines and laid them out in relays, took down the light spars, disposed of top hamper, and stoppered the standing rigging. They polished brasswork and holystoned the decks as for a ball, and while they worked they roared out a chantey a British seaman composed for the occasion:

> *We're homeward bound, homeward bound,*
> *And soon shall stand on English ground.*
> *But ere that English land we see*
> *We first must fight the Kearsargee!*

Such work continued through Saturday, June 18, when Semmes, aware that "the issue of combat is always uncertain," put ashore four sacks

containing 4700 gold sovereigns, the ransom bonds of ten ships he had
released for lack of space for their crews aboard the *Alabama*, and the
large collection of chronometers taken from his victims, which he
periodically wound by way of keeping tally or counting coup. After
notifying the port authorities that he would be steaming out next
morning, he went ashore for Mass, then came back and turned in early
as an example for his officers and men, who did so too, despite many
invitations to dine that night in Cherbourg with admirers.

Sunday dawned bright and nearly cloudless, cool for June, with a
calm sea and a mild westerly breeze to clear the battle smoke away.
After a leisurely breakfast, the crew weighed anchor at 9.45 and headed
out, cheered by crowds along the mole and in the upper windows of
houses affording a view of the Channel and the *Kearsarge*, still on station
beyond the breakwater. News of the impending duel had been in all the
papers for the past three days and excursion trains had brought so many
spectators from Paris and other cities that there was no room left in the
hotels; many sportsmen-excursionists had slept on the docks, as if at the
entrance to a stadium on the night before a game between archrivals.
They fluttered handkerchiefs and cheered, some waving small Confederate flags hawked by vendors along with spyglasses and camp stools.
"Vivent les Confederates!" they cried, looking down at the trim and
polished raider, all of whose sailors were dressed in their Sunday best
except the gun crews, who were stripped to the waist, like athletes
indeed, and stood about on decks that had been sanded to keep them
from slipping in their blood when the contest opened. "Vivent les
Confederates!" the crowd shrilled, flourishing its home-team pennants
triumphantly when the *Kearsarge*, seeing the *Alabama* emerge from
around the western end of the breakwater, turned suddenly and steamed
away northeastward, as if in unpremeditated flight.

Semmes knew better: knew, indeed, that this maneuver signified
that his adversary meant to give him the fight-to-a-finish he was seeking.
Engaged in reading the Sunday service when a yardarm watchman sang
out the warning, "She's coming out and she's headed straight for us!"
Winslow closed the prayer book, ordered the drum to beat to quarters,
and brought his ship about in a run for bluer water, his intention being to
lure the rebel well beyond the three-mile limit, inside which she could
take sanctuary in case she was disabled. This applied as well to the
Kearsarge, of course, but Winslow was thinking of punishment he
would inflict, rather than of damage he might suffer; his aim was not just
to cripple, but to kill.

The warning had been given at 10.20; at 10.40, some seven miles
out, he once more came about and bore down on the *Alabama*, just
over two miles away, wanting to bring his two big Dahlgrens within
range of his adversary.

Semmes held his course, closing fast. Resplendent in a new gray uniform, long-skirted and with a triple row of bright brass buttons down the breast, epaulets and polished sword making three fierce glints of sunlight, he had had all hands piped aft as soon as he cleared the breakwater, then mounted a gun carriage to deliver his first speech since setting out from the Azores. "Officers and seamen of the *Alabama*!" he declaimed, pale but calm behind the fantastical mustache whose spike-tips quivered as he spoke. "You have, at length, another opportunity of meeting the enemy — the first that has been presented to you since you sank the *Hatteras*.... The name of your ship has become a household word wherever civilization extends. Shall that name be tarnished by defeat? The thing is impossible! Remember that you are in the English Channel, the theater of so much of the naval glory of our race, and that the eyes of all Europe are at this moment upon you. The flag that floats over you is that of a young Republic who bids defiance to her enemies, whenever and wherever found; show the world that you know how to uphold it. Go to your quarters!" Having said as much, he set the example, while the crew still cheered, by taking station on the horseblock abreast the mizzenmast, a vantage point from which he could see and be seen by the enemy throughout the fight to come.

Watch in hand, he waited until there was barely a mile between the two ships bearing down on each other, then at 10.57 turned to his executive, Lieutenant John Kell, a six-foot two-inch Georgian who, like himself, was a veteran of the old navy: "Are you ready, Mr Kell?" Kell said he was. "Then you may open fire at once, sir."

The Blakely roared. Its 100-pound shell raised a sudden geyser, well short of the target, and was followed within two minutes by another, which, overcorrected, went screaming through the Federal's rigging. By now the other guns had joined, but their shots too were high, fired without proper calculation of the reduction of space between the rapidly closing vessels. Not until the range was down to half a mile did Winslow return fire, sheering to bring his starboard battery to bear. All the shots fell short, but Semmes had to port his helm sharply to keep from being raked astern. He succeeded, though at the cost of having *Kearsarge* close the range. As the Confederate swung back to starboard, Winslow followed suit and the two warships began to describe a circle, steaming clockwise around a common center and firing at each other across the half-mile diameter.

Alabama drew first blood with a shell that exploded on the Union quarterdeck and knocked out three of the after Dahlgren's crew. Then came what Semmes had prayed for, ashore at church last night. A shell from the Blakely struck and lodged itself in the sternpost of the *Kearsarge*. But as he watched through his telescope, awaiting the explosion that would signal the end of the enemy vessel — "Splendid! Splendid!" he exclaimed from his perch on the horseblock — the long moment passed with no sign of smoke or flame in that vital spot. The projectile, a dud, accomplished nothing except to make the helmsman's job a little harder by binding the rudder, which was already set to starboard anyhow. *Alabama*'s gunners kept hard at it, firing fast while straining for another, luckier hit.

Winslow's gunnery was methodical by contrast, and a good deal more effective; he would get off a total of 173 shots in the course of the engagement, only about half as many as Semmes, but the accuracy in both cases, a tally of hits and misses would show, was in inverse ratio to the rate of fire. As the two sloops continued their wheeling fight, churning along in one another's wake, a three-knot current bore them westward so that they described a series of overlapping circles, each a little tighter than the one before, with the result that the range was constantly shortened, from half a mile on the first circle, down to little more than a quarter-mile on the seventh, which turned out to be the last.

From the outset, once the blue crews got on target, the damage inflicted by the 11-inchers was prodigious; *Alabama* was repeatedly hit and hulled by the 135½-pound shells aimed at her waterline by the Dahlgrens, in accordance with Winslow's orders, while the 32-pounders swept her decks. The combined effect was devastating: as for example when a projectile breached the 8-inch smoothbore's port, disemboweling the first man it struck, then plunging on to mangle eighteen others when it blew. Survivors and replacements cleared away the wounded and heaved the corpses overboard, but resumption of fire had to wait for a shovel to be used to scrape up the slippery gobs of flesh and splinters of bone; only then, with the deck re-sanded, could the crew secure a proper footing for its work. Meantime, Semmes had seen the most discouraging thing he had encountered since the shot lodged in the enemy sternpost failed to explode. Observing that shells of all sizes were bouncing ineffectively off the Federal's sides, like so many tennis balls, he told Kell to switch to solids for better penetration. Yet these too either splintered or rebounded, and it was not until after the battle that he found out that the cause lay in anything more than the weakened condition of his powder. *Kearsarge* was armored along her midriff with 120 fathoms of sheet chain, suspended from her scuppers to below her waterline, bolted down and boxed out of sight with one-inch planking. Indignant at the belated disclosure that his adversary was "iron-clad," Semmes protested that this violation of the code duello had produced an unfair fight. "It was the same thing as if two men were to go out and fight a duel, and one of them, unknown to the other, were to put on a suit of mail under his outer garment."

However true or false the analogy — and Old Beeswax, one of the trickiest skippers ever to prowl the sea lanes, was scarcely in a position to protest the use of a stratagem that had been common in all navies ever since Farragut employed it, more than two years ago, to run past the forts below New Orleans — the *Alabama*, with all her timbers aquiver from the pounding being inflicted by the *Kearsarge*, was clearly nearing the end of her career. Semmes, nicked in the right hand by a fragment of shell as the raider went into her seventh circle, had a quartermaster bind up the wound and rig a sling, never leaving his perch on the horseblock. From there he could see better than anyone the damage being done his ship and the ineffectiveness of his return fire. This seventh circle must be the last. The only course left was to attempt a run for safety. Accordingly, he told the exec: "Mr Kell, as soon as our head points to the French coast in our circuit of action, shift your guns to port and make all sail for the coast."

Kell tried, but Winslow quickly interposed the *Kearsarge*, slamming in shots from dead ahead and at a shorter range than ever. At this point the *Alabama*'s chief engineer came topside to report that his fires were being flooded by rising water from holes the Dahlgrens were blasting in the hull. "Go below, Mr Kell," Semmes said grimly, "and see how long the ship can float."

The Georgian went, and on his way through the wardroom saw a sight he would never forget. Assistant Surgeon David Llewellyn, a Briton and the only non-Southerner among the two dozen officers aboard, stood poised alongside where his operating table and patient had been until an 11-inch solid crashed through the adjoining bulkhead, snatching table, wounded seaman, and all his instruments from under the ministering hand of the doctor, who stood there, abruptly alone, with a dazed expression of horror and disbelief. Kell continued down to the engine room, where he saw through the steam from her drowned fires that the ship could scarcely remain afloat another ten minutes. He picked his way back up, through the wreckage and past the still-dazed surgeon, to report to the captain that the *Alabama*'s ordeal was nearly over.

"Then sir," Semmes replied, "cease firing, shorten sail, and haul down the colors. It will never do in this nineteenth century for us to go down, and the decks covered with our gallant wounded."

Across the water, less than 500 yards away, Winslow saw the rebel flag come down, but being, as he later explained, "uncertain whether Captain Semmes was using some ruse," called out to his gun crews: "He's playing a trick on us. Give him another broadside." They did just that, adding to the carnage on *Alabama*'s bloody, ripped-up decks with every gun that could be brought to bear; whereupon a white flag was run up from the stern. "Cease firing!" Winslow cried at last.

Through his telescope he observed on board the sinking raider a pantomime that called up within him, in rapid sequence, mixed emotions of pity, mistrust, sympathy, and resentment. Settling fast, with only a thread of smoke from her riddled stack, the *Alabama* had lost headway; Semmes, though still on his horseblock, obviously had given the order to abandon ship. While some of the crew milled about in confusion, engaging Winslow's pity by their plight — which, after all, might have been his own if the 100-pound shell lodged in his sternpost had not turned out to be a dud — others aroused his mistrust by piling into a dinghy and shoving off, apparently in an attempt to avoid capture. This was disproved, however, when the dinghy made for the *Kearsarge* and he saw, when it came within hailing distance, that it was filled with wounded men, including a master's mate who shouted up a request that boats be sent to rescue survivors gone over the side and thrashing about in the water.

Winslow had only two boats not smashed in the course of the fight, but he ordered them lowered without further delay and gave permission, moreover, for the rebel dinghy to be used as well, once the wounded had been unloaded. Obviously, though, these three small boats would not hold all the men in the water; so he called through his speaking trumpet to a nearby English pleasure yacht whose owner had sailed out of Cherbourg that morning for a closeup view of the duel: "For God's sake, do what you can to save them!" The yacht responded promptly, and as she did so Winslow turned his telescope back to the final scene of the tableau being enacted on *Alabama*'s canted deck.

The rebel skipper by now had descended from his perch, and he and another officer, a large, heavily bearded man — John Kell — began to undress for their leap into the Channel. The big man stripped to his underwear, but Semmes, apparently mindful of his dignity, retained his trousers and waistcoat. He seemed to part reluctantly with his sword. After unbuckling it rather awkwardly with his unhurt left hand, he held it above his head for a long moment, flashing brightly in the noonday sunlight, before he did the thing that brought Winslow's resentment to a boil. He flung it whirling and glinting into the sea, thereby making impossible the ceremony of handing it over to his vanquisher. Winslow could scarcely expect him to bring it along while he swam one-handed across four hundred yards of choppy water to the *Kearsarge* to surrender, but it seemed to the Federal captain that his adversary took a spiteful pleasure in this gesture which deprived him of a customary right.

Semmes followed Kell and his sword into the Channel, and the two men struck out as best they could, the former clutching a life preserver, the latter a wooden grating, to avoid the suction that might pull them under when the *Alabama* sank. She was filling fast now, air gurgling, hissing, chuckling under her punctured decks while the sea poured in through rents in her hull. Her stern awash, her prow was lifting, and suddenly it rose higher as her guns, still hot from battle, tore loose from their lashings and slid aft. The breeze freshening, she recovered a little headway with her sails, and as she moved she left behind her a broad ribbon of flotsam, broken spars and bodies, bits of tackle and other gear. Fifty yards off, Semmes turned to watch her die. Backward she went, beginning her long downward slide, anchors swinging wildly in the air below her bow; the main-topmast, split by a solid in the fight, went by the board when she paused, nearly vertical; then she was gone, the Channel boiling greenly for a time to mark the place where she had been.

It was 12.24, just under ninety minutes since she fired her first shot at the *Kearsarge*. For all his grief, Semmes was glad in at least one sense that she was on the forty-fathom bottom with his sword. "A noble Roman once stabbed his daughter, rather than she should be polluted by the foul embrace of a tyrant," he later wrote. "It was with a similar feeling that Kell and I saw the *Alabama* go down. We had buried her as we had christened her, and she was safe from the polluting touch of the hated Yankee!"

By now the trim British yacht *Deerhound* — whose captain-owner John Lancaster, a wealthy industrialist on vacation with his family, had had her built up the Clyde by the Lairds two years ago, at the same time they were at work on the sloop that became the *Alabama* — was within reach of the crewmen bobbing amid the whitecaps. She lowered her boats and began fishing them out, including Semmes and Kell and Marine Lieutenant Beckett Howell (Varina Davis's younger brother) but not Dr Llewellyn; a nonswimmer, he had drowned. Forty-two men were saved in all by the *Deerhound* in response to Winslow's plea; another dozen by the captains of two French pilot boats, who needed no urging; while seventy more were taken and made captive aboard the *Kearsarge*. Semmes himself might have been among these last except for Kell's quick thinking. Exhausted, the Confederate skipper was laid "as if dead" on the sternsheets of one of *Deerhound*'s boats when the *Kearsarge* cutter came alongside. "Have you seen Captain Semmes?" a blue-clad officer asked sharply. Kell, who had put on a *Deerhound* crewman's cap and taken an oar to complete the disguise, had a ready answer. "Captain Semmes is drowned," he said, to the Federal's apparent satisfaction. Aboard the yacht, after the shipwrecked men had been given hot coffee and shots of rum to counter the chill and exhaustion, Lancaster put the question: "Where shall I land you?" This time it was Semmes who had the answer that meant salvation. "I am now under English colors," he said, "and the sooner you put me, with my officers and men, on English soil the better."

Well before nightfall the *Deerhound* put in at Southampton, where, news of the battle having preceded them, Semmes and his men were given a welcome as hearty as if they had won; "A set of first-rate fellows," the London *Times* pronounced them. As soon as he had rested from his ordeal, the Maryland-born Alabamian used the gold left at Cherbourg to pay off the survivors and send allotments to the nearest kin of the nine men killed in action and twelve drowned. He was banqueted by admirers, including officers of the Royal Navy, who united to present him with an elegant, gold-mounted sword, engraved along the blade to signify that it was a replacement for the one he had flung into the Channel after his "engagement off Cherbourg with a chain-plated ship of superior power, armament, and crew." However, when Confederate officials tendered him a new command with which to continue the record begun aboard the *Sumter*, he declined, needing time to absorb the shock of his "impossible" defeat. Though he was promoted to rear admiral and eventually made his way, via Cuba and Mexico, back to the Confederacy (none of whose ports the *Alabama* ever touched) he had done all he would do afloat. Other raiders would continue to strike at Yankee shipping around the globe, but not Raphael Semmes. "I considered my career upon the high seas closed by the loss of my ship," he later explained.

As for Winslow, he too was being lionized by now as the man who had abolished in single combat the myth that the *Alabama* was invincible. After clearing his decks and assembling the crew for thanks-giving prayers — which helped to ease his dudgeon at having seen the British yachtsman make off with his prize of prizes, Semmes — he steamed into Cherbourg, flags aflutter from every mast of the *Kearsarge*, and was promptly surrounded by boatloads of people out to greet the ship whose victorious crew had somehow been transformed into the home team.

Her casualties were limited to the three men hit early in the duel, one of whom died a few days later; *Alabama*'s came to 43, just under half of them drowned or killed in action. Once he had paroled his pris-oners and patched up superficial damage, Winslow went to Paris to consult a specialist about his failing eye, only to learn that he had waited too long for treatment to be of any use. A victory banquet, tendered by patriotic fellow countrymen in the French capital, helped to dispel the medical gloom of the occasion, and a letter from Gideon Welles was even more effective in that regard. "I congratulate you," the Secretary wrote, "on your good fortune in meeting the *Alabama*, which had so long avoided the fastest ships and some of the most vigilant and intelli-gent officers of the service, and for the ability displayed in the contest you have the thanks of the Department. . . . The battle was so brief, the victory so decisive, and the comparative results so striking that the country will be reminded of the brilliant actions of our infant Navy, which have been repeated and illustrated in the engagement."

Presently this was followed, upon the President's recommendation, by a vote of thanks from Congress and a promotion to date from June 19. Commodore Winslow returned to the United States by the end of the year, and while the *Kearsarge* was being refitted in the Boston Navy Yard carpenters removed a section of her sternpost, still with the 100-pound dud embedded in the oak, and boxed it for shipment to

Washington, the Commander in Chief having expressed a desire to see for himself what a close call the ship and all aboard had had on that famous Sunday, six miles out in the English Channel, when she sank the *Alabama*.

Lincoln was indeed glad to learn that the most famed of rebel raiders had been struck from the list of woes to be endured until the war had run its course. Lately, though, he had begun to perceive that while striving to keep up national morale he would also have to deal with national impatience, which mounted with every indication, true or false, that the end might not be far off. Earlier that week, on June 14 — the day Bishop Polk was cannon-sniped on Pine Top and Grant began crossing the James — he had confessed to a friendly newsman that the country's tendency to "expect too much at once" was, for him, a matter of considerable private anxiety: "I wish, when you write or speak to people, you would do all you can to correct the impression that the war in Virginia will end right off and victoriously. . . . As God is my judge, I shall be satisfied if we are over with the fight in Virginia within a year. I hope we shall be 'happily disappointed,' as the saying is; but I am afraid not. I am afraid not."

This was something new, this concern lest the public, in its ebullience, demand an end to the war before it was won, and Lincoln bore down to counteract it two days later, nine days after his renomination, when he went to attend and address a sanitary fair in Philadelphia. "It is a pertinent question often asked in the mind privately, and from one to the other: When is the war to end? Surely I feel as deep an interest in this question as anyone can, but I do not wish to name a day, or month, or a year when it is to end. I do not wish to run any risk of seeing the time come, without our being ready for the end, and for fear of disappointment because the time had come and not the end. We accepted this war for an object, a worthy object, and the war will end when that object is attained. Under God, I hope it never will until that time."

Cheers went up at this, and he pressed on to warn his hearers that the approach of victory might call for more, not fewer sacrifices. "If I shall discover that General Grant and the noble officers and men under him can be greatly facilitated in their work by a sudden pouring forward of men and assistance, will you give them to me?"

"Yes! Yes!" the crowd roared, catching fire.

"Then I say, stand ready," Lincoln told the upturned faces about the rostrum, as well as those that would be downturned over tomorrow's newspapers all across the land, "for I am watching for the chance."

✼ 3 ✼

Now that Johnston had relinquished Pine Top, retiring down its rear-ward slope with the corpse of Bishop Polk, Sherman followed close on his heels, determined to keep up the pressure which, so far, had gained him eighty of the critical hundred air-line miles between Chattanooga and Atlanta, his base and his objective. He did so with caution, however, being confronted on the left and right by the loom of Brush and Lost mountains, both occupied by butternut marksmen who asked nothing more, in the way of compensation for their pains, than one quick glimpse down their rifle barrels at blue-clad soldiers moving toward them, within range and without cover. "We cannot risk the heavy loss of an assault at this distance from our base," the red-haired Ohioan had wired Halleck on the day before Polk's mangling. But on June 16, two days after that event, he changed his mind and began to consider trying what he had said he could not risk. "I am now inclined to feign on both flanks and assault the center," he told Old Brains. "It may cost us dear, but in results would surpass any attempt to pass around."

Presently, though, he changed his mind again — or, more strictly speaking, had it changed for him by Johnston, who gave him the slip the following night with another of his "clean retreats." This one was not so much an outright withdrawal, however, as it was a rectification, an adjustment whereby the foxy Confederate not only shortened his rather extended line but also shored up the sagging center Sherman had planned to assault. Turning loose of the high ground on his flanks, he fell back to Kennesaw Mountain, two miles in rear of the abandoned Pine Top salient. Polk's corps — temporarily under Major General W. W. Loring, the senior division commander — was posted there, dug in along its northern face, with Hood on the right, astride the Western & Atlantic, and Hardee on the left, denying the Federals access to Marietta by blocking the roads coming in from Dallas and Burnt Hickory. Johnston's line, which had been concave after he gave up Pine Top, was now convex, and its center, which had been its weakest element when Sherman contemplated launching a headlong strike, was now its stoutest part. In point of fact, the graybacks had occupied no stronger position in the course of their six-week retreat.

"Kennesaw Mountain is, I should think, about 700 feet high," an Illinois major wrote home in reaction to his first sight of this for-bidding piece of geography reared up in the army's path, "and consists of two points or peaks, separated by a narrow gorge running across the top. The mountain itself is entirely separated from all mountain ranges, and swells up like a great bulb from the plain." Sherman too was im-pressed and given pause by what he called "the bold and striking twin mountain." Rebel signalmen were at work on its two bulbous peaks, both of which were "crowned with batteries," while "the spurs were alive with men busy felling trees, digging pits, and preparing for the grand struggle impending." As he stood and looked, awe gave way to determination. "The scene was enchanting; too beautiful to be disturbed by the harsh clamor of war," he was to say, years later; "but the Chattahoochee lay beyond, and I had to reach it."

He had to reach it; but how? In an attempt to find some easier means than a headlong assault, which seemed foredoomed, he brought up his guns and began to pound away at the fortified slopes of the mountain, hoping to fix the enemy in position there while he probed both flanks of the rebel line in search of a way around it, one that would enable him to menace the railroad in Johnston's rear and thus provoke him into abandoning his present all-but-impregnable position, as he had done so many others in the course of his long retreat, rather than risk a fight whose loss would mean the severance of his supply line. The result was a series of skirmishes, some of which attained the dignity of engagements, first at Gilgal Church, where the graybacks fought a holding action to cover their withdrawal, and then along Mud and Nose (or Noyes) creeks, both of which had to be crossed if Sherman was to turn the rebel left for a strike at Marietta, Johnston's base, two miles back of Kennesaw, or at Smyrna Station, another four miles down the railroad. While Schofield, reinforced by Hooker, was doing all he could in that direction, McPherson, strengthened by Blair's return the week before, was feeling out the Confederate right, but with little success, being under the guns and surveillance of the enemy on the taller of Kennesaw's two peaks. Thomas meantime kept up the pressure dead ahead, firing so many rounds from his massed batteries — he had 130 guns in all: half a dozen more than McPherson and Schofield combined — that his soldiers, watching the bombardment from dug-in positions on the flat, began to tell each other that Uncle Billy was determined to take the double-crested mountain in their front, or else "fill it full of old iron."

For three days this continued, neither Thomas nor McPherson achieving much with their pounding and probing, and then on June 22, having proceeded well to the south around Kennesaw's western flank, Schofield too was brought to a sudden halt.

It happened at a place called Culp's (or Kolb's) Farm, four miles southwest of Marietta on the road from Powder Springs, and it came about because Johnston, in reaction to Sherman's continuing effort to reach around his left, had issued instructions the night before for Hood, whose intrenchments on the right would be occupied temporarily by Wheeler's dismounted troopers, to march at daylight across the rear of Kennesaw and go into position beyond Hardee on the far left, south of the mountain's western flank, in order to block the Federal turning movement. Hood did this, and more. Within a mile of his objective by midday, he encountered troops from Schofield's corps advancing up the Powder Springs Road, and with soldierly instinct, but without taking time for reconnaissance, attacked at once.

Assuming he had the flankers outflanked, he figured that a prompt assault would "roll them up," drive them back with heavy casualties, and abolish this threat to Johnston's lifeline. The result was heavy casualties, all right, though not for Schofield, who had taken the precaution of having his and Hooker's men dig in while awaiting reports from patrols sent out to find the best route up the valley of Olley's Creek for a strike at the Western & Atlantic above Smyrna, three miles across the way. Hood drove these forward elements rapidly back, giving chase with the two divisions on hand, but at Culp's Farm the pursuers came unexpectedly upon the enemy main body, stoutly intrenched, and were bloodily repulsed. A second assault, launched near sundown, only added to the carnage; Stevenson's division alone lost more than 800 men, and Hindman's brought the total to better than 1000. Schofield and Hooker, whose soldiers did their fighting behind earthworks for a change, suffered less than a third that many casualties in breaking the two attacks. Then at nightfall, while the graybacks dug in too along the line where the fighting stopped, Schofield and Hood sent word to their superiors at Big Shanty and Marietta of what had happened.

Johnston's anger at this loss of a thousand badly needed veterans, once more as a result of Hood's impetuosity, was exceeded by Sherman's when he received an out-of-channels dispatch that evening from Hooker, proudly reporting that he had "repulsed two heavy attacks" and calling urgently for reinforcements before he was overrun. "Three entire corps are in front of us," he added by way of lending weight to his proud cry for help. "Hooker must be mistaken; Johnston's army has only three corps," Sherman noted in passing the message along to Thomas, who, knowing only too well that Hardee and Loring were still in position to his and McPherson's front, replied rather mildly: "I look upon this as something of a stampede." Sherman agreed and next morning, still miffed, rode down to Culp's Farm in a pouring rain to tell Fighting Joe he wanted no more of his boasts and misrepresentations. In reaction, Hooker went into a month-long pout; or, as his superior later put it, "From that time he began to sulk."

This would have its consequences for all concerned; but the fact was, Sherman's anger had its source in something far more irksome than Hooker's inability to avoid exaggeration. Daylight showed the graybacks intrenched across Schofield's front. This meant that the army had gone as far as it could go in that direction without turning loose of its supply line, already under threat from rebel horsemen, and the drowned condition of the roads precluded any movement on them so long as the rain continued.

Confronted thus with the probability of a stalemate — which was not only undesirable on its own account, here in Georgia, but might also give Richmond the chance to reinforce Lee's hard-pressed Virginia army from Johnston's, biding its time north of the Chattahoochee — Sherman reverted to his notion, expressed a week ago, "to feign on both flanks and assault the center." The trouble was that the center now was Kennesaw Mountain, and Kennesaw seemed unassailable. But there, perhaps, was just the factor that might augur best; an attacker would greatly increase his chance for success by striking where the blow was least expected. Besides, continued probes by McPherson today showed that Loring's corps had been extended eastward to include a portion of the works abandoned yesterday by Hood when he set out westward to counter Schofield's flanking threat. That march, with its extension of the Confederate left while Loring spread out to cover the right, stretched Johnston's line to a width of about eight miles, exclusive of the cavalry on his flanks. It must be quite thin somewhere, and that somewhere was likely to be dead ahead on Kennesaw, whose frown alone was enough to discourage assault. So Sherman reasoned, at any rate, in his search for some way to avoid a stalemate. Moreover, he explained afterwards, he conferred with his three army commanders, "and we all agreed that we could not with prudence stretch out any more, and therefore there was no alternative but to attack 'fortified lines,' a thing carefully avoided up to that time."

Such a change in tactics, abruptly sprung, would also serve to increase the element of surprise, which figured largely in Sherman's calculations. But the outlook remained grim, if not downright awesome. "The whole country is one vast fort," he informed Halleck on June 23. "Johnston must have full fifty miles of connected trenches, with abatis and finished batteries.... Our lines are now in close contact and the fighting incessant, with a good deal of artillery. As fast as we gain one position, the enemy has another all ready."

These were minor adjustments, permitting no more than a closer look at the honeycombed slopes of the mountain up ahead, and a closer look only magnified the original impression of impregnability. One-armed Howard, studying the rebel line from a position well to the front, pronounced it "stronger in artificial contrivances and natural features than the cemetery at Gettysburg," which he had helped to hold despite Lee's all-out efforts to oust him. But Sherman refused to be distracted, let alone dissuaded. Determined, as he had told Grant the week before, to "inspire motion into a large, ponderous and slow, by habit, army," he believed that his soldiers, weary of roundabout marches that never quite managed to bring the enemy to bay, needed the stimulus the pending assault would provide, even if most of the blood that was shed turned out to be their own — and he was concerned, as well, lest Johnston's habitual caution, which had led him to give up so many stout positions in the course of the past seven weeks, should be replaced by a conviction that the Federals would never attack him once he was snugly intrenched. Both of these things counted heavily in the red-head's calculations, as did the promise of all that would be gained if the attack was anything like as successful as the one up Missionary Ridge, seven months ago, by many of these same men against many of these same opponents, with the difference that there had been no unfordable Chattahoochee in the rebel rear on that occasion.

Other factors there were, too, no less persuasive because Sherman himself — defined by Walt Whitman as "a bit of stern open air made up in the image of a man" — was perhaps not even aware of their influence on him. For one, the Union army in Virginia was not only doing most of the bleeding in the double-pronged offensive, it was also getting most of the headlines, and despite his dislike of journalists, and indeed of the press in general, he could see that his troops would be heartened by a more equitable distribution of praise, such as the over-running of Kennesaw would secure. Moreover, back in Nashville and Chattanooga, while preparing for the campaign, he had learned that certain observers snidely characterized him as "not a fighting general." He dismissed the charge without exactly denying it, saying: "Fighting is the least part of a general's work. The battle will fight itself." Still, the imputation rankled, containing as it did some grains of truth, and he welcomed the opportunity, now at hand, to refute it for once and for all. On June 24 he issued a special field order directing his army commanders to "make full reconnaissances and preparations to attack the enemy in force on the 27th instant, at 8 a.m. precisely."

That left two full days for getting set; Sherman, having decided to be rash, had also decided to go about it methodically, even meticulously, so as to minimize the cost if the breakthrough failed. For one thing, he would limit the weight of his assault to less than a fifth of the troops on hand, and for another, despite its regrettable but inevitable detraction from the element of surprise, the jump-off would be preceded by an hour-long bombardment from every gun that could be brought to bear on the critical objectives. Of these there were two, main and secondary, neither of them, properly speaking, on the mountain that would give the battle its name, although the secondary effort, assigned to McPherson, would be made against — and, if successful, across — the gently rolling southwest slope of the lower of the two peaks, called Little Kennesaw to distinguish it from Big Kennesaw, the taller and more massive portion of the mountain to the east, overlooking the slow curve of the Western & Atlantic on that flank. This attack

would be launched astride the Burnt Hickory Road, simultaneously
with Thomas's main effort, along and to the right of the Dallas Road,
one mile south; both commanders would assault with two divisions,

their others standing by to exploit whatever progress was
achieved. Schofield and Hooker
would feint on the far right,
Garrard's cavalry on the left, all
at the same prearranged hour,
hard on the heels of the soften-
ing-up artillery bombardment, so
as to prevent Johnston from
knowing which part of his line to
reinforce from any other, or
from his reserves if he had them,
before it was swamped. "At the
time of the general attack," the
special order ended, foreseeing a
happy outcome to the rashness
so meticulously prescribed, "the

skirmishers at the base of Kennesaw will take advantage of it to gain, if
possible, the summit and hold it. Each attacking column will endeavor
to break a single point of the enemy's line, and make a secure lodgment beyond, and be prepared for following it up toward Marietta and the railroad in case of success."

Throughout that two-day interim, although few along the eight-
mile curve of intrenchments knew what they were waiting or getting
set for — "All commanders will maintain reserve and secrecy even from
their staff officers," the field order had cautioned — fire fights, picket
clashes, and sudden cannonades would break into flame from point to
point, then subside into sputters and die away, sporadic, inconclusive,
and productive of little more than speculation. Whether off on the flanks
or crouched near the critical center, men listened and wondered, unable to find a pattern to the action. The crash of guns would come
from somewhere up or down the line, an Indiana soldier would recall,
"then the hurrahing, sometimes the shrill, boyish rebel yell, sometimes
the loud, full-voiced, deep-toned, far-sounding chorus of northern
men; then again the roar of cannon, the rattle of musketry and the
awful suspense to the listeners. If, as the noise grew feebler, we caught
the welcome cheer, answering shouts ran along. But if the far-off rebel
yell told of our comrades' repulse, the silence could be felt."

Across the way, within the horseshoe curve of works containing
Kennesaw and Marietta, the reaction was much the same, but in reverse.
No one there could discern a pattern either, including the men of
Major Generals Samuel French's and Benjamin Cheatham's divisions

of Loring's and Hardee's corps, respectively astride the Burnt Hickory and Dallas roads, up which the two Union assaults were to be delivered on Monday morning, June 27, one week past the summer solstice.

The rain left off on Sunday and the sun came up in a cloudless sky next morning at 4.40 to begin its work of drying the red clay roads, the sodden fields and breathless woods. By the time it was three hours high the day was hot and steamy with the promise of much greater heat to come. Twenty minutes later, precisely at 8 o'clock and without preamble, 200-odd Union cannon roared into action, pounding away at the rebel line on the mountainside and across the flats beyond. Crouched in their pits and ditches, jarred and shaken about by the sudden hurtle of metal exploding over and around them, the defenders marveled at the volume and intensity of the fire, which was to them still another manifestation of Yankee ingenuity and wealth. "Hell has broke loose in Georgia, sure enough!" one grayback shouted amid shellbursts, and as the bombardment continued, sustained by an apparently inexhaustible supply of ammunition, they began to snatch down the blankets pegged for shade across the open tops of their trenches, preparing for what they knew would come when the guns let up. Finally, close to 9 o'clock, the uproar reached a spasmodic end; the cannoneers stepped back from their pieces, panting, and the blue infantry started forward in two clotted masses, about a mile apart, to assail the Confederate center.

For a time they advanced in relative security, protected by the intervening woods and the butternut pickets trotting back to join their comrades along the main line of resistance. Then the attackers emerged into brilliant sunlight, silhouetted against the bright green backdrop of trees, and the rebel headlogs seemed to burst spontaneously into flame along their bottoms, all up and down that portion of the line. Sam French, whose left-flank division of Loring's corps was challenged first on Little Kennesaw's lower slopes, said later that the rattle and flash of musketry, combined with the deep-voiced boom of guns whose crews had held their fire till now, produced "a roar as constant as Niagara and as sharp as the crash of thunder with lightning in the eye."

Such was the fury of the sound that accompanied McPherson's attack, launched astride the Burnt Hickory Road by Brigadier General Morgan Smith, whose division was reinforced for the effort by a brigade from another division in Major General John A. Logan's corps. Sound and fury were all it came to, however, in the end. In the course of their plunge across a rocky, brush-choked gully, unexpectedly encountered in rear of the line abandoned by the gray pickets, 563 of the 4000 attackers fell before they could get to grips with the defenders intrenched on the far side. At one point "within about thirty feet of the enemy's main line," Smith reported, they came close; but there, receiving the full blast of massed rifles, they "staggered and sought cover as best they could behind logs and rocks." Stalled ("It was almost sure death to take your face out of the dust," one prone Federal declared, while another expressed a somewhat less gloomy view of the consequences, saying: "It was only necessary to expose a hand to procure a furlough") they were no longer much of a threat to French, who turned his high-sited batteries a quarter circle to the left and added the weight of the metal to Hardee's resistance, a mile away, astride and beyond the Dallas Road.

There Thomas was making a sturdier bid for a breakthrough, and Cheatham's division had all it could do to keep from being overrun by nearly twice as many Federals as French had had to deal with. "They seemed to walk up and take death as coolly as if they were automatic or wooden men," one defender was to say of these troops from two divisions under Jeff Davis and Brigadier General John Newton, respectively of Palmer's and Howard's corps.

Two of Cheatham's four brigades were posted where Hardee's line bent sharply to the south, creating a somewhat isolated salient, and it was here at the hinge, known thereafter as the Dead Angle, that Thomas struck. "The least flicker on our part would have been sure death to all," a Tennessee private who helped to hold it later declared. "We could not be reinforced on account of our position, and we had to stand up to the rack, fodder or no fodder." They did stand up, inflicting in the process — with the help of French's guns and Cleburne, whose marksmen brought their rifles to bear from up the line — a total of 654 casualties on Newton and 824 on Davis, both of whom notified their superiors that they hoped they could hang on where they were, if that was what was wanted, but that there was no further hope of carrying the position. Howard put it strongest, some time later, looking back. "Our losses in this assault were heavy indeed," he wrote, "and our gain was nothing. We realized now, as never before, the futility of direct assault upon intrenched lines already well prepared and well manned." Thomas agreed, sending word around 11 o'clock for those who could fall back to do so at once, while those who could not were to dig in where they were and wait for darkness.

The sudden resultant drop in the intensity of the fighting came none too soon for the defenders of the Angle, one of whom was to testify that he fired no less than 120 rounds in the course of the repulse. "My gun became so hot that frequently the powder would flash before I could ram home the ball," he said, adding: "When the Yankees fell back and the firing ceased, I never saw so many broken down and exhausted men in my life. I was sick as a horse, and as wet with blood and sweat as I could be, and many of our men were vomiting with excessive fatigue, overexhaustion, and sunstroke; our tongues were parched and cracked for water, and our faces blackened with powder and smoke, and our dead and wounded were piled indiscriminately in the trenches."

Cheatham's loss came to 195, French's to 186; between them, they had shot down 2041 of the 12,000 Federals thrown against their works. Other losses, elsewhere in Loring's and Hardee's corps, as well as in Hood's, which had been skirmishing with Schofield all the while, brought the Confederate total to 552. Sherman put his at 2500 — a figure Johnston vowed was a good deal less than half the true one — but later revised it upward to "about 3000."

Even so, and despite the shock of the sudden double repulse, he had been willing to drive it still higher at the time. From Signal Hill, his command post on the left, he could see that McPherson had shot his wad, and word had come from Schofield that little could be done on the far right. That left Thomas, the Rock of Chickamauga. He too had been checked, losing two of his best brigade commanders in the process, but he might be willing to try again for a repetition of what he had achieved on Missionary Ridge despite conditions even more unfavorable. "McPherson and Schofield are at a deadlock," Sherman wired him at 1.30. "Do you think you can carry any part of the enemy's line to-day? ... I will order the assault if you think you can succeed at any point." Thomas replied: "We have already lost heavily today without gaining any material advantage. One or two more such assaults would use up this army."

He recommended a change to siege methods, the digging of saps for a guarded approach. But Sherman, wanting no part of such a time-consuming business, preferred to maneuver the rebels out of position, as before. Encouraged by the let-up of the rain and the fast-drying condition of the roads, he telegraphed Thomas that evening: "Are you willing to risk [a] move on Fulton, cutting loose from our railroad?" Fulton was two miles beyond Smyrna Station, within three miles of the Chattahoochee and about ten miles in Johnston's rear; Sherman proposed to move by the right flank "with the whole army." Thomas considered the venture highly risky, exposing as it would the Union life line to Confederate seizure while the wheeling movement was in progress; but in any case, he replied before turning in for the night, "I think it de-cidedly better than butting against breastworks twelve feet thick and strongly abatised."

While waiting for the roads to finish drying Sherman worked on plans for his newest sidle and, eventually, on securing a truce for the burial of the unfortunates who had fallen in the double-pronged repulse. Undaunted — at least on paper — he took the offensive in defending his decision to strike at the rebel center, even though all it had got him was a lengthened casualty list. "The assault I made was no mistake; I had to do it," he wired Halleck, explaining that after nearly eight weeks of gingerly skirmishing, all the time conforming to a pattern about as precise as if he and Johnston were partners in a classic minuet, Federals and Confederates alike "had settled down into the conviction that the assault of lines formed no part of my game." Now that both sides knew better, having seen the dance pattern broken as if with a meat ax, he expected to find his adversary "much more cautious." That was his gain, as he saw it, and he continued to pursue this line of consolation. "Failure as it was, and for which I assume the entire responsibility," he would assert in his formal report of the lost battle, "I yet claim it produced good fruit, as it demonstrated to General Johnston that I would assault, and that boldly."

Earlier, while smoke still hung about the field and the wounded mewled for help between the lines, he had reminded Thomas: "Our loss is small compared with some of those in the East. It should not in the least discourage us. At times assaults are necessary and inevitable." However, his most forthright statement with regard to losses was reserved for his wife, to whom he wrote two days after the Kennesaw repulse. " I begin to regard the death and mangling of a couple of thousand men as a small affair, a kind of morning dash," he told her, adding: "It may be well that we become hardened. . . . The worst of the war is not yet begun."

That might well be, though there could be no denying that for a considerable number of his soldiers — young and old, recruits and veterans alike — the best was over, along with the worst. Their interment was a grisly thing to watch. "I get sick now when I happen to think about it," a Confederate wrote years later, remembering the June 30 burial armistice that was asked and granted "not for any respect either army had for the dead, but to get rid of the sickening stench." Although three days of festering midsummer Georgia heat had made the handling of the corpses a repugnant task, he recalled that Yankee ingenuity once more had measured up to the occasion. "Long and deep trenches were dug, and hooks made from bayonets crooked for the purpose, and all the dead were dragged and thrown pell mell into these trenches. Nothing was allowed to be taken off the dead, and finely dressed officers, with gold watch chains dangling over their vests, were thrown into the ditches. During the whole day both armies were hard at work, burying the Federal dead."

Thus June ended, bringing with it another pause for a backward look at the casualty count in each of the two armies. In both cases these were lower than they had been the month before, and they were similar in another way as well. Just as New Hope Church and Pickett's Mill, engagements fought near the bottom of the previous calendar leaf, had reversed the May tally, raising Sherman's losses above Johnston's, which had been higher than his opponent's before the clashes around Dallas, so now did Kennesaw Mountain reverse the count for June, which had been lower for the Union up till then. Sherman's loss for the past month was 7500, Johnston's around 6000. This brought their respective totals for the whole campaign to just under 17,000 and just over 14,000. Roughly speaking, to put it another way, one out of every four Confederates had been shot or captured, as compared to one out of seven Federals.

In time, when the guns had cooled and approximate figures from both sides became available in books, Sherman would take great pride in this reversal of the anticipated ratio of losses between attacker and defender (as well he might: especially in reviewing a campaign fought on ground as unfavorable to the offensive as North Georgia was, against an adversary he admired as much as he did Joe Johnston) but just now there was the war to get on with, the wheeling movement he had designed to flank the rebels off their impregnable mountain and back across the only remaining river between them and his goal, Atlanta. By July 1 the roads were baked about hard enough for marching; the sidle began next day.

Garrard's dismounted troopers replaced the infantry in the trenches astride the Western & Atlantic, blocking a possible track-breaking sortie by the graybacks on that flank, and McPherson set out across Thomas's rear to join Schofield for a lunge around Hood's left the following day. If successful, this would not only sever Johnston's life line, it would also oblige him to fight without the protection of intrenchments when he fell back, through Marietta and Smyrna, to where the flankers would be waiting around Fulton, three miles short of the Chattahoochee and better than 50,000 strong. McPherson thus was given a chance to redeem his Resaca performance by repeating it without flaws, although Sherman's expectations were by no means as great as they had been eight weeks ago, some eighty miles back up the railroad. Warned by lookouts high on Kennesaw, which afforded a panoramic view of the country for miles and miles around, Johnston would probably choose to give up his present position rather than risk the consequences of fighting simultaneously front and rear, with a force about as large as his own in each direction. Anticipating this reaction the night before, Sherman told Garrard and Thomas to advance their pickets at daylight, July 3, and determine whether the Kennesaw trenches were occupied or abandoned; whether Johnston had chosen to stand his ground, despite the menace to his life line, or fall back, as he had always done in the face of such a threat.

On Signal Hill before dawn next morning, while the skirmishers were groping their way forward through the brush, Sherman waited impatiently for the light to grow enough to permit the use of a large telescope he had had mounted on a tripod and trained on the double-humped bulk of Kennesaw, looming blacker than the starless sky beyond it. Presently the sun broke clear and he saw, through the high-powered glass, "some of our pickets crawling up the hill cautiously. Soon they stood upon the very top, and I could see their movements as they ran along the crest."

Not a shot had been fired; the works were empty; the rebels had pulled out southward in the night.

The red-haired Ohioan caught fire at the notion that now they were out in the open, somewhere between the abandoned mountain and the river ten miles in its rear — his for the taking, so to speak, if he could overhaul them with his superior numbers before they reached whatever sanctuary their commander had it in mind to fortify. "In a minute I roused my staff, and started them off with orders in every direction for a pursuit by every possible road, hoping to catch Johnston in the confusion of retreat, especially at the crossing of the Chattahoochee River." Thomas could be depended on to descend at once on Marietta, but what was needed most just now, if the pursuers were to overcome whatever head start the Confederates might have gained, was cavalry. Sherman told Garrard to get his three brigades remounted and ride hard to bring the enemy to bay, short of the Chattahoochee, while McPherson and Schofield caught up to close in for the kill.

Events moved fast now, but not fast enough for Sherman. Without waiting for Garrard, he rode ahead with a small escort, around the eastern flank of the mountain and on into Marietta, nestled in its rear. He got there by 8.30 and was pleased to find that, although the graybacks had made a clean getaway with all their stores and had torn up several miles of railroad to the south, Thomas already had soldiers in the town. As the minutes ticked off, however, and no troopers appeared, his impatience mounted. "Where's Gar'd?" he began to storm. "Where's Gar'd? Where in hell's Gar'd?" Finally the cavalryman — a fellow Ohioan, seven years his junior in age and eleven years behind him at West Point — arrived, explaining that it had taken time to bring his horses forward and get his men into column on the road. Dissatisfied to find still more time being wasted on excuses, Sherman yelled at him: "Get out of here quick!" Garrard was flustered. Transferred from the East on the eve of the present campaign, he was not yet accustomed to being addressed in this manner. "What shall I do?" he asked, and his red-haired chief barked angrily: "Don't make a damned bit of difference so you get out of here and go for the rebs."

Despite such urgency it was midafternoon before contact was reëstablished near Smyrna, five miles down the line, and reconnaissance used up the daylight needed for mounting an assault. Fortified in advance for ready occupation, its flanks protected east and west by Rottenwood and Nickajack creeks, the rebel position astride the railroad, midway between Marietta and the river crossing five miles in its rear, obviously called for caution if the Federals were to avoid blundering into a bloody repulse. Sherman was convinced, however, that his adversary had occupied it only in hope of delaying the blue pursuit, and he said as much in a message to Thomas near sundown: "The more I reflect the more I know Johnston's halt is to save time to cross his material and men. No general, such as he, would invite battle with the Chattahoochee behind him. . . . I know you appreciate the situation. We will never have such a chance again, and I want you to impress on Hooker, Howard, and Palmer the importance of the most intense energy of attack tonight and in the morning. . . . Press with vehemence at any cost of life and material. Every inch of line should be felt and the moment there is a give, pursuit should be made."

But there was no give, and no pursuit. In fact there was no attack. Vehemence yielded to prudence next morning — July 4: the first anniversary of Vicksburg's fall, Lee's retreat from Gettysburg, and Holmes's drubbing at Helena — when Sherman found the works in his front still a-bristle with bayonets and Johnston apparently desirous of nothing so much as he was of a blue assault that would permit a repetition of what had happened on the slopes of Little Kennesaw a week ago today.

On second thought, the Ohioan cancelled his sundown instructions to Thomas, which had called for "the most intense energy of action," and reverted instead to his time-tested method of attempting to maneuver, rather than knock, the graybacks out of fortifications established in his path. While the Cumberlanders kept up a noisy demonstration in front, banging away with all their guns as if in celebration of the Fourth, McPherson set out on another of his whip-lash marches, down the near bank of Nickajack Creek, to threaten the Confederate left rear. Darkness fell before his troops were in position, and the following sunrise proved Sherman right after all. The Smyrna works yawned empty; the rebs once more had stolen away in the night. Eager as ever to catch them amid the confusion that always attended a river crossing, the northern commander took off fast, making excellent time on a march of about three miles; which ended unexpectedly, within two miles of the Chattahoochee, when he came upon Johnston, just beyond Vining Station, in occupation of what Sherman frankly called "the best line of field intrenchments I have ever seen."

Looking back on the experience, years later — mindful no doubt of what he had said, two nights before, about his adversary's unwillingness to "invite battle with the Chattahoochee behind him" — he expanded the compliment: "No officer or soldier who ever served under me will question the generalship of Joseph E. Johnston. His retreats were timely, in good order, and he left nothing behind."

One exhilarating gain there was at any rate, available from the crest of a hill inclosed by a loop of the railroad as it approached the Chattahoochee beyond Vining's. "Mine eyes have beheld the promised land," an Illinois major wrote home to his wife. "The 'domes and minarets and spires' of Atlanta are glittering in the sunlight before us, only eight miles distant." Sherman and Thomas were both on the hilltop for a Pisgah view of the prize beyond the river, and though the

Union-loyal Virginian took it calmly, as always — to look at his deep-set eyes and massive brow, a newsman declared, "made one feel as if he were gazing into the mouth of a cannon; and the cannon said nothing" — the volatile Ohioan, as usual, let his exhilaration show. "Stepping nervously about, his eyes sparkling and his face aglow, casting a single glance at Atlanta, another at the river, and a dozen at the surrounding valley," he seemed to the major to be studying the rebel dispositions in order to "see where he could best cross the river, how best he could flank them."

Clearly this would take some doing: Johnston once more had chosen well. Faced with the problem of defending a stream whose low south bank was dominated by high ground on the side which a crossing would leave in enemy control, he had intrenched in advance a six-mile line along the north bank, above and below the critical railroad span. With this and five other bridges at his back — a pair for each of his three corps — he could withdraw quickly in case of a break-through, left or right, or counterattack without delay if the Federals were repulsed. His wagons were already over the river, parked in safety beyond a secondary line of south-bank works, preconstructed for instant occupation if needed, and so was his cavalry, posted up-stream and down to guard against probes in either direction. Sherman, after a look at these canny dispositions from the Vining's hilltop, wired Halleck that he would have to "study the case a little" before proceeding. He foresaw delays and he wanted Washington braced for the disappointment they would bring.

"I am now far ahead of my railroad and telegraph, and want them to catch up," he explained; "[I] may be here some days. Atlanta is in plain view, nine miles distant.... The extent of the enemy's parallels already taken is wonderful, and much of the same sort confronts us yet, and is seen beyond the Chattahoochee."

Still, he was not long in deciding that he "could easily practice on that ground to better advantage our former tactics of intrenching a moiety in [Johnston's] front, and with the rest of our army cross the river [above or below] and threaten either his rear or the city of Atlanta itself." Accordingly, while repair gangs were hard at work restoring the railroad down to Vining's, he confronted the north-bank rebel *tête-du-pont* (as he called it) with the forces of Thomas and McPherson, posted Schofield rearward in reserve, under instructions to be ready to march at a moment's notice, and sent a division of cavalry in each direction, upstream and down, in search of a likely point or points for crossing.

Stoneman, who led the downriver column, found all the bridges destroyed and their sites covered by horse artillery on the opposite bank. Although Garrard, who rode all the way to Roswell, nearly twenty miles above, had no better luck with regard to bridges, in other respects he was fortunate indeed. Roswell was a manufacturing center; or it had been, anyhow, until Garrard's troopers put in a hard day's work with sledges and torches, wrecking and burning. One problem there was, of a somewhat diplomatic nature, but not for long. He came upon a cotton mill running full tilt, still turning out gray cloth for the rebel armies; a French flag flew above it and the Gallic owner claimed immunity from damage or interference on the grounds that he was not only not a Confederate but was of foreign allegiance. Feeling rather beyond his depth in international waters, the cavalryman referred the claim to Sherman, who reacted with predictable indignation. "Such nonsense cannot deceive me," he wired Halleck, a specialist in such matters. "I take it a neutral is no better than one of our own citizens." And to Garrard went instructions to proceed against the foreign-owned mill as he had done against the others. As for the Frenchman himself, Sherman was specific as to how he might be dealt with. "Should you, under the impulse of natural anger, natural at contemplating such perfidy, hang the wretch," he told Garrard, "I approve the act beforehand."

But there was neither a hanging nor another burning; Garrard let the Frenchman go and tore down his mill to provide material for rebuilding the nearby bridge, destroyed the week before. This took three days, which allowed plenty of time for one of McPherson's corps to arrive for a crossing on July 10, dry-shod and without rebel opposition, Schofield having crossed two days earlier, about midway between Roswell and the Confederate right at Pace's Ferry, and driven the butternut vedettes away from their picket posts on the south bank. Sherman thus had been quick to solve the Chattahoochee problem, and Johnston's stand with his back to the river was correspondingly brief. Much of the credit went to Stoneman, whose downriver excursion had drawn the enemy's attention in that direction, but most of it went to Schofield, who showed for the first time in the campaign what he could accomplish when left to his own devices.

Ordered to carry out an upstream crossing, the New-York-born West Pointer — he had been a schoolteacher and a surveyor on the western plains by the time he was seventeen, and even now, though balding fast, was two years less than twice that age — arrived at daylight, July 8, reconnoitered briefly, and decided to cross where Soap Creek emptied into the river, seven miles below Roswell, the opposite bank being held at that point by a light force of gray cavalry, apparently not over-vigilant and equipped with only one gun. Silently he brought up his batteries, screened by brush along the north bank, and loaded infantry assault teams into pontoon floats launched well back from the creek mouth. "At the appointed time," he later reported, "the artillery was pushed quickly into position and opened fire, a line of battle advanced, rapidly firing, to the river bank, while the batteaux, loaded with men, were pulled down the creek and across the river.... The astonished rebels fired a single shot from their single gun, delivered a few random discharges of musketry, and fled, leaving their piece of artillery in our possession. The crossing was secured without the loss of a man." By dawn of July 9, the pontoon bridge having been installed the night before, "two divisions occupied a secure tête-de-pont a mile in depth, giving ample room for the *debouché* of the whole army."

Johnston reacted to Schofield's upstream crossing as expected, and with all his accustomed stealth and skill. Destroying or dismantling the six bridges in his wake — and, incidentally, provoking Sherman's one uncomplimentary postwar comment on the quality of his generalship throughout the long campaign: "I have always thought Johnston neglected his opportunity there, for he had lain comparatively idle while we got control of both banks of the river above him" — he withdrew his main body across the Chattahoochee that night, and after temporarily occupying the south-bank works, prepared in advance for just such an emergency, continued the pull-back the following day, July 10, to a line in rear of Peachtree Creek, apparently prompted by concern that if he took up a position any closer to the river the Federals might cut in behind him and seize the city. In any case he now was less than five miles from the heart of Atlanta.

Grateful though Sherman was for this development, which meant that he would be able to cross this last of North Georgia's three broad rivers without a battle that had seemed likely to prove costly both in casualties and time, he once more found himself confronted with the problem that had loomed with every major gain: What now? — meaning *how?* Should he swing left or right, upstream or down, for the accustomed flanking effort, or bull straight ahead for an end-all strike at an opponent whose back was at last to the gates of the city in his charge, with little room for maneuver unless he chose to give it up without a fight?

While the red-haired general pondered and pored over maps and reports, his troops moved up to the unguarded Chattahoochee, anticipating their first leisurely bath in ten weeks. Admiration for their commander had grown with every tactical leap or sidestep, and now it reached a climax in which almost anything seemed possible. "Charley," one dusty infantry man told a comrade as they approached this last natural barrier and saw smoke rising from the buildings along its banks, "I believe Sherman has set the river on fire." Nor was the wonder limited to wearers of the blue. A butternut prisoner, conducted rearward past exuberant Federals in their tens of thousands, was so impressed by their multitude that he said to his captors: "Sherman ought to get on a high hill and command, 'Attention! Kingdoms by the right wheel!' " The general, in point of fact, was squatting naked in the

Chattahoochee at the time, discussing the temperature of the water with a teamster who admired him from the bank, while all around them other soldiers lolled neck deep in the river, soaking away the grime of more than a hundred red-clay miles of marching and fighting and the caked sweat of seventy days of exertion and fear, or else whooped and splashed in pure delight at having nothing else to do.

But not for long. After the brief time-out for his dip in the Chattahoochee, Sherman returned to his maps and reports, designing the next, and he hoped final, move in the campaign to whip Joe Johnston and take Atlanta. With the two-weeks-old repulse at Kennesaw fresh in mind, he quickly rejected the notion of mounting an all-out frontal attack on the Confederates dug in behind Peachtree Creek — attractive though that would be as a slam-bang finish, if successful — and reverted instead to his accustomed practice of operating on or around one of the enemy flanks.

Mostly, before, he had moved by his right, in a series of mirror images, so to speak, of Grant's leftward sidles in Virginia; but in this case the choice was by no means simple. It was true, a downstream crossing would not only give him ground that favored the offensive (the south-bank creeks, below, ran into the Chattahoochee at right angles, affording Johnston no perpendicular ridges to defend but many to cross in changing position to meet the challenge, while permitting Sherman to advance on the city by moving up the ravines, unhindered in front and sheltered on the flanks); it would also place him in rear of his objective from the outset, within easy striking distance of the railroads leading southwest through Montgomery to Mobile and southeast through Macon to Savannah, without which Atlanta could not long survive a siege. An upstream crossing, on the other hand, would give the advantage of terrain to the defenders; for there the creeks ran more or less parallel to the Chattahoochee, presenting Sherman with ridges to cross while advancing and Johnston with ravines to shelter his army while shifting to meet the threat. Geography clearly favored a downriver flanking operation. Yet there was a good deal more to the problem than geography per se. For one thing, there was the risk of exposing the all-important Union supply line to depredations, and this would be a far greater danger if the crossing was made below the railroad bridge. Just above there, after receiving the waters of Peachtree Creek, the Chattahoochee swerved northward (on the map, that is; the flow, of course, was south) and ran alongside the Western & Atlantic all the way beyond Vining Station, the newly established Federal railhead and supply dump, which would be within easy reach not only of rebel cavalry but also of rebel infantry, launched across the nearby river on a track-breaking sortie that could scarcely be blocked if most of the blue army moved below. This gave Sherman pause, as well it might, and so did something else. Recent dispatches from Grant indicated that their previous concern, lest Johnston reinforce Lee for a blow at Meade, was now reversed; Lee's current problem, Grant explained, was not how he could get more troops, but rather how he could feed the ones he had, and under such circumstances it was not unlikely that he might detach a sizeable portion of them for service in far-off Georgia, just as he had done the year before, on the eve of Chickamauga. If he did so, they would come by rail: specifically, by way of Augusta on the Georgia Railroad, the one line into Atlanta that would not be threatened, let alone broken, if Sherman crossed downriver to close in on the city from the west.

Thus to define the problem was to solve it, so far at least as the choice of directions was concerned: Sherman decided to break the pattern of his campaign and move by the left, crossing the river well upstream for a preliminary strike at the Georgia Railroad. Schofield in fact had already begun the movement three days ago, when his improvised amphibious assault teams emerged from the mouth of

Soap Creek to surprise the rebel pickets across the way, and Sherman had followed through by sending one of McPherson's corps to join Garrard at Roswell, seven miles beyond Schofield. On July 13, having reached a firm decision the night before, he continued the buildup by ordering McPherson to take his second corps upriver and reinforce the first, leaving the third in position on Thomas's right to maintain the downstream feint until Stoneman got back from the ride designed to mislead Johnston still further into thinking that the Federals were about to cross below.

"All is well," Sherman wired Halleck next day. "I have now accumulated stores at Allatoona and Marietta, both fortified and garrisoned points. Have also three places at which to cross the Chattahoochee in our possession, and only await General Stoneman's return from a trip down the river, to cross the army in force and move on Atlanta."

Stoneman got back the following night and McPherson's third corps set out for Roswell next morning, July 15. Reunited, the whiplash Army of the Tennessee would thus be on the rim of what Sherman described as "a general right wheel," designed to roll down on the city from the north and east, with Schofield about midway out the twelve-mile radius and Thomas holding the hub, or pivot, to confront and fix the Confederate main body in position for the crunch. McPherson would cross the river and march south to strike the railroad near Stone Mountain, six miles east of Decatur, Schofield's preliminary objective, about the same distance east of Atlanta. The two commands would then advance westward in tandem along the right-of-way, tearing up track as they went, and link up with Thomas for the final push that would assail Johnston along his front, outflank him on his right, and drive him back through the streets of the city in his rear.

"Each army will form a unit and connect with its neighbor by a line of pickets," the warning order read. "Should the enemy assume the offensive at any point, which is not expected until we reach below Peachtree Creek, the neighboring army will at once assist the one attacked. . . . A week's work after crossing the Chattahoochee should determine the first object aimed at, viz, the possession of the [Georgia Rail]road east of Decatur, or of Atlanta itself."

July 17 was the jump-off date, a Sunday, and everything went as ordered for all three armies involved in the grand wheel. Crossing with Schofield in the center, Sherman grew concerned, as usual, about what was happening out of sight: particularly in Thomas's direction, where the going was likely to be slow. "Feel down strong to Peach Tree and see what is there," he urged the Virginian. "A vigorous demonstration should be made, and caution your commanders not to exhibit any of the signs of a halt or pause." Next morning he rode over to check on the progress of the Cumberlanders, and found them crossing Nancy's

Creek on schedule to descend on Buckhead, a crossroads hamlet where Thomas would set up headquarters before sundown, within a mile of Peachtree Creek and its intrenched defenders.

"I am fully aware of the necessity of making the most of time," Sherman wired Halleck, "and shall keep things moving." Accordingly, he kept prodding Thomas: "I would like you to get to Buckhead early today and then to feel down strong on Atlanta," meantime fretting about McPherson's progress on the far left: "I want that railroad as quick as possible and the weather seems too good to be wasted."

Informed after nightfall that both Schofield and McPherson had reached their objectives and would begin their wrecking marches westward along the railroad at daybreak, Sherman exulted: as well he might, having accomplished within two days what he had predicted would require "a week's work after crossing the Chattahoochee." He had control of the Georgia Railroad from Stone Mountain through Decatur, and now, secure against reinforcements sped from Virginia by Lee, he was out to take Atlanta by bringing his combinations to bear on its outflanked defenders. The question was whether Johnston would stand, as he had done at Kennesaw, or skedaddle, as he had done everywhere else in the course of the seventy-seven-day campaign.

Riding out to confer on the matter with Thomas next morning, July 19, the red-haired Ohioan encountered an answer of sorts in a copy of yesterday's newspaper, brought out of the semi-beleaguered city by a spy. Johnston, it seemed, would neither stand nor skedaddle. "At this critical moment," Sherman later put it, looking back, "the Confederate Government rendered us most valuable service."

✗ 4 ✗

In Atlanta, all this time, there had been growing consternation as Sherman's "worse than vandal hordes" bore down on the city, preceded by a stream of refugees in wagons and on foot, mostly old men and boys, below or beyond the conscription limits of seventeen and fifty-two, and "yellow-faced women and their daughters in long-slatted sunbonnets and faded calico," who had fled their upcountry farms and hamlets at the approach of the blue outriders. City parks were no longer parks; they bloomed instead with gray-white clusters of hospital tents, where the reek of disinfectants competed with the morbid stench of gangrene, and both combined to rival the predominant smell of horses. Trains chuffed into the station, day and night, loaded with sick and wounded soldiers, many of them dying, many dead before they got there. "Embalming: Free from Odor of Infection," signs proclaimed, soliciting business, and Bohnefield's Coffin Shop on Luckie Street had more orders than it could fill. "Give us this day our daily bread," the Second Baptist minister had taken as his text the previous Sunday, when news came that Marietta had been abandoned in still another retreat. And before the dawn of another sabbath, so quickly did things move at this late stage of the campaign, word arrived that the gray army had retired across the Chattahoochee, burning in its rear the bridges spanning the last natural barrier between Atlanta and destruction. "Stay a few days longer," a member of Hardee's staff advised a family he joined in town that afternoon for Sunday dinner. "I think we will hold this place at least a week."

They did not take the colonel's advice, but left next morning, scrambling with others like themselves for places on a southbound train. Places were hard to get now, for the military had commandeered most of the cars for removal of the wounded, along with all government stores and the vital machinery taken from outlying mills and factories, a salvage project assigned by Johnston to a high-ranking volunteer aide, Major General Mansfield Lovell, who presumably was experienced in such matters, having given up New Orleans two years back. Atlanta had not expected to share the fate of the Crescent City, but as the fighting grew nearer, week by week, the possibility seemed less and less remote, until finally even diehards had to admit that it had developed into a probability. Loyal admirers of Old Joe — including an editor who maintained, even now, that his reputation had "grown with every backward step" — were hard put to defend the general from charges that he intended to give up the city without a fight. For the most part, he retained the confidence and above all the devotion of his soldiers, but there were those who questioned his Fabian strategy, which they saw as leading only to one end: especially after he turned loose of Kennesaw and fell back to the Chattahoochee.

"There was not an officer or man in this Army who ever dreamed of Johnston falling back this far," a young artillery lieutenant, whose home in Atlanta was then only seven miles in his rear, wrote his mother from the north bank of that river, "or ever doubted he would attack when the proper time came. But I think he has been woefully outgeneraled and has made a losing bargain."

Official concern had been growing proportionately as the Union forces closed down on Atlanta. "This place is to the Confederacy as important as the heart is to the body. We must hold it," Joe Brown wrote Jefferson Davis in late June, appealing for strategic diversions and substantial reinforcements to help Johnston avert what seemed certain to happen without them. The governor was in touch with other prominent men throughout the South, and he urged them to use their influence on the President to this end.

His chief hope was in a fellow Georgian, Senator Benjamin Hill, who occupied the unusual position of being the friend of both Davis and Johnston, a relationship they could scarcely be said to enjoy in reference to each other. Brown's hope was that Hill could serve as a go-between, if not to bring the two leaders together, then in any case to improve communications — particularly at the far end of the line, where Brown believed the messages were having the greater difficulty in getting through. He suggested that the senator write at once to the Commander in Chief, urging a more sympathetic response to the general's pleas now that the crisis was at hand. Hill said he would do better than that; "Time is too precious and letters are too inadequate"; he would go to Richmond and talk with Davis face to face. First, though, he thought it best to confer with Johnston for a clearer understanding of the hopes and plans he then would pass along. Accordingly, he rode up to the general's headquarters at Marietta next morning, July 1, and had what he later called a "free conversation" along these lines with the Virginian.

Reviewing the situation, Johnston declared that his principal aim, up to now, had been to defeat Sherman by obliging him to attack Confederate intrenchments, but after the limited effort which had been so decisively repulsed, four days ago at Kennesaw, he doubted that his adversary could be persuaded to try the thing again. As for himself, he certainly had no intention of wasting his outnumbered veterans in any such attempt. All he could do with his present force, he said, was block the direct path to Atlanta, thus delaying another Union advance until such time as Sherman again compelled his retreat by "ditching round his flank." Aside from the long-odds chance that the enemy mass would expose itself to piecemeal destruction by dividing into segments he could leap at, one by one, he saw but a single hope for reversing the blue tide, which even then was lapping the flanks of Kennesaw and would otherwise in time no doubt roll down to the Chattahoochee and beyond. This was that 5000 cavalry be thrown without delay against Sherman's life line up in Tennessee, either by Forrest or John Morgan; in which case, Johnston said, the Federals would have to accept battle on his terms — that is, attack him in his intrenchments — or else retreat to avoid starvation. Asked why he did not use his own cavalry for such a profitable venture, the general replied that all his horsemen were needed where they were. Observing that "I must go to Richmond, and Morgan must go from Virginia or Forrest from Mississippi, and this will take some time," Hill expressed some doubt whether either body of gray cavalry could reach the Federal rear before the Federals reached Atlanta. "How long can you hold Sherman north of the Chattahoochee River?" he pointedly asked Johnston, who replied somewhat evasively that the bluecoats had covered less than a dozen southward miles in the past month, shifting their ground from around New Hope Church to Kennesaw Mountain, where they had made no progress at all in the past two weeks; Hill could figure for himself, the general said, how long it would take them to reach the river at this rate.

Hill calculated, accordingly, that the Confederates could remain north of the Chattahoochee "at least fifty-four days, and perhaps sixty."

Johnston assented, but not Hood, who though present throughout the interview had held his peace till now. He disagreed, saying: "Mr Hill, when we leave our present line, we will, in my judgment, cross the Chattahoochee River very rapidly." Johnston turned on the tall blond Texan, who was twenty-four years his junior in age, as well as in length of service. "What makes you think that?" he asked, and Hood replied: "Because this line of Kennesaw is the strongest line we can get in this country. If we surrender this to Sherman he can reconnoiter from its summit the whole country between here and Atlanta, and there is no such line of defense in the distance." Johnston demurred. "I differ with your conclusion," he said. "I admit this is a strong line of defense, but I have two more strong lines between this and the river, from which I can hold Sherman a long time."

Hill took his leave, pleased to learn that two more stout positions had been prepared for the army to defend before it retired across the Chattahoochee, some fifty-four to sixty days in the future, according to his Johnston-approved calculations, or in any case "a long time" from now. Delayed by personal matters, he took a train for Virginia before the end of the following week, passing en route a group of public men proceeding by rail on a mission similar to his own, except that the two were headed in opposite directions toward diametric goals. Hill was going from Atlanta to Richmond in hope of impressing Johnston's views on Davis, while they were going from Richmond to Atlanta in hope of impressing Davis's views on Johnston. Congressmen all, they had been delegated by their colleagues, as friends of the general, to warn him that his conduct of the Georgia campaign was under heavy attack in the capital and to urge him to disarm these rearward critics by taking aggressive action against the enemy in his front.

Reaching Atlanta on the evening of July 8 they proceeded next morning to army headquarters for a conference with Johnston, who by then had fallen back through Smyrna, the first of his two stout positions south of Kennesaw, to his bridgehead on the north bank of the Chattahoochee, which was his second. The Virginian received them graciously, heard them out, and replied, alas, as if they had been dispatched for irksome purposes by the President himself: "You may tell Mr Davis that it would be folly for me under the circumstances to risk a decisive engagement. My plan is to draw Sherman further and further from his base in the hope of weakening him and by cutting his army in two. That is my only hope of defeating him."

There was silence at this until one delegate, a Missourian, remarked that what was required, both for the country's sake and the general's own, was for him to strike the Yankees "a crushing blow," and then went on — tactlessly, but apparently in hope of jogging

Johnston into action — to say that lately he had heard the President quoted to the effect that "if he were in your place he could whip Sherman now." The general was jogged into action, all right, but not of the kind intended. He bridled and did not try to hide his scorn.

"Yes," he said icily, "I know Mr Davis thinks he can do a great many things other men would hesitate to attempt. For instance, he tried to do what God failed to do. He tried to make a soldier of Braxton Bragg, and you know the result. It couldn't be done."

This might have wound up the matter then and there, to no one's satisfaction, but a courier arrived at that point with news of a development to which Johnston's response provided the conference with an upbeat ending. Schofield had effected a south-bank lodgment yesterday, seven miles upriver, the courier reported, and this morning he had continued the crossing with what appeared to be most, if not all, of his command. . . . If the general's visitors expected him to react with dismay to this information that he had been flanked, they were agreeably disappointed. Pointing out that Sherman had thus divided his army, north and south of the deep-running Chattahoochee, Johnston declared that the time at last had come to strike and "whip him in detail."

The delegates returned to Atlanta expecting to hear before nightfall the roar of guns that would signal the launching of the attack. It did not come, either then or the following morning, July 10, when all that broke the sabbath stillness was the peal of church bells, summoning the city's dwindling population to pray for a deliverance which Johnston himself seemed less and less willing to attempt.

Bells were tolling that Sunday morning in Richmond, too, when Benjamin Hill stepped off the train from Georgia. He went straight to his hotel and stayed there only long enough to wash up before going to the White House for the appointment he had secured by wiring ahead. Having, as he said, "repelled the idea that any influence with the President was needed, if the facts were as General Johnston reported them," the senator was convinced that all the situation required was for him to relay the general's requests to Davis; "I did not doubt he would act promptly."

He was ushered without delay into the Chief Executive's residential office, and as he advanced across the white rug that was said to provoke temerity in the breasts of men who called in unscraped boots, the Mississippian rose to greet him with a geniality that matched the Virginia general's own, nine days ago in Marietta. Davis heard him out, his smile fading when Hill spoke of Morgan and Forrest as presumably lying more or less idle in Southwest Virginia and North Mississippi. As for Morgan, he replied, it was true that he was where Johnston said he was, having just returned, sadly depleted, from just such an expedition as Johnston recommended, whipped and in no condition for anything more than an attempt to pull his few survivors together for operations necessarily weeks in the future. Forrest too was unavailable, Davis said, although for different reasons. Having disposed of Sturgis at Brice's Crossroads in mid-June, he now was engaged in opposing a 15,000-man Union force that had left Memphis two weeks ago under A. J. Smith, bound either for Georgia to reinforce Sherman, in front or in rear of Atlanta, or for Mobile in conjunction with an even larger blue column reported to be on the march from New Orleans under Canby; he not only could not be spared for the proposed raid into Middle Tennessee, but his superior, Polk's successor Stephen Lee, was protesting hotly — as Johnston had only recently been informed — that he needed "his troops now with Johnston more than the latter can need Forrest."

Hill's hopes, which had been so high on the ride east, declined rapidly while he listened to this double-barreled refutation of the "facts" behind them. But presently they took an even sharper drop when Davis paused and asked: "How long did you understand General Johnston to say he could hold Sherman north of the Chattahoochee River?" Fifty-four to sixty days, the senator replied; whereupon Davis took up and read to him a telegraphic dispatch received just before his arrival. It was from Johnston and it announced that, a part of Sherman's army having crossed upriver two days ago, several miles beyond his right, he had begun his withdrawal across the Chattahoochee last night and completed it this morning.... Hill retired in some confusion, which was increased next day when the Secretary of War called on him "to reduce my interview with General Johnston to writing, for the use of the Cabinet."

He perceived now that his trip to Richmond, designed to help the Atlanta commander, had resulted instead in furnishing the general's Confederate foes with ammunition they could use in urging his removal from command. Three days later, after taking a still closer look at the attitude of those in high positions at the capital, he wired Johnston by way of warning: "You must do the work with your present force. For God's sake do it."

Just as the pressure had been greater, so now was Johnston's time even shorter than Hill knew — unless, that is, the general was somehow able to follow his friend's advice and "do the work." Atlanta, with its rolling mill and foundries, its munition plants and factories, its vital rail connections and vast store of military supplies, was the combined workshop and warehouse of the Confederate West, and as Sherman closed down upon it, Davis later wrote, the threat of its loss "produced intense anxiety far and wide. From many quarters, including such as had most urged his assignment, came delegations, petitions, and letters," insisting that the present army commander be replaced by one who would fight to save the city, not abandon it to the fate which Johnston seemed to consider unavoidable without outside help. "The clamor for his removal commenced immediately after it became known that the army had fallen back from Dalton," Davis added, "and it gathered volume with each remove toward Atlanta."

Nowhere was this clamor more vociferous than at meetings of the cabinet, not one of whose six members was by now in favor of keeping the Virginia general at his Georgia post. Some had advised against sending him there in the first place: including the Secretary of State, who afterwards told why. "From a close observation of his career," the shrewd-minded Benjamin declared, "I became persuaded that his nervous dread of losing a battle would prevent at all times his ability to cope with an enemy of nearly equal strength, and that opportunities would thus constantly be lost which under other commanders would open a plain path to victory." Still, those who had opposed his selection were not nearly so strident in their demands for his removal, at this stage, as were those who had been his supporters at the outset. The Secretary of War, for example, explained that, having made "a great mistake" seven months ago, "he desired to do all he could, even at this late date, to atone for it."

Davis resisted — now as in the case of that other Johnston, two and a half years ago, after Donelson and on the eve of Shiloh — both the public and the private clamor for the general's removal; Seddon later revealed that though "the whole Cabinet concurred in advising and even urging" the change, the President moved toward a decision "slowly and not without much hesitation, misgiving and, even to the last, reluctance." His concern was for Atlanta, for what it contained and for what it represented, not only in the minds of his own people, but also in the minds of the people of the North, who would be voting in November whether to sustain their present hard-war leader or replace him with one who might be willing, in the name of peace, to let the South depart in independence. A military professional, Davis knew only too well, as he put the case, "how serious it was to change commanders in the presence of the enemy," and he told Senator Hill flatly, in the course of their Sunday conference at the White House, that he "would not do it if he could have any assurance that General Johnston would not surrender Atlanta without a battle."

In this connection, he had sent his chief military adviser, Braxton Bragg, to determine at first hand, if possible, what the intentions of the western commander were. Bragg had left the previous day, July 9, but before he reached Atlanta — a three-day trip, as it turned out — the War Department received from Johnston himself, on July 11, a telegram which seemed to some to answer only too clearly the question as to the city's impending fate: "I strongly recommend the distribution of the U.S. prisoners, now at Andersonville, immediately."

Andersonville, a prisoner-of-war camp for enlisted personnel, established that spring near Americus, Georgia, and already badly crowded as a result of the northern decision to discontinue the exchange of prisoners, was more than a hundred miles due south of Atlanta. That distance, combined with the use of the word "immediately," gave occasion for alarm. For though Davis knew that what mainly caused Johnston to recommend the camp's evacuation was fear that Sherman, finding it within present cavalry range, might send out a flying column to liberate its 30,000 Federal captives — and thus create, as if by a sowing of dragon teeth, a ferocious new blue army deep in the Confederate rear — still, following hard as it did on the heels of news that Atlanta's defenders had retired in haste across the Chattahoochee, the telegram was an alarming indication of the direction in which Johnston's mind had turned now that Sherman was about to leap the last natural barrier in his path. For the first time since the clamor for the Virginian's removal began, two months ago, Davis agreed that his relief seemed necessary, and he said as much next day in a cipher telegram asking R. E. Lee's advice in choosing a successor: "General Johnston has failed and there are strong indications that he will abandon Atlanta. . . . It seems necessary to remove him at once. Who should succeed him? What think you of Hood for the position?"

Lee replied, also by wire and in cipher: "I regret the fact stated. It is a bad time to relieve the commander of an army situated as that of Tenne. We may lose Atlanta and the army too. Hood is a bold fighter. I am doubtful as to other qualities necessary." That evening he expanded these words of caution and regret in a follow-up letter. "It is a grievous thing," he said of the impending change. "Still if necessary it ought to be done. I know nothing of the necessity. I had hoped that Johnston was strong enough to deliver battle." As for the choice of his former star brigade and division chief as his old friend's successor out in Georgia, second thoughts had not diminished his reservations. "Hood is a good commander, very industrious on the battlefield, careless off, and I have had no opportunity of judging his action when the whole responsibility rested upon him. I have a high opinion of his gallantry, earnestness, and zeal." Further than this Lee would not go, either in praise or detraction, but he added suggestively: "General Hardee has more experience in managing an army. May God give you wisdom to decide in this momentous matter."

A series of telegrams and letters from Bragg, who reached Atlanta next morning, July 13, confirmed the need for early action, either by Johnston or the government. "Indications seem to favor an entire evacuation of this place," he wired Davis on arrival, and followed with a second gloomy message a few hours later, still without having ridden out to the general's headquarters in the field: "Our army is sadly depleted, and now reports 10,000 less than the return of the 10th June. I find but little encouraging." Two days later he was able to report more fully on conditions, having paid two calls on Johnston in the meantime. "He has not sought my advice, and it was not volunteered," Bragg wired. "I cannot learn that he has any more plan for the future than he has had in the past. It is expected that he will await the enemy on a line some three miles from here, and the impression prevails that he is now more inclined to fight.... The morale of our army is still reported good."

In a letter sent by courier to Richmond that same day he went more fully into this and other matters bearing on the issue. Johnston's apparent intention, now as always, Bragg declared, was to "await the enemy's approach and be governed, as heretofore, by the development in our front." What was likely to follow could be predicted by reviewing what had happened under similar circumstances at Dalton, Resaca, Cassville, and Marietta — or, indeed, by observing what had happened in and around Atlanta just this week; "All valuable stores and machinery have been removed, and most of the citizens able to go have left with their effects.... Position, numbers, and morale are now with the enemy." Which said, Bragg moved on to the problem of choosing a successor to the general who had brought the army to this pass. Hardee had disqualified himself, not only because he had declined the post seven months ago (and thereby brought on Johnston) but also because he had "generally favored the retiring policy" of his chief. Alexander Stewart, who had been promoted to lieutenant general and given command of Polk's corps on the retreat to the Chattahoochee, was too green for larger duties yet, despite the commendable savagery he had displayed at New Hope Church. That left Hood, who had "been in favor of giving battle" all the way from Dalton and who, in fact — aside, that is, from the peculiar circumstances that prevailed at Cassville — had done just that whenever he was on his own. By way of evidence that this was so, Bragg included a letter he had received from the young Texan the day before, expressing regret that the army had "failed to give battle to the enemy many miles north of our present position."

"If any change is made," Bragg concluded, "Lieutenant General Hood would give unlimited satisfaction." Then, as if aware of the misgiving Lee had expressed three days ago, he added: "Do not understand me as proposing him as a man of genius, or a great general, but as far better in the present emergency than any one we have available."

Davis agreed that Hood was the man for the post, if its present occupant had to be replaced, but he would not act without giving Johnston one last chance to commit himself to a fight to save Atlanta, in which case he would keep him where he was. Accordingly, in a wire next day, July 16, he put the case to the general in no uncertain terms: "I wish to hear from you as to present situation, and your plan of operations so specifically as will enable me to anticipate events."

Johnston felt no more alarm at this than he had done at Hill's

"For God's sake do it" telegram, received the day before. Busy with tactical matters, he did not take the time or trouble to outline for the Commander in Chief what he afterwards claimed was his plan for the overthrow of the blue host in his front: which — as he would set it forth some ten years later, after the guns had cooled but not the controversy — was to engage the enemy "on terms of advantage" while they were divided by Peachtree Creek. If this did not work he planned to hold the intrenchments overlooking the creek with 5000 state militia, lately sent him by Governor Brown, "and leisurely fall back with the Confederate troops into the town and, when the Federal army approached, march out with the three corps against one of its flanks." If this was successful, the bluecoats would be driven back against the unfordable Chattahoochee and cut to pieces before they could recross; if not, "the Confederate army had a near and secure place of refuge in Atlanta, which it could hold forever, and so win the campaign." So he later said — "forever" — but not now. Now he merely responded, as before, that he would have to be governed by circumstances; circumstances which it was clear would be of Sherman's making. "As the enemy has double our number, we must be on the defensive," he replied to Davis's request for specific information. "My plan of operations must, therefore, depend on that of the enemy. It is mainly to watch for an opportunity to fight to advantage. We are trying to put Atlanta in condition to hold it for a day or two by the Georgia militia, that army movements may be freer and wider."

On the defensive. A day or two. The Georgia militia. Freer and wider movements.... Johnston would later maintain that just as he was about to deliver the blow that would "win the campaign," and which he had had in mind all along, his sword was wrenched from his grasp by the Richmond authorities; but the fact was, he signed his own warrant of dismissal when he put his hand to this telegram declaring, more clearly than anything else it said, that he had no plan involving a battle to save Atlanta.

Word came next morning — July 17, another Sunday — that Sherman's whole army was over the Chattahoochee, apparently engaged in an outsized turning movement designed to close down on the city from the north and east. After nightfall Johnston was at his head-quarters three miles out the Marietta Road, conferring with his chief engineer about work on the Atlanta fortifications, when a message for him from Adjutant General Samuel Cooper clicked off the telegraph receiver:

> Lieutenant General J. B. Hood has been commissioned to the temporary rank of General under the late law of Congress. I am directed by the Secretary of War to inform you that as you have failed to arrest the advance of the enemy to the vicinity of Atlanta,

far in the interior of Georgia, and express no confidence that you can defeat or repel him, you are hereby relieved from the command of the Army and Department of Tennessee, which you will immediately turn over to General Hood.

Old Joe spent most of the rest of the night in the throes of composition, preparing first a farewell address, in which he expressed his affection for the troops who had served under him, and then a response to his superiors, in which he managed to vent a measure of the resentment aroused by the backhand slap they had taken at him in the order for his removal. "I cannot leave this noble army," he told its members, "without expressing my admiration of the high military qualities it has displayed. A long and arduous campaign has made conspicuous every soldierly virtue, endurance of toil, obedience to orders, brilliant courage. The enemy has never attacked but to be repulsed and severely punished. You, soldiers, have never argued but from your courage, and never counted your foes. No longer your leader, I will still watch your career, and will rejoice in your victories. To one and all I offer assurances of my friendship, and bid an affectionate farewell."

The other document was briefer, if no less emotional under its surface of ice. "Your dispatch of yesterday received and obeyed," it began, and passed at once to a refutation of the charges made in the dismissal order: "Sherman's army is much stronger compared with that of Tennessee than Grant's compared with that of Northern Virginia. Yet the enemy has been compelled to advance much more slowly to the vicinity of Atlanta than to that of Richmond and Petersburg, and has penetrated deeper into Virginia than into Georgia." Then at the end came the stinger. "Confident language by a military commander is not usually regarded as evidence of competency. J. E. Johnston."

Hood too got little if any sleep after he received at 11 p.m. the War Department telegram which, he said, "so astounded and overwhelmed" him that he "remained in deep thought throughout the night." He had in fact much to ponder, including a follow-up wire from Seddon: "You are charged with a great trust. You will, I know, test to the utmost your capacities to discharge it. Be wary no less than bold. . . . God be with you." His appointment was plainly an endorsement of the aggressive views he had been propounding all the way south from the Tennessee line, and he was clearly expected to translate them into action. But he perceived that to do so here on the flat terrain south of the Chattahoochee, with his back to the gates of the city in his care, was a far more difficult undertaking than it would have been in the rugged country Johnston had traversed in the course of his long retreat from Dalton. "We may lose Atlanta and the army too," Lee had warned Davis five days ago, and though Hood had not seen the message, he was altogether aware of the danger pointed out — as well as of his own shortcomings, which Lee had by no means listed in full.

For one, there was his youth. He had just last month turned thirty-three, the crucifixion age, which made him not only younger than any of his infantry corps or division commanders, but also a solid ten years younger than the average among them. Then too there was his physical condition; Gettysburg had cost him the use of his left arm, paralyzed by a fragment of bursting shell as he charged the Devil's Den, and at Chickamauga his right leg had been amputated so close to the hip that from then on he had to be strapped in the saddle to ride a horse. Worst of all, though, was the timing of the change now ordered by the War Department. Sherman's final lunge at Atlanta was in full career, and only Johnston knew what plans had been made, if any, to meet and survive the shock. Certainly Hood knew nothing of them, except as they applied to the disposition of his corps on the Confederate right, astride the Georgia Railroad. Emerging at last from the brown study into which the telegram had plunged him, the blond, Kentucky-born Texan came out of his tent before dawn, mounted his horse with the help of an orderly, and set out for Johnston's headquarters near the far end of the line.

On the way there, about sunrise, he encountered Stewart on the way there too. Old Straight, who had led a division under Hood until his recent promotion to head the corps that had been temporarily under Loring, was also disturbed by the untimely change. He proposed that they unite with Hardee "in an effort to prevail on General Johnston to withhold the order and retain command of the army until the impending battle has been fought." Hood readily agreed, and they rode on together.

At headquarters, where a candle flickered atop a barrel with the telegram beside it, Johnston received them courteously, but when Hood appealed to him to "pocket that dispatch, leave me in command of my corps, and fight the battle for Atlanta," the Virginian would have no part of such an irregular procedure. He was off the hook and he intended to stay off. "Gentlemen, I am a soldier," he said. "A soldier's first duty is to obey." So that was that.

Or perhaps not. Hardee having arrived by now, the three lieutenant generals dispatched a joint telegram to the President requesting that he postpone the transfer of command "until the fate of Atlanta is decided."

Davis's answer was not long in coming, and it was a flat No: "A change of commanders, under existing circumstances, was regarded as so objectionable that I only accepted it as the alternative of continuing a policy which had proved so disastrous. . . . The order has been executed, and I cannot suspend it without making the case worse than it was before the order was issued."

Hood made one last try, returning to plead a second time, "for the good of the country," that Johnston "pocket the correspondence" and remain in command, "as Sherman was at the very gates of the city." Old Joe again declined: whereupon Hood launched into a personal appeal, referring to "the great embarrassment of the position in which I had been placed." Not only was he in the dark as to such plans as had been made for meeting the enemy now bearing down on Atlanta and its defenders, he did not even know where the other two corps of the army were posted. "With all the earnestness of which man is capable," Hood later wrote, "I besought him, if he would under no circumstances retain command and fight the battle for Atlanta, to at least remain with me and give me the benefit of his counsel whilst I determined the issue." Touched at last, and "with tears of emotion gathering in his eyes," Johnston assured his young successor that, after a necessary ride into Atlanta, he would return that evening and help him all he could. So he said. According to Hood, however, "he not only failed to comply with his promise, but, without a word of explanation or apology, left that evening for Macon, Georgia."

There was some fear, according to a number of observers, that the men in the ranks "would throw down their muskets and quit" when they learned of the transfer of command: not so much from distrust of Hood, who at this stage was little more than a damaged figurehead to most of them, as because of their "love for and confidence in Johnston," who many said "had been grievously wronged" by his superiors in Richmond. "A universal gloom seemed cast over the army," a lieutenant on Hood's own staff declared, and a Tennessee private — a veteran who remembered Bragg and the aftermath of Missionary Ridge — later told why the news was received with so much sorrow and resentment: "Old Joe Johnston had taken command of the Army of Tennessee when it was crushed and broken, at a time when no other man on earth could have united it. He found it in rags and tatters, hungry and broken-hearted, the morale of the men gone, their manhood vanished to the winds, their pride a thing of the past. Through his instrumentality and skillful manipulation, all these had been restored.... Farewell, old fellow!" he cried, breaking into an apostrophe of remembered grief as he approached the end of this "saddest chapter" of the war; "We privates loved you because you made us love ourselves."

Not all who felt that way about the Virginia general had to say goodbye from such a distance, either of time or space. Between the reading of his farewell address that Monday morning and his actual departure for Macon that afternoon, several units passed his head-quarters on their way up to the lines on Peachtree Creek, and thereby got the chance to demonstrate their affection in his presence. A Georgia regiment happened to march out the Marietta Road, for example, and the colonel left a record of how he and his men reacted to what they thought would be their last look at their former commander, who came out of the house and stood by the gate to watch them pass. "We lifted our hats. There was no cheering. We simply passed silently, our heads uncovered. Some of the officers broke ranks and grasped his hand, as the tears poured down their cheeks."

Higher up the ladder of rank, the reaction was scarcely less emotional. Hardee, upset at having someone more than a year his junior in grade promoted over his head, promptly asked to be relieved, complaining that the President — who in the end persuaded him to withdraw his application for a transfer — was "attempting to create the impression that in declining the command [six months ago] at Dalton, I declined it for all future time." He doubted Hood's ability to fill the position to which he had been elevated, and others felt, as one of them put it, that the appointment was an "egregious blunder." Sam French called at headquarters that evening to assure the new commander of his full coöperation, but did not fail to add, with his usual forthrightness, that he regretted the change. "Although he took my hand and thanked me," he later said of Hood, "I was ever afterwards impressed with the belief that he never forgave me for what I said." Still others, aware of the reason behind the shift, foresaw hard fighting and had mixed opinions concerning the fate of Atlanta, as well as their own. Undoubtedly, Hood being Hood, they were about to go over to the offensive; Pat Cleburne, for one, believed that this was likely to take them far — in miles, at any rate. "We are going to carry the war to Africa," he predicted, "but I fear we will not be as successful as Scipio was."

Across the way, on the far side of Peachtree Creek and eastward out the Georgia Railroad, the reaction among Federals of rank was not dissimilar, so far as expectation of a step-up in the scale of fighting went, when it became known next day that the Confederates, in Lincoln's current campaign phrase, had "swapped horses in midstream."

McPherson and Schofield had been West Point classmates of Hood's, standing first and seventh respectively in a class of fifty-two, while he stood forty-fourth — ten places below even Sheridan, who had been held back a year for misconduct. Schofield in fact had been his roommate, and by coaching him in mathematics, which gave the Kentucky cadet a great deal of trouble, had managed to keep his military career from ending in academic failure and dismissal. "I came very near thinking once or twice that perhaps I had made a mistake," the Illinois general would remark in later years, though for the present he simply warned his chief: "He'll hit you like hell, now, before you know it." McPherson agreed, and so did Thomas, under whom Hood had served five years ago in Texas. But perhaps the most convincing testimony as to this new opponent's boldness came from a Union-loyal fellow Kentuckian who had watched him play old-army poker. "I seed Hood bet $2500," this witness declared, "with nary a pair in his hand."

Warned from all sides that his adversary was "bold even to rashness, and courageous in the extreme," Sherman took the precaution of advising his unit commanders to keep their troops "always prepared for battle in any shape."

Not that he regretted the predicted shift in rebel tactics. His casualties would undoubtedly mount, but there was plenty of room for taking up the slack that was evident from a comparison of Union losses, east and west. In the eleven weeks of his campaign against Johnston and Atlanta, he had lost fewer men than Meade had lost in the two-day Wilderness battle that opened his drive on Lee and Richmond. Besides, as Sherman saw it, the heavier the casualties were — provided, of course, that they could be kept in ratio, Federal and Confederate — the sooner the fighting would end with him in occupation of his goal. That was what he meant, in part, when he wrote home the following week: "I confess I was pleased at the change."

LIST OF MAPS

*Maps drawn by Rafael Palacios, from originals
by the author. All are oriented north.*

BIBLIOGRAPHICAL NOTE
The following bibliographical note was included with the full text of
THE CIVIL WAR: A Narrative—Red River to Appomattox.

So there now. Twenty years have come and gone and I can say with
Chaucer, "Farwel my book and my devocion." All through the second of
these two decades—the drawn-out time it took to write this third and
final volume—my debt to those who went before me, dead and living, continued to mount even as the Centennial spate diminished to a trickle and
then ran dry. Previous obligations were enlarged, and new ones acquired,
on both sides of the line defining the limits of the original material: especially on the near side, where the evidence was assembled and presented in
general studies, biographies, and secondary accounts of individual campaigns. Chief among these last, to take them in the order of their use, were
the following: *Red River Campaign* by Ludwell H. Johnson, *Lee's Last
Campaign* by Clifford Dowdey, *Autumn of Glory* by Thomas L. Connelly,
Jubal's Raid by Frank E. Vandiver, *The Decisive Battle of Nashville* by
Stanley F. Horn, *Sherman's March Through the Carolinas* by John G. Barrett,
and two recitals of the Appomattox chase, *An End to Valor* by Philip Van
Doren Stern and *Nine April Days* by Burke Davis. Similarly, my long-term
obligation to works on naval matters was extended by Virgil Carrington
Jones's *Civil War at Sea: The Final Effort* and Edward Boykin's *Ghost Ship
of the Confederacy.*

No one who has read or even scanned these books can fail to see my
debt to them, as well as to the biographies cited earlier, two of which had
concluding volumes that came out just as the need for them was sorest:
Hudson Strode's *Jefferson Davis: Tragic Hero* and Bruce Catton's *Grant
Takes Command.* Having had them, I cannot see how I could have managed
without them, and the same applies to J. G. Randall's *Lincoln the President,*

completed after his death by Richard N. Current in *Last Full Measure,* and Jim Bishop's *Day Lincoln Was Shot.* Clifford Dowdey's *Lee* brought his subject into sharper focus, and T. Harry Williams filled a sizeable gap with his *Hayes of the Twenty-third,* as E. B. Long did many others with *The Civil War Day by Day: An Almanac.* Nash K. Burger's and John K. Bettersworth's *South of Appomattox* helped get me down to the wire, and Kenneth M. Stampp, who was with me at the start in *And the War Came,* was also with me at the finish in *The Era of Reconstruction,* another old friend among the many I know only through their work.

To all these I am grateful, as I was and am to those mentioned in the end notes to the first two volumes of this iliad, most of whom continued their contribution through the third. Originally I intended to list my obligations in a complete bibliography here at the close of the whole, but even this chore has been spared me—along with a considerable added bulkiness for you—by Ralph G. Newman and E. B. Long, whose 1964 pamphlet, *A Basic Civil War Library,* first published in the *Journal of the Illinois State Historical Society,* enumerates by category the 350-odd books I owe most to, old and new and in and out of print. Other such compilations are readily available, including a much fuller one in Long's own *Almanac,* yet this one is to me the best in its inclusion of the works I mainly relied on, at any rate up to its date of issue. While I hope I have acknowledged my heaviest contemporary debts in this trio of notes, there are two I would like to stress in particular. One is to Bruce Catton, whose *Centennial History of the Civil War* was finished in time for its third volume, *Never Call Retreat,* to be available, together with his earlier *Stillness at Appomattox,* as a source and guide all through the writing of my own third volume. I was, as Stonewall Jackson said in another connection on his deathbed, "the infinite gainer" from having him thus meet his deadline even as I was failing to reach mine. My other chief debt is to the late Allan Nevins, whose close-packed *Organized War to Victory,* the last in his four-volume *War for the Union,* was similarly available during the past two years. Both gave me a wealth of useable material, but at least as valuable was their example of dedication and perseverance, double-barreled proof that such an undertaking could be carried to a finish. In that sense my debt to them is personal, though not as much so, nor as large, as the ones I owe my editor, Robert Loomis, and my wife, Gwyn Rainer Foote, both of whom bore with me all the way.

Perhaps in closing I might add that, although nowhere along the line have I had a "thesis" to argue or maintain—partly no doubt because I never saw one yet that could not be "proved," at least to the satisfaction of the writer who advanced it—I did have one thing I wanted to do, and that was to restore a balance I found lacking in nearly all the histories composed within a hundred years of Sumter. In all too many of these works, long and short, foreign and domestic, the notion prevailed that the War was fought in Virginia, while elsewhere—in an admittedly large but also rather empty region known vaguely as "the West"—a sort of running skirmish wobbled back and forth, presumably as a way for its participants, faceless men with unfamiliar names, to pass the time while waiting for the issue to be settled in the East. I do not claim that the opposite is true, but I do claim that it is perhaps a little closer to the truth; that Vicksburg, for example, was as "decisive" as Gettysburg, if not more so, and that Donelson, with its introduction of Grant and Forrest onto the national scene, may have had more to do with the outcome than either of the others had, for all their greater panoply, numbers, and documentation. In any case, it was my hope to provide what I considered a more fitting balance, East and West, in the course of attempting my aforesaid purpose of re-creating that war and making it live again in the world around us.

So, anyhow, "Farwel my book and my devocion," my rock and my companion through two decades. At the outset of this Gibbon span, plunk in what I hope will be the middle of my writing life, I was two years younger than Grant at Belmont, while at the end I was four months older than Lincoln at his assassination. By way of possible extenuation, in response to complaints that it took me five times longer to write the war than the participants took to fight it, I would point out that there were a good many more of them than there was of me. However that may be, the conflict is behind me now, as it is for you and it was a hundred-odd years ago for them.

—S.F.

INDEX

ABOUT THE AUTHOR

Shelby Foote was born in Greenville, Mississippi, and attended school there until he entered the University of North Carolina. During World War II he served in the European theater as a captain of field artillery. In the period after the war he wrote five novels: *Tournament, Follow Me Down, Love in a Dry Season, Shiloh,* and *Jordan County.* He was twice awarded a Guggenheim fellowship. A longtime resident of Memphis, Tennessee, he died in 2005 at the age of 88.

SHERMAN vs JOHNSTON
Dalton to Peachtree Creek
7 May–17 July

1. Outflanked via Snake Creek Gap, May 12, Johnston withdraws southward fifteen miles.
2. Sherman is repulsed, May 14, but Johnston, hearing that the Federals are over the Oostanaula five miles in his rear, begins a thirty-mile displacement.
3. Bypassing Calhoun and Adairsville, the Confederates occupy Cassville, May 18, while the Federals converge mistakenly on Kingston. Johnston plans, then cancels, an attack; when Sherman comes up, withdraws across the Etowah to Allatoona, May 19, and shifts his base to Marietta.
4. Sherman cuts loose from the railroad, May 23; heads due south for Burnt Hickory and Dallas.
5. Johnston conforms; blocks Union advance at New Hope Church, May 25. Both extend lines eastward; clash again, May 28. Johnston cancels planned attack.
6. Sherman shifts to Acworth; Johnston takes up position, June 4, on Lost Mountain and Pine Top, then sidles eastward to Brush Mountain, covering railroad.
7. When Sherman advances, June 14-15, Johnston falls back to a new and shorter line next day on Kennesaw.
8. Skirmishing begins June 19. Hood attacks Federal right, June 22; is repulsed. Thomas attacks Confederate center, June 27; is bloodily repulsed.
9. Sherman resumes flanking movement, July 2, shifting McPherson westward. Johnston falls back to Smyrna.
10. Again Sherman advances; Johnston falls back to the north bank of the Chattahoochee. Sherman continues his advance; sends McPherson far to the left, upstream, for a crossing July 8, near Roswell. Johnston falls back across the river next day, then shifts to Peachtree Creek to cover Atlanta, now only six miles in his rear. July 17, still in that position, he receives notice that he is relieved of command.

SHERMAN vs HOOD
Peachtree Creek to the Fall of Atlanta
17 July–2 Sep.

1. Hood attacks Thomas, July 20, near the Chattahoochee crossing; is repulsed.
2. Hood attacks Federal left, July 22; is repulsed.
3. Sherman sidles south around the west side of Atlanta, reaching for the Confederate rail supply lines. Hood strikes him, July 28, at Ezra Church; is repulsed.
4. Schofield breaks the Macon railroad, Aug. 30, then is joined by Thomas for the march on Jonesboro, wrecking track as they move south.
5. Hardee attacks Federal concentration; is repulsed; then escapes encirclement, one corps moving south to Lovejoy Station while the other rejoins Hood in Atlanta—in time to assist in the evacuation and act as rear guard on the march to rejoin Hardee at Lovejoy's. The Federals march into the evacuated city next morning, Sep. 2; Sherman notifies Washington, "Atlanta is ours, and fairly won."